Masterpieces and Dramas
of the Soviet Championships

Volume III (1948-1953)

Sergey Voronkov

Masterpieces and Dramas of the Soviet Championships: Volume III (1948-1953)

Author: Sergey Voronkov

Translated from the Russian by Alexei Zakharov

Typesetting by Andrei Elkov (www.elkov.ru)

Photos provided from the archives of the Russian Chess Museum, magazines *Chess in the USSR (Shakhmaty v SSSR), 64* and *Chess Review*, and personal archives of the author, Yuri Averbakh, Aron Bogatin, Isaak Boleslavsky, Mikhail Botvinnik, David Bronstein, Viktor Chepizhny, German Friedstein, Mykola Fuzik, Ratmir Kholmov, Paavo Kivine, Alexander Kotov, Efim Lazarev, Ivan Lyskov, Yakov Neishtadt, Alexander Nikitin, Ruslan Ponyaev, Vasily Smyslov, Mikhail Volkovysky, Lyubov Yakir, Ivan Yaremko, and Anatoly Zlobovsky.

Front cover: photo by G. Yablonovsky of the third round of the 17th Soviet Championship, 1949

Follow us on Twitter: @ilan_ruby

www.elkandruby.com

ISBN 978-5-6044692-1-7 (paperback), 978-5-6045607-1-6 (hardback)

CONTENTS

Index of Games

Game	White	Black	Opening	Year
231	Keres	Petrosian	Fragment	1950
232	Boleslavsky	Tolush	Fragment	1950
233	Averbakh	Keres	Fragment	1950
234	Moiseev	Simagin	King's Indian Defense	1951
235	Taimanov	Geller	Queen's Pawn Game	1951
236	Smyslov	Simagin	English Opening	1951
237	Geller	Keres	Ruy Lopez	1951
238	Bronstein	Geller	Ruy Lopez	1951
239	Bronstein	Botvinnik	Semi-Slav Defense	1951
240	Petrosian	Smyslov	Fragment	1951
241	Botvinnik	Kopylov	Dutch Defense	1951
242	Kopylov	Keres	Fragment	1951
243	Botvinnik	Keres	Fragment	1951
244	Taimanov	Averbakh	Fragment	1951
245	Averbakh	Bondarevsky	Fragment	1951
246	Smyslov	Bronstein	Fragment	1951
247	Bronstein	Kotov	Fragment	1951
248	Lipnitsky	Terpugov	Fragment	1951
249	Petrosian	Kopylov	Nimzo-Indian Defense	1951
250	Taimanov	Bronstein	King's Indian Defense	1952
251	Botvinnik	Taimanov	Nimzo-Indian Defense	1952
252	Geller	Keres	Nimzo-Indian Defense	1952
253	Tolush	Smyslov	Slav Defense	1952
254	Botvinnik	Keres	Fragment	1952
255	Simagin	Goldenov	Fragment	1952
256	Byvshev	Boleslavsky	Sicilian Defense	1952
257	Byvshev	Smyslov	Ruy Lopez	1952
258	Smyslov	Korchnoi	Fragment	1952
259	Suetin	Kasparyan	Fragment	1952
260	Boleslavsky	Taimanov	Fragment	1952
261	Botvinnik	Byvshev	Fragment	1952
262	Geller	Taimanov	Fragment	1952
263	Suetin	Botvinnik	Fragment	1952
264	Taimanov	Botvinnik	Fragment	1953
265	Botvinnik	Taimanov	Fragment	1953
266	Taimanov	Botvinnik	Dutch Defense	1953
267	Botvinnik	Taimanov	Nimzo-Indian Defense	1953
268	Taimanov	Botvinnik	Nimzo-Indian Defense	1953

Introduction: Chess of the Red Propaganda

After World War II, a new, powerful and exciting generation of masters came to the fore in Soviet chess: including David Bronstein, Efim Geller, Tigran Petrosian, Yuri Averbakh, Mark Taimanov, and Viktor Korchnoi... However, there was an equally powerful and exciting pre-war generation blocking their way to the chess pinnacle – in their prime and still progressing, too: including grandmasters Mikhail Botvinnik, Paul Keres, Vasily Smyslov, Isaak Boleslavsky, Alexander Kotov, and Igor Bondarevsky... Simply listing these names is breathtaking: every player here was a star! The Soviet championships back then truly were the "tournaments of stars".

It was then that the decades-long period known as "the golden age of Soviet chess" began. The Soviet world champions took turns on the throne, Soviet grandmasters dominated international matches and tournaments, their annotations were considered the best training material for the whole world, and Soviet chess books and magazines were deemed the gold standard for quality.

The status of chess players also changed. In 1948, grandmasters and masters started receiving stipends, which allowed them to concentrate fully on chess, without thinking how to make ends meet. A gold medal for the national champion was introduced in the same year. Chess players were granted the right to travel abroad – a privilege which was previously reserved only for Botvinnik (apart from him, only Ragozin was allowed to compete in an international tournament before the war) and of which, I should remind Western readers, almost all Soviet citizens were deprived. On the one hand, this meant that the best Soviet grandmasters joined the country's elite, but, on the other hand, they became highly dependent on the state. They knew: one careless word said abroad, any unsanctioned contact with a foreigner, the smallest attempt to disobey a superior's orders during a trip, and that was it – you were added to the no-foreign-trip list for a long time, with all the material and other consequences that this entailed.

David Bronstein once told me that in 1954, when he was in New York during the USSR – USA match, he found a cartoon in the *New York Times*, called "Kremlin's Puppets": "Below, we were all gathered there: Smyslov, Bronstein, Keres, Averbakh, Geller, Kotov, Petrosian, and Taimanov, and above were the Kremlin higher-ups headed by Khrushchev, pulling our strings. This looked like a slap in the face. But now I think that this cartoonist was essentially right: we were indeed puppets, but didn't realize it." Indeed, all our greats had to play the role of "Soviet chess players" abroad, not allowed to act independently. Even at the chess board, too – if the party "gave an order". The stakes in this black and white theater were incredibly high: in Stalin's time, any tournament place other than first was considered a failure for Soviet grandmasters.

The contemporary reader most probably doesn't know that it was no accident that chess experienced such hypertrophied attention and development in the Soviet Union: it was an important instrument of propaganda. In 1929, Nikolai Krylenko, the boss of Soviet chess (as well as being the Russian SFSR chief prosecutor and future Soviet People's Commissar for Justice), reacted to the "bourgeois" call "Down with politics in chess" with proletarian straightforwardness, coming up with the slogan "Chess is a weapon of politics", and Soviet chess players lived under that slogan ever since. The fact that we were "ahead of the whole planet" not only "in the area of ballet"[1], but in the most intellectual of all games too, was supposed to be a symbol of the communist system being superior to the capitalist one.

The country caught "chess fever" back in 1925, when a huge tournament was staged in Moscow featuring Capablanca, Lasker, Rubinstein, Marshall and other stars of the West. The Soviet government, urged by Krylenko, funded it handsomely (this was the first tournament in the world to be directly sponsored by a state), but it was worth it. The breakthrough of the cultural blockade had to become – and it did become! – a preface to the breakthrough on other, much more important frontlines: economic and political. And the tournament itself was, possibly, the first attempt to engage in "team play", of which the Soviet players were later repeatedly accused.

The tournament was won by Efim Bogoljubov. Back then, he was not yet "the renegade" who renounced his Soviet citizenship – he was the Soviet champion, so Krylenko was highly invested in his victory. The key to Bogoljubov's success was his phenomenal score against other Soviet players – 8/9; it's usually explained by the fact that he knew their game very well. Yes, this is true. But the opposite was also true: they had also adapted to his play – in the 1924 Soviet championship, Bogoljubov's score was close to perfect, but in 1925, he lost two games and drew six. Yet, in this tournament, the Soviet masters went down against him without much fight, even though they didn't fear Capablanca or Lasker, whom they were facing for the first time in their life! I'm sure that Bogoljubov did not play any active part in this, but Krylenko, as we shall see later, didn't exactly restrain himself in his methods of achieving the aim...

The 1933 match between Salo Flohr and the leader of Soviet chess, Mikhail Botvinnik, was held in both Russian capitals, Moscow and Leningrad, with

---

[1]   Quote from a satirical song by Yuri Vizbor. – *Translator*

top-notch arrangements. "Krylenko organized the match in grandiose style," we read in Botvinnik's memoir. "We played in the Column Hall of the House of the Unions. The participants were housed in the National Hotel, we had an open tab in the restaurant. (...) Flohr was surprised by all that. He probably thought that all Soviet chess players lived like that." There was a food stamp system operating in the country at the time, but the Soviet government was always adept at showing off before foreign guests.

The Moscow half of the match went quite badly for Botvinnik: he lost two games out of six. "Botvinnik, a very nice young man, was sure that he would lose the match from the outset. What happened later, I think, was a big surprise for him and the entire Soviet chess society" (Flohr). Indeed: the Soviet master won two games in a row and drew the match! At the closing banquet, Krylenko commented, "Botvinnik showed the qualities of a true Bolshevik in this match..."

And what about Flohr? He never allowed himself to say anything out of line – or at least only with people very close to him. Writer Vladimir Moschenko was a long-term friend of Flohr and, what's more important, recorded his conversations with him, which became the foundation of the book *Salo Flohr. Bitter Czech Chocolate* (Moscow 2015). Flohr once said, "Well, I will say this: I showed my gratitude to my hosts for their hospitality." When questioned what kind of "gratitude" he was talking about, he replied, "I wanted this to be a real celebration. For everyone, not only for me – for Botvinnik, for Comrade Krylenko, the chief of Soviet chess. I told Raisa *(his future wife; Flohr met her in Moscow – she approached him herself at the Bolshoi Theater and asked if he had an extra ticket – S. V.)* [2] that I expected to receive more invitations to Moscow! She liked that, and, if I'm being honest, so did I."

And what is more, "Smyslov, Bronstein, Spassky and Korchnoi were quite skeptical about Flohr losing two games in a row," Genna Sosonko wrote in his book *My Testimony*. In *Smyslov on the Couch* (Elk and Ruby, 2018), he quotes Vasily Vasilyevich: "You should have heard Flohr tell us about how he lost his final two games in his 1933 match against Botvinnik and then got a really fancy gift. A fur coat! Not just any fur coat, but a sable one! Well actually, a furrier in Prague told him it was weasel fur, not sable, but that's beside the point..."

The 1935 and 1936 Moscow tournaments were even more expensive and pompous – they were organized to test the strength of the masters growing up in the Soviet state. The arrival of global chess stars, headed by Lasker, Capablanca and Flohr, caused a new bout of "chess fever" and sprouted an

---

[2]   Henceforth, all italic text in parentheses is mine. All small-font insertions, including those in quotes, are also mine (S.V.)

entire generation of young talents... The goal set by Krylenko in the mid-1930s and approved at the very top would be finally achieved in 1948, when Mikhail Botvinnik won the world championship!

The foreign luminaries took a rather pragmatic position from the start: down with the politics, it only interferes with making money. Thus, they gladly visited the "chess Eldorado" and then warmly complimented their hosts. It's totally understandable: they were treated like royals, accommodated in the best hotels, had open tabs in the restaurants, and the prizes were paid in hard currency – what else could you wish for?! After the war, the chess boom in the USSR didn't subside, and the Western grandmasters, who made their living from modest tournament prizes, could only envy the status of their Soviet colleagues who were supported by the state...

The first player to highlight the underside of this blissful picture and to call on the West not to allow communists to use chess for political purposes was the ex-Soviet champion Fyodor Bogatyrchuk. After emigrating to Canada in 1949, he immediately sent a letter to *CHESS* magazine under the headline "Chess of the Red Propaganda" (the headline was omitted in the magazine for some reason). This was the first public attempt to open Western society's eyes to the state of affairs in Soviet chess, which, like all Soviet sports, supposedly featured only amateurs and no professionals. In actuality, if you wanted to achieve success, you generally had to drop your day job altogether and fully dedicate yourself to chess. Only after that did the state take financial responsibility for you – granting a stipend, organizing training camps, and paying for travels abroad. Chess in the Soviet Union turned into a matter of state importance, which was funded handsomely.

"The declarations of red propagandists about the contribution of chess to the cultural development of the younger generation are only a camouflage, under cover of which red propaganda pursues other aims. (...) Abroad, chess is used as a method of impressing intellectuals. The enormous diffusion of chess in the USSR is pictured as one indication of the high intellectual level of the masses which is, of course, 'only possible in the Soviet state.' (...) Chess in the Soviet Union has ceased to be a game but is planned, directed, ordered by communist super-brains."

The reaction to the letter was predictable: some, like Andre Gide, clearly saw the totalitarian essence of the Soviet system and were not deceived by the achievements "in the area of ballet", while others, like Lion Feuchtwanger, still took Stalin's facade at face value and dreamed of a similar "bright future". Thankfully, this interest in leftist ideas, which were rather popular among Western intellectuals after the war, slowly faded away. Some were cured by the Slansky trial (1952), when the top officials of the Czech communist party were executed, others by the bloodbath in Budapest (1956), while others still held on to their illusions up until the Soviet tanks showed up on the streets of Prague in 1968...

The most interesting part of Bogatyrchuk's letter was his story about the consequences of his win against Botvinnik at the Moscow 1935 tournament, which he described in more detail later, in an article for the Ukrainian-language emigre monthly magazine *Federalist Democrat* (Canada 1953). "Didn't you know that by winning a game against Botvinnik **you were indirectly undermining the prestige of the proletarian state** *(emphasis by Bogatyrchuk – S. V.)*, which Botvinnik was defending at the time?" the master was asked a year (!) later, in the Communist Party propaganda department. When he tried to argue that "a good win against the Soviet champion by another Soviet master only raised the prestige of Soviet chess art," he was told, "We worry not about Soviet chess art, but rather about the world's first proletarian state, and to support its prestige, we should be ready to sacrifice everything, not just a win in a chess game."

Even in the mid-1930s, there were suspicions that Soviet chess players could throw games or pre-arrange draws "in the interests of the state". However, there were no leaks and no direct evidence, so Bogatyrchuk's testimony was the first concrete proof. Later, strangely, it was Botvinnik of all people who opened up on that topic. There are two telling episodes in his book *Achieving the Aim*. In the first, Krylenko was the one who proposed throwing a game, while in the second, it was Andrei Zhdanov, a member of Stalin's inner circle.

In the 1935 tournament, Botvinnik and Flohr were on equal points before the last round. "There was a knock at the door, and Nikolai Vasilyevich Krylenko entered. 'What would you say,' he asked, 'if Rabinovich loses to you?'" Botvinnik wrote that he angrily rejected the proposal, and answered the question "What should we do then?" with, "I think that Flohr himself will suggest that we draw both games; he did a similar thing during our match..." And then he added, "Besides, he might be worried that Rabinovich is going to throw his game against me." It would have been better not to write anything at all! That way, the sentence, "And then, S. Vainstein entered the room: *Flohr proposes two draws*" would not have sounded too revealing. So Flohr really was worried about "foul play"...

The second episode is even more egregious. Before the second, Moscow half of the 1948 match tournament, Botvinnik was summoned to a Central Committee secretariat meeting. He tried to assure everyone that there was no reason to worry. "But still, we fear that Reshevsky might become the world champion," Zhdanov said. "What do you think of the idea of Soviet players losing to you on purpose?" Botvinnik refused outright, but Zhdanov insisted, and then Botvinnik proposed, "OK, let's leave this an open question – maybe we won't need it at all?" Zhdanov gladly agreed, and added, "We wish YOU (he put a particular accent on this word) victory!"

It seems that all was fair in such an important state matter. Lev Alburt, the most famous chess defector after Korchnoi, wrote, "Jotters with chess notes *('secret opening analysis,' Botvinnik clarified)* were confiscated from ex-world champion Max Euwe in Brest, on his way to Moscow. The customs officials allegedly mistook the notes as some kind of cipher. At Botvinnik's request, the notebooks were later returned (Euwe was moved and thanked Botvinnik heartily), but copies of these notes somehow wound up in the possession of Soviet grandmasters. The powers that be played their game in great style..." (*Strana i Mir*, Munich, 1986).

The results of the match tournament caused a new wave of rumors about "pre-arranged" games. Botvinnik's absolute destruction of Keres (four wins in a row!) looked especially suspicious. However, Bogatyrchuk's main accusation was different: how could FIDE have allowed three Soviet players to face just two foreigners? The 1948 match tournament was the first time that the world championship was not contested in a one-on-one match. The reason was Alekhine's death. In old times, world champions could choose their opponents, but now the situation had changed. After joining FIDE in 1947, the Soviets managed to push through the new world championship system developed by Botvinnik. Zonal Tournaments, then the Interzonal, and finally the Candidates Tournament, with the winner facing the world champion.

In conditions where almost half of the qualifying tournament participants were Soviets, Western players had no chance of breaking through the "red wall". The 1952 Stockholm Interzonal was most telling in this regard: the Soviet participants played short draws against each other, not even trying to pretend that they were playing competitive games (ultimately, all five qualified for the Candidates Tournament). When I asked Averbakh about the reasons for such "pacifism", he said that there were no orders from Moscow. I do believe him, but such conduct can hardly be called "sporting"...

There were many other similar cases after Stalin's death, but they are beyond the scope of this book. At any rate, the issue is not the quantity of cases of cheating, but rather the system that was put in place in Soviet chess during Stalin's time and that helped Soviet grandmasters to reside on the chess Olympus for the next quarter of a century.

Anyway, this is just some background. The real story is quite different.

Stalin's desire to obtain the world chess champion's title for the USSR was not just based on vanity. Sometimes, the Soviet "coat-of-arms" would appear with an Earth-sized hammer and sickle. This was not simply an image: it was a call to action. The Bolsheviks strove for world domination from the very outset. Their outward "fight for peace" was a cover for their aggressive plans to destroy the hated West. It doesn't matter whether Churchill actually said "The fascists of the future will call themselves anti-fascists": whoever really coined this phrase was a prophet. In this book's chapter "The End of an Era", you'll find a cartoon from the *Krokodil* magazine where the future US President Eisenhower is pictured with Hitler's portrait under his arm. Soviet newspapers were now branding their former allies in the fight against Nazism as fascists! Stalin's true plans were revealed by his close confidant Vyacheslav Molotov in his speech at the Communist Party conference in autumn 1952: "We cannot ignore the facts of the past. The facts say that after World War I, Russia broke away from the capitalist system, and after World War II, a number of European and Asian countries broke away from that system, too. There is every ground to believe that a third world war will destroy the global capitalist system altogether." The Korean War was supposed to be the trigger, but, thankfully, Stalin died before he managed to start a new worldwide bloodbath...

But his ideas, as we see, did not die with him. Will the war in Ukraine devolve into World War III? I sincerely hope not. But the conflict there is of a truly existential nature. Its outcome will determine whether Russia is finally able to climb out of the imperial rut of simultaneous feelings of superiority and servility that have led it into a dead end and turned it into a threat to the entire world. When the Maidan uprising started in Kiev in autumn 2013, and the protesters started to demolish Lenin statues, I noted that the "nationalism" employed there was merely rhetoric, and that the events were really an anti-Soviet revolution. The Ukrainians (and not only them) associate the former USSR with the totalitarian past that Russia is still stubbornly trying to enforce as the image of the future.

When I delivered a lecture in November 2014 at a Prague conference marking the 70th anniversary of the signing of the Prague Manifesto, I quoted Bogatyrchuk's article written in the late 1940s: "To be honest, I can't imagine an independent Ukraine if there is a totalitarian regime in Russia. It's clear to me that such a regime will quickly gobble up Ukraine and other states which, like Ukraine, might emerge on the outskirts of the former Russia *(the USSR, to be more precise)*. Thus, I think that the only way to a democratic Ukraine lies through a democratic Russia." Even back then, I saw that this was a Utopia, and I made a comment that I still place my hopes on now: "Knowing about the recent events in Ukraine, I really don't want Bogatyrchuk's words to become prophetic. Maybe it's vice versa – the way to a democratic Russia lies through a democratic Ukraine?"

***

I'm often asked if I'm intending to continue *Masterpieces and Dramas of the Soviet Championships* beyond the initial three volumes. I must admit that this was not in my plans. I can't perpetually postpone my other projects, which are of equal importance for me. The first and foremost of these is a series about my senior friend, the genius David Bronstein. It will be a three-volume work – one book will clearly not be enough. His entire archive is in my possession, and there are so many materials that even looking and reading through them might take months...

In other words, I was not going to continue the project. But then the 100th birthday of Yuri Averbakh came about, and I remembered that I promised him to write an article about the 21st Soviet Championship, where he won his only title. There's no better gift than that... I'm happy that the article was published on the Chesspro site precisely on the day of his jubilee, 8th February 2022, while he was still alive. When I wished Yuri Lvovich a happy birthday on the phone, I told him about the article, and he said, "Thank you, Seryozha."

And so, the die is cast. One championship has already been completed. Only four to go... but *what* four they are! Especially the 25th, with its fantastic denouement where a masterpiece intertwines tightly with drama.

My greatest words of thanks go to Yuri Lvovich Averbakh, who blessed me in my career as a chess historian and provided me with boundless help throughout my life. His loss will never be compensated! I will also really miss Mikhail Sokolov, who proved to be a treasure trove of invaluable information across the spectrum of chess culture. I am sincerely grateful to Artur Avetisyan, the creator and editor of the Chesspro website and to whom the Masterpieces and Dramas project owes its birth. My gratitude extends to my old friend and erstwhile co-author Dmitry Plisetsky, whose fundamental knowledge ensured high quality of the chess part of this project. The keeper of the Central Chess House's library and museum Tatiana Kolesnikovich and bibliophile Vladislav Novikov made sure that I was supplied with periodicals from the archives. Yakov Neishtadt, Viktor Chepizhny and the sadly departed Alexander Nikitin gave me access to their rich archives of photos, while Dmitry Oleinikov shared photos from the Russian archives. Mykola Fuzik of Kiev helped me to access materials from the Ukrainian Security Service's archives. Alexei Zakharov delighted me with his interesting findings in western periodicals. Anatoly Zlobovsky (Moscow), Paavo Kivine (Tallinn), Ariadna Kornilova and Ruslan Ponyaev (both from Izhevsk), Andrey Terekhov (France), Elena Kotova and Ilya Lobashov (both from Moscow) also deserve to be mentioned.

Sergey Voronkov
Moscow, September 2022

Gold for the Cosmopolitans

16th Soviet Championship: Moscow, 10th November – 13th December 1948

It is a law of history that the winning nation
Always embraces the idea of those
Whom it defeated.
A. Mezhirov, "Because the Border Is Insurmountable..."

Although the championship was scheduled for early 1948, it only took place in November. It's understandable – the year was intense: the world championship match tournament, triumphantly won by Mikhail Botvinnik, was played in the spring, and the first ever Interzonal tournament took place in the summer, with David Bronstein emerging as the winner. From now on, these two names would be constantly mentioned together, as though confirming the old adage that opposites attract.

Botvinnik found a dangerous adversary in that puny, smiley youth. He felt it immediately when he lost to him in the 13th championship and barely managed to make a draw in the 14th, so he did everything he could to avoid meeting him in the future. Probably that's why Bronstein wasn't invited to the Chigorin Memorial in December 1947, even though his participation would have surely raised the tournament's level even further. "I know that Botvinnik was a little afraid of me," David Ionovich told me. "And when I wasn't allowed to play somewhere, I took it as par for the course." He even only made it to the Interzonal because of foreign chess federations' intervention, as the Soviet Federation didn't even include him in the candidates list!

But that's all by the way. There's another, more important question. If Botvinnik intended to create a consistent world championship system, why did he hurry so much with the match tournament, the line-up for which was assembled without any qualification?

Ten years had passed since the AVRO tournament, and Smyslov was not the only one to join the chess elite. "Of course it was unfair to exclude Najdorf from the tournament *(he was fourth in Groningen, defeating Botvinnik in line with a bet that he made)*, especially after Fine's withdrawal," Bronstein insisted. "Why didn't they invite Boleslavsky, who finished as a runner-up in two Soviet Championships in a row, in 1945 and 1947? *(For context: Smyslov shared 10th–11th and 3rd–4th places there.)* Of course it would have been more logical to hold an Interzonal tournament, and then, half a year or a full year later, a Candidates Tournament. I'm not saying that Boleslavsky, Najdorf or I would've won, but the results would have surely been different."

In spring 1948, Mikhail Botvinnik became the world champion. Unlike the "mere mortals", he was allowed to travel abroad with his wife and daughter. On the photo: with Vasily Valkov, the Soviet ambassador to The Netherlands, before the world championship tournament in The Hague.

Bogatyrchuk: "An example of FIDE's simplemindedness is the organization of the first tournament for the world championship. In this tournament, as it is known, three representatives of the USSR and two of other countries participated. Everybody but an extreme simpleton knows now very well that chess in the USSR is subordinated to politics and all the chess masters are no more than pawns in the hands of the Communist propaganda machine. According to this fact FIDE had a right to assume that in such an important political (from the point of view of Soviet propaganda) event as the world championship a sort of team work may exist among Soviet chess masters. **And if in a tournament of five players a team of three good masters would act together, then no Capablanca, Alekhine or Lasker would have the slightest chance of becoming champion** *(emphasis by me – S.V.).* I looked through all the games of this tournament, and some of the games of Soviet masters between themselves astonished me with their lack of ideas.

In particular, Keres, against Botvinnik, did not demonstrate any of his skill. The same Keres played with Euwe and Reshevsky in his old manner with striking geniality. Of course, this fact may be explained by Botvinnik's superiority, but I know the play of both and I am far from being sure of this superiority. The play of Smyslov with Botvinnik was also not as impressive as it was sometimes in the games with other masters.

Being aware of methods of Soviet propaganda I have no doubt that this weak play is rather the result of proper instruction than playing supremacy of Botvinnik. Other tournaments with the participation of Soviet masters permit to suspect the same teamwork. It is quite natural. Sporting achievement may only be based on skill, genius and experience when it is free from all influences, and especially from the pressure of politics, which, in Stalin's words, 'have the sole aim of benefit of one's state, and this

Autograph on the reverse side: "USSR chess master D. I. Bronstein before going to Stockholm to play in his first international tournament. Moscow, 12th July 1948." From D. Bronstein's archive. Published for the first time.

aim justifies the means.'" (*Canadian Chess Chat*, No. 12, 1950, edited version.)

Fyodor Parfenyevich had tried to open Western society's eyes to the true state of affairs in Soviet chess in 1949, in his letter to *CHESS* – the most influential chess magazine of the time (see also the chapter "Chess of the Red Propaganda" in the second volume of *Dr. Zhivago of Soviet Chess[3]*).

Speaking of Boleslavsky, I remember David Ionovich saying bitterly, "Isaak never complained to me: he also realized that he had certain weaknesses in the eyes of Botvinnik, and perhaps the whole of society, too..." The hint is too transparent to fail to understand. Back then, the campaign against "rootless cosmopolitans" had started.

The myth of the dangers of cosmopolitanism had been actively promoted in society since the second half of 1947. The wheels of the Cold War had started turning, siege mentality was rampant in the country, and the newspapers

---

[3]   The full bibliography and championship tables are included at the end of the book. (S.V.)

created a new image of an enemy, "reactionary American imperialism" that "made cosmopolitanism its ideological banner". Of course, common Soviet people didn't know who "cosmopolitans" were, but they were handed an explanation: cosmopolitans are all those eggheads and Jews who don't like the Russian people, don't value our achievements and engage in "sycophancy before the West". In one word, anti-patriots. And then it started...

In January 1948, upon Stalin's personal order, the famous actor and film director Solomon Mikhoels was secretly killed (hit by a truck), and then the Jewish Anti-Fascist Committee, which he chaired, was destroyed. The arrests started in December of that year. Professor Solomon Lozovsky, the former head of the Soviet Information Bureau, was one of those arrested. "On the way back from the courtroom, when the 70 year-old Lozovsky was stretchered out to the 'black raven' *(a prisoner transport vehicle)*, the captain caught up with them, grabbed the defendant by the beard and, shaking a fist which was bigger than Lozovsky's face before his nose, said, 'Hey, Solomon, you damn Jew. If you say again one thing to me and another to the judges, if you again turn the whole process in the wrong direction, I'll disembowel you, strangle you with your own guts, and there'll be enough to hang your

The top five players of the Tournament of Slavic Countries: Mikhail Botvinnik, Alexander Kotov, Vyacheslav Ragozin, Vasily Smyslov and Isaac Boleslavsky. Thankfully, the pogroms against "rootless cosmopolitans" hadn't reached the chess world... From the author's archive.

children who still walk free. Do you understand? Stop getting on my nerves, I'm getting tired of fighting you.'" (This testimony of a sergeant who carried Lozovsky was quoted in an article by the well-known historian and philosopher Dmitry Volkogonov.)

Life came full circle: the country that had defeated Nazism turned towards Nazism itself (see the epigraph; a similar thought was later expressed by writer Vladimir Tendryakov: "It's been long known that the winners imitate their defeated enemies."). In the same year, cybernetics was declared a pseudoscience, and the "people's academician" Lysenko, with Stalin's approval, damned "Weismannism – Morganism – Mendelism" in biology. There were also ideas of attacking

When Viktor Korchnoi was issued his first passport at the age of 16, he asked to list his nationality as Jewish. Photo by M. Volkovysky. From Y. Neishtadt's archive.

"Einsteinism" in physics, but Kurchatov managed to explain to Beria that if they renounce the theory of relativity and quantum mechanics, they wouldn't be able to create atomic bombs...

Thankfully, chess players weren't targeted during the pogrom of the "rootless cosmopolitans". However, the rushed and illogical organization of the "M. I. Chigorin Chess Memorial Tournament of Slavic Countries" – honoring the 40th anniversary of his death(?) – was quite symptomatic. Why wasn't chess struck by the wave of state antisemitism? It probably got an exception because of impressive successes in the international arena: the world championship was won by Botvinnik, a Jew, and two other Jewish players, Bronstein and Boleslavsky, won the Interzonal. If, say, Reshevsky had become world champion, and the Stockholm tournament had been won by Najdorf, then the Sports Committee might have received a memo that there were "too many Jews" in Soviet chess (and the Sports Committee would have taken the memo to heart: in April 1948, state security Colonel-General Arkady Apollonov was appointed chairman).

But on the everyday level, ethnicity-based troubles were, of course, unavoidable. Here are two very telling accounts.

Korchnoi: "At the age of 16 *(in 1947)*, I was due to receive my first passport *(the Soviet ID document, not a travel passport)*. I went to the building's superintendent. In the fifth column of the passport, I had to state my ethnicity. I thought that since my mother was Jewish, I was clearly 50% Jewish as well; the other percentage, from my father's side, was less convincing. And so, I asked the superintendent to write that I was Jewish. When I came home, my Jewish stepmother made a huge scene, screamed at me that I was a fool, ran to the building's superintendent and convinced him to write that I was Russian in my passport." (From the book *Chess Without Mercy*.)

Averbakh: "In 1949, when antisemitism was rampant in the country, I was due to travel abroad for the first time, to take part in the Moscow – Budapest match. The Sports Committee personnel department gave me a large questionnaire, in which I had to describe my background and that of my closest relatives going back three generations. The official, his surname was Pavlov as I recall, looked through my answers and asked, 'May I ask you confidentially: why do you state that your ethnicity is Jewish?'

I explained that in the first passport, issued back in school, it was written: 'Father is Jewish, mother is Russian'. But then, when I came of age and had to change my passport, I was told that I couldn't do that, and I had to specify one ethnicity. Ethnicity was never an issue for me – I was brought up as an internationalist, both at home and in school – and so I said, 'I'll take my father's ethnicity.'

'But your mother is Russian!' Pavlov exclaimed. 'Do you want advice from an old, seasoned man? Change your ethnicity immediately. The law allows you to choose.'

When I came home, I told my parents about this conversation. My mother supported the idea of changing my ethnicity. My father said nothing, but it seemed to me that he was upset.

Soon I went to the militia precinct with an application. The chief, a big-faced colonel, read it and grinned.

'Why do all the Jews suddenly want to become Russian?'

'Am I doing something illegal?' I asked in return.

'No, no, it's all right!' he said quickly, writing down his resolution..." (From the original Russian version of the book *Centre-Stage and Behind the Scenes*.)

When I was writing an article on the matter, I asked Yuri Lvovich whether antisemitism was felt in the chess milieu. He answered, "In chess, the fight against cosmopolitanism wasn't as harsh as in other areas of culture. Perhaps it was because chess, unlike literature or music, where much depends on personal taste, has strict criteria: he who is stronger wins, and you can't argue against points in the table. Still, there was antisemitism in chess as well. For instance, Kotov, even though our relationship was very good, reproached me after the championship for defeating him and losing to both his main competitors – Bronstein and Furman. He didn't say it directly, but there was a certain ethnic subtext in his words."

The Secret Weapon

Before the war, there were no medals in our sport. The winners were usually awarded diplomas, tokens, letters or "valuable prizes" such as clocks, radios, bicycles, busts of the rulers, etc. But after the war, when the Soviet Union joined a number of international sports organizations, including FIDE (in 1947, after pointedly ignoring it for a quarter of a century), the situation changed. Now, Soviet sport had to be the best in the world, demonstrating the advantages of the Soviet way of life. In summer 1947, a resolution was adopted that was called "clear evidence of the great care for the development of Soviet physical education and sport on the part of the party, government and Comrade Stalin personally" by *Shakhmaty v SSSR*. Among other items, the resolution stated: "With the purpose of rewarding the successes of Soviet sportspeople, the USSR Council of Ministers decrees to establish gold and silver (gilded) medals and silver and bronze tokens... In chess, the winner of the men's Soviet Championship will be awarded

ЗОЛОТАЯ МЕДАЛЬ
ЧЕМПИОНА СССР

Лицевая сторона

ЖЕТОНЫ ЗА 2-е и 3-е МЕСТА НА
ПЕРВЕНСТВЕ СССР
(Натуральная величина)

Since 1948, the winners of the Soviet chess championship were awarded gold medals and (for 2nd and 3rd places) silver and bronze tokens. In addition, special stipends were established for the best players. From the Shakhmaty v SSSR magazine (No. 8, 1947).

a **gold medal**, and the winner of the women's Soviet Championship will receive a silver medal..."

Let's put aside the "metallic discrimination" of women (especially since, according to Kira Zvorykina, the championship medal she won in 1951 was actually gold) and discuss the matters that the press stayed silent about. It turns out that the resolution contained a "hidden component".

> **Averbakh:** "There was also a secret resolution (which, of course, wasn't published in the press) concerning the funding of sport. The best sportspeople received **special stipends** *(emphasis by me – S.V.)* that allowed them to fully dedicate themselves to sport, without worrying about how to earn a living. The decision on state funding of sport led, of course, to great progress, even though, strictly speaking, it was contrary to the position of the International Olympic Committee that considered sport an amateur endeavor. That's why only amateurs could compete at the Olympic Games... But, as we all know, you can't hide a cat in the bag, and our sportspeople had already got the nickname 'state amateurs' by the time of the 1952 Helsinki Olympics!" (From the books *What the Pieces Don't Mention* and *A Chess Player's Life in the System.*)

Yuri Lvovich recalled that grandmasters received a stipend of 2,000 rubles (3,000 for a world champion), and masters got 1,200 rubles. Was that a big sum? Judge for yourselves: the average engineer's salary was 1,400 rubles, and starting wages were just 800... However, not all masters received a stipend – only the best and most promising. In addition, the stipend could be reduced or fully revoked for poor performance.

Berger's Surprises

Even though grandmasters were exempt from qualifying, the semi-final battles were even more intense than in the previous championship. Small wonder: now, only the top three players from each of the Moscow and Leningrad semis qualified instead of five, and just two qualified from the Sverdlovsk event. Ilya Kan warned on the magazine pages: "Now we have 11 grandmasters, and this number will only grow in the future. If we personally invite all of them straight to the final, the semi-final qualifying system, which increasingly resembles a lottery, may become totally useless."

The brutal fight among 38 masters and 7 candidate masters was no walk in the park for the seasoned veterans: Kan, Dubinin, Chekhover, Sokolsky, Mikenas, Goldberg, Veresov, Kasparyan, Ravinsky, Chistiakov, and Ufimtsev all failed to qualify. And all three semi-finals were won by young masters!

Candidate Master Ratmir Kholmov qualified for the final from the Moscow group. From R. Kholmov's archive.

Yudovich: "The fate of the **Moscow semi-final** was decided long before the end. After a modest start (1.5/3), Averbakh won six games in a row, which left him almost unreachable: 1. Averbakh – 11.5/15; 2. Panov – 10; 3–4. Konstantinopolsky, Kholmov – 9 *(both qualified for the final because their Berger coefficients – a rare occurrence – were absolutely equal as well)*; 5. Petrosian – 8.5; 6. Ravinsky – 8; 7–9. Kan, Kasparyan, Simagin – 7.5; 10. Veresov – 7; 11–12. Kamyshov, Podolny – 6.5; 13–14. Zagoriansky, Liublinsky – 6; 15. Fridstein – 5; 16. Abramov – 4.5.

In addition to great theoretical preparation, Averbakh showed exceptional skills both in maneuvering positional play and sharp attacks. We think that the young master's main shortcoming is his tendency to play only familiar development set-ups. When faced with an unexpected position, his play weakens..."

By the admission of **Averbakh** himself, his playing style and overall attitude to chess were hugely influenced by Vladimir Alatortsev:

"In 1940, I was a member of the Zenit society. The society sent me and Misha Bonch-Osmolovsky, a candidate master back then, as apprentices to Master V. A. Alatortsev, who was also a member of Zenit. We started training sessions with him. No chess player ever impressed me as much as Alatortsev

ХОЛМОВ

От турнира до турнира
Крепнут силы у Ратмира.
На пути твоем, Холмов,
Нет ни кочек, ни холмов.

Дружеский шарж
Н. ЛИСА.
Текст
Мих. ПУСТЫНИНА.

KHOLMOV

From tournament to tournament
Ratmir grows stronger and stronger.
On your way, Kholmov,
There are no hummocks or hills.
[The surname Kholmov literally means "of
the hills".]

ПЕТРОСЯН

Силен и смел. Играет славно.
Быть мастером — его удел.
А ведь еще совсем недавно
На школьной парте он сидел!

Дружеский шарж
Н. ЛИСА.
Текст
Мих. ПУСТЫНИНА.

PETROSIAN

Strong and bold. Plays nicely.
His fate is to become a master.
Even though just a short while ago
He was still sitting at the school desk![4]

Ratmir Kholmov qualified for the final, while Tigran Petrosian would only make his debut the following year. Cartoons by N. Lis. Poetry by Mikh. Pustynin. From the semi-final bulletin (21st October 1947).

did during these sessions. All young players – I was 18 at the time – usually show their tactical skills first and foremost. I was no exception. And suddenly, we got deeply immersed in the games played by Alatortsev based on a single strategic plan, where everything flowed very logically... This revolutionized

---

[4]   As in previous volumes of this work, the original rhymed. This is also the case for all other verses mentioned in the present volume.

my understanding of chess. I saw that the greatness of chess was in the strategy, in positional play.

This meeting played an exceptional role in my development as a chess player, I completely revised my understanding of chess thanks to Vladimir Alexeevich." (From the book *Two Lives of Grandmaster Alatortsev*.)

Among each other, chess players called Alatortsev "The Strategist". Petrosian signed a photo for him: "To the Old Strategist from the Young Petrosian. 26.07.1952. Moscow". Spassky held the same opinion: "Alatortsev was a good strategist. We learnt from his games." And here's a confession from another world champion, Smyslov: "His advice, experience and depth of understanding of the position greatly helped me to improve my style."

Kholmov's success is quite remarkable. We have a good system in place that allows young players to develop: all-Union first-category tournaments and candidate master tournaments have turned into a true school of mastery. Ratmir Kholmov completed this school and played as well as any renowned master in the semi-final. He's still behind in opening subtleties, but wins because of his inventive ideas and the strength of his imagination.

Tigran Petrosian also scored enough points for a master's norm. He still needs a lot of work to prove his master's level. First of all, he has to play more boldly..." (*Three Tournaments. Semi-Finals of the 16th Soviet Championship* bulletin, 14th November 1947.)

Alatortsev: "The struggle in the **Leningrad semi-final** was intense from the very beginning. You couldn't predict the winner until the very end, there were seven players in the group of leaders... Ultimately, Aronin (11/15), Taimanov (10.5) and Lisitsin (9.5), whose Berger coefficient was better than Bronstein's, qualified for the final. Other participants: 5–6. Vasiliev, Zagorovsky – 9; 7. Chekhover – 8; 8–9. Zhukhovitsky, Sokolsky – 7.5; 10–11. Kopylov, Mikenas – 6.5; 12–13. Batuev, Kuzminykh – 6; 14. Goldberg – 4.5; 15–16. Kirillov, Klaman – 4.

Master Aronin played very strongly during the whole tournament, winning nine games. He's grown both as a practical player and theoretician in the last year.

Mark Taimanov from Leningrad qualified for the final for the very first time. At 21 years old, he's the youngest semi-final participant. Taimanov is a pupil of Botvinnik and Sokolsky. He was the only one to finish the tournament without losing. We can expect more successes from him...

The numerous fans of Bronstein's chess talent wanted him to win the competition. He played very well in the first half of the tournament, showing his high class. At the end, the future grandmaster faltered." (Ibid.)

In the Leningrad semi-final, luck smiled on the youngest participant, Mark Taimanov. From D. Bronstein's archive.

Taimanov: "I think that there are now elements of tenacity and patience in my play, which I often lacked in previous competitions. The game against Kopylov is very telling in this regard. In a position that cried out for an attack, I preferred a sober transposition into a 'boring' but better endgame, which I managed to win." (*16th Soviet Championship. Leningrad Semi-Final* bulletin, October 1947.)

Bronstein: "Had I not won the Stockholm Interzonal, I wouldn't have played in that Soviet Championship final, because I didn't perform particularly well in the semi-final... But when I was awarded the grandmaster's title after winning the Interzonal, the federation managed to find me a place in the final." (From the book *The Sorcerer's Apprentice*.)

Bonch-Osmolovsky: "And so, the struggle in the **Sverdlovsk semi-final** is over: 1. Furman – 9.5/12; 2–3. Ilivitsky, Novotelnov – 8.5; 4. Chistiakov – 8; 5–6. Geller, Saigin – 7; 7. Shamaev – 6; 8. Ufimtsev – 5.5; 9. Dubinin – 5; 10. Koblencs – 4; 11. Rovner – 3.5; 12. Vistaneckis – 3; 13. Grechkin – 2.5.

Master Semyon Furman achieved great success. A positional player, he knows openings very well and calculates lines far ahead and subtly. He really played better than everyone else...

МАСТЕР
В. ЧЕХОВЕР

Талант его бесспорен,
Наш мастер — феномен!

Он в музыке — Чигорин,
А в шахматах — Шопен!..

Дружеский шарж В. ГАЛЬБА,
текст А. МОДЕЛЯ

MASTER V. CHEKHOVER
His talent is doubtless.
Our master is a phenomenon!
He's the Chigorin of music
And the Chopin of chess!..

A famous epigram. However, Vitaly Chekhover never got to play in a Soviet championship final again. Cartoon by V. Galba. Poetry by A. Model. From the Leningrad semi-final bulletin (November 1947).

The performance of Sverdlovsk candidate master Georgy Ilivitsky was a pleasant surprise. He's tenacious in defense, and his endgame play is very good. I hope the young master attains a wider outlook on chess.

The *(1947)* Russian SFSR champion Nikolai Novotelnov prepared well for the tournament. He's an inventive player who's equally good at all stages of the game *(but he didn't take part in the final due to his worse Berger score)*. Master Chistiakov, who hasn't been playing in tournaments lately, managed to show the best sides of his creativity in the semi-final. He was the tournament's leader in interesting ideas...

Candidate Master Efim Geller is an attacking player with good tactical skills, but a lack of experience showed up in some of his games. Instead of a simple path to a win, he sometimes chooses more complicated and risky ones." (Ibid.)

The prizewinner of the Sverdlovsk semi-final, Russian SFSR champion Georgy Ilivitsky. From the book Georgy Ilivitsky's Chess Odyssey.

Without Botvinnik and Smyslov

From the press: "The 16th Soviet Championship, starting today, is the new great stepping stone in the further development and growth of the Soviet chess art. The tournament will conclude the year-and-a-half period that has passed since the previous championship.

> **Levenfish:** "Several important competitions were played in these months: a training tournament in Parnu *(1. Keres, 2. Kotov, 3. Lilienthal, 4–6. Boleslavsky, Bronstein, Smyslov)*, the USSR – England match, the Chigorin Memorial *(1. Botvinnik, 2. Ragozin, 3–4. Boleslavsky, Smyslov, 5. Kotov, 6–7. Keres, Novotelnov)*, the world championship match tournament, the Stockholm tournament... Most of the participants of the 16th championship either played in those competitions or worked as coaches there, gaining deep theoretical preparation in the process."

The line-up of the tournament is very interesting. In addition to the Soviet champion P. Keres, the Soviet chess veteran G. Levenfish who's playing in his eleventh national championship *(according to M. Beilin, he was the only grandmaster who didn't get a stipend: "As the guys said, because he was too clever"),* and world-famous grandmasters D. Bronstein, A. Kotov, A. Lilienthal, I. Bondarevsky, S. Flohr and V. Ragozin, there's a big group of young talented chess players who have earned the right to compete for the Soviet Championship for the first time. It consists of the 22 year-old Leningrad champion M. Taimanov, Russian SFSR champion G. Ilivitsky, Y. Averbakh from Moscow, S. Furman from Leningrad and R. Kholmov, who took part in the Chigorin Memorial; L. Aronin, who already played in the previous championship, should be placed in this group as well. The middle generation of masters is represented by the seasoned tournament fighters V. Alatortsev, A. Konstantinopolsky, G. Lisitsin, V. Panov and A. Tolush." (*16th Soviet Chess Championship* bulletin, 11th November 1948.)

Keres: "Unfortunately, not all the strongest players are taking part in the Soviet Championship this time. I mean the world champion Botvinnik first and foremost, and also grandmasters Smyslov and Boleslavsky, who couldn't play. But still, I think that the tournament will be interesting, and the struggle intense.

The participation of young players and old, experienced masters Alatortsev and Tolush makes the championship even more interesting. Alatortsev worked as Smyslov's coach at the world championship, and Tolush worked with me *(for this reason they were given places in the tournament without needing to take part in the semis; but in this case, why didn't they still include Novotelnov, to make an even number of 20 competitors?).* Both masters of course gained a lot during these training sessions.

I personally have rested well after the world championship match tournament and am ready for the chess battles." (Ibid.)

The Anti-Draw Revolt

The championship bulletin, with a press run of 25,000 copies (according to *CHESS* magazine), wasn't much better than the previous one, with the exception of one innovation that was probably well-received by the readers: each round review was written by a different author. Such a diverse palette of names and opinions! Half of the reviews were written by participants themselves: Levenfish, Flohr, Ragozin, Lisitsin, Panov, Furman, Aronin, Taimanov, and Kholmov... We shall see whether this idea took hold in the subsequent championships.

The role of "spectator B. Sergeyev" from the Leningrad bulletin was assumed by Boris Galich. His *Izvestia* colleague, writer Dmitry Mamleyev, remembered Galich as a "newspaper ace". Boris Drozdov also praised him in his book *Gone with the Vodka (On Russian Writers' Drunkenness)*: "When I worked for *Izvestia*, I was friends with Boris Galich, Evgeny Kriger, Yuri Feofanov – they were renowned, well-known journalists back then. They

К ОТКРЫТИЮ ЗИМНЕГО ШАХМАТНОГО СЕЗОНА

Сильна спортивная сноровка
И колоритен сбор фигур!
Сегодня — только тренировка,
А завтра — первый зимний тур!

Пылают взоры возбужденно,
И стар, и млад — все нынче тут!

Открытья зимнего сезона
Все шахматисты жадно ждут.

Каких они добьются взлетов?
Кто более и смел и скор?
БРОНШТЕЙН, ЛИСИЦЫН или
                          КОТОВ?
РАГОЗИН, КЕРЕС или ФЛОР?

Мы с интересом наблюдаем
Парад на шахматном катке
И от души им пожелаем —
Не поскользнуться на… доске!

Мих. Пустынин.

Дружеский шарж Н. ЛИСА.

TO THE OPENING OF THE WINTER CHESS SEASON

The sporting skills are great,
And the collection of pieces is colorful!
Today is just practice,
And the first winter round is due tomorrow!
The gazes are burning excitedly,
The old and the young – everyone is here!
The opening of the winter season
Is eagerly awaited by the chess players.

What heights will they reach?
Who's the boldest and quickest of all?
Bronstein, Lisitsin or Kotov?
Ragozin, Keres or Flohr?
We're watching with great interest
The parade on the chess rink,
And we wish them with all our hearts:
Not to slip up… on the board!

Many will indeed bruise themselves on this slippery ice. But how did the artist predict the winners so perfectly? Kotov and Bronstein, the future co-champions, stand at the front, holding hands! Cartoon by N. Lis. Poetry by Mikh. Pustynin. From the tournament bulletin (11th November 1948).

drank a lot, but they always knew when to stop." By the way, according to Drozdov, Galich's real last name was Galachyants.

All in all, Galich did very well; the only thing that somewhat lacked in comparison with his "predecessor" was humor. But compared with the sickly articles in *Shakhmaty v SSSR* (there's literally nothing quotable here!), Galich's reports are a true oasis of the living word. His "anti-draw revolt", supported by Peter Romanovsky, got under the players' skin so well that the overall draw percentage in this championship (45) was even smaller than in the previous one (49).

B. Galich: "They say that first impressions are indelible. I don't know. I haven't noticed that yet. The air of the cozy hall of the Central Railway Workers House of Culture (TsDKZh) is rather chilly, and you can't blame only the stokers and management. The temperature in the hall that hosts the All-Union chess championship is determined by the intensity of the struggle. Heated fights warm the souls of fans and make the chess weather great at any time of year. Whereas,

Before the battle. Chief arbiter Nikolai Zubarev is in the umpire's tower. Cartoon by N. Lis. From the Ogonyok magazine (No. 48, 1948).

by contrast, dry draws turn the chess climate arid. And when they are agreed upon on move 19, the spectators are left with cold disappointment.

Millions of fans are waiting for the days that will determine the best chess player in the country. No international tournament abroad can boast of such a mighty line-up. Just remember Stockholm this summer. The Swedish capital welcomed the top 20 players of the world. Who didn't take part? Only Botvinnik, the world champion, Smyslov, the world's second-strongest player, Keres, Reshevsky and Euwe. Everyone else was present.

And what did we see? After the tournament, some grown-up men ran to the International Chess Federation like little kids run to their mom: 'They beat us like children!' But you can't do anything about the tournament table: it shows the true balance of strength. Out of seven players representing the Soviet Union, six finished in the winning group *(1. Bronstein, 3. Boleslavsky, 4. Kotov, 5. Lilienthal, 6–9. Bondarevsky, Flohr, 14. Ragozin).*

Now we see the winners of the Stockholm tournament, led by Bronstein, on the TsDKZh stage. Bronstein looks more mature now. This year, he became one success older, and this success would be the highlight of any strong player's CV. The promising master didn't fail to meet expectations. Now we want to see how the world's youngest grandmaster is playing.

In the first round, he sits at the table against the oldest holder of the highest title. It's interesting, what will they show us? While the young Bronstein has grown up, we can happily say that our veteran Levenfish doesn't let his age stop him: he took part in the first All-Russian Olympiad back in 1920, and he's now playing in the 16th Soviet Championship in 1948. He rightfully gets the first move: Grigory Yakovlevich moves his king's pawn forward – e2-e4, and we recognize the old tournament fighter – he likes to fight openly *(these opponents had already met twice at the board: in the semi-final of the 15th championship Bronstein, playing white, had preferred d2-d4, and he had won both games)*. Bronstein seems to accept the challenge – e7-e5. Then the cavalry gets into the fight – all four knights have joined the fray. Great! What's to come next? Next came... nothing. The 'opponents' peacefully exchanged queens on move 9. Then they make another dozen moves, trade some more pieces and, with the same calm as they felt at the start, get up from the table and shake hands.

Why did this happen? Where's that indelible impression? OK, let's not be so impatient. We shall see what happens next. Moscow chess fans know very well those exciting, captivating minutes when it seems that a wave sweeps the hall, getting higher and higher: there's a sharp battle on the board, knights and pawns pile up, and the spirit of the fight hovers over the heads of the warlords who lean close over their chess armies. There are heated debates

The youngest and the oldest grandmasters, David Bronstein and Grigory Levenfish, were drawn to face each other in the very first round. From D. Bronstein's archive.

in the lobby, with chessmen flashing over the board, and the most avid fans play 'fantastic' combinations on the demonstration boards.

> Modern young fans probably don't even know what a pocket chess set is. Now, if you want to analyze a position, you always have a smartphone on hand. But back then, any chess fan worth their salt wanted to get a pocket chess set – either in a cheap calico folder or a more sturdy leather one. I don't know what pocket chess sets the fans possessed at that championship, but a leather goods factory made 1,000 elegant chess sets for the 19th championship, which were sold in the Column Hall: "Pictures were embossed on the front side: the Spasskaya Tower of the Kremlin, the Moscow State University skyscraper, the Bolshoi Theater and other Moscow landmarks. Inside the folder, on a small, 12x12 cm piece of leather, there are 64 squares of the chess board. There are slits between the squares. Chess pieces made of celluloid are inserted into those slits. Small pockets for pieces are at the sides." (*19th Soviet Chess Championship* bulletin, 28th November 1951.)

We love our grandmasters and masters very much. But as of now, they are rather stingy with such exciting moments. In the second round, Lisitsin agrees to a draw with Taimanov after 20 moves, while in the third round, Bondarevsky drew with Tolush in 21 moves. But even these 'records' were surpassed by Konstantinopolsky and Bronstein. They quickly make 19 moves and declare peace...

Why did this happen? I ask again. Perhaps the newly anointed grandmaster is playing too many 'grandmaster draws'? I feel for Bronstein. I feel for us, fans of his chess talent, as well. He has got older and more solid – that's good, but why is he so dry and calm?.." (Tournament bulletin, 18th November.)

Romanovsky: "An incredible tournament! Everything is unusual, from the line-up to its peculiar course, which has already raised questions from dozens of perplexed Moscow spectators. Botvinnik, Smyslov and Boleslavsky aren't taking part in the tournament – those great chess fighters and artists who always set the spirit of the tournaments where they played. And now, watching the events of the first eight rounds, the spectators probably remembered the glorious names of the Soviet Union's best chess players and regretted their absence many times. Had they taken part, some players wouldn't have had such an easy time building endless fences of coveted half-points.

The First Draw. The same game through the eyes of a cartoonist. Zubarev is at the bottom. (Sovietsky Sport, 13th November 1948).

Goldberg: "Many regret the fact that Botvinnik isn't playing in this championship. Such regret is quite reasonable, but, on the other hand, the competitive tension is much higher without the world champion – it's completely unclear who's going to win the tournament." (Ibid., 27th November.)

By the way, the tournament schedule was rather sparing, if you didn't accumulate a lot of adjourned games of course: two rounds, then a play-off day, two more rounds and a play-off day, and then a rest day. All the conditions for great creative achievements!

One of the most unusual aspects of the tournament is the fact that the tone for this compromising, drawish approach has been set by none other than Keres *(he started the tournament with five draws, repeating Bronstein and Levenfish's "achievement" from the previous year)*. We can't say that the Soviet champion plays all those games with an intention to draw. In most games, Keres even managed to get an initiative, but, alas, nothing came of it. In the game against Kholmov, he constantly pressurized his inexperienced opponent, and he did it by all the rules. The game with Averbakh was similar. But in the former, Keres blundered a simple stalemate *(see game 198)*, while in the latter he transitioned to a drawn knight endgame...

Flohr: "Master Tolush cheerfully sits down at the table and tells his opponent, Soviet champion Keres, 'Here in this hall, I first played you 10 years ago. We have played four games since then, I always had white...'

However, judging by the results of those games, it's not that big an advantage to have white against Keres – Tolush lost all four games.

'You have white today as well, why don't you continue the trend?' Keres jokes.

His ex-second showed little 'respect' to his formidable opponent in the Queen's Indian and launched a kingside attack. However, Keres managed to close the position and trade off the major pieces, and a draw was agreed afterwards.

'The first draw! It seems that I did learn something from you during the world championship match tournament, Paul,' the happy Tolush says." (Ibid., 14th November.)

Bondarevsky's start is unusual: seven draws! But in this case, we again can't say that the grandmaster intended to get such a result. In several games, he played with subtlety, determination and a will to win. But he did all that without taking risks, always having a failsafe plan on hand.

Борода
гроссмейстера
Бондаревского.
Дружеский
шарж
Н. ЛИСА.

Caption to N. Lis' cartoon: "Grandmaster Bondarevsky's Beard". Seven draws in a row were obviously too much and it was time to shave! From the tournament bulletin (25th November 1948).

The third player possessed by the drawing spirit is, without a doubt, Flohr. However, he assumed that role years ago, and so his six draws out of seven games surprised exactly nobody.

We, together with the spectators, resolutely disapprove of this cascade of half-points; the famous Russian chess player Chigorin was always a sworn enemy of draws...

There were a lot of unusual happenings, you can't list them all! Let's just mention that Kotov retained his leadership despite losing two games in a row *(to Tolush – see game 196 – and Averbakh)*, while Ragozin and Lilienthal, whose strong chess always drew praise from their numerous fans, started the tournament rather modestly.

It's good that there were also many common phenomena and events, characteristic of any Soviet competition *(what a turn of phrase!)*, and they, thankfully, allow us to project a rosy future for the championship. The first and foremost of those common phenomena is Levenfish's fresh, creatively deep play. His great wins against Lilienthal and Tolush are reminiscent of the best achievements of his younger days. Kotov's five wins in a row also aren't unusual – each win is better than the previous one; his creative credo contrasts sharply with the attempts to create a 'kingdom of draws' in the championship.

Panov: "The very style of Kotov's wins deserves praise. Many of our grandmasters and masters tend to overestimate the role of chess logic compared with chess imagination. They don't think – they calculate; they don't try to win as much as they try to avoid mistakes. Kotov, however, is playing in the true sense of the word: his games may be risky and not mistake-free, but creative and interesting as well.

ЛИХА БЕДА НАЧАЛО

Гроссмейстер А. Котов выиграл в первых четырех турах все четыре партии.

Он на турнирах лидер не впервые,
Его ходы незыблемо тверды, —

И видят шахматисты молодые,
Что «старый конь не портит борозды»...

Стихи **В. ГРАНОВА** и Мих. **ПУСТЫНИНА**.
Дружеский шарж Н. ЛИСА.

A GOOD BEGINNING IS HALF THE BATTLE

Grandmaster A. Kotov won all four games out of the first four.
It's not the first time he leads a tournament,
His moves are unshakably firm,
And the young chess player can see
That the old horse doesn't ruin the furrow...

Alexander Kotov had such a big lead (5/5!) that he still kept his first place even after two losses. Cartoon by N. Lis. Poetry by V. Granov and Mikh. Pustynin. From the tournament bulletin (25th November 1948).

Levenfish makes the same fundamental mistake as Keres. They are both great masters of combination and know theory very well. And this knowledge of theory, as strange as it may sound, can sometimes be detrimental. The grandmasters follow the latest trends in chess science that demand 'equalizing the position', but because of that, they lose their opportunities to create complicated situations that can fully and clearly show the individuality of their chess talent." (Ibid., 18th November.)

Still, many players also got fed up with this drawing spirit. For what it's worth, Konstantinopolsky won two games after five draws in a row, Bronstein started winning after three draws, several draws inspired Averbakh's winning streak, and it seems that sooner or later, every player will have at least one win under his belt...

Mark Taimanov, the youngest participant, is not playing particularly well yet: when it's your first time in such dangerous company, it's not that simple to find your bearings and select the correct battle strategy. Be bolder, Mark! That's what I want to recommend him.

> The desire to encourage the debutant is also seen in the jovial comments of **G. Goldberg:**
>
> "In a well-known theoretical position, Taimanov spent 1 hour 10 minutes on his 10th move. It's unlikely that he calculated everything until the very end of the game. But in such a long time, you could have recalled the entire history of the Nimzo-Indian Defense ..."

The games of Ilivitsky and Furman leave an impression of clever, well-planned play. Averbakh's play is good – you can't really find a word other than 'good' to describe it, but isn't it too cautious? Kholmov is inventive, and Aronin's games are subtle, if somewhat routine-like..." (Tournament bulletin, 25th November.)

Verlinsky: "I, an old master, am particularly pleased at the great and indubitable progress of the chess youth. Furman is playing especially well. He's already a full-fledged chess player. Ilivitsky's playing style is less pronounced, even though he has played some very good games already. Averbakh's performance is excellent as well.

I think that Kotov has the best winning chances. Flohr has never played as well as now in the last ten years. Ragozin's lack of success is unexpected – only recently, he was

Peter Romanovsky watching the debutant Averbakh's game. From D. Bronstein's archive. Published for the first time.

known as the 'scourge of grandmasters'. Keres is clearly playing below his level in the first half of the tournament." (Ibid., 30th November.)

Standings after round 7: Kotov – 5/7; Bronstein, Ilivitsky – 4/6; Aronin, Tolush, Furman – 4/7; Averbakh, Flohr – 3.5/6; Konstantinopolsky, Levenfish, Lisitsin – 3.5/7; Bondarevsky – 3/6; Alatortsev, Kholmov – 3/7; Keres, Panov – 2.5/6; Ragozin – 2.5/7; Lilienthal, Taimanov – 2/7.

An Ode to the Middlegame

B. Galich: "The tournament has entered the blessed middlegame. Now you have to do away with caution, whether you like it or not. Anticipating big time trouble, when it will be too late to 'catch up', those who have fallen behind now boldly give chase. And the leaders in particular mustn't slow down either: each game is now as valuable as each move in the middlegame, when, as we know, one tempo can decide much, if not everything!

The game between Bondarevsky and Kotov in round 10 is a brilliant illustration of that. It caused much anxiety for the spectators – and we can only imagine what the players themselves must have felt. When Kotov, whose ironclad calmness is remarkable, got up from the table, his cheeks were completely bloodless. He won, but this win took a toll. Still, the earned point was all the more precious and valuable for him: it helped him to reinforce his leadership. However, the game's fate was hanging by a thread. It's up to the specialists to determine what exactly happened: either Bondarevsky lost an important tempo in attack, or Kotov gained it with his inventive defense. For us, the most important thing is Kotov's psychological win. His incredible tenacity and ability to keep calm won again. It's a very important quality for a tournament fighter. Kotov didn't falter before the danger – and just like in the previous round, against Keres, he didn't get dazzled by success.

This was also a highly intensive game. At the start of the fifth hour, both players had less than half an hour left for 20 moves. Kotov was on the attack. He had the initiative. He needed to find ways to win. This is a pleasant situation to be in, but it requires time to think: which way to choose to achieve the goal with greatest certainty?

Time trouble was growing: Kotov's flag was hanging. Keres, however, had just a minute more. The spectators watched with bated breath. The demonstrator couldn't keep up with the game. The tension was incredible. And only one person seemed to remain completely calm – it was Kotov himself. He wasn't just making the moves – he carefully wrote them down. And only after the 40th time-control move, when the grandmaster got up and sighed in relief, could we see the value of that calmness. He walked around

David Bronstein's finishing spurt began after his win against Tolush in round 12. On the far right – the future master Mikhail Bonch-Osmolovsky. Flohr and Lisitsin are also standing. From D. Bronstein's archive.

the stage, holding back a smile: the game was won. And indeed, the Soviet champion resigned on the next move.

Yes, big days have come for the tournament. We complained about draws in the first rounds, but now chess fans face a different difficulty – there's too much to watch. It was a very combative week. The TsDKZh hall, filled to the brim, saw fierce battles. 'The clash of swords' of sharp chess thought got mixed with the dry thuds of pieces flying off the demonstration boards and the excited whispers of spectators who buzzed like a huge beehive.

What's especially pleasing now? The sharp fights in the middlegame. Of course, openings are openings and endgames are endgames. We pay our dues to both. But this is paying respect to the great theoretical knowledge that is required for the starting and ending stages of a chess game. Our hearts and souls, however, are attracted to the middlegame, we give it the most love: this is the element of creativity, the stormy flights of fantasy, the promised land of the true art where not everything can be calculated precisely, and unlimited possibilities open up before the chess player's talent. Here, conquering death by draws, the eternal tree of life, struggle, and evergreen combinations blooms. That's why the Moscow fans hurry to look at the middlegames, trying to go through the opening as quickly as possible and not

Championship leader Kotov and his coach Vladimir Simagin as spectators. From D. Bronstein's archive. Published for the first time.

The chess broadcast of Latest News began at 00.05. It was presented by the famous radio commentator Vadim Sinyavsky. Photo by M. Volkovysky from his archive. Published for the first time.

ИНТЕРЕСНАЯ ПАРТИЯ!

A poster from the late1940s titled "An interesting game". It portrays a typical Soviet family getting the chess news: Grandfather is tuning the radio, his daughter is noting down the adjourned position, and his pioneer grandson is analyzing after setting up the pieces.

willing to look into the misty distances of the endgame. Here, we are like fish in water, and even though sometimes we 'float' helplessly in our evaluation of the hidden possibilities of the position, we still immerse ourselves in the very depths of the passions and sincerely admire the denouement, when everything becomes clear, and the game is laid before us as a complete work of art.

The last rounds were rather prolific in that regard. They had everything that's needed, up to the beautiful, spectacular sacrifices that were generously offered by players and made the fans truly happy. It all began with a 'gift' from Levenfish, who sacrificed a queen to Lilienthal and won with several brilliant moves *(see game 195)*. In another game, master Alatortsev made an equally great sacrifice and destroyed Averbakh's position *(game 205)*...

There's a good old adage: 'He who wants to win the most, wins'. As long as your will is not crushed, not everything is lost. You can lose points – it's bad, but still fixable. But you cannot lose your belief in yourself – this drops your morale and can often be irreparable.

On the pages of this bulletin, Flohr complained that he forgot how to win. 'Am I growing old?' he asked perplexedly. I think that it was only a temporary loss of heart. 'Grow up until you're a hundred without growing old' *(a quote from Mayakovsky)*, dear grandmaster! Flohr himself proved my assumption with his great games against Furman *(see game 201)* and Levenfish." (Tournament bulletin, 30th November.)

Standings after round 14: Bronstein, Kotov, Furman – 9/13; Tolush – 8.5/14; Flohr – 7.5/13; Lisitsin – 7/13; Konstantinopolsky, Kholmov – 7/14; Averbakh, Bondarevsky, Ilivitsky – 6.5/13; Keres, Lilienthal – 6/13; Alatortsev, Levenfish – 6/14; Panov, Ragozin – 5/13; Aronin – 4.5/13; Taimanov – 4/13.

The Hot Breath of the Finale

Romanovsky: "As we predicted, the middle part of the tournament saw some fierce struggles. There are no players left who haven't won a single game, and no players who haven't lost, either.

В НОЛЬ ЧАСОВ 13 МИНУТ

— Тов. Синявский, умоляю — повторите ходы! Я не успел записать положения!.. Рис. А. ЗУБОВА.

The night radio report ended at 12:10 a.m. Caption to A. Zubov's cartoon: "At 12:13 a.m.: 'Comrade Sinyavsky, I beg you, please repeat the moves! I didn't have enough time to write down the position!..'" From the tournament bulletin (16th November 1948).

Flohr and Bronstein held out the longest. In round 14, when they shook hands after a draw, they were smiling happily and didn't suspect what awaited them the following day. In round 15, both Flohr and Bronstein lost heavily *(to Ragozin and Keres respectively – see game 200).*

Furman also lost in round 15, to Ilivitsky, while Kotov coolly accepted a piece sacrifice from Alatortsev and won a very important game – perhaps even more important than he realized. At any rate, after that lucky round, Kotov reinforced his leading position once again and pulled a full point ahead of his main competitors, Bronstein and Furman.

However, a disaster awaited Kotov in round 16. He had white against Konstantinopolsky,

ФИНИШ БЛИЗКО...

Дружеский шарж Н. ЛИСА.

"The finishing line is close..." After round 15, Kotov was a full point ahead of his main competitors, Bronstein and Furman. Cartoon by N. Lis. From the tournament bulletin (7th December 1948).

Мастер С. ФУРМАН
Дружеский шарж Н. ЛИСА.

Semyon Furman caught up with Kotov after round 17. Cartoon by N. Lis. From the tournament bulletin (30th November 1948).

underestimated his opponent's chances in the center in a King's Indian and had to give up an exchange after a counter-attack by black's e- and f-pawns. In a difficult and tense endgame, Kotov lost despite all his heroic resistance.

Bronstein made only a draw that day, but Furman won, and the intrigue escalated again in the championship: Lisitsin quietly crept up towards the leaders, on 9 points; Bronstein only had 9.5, and Furman and Kotov 10 (isn't that rather few after 15 games?).

All leaders have three games left; Lisitsin will have it especially hard – he's going to play against three grandmasters, Flohr, Keres and

Bondarevsky, and their intentions are unlikely to be peaceful *(Peter Arsenyevich was right: Lisitsin only scored another half point)*... Kotov will play Ilivitsky (a tough nut!), Panov (you can always expect an unpleasant surprise from him) and... Bronstein (in the last round). Bronstein will have to overcome Furman *(he did, and this game was one of the highlights of the whole tournament – see game 192)*, and the latter also faces Ragozin, who, by the way, handed out quite a beating to both Flohr and Keres.

In addition to the top four, Tolush, Konstantinopolsky, Flohr and Ilivitsky also have good chances. Kholmov has improved considerably and managed to reach a 50-percent score, but the grandmaster group – Bondarevsky, Lilienthal, Levenfish, Keres, and Ragozin – still can't emerge from the depths and at least equalize their chances with those of... the inspired representative of Lithuanian chess *(Kholmov played for Vilnius in the championship)*.

We should single out Levenfish

БРОНШТЕЙН

Играет сдержанно, без спешки,
В цейтнотах обвинить нельзя.
Следит, чтоб превратились пешки
По меньшей мере хоть... в ферзя!

His play is restrained, without hurry,
You can't accuse him of getting into time trouble.
He's watching his pawns to ensure their promotion
At the very least to a... queen!
Even in blitz, Bronstein never banged on the clock. Cartoon by N. Lis, poetry by Mikh. Pustynin. From the semi-final bulletin (31ˢᵗ October 1947).

from this group – not only because, as they like to say, he is a 'chess veteran', but because of his interesting, rich play in all games, regardless of the result. His brilliant wins against Kotov and Bondarevsky were admired by numerous fans, the true and best connoisseurs of the Soviet chess art. Of course, we can and should criticize some things in the famous grandmaster's play, but in such a tumultuous tournament, nobody, not even the leaders, is exempt from criticism.

Isn't it bad when such a young and talented player as Bronstein, who is only 24, already speaks with a note of skepticism? At this rate, he might soon say 'I'm already from the past'. Kotov's deep, interesting style is marred by the occasional strange hope that his opponent will make a mistake. Furman can be too naive at times, but still, he probably played more well-planned and attractive attacks than anyone else…

One of the characteristics of the finishing stage is every player feeling the urgent necessity to improve their results. Nobody, with maybe a couple of exceptions, is satisfied with their score.

Partially because of that, but mostly by default, the remaining three days will surely be filled with creative, sharp and rich struggle. These days will be the best in the whole tournament." (Tournament bulletin, 9th December.)

David Versus Goliath

B. Galich: "Round 19. The decision to go to the tournament hall was made when Vadim Sinyavsky said on the radio at 7 p.m. *(the games started at 5:30)* that Bronstein had sacrificed a pawn to Kotov on move 6. The sacrifice was declined, but Sinyavsky added that there was one of the sharpest Queen's Gambit lines on the board, and that the masters in the hall were predicting a fierce struggle.

I couldn't hesitate any more. Many predicted that the game would end with a peaceful grandmaster draw, but these predictions were dashed, which made everyone rather happy, especially the 'forecasters' themselves. It's better to make a wrong prediction than to deprive yourself of seeing a truly furious battle between these two chess titans.

It was quite hard to get into the TsDKZh hall. We felt like hopelessly blockaded passed pawns at the entrance, hearing the dozens of disappointed fans asking, 'Have you got a spare ticket?' Someone cried out, 'Call the Distinguished Master of Sports Peter Arsenyevich Romanovsky to see me!' Someone muttered almost unintelligibly, trying to convince everyone around and probably himself as well, 'My friend is late, but he will surely come. I called him, he's already on his way.' But, strange as it sounds, everyone knew quite well what was going on in the hall.

'Bronstein is pressing!' some would say.

'But why doesn't he play c5?' others asked.

'Don't worry,' still others replied. 'But don't forget about the black knight.'

In the lobby, waves of loud voices washed upon the demonstration board. After each new move relayed by the breathless demonstrator, someone would exclaim triumphantly, 'A-ha! Told you so!'

And an obligatory flurry of replies followed: skeptical ('We'll see'), ironic ('I see you're a grandmaster-strength player?'), polemic ('And now we're going to move a bishop in reply'), or approving ('And still, Kotov

Aronin versus Furman. Unlike the drawn game from the 15th championship (on the photo), this direct encounter decided the fate of the third prize. From D. Bronstein's archive. Published for the first time.

made the right move, he doesn't care about your bishop, his own bishop is strong.').

Hoping to see the strong bishops, we hurriedly push our way into the hall. It was permeated with the hot air of battle. I couldn't help but recall the first rounds, when the atmosphere was rather chilly. There were fewer spectators, the heating in the hall was maybe worse, and a lot of quiet draws made in the first rounds also cooled the mood.

But, as it turns out, it was just a sluggish opening. And this opening was followed by a fiery middle part, with explosion after explosion, pieces and pawns ascending and falling, crushing attacks destroying kings after cunning sacrifices. The ground under the players' legs shook, too; fate was raising them high and then throwing them into the abyss of defeat...

So, only two are left. Bronstein and Kotov. Kotov or Bronstein? Or, maybe, *both* Kotov and Bronstein?

Can you imagine the pandemonium in the hall? Furman made a draw with Aronin and guaranteed third place for himself. Flohr 'squeezed out' Kholmov and won fourth prize. Tolush confused Averbakh, won a spectacular game and finished fifth. But the main game, the game that determined the tournament winner, was still on.

The flag is hanging. The decisive game of the championship is watched by Alexander Tolush, Paul Keres and arbiter Peter Romanovsky. From D. Bronstein's archive. Published for the first time.

It was a fight to the death. Like his legendary namesake, David Bronstein tried to hit his mighty adversary with the c4 pawn, a shot from a sling. *When will he move it?* we all wondered. But the cautious David didn't hurry. He wanted to play with certainty, but black's position looked as solid as a rock. 'They shall not pass!' – this motto might have been written on Kotov's banner as he looked at Bronstein's menacing pawns that threatened to become queens.

And they didn't indeed pass! Kotov was a Goliath of tenacity and cold-bloodedness, and David couldn't topple him. For a moment, it seemed that everything would fall apart: in addition to the formidable white pieces, black's position was threatened by severe time trouble. The arbiter had already sat down at the table and was looking hypnotically at the clock, where Kotov's flag was hovering on the very edge of the thin minute hand.

And Kotov again showed his ironclad will. He made his time-control move literally at the last second, got up and steadily walked off the stage.

Nothing is certain yet. Bronstein is still thinking over his sealed move. But there's already applause in the hall: the fans have already assessed the outcome of the intense fight *(see game 206)*.

And they were right. The grandmasters agreed to a draw without resuming the game in the morning. But you can't call this game a 'grandmaster draw'. No, it was a draw of Soviet grandmasters, grandmasters of the USSR *(the author would have probably written "true Bolsheviks" as well if he could, but David was nonpartisan, and so hitting this high note was impossible)* who fight until the end, using the full strength of their talent, with an unyielding will to win.

We can say that white deserved to win the game, but black showed that he was undefeatable. A brilliant conclusion to the All-Union championship, which didn't give us a champion, but regaled us with many great games, and the future match between Kotov and Bronstein also looks quite promising in this regard." (Tournament bulletin, 17th December.)

The Tournament Through the Eyes of Champions

Final standings: 1–2. Bronstein, Kotov – 12/18; 3. Furman – 11; 4. Flohr – 10.5; 5. Tolush – 10; 6–9. Bondarevsky, Keres, Konstantinopolsky, Lisitsin – 9.5; 10–11. Ilivitsky, Lilienthal – 9; 12. Kholmov – 8.5; 13–15. Averbakh, Levenfish, Ragozin – 8; 16–17. Alatortsev, Panov – 7.5; 18–19. Aronin, Taimanov – 6.

Bronstein: "In the last two years, Soviet grandmasters have successfully defended the sporting honor of the USSR in international tournaments, but

Moscow, 14th December, the famous Central Railway Workers House of Culture where many chess competitions were held. The closing ceremony of the championship... First page of the tournament bulletin (No. 21, 1948).

have played relatively rarely in all-Union competitions. There were concerns that the playing level of our masters, who don't play against grandmasters on a regular basis, would decrease.

The 16th Soviet Championship dispelled any doubts. There are more than 50 masters in our country, and the best of them faced the top ten, the USSR national team, in the recently finished championship. The masters performed very well, and the grandmasters got hurt somewhat. The tournament showed that the overall playing level has increased dramatically, and the difference between the grandmasters and the best masters is now minimal. This pleasant phenomenon allows us to hope that the family of Soviet grandmasters will grow in the near future.

It's good to see that, in addition to the success of the youngsters – Furman, Kholmov, Ilivitsky, and Averbakh – such seasoned masters as Tolush and Lisitsin also finished among the leaders. As for my first teacher in the Kiev Young Pioneers Palace and my regular coach, Master Konstantinopolsky, I think that his result could surely have been better. His writing and coaching workload stopped him from being more consistent in the tournament.

> **Simagin:** "Konstantinopolsky achieved a paradoxical result: 6 points out of 8 against grandmasters and only 3.5 out of 10 against masters. He joked that there were too few grandmasters in the tournament. But what would have happened if there were candidate masters among the participants?" (Ibid., 11th December.)

The young Leningrad master Furman achieved the most significant success. He fought for a win in every game, not deterred by setbacks. If Furman continues to play like that, he'll achieve great things.

Grandmaster Kotov experienced the progress of the Soviet masters firsthand – they handed him some painful defeats. However, his great tenacity and self-control allowed him to finish the tournament successfully. The great start, of course, played a role too – five wins in a row!..

I started the tournament too quietly and peacefully. I only caught a fighting mood in the middle of the distance, and so I'm fully satisfied with sharing first place.

Now I'm starting to prepare for future competitions. First of all, I'm going to play an important match for the honorable title of Soviet champion with Kotov. Such matches usually consist of at least ten games. I foresee a serious struggle against a dangerous opponent, who is probably preparing for the match too." (Tournament bulletin, 21st December.)

> The match was announced in the press: "The Council of Ministers of the Soviet Union's Physical Education and Sports Committee has made a decision to hold a six-game play-off match between the winners of the 16th Soviet Championship. In case of a draw, Bronstein and Kotov shall play four more games. The first game is scheduled for 20th January." (*Vechernaya Moskva*, 4th January 1949.)

The top three – Semyon Furman, Alexander Kotov and David Bronstein – with their Sports Committee diplomas. Photo by G. Yablonovsky. From D. Bronstein's archive. Published for the first time.

But something went wrong. A week later, the newspaper reported that the Sports Committee had decided to hold a jubilee Russian SFSR championship in Moscow to commemorate the 50th anniversary of the first All-Russian Championship (1899) "won by the great Russian player M. I. Chigorin." Grandmasters Boleslavsky, Bondarevsky, Kotov (!), Ragozin and Smyslov and ten masters were invited to take part. Nenarokov, a participant of the first All-Russian Championship, was appointed chief arbiter. Special prizes were to be awarded by a jury headed by Botvinnik. "The tournament shall start on 10th February and continue for a month. The games will be played in the October Hall of the House of the Unions and in the TsDKA *(Central House of the Red Army)* Concert Hall."

And then what? The jubilee Russian SFSR championship was never mentioned again. Instead of it, an "ordinary" Russian SFSR championship started on 8th February in Yaroslavl, and on 2nd March, both co-champions traveled to Hungary, for a Moscow – Budapest match tournament...

Ultimately, the play-off match never took place. In Averbakh's opinion, Kotov might have been the one who initiated the cancellation – unlike Bronstein, he said nothing about the impending match. At the very least, if he did want to play, the match would have been played: Alexander Alexandrovich was quite chummy with the Sports Committee higher-ups, and they listened to his opinions...

Bronstein: "At first, they suggested that Kotov and I play a Soviet Championship match, but then decided to award us both gold medals. Furman received a bronze medal (*a bronze token, to be more precise*) and scored his first grandmaster norm." (From the book *Sorcerer's Apprentice*.)

Kotov: "David Bronstein's result served as confirmation of sorts of his recent brilliant victory at the Stockholm Interzonal tournament. The world's youngest grandmaster has scored a very good 'brace' this year.

Interestingly, he used the same means to achieve success both in Stockholm and Moscow. A modest start, which barely allowed him to reach the top 5, then a strong 'middlegame' and a tempestuous finish. In both tournaments, the final standings were decided by the

The first ever gold medal of the Soviet championships is on the lapel of Bronstein's jacket. From D. Bronstein's archive. Published for the first time.

results of the last two games. And Bronstein passed the final tests with flying colors. Such a gradual acceleration shows his will to win; youthful freshness plays a role here as well, of course.

The evolution of Bronstein's playing style over the course of just one year is staggering. Today's Bronstein is not just a fervent master of puzzling combinations, like in previous years. Bronstein is now a calm grandmaster with a big tendency towards positional, maneuvering struggle. He has got almost invincible: out of 37 games of the two most recent tournaments, Bronstein lost only one – to Keres. However, he's now making a lot of draws: he made 21 draws in Moscow and Stockholm, while even the 'world draw champion' Flohr made 'just' 28 of them in the same tournaments. It has become harder to defeat Bronstein, but wins also come harder to him now. He discovered the truth of tournament victories – 'lose as little as possible' – and holds fast to this truth.

Kholmov: "Of all the chess players of the past, Alekhine's play strikes me as the strongest. I use him as a benchmark to evaluate the players of the 16th Soviet Championship. I like Furman the most, and then some wins by Bronstein. The play of the young master and young grandmaster looked most similar to Alekhine's style to me." (Tournament bulletin, 7th December.)

The abundance of draws wasn't caused solely by the "evolution of playing style". Here's what Bronstein wrote in the notebook we've already encountered in the second volume of this work ("Chess Games of D. Bronstein. No. 1 – All-Union Championships") about the game with Kholmov: "I offered a draw when everyone thought that I had an advantage, even though my **prospects** were **worse in every line**. Mikenas was so angry with him... 'Lad, don't you realize that D. would never offer you a draw in a better position?!'"

Semyon Furman's third place is a sensation for the whole chess world. But it's not a random occurrence. On the contrary, only a random slip at the finish stopped him from taking an even higher place. Bold, imaginative play, precise calculation of even the most complicated lines, natural modesty – all that brought deserved glory to Furman. The practice of Soviet Championships has shown that such high ascents are never random. Such an achievement is only possible for someone who possesses great chess technique and has studied all the subtleties of chess art.

The impenetrable Salo Flohr: like Bronstein, he lost only one game. From Y. Averbakh's archive.

Ragozin: "Semyon Furman was born in 1922 *(actually, in 1920)*. He studied chess under one of the greatest Soviet masters and methodologists, Ilya Leontyevich Rabinovich, who possessed excellent positional skills. Recently, grandmaster Grigory Yakovlevich Levenfish, whose style is bold and original, became Furman's second teacher. Furman has become a worthy pupil to both teachers, managing to develop both his positional skills and love for combinations." (*Smena*, No. 3, 1949.)

Fourth place was taken by 'veteran of chess battles' Salo Flohr. It's a very good place, but I wouldn't dare to call it an 'achievement' for Flohr *(a stab at Ragozin, who wrote in his review "Flohr can list this fourth place in such a strong tournament among his best achievements")*. We still remember his unforgettable wins of old. I think that we'll still see the 'old' Flohr at the very top of chess... He remembers well how not to lose, but still hasn't quite recovered his old ability to win.

> The grandmaster confirmed the character description given to him in the Stockholm Interzonal bulletin: "Flohr's positional feeling is quite developed; even the strongest players have a hard time defeating him because he foresees the possible danger long before it actually materializes and steers the game in another direction. We should add intricate technique to that – he has almost no equals in that regard."

The Leningrad master Alexander Tolush will probably soon consider fifth place in the Soviet Championships his property – he has now taken it twice, in the 15th and 16th championships. Tolush's playing style is the same as it was ten years ago, but he's playing much better. The same confidence in better positions, leading to quick and easy crushing wins, and the same sluggishness in defense that often leads to inglorious defeats.

Defense is not a strong aspect of Tolush's personality, he doesn't like to defend, and he defends poorly. But attack is his element, he can explode into a series of dazzling combinations at any minute. Tolush's new success places him among the ranks of the Soviet Union's strongest masters. *(Illness stopped him from achieving even greater successes: Tolush scored just 3/8 at the finish!)*

The most unexpected outcome of the tournament is the Soviet champion Paul Keres' poor performance. I think that there are two reasons for that. The first one is internal discord in Keres' play: there's a struggle between his combinational desires of old and his tendency towards simple setups and waiting for his opponent to make mistakes, which are characteristic of his current style *(Kan, on the other hand, saw "underestimating the strength of masters – especially the young ones" as the main reason for Keres' failure).* Another reason is his distress after his unsuccessful performance in the world championship match tournament that was a lifelong dream for Keres. But the last few games in the championship, filled with freshness and energy, tell us that the spirit of the old Keres – a master of complicated combinational play – is still alive in the creative output of the talented Tallinn grandmaster.

> **Keres:** "There are periods in the life of every chess player when he plays either very well or rather mediocrely, and it's only natural. I think that the slump in my form started at the Chigorin Memorial tournament and then continued in other competitions. For instance, I just couldn't do anything properly at the 16th Soviet Championship. The bad luck started in the first round, when I overlooked an inventive stalemate combination against Kholmov... Only at the finish, mustering all my strength, did I manage to improve my position and play some good games. The game against Bronstein, without a doubt, was the most interesting..." (From the book *One Hundred Games.*)

Grandmaster Igor Bondarevsky is looking much like Keres. There's much less fighting spirit left in him than in previous years. Only when the going gets tough does he turn to his old weapons – pressure, attack, desire to win with any means necessary. But even a great finish couldn't fully compensate for a bad start – either in Stockholm or in Moscow.

> **Kan:** "Bondarevsky is probably going through a particular creative crisis, caused by his transition from tactical style to a positional one. That's why his results have been so inconsistent in recent years." (*Shakhmaty v SSSR*, No. 1, 1949.)

Мастер Л. Аронин.
Дружеский шарж Н. ЛИСА.

Lev Aronin's finest hour in the Soviet championships was still to come... Cartoon by N. Lis. From the tournament bulletin (7th December 1948).

Alexander Konstantinopolsky is one of our best theoreticians. This very strong master is dangerous to any chess player in the world. Only the lack of full concentration stops him from achieving the greatest heights.

Master Georgy Lisitsin has returned to form after several years of 'slumber'. He amazed everyone before the tournament by saying that he'd analyzed 3,000 games. Someone joked that this was enough only for 9.5 points in the Soviet Championship, and had Lisitsin analyzed a couple of thousand games more, he would have surely won it! Lisitsin's playing style is very well known, and I think that it hasn't changed much following his hiatus. He's a very solid and strong master who fights intensely for any half-point.

Grandmaster Andre Lilienthal's result is quite modest. I think this is a result of a haphazard regimen during the tournament *(a puzzling phrase that everyone is free to interpret according to their own... imagination)*. There is no other way to explain why his creative achievements alternated with upsetting failures. Nevertheless, despite everything, Lilienthal is still one of the strongest players in our country.

The Russian SFSR champion, Georgy Ilivitsky, showed that he is a mature master who has every right to challenge the strongest players in the world. Without a doubt, he has a bright chess future ahead of him.

Master Ratmir Kholmov has grown noticeably since the Chigorin Memorial. The influence of his experienced coach, Lithuanian master Mikenas, is clearly seen.

Мастер Г. ИЛИВИЦКИЙ
Дружеский шарж Н. ЛИСА.

Not many players managed to beat the debutant Georgy Ilivitsky from Sverdlovsk. Cartoon by N. Lis. From the tournament bulletin (30th November 1948).

Ragozin: "Georgy Ilivitsky started to study chess seriously in 1935, at the age of 15. There were no grandmasters or masters in Sverdlovsk at the time. He had to study theory on his own, without an experienced coach. In 1941, Ilivitsky earned 1st category. Soon afterwards, Boleslavsky moved to Sverdlovsk as a permanent resident. The alliance with one of the strongest Soviet grandmasters was fruitful: Ilivitsky won the master's title in 1947... Ilivitsky prefers quiet, maneuvering games, but, despite his relatively short experience, already possesses good technique.

Yuri Averbakh was essentially still an amateur at this point: he worked as an engineer in a research institute and was preparing to write his thesis. From Y. Averbakh's archive.

While a Komsomol member, Ratmir Kholmov learned to play chess in the Arkhangelsk Young Pioneers Palace, achieving his first successes there. During the Great Patriotic War, he went to sea as a sailor on a trading ship. In 1947, in his first Soviet Championship semi-final, Kholmov earned his master's title. He's only 23 years old... Kholmov's chess knowledge is not too great, but he possesses fine tenacity and fighting spirit." (*Smena*, No. 3, 1949.)

So much is hidden behind the words "went to sea as a sailor"! Ratmir Kholmov's childhood and youth are very similar to an adventure novel. Open the book *Dialogues with the Chess Nostradamus* and read the chapter "A Miracle" – it's one of Genna Sosonko's greatest and most poignant essays.

Grandmaster Vyacheslav Ragozin was, I think, overburdened with his coaching and public duties as a FIDE vice president. This clearly affected his performance both in Stockholm and this championship.

The Moscow master Yuri Averbakh simply didn't have enough drive to win even won games.

Ragozin: "A pupil of the Moscow Young Pioneers House, Yura Averbakh studied in a good school – even before becoming a master, he faced grandmasters in the capital city's championship. He's more of a player than a theoretician. His main strength is defending difficult positions, which says a lot about his strong will. Averbakh works as an engineer in a research institute. He performs a lot of mathematical calculations, and he feels great in positions that need precise calculations far ahead. Before the tournament, many thought that Averbakh would be the most dangerous opponent for the seasoned masters and grandmasters. These hopes weren't justified. Averbakh's lack of theoretical preparation showed. But Averbakh is objective. He won't stop at his achievements and will work to improve." (Ibid.)

Botvinnik: "Averbakh is one of the most talented young masters. In addition, he's constantly improving and growing creatively. The art of chess has reached a level so high today that a systematic, scientific approach is necessary to master it. I think that Averbakh's scientific studies only help him in his chess achievements." (*27th Moscow Chess Championship* bulletin, 22nd April 1949.)

The games of the country's oldest grandmaster, Grigory Levenfish, were fresh and very rich in content. However, physical strength often failed him, preventing him from achieving a better result.

Master Vasily Panov was clearly tired and faltered at the finish.

The failure of the talented master Vladimir Alatortsev is quite upsetting. Non-chess reasons *(another thinly-veiled hint)* prevent him from reaching higher places in the tournaments.

This national championship final was the last for Vasily Nikolaevich Panov. He tried to qualify through the semi-finals four more times, but to no avail.

Panov: "My poor performance in the 1948 Soviet Championship showed me that I couldn't juggle two jobs as effortlessly as in the past, I couldn't combine intensive journalism with successful chess performances..." (From the book *Forty Years at the Chessboard.*)

Chekhover: "Alatortsev and Tolush only recently worked as seconds at the world championship match tournament. However, while Tolush, judging by many of his games, took many useful lessons from his work with Keres, Alatortsev failed to do so at his training sessions with Smyslov." (Tournament bulletin, 11th December.)

Alatortsev's consistency was amazing: he scored exactly 7.5 points in three championships in a row (14th, 15th and 16th). As though he had made some promise.

Master Lev Aronin got confused when he needed self-control the most, while the talented Leningrad champion, Master Mark Taimanov, felt doomed from the start.

Some words about my own result. Previously, I tried to play in tournaments during intense industrial work and failed miserably. Thus, I had to be very careful in the postwar tournaments to justify and rehabilitate myself for past failures in the eyes of the chess world. I think I did manage that in a number of tournaments, including the Stockholm one, by consistently achieving good results.

Photo of Vladimir Simagin taken during the semi-final of the 15th Soviet Championship by M. Volkovsky from his archive. Published for the first time.

In the 16th Soviet Championship, I wanted to play more boldly, taking more risks and not fearing to lose, especially now that my friendship and training with the talented Moscow champion Vladimir Simagin has enriched my playing style with fresh ideas. At the start, I won five complicated and interesting games, but then made a tactical error. Instead of making a few draws and 'resting' before the finish, I continued to play for a win. Ultimately, I simply got tired, which explains my gross blunders against Levenfish, Konstantinopolsky and Panov. Still, I'm glad to have kept my leadership from the first round to the last.

There were many attacks on draws in our press. I, who suffered from a lack of them in this championship, now vote for the reasonable 'rest at a distance' – for timely, necessary draws." (Tournament bulletin, 21st December.)

The Heavy Burden of Choice

Why can't I be sure of anything anymore? Encouraged by the lists of best games at the previous championship, I was sure that the exhausting work of choosing the masterpieces (I can select the dramas myself) would henceforth be carried out by a competent jury. They'll sort everything out, explain their opinions, and I'd just have to listen to them... Oh, sweet dreams. What lists was I talking about? There wasn't a single brilliancy prize this time! Desperate, I leafed through the bulletin again, but only found B. Galich's lone voice crying out in the wilderness: "From our point of view, it's completely inexplicable why the All-Union Committee for Physical Education and Sport only established prizes for the greatest sporting achievements. How about for the beauty of the games, the depth of ideas, the innovations? The tournament regulations don't mention these qualities in any way. But wouldn't it be even more fitting for the very spirit of our Soviet chess art?"

Yes, of course it would have been. But why did he address the Sports Committee? In the 15th championship, one special prize was established by the Leningrad City Council, and two more by *Shakhmaty v SSSR*. What stopped the Moscow authorities and the magazine editorial board (headed by Comrade Ragozin) from doing the same? Even if they hadn't come up with the idea before the tournament, perhaps they would have done so during it? There were more than enough beautiful attacks, opening revelations and subtle endgames...

To cut a long story short, I had to spend quite some time just looking through the annotated games because of those slackers in high places. And I must say that between the tournament bulletin, magazine and the *Chess in 1947–1949* compilation book, there were a whole lot of them – 85, twice the amount of a year earlier. Strict selection stripped down this list to a bare minimum, but even that was too much. Ultimately, I had to cut it even more; I hope I haven't cut anything truly valuable from Soviet chess in the process.

Precursor to the Rubik's Cube

B. Vainstein: "Boleslavsky rightfully said that this game was the most complicated and puzzling of all in the 16th Soviet Championship. If there were some objective criteria for 'complicatedness', I think that it would have taken that prize among all the games of all the 16 championships, not only this one."

The game was played two rounds before the finish and decided which of the two opponents would continue the race for the title. Bronstein was half a point behind Kotov and Furman, and he had nothing to lose. Furman did have something to lose, and sometimes that makes players less bold...

Strangely enough, Bronstein only annotated the fateful game in the book *Sorcerer's Apprentice*. But, since he obviously based his annotations on Boleslavsky's analysis carried out half a century earlier, it would be more appropriate to use the original source.

No. 192. Nimzo-Indian Defense E51
Bronstein – Furman
Moscow 1948, round 17
Annotated by I. Boleslavsky
1.d4 ♘f6 2.c4 e6 3.♘c3 ♗b4 4.e3 d5 (*4...♘c6 – see game No. 251; 4...b6 – see game. No. 252*) **5.a3 ♗e7 6.♘f3 0-0 7.♗d3 b6 8.0-0 c5 9.b3 ♗b7 10.♗b2 ♘c6.** The game has transposed into a line of the Queen's Gambit, but with the white pawn on a3. This has its advantages and disadvantages: the black knight cannot get to b4, but the b3 square is somewhat weak, and the natural 11.♕e2 is met with 11...♘a5, attacking the b3 pawn.

11.♕c2 was worthy of consideration.

11.cxd5 exd5? A serious positional error. With the c- and d-pawns hanging, the knight's position on c6 becomes quite bad. The knight obstructs the way both for the a8 rook to protect the c5 pawn and the b7 bishop to protect the d5 pawn, and if the knight goes, say, to a5, then white will control the important e5 square. When the pawns are hanging, d7 is the best square for the knight – it protects both the c5 pawn and the e5 square from there.

Black, of course, had to play 11...♘xd5, and after 12.♘xd5 ♕xd5 13.♕c2 ♕h5, his position wouldn't have been much worse.

12.♘e2!

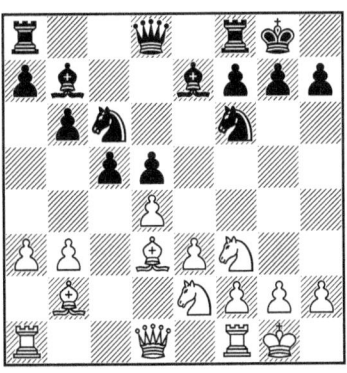

This subtle move strengthens the d4 square and threatens to transfer the knight to f5, which is rather unpleasant for black; it's hard for him to create counterplay. It seems that the best move was 12...a5, with a subsequent pawn sacrifice on a4; in this case, the c-pawn becomes passed, and there is some counterplay for black.

After the natural, but bad knight move, black's situation becomes even worse.

12...♘e4 13.dxc5 bxc5 14.♕c2 ♕b6 15.♘g3. *"If 15.♘f4 ♘a5 16.♘xd5 ♗xd5 17.♗xe4 ♗xe4 18.♕xe4, then black regains the pawn with 18...♖fe8." (Bronstein)*

15...f5 16.♘h5 ♖f7 17.♖ab1! Before exerting the decisive pressure on the d5 pawn, white deprives black of his last counterchance – the attack on the b3 pawn. Now, b3-b4 can even be a threat in some lines.

17...♖d8 18.♖fd1 ♖d6 19.♘f4 ♔h8? This prophylactic move is a tactical mistake. 19...a5 was worthy of consideration, preventing at least the b3-b4 threat.

This is bad because of the same reply 20.♗f1. It seems that the best chance was 19...♗f8!, freeing up the e7 square for the rook, for instance: 20.♗f1 ♕d8 21.♘e5 (the capture on d5 gains nothing) 21...♘xe5 22.♗xe5 ♖dd7 23.♗b5 ♖de7 etc.

20.♗f1 ♕d8. Loses a pawn, but black's position is already hopeless. 20...♘d8 was met with 21.b4 c4 22.♗e5 ♖d7 23.♗d4 and ♘e5.

21.♘xd5. 21.♖xd5 was even simpler – after two captures on d5, there was, of course, ♗c4.

21...♗h4. Black executes his only threat. It's very unlikely that he could exploit the weakening of the a8-h1 diagonal after the simple 22.g3, but white prefers another move that leads to simplifications by force.

22.♘xh4 ♕xh4 23.♘f4 ♖fd7 24.♘h3. This is obviously not the strongest move. Now black manages to create great complications.

Meanwhile, 24.♖xd6 ♖xd6 25.♘h3 won rather easily. For instance: 25...♖d2 26.♕c4 ♖xf2 27.♕f7 or 25...♖g6 26.♕c4, and after 26...♕xh3, there's 27.♕f7.

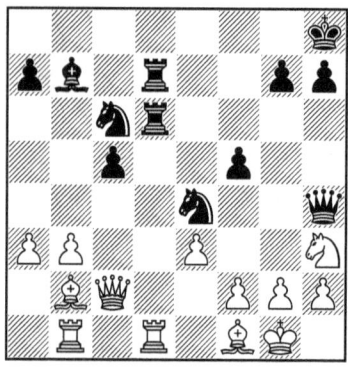

24...♘d2! 25.♕xf5. *"The queen is heading to c8, but 25.♕xc5 was stronger. In this case, the knight wouldn't be able to capture any piece, because the d6 rook would've been attacked twice. Meanwhile, white would now have a threat 26.♖xd2." (Bronstein)*

25...♘e7 26.♕f7! 26.♕f8+? ♘g8 27.♖bc1 is wrong, since after 27...♖g6, black's attack is unstoppable.

Instead of 27.♖bc1?, 27.♗c3 is stronger, but after 27...♘xf1! (27...♖g6? 28.♖xd2 ♖xd2 29.♗xd2 ♕xh3 30.g3) 28.♖xd6 (28.♗xf1? ♕xh3) 28...♕e4! 29.♘f4 ♕xb1 30.h3 ♘g3+, black has a perpetual check.

26...♕h6. *Neither the players nor the commentator noticed the reply 26...♕g4!, forcing an exchange sacrifice*

— 27.♖xd2 (otherwise ♘f3+) 27...♖xd2. If now 28.♘f4 ♘g8 29.♕f8 ♗e4! 30.f3 (30.♖e1 ♖d8! is unclear, but not 30...♖xb2? 31.♗c4), then black has a perpetual check again: 30...♗xf3 31.♗c3 ♖c2 32.♗c4! ♖xg2+ 33.♔f1 ♖g1+ etc.

27.f4! Since the black pieces are pinned into place (27...♘xb1? 28.♖xd6 ♖xd6 29.♕xe7 with an easy win), white obtains the important g5 square for his knight.

A mistake in return! The computer wants to sacrifice the queen for rook and bishop – 27.♗e5! ♘g8 28.♗xd6 ♖xf7 29.♖xd2 ♖f5 30.♖c1, with great compensation.

27...♘g8. *By exchanging queens with 27...♕g6!, black even seizes the initiative, for instance: 28.♕xg6 hxg6 29.♘f2 ♘xb1 30.♖xb1 ♖d2, and now it's white who has to be precise in defense.*

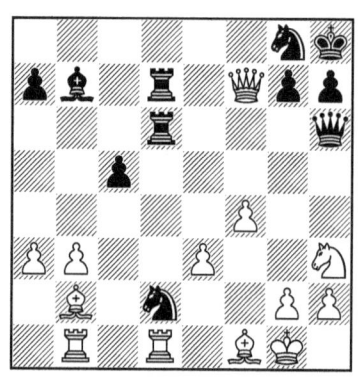

28.♕f8? This prosaic retreat misses the win, which, as the following lines prove, could be achieved after the tactical lunge 28.♘g5! For instance:

Boleslavsky called the Bronstein versus Furman game "the most complicated and puzzling of all in the 16th Soviet Championship". To the left is Flohr. From D. Bronstein's archive. Published for the first time.

1) 28...♘xb1 29.♖xd6 ♖xd6 30.♕xg7+ ♕xg7 31.♘f7#;

2) 28...♕xg5 29.♕xd7, and white wins;

3) 28...♗d5 29.♗xg7+ ♕xg7 30.♕xg7+ ♔xg7 31.♖xd2;

4) 28...♕g6 29.♕xg6 hxg6 30.♗e2 ♘h6 31.♗e5! ♖d5 32.e4 ♘xe4 33.♘xe4 ♖xd1+ 34.♖xd1 ♖xd1+ 35.♗xd1 ♗xe4 36.♗d6;

5) 28...♘xf1 29.♕xg7+! ♕xg7 30.♖xd6 ♘f6 (30...♕xb2 31.♖xb2 ♖xd6 32.♘f7+ ♔g7 33.♘xd6 ♗a6 34.♘e8+ ♔f7 35.♘c7 ♗d3 36.♖f2 ♘xe3 37.♖f3) 31.♗xf6 ♖xd6 32.♗xg7+ ♔xg7 33.♔xf1 with an easy win.

"We had less than two minutes for 13 moves. And so, I didn't dare to play 28.♘g5!, which required precise calculations. This is a rare case when I didn't listen to my intuition." (Bronstein)

28...♘xb1. The rook capture is much more dangerous for black than it seems. Considering the severe time trouble, it was more sensible to play 28...♘xf1, which, after 29.♖xd6 ♖xd6 30.♖xf1 ♖d2 31.♔f2 ♖d1+, led to a draw by repetition.

The subsequent moves until time control were made at lightning speed.

29.♖xd6 ♖xd6 (of course, not 29...♕xd6? 30.♗xg7+) **30.♘g5 ♗d5.** Not 30...♖d7 31.♘f7+! ♖xf7 32.♕xf7 with a double threat of ♕xb7 and ♗c4.

31.e4! *"Beginning a psychological attack." (Bronstein) There was a solid move 31.♗xg7+ ♕xg7 32.♕xd6 ♗xb3 33.♕xc5, with three pawns for a piece. But white can't afford a draw!*

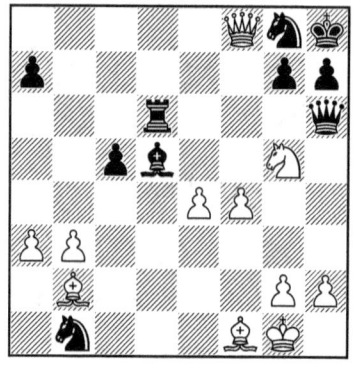

31...♗xb3? The very fact that this natural move loses proves how risky capturing the rook on move 28 was. *(You'll find the solution to this puzzle in the annotations to move 32.)*

Perhaps, if black had more time, he would have found the problem-like move 31...♖f6!, which drastically changes the course of the game. In this case, white can either capture the rook immediately, which after 32.♗xf6 gxf6 33.♕xh6 ♘xh6 34.exd5 fxg5 35.fxg5 ♘f7 leads to an endgame with good drawing chances for white, or play 32.♕b8, which looks very dangerous for black, since the d5 bishop has no good squares to retreat to.

However, the second problem-like move *(after 32.♕b8)*, 32...♘d2! (33.exd5? ♕xg5), forces white to capture the rook. After 33.♗xf6 gxf6

34.exd5 fxg5 35.♕e5+ ♕g7 36.d6 ♘f6 37.fxg5 ♘d7 38.♕e8+ ♕f8, there's a similar endgame with good drawing chances for white.

However, after 35...♕f6! 36.d6 gxf4, the second line is dangerous for white. Instead of 32.♕b8, 32.♕xc5! ♗xb3 33.♕e3! gives a clear draw.

32.e5 ♖d1. If black had a minute more, he would have probably played 32...♖d7. Even though after 33.♕f5 ♖e7 34.♕xb1 white had a better position, play wouldn't have been so forced.

White's risky tactic worked! As Vainstein demonstrated later,

after 33...♖d1! 34.e6 ♗xe6 35.♘xe6 ♘d2! black won. Thus, the move 31...♗xb3 deserves an exclamation mark, not a question mark!

33.e6! The pawn's march from e3 to e6 with constant threats is fascinating.

33...♗xe6   34.♘xe6   ♖d4. Desperation! After 34...♖d7, there's 35.♘xg7 ♖xg7 36.♗c4, winning.

35.♗xd4 cxd4 36.♘g5. Black lost on time.

"Syoma got unlucky – we weren't on friendly terms yet, and I played

quite aggressively. When he got his chances, he didn't take them. After the game, I wanted to invite him for dinner, but he walked like he was mesmerized, not really noticing anything, and I quietly moved away, spooked. It's actually one of my best intuitive achievements; when I played e3-e4, there was no time to think, I blitzed out every move until the end, and the public cried 'Encore!!' for the first and last time in my life, demanding that the demonstrator repeat the moves." (From Bronstein's notebook.)

Compare this with an entry from Botvinnik's "secret" notebook that contained short evaluations of Bronstein's games which he studied before their 1951 match:

"Furman played weakly, got a hanging center, and had 'Br' played 15.♞f4, it would've been hopeless for him. Then, he just shuffled around, harassing his opponent Reshevsky-style! And he got a clear win on move 21. Two weak moves by 'Br', and then trying to flag. A patzer-like rook sacrifice – had Furman played 32...♖d7, everything would've been clear, but he didn't and then lost on time in a hopeless position four moves later. Embarrassing. But what a game!" (From the book Botvinnik – Bronstein Match.*)*

So Was it a Study?

Flohr: "Kotov's position was critical. Both opponents were in time trouble by then. Aronin is considered a brilliant blitz player. But playing five-minute games in a chess club is one thing, and playing them in the Soviet Championship is very different. Kotov outplayed his opponent and has a better endgame before the adjournment. In the opinion of some players, Kotov should win. But Aronin claims that he doesn't see any loss yet."

No. 193
Aronin – Kotov
Moscow 1948, round 2
Annotated by A. Kotov

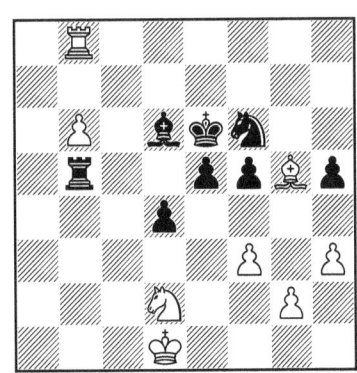

41.♖h8! The only chance. White lost after 41.♖b7 ♞d5 *(41...♞d7!, like in the game, is more precise)* 42.♞c4 ♝c5!

41...♞d7! It's necessary to keep the active knight. After 41...♞d5? 42.♞c4!, white's chances are no worse *(and after 42.♖h6+! ♚d7 43.♞c4, it's now black who should go for a draw!).*

42.♖xh5 ♚d5! Black's plan is simple: despite the material losses, he goes for an all-out attack.

43.g4! Best. White is trying to eliminate the dangerous black pawns by sacrificing a piece.

After 43.♗d8, black had a study-like win: 43...♘xb6 44.♗xb6 (44. ♖xf5 ♘c4! is even worse for white) 44...♖xb6 45.♖xf5 ♖b2! 46.f4 d3! 47.fxe5 ♗b4 48.e6+! ♔xe6 49.♖f2 ♔d5 (49...♗xd2 50.♖f3!, *but 49... ♖a2! 50.♔c1 ♗a3+ 51.♔b1 ♖b2+ 52.♔a1 ♖c2 is even more precise*) 50.♖f5+ ♔c6! (50...♔d4 51.♖f4+ ♔e5 52.♘c4+) 51.♖f6+ ♔b5 52.♖f5+ ♔a4 53.♖f2 ♗c3! *(53...♖a2! was the winning moove, as now white has a draw with 54.h4! ♗xd2 55.♖f3 and ♖xd3=)* 54.♖f4+ (54.♔c1 ♖c2+ 55.♔d1 ♖a2) 54...♔b5 55.♖f5+ ♔c6 56.♖f2 ♔d5 57.♖f5+ ♔d4 58.♖f4+ ♔e5! etc.

Alas, the machine coldly destroys all those study beauties.

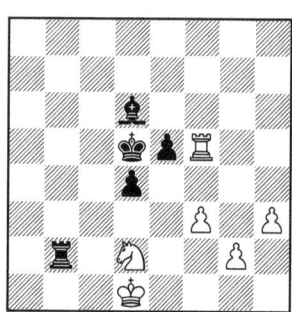

Instead of 46.f4?, white draws with 46.♖g5! For instance: 46...d3 47.♖g8! ♖a2 48.♖c8 or 46...♖a2 47.♖g8! ♗b4 48.♖d8+ ♔e6 49.♘c4! ♖xg2 50.♖e8+ ♔f6 51.♘xe5 d3 52.♘xd3 ♖d2+ 53.♔e1 ♖xd3+ 54.♔e2 etc.

43...e4 44.♗h6. After 44.gxf5,

there's 44...e3!

And after that 45.♗xe3? dxe3 46.f6+ ♘e5! is bad, but 45.♘e4! still holds.

44...e3 45.♖xf5+ ♘e5.

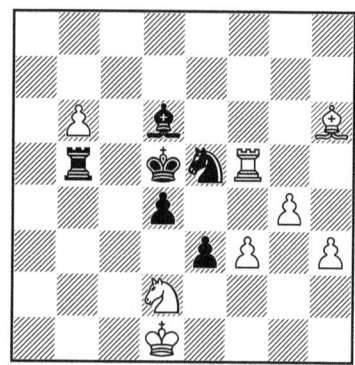

46.♗xe3! The only move. If 46.f4, then 46...♖b2!, winning.

46.♘e4! also gave some drawing chances. For instance: 46...♖b1+ 47.♔c2! e2 48.♗d2 e1=♕ 49.♗xe1 ♖xe1 50.b7 d3+ 51.♔b2 ♗c7 52.g5 etc.

46...dxe3 47.f4 ♖b2 48.♘f3 ♔e4! 49.fxe5 ♗a3!! Creating a discovered attack on the c1 square.

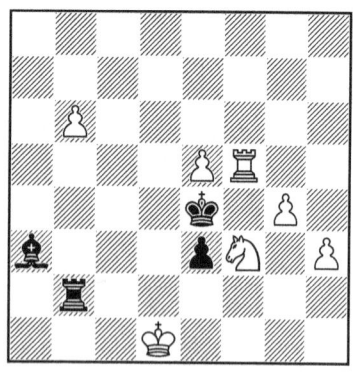

50.e6. Loses immediately. 50.b7

was more resilient. In this case, 50...e2+ 51.♔c1 ♖xb7+ 52.♔c2 ♖b2+ 53.♔c3 ♚e3 54.♘e1! ♝b4+! 55.♔xb2 ♝xe1 56.e6 ♝c3+ 57.♔xc3 e1=♕+ 58.♔c4 is quite unclear, with drawing chances for white, but 50... ♖xb7! 51.e6 ♖b1+ 52.♔c2 ♖c1+ 53.♔b3 ♝e7 gives black a decisive advantage.

The move 50.b7 isn't just "more resilient": it could have saved the game for white! The final position of the first line is indeed losing for him: after 58...♕d2 59.♔c5 ♚e4 60.♔c6 ♕d8 61.♖h5 ♕e7 62.♖h6 ♚e5 63.♖h5+ ♚xe6 64.♔b5 ♕c7, the queen stalemates the white king, forcing the rook to leave h5, and then captures both pawns.

Still, after 50...e2+, there's a way to draw:

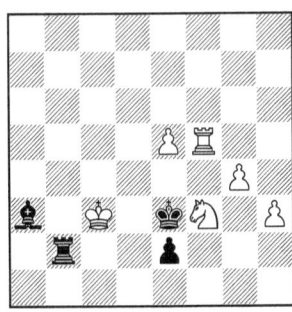

Position after 50.b7 e2+ 51.♔c1 ♖xb7+ 52.♔c2 ♖b2+ 53.♔c3 ♚e3

54.g5!! (instead of 54.♘e1?), for instance: 54...♖b1 55.g6 ♖f1 56.g7 ♖xf3 57.♖xf3+ ♚xf3 58.g8=♕ e1=♕+ 59.♔b3 etc.

In the second line, the draw is even

simpler:

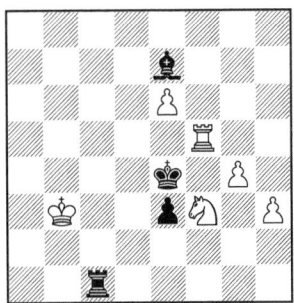

Position after 50.b7 ♖xb7! 51.e6 ♖b1+ 52.♔c2 ♖c1+ 53.♔b3 ♝e7

54.♔b2! ♖c6 55.h4 ♖xe6 56.h5 ♖f6 57.♖e5+! ♚xf3 58.♖xe7 e2 59.g5 or 54...♖h1 55.♔c2! ♖xh3 56.♘g5+ ♝xg5 57.♖xg5 etc.

50...e2+! 51.♔c1 (51.♔e1 ♚e3! 52.♘d2 ♖b1+! 53.♘xb1 ♝b4+, mating) **51...♖b5+ 52.♔d2 ♖xf5 53.gxf5 ♚xf3 54.b7 ♝b4+!** The last subtlety! Pushing the king away from the e1 square.

55.♔c2 ♝d6. White resigned.

A Novelty
Uncorked After Two Years

Panov: "The game Lilienthal – Kotov was the highlight of the fourth round. The opponents chose a line of the Slav Defense *(in Russian there is no separate name for the Semi-Slav)* first introduced by Botvinnik. This system, intended for those who like double-edged, complicated play, was evaluated in white's favor. However, as Kotov told the gloomy Lilienthal after the game, smiling happily, he had developed his radical improvement for black about two years earlier."

No. 194. Semi-Slav Defense D44
Lilienthal – Kotov
Moscow 1948, round 4
Annotated by A. Kotov
1.d4 d5 2.c4 e6 3.♘c3 c6 4.♘f3 ♘f6 5.♗g5 *(5.cxd5 – see game 208)* **5...dxc4 6.e4 b5 7.e5 h6 8.♗h4 g5 9.♘xg5** *(9.exf6 – see game 239)*

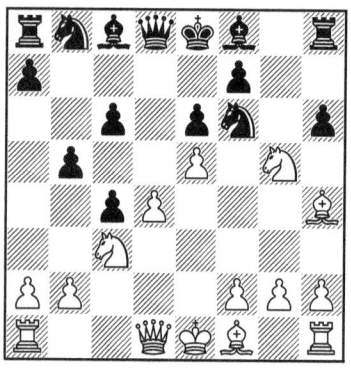

9...hxg5. The line 9...♘d5 10.♘xf7 ♕xh4 11.♘xh8 *(see game 112 in volume 2),* used by Ragozin (black) against Smyslov and Lilienthal in the previous Soviet Championship, didn't pay off.

10.♗xg5 ♘bd7 11.g3. Lilienthal played that move against Botvinnik in the game that introduced it to tournament practice (in the 13th Soviet Championship). There followed: 11...♗b7 12.♗g2 ♕a5 13.exf6 0-0-0 14.♕f3 ♘b6, and black ultimately won. Subsequently, in the 1946 Moscow championship, Lilienthal played 11.exf6 ♗b7 12.♗e2 *(12.g3! is now considered*

Alexander Kotov led the championship from start to finish. From A. Kotov's archive. Published for the first time.

the best move) 12...♕a5 13.0-0 0-0-0 14.♕c2 ♕c7 15.f4 against me, but unsuccessfully as well.

Now he's going back to his old continuation – he probably found an improvement in his home analysis.

11...♗b7 12.♗g2 ♕b6. This move was never played in high-level tournaments before. Black is preparing to open up the center immediately.

13.exf6 c5 *(13...0-0-0 14.0-0 c5 is more precise, and if 15.dxc5, then 15...♘xc5=)* **14.dxc5!** The best! The tempting 14.d5 is bad because of 14...0-0-0.

It's not that bad for white: 15.0-0 b4 16.♘a4 is the current main line.

14...♗xc5 15.0-0 0-0-0!

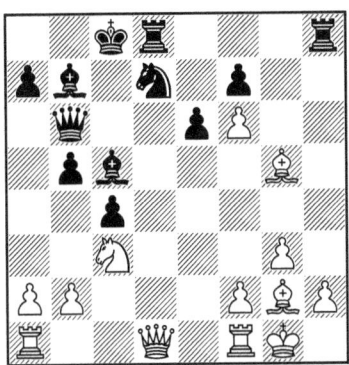

A paradoxical position. Black has sacrificed a pawn, his castle position is weak, but it soon becomes clear that he has good counterchances in the center and on the queenside.

16.♕e2 ♗d4! Black's whole strategy is based on this maneuver. The knight is preparing to jump to d3.

That said, despite the exclamation marks for black's moves, white still has the advantage.

17.♖ad1. 17.a4 was worthy of consideration. There could follow 17...♗xc3 18.bxc3 ♗xg2 19.♔xg2 ♕c6+ 20.♔g1 *(20.f3!?)* 20...bxa4 and ♘b6 with a complicated game.

It's necessary to play 17...♗xg2 first, because 17...♗xc3? is bad due to 18.♗xb7+! ♕xb7 19.bxc3, and black is losing.

17...♘c5. 17...♘e5 18.♖xd4 ♕xd4 19.♘xb5 was worse: white has sacrificed an exchange, but has gained a strong attack.

17...♗xg2! 18.♔xg2 ♘c5 was necessary.

18.♗xb7+ ♕xb7 19.♖xd4. The correct decision! Otherwise, black

could bolster the d4 bishop's position with e6-e5.

19...♖xd4.

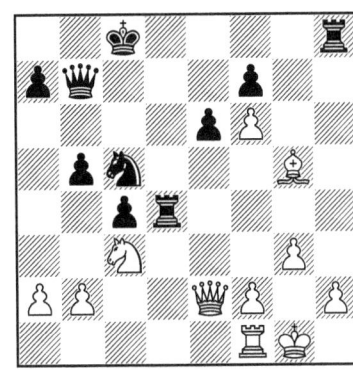

20.♕e5? This is a mistake. The correct move is 20.♗e3! ♖e4 (20...e5 21.♗xd4 exd4 22.♕e5! is bad) 21.♘xe4 ♕xe4 22.♕d2 *(22.b3! ♘d3 23.♕c2 is clearly better for white)* 22...♘d3 23.f3 ♕c6 24.b3 with double-edged play. Now black seizes the initiative.

20...♖d5 21.♘xd5 ♕xd5 22.♖e1. In case of 22.♕xd5, the endgame is better for black, for instance: 22...exd5 23.♗e3 ♘d3 24.♗d4 ♔d7. He has an active knight and, what's more important, an active king, while it's hard for white to convert his kingside pawn advantage.

22...♕c6! (threatening ♘d3) **23.♕e3** *(23.♖d1! ♘d3 24.♕e2 is somewhat better)* **23...♘d3 24.♖b1 ♖d8 25.h4?** The decisive mistake *(actually, it isn't – see the note to move 27).*

White should have played 25.f3 ♔b7 26.♕e4, and even though

black has an advantage after 26...
♖d5, white could still put up a good
fight. 26...♛xe4 27.fxe4 ♖d4 was
also possible, regaining the pawn and
getting a good endgame.

25...♞xb2! (capturing the most
important pawn with impunity)
26.♛xa7 ♞d3.

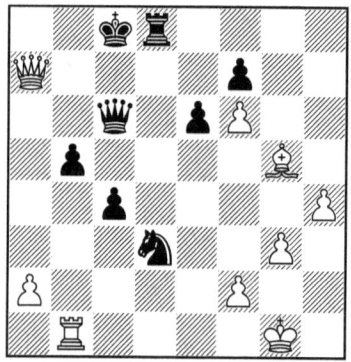

27.♖d1? Loses immediately.
White couldn't play 27.♛xf7 ♞e5!
28.♛e7 (threatening ♛xd8+) 28...
♞f3+ 29.♔f1 ♞xg5 30.hxg5 ♛h1+
31.♔e2 ♛e4+ etc.

*But instead of 28.♛e7?, white
can save the game with 28.♛h7!!,
controlling the e4 and c2 squares.
Black has nothing better than
a perpetual check: 28...♞f3+
29.♔f1 c3 (it's bad to capture on
g5) 30.f7 ♞d4 31.♔g1 ♞f3+ or
30...c2 31.♗xd8 ♞h2+ (both 31...
cxb1=♛+? and 31...c1=♛+? are
bad).*

27.♛e3 was best, even though
black should still win by pushing the
c-pawn *(for instance: 27...c3 28.♖d1
c2 29.♖xd3 c1=♛+ 30.♛xc1 ♛xc1+
31.♗xc1 ♖xd3 etc.).*

27...♖d7! Lilienthal probably
missed this move. Now, if the queen
retreats, black immediately wins
with 28...♞f4!!, threatening to mate
on d1 or g2. White resigned.

If You're Going to Sacrifice,
Sacrifice the Queen!

Goldberg: "Levenfish's play was
explosive, just like in the old days.
The spectators warmly greeted the
first, but very elegant win of the
oldest grandmaster. It's probably the
best game of the first five rounds."

No. 195. Grunfeld Defense D70
Levenfish – Lilienthal
Moscow 1948, round 5
Annotated by G. Levenfish
**1.c4 ♞f6 2.d4 g6 3.♞c3 d5 4.cxd5
♞xd5 5.e4 ♞b6.** The continuation
5...♞xc3 6.bxc3 c5 7.♗e3 ♗g7
8.♗c4 leads, in my opinion, to a
difficult position for black. *Later,
Grigory Yakovlevich admitted that 5...
♞xc3 6.bxc3 c5 was "preferable" (see
games 196 and 209).*
6.♞f3 ♗g7

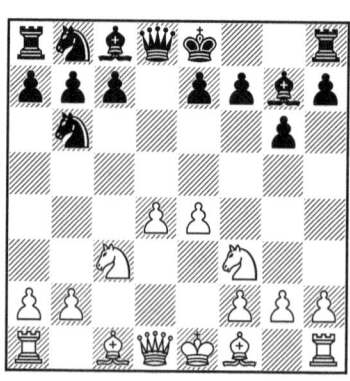

Spectators applauded the beautiful win by Grigory Levenfish, the elder of Soviet chess, against Lilienthal. From the author's archive.

7.h3. Preventing 7...♗g4, which would have immediately made black's position easier.

At the previous championship, the same opponents played 7.♗e2 0-0 8.♗e3 ♗g4 9.♕d2 ♘c6 10.♖d1 ♗xf3 11.♗xf3 ♘c4 12.♕e2 ♘xe3 13.fxe3 e5=.

7...0-0 8.♗e3 ♘c6. A bad maneuver. 8...♗e6 and ♗c4 was better, intending to weaken the light squares in the opponent's camp (and if 9.d5, then 9...♗d7 and c7-c6).

9.♗e2 e5. In the Grunfeld Defense, c7-c5 is the liberating move, while after e7-e5, black's position always gets quite cramped.

10.d5 ♘b8 11.a4 a5 12.0-0 ♘a6 13.♕b3 ♘d7. Black intends to play ♘dc5, b7-b6 and ♕e7, getting a

solid defensive position. This should be prevented.

14.♗xa6! bxa6. After 14...♖xa6 15.♖ac1 and ♘b5 black would have been cramped, but now he gets some counterplay along the b-file.

15.♖fd1 ♖b8 16.♕a2 ♘b6 17.♖ac1 ♖e8 18.♘b1. White is targeting the a5 pawn, so black has to force matters.

18...♗d7. 18...♗f8 is bad: 19.♗d2 ♗b4 20.♗xb4 axb4 21.a5 ♘d7 22.♕c4 ♖b5 23.♕xc7 ♕xc7 24.♖xc7 ♖xa5 25.♖dc1 etc.

19.♗g5! ♕c8. 19...f6 is met not with 20.d6+ ♗e6!, but rather 20.♗d2.

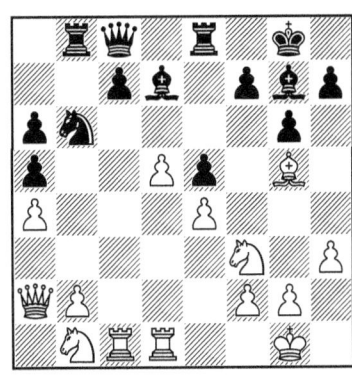

20.d6. *In the bulletin, Levenfish doesn't annotate this move, but in* Selected Games and Memories *he agreed with Panov:* "This hurry is completely unnecessary. 20.b3 ♗f8 *(20...♕b7!? 21.♕c2 ♖ec8)* 21.♗f6! ♗d6 22.♕d2 ♗b4 23.♕g5 won a pawn. Now, the game gets complicated.

20...c5 21.♗e3 ♗e6! 22.b3 ♘d7 23.♘bd2 ♕c6 24.♘c4! *"The immediate 24.♘g5! ♕xd6 25.♘c4 ♕c7 26.♘xe6 ♖xe6 27.♕d2 ♖e7*

28.♞xa5 was probably stronger" (*Panov*). *The computer agrees, but instead of the sluggish 27...♖e7, it offers 27...♞f6! with counter-threats.*

24...♕xe4. "After 24...♝xc4 25.♖xc4 ♖e6, there could follow 26.♕d2, and if 26...♖b6, then 27.♝xc5 ♞xc5 28.d7," *Levenfish writes in his book, missing the reply 26...♝f8! The immediate 26.♝xc5! ♞xc5 27.♕c2 ♖xd6 28.♖xd6 and ♖xc5 led to an advantage.*

25.♞g5   ♕c6   (25...♕a8!? 26.♞xe6   ♖xe6   27.♞xa5   ♝f8!) 26.♞xe6 ♖xe6 27.♞xa5 ♕b6.

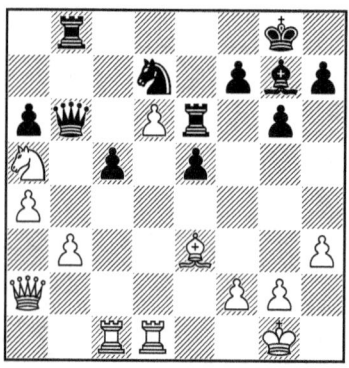

28.b4! The point of the combination planned by white on move 24.

28...♕xb4. Black goes for the main line of the combination. Still, even after 28...♖xd6 29.♖xd6 ♕xd6 30.bxc5 ♕c7 31.c6!, the c-pawn should win the game.

29.♞c6 ♕b3. This move saves the exchange, but not the game.

30.♞xb8!! White gets only a rook and a knight for the sacrificed queen, but the d-pawn becomes very strong.

30...♕xa2 31.♞xd7 ♖e8 32.♝g5! Threatening to give a deadly check on f6. There's no salvation.

32...♖a8 33.♞b6 ♖a7 34.d7 ♖xd7 35.♞xd7 h6 36.♞f6+ ♚f8 37.♖d8+ ♚e7 38.♖e8+ ♚d6 39.♞e4+. Black resigned: 39...♚d7 40.♖e7+ ♚c6 41.♖xc5+ ♚b6 42.a5+ etc.

The Leader Stumbles

Kotov's incredible start – 5/5! – caused quite a stir. He defeated Ragozin, Aronin, Lisitsin, Lilienthal and Kholmov. But he faltered in round 6. The loss to Tolush affected Kotov so much that he lost to Averbakh "mechanically" in the next round as well, giving the competitors some hope of catching up...

No. 196. Grunfeld Defense D87
Tolush – Kotov
Moscow 1948, round 6
Annotated by A. Tolush
1.d4 ♞f6 2.c4 g6 3.♞c3 d5 4.cxd5 ♞xd5 5.e4 ♞xc3 6.bxc3 c5 7.♝c4 ♝g7 (*7...cxd4 – see game 209*) **8.♞e2 0-0 9.0-0 ♞d7.** The defensive system chosen by black was introduced by Botvinnik.

"As it turned out after the game," G. *Lisitsin writes in the opening review* (Shakhmaty v SSSR, *No. 3, 1949*), *"Kotov didn't know about D. Rovner's system that made his chosen line dubious, and so he didn't see the impending danger."*

10.♝e3. *In the match against Botvinnik (1951), Bronstein deployed*

Photo of Tolush taken during the semi-final of the 15th Soviet Championship by M. Volkovysky from his archive. Published for the first time.

the move 10.♗g5!, shown by his coach Furman. This move was praised by the world champion: "Very good! White usually plays 10.♗e3, allowing black some counterplay."

10...♕c7 11.♕c1. An original maneuver of the Leningrad master Rovner. The purpose of this move is to protect the c4 bishop from the threat 11...cxd4, prepare the dark-squared bishop trade that will weaken the black king's position, and, finally, free up a square for the rook, which is rather important.

11...b6 12.♘f4 e6 13.d5. After 13.♗xe6, there could follow 13...cxd4!, but not 13...fxe6 14.♘xe6 ♕d6 15.♘xg7 ♔xg7 16.♗h6+ ♔g8 17.♗xf8 ♘xf8 18.♕e3, and white

has a rook and two pawns versus two minor pieces in a good position.

13...e5. After 13...♘e5, white would have played 14.♗e2 and c3-c4, creating a strong pawn center. If black plays 14...c4 himself, white will reply 15.♗d4 with an active position.

In the game Borisenko – Lilienthal (1950 Soviet Championship s/f), black equalized with 15...♖e8 16.dxe6 fxe6, and the move 11.♕c1 was mothballed afterwards.

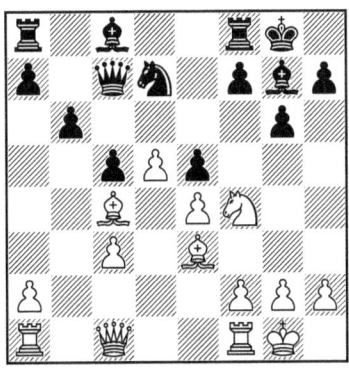

14.d6! 14.♘e6 fxe6 15.dxe6 ♘f6 16.e7+ ♖f7 achieved nothing.

14...♕b8? It was necessary to capture the pawn, like in the game Rovner – Tolush (1947 Leningrad championship). Even though white won that game, it would be interesting to test again if the pawn sacrifice is correct. I think that refusing to accept the sacrifice immediately was Kotov's decisive mistake.

15.♘d5 ♕xd6 16.♗g5. Here's the point. It turns out that black has only one reply now – to move the queen back.

Why only one? The computer

insists on 16...♗f6. *In any event, it's unlikely someone would try to test the "Kotov maneuver" in practice...*

16...♕b8 17.♖d1 ♔h8 18.♗e7. 18.♖d3 was probably even stronger, with 18...f6 losing to 19.♘e7!

Tolush shouldn't worry – the text move was the strongest one!

18...♖e8 (or 18...♖g8 19.♗b5) **19.♗b5 ♕b7.** After 19...a6, there was 20.♗c6 ♖a7 21.♖b1 b5 22.a4, and black has nothing to move.

20.♖b1   a6   21.♗xd7   ♕xd7 22.♗f6! Winning an exchange after 22.♘xb6 ♕xe7 23.♘xa8 was too small an achievement due to the opponent having the bishop pair, whereas the game move wins very quickly.

22...♖b8 23.♕h6 ♖g8.

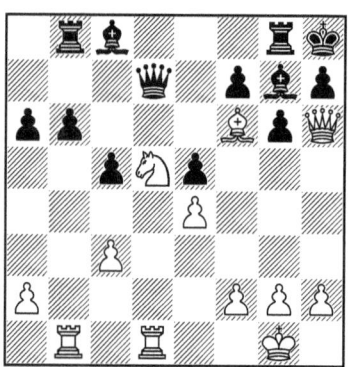

24.♕h4. It was also fine to play 24.♘e7   ♕xe7   25.♕xg7+   ♖xg7 26.♗xe7, winning an exchange in a good position. But I wanted to finish the game with an attack on the king.

24...♕e6 25.♖d3! ♖f8. After 25...h5, white forces a win with 26.♕g5 ♔h7 27.♗xg7 ♔xg7 28.♘e7 ♖e8 29.♘f5+ ♔g8 30.♖d6 and ♖xg6+.

26.♖h3 h5 27.♕g5 ♕xf6 (there was a checkmate threat after 28.♕h6+, while after 27...♔g8, white wins with 28.♘e7+) **28.♘xf6 ♗xh3 29.gxh3.** Black resigned.

The Mate in Five

This analysis alone shows that Averbakh loved endgames – and a few years later, he started his fundamental work, *Chess Endgames*. The interest in endgames was sparked by... his opponent in this game! From Beilin's book *My Encounters in the Chess Kingdom*: "In 1939–40, A. Kotov organized endgame tournaments in a chess club. They would set up a roughly equal endgame position before the tournament. Then they played and analyzed it. Not many people realized that it was a good area for improvement. But Averbakh saw its true worth, and this was the start of his faithful love of endgames."

No. 197
Kotov – Averbakh
Moscow 1948, round 7
Annotated by Y. Averbakh

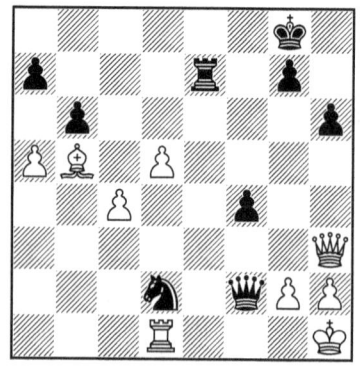

42.♖g1. The sealed move. If now 42...♖e1, then 43.♕c8+ ♔f7 44.♕f5+ ♔e7 45.d6+ ♔xd6 46.♕f8+, and after 46...♔c7, black has to settle for a perpetual check, because otherwise he even risks losing (46...♖e7 47.c5+! bxc5 48.♖d1!).

42...♘e4! 42...♕c5 is met with 43.d6! ♘e4 (if 43...♕xd6, then 44.♕c8+ ♔h7 45.♗a4 with sharp play) 44.♕f3 ♕xd6 (44...♘f2+? 45.♕xf2 ♕xf2 46.dxe7 is a mistake) 45.h3, and, despite his extra pawn, it's not so simple for black to win because of his king's compromised position.

43.♕c8+. Loses by force. 43.♕f3 couldn't save the game either because of 43...♕h4! 44.♖a1 (if 44.h3, then 44...♘f2+ 45.♔h2 ♖e3, winning) 44...♘f2+ 45.♔g1 ♘g4.

Now, after 46.h3, black wins with 46...♖e1+ 47.♖xe1 ♕xe1+ 48.♕f1 ♕e3+ 49.♔h1 ♘f2+ 50.♔h2 ♕g3+ 51.♔g1 ♘xh3+ 52.♔h1 ♘f2+ 53.♔g1 ♘g4 54.♕f3 ♕e1+ 55.♕f1 ♕e3+ 56.♔h1 ♕g3.

If 46.♕xf4, then 46...♖e1+ 47.♖xe1 ♕xe1+ 48.♕f1 ♕e5! 49.♕d3 (49.g3 ♕d4+ 50.♔h1 ♘e3!, winning the queen, or after 49.♕f3,

black wins with 49...♕d4+) 49...♕f4! 50.c5 ♕c1+ 51.♕f1 ♕xc5+ 52.♔h1 ♘f2+ 53.♔g1 ♘d3+ 54.♔h1 ♕xb5 with an extra piece.

"The coordination between the black queen and knight is astonishing, while the white bishop is totally passive," *Averbakh writes in the book* Centre-Stage and Behind the Scenes. "However, the more prosaic 44...♘g3+ 45.♔g1 ♘e2+ 46.♔h1 ♖e3 also won (pointed out by the English player Ken Neat)."

The best move was 43.d6, transitioning into a rook ending:

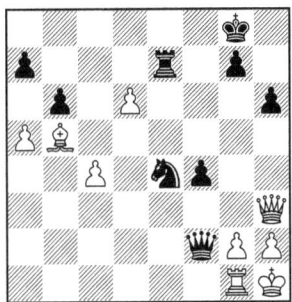

43...♘xd6 44.♕f3 (or else ♖e1) 44...♕xf3 45.gxf3 ♘xb5 46.cxb5 ♖e3! 47.axb6 axb6 48.♔g2 ♖b3 49.♖d1 ♖xb5 50.♖d4 ♖b2+ 51.♔h3 g5, and black should win, albeit with some difficulties.

But after 48.♖g6! ♖xf3 49.♖xb6 ♖b3 50.♔g2, the position is drawn! Later, Averbakh found a clearer way to win: 46...♖e5! 47.axb6 axb6 48.♖b1 ♔f7 etc.

43...♔h7 44.c5. After 44.♗d7, there was 44...♘d6 45.♗f5+ g6 46.♗xg6+ ♔xg6 47.♕g8+ ♔h5 48.h3 ♕g3 49.♕f8 ♕g5 with an extra piece.

In the book, Averbakh added: "44. ♕f5+ g6 45.♕f8 ♖g7 *didn't help either because of the unstoppable threat* ♕e3." *Technically, it can be stopped with* 46.♕a3 *(46...♕e3? 47.♕xe3=), but black still wins with* 46...♕e2.

44...♕e3 45.g3.

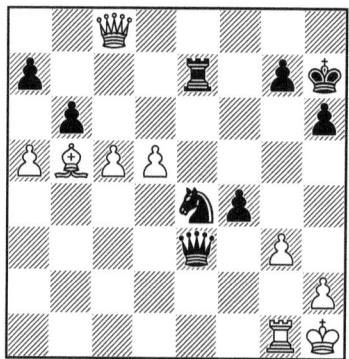

"Here, I couldn't stop myself," *Yuri Lvovich would write years later,* "and announced, 'I can mate you in five!' Then I played **45...♕f3+ 46.♖g2 ♘f2+ 47.♔g1 ♖e1+.** White resigned: 48.♗f1 ♘h3+ 49.♕xh3 ♕(♖)xf1#.

After signing the game score, Kotov sneered back, 'Some checkmater you are. There was another mate, simpler and in just three moves!' Indeed: 45...♘f2+ 46.♔g2 f3+ 47.♔f1 ♕e1#. That was the last time I ever declared mate at the board!"

Stalemate out of Nowhere

E. Ilyin: "When the arbiters opened the envelope on the play-off day, Keres shrugged and gave a naturally-looking check. The Estonian grandmaster probably thought that his inexperienced opponent had simply sealed a weak move. Keres had only thought about how to best protect his passed pawn in his home analysis."

No. 198
Keres – Kholmov
Moscow 1948, round 1
Annotated by R. Kholmov

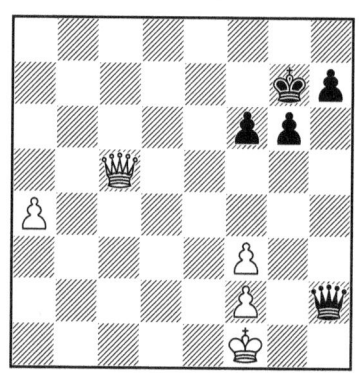

44.♕e7+ ♔h6 45.♕xf6 ♕h3+ 46.♔g1? Missing black's cunning reply. After 46.♔e2, white still had every chance to win, even though it was hard to convert the advantage after 46...♕d7.

46...♕g4+!! Out of nowhere! Now black has a draw.

47.♔h2. White isn't satisfied with the stalemate after 47.fxg4, and he still tries to win.

47...♕h5+ 48.♔g2 *(a pretty dual:* 48.♔g3 ♕g4+!) **48...♕g4+ 49.♔f1 ♕xa4 50.♕f8+ ♔g5 51.♕e7+ ♔h6 52.♕e3+ ♔g7 53.♕e5+ ♔f7 54.♔g2**

♕e8 **55.♕f4+ ♔g8 56.♔g3 ♕e7 57.♕c4+ ♔g7 58.f4 ♕d7 59.♕c3+ ♔g8 60.♕e5 ♔f7 61.♕h8 ♕d3+ 62.♔h4 h5 63.♕c8 ♕d5.** Draw.

This curious endgame made the rounds in the world's chess magazines... and threw the Soviet champion off balance: after this setback at the start, Keres only managed to score 2.5 points in the next seven games!

The Third Knight

Romanovsky: "After drawing his first five games, Keres tried to break this drawing run with very original, but clearly positionally flawed play against Furman. The Leningrad master of course punished his opponent for that, crushing him with several mighty blows."

No. 199
Furman – Keres
Moscow 1948, round 7
Annotated by S. Furman

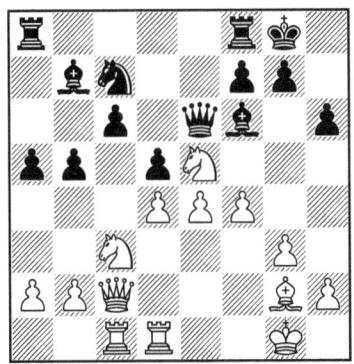

19.♘xd5! This small, but very important exchange combination

Semyon Furman won a bronze token in his first championship. Photo by J. Berland. From the author's archive. Published for the first time.

allows white to clear the c-file and invade his opponent's camp.

19...♘xd5 20.exd5 cxd5 21.♕c7 ♖a7. There's nothing better:

1)   21...♕e7? 22.♕xe7 ♗xe7 23.♖c7;

2)   21...♕a6 22.♘d7 *(this is bad due to 22...♗xd4+! 23.♖xd4 ♖fc8; the correct move is 22.♖c5! ♖ac8 23.♕d7)* 22...♖fc8 23.♘xf6+ gxf6 24.♕d7;

3) 21...♖fb8 22.♖c5! (Not 22.♘d7? ♗d8!, but not 22...♕e3+ 23.♔h1 ♖c8 24.♕xb7 ♖xc1 25.♕xa8+ ♔h7 26.♘xf6+ gxf6 27.♖f1 etc.) 22... b4 23.♖b5 ♗d8 24.♕d7, and black inevitably loses material.

22.♕c5! Bypassing the traps:

1) 22.♘c6 ♖c8 23.♕b6 ♖a6 with counterplay *(24.♕xb7 ♖axc6 25.♖xc6 ♖xc6 26.♕xb5=);*

2) 22.♘d7 ♕e3+ 23.♔h1 ♖c8, and white has to force a draw with 24.♕xc8+ ♗xc8 25.♖xc8+ ♔h7 26.♘f8+, giving a perpetual check.

22...♖a6 23.♕xb5 ♖b6 24.♕e2 (but not 24.♕xa5 ♖a8 with counterplay) **24...♗e7 25.♖c2 ♖d8 26.♕h5.** Winning a pawn, white launches his kingside attack.

26...♗d6 27.♗h3.

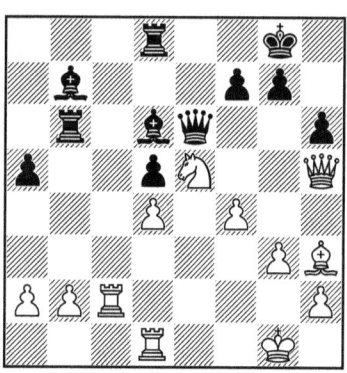

27...♕f6? *"Black essentially resigns the game with this move. It was necessary to play 27...♕e7 28.♖e2 ♗xe5, even though white still had a dangerous attack."* (Panov)

28.♘g4. White is not tempted with 28.♘d7, winning an exchange, since after 28...♖xd7 29.♗xd7 ♕e7, black could complicate matters.

But how? It's enough to play 30.♗a4, and black's position is hopeless (30...♕e3+ 31.♔g2!; 30...♖b4 31.♖e2!). Now, the struggle is prolonged.

28...♕e7 29.♖e2 ♕f8 (29...♕xe2?? 30.♘xh6+) **30.♘e5 ♗a6.** Defending against the threats 31.♘xf7 ♕xf7 32.♗e6 and 31.♘d7.

31.♖f2 ♗b5 32.♖c1 ♗b8 33.♖fc2 g6. *Weakening the king's position. 33...a4!? was more solid.*

34.♕h4 ♔g7 35.a3. Preventing the queen from reaching b4.

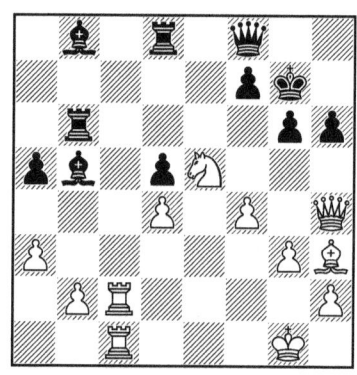

35...♗xe5. *The suicidal-looking 35...f6!! actually saved the game. For instance: 36.♖c7+ ♗xc7 37.♖xc7+ ♗d7!! 38.♗xd7 (with the idea 38...fxe5? 39.♗e8+) 38...♕e7 and ♖d6 or 36.♘c6 ♗xc6 37.♖xc6 ♕e7! 38.♖xb6 ♕e3+ with a perpetual check.*

36.fxe5 ♗d3. *Simplifies things for white (36...♗c4!?).*

37.♖c6! ♖xb2. There's no defense against the decisive threat ♕f6+, but black tries to create at least some counterplay.

38.♕f6+ ♔g8 39.e6! ♖db8 40.♖c8. It was possible to win with the simple 40.e7 ♕e8 41.♖c8, but white was tempted by a combination with a spectacular pawn promotion to a knight.

40...♖xc8   41.♖xc8   ♖b1+
42.♔f2 ♕xc8 43.exf7+ ♔h7.

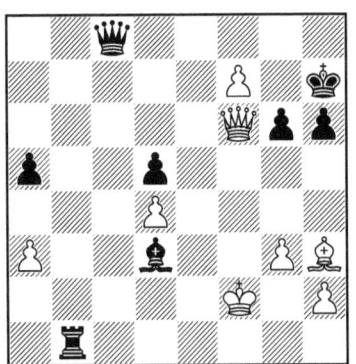

44.f8=♘+! All other moves were losing for white.

**44...♔g8   45.♗e6+   ♕xe6
46.♕xe6+   ♔xf8   47.♕xd5.** The game was adjourned here, and black could have easily resigned. Keres probably decided to test his young opponent's technique "just in case".

**47...♗f5   48.♕xa5   ♔f7   49.a4
♔e6   50.♕e5+   ♔d7   51.g4   ♖b2+
52.♔g3   ♖b3+** (the last trap:
53.♔h4?? g5+ 54.♔h5 ♖h3#)
**53.♔f4   ♗e6   54.♕g7+   ♔d6
55.♕f8+   ♔d7   56.♕xh6.** Black resigned.

The Art of Counter-Attack

Romanovsky: "Bronstein got an excellent position and even won a pawn. The Estonian grandmaster, however, didn't get confused – he launched a brave, energetic counter-attack, and the 'old' Keres of the 1930s shone through. The Soviet champion got an extra pawn in the endgame, played very well and defeated David who hadn't suffered losses for quite a while."

No. 200
Bronstein – Keres
Moscow 1948, round 15
Annotated by P. Keres

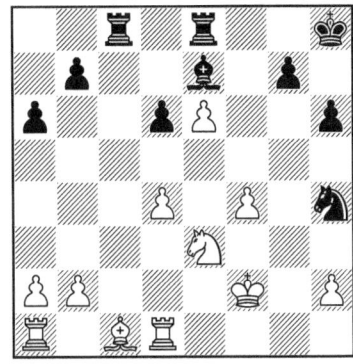

29...d5! With this new pawn sacrifice, black ruins white's plans (to play d4-d5); black pieces are dominating now. Despite the two extra pawns, white can't keep his advantage.

30.♘xd5 ♗d6 31.♗d2. White is still hoping to maintain his advantage and passes up an opportunity to equalize with 31.♖e1 ♖c2+ 32.♖e2 ♖xe2+ 33.♔xe2 ♖xe6+ 34.♔f2 ♘f5 35.♗d2 etc. Keeping both rooks on the board is advantageous for black, who has got a strong attacking position.

**31...♖xe6 32.♖ac1 ♖f8 33.♖e1
♖g6 34.♖g1 ♖f5 35.♖xg6 ♘xg6
36.♘c3.** 36.♘b6 was more precise, supporting the d4-d5 pawn push; the knight can also reach c4 from there.

The victory against one of the leaders was a small consolation for ex-Soviet Champion Keres. From D. Bronstein's archive. Published for the first time.

In One Hundred Games, Keres came up with another recommendation: 36.♖c8+ ♔h7 37.♘c3. The computer approves of both moves.

36...♘xf4 37.♔e3? Now white loses a pawn himself and gets a worse position. After 37.♗xf4 ♗xf4 38.♖c2 or 38.♖d1, he lost a pawn as well, but still retained good counterchances because of his passed d-pawn.

"The best move was the bold 37.♔f3!, because the knight has no good retreat squares." (*One Hundred Games*).

37...♘g2+ 38.♔d3 ♗xh2 39.d5 ♖f3+. Mutual inaccuracies in time trouble. The immediate 39...h5 or 39...♔g8 were better.

40.♔e4 ♖f2 41.♖d1.

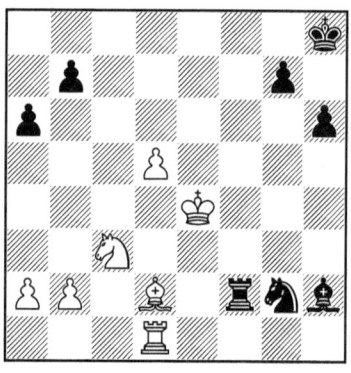

Black sealed his move here. The position is probably won, even though winning would be difficult. The white d-pawn is very dangerous.

"*The play-off was quite comical,*" *Botvinnik wrote in his red notebook. "After Keres' inaccuracies, 'Br' played for a win (his king was centralized) and... lost! Missed a simple move. So, does he overestimate his positions? Does he even analyze??"*

41...♔g8. The immediate 41... ♘h4, getting the knight into play, was better. The game move gives white some counterchances.

42.♘a4. I think that 42.♗e3 gave black the most trouble. He, of course, wouldn't be able to play 42... ♖xb2 due to 43.d6. After 42...♘xe3 43.♔xe3, the endgame is probably not won for black, because the passed d-pawn is very strong *(later, Keres came to the conclusion that "black had a promising endgame").*

42...♘h4 43.♗e3 (43.♘c5 ♖e2+) **43...♖g2.** This move is not bad, because black wins another pawn due to the threat ♖g4+. Still, there was a simpler win after 43... ♖f7, because the passed pawn was blocked (44.d6 ♗xd6 45.♖xd6 ♖e7+ 46.♔d3 ♖xe3+).

44.♘c5! Probably the best practical chance.

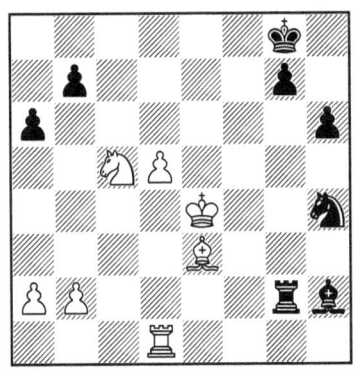

44...♖xb2? This pawn capture makes winning much more difficult

for black; his pieces are now forced to take up passive positions, while white's d-pawn becomes very dangerous. The correct move was 44...b6, and after 45.♘xa6 ♖g4+ 46.♔d3 ♗g3, black has an easily-won endgame; if 45.♘d7, then 45... ♖g4+ 46.♔d3 b5, and the d-pawn is stopped.

When Keres worked on his game collection, he noticed that 46... ♗g3? in the first line was bad due to 47.♗xb6 ♖g6(a4) 48.♗c7!, and corrected the evaluation of this line: 46...♖a4 47.♖h1 ♗g3 48.♖h3 ♘f5 49.♖xg3! ♘xg3 50.d6 "with great drawing chances".

45.♖d2! Of course, not 45.d6? ♖b4+ 46.♔d5 ♗xd6. If black now trades rooks, he loses any real winning chances.

45...♖b4+ 46.♖d4 ♖b6 47.♘e6 ♗d6? Losing a tempo. 47...♔f7 was much better.

48.♗f4! It's necessary to kick the bishop from the d6 square. 48.♖c4 ♖b1 49.♖c8+ ♔f7 50.♖d8 ♗e7 51.♖d7 ♖e1! gained nothing.

48...♘g6 49.♗xd6 ♖xd6.

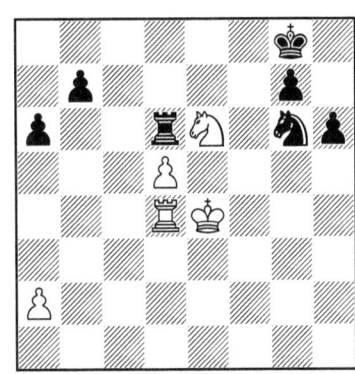

50.♔f5? A weak move that nullifies all of white's previous efforts. Of course, he had to play 50.♖c4! with great drawing chances. If, for instance, 50...♘e7, then 51.♖c7 ♘xd5 (51...♔f7 52.♘xg7) 52.♖xg7+ ♔h8 53.♖g6 with a draw. If 50...♖d7, then 51.♘c5 ♖e7+ 52.♔d4 (not 52.♘e6 ♔f7 and ♖d7; *this is a draw as well*), and black has no choice other than to go for difficult defense with 52...♘f8 (*52...♘e5!?*) 53.d6 ♖f7.

After the game move, there's no real struggle left.

50...♔f7 51.♘c5. *The last mistake: 51.♖d1! still retained good drawing chances.*

51...♖f6+ 52.♔e4 b6 53.♘xa6 ♔e7 54.♘c7 ♘f8 55.♘b5. *If white plays 55.d6+ immediately, trying to get one of the black pawns in exchange (55...♖xd6 56.♖xd6 ♔xd6 57.♘e8+ or 55...♔d7 56.♘d5! ♖xd6 57.♘xb6+), black has the simple 55... ♔d8!*

55...g5 56.d6+ ♔d7 57.♔e3 ♘e6 58.♖b4 (after 58.♖a4, there's the preliminary 58...♔c6) **58...♘g7.** Now the d-pawn, which caused so much trouble for black, finally falls.

59.♘d4 ♖xd6 60.♖a4 ♔e7 61.♖a6 (or 61.♖a7+ ♔f6 62.♖xg7 ♖xd4) **61...♔f6 62.a4 ♘f5+ 63.♘xf5 ♔xf5.** 64.a5 is met with 64...♖e6+. White resigned.

This loss almost destroyed Bronstein's hopes for the championship medal. He and Furman had just caught up with the leader the previous day, but they both lost in round 15, and Kotov got ahead again after defeating Alatortsev. They had to catch up once again!

The Ovation that Never was

Mikenas: "In the game against Furman, which, by the way, was the best one in round 6, we saw the old Flohr, who's not only strong in the positional skirmishes, but also possesses a great tactical vision."

No. 201
Flohr – Furman
Moscow 1948, round 6
Annotated by S. Flohr

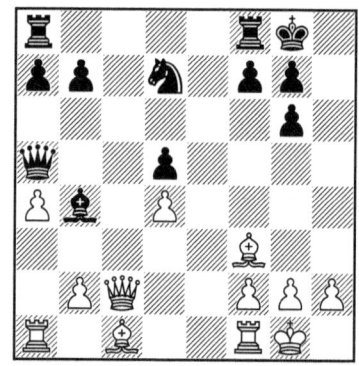

17.h4! A very strong move. If the game was quieter, black would have had enough time to put his rooks on c8 and e8 and play ♘f6-e4. White correctly saw that black's kingside was weakened (g6) and it was time to attack the poorly defended king's position.

17...♖ac8 18.♕d3 ♖c4. 18...♘f6 19.♗g5 ♖fe8 was probably better:

black had an extra tempo, and the c8 rook would have taken part in defense.

19.♗g5 ♘f6 20.g3 ♖e8 21.♗xf6 gxf6 22.h5 ♔g7 23.♔g2. White has many resources for the attack, which, as often happens with opposite-colored bishops, is very dangerous.

23...♗d2. If 23...♖h8, then 24.♖h1 ♖cc8 25.♕b3!, and white wins a pawn or seizes the h-file.

After 24.♖h1, there's the reply 24...♕b6! 25.♖ad1 ♕e6, so there's a more precise move: 24.hxg6 fxg6 25.♖h1 etc.

24.♖h1 ♕b4 25.hxg6 fxg6 26.♖h4! ♗g5. Otherwise, white would have doubled rooks along the h-file.

27.♗xd5 ♖c7 28.♖h2.

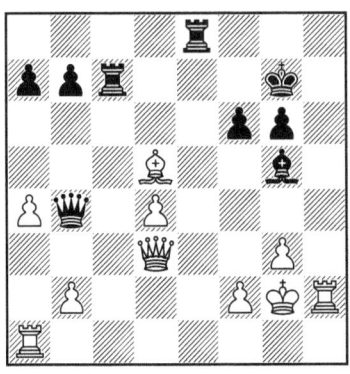

28...♖e1. There was also the tempting 28...♖e3. White had the spectacular 29.♖ah1! ♖xd3 30.♖h7+ ♔f8 31.♖h8+ ♔e7 32.♖1h7+ ♔d6 33.♖d8+, mating.

The first critical moment! 28...f5! 29.♖ah1 ♔f6 repelled the attack, and

the doubled rooks shoot in the dark (30.f4 ♕xb2+ 31.♔f3 ♕c3!=).

The game move, however, could have got Flohr an ovation after 29.g4!! The rook is untouchable (29...♖xa1? 30.♕h3, mating), and after 29...♕d6 30.♖xe1 ♕xd5+ 31.♕f3, black might as well resign.

29.♖xe1 ♕xe1 30.♖h1 ♕b4 31.b3 ♖d7 32.♗c4.

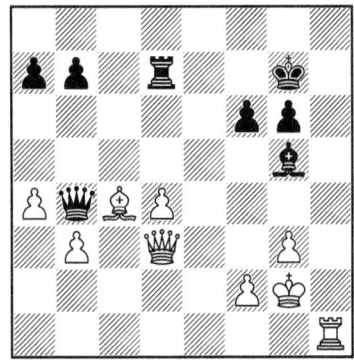

32...♕d2. Loses quickly, but black's position is already hopeless. 32...♕e7 was the most resilient move, but after 33.f4 ♗h6 34.♔f2 and ♖e1, the black bishop is out of play.

After 32...♕e7, there's a pretty win: 33.♖h8! ♔xh8 34.♕xg6 ♖g7 35.♕e8+ ♔h7 36.♗d3+ ♔h6 37.♕h8+ etc.

The second critical moment! Here, 32...f5! was actually the most resilient move, for instance: 33.g4 ♕d2 34.♕h3 ♗h6 35.♕g3 ♕f4! 36.gxf5 ♕xg3+ 37.fxg3 gxf5 38.♗e6 etc.

33.♕e4! ♕a5 34.♖h8 (34.♕e6 ♕d8 35.♕h3 won quickly as well) **34...♖d8.** Or 34...♔xh8 35.♕e8+

♔h7　36.♕xd7+　♚h6　37.♗g8, mating.

35.♖xd8 ♕xd8 36.♕xb7+ ♚h8 37.♕xa7 ♗d2 38.♕f7 g5 39.♕h5+ ♚g7 40.♕f7+ ♚h8 41.♗d3. White repeated moves in time trouble "just in case", because I didn't know if 40 moves had already been made. Now, the time trouble was over, and black resigned.

The Press Bureau's Mistake

Lisitsin: "Alatortsev managed to activate his queenside pieces and pawns in the endgame. Bondarevsky's counterplay led to a complicated, double-edged position that needs precise analysis to evaluate it correctly."

No. 202

Bondarevsky – Alatortsev
Moscow 1948, round 12
Annotated by I. Bondarevsky

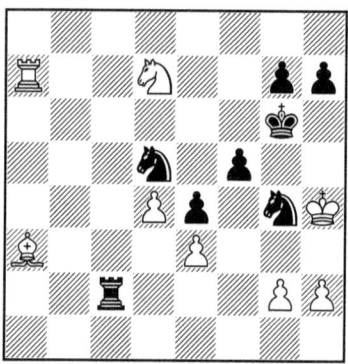

Leningrad, July 1948. Bondarevsky with Tolush before he left for the Stockholm Interzonal, where, like in the Soviet Championship, he shared 6th to 9th places. Photo by M. Volkovysky from his archive. Published for the first time.

With the time-control move (40...♘f2-g4), black defends against 41.♘e5+ and ♖a6+, which would lead to mate. At first glance, it might seem that the counterplay was successful, and that black has managed to win a pawn and even get a better pawn position. Interestingly, even the press bureau's report said that black was better!

41.h3! The sealed move that leads to a forced win.

41...♘gf6. Not 41...♘gxe3 because of 42.♘e5+ ♔h6 (42...♔f6 43.♖a6+, mating) 43.♖a6+ ♘f6 (43...g6 44.♗f8#) 44.♖xf6+ gxf6 45.♗f8#.

The best chance was to sacrifice a knight for two pawns: 41...♖xg2 42.hxg4 fxg4. However, after 43.♘f8+ ♔f5 44.♗d6, white should still win *(for instance: 44... g5+ 45.♔h5 ♖g1 46.♗f7+ ♘f6+ 47.♔h6 g3 48.♔g7 ♔g4 49.♖xf6 ♖e1 50.♗xg3 etc.).*

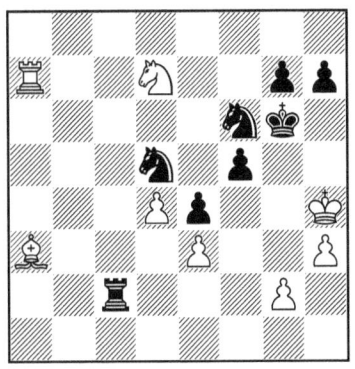

42.♘e5+ ♔h6 43.♗f8 ♘c7. After 43...♖c7, there's 44.g4. White has a beautiful win after 43...♖xg2

44.♘g4+!!, for instance: 44...♘xg4 45.♖xg7, and there's no defense to the checkmate. 43...♘h5 loses as well: 44.g4 fxg4 45.♗xg7+!! ♘xg7 46.♖a6+ ♘e6 47.♖xe6+ ♔g7 48.♘xg4 etc.

44.g4 fxg4 45.hxg4 *(white had an even quicker win: 45.♖xc7! ♖xc7 46.hxg4, and we reach the position after white's 48th move)* **45...♖h2+ 46.♔g3 ♖c2.**

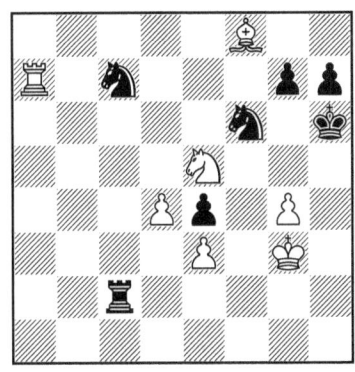

47.♖xc7! ♖xc7 48.♔h4 ♘xg4. The only defense against 49.g5#. Now white wins easily because of his passed pawn.

49.♔xg4 ♖c1 50.♗e7 ♖g1+ 51.♔f4 ♔h5 52.d5 g5+ 53.♔xe4 g4 54.d6 ♖f1 55.d7 g3 56.d8=♕ g2 57.♕g8. Black resigned.

Five Queens

Simagin: "Levenfish played excellently in the first part of the game and had a clearly better position because of two strong bishops. However, he went for complications in the middlegame, and they didn't turn out in black's favor..."

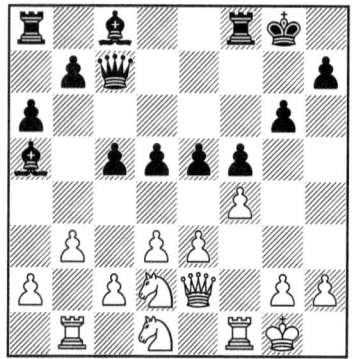

No. 203

Konstantinopolsky – Levenfish
Moscow 1948, round 17
Annotated by A. Konstantinopolsky

18.c4. One of the bishops is out of play, and the other one isn't developed yet, so white attacks in the center to block the pawn position.

18...d4. *The pawn "solitaire" could have been resolved with 18...exf4 19.exf4 b5! 20.cxd5 ♗b7, activating the bishop.*

19.♘f3 exf4. *But now this move only benefits his opponent. Black could keep a small plus with 19...e4 20.♘e5 exd3 and ♖d8.*

20.exd4 ♗d7. Black is trying to put the rook on the e-file and attack white's weak e3 square quickly. After 20...cxd4 21.b4 ♗b6 22.c5 ♗a7 23.♘xd4, white has a good position.

With 23...b6! 24.♕f3 ♗b7 25.c6 b5! (the point!) or 24.♘b3 bxc5, black gets good counterplay and separates

the white pawns (so 23.♖e1= is better). That's how black had to play. The game move is in white's favor.

21.dxc5 ♖fe8 22.♕f2 ♗b4 (23. a3 was a threat) **23.d4 ♗c6 24.a3!** Of course, 24.d5? ♗xd5 25.cxd5 ♗xc5 26.♘d4 ♕b6 is bad. Instead, white sacrifices a pawn to free the path for his d1 knight.

24...♗xa3 25.♘c3. 25.b4 a5! 26.b5 ♗e4 gained nothing.

25...♖e3 26.♘d5 ♗xd5 27.cxd5 ♗b4. Preventing b3-b4, with the threat ♕a2. After 27...♖ae8, there could follow 28.♕h4 and d5-d6 or even ♘g5 *(there's an even cooler line: 28.b4! ♖e2 29.♖fe1!! ♖xf2 30.♖xe8+ ♔f7 31.♖be1).*

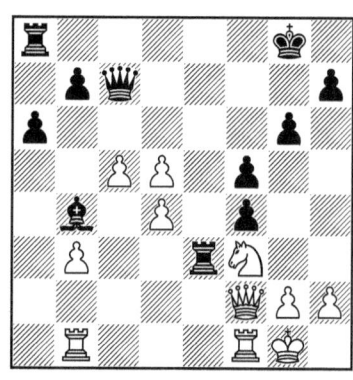

28.d6. 28.♕h4 was stronger, threatening d5-d6 and ♕xf4. If 28...♖e4, then 29.♘g5 ♖xd4 30.♘e6 ♕e5 31.♘xd4 ♕xd4+ 32.♔h1 ♕xd5 33.♖bd1!, with an advantage for white.

28...♕c6   29.♖bc1. Here, 29.♕h4 was better as well. White hoped to use the queen for tactical blows along the a2-g8 diagonal, but black, of course, could parry these threats.

29...♕d5! An excellent square for the queen, it's virtually invincible here.

30.♖c4. A trap; black, however, thought it was a blunder.

30...♖xb3? It was necessary to play 30...a5 31.♘e5 b5 32.♖cc1 ♗c3 33.♖cd1 ♗xd4 34.♘f3 ♖xf3 35.♖xd4 ♖xf2 36.♖xd5 ♖c2 37.♖xf4 ♖d8 38.d7 ♔f7 39.♖fd4 ♔e7 40.♖d3 a4 41.bxa4 bxa4.

However, after 37.♖e1! (doubling on the e-file, rather than the d-file!), black's days are numbered as well, for instance: 37...♖d8 38.♖de5 ♖d2 39.c6 ♖8xd6 40.c7 ♖c6 41.♖e8+ with an extra rook.

So, was there no salvation then? There was: instead of 31...b5?, black should play 31...♖xb3! The lines are just incredible: 32.♕xf4 a4 33.♕g5 ♖b2! (creating a mate threat; 33...a3? 34.♘g4) 34.d7 a3 35.c6 ♗e7! (this would be impossible without 33...♖b2!) 36.♕g3 a2 37.c7 a1=♕ 38.c8=♕+ ♔g7! 39.d8=♕.

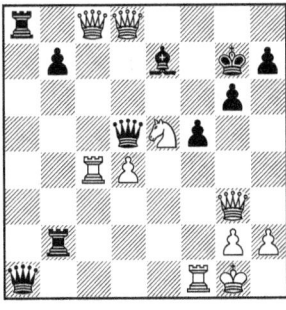

Fantastic: there are five queens on the board! And, unlike the Alekhine

masterpiece, all the moves were the strongest (and sometimes the only possible ones). The last move is also not just an aesthetic whim – it's the start of a spectacular... drawing finale: 39...♗xd8 (39...♖xd8? 40.♕xf5) 40.♖c7+! ♗xc7 41.♕xc7+ ♔g8 42.♕xh7+ ♔xh7 43.♕xg6+ etc.

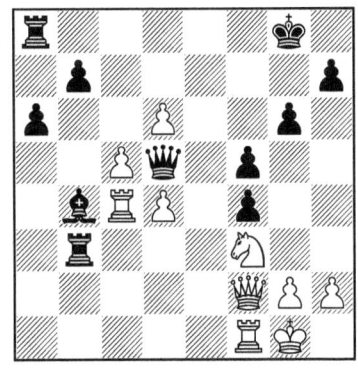

31.♕c2! **♖xf3.** There's no other move. 31...♖b2 32.♕xb2 ♕xc4 33.♘e5! ♕c3 34.♕a2+ ♔h8 35.♕d5 ♕e3+ 36.♔h1 ♕e2 37.♖g1 loses.

32.gxf3 ♗d2 33.♕xd2 ♕xc4 34.♖e1. After 34.♕xf4 ♖e8, black can defend.

34...g5 35.♖e5. Perhaps 35.♔h1 was stronger, and if 35...♕d5, then 36.♕e2! ♕xd4 37.♕e6+ ♔h8 38.d7, and white wins.

35...♖f8 36.♖e2 ♖f7 (♖g2 was a threat) **37.♖g2 h6 38.h4.** 38.♕xf4 is worse – the f4 pawn is not important at all.

38...♖g7. After the queen trade, the game is lost, but what is black supposed to do? If 38...♔f8, then 39.hxg5 hxg5 40.♖xg5 ♖g7 41.♖xg7 ♔xg7 42.♕xf4, and there's no 42...

♕d5 due to 43.♕e5+ ♕xe5 44.dxe5 ♔f7 45.♔f2 etc. Otherwise, the queen endgame is lost.

39.♕a2! ♕xa2 40.♖xa2 ♖d7. White is threatening ♖c2, d4-d5 and c5-c6. There's no defense.

41.hxg5 ♖g7. Or 41...hxg5 42.♖c2 ♔f7 43.d5 ♔e8 44.c6 bxc6 45.dxc6 ♖d8 46.d7+, winning *(46.♖e2+ and c6-c7 is even more technically sound).*

42.d5 ♔f7 43.♖e2 ♖xg5+ 44.♔f1. Black resigned.

No Escape for the King

Lisitsin: "The grandmaster skillfully exploited the bishop pair advantage, even though Aronin defended tenaciously. Lilienthal gradually, move by move, increased the pressure on his opponent's position and got a decisive advantage... I think that it was the best game of round 12."

No. 204
Lilienthal – Aronin
Moscow 1948, round 12
Annotated by A. Lilienthal

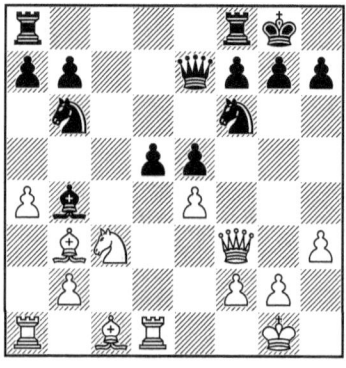

16.a5! An interesting pawn sacrifice 16.♘xd5 ♘bxd5 17.♗xd5 (17.exd5 e4!) 17...♘xd5 18.♖xd5 ♖fd8 only led to simplifications.

16...d4? 16...dxe4 17.♘xe4 ♘xe4 (17...♘bd7? 18.♗g5) 18.♕xe4 ♘c8 19.♕g4 is dangerous for black: white gets an unstoppable attack for the sacrificed pawn.

I think that the best move here was 16...♗xc3 17.bxc3 ♘bd7! (but not 17...dxe4? 18.♕e3 and ♗a3). Even though white retains his bishop pair, it's hard to use them effectively.

Nevertheless, the computer gives 16...d4 as the first line.

17.axb6 dxc3 18.bxc3 ♗c5 19.♖xa7. *In the game Kholmov – Geller (1954 Soviet Championship)*

Andre Lilienthal. From V. Chepizhny's archive. Published for the first time.

white preferred 19.bxa7, and after 19...h6? (19...♗xa7) 20.♗e3 b6 21.♗d5 ♖xa7 22.♖xa7 ♕xa7 23.♗xh6, he ultimately won.

19...♖xa7. Black could have put up a better defense with 19...♗xb6.

20.bxa7 ♗xa7 21.♗g5 ♖d8 22.♗d5 ♖d6 23.♖b1! White could win a pawn, but probably not the game after 23.♗xb7 ♖xd1+ 24.♕xd1 h6 25.♗xf6 ♕xf6, and black has good drawing chances because of the opposite-colored bishops.

23...♗b6. *23...♖b6! (24.♖a1 ♖a6) was more tenacious, with the same idea as in the previous line. With the rooks still on board, black loses quickly.*

24.c4 ♕c7.

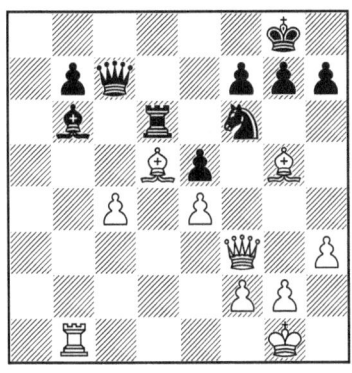

25.c5! Opening the c-file creates decisive threats along the 8th rank.

25...♕xc5 26.♖c1 ♕a5 27.♗xf6 ♖xf6. 27...gxf6 28.♖c8+ ♖d8 *(or 28... ♗d8 29.♕h5 ♖xd5 30.exd5 ♕xd5 31.♕h6! ♕d6 32.♖c3)* 29.♕h5! ♕xd5 30.exd5 ♖xc8 31.♕g4+ couldn't save black either.

28.♖c8+ ♗d8 29.♕c3 *(29.♕d1!)* **29...♕b6 30.♕b2!** ♕d6 *(30...♕a5 31.♕b5!)* **31.f4!** After 31.♕xb7 ♔f8 32.♕a8 ♔e7, white would have faced certain difficulties. *The computer doesn't: after 33.♔h2!, it easily finds the maneuver ♖b8-b7+, then ♗b3-a4+ and ♖d7.*

31...exf4 (of course, after 31... ♖xf4 32.♕xe5 white wins) **32.e5 ♕d7 33.♕xb7 ♕e8 34.♕b8 ♖d6.** The last chance. If 35.exd6?, then 35...♕e1+ with perpetual check.

35.♕xd6 ♗b6+ 36.♕xb6 ♕xc8 37.e6 g5 38.e7 ♔g7 39.♗c6. Black resigned.

"Didn't Notice the Rook..."

While the queen only offered itself for sacrifice in the previous game, it was actually sacrificed here. The combination's motif is the same – the weakness of the 8th rank.

No. 205
Alatortsev – Averbakh
Moscow 1948, round 9
Annotated by V. Alatortsev

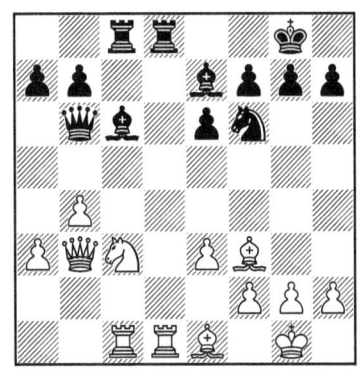

20.♘a4. Of course, 20...♗xa4 21.♕xa4 is now bad: the f3 bishop could cause a lot of trouble afterwards. The best move was 20...♖xd1 21.♕xd1 ♕b5, because after 22.♗e2, there's a strong maneuver 22...♕g5!

20...♕b5 21.♖xd8+ ♗xd8? Averbakh thought on this position for a long while, but failed to notice white's main threat (22.♖c5!). It was necessary to play 21...♖xd8; white could meet this with 22.♗xc6, creating a weak isolated pawn on c6.

22.♖c5! ♗d5. The best chance. The knight can't be captured because of the pin on the rook. The queen has no good squares: after 22...♕a6, there's 23.b5, winning a piece.

Black now hoped for 23.♗xd5 ♖xc5 24.bxc5 ♕e2!, attacking both bishops. However, white can force a win with a queen sacrifice.

23.♖xc8! ♗xb3 24.♖xd8+. Black resigned. After 24...♘e8 there's 25.♘c3, and the queen has no good squares to retreat to.

The Finishing Drama

Ragozin: "Before the round started, Kotov told me with his characteristic optimism, 'I already have experience of deciders. In the 11th Soviet Championship, both Botvinnik and I had 11.5 points before the last round. Back then, I was a novice and failed to pass the exam. Botvinnik won. This time, Bronstein is the novice, it's his first challenge for the Soviet Championship. Let's see if his nerves can withstand such an intense struggle.' This deep game justified Kotov's prediction and lived up to the expectations of numerous *(two thousand!)* spectators who filled the tournament hall to the brim."

No. 206. Slav Gambit D31
Bronstein – Kotov
Moscow 1948, round 19
Annotated by D. Bronstein

1.d4 d5 2.c4 e6 3.♘c3 c6. This move order had occurred in Chigorin's games. Most opponents played 4.e3 or 4.♘f3 against Kotov in this championship.

4.e4! I am totally sure that this is the only way to counteract the passive moves 2...e6 and 3...c6.

If 4.♘f3 Kotov had evidently planned 4...dxc4 5.e4 b5, just like in his games with Flohr and Alatortsev. But Bronstein had prepared a sharp and little-known variation" (Alatortsev).

4...dxe4 5.♘xe4 ♗b4+ 6.♗d2. Of course, the loss of the d4 pawn does not deter white. However, this is the very reason why the move 4.e4! is considered incorrect by theory.

6...♗xd2+. If black chooses the line with 3...c6, he should be ready to repel the attack. The fact that Kotov refuses to accept the sacrifice of two pawns (d4 and g2), or even one (d4), after 6...♕xd4 7.♗xb4 ♕xe4+ etc., despite the game's importance, speaks in white's favor. It seems that it's impossible to find completely safe paths for black!

With 6...♗xd2+, black settles for a long, difficult defense.

Bronstein held something back when he annotated the game in the magazine. We see what exactly he prepared for Kotov in his notebook entry: "Alas, Kotov, after thinking for 15 minutes, didn't walk into the trap. Even though he was sure that he could play ♘h6. But still, he believed that I knew something. Simagin criticized him so much! But Kotov was very happy when Simagin and Syoma *(Furman)* spent three days in the spring to try and find what I had prepared and finally found ♗xf6!."

Here's what "crafty Davey" had prepared: 6...♕xd4 7.♗xb4 ♕xe4+ 8.♗e2 ♘a6 9.♗c3 f6 10.♕d6!

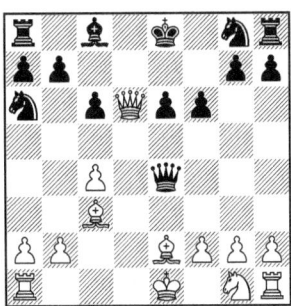

"The opening handbooks of the time preferred the maneuver 10... ♘h6 with the subsequent transfer of the knight to f7," Boris Vainstein

Just like in the 11th championship, the title was decided in a last-round head-on encounter. This time, Kotov stood his ground against Bronstein! In the center – Semyon Furman. From D. Bronstein's archive. Published for the first time.

wrote in his book Improvisation in the Art of Chess. *"They say that Kotov regretted not taking Bronstein's gambit pawn. But he probably didn't know that after 11.♗xf6!! gxf6 12.0-0-0 ♘f7 13.♗h5 he wouldn't be able to win the championship..." However, instead of 12...♘f7?, Kotov could have played 12...♕g6! 13.♕d8+ ♔f7 14.♕xh8 ♘b4 15.♗h5 ♘xa2+ 16.♔d2 ♕xh5 17.♕xh7+ ♔f8 (Nakamura – Tomashevsky, Paris 2013), still securing the draw.*

10...♘e7 or 10...♗d7 are not bad for white either. And in addition to 9...f6, black has the sharp 9...♘e7, which was soon tested in the games Lilienthal – Bronstein (Soviet Championship 1949) and Bronstein – Kotov (Budapest 1950).

7.♕xd2 ♘f6 8.♘xf6+ ♕xf6 9.♘f3 0-0 10.♗e2. White has a small development advantage. Black will play c6-c5 sooner or later. In this case, the bishop will be positioned better on e2 than on d3.

10...♘d7. It's dangerous to lose a tempo for 10...♖d8. White could reply 11.0-0-0! with a dangerous attack.

11.♕e3 b6 12.0-0 c5. There was no need to hurry with this move. Perhaps black, after 12...♗b7, didn't like the reply 13.c5?

13.♖ad1 ♗b7 14.dxc5 ♘xc5 15.b4 ♘a6 (15...♘a4 16.♘e5 or 15...♘e4? 16.♖d7 are bad) **16.a3 ♖fd8 17.♘e5.**

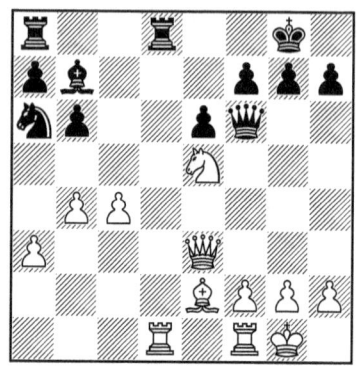

Black has managed to solve his development problem, but now white gets new advantages: firstly, his pieces are placed better, and, secondly, as the number of pieces on the board decreases, white's queenside pawn majority becomes increasingly important.

White's subsequent play was harshly criticized by Botvinnik in his "secret" notes: "There followed very unconvincing, cautious play with shuffling, trades, but still retaining an advantage. He forgot to bring the king closer after trading queens! Draw. Some decider! Does he really have proper, grandmaster-level technique?"

17...♘c7 18.♗h5. Forcing black to weaken his pawn structure: he won't be able to withstand the e5 knight's pressure for long, and so the move f7-f6 is inevitable, weakening the 7th rank. In this case, it's better for white to go for a queen endgame: in such endings, the king's compromised position often allows his opponent to force the movement of a passed pawn with checks.

18...g6 19.♗e2 ♘e8 20.f3 (restricting the b7 bishop) **20... ♕e7 21.♖xd8 ♖xd8 22.♖d1 ♖xd1+ 23.♗xd1 f6 24.♘d3.**

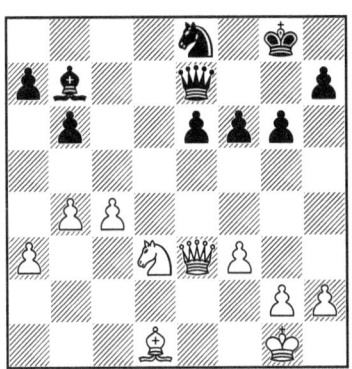

24...♘c7. *Black could have gone for more active defense: 24...♘d6!? 25.c5 ♘f5 26.♕f4 ♕d8 etc.*

25.♗b3 ♔g7. The king is already feeling somewhat uncomfortable. It's relatively safe on g7, but now black's entire kingside is frozen, because any pawn movement can be dangerous.

26.a4 ♕d6 27.c5 bxc5 28.♘xc5 ♗c8? Black voluntarily "kills" his bishop, worsening his position considerably. It was necessary to play 28...♗d5!, offering a bishop trade and maintaining his defensive resources. It would be much harder for white to organize the movement of the passed b-pawn.

29.b5. Pinning down the a7 pawn to its place, since now black can't play a7-a6? because of b5-b6!

29...e5. This extends the white pieces' range even more, but what more could black do? After the

mistake on the previous move, his position is quite difficult.

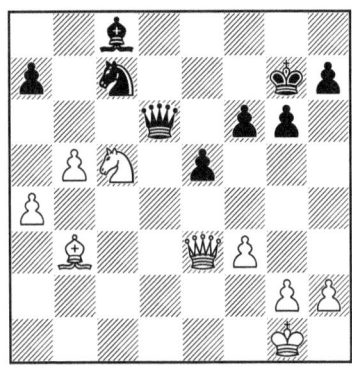

30.♘e4? White makes a big mistake in return. He's sure of his win, so he gets tempted by a forced line that wins a piece.

The simple 30.♔f2 was the correct move. Black can do nothing to counter the white king's march to the queenside, because his pieces are essentially in zugzwang. For instance, both 30...♕b6 31.♔e2 and 30...♘d5? 31.♘e4! are bad.

According to Alatortsev, immediately after the game Bronstein demonstrated the variation 30.♔f2! ♘d5 31.♗xd5! ♕xd5 32.♕c3! "with the queen then transferred to b4 and an advance of the a- and b- pawns," but the right move was nevertheless 32.♘e4! (due to 32.♕c3 ♕a2=).

30...♕b6! The only move. Not 30...♕b4? 31.♔f2 with the threats ♕xa7! and ♕c1!

31.♕xb6. It's now too late to play 31.♔f2 because of 31...♗e6 32.♗xe6 ♘xe6, and the black king comes to the rescue in time *(32.♕xb6 axb6*

33.a5 bxa5 34.b6 ♗xb3 35.♘c5 ♘a6= achieves nothing either).

31...axb6 32.♘d6 ♗d7 33.♗c4 ♘a8. White threatened a4-a5, and 33...♔f8 wasn't an adequate defense due to 34.a5 ♔e7 35.axb6! ♔xd6 36.b7!!.

34.♗d5 ♘c7.

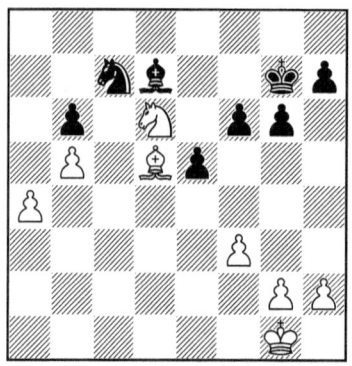

Only now did white notice that the "planned" win of a knight with 35.♗b7 ♗e6 36.a5 bxa5 37.b6 ♘d5 38.♗xd5 ♗xd5 39.b7 ♗xb7 40.♘xb7 leads, after 40...a4 41.♔f2 a3 42.♘c5 a2 43.♘b3 ♔f7 44.♔e2 ♔e6 45.♔d3 ♔d5, only to a draw: the knight is shackled to the a2 pawn, and if white wants to eliminate it with his king, the black king will break through to the white pawns.

35.♗c6 ♗e6. After 35...♗xc6 36.bxc6, white should win the resulting knight endgame *(actually a pawn endgame: 36...♔f8 37.♘b5 ♘xb5 38.axb5).*

36.♘b7 ♔f7 37.a5 bxa5 38.♘xa5. Now "winning" the knight is outright bad: 38.♘c5? ♘d5! 39.♗xd5 ♗xd5 40.b6 ♔e7 41.b7 ♗xb7 42.♘xb7 a4, and black wins.

An obvious mistake: after 43.♘c5 a3 44.♔f2, there's a draw on the board!

38...♔e7 39.♔f2 ♗d7. The simplest way to draw was 39...♔d6 40.♘b7+ ♔e7 41.♘a5 ♔d6 42.♘b7+ etc.

Now, after **40.b6 ♘a6,** white could have traded on d7 and got a slightly better knight endgame, which, nevertheless, should still end in a draw with the best defense (41.♗xd7 ♔xd7 42.♔e3 ♘c5 43.f4 exf4+ 44.♔xf4 ♔d6!). However, the struggle was too exhausting, and so white decided to seal a calm, non-committal move to think everything through thoroughly.

41.♗b7. Draw.

Black can't get to the b6 pawn, but white can't improve his position either. And if black does try to eliminate the b6 pawn, he risks losing a couple of pawns on the kingside and then the game.

Cossacks of the Kuban

17th Soviet Championship: Moscow, 16th October – 20th November 1949

> How do you live, the great Motherland of Fear?
> How many times has fear got you reborn!..
> We learned to fear even before being born.
> The state fear was cultivated like a plant.
> *R. Rozhdestvensky, "Fear"*

This Soviet Championship was played in a year when the country's collective brain was completely frazzled – by the frenzied fight against "cosmopolitanism" and the super-fertilized soil of the cult of personality. The thoughts of millions of people seemed to be embodied by a rather short, pockmarked man in a military tunic, who walked around the Kremlin in his soft boots, with a pipe in hand, looking at the world like a predator from behind the crenellated walls. The newspapers and radio shows competed in how frequently they would mention his name, or, to be precise, his party pseudonym, which caused a paroxysm of delight in one part of the population and made the other part (a minority, as always happens in Russia) gnash their teeth in hatred. Nobody knew that very soon, these two Russias would meet and never love each other again...

In case you hadn't realized, this was the year of the 70th birthday of the "genius successor of V. I. Lenin, the chairman of the Bolshevik party and Soviet state, the leader of the workers of the whole world – Iosif Vissarionovich Stalin". That's how, with a gasp of admiration, you were supposed to call the "best friend of athletes" – even in the *Shakhmaty v SSSR* magazine that I've just quoted (the article "Great Leader and Teacher – Our STALIN" was written to honor his birthday). Preparations for the national celebrations began long before the actual round number birthday (21st December), and it was amazing that none of the 20 issues of the 17th Soviet Chess Championship bulletin featured a photo of the glorious leader or even mentioned his name!

That was despite the fact that more than 100,000 gifts were sent to the Kremlin from all corners of the Soviet Union and from brotherly countries. According to eyewitnesses, this endless stream resembled an offering to some god. The exhibition, opened on 22nd December and closed only after Stalin's death, was hosted by the Museum of the Revolution and the Museum of Fine Arts. There were chess sets among those gifts as well.

Y. Razumovsky: "The Tula gunsmith V. B. Sokolov also timed his gift for that day. He sent a decorated, crafted chess set dedicated to the victory of the Russian nation against the Teutonic knights on Chudskoe Lake. G. L. Lebedev, Stakhanovite worker of the Molotov Furniture Factory in Minsk, also sent a chess set. His chess set is composed of several thousand pieces of various types of wood. The workers of the Karbolit factory (Orekhovo-Zuevo) sent comrade Stalin a chess table with a board and pieces made of organic glass." (*Shakhmaty v SSSR* No. 12, 1949.)

All famous writers and poets felt the need to "respond" to the big birthday. Even Anna Akhmatova, who, together with Mikhail Zoschenko, was defamed in the notorious 1946 report by Zhdanov, had to cobble together a panegyric that started with the following words: "Let the world remember this day forever, let this hour be bequeathed to eternity. The legend tells about a wise man who saved all of us from a horrible death..." You can't do anything with that – in a totalitarian state, any artist will eventually create something similar.

Why, I think that even the first nuclear test in the USSR, on 29th August 1949 at the Semipalatinsk range, was also held to honor that

The Battle on the Ice chess set commemorating Russia's victory against the Teutonic knights on Chudskoe Lake in 1242. A present to Stalin from hereditary Tula gunsmith Vasily Sokolov. Indeed, back in 1923 he carved a rifle that was gifted by the people of Tula to Lenin.

big birthday. Of course, no details were given, but the very fact bolstered people's self-esteem and their love for the leader. By the way, the events of Alexander Solzhenitsyn's novel *In the First Circle* happen in December of that year; they begin when a Soviet diplomat calls the American embassy, saying that "soon, in New York, the Soviet agent Georgy Koval will obtain important technological parts to create an atomic bomb in the radio equipment shop". The imprisoned engineers from the *sharashka* – a specialized prison of the MGB – help identify the caller.

> Preparations for a nuclear war were hidden by calls for peace. And the greater the preparations, the louder the calls. Cultural workers were an important part of the propaganda choir. Here is an excerpt from **Botvinnik**'s speech on Moscow radio: "I call on sportsmen all over the world to follow the example of sportsmen of the Soviet Union, and to support firmly the appeal for a ban on atomic weapons. Let the army of world athletes become an army of peace supporters and the vanguard of fighters for happiness and a brighter future for all mankind." But such calls could hardly deceive anybody. Baruch Wood, printing the champion's speech in his *CHESS* magazine (No. 9, 1950, quoted from here with minor edits), added only one short sentence: "Comment is unnecessary".

Dread and desperation fill the pages not only of the famous novel but also of the diary of a seemingly free person – the head of the Ancient Languages Department of Leningrad University, Olga Freidenberg (Boris Pasternak's cousin). Her diary was partially published in the book *The Correspondence of Boris Pasternak and Olga Freidenberg* (New York – London 1981), which was published in Moscow in 1990, during perestroika, as part of a huge volume *The Correspondence of Boris Pasternak*. I was quite taken aback when I failed to find a letter that I remembered well – one written in August 1949... Oh, Soviet censorship! Thankfully, I had a photocopy of the original.

> **Olga Freidenberg:** "All the cities of the long-bodied Russia are hit by the plague of moral and intellectual pogroms.
> The people of thinking professions have lost their faith in logic and hope. The entire latest campaign had the purpose of causing concussion, vomiting and dizziness. Cultural workers with Jewish surnames are being morally lynched.
> You have to see the environment of pogroms at our department: groups of students are walking around, delving into the works of Jewish professors,

listening in to their private conversations, whispering in the corners. We see all that activity before our eyes.

Jews cannot get an education, they aren't being admitted to universities and postgraduate studies.

This cartoon by K. Eliseev was printed on the cover of the Krokodil magazine in the year of Stalin's jubilee (No. 8, 1949). It depicts, in movie director Mikhail Romm's words, "a 'rootless cosmopolitan' with a distinctive Jewish appearance", and on the small sheets sticking out of his rucksack we can see the phrases, "Slander against Soviet culture" and "Slander against Russian art". The brief-case stickers bear the names Andre Gide, Sartre, Somerset Maugham, Lippman, Griffith and Andre Malraux.

The university is being destroyed. All the senior professors have been sacked. The murder of the remains of the intelligentsia is progressing non-stop. Students, teachers, doctors, professors are burdened with unbearable, senseless work. Everyone is forced to learn, pass political exams, all the old men, all the old women.

Academics are attacked mercilessly. They get removed from work, sacked, they're punitively thrown into non-being. The professors who suffered in the nationwide pogroms last year are dying, one after the other. They're getting killed by strokes and heart attacks... The most cynical thing is expensive wreathes and big funerals: the Soviet government knows how to pay respects to its academics."

Someone might ask: what does all this have to do with chess, and the Soviet Championships in particular? It has everything to do with it. David Bronstein's father, who was arrested on the last day of 1937 and released from a camp in 1944 due to ill health (he lost an eye and got a heart condition there), first lived in Kazakhstan in exile, and then rented a room in Podolsk (outside Moscow) – he was not allowed to live in big cities. He would occasionally come to Moscow to visit his son.

Bronstein: "He couldn't understand what was going on in the country. Nobody could, to be honest... My father wanted to find some of his old colleagues in Moscow. I barely managed to dissuade him, because many got arrested for a second time back then. He would go to a cafe with my mother, have a shot of vodka and then say loudly, 'In our camp...' She would shake and ask him to speak more quietly, and he would reply calmly, 'What's wrong with that?' I was so sorry for him... God, what could I do for him? Nothing...

I even went to the higher ups in my efforts to help my father. The Moscow council of the Dynamo society was headed at the time by KGB lieutenant general Solomon Milstein, an avid sports fan. I was told that he was very happy when I won the Moscow championship. I decided to take a risk: I called him and asked to meet. 'Come,' he said laconically. The general met me in a military tunic worn over a naked torso, smiling affably, 'So, what's the matter?'

'I came to ask you to help my father.'

'What's up with him?'

'He was arrested in '37.'

'Where is he now?'

'In Moscow.'

The general's face changed. He asked quietly, 'In Moscow?'

'Yes.'

'Alive?'

'Yes.'

'What do you want from me then? Should I exile him beyond the 101st kilometer?' he whispered, barely audible. I understood and said, 'Thank you.'" (*Shakhmaty v Rossii*, No. 5–6, 1996.)

Neither *Shakhmaty v SSSR* nor the tournament bulletin mentioned anything regarding the dramas happening in the country at the time. Everything was well and good, all championship participants were only concerned with playing decent games worthy of the progressive Soviet chess school and taking a prize place. If there were some conflicts and dramas, they only happened on the chessboard... What more can we say? Watch the movie *Cossacks of the Kuban*, it was made in 1949![5]

Qualification pains

Vasily Panov surprised me when he wrote in an article (see the section "Thoughts on the Equator") that "all our grandmasters, except for the world champion, had to and could play in the semi-finals of the Soviet Championship". If they "had to", why did almost everyone collectively shirk that duty? It turned out that Panov (probably confused by two grandmasters playing in one of the semi-finals) engaged in wishful thinking: this "democratization" only happened in the next cycle! I learned that from the tournament book *17th Soviet Chess Championship* – the tradition of publishing such books resumed for the first time since 1939. "By the decree of the All-Union Committee for Physical Education and Sport, all grandmasters except the world and Soviet champions are now asked to take part in the semi-final tournaments, whereas they were seeded directly into the finals before."

This time, there were four semi-finals in total, with the top three players progressing. Overall, there were 2 grandmasters, 44 masters and "26 of our best candidate masters whose playing skill is better than an average West European master. No country in the world has such strong qualifying competitions." (Botvinnik)

---

[5] A famous Soviet-era film whose name gained negative connotations – it was propaganda about happy lives on a collective farm that had no relation to reality. Similarly, chess magazines and tournament bulletins of the time portrayed pure happiness, in which reality was sterilized and painted over. The film can be found online with English subtitles, e.g. on YouTube

Leningrad semi-final: 1–2. Bondarevsky, Taimanov – 10.5/17; 3. Levenfish – 10; 4. Kopylov – 9.5; 5–8. Zagoriansky, Kuzminykh, Tarasov, Ufimtsev – 9; 9–11. Koblencs, Lisitsin, Ravinsky – 8.5; 12–15. Dubinin, Krogius, Randviir, Shamaev – 8; 16–17. Zamikhovsky, Zagorovsky – 7; 18. Estrin – 5.

Tbilisi semi-final: 1. Geller – 11.5/16; 2. Petrosian – 11; 3. Kholmov – 10; 4–5. Novotelnov, Chistiakov – 9; 6–9. Grechkin, Ilivitsky, Makogonov, Ebralidze – 8.5; 10. Vasiliev – 8; 11. Klaman – 7.5; 12. Nezhmetdinov – 7; 13. Kasparyan – 6.5; 14–15. Lubensky, Solmanis – 6; 16. Pogrebyssky – 5.5; 17. Aramanovich – 5.

Moscow semi-final: 1. Aronin – 11/16; 2–3. Goldberg, Liublinsky – 10.5; 4–5. Kan, Moiseev – 10; 6–7. Alatortsev, E. Poliak – 9.5; 8. Fridstein – 9; 9–10. Abramov, Kamyshov – 8.5; 11. Khasin – 8; 12.

Despite his work in the technical department of the Power Plant Ministry and preparation for his doctoral thesis, world champion Mikhail Botvinnik hadn't forgotten about chess. He even wrote an article about the semi-finals and often visited the final tournament. From M. Botvinnik's archive.

Beilin – 7; 13. Cherepkov – 6.5; 14–15. Batuev, Lyskov – 5.5; 16. Bonch-Osmolovsky – 3.5; 17. Khavin – 3.

Vilnius semi-final: 1–3. Mikenas, Sokolsky, Furman – 11.5/17; 4. Bannik – 11; 5–6. Bastrikov, Byvshev – 10; 7. Chekhover – 9.5; 8. Simagin – 9; 9–10. Vistaneckis, Kirillov – 8.5; 11. Ratner – 8; 12–13. Kopaev, Rovner – 7.5; 14–15. Arulaid, Duz-Khotimirsky – 7; 16. Aratovsky – 6; 17. Podolny – 5.5; 18. Vatnikov – 3.5.

Botvinnik: "About twenty years ago, the chess players of my generation started to storm the positions that were previously completely occupied by the 'chess old guard'. It would be useful to recall that because of the young players' success in the semi-finals. Among the winners who earned the right to take part in the national championship finals, we see the names of young players Geller, Petrosian, Taimanov and Kholmov, in addition to Aronin, Liublinsky, Kopylov and Furman, who also should be considered part of the young generation.

Kholmov: "I was thoroughly impressed with the play of candidate master Geller. He's a mature player who possesses great endgame technique. His theoretical knowledge is also very good. Young master Petrosian is playing with exceptional ease. There's probably still not enough necessary depth in his play, but he's very skillful in tactical complications." (*Four Semi-Finals* bulletin, 5th July 1949.)

Levenfish: "Kopylov possesses a very remarkable and original chess talent. His play is purely tactical as of now. If Kopylov manages to create a suitable situation on the board, he can be dangerous to anyone in the middlegame." (Ibid., 18th June.) *(Kopylov failed to qualify from the semi but nevertheless played in the final instead of the ill Bondarevsky – see below.)*

Duz-Khotimirsky: "We can say for sure that Furman confirmed his high class in Vilnius. His play is reminiscent of M. M. Botvinnik in his old days. Great opening knowledge and chess understanding, skillful exploitation of his opponents' positional mistakes and occasional deep combination ideas are all characteristic of the style of this talented master." (Ibid., 14th July.)

It's telling that such seasoned chess 'fighters' as Alatortsev, Kan, Lisitsin, Makogonov and Chekhover failed to qualify. These players, who have taken part in numerous Soviet Championship finals and international tournaments, lacked the necessary stamina this time.

However, not all the players of the old generation have fallen under the youth's onslaught. Grandmaster Bondarevsky, and masters Mikenas, Sokolsky and Goldberg, have withstood the intense battles and earned the right to qualify. The success of Grandmaster Levenfish is especially remarkable: at the age of 60, he's managed to perform at full strength in such a lengthy tournament...

Mikenas: "After a relatively long absence, I'll take part in

Мастер Е. ГЕЛЛЕР
(Одесса)
Дружеский шарж Н. ЛИСА.

Efim Geller, the winner of the Tbilisi semi-final. Cartoon by N. Lis. From the tournament bulletin (20th November 1949).

my third Soviet Championship final. Of course, I'm not counting on great success, but I'll try to play in a sharp tactical style. I was once called 'the scourge of grandmasters', now I'm 'the scourge of candidate masters' – what if the old times return?" (Ibid., 20th July.)

Duz-Khotimirsky: "I've known Sokolsky since 1926 when I met him in Penza – the boy who amazed me with his chess talent. I was always happy at his successes, which were numerous. Unfortunately, he has suffered some resounding failures as well, which can only be explained by his poor health." (Ibid., 14th July.)

Taimanov is one of the most talented young players. His success in the Leningrad semi-final proved that his poor performance in the 16th Soviet Championship was a fluke. The success of the Odessa University student Geller has attracted everyone's attention... His first place in the Tbilisi semi-final suggests that the talented master may become one of the best players in the country.

He only got his master's title for winning the semi-final, and when he came to Moscow, he was technically still a candidate master: the title papers were signed literally days before the championship draw!

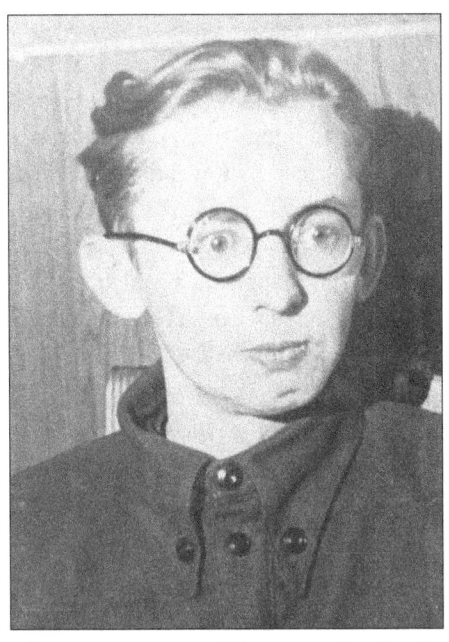

The tournament in Tbilisi proved to be the last for the talented master Viktor Andreevich Vasiliev: he died in 1950 at the age of just 34 from wounds that he suffered at the front during WWII... This photo was taken during the Leningrad championship of 1940 where he shared 2nd to 4th place. Photo by M. Volkovysky from his archive. Published for the first time.

Дружеский шарж
М. ВАДБОЛЬСКОГО
(Тбилиси)

Ratmir Kholmov giving Tigran Petrosian an exam. Cartoon by M. Vadbolsky. From the semi-final bulletin (3rd July 1949).

Geller: "I grew up on the traditions of the Soviet chess school. I was largely influenced by the games of Chigorin, Alekhine, Botvinnik, Smyslov, Bronstein. I owe my success in Tbilisi to them." (Ibid., 3rd July.)

Botvinnik didn't mention the poor result of Yakov Estrin, whose failure was explained by **Levenfish:** "Estrin was the only semi-final participant who wasn't concerned with his score. He experimented in every game: either offering a gambit, or accepting one, or going for some complicated continuations that were all but impossible to calculate. As a result, Estrin earned few points, but a lot of useful knowledge about playing in sharp positions." (Ibid., 16th June.) The result is well-known: Yakov Borisovich got to become world correspondence champion (1972-1976), as well as a renowned theoretician, the author of many opening books, gambits included, and the co-author of the famous *Opening Course*.

Petrosian and Kholmov are playing well. Furman is also very talented. The young Leningrad master amazed everyone in the 16th championship, taking third place. Some thought that it was a fluke. Now, Furman has proved with his performance in Vilnius that his third place in the national championship was no accident." (*Four Semi-Finals* bulletin, 1st July.)

An Unprecedented Championship!

From the press: "The opening ceremony of the 17th Soviet chess championship took place in the evening of 15th October. Tournament participants, arbiters, chess community leaders and reporters gathered in the conference room of the USSR Council of Ministers' Committee for Physical Education and Sport.

Committee deputy chairman D. V. Postnikov declares the 17th Soviet Championship officially open.

'Nine grandmasters,' comrade Postnikov says, 'who were recently awarded the titles of international grandmaster, are joined by the winners of the recent semi-finals. The tournament attracts a lot of interest both in our country and from the entire world...'

Have you noticed? It's still 1949, but he refers to those "recently awarded the titles of international grandmaster", even though the official date of the award is listed everywhere as 1950 (including in the *Shakhmaty* encyclopedia)... But there's no mistake. The international titles were established by the Paris FIDE congress (1949), and it was already clear who met the requirements, but the titles were only officially awarded at the 1950 congress in Copenhagen.

Then, the chief arbiter, V. A. Goglidze, read out the championship statute and regulations for the players. The winner is awarded the Soviet champion's title, a gold medal, a first-degree diploma and a prize. The runner-up receives a silver token, a second-degree diploma and a prize. The player who takes third place gets a bronze token, a third-degree diploma and a prize. The players who take fourth, fifth and sixth get a Sports Committee certificate.

If first place is shared between two players, they will play a six-game match. In the event that first place is shared between three or more players, the question of the champion's title shall be resolved in a double round-robin match tournament.

> This is obviously an echo of the previous year's story, when Bronstein and Kotov were asked to play a Soviet Championship match, but were ultimately both awarded gold medals. The tournament schedule was the same as the previous year's: two rounds, then a play-off day, then two rounds, a play-off day and a rest day.

Eventually, the draw was held *(grandmasters in italic)*: 1. S. Furman (Leningrad), 2. A. Sokolsky (Lvov), 3. N. Kopylov, 4. M. Taimanov (both Leningrad), 5. *V. Ragozin* (Moscow), 6. V. Liublinsky (Moscow Oblast), 7. *A. Kotov*, 8. *V. Smyslov*, 9. *S. Flohr* (all Moscow), 10. E. Geller (Odessa), 11. *P. Keres* (Tallinn), 12. *A. Lilienthal* (Moscow), 13. L. Aronin (Moscow Oblast), 14. T. Petrosian (Yerevan), 15. V. Mikenas (Vilnius), 16. G. Goldberg (Leningrad), 17. *D. Bronstein* (Moscow), 18. *G. Levenfish* (Leningrad), 19. *I. Boleslavsky* (Sverdlovsk), 20. R. Kholmov (Vilnius)." (*17th Soviet Chess Championship* bulletin, 18th October 1949.)

Goglidze: "I am deeply convinced that the 17th championship is the strongest of all the Soviet Championships. It's a pity that we don't see the greatest chess player of the present time, world champion M. M. Botvinnik, among the participants – he couldn't play because he was too busy with his academic work. Unfortunately, A. Tolush, whose sharp, tactical play always livens up the struggle, and I. Bondarevsky aren't playing either. But all the other outstanding chess players will take part in this championship...

I got to play in the second Moscow International Tournament in 1935. Botvinnik, Capablanca, Lasker, Flohr and others played there. And still I think that the lineup of this championship is stronger than that outstanding competition.

Chekhover: "I played in five national championships and have thoroughly studied the materials of other championships, and I can say for sure that there has been no stronger national tournament than this one." (Ibid., 5th November.)

It's hard to say who's going to win. But there's no doubt that Bronstein and Kotov will have a hard time defending the honorable title of Soviet champion that they won last year." (Ibid., 22nd October.)

Predictions from Flohr

Flohr, like Tartakower, the inventor of the "prediction genre", didn't have a specific aim of predicting anything. Why risk taking wild shots in the dark when you can just amuse readers and have some fun yourself? Of course, their joking hints also had a grain of rationality, but still... It's highly unlikely that the readers of this essay (written after round 9) actually wanted to know whether the author would really be able to answer the question in the title of his article, "So, Who's Going to Be the Champion?"

Flohr: "I would like to give some clarity on the most pressing question, even though, of course, I won't be able to give a precise answer. One thing is clear: there's not a single grandmaster who doesn't want to win. Our grandmasters are modest people. Every one of them is secretly hoping to become the national champion...

Soviet champions Bronstein and Kotov. Both of them have proved that they could win both together and separately. At the very least, they'll definitely be glad to repeat last year's achievement.

Boleslavsky. Will he again be 'only' a runner-up? That would not be bad, of course. But the big jump from second place to first should eventually happen.

Гроссмейстер
С. ФЛОР

Дружеский шарж
Н. ЛИСА.

Salo Flohr. Cartoon by N. Lis. From the tournament bulletin (6th November 1949).

Keres. He played solidly and convincingly in the 15th championship and became Soviet champion. In the 16th championship and the world championship match tournament he overthought things too much. 'Enough of that!' says Keres. A new success could well be on the cards.

Smyslov. His situation is most unenviable. In theory, the world's second-best player should win the national championship. But in practice, it's not that simple. The chess players of one-sixth of the world are stronger than all the chess players of the rest of the world taken together. If Vasily Vasilyevich wins, everyone will say that that's how it should've been. If someone else wins, Smyslov will let himself down. But that's only half of the problem. He'll let down his incalculable number of fans who are sure of his victory. Yes, it's Smyslov who should really give his all!

Levenfish. 'It would be nice to give them a little beating. I don't like all this talk about 'old', 'the oldest'. Can't they call me an old man after I turn 90, like Mieses? In the sixth round, Vadim Sinyavsky came to the conclusion that I lost to Kotov because he was 24 years younger than me. In the seventh round, I defeated Smyslov – obviously, that was because I'm 30 years older than him!'

Lilienthal. Of course, he would've 'shown' everyone if everything was normal. But one thing is not normal: Lilienthal quit smoking several years

МОСКВА – БУДАПЕШТ

МАТЧ-ТУРНИР ДРУЖБЫ

КОМАНДА МОСКВЫ: Котов, Смыслов, Бронштейн, Рагозин, Авербах, Флор, Симагин и Лилиенталь.

Six of the eight participants of the Moscow vs. Budapest match again took the stage at TsDKZh to play in the 17th Soviet championship. "Moscow – Budapest Friendly Match Tournament. Moscow team: Kotov, Smyslov, Bronstein, Ragozin, Averbakh, Flohr, Simagin and Lilienthal." From the Ogonyok magazine (No. 17, 1949).

ago. This role as a non-smoker is hampering him. This tournament will surely serve as serious preparation for the non-smoking Lilienthal before the Budapest tournament. By the way, there are only two smokers left among our 11 grandmasters – Bondarevsky and Ragozin. Maybe they'll quit smoking too, out of solidarity with the majority?

Ragozin. His status – international grandmaster, FIDE vice president, Botvinnik's coach, *Shakhmaty v SSSR* editor – more or less forces him to strive for creative and sporting successes. A fan asked me the other day: 'I like Ragozin's original style. Tell me, Grandmaster, if Ragozin managed to help Botvinnik become world champion, why can't he help himself become Soviet champion?'

A reasonable question. But my answer was obvious as well. You see, 'something' depended on Botvinnik, too!

Flohr. It's hard to live only on memories of past glories. I'm in desperate need of success. I want to win so much! And I really don't want to lose! And I'm so tired (together with you, dear readers) of draws! What should I do, what should I do? Dear supporters, please help me!..

It would be, of course, impolite not to ask the masters for their opinion as well. But I don't think we need to ask every one of them to speak individually. All eleven say as one, 'It would be quite funny if one of us took first place. It's unlikely to happen, but, at the very least, we have already ruined the mood of some grandmasters at the start. And we are sure that there'll be more surprises in the table!'" (Tournament bulletin, 1st November.)

The First Storms

This is the title of Boris Galich's report. I don't know why, but this was his only report in the tournament bulletin. A couple of scanty "spectator's essays" couldn't compensate for this loss, and neither could the "Our Questions" column (previously tested back in the semi-final bulletin), where tournament participants and guests shared their opinion on every issue. The impression was somewhat brightened by the photos and rare cartoons, mostly by "N. Lis". We have already seen this name on the pages of chess bulletins, and we'll see it again. Naum Moiseevich Lisogorsky, an outstanding master of political caricature, worked at *Krokodil* for half a century. In the wartime years, he bolstered soldiers' morale in the frontline newspapers, publishing a satirical column "Fun Katyusha" that became very popular.

The picture was also somewhat livened up by occasional epigrams from another *Krokodil* staff member, **Yakov Bylanin**. His verse about Kopylov's attempt to catch Levenfish in a half-forgotten line of the Giuoco Piano probably pleased Grigory Yakovlevich:

What's new for Kopylov here	Bishops, queens, rooks, knights
Is not new for Levenfish.	He keeps in his mind,
All the tricks of kings,	From Romulus up to the present day.

I referred to Galich's reports as "a true oasis of the living word" earlier. This one deserves a similar designation, and the only element that's lacking is humor; but back then, humor was generally in short supply in the country...

B. Galich: "The Central Railway Workers House of Culture, TsDKZh, is increasingly and frequently referred to jokingly by Moscow fans as TsDKSh, with the last letter meaning *'shakhmatisty' (i.e. The Central Chess Players House of Culture)*. I don't think that the railway workers would complain: they have been very hospitable, opening their doors to many great tournaments these last years. The 16th Soviet Championship was played there. The captivating friendly match Moscow – Budapest was too... And now, twenty of the strongest players of the world's strongest chess country are doing battle here again.

No wonder that this luminous white-stone hall, wrapping round the stage in a crescent, has become familiar and almost homely for Moscow fans of this wise and ancient, yet ageless and young thrilling game. Everything is pleasing to the eyes here: the checkered ceiling, the gentle light from the chandeliers, the open ranks and files of comfortable chairs, the lush beauty of the fresh autumn flowers that bloom in the hall like the best 'evergreen' chess combinations.

Another thing is yet more surprising: why have the tournament organizers decorated the entrance to the building that hosts the biggest event in the country's chess life so bleakly and unlovingly? The facade is dark, there's not a single light by the door, and the one sign advertising the tournament can only be read in the street lights. The organizers lacked a certain 'fire' there...

But it's just a small quirk. A little comment on a 'bad move'.

Let's get back to the hall, where 'every evening, at the appointed hour', a sharp, exciting struggle is happening. There's enough fire to warm the hearts of fans, make their blood boil, sharpen their thought. Not only those twenty who lean over the board are playing and creating – everyone in the hall who watches the games on demonstration boards also plays, comes up with combinations, finds 'best moves'. This is what makes the atmosphere in the hall especially pleasant – this feeling of everyone's commitment, everyone's participation in the events happening on stage.

The third round's opening had just ended. Nothing yet foretells the sharp struggle at the finish...
Photo by G. Yablonovsky. From D. Bronstein's archive. Published for the first time.

'Mikenas' exchange sacrifice was unnecessary,' someone to my right whispers.

'Nonsense, you should look deeper,' a spectator from the row in front of me says quietly, turning to us.

'You want to say that you can see further than Kotov?' the offended fan hisses.

'We shall see,' the other says apologetically.

'That's just it!' my neighbor to the right says menacingly, even though it's unclear what satisfaction he gets from such a philosophical conclusion.

As a matter of fact, nobody follows the 'friendly advice': everyone plays combinations, gets into fights, guesses the secret ideas of grandmasters, and, of course, nothing is nicer for a fan than seeing Smyslov or Keres make a move they predicted.

'I told you so!' they say with delight, looking condescendingly at someone who proposed a different move.

And then, we again hear the skeptical, 'We shall see!..'

And we do see: the first rounds have been quite intense – a good omen, a proper start, no matter what openings we see on the boards. This time, the start of the tournament wasn't as cold as in the previous year. On the contrary,

Vasily Smyslov, the hero of the start. After winning this game against Bronstein, his score was 4.5/5! Photo by G. Yablonovsky. From D. Bronstein's archive. Published for the first time.

the swords have been 'rattling' since the first moves, and the first king was dethroned in record time – in the 50th minute, after 13 moves *(Petrosian lost to Kotov)*. The king, of course, stumbled and fell almost by itself, without much help from the opponent, but there's nothing you can do – you have to stay on your feet, especially when you make your first moves.

Self-confidence of the youth is a good quality, if you don't abuse it. It's better than the complacency of the famous. But this confidence shouldn't turn into confusion. The art of winning owes much to the ability to bounce back after bitter losses. This is the expression of willpower of great chess players, and the incumbent world champion is the best example. He always improved his play after the rare and somewhat relative setbacks in his chess career.

It's not a bad thing that Petrosian and Geller lost in the first two rounds. Losing two points is, of course, unpleasant. But losing your fighting spirit and balance is much worse. And so, we should wish the two youngest participants to stay calm inside. Let them think of each subsequent game as the only one they'll get to play in Moscow. No matter how many points they score – our young players have their lives ahead of them; what's important is the number of truly beautiful works of chess art they create, new, interesting ideas and fresh solutions they come up with to please the fans of this inexhaustibly deep and beautiful game.

And Smyslov, Kotov, Keres, Lilienthal and other grandmasters are the first line of the best chess players in the world, the candidates for a match with Botvinnik *(Bronstein was still "backstage": because of an illness, he only entered the fray in round 4)*. It's not shameful to lose to them, but defeating them is an honor, a sign of great success.

The grandmasters' predicament is somewhat worse. If a grandmaster wins, everyone says 'It's only natural'. If he loses, then everyone sighs in pity.

Kotov had already experienced this pain. When he defeated Petrosian, nobody gave him much praise. However, when he got into a difficult position the next day and ultimately had to resign to Mikenas, the skeptics immediately said, 'Some strong player he is!'

It seems that you have to face a lot of suffering to become a strong tournament fighter, with resilience becoming an integral part of a player's personality. And still, we can only praise those players who aren't afraid to lose in their relentless will to win.

Active, attacking strategy has long been a calling card of the Soviet chess style. Chigorin's principle, his attacking spirit has found worthy successors in a whole army of brilliant masters of our time. The dream of the Russian school's founder has come true: our Motherland boasts both the individual and team world champions.

At the Candidates Tournament that's going to take place in Budapest in the spring, eight out of fourteen players represent the Soviet Union. Seven of them (except for Bondarevsky, who is ill) are taking part in the Soviet Championship.

What illness struck Bondarevsky? It's unknown. Allegedly, this same illness prevented him from taking part in the Candidates Tournament as well. Why "allegedly"? Because, according to Averbakh, illness played no part in that. After Euwe and Fine declined to play, and the U.S. State Department refused to issue an exit visa to Reshevsky to travel to communist Hungary, Trifunovic was the next in line to play in the tournament. But in September 1949 (before the Soviet Championship!), the USSR broke off relations with Yugoslavia, and to prevent the "enemy" from playing in the tournament, the Soviet side... sacrificed Bondarevsky!

Averbakh: "Officially, it was declared that he suddenly got ill, and the competition started with ten players. However, the Sports Committee decided to make amends with Bondarevsky afterwards and sent him to Budapest two weeks later, as a spectator.

When Igor Zakharovich entered the tournament hall, one of the participants, Miguel Najdorf, approached him, poked him in the ribs and said wonderingly, 'They said that you were seriously ill, but I see that you're as strong as an ox!'

Bondarevsky only smiled wryly." (From the book *What the Pieces Don't Mention.*)

Of course, their play attracts the most attention. And they have lived up to expectations. Vasily Smyslov has already pleased us with deep, original, interesting games – the commentators will probably reveal all the subtleties to us later. Boleslavsky, who was reproached for being too peaceful in the first round, satisfied the desires of the most 'bloodthirsty' fans the next day, crushing Kopylov in just 25 moves. Keres choked Geller in his stranglehold, the Odessa player couldn't do much about it. Even Flohr and Lilienthal, who are usually 'amicable' towards each other, created a real storm on the chessboard this time, pleasing the fans with a sharp, beautiful game.

Therefore, we fans don't have much to complain about now. The course seems to be correct – play as many decisive games as possible.

'Keep it up!' – that's everything we can wish to the strongest players.

And while there are beautiful, clear autumn days outside, we want to see a flow of storms, whirlwinds and hurricanes inside the spacious hall on Komsomolskaya Square, reaching their peak strength towards the end of the tournament. Because these storms – we won't hide that – is where the chess fans seek and find the calm of true pleasure." (Tournament bulletin, 22nd October.)

Thoughts on the Equator

I was happy to see that the tradition of having different authors write round reports had taken root. The constellation of names was even brighter this time around. While there were only "spectators" among the masters – Romanovsky, Tolush, Alatortsev, Abramov, and Lisitsin – four grandmaster participants wrote reports: Levenfish, Bronstein, Kotov and Boleslavsky!

But this approach has one problem: there was no consistent picture of the competition. The game descriptions were thorough and professional, but one element was lacking: the bigger picture. Thankfully, the bulletin editors saw that problem as well and asked Vasily Panov to describe the state of play after round 10, which he did wonderfully.

As an epigraph, let's look at the standings at this moment: Keres – 7/10; Geller, Kotov, Flohr – 6.5; Boleslavsky, Smyslov, Taimanov – 6; Bronstein,

Kholmov – 5.5; Aronin, Sokolsky – 5; Kopylov, Ragozin, Furman – 4.5; Levenfish, Mikenas – 4; Goldberg, Lilienthal – 3.5; Liublinsky, Petrosian – 3.

Panov: "Half of the tournament has passed, but there's no leader – if by leader we mean a player who has amassed a substantial lead over the others, a player whose victory is beyond doubt.

Considering the probable results of the adjourned games, we should consider grandmasters Keres, Kotov, Boleslavsky and Smyslov as the players comprising the leading group. Unlike last time, all of them started the tournament under the banner of a sharp, intense creative struggle, and this strategy seems to have justified itself.

Indeed, a draw both gains half a point and loses half a point. If a draw is 'half a win', then it's also 'half a loss'. Thus, there's no reason to prefer the strategy of cautious progress through numerous draws and occasional wins. Even Grandmaster Flohr, the known adherent of such a strategy and a seasoned tournament fighter, has still played a number of games in a lively, fighting style and got good results. By contrast, we should note that those players who tried to apply this seemingly reliable tactic have only devalued

Rookie Viktor Liublinsky. To the right, Lev Aronin and Vasily Smyslov. In the background, Andre Lilienthal and Grigory Levenfish. Photo by G. Yablonovsky. From D. Bronstein's archive. Published for the first time.

their chances. Liublinsky and Aronin's series of draws, Aronin's draw offer to Keres in a clearly better position, and Petrosian and Kholmov's draw agreement with a board still full of pieces, are the unfortunate 'blots' on creativity, and they're especially harmful for young players.

> The overall draw percentage in this championship was close to the previous one (45%; in the 15th championship, that statistic was 49%). I wanted to praise Galich's "anti-draw revolt" that started the previous year, but then decided to look at the trend and calculated the draw percentage for the 14th championship. I wish I hadn't done that: 35%!! It's unlikely we will ever see such an "anti-draw" championship again...

Yes, the championship leaders have lost some games because of their tendency to play complicated, intense, double-edged games. This only shows the high level of the championship, the strength of the line-up – the majority of participants also chose the way of conscious creative risk instead of dull draws that are characteristic of competitions abroad. And the reason why we now have several leaders instead of one is precisely the fact that this strategy works both in creative and sporting regards; the fight for the honorable title of Soviet champion will probably last until the final rounds.

Analysis of Keres' games is quite instructive. In the last couple of years, his playing style underwent a bit of a crisis. It was clear that this great master of brilliant attacks and deeply calculated combinations was artificially trying to steer his picturesque style towards dry, purely rationalistic positional play. As a result, his games sometimes made us forget about the winner of some of the greatest international tournaments and the 15th Soviet Championship, about the Keres who defeated the ex-world champion Euwe when the latter was at his peak strength during their match.

But the first games of the 17th championship have already shown that the Estonian grandmaster has 'found himself' again. A spectacular 20-move win against Mikenas, and fighting games against Geller and Lilienthal show that Keres is in his best form. Even his loss to Bronstein, which can be mostly explained by poor opening play, shows his great tenacity in defense and his resourcefulness and inventiveness in the middlegame *(see game 215)*.

> **Keres:** "I had 5.5 points after the first seven games, and it seemed that I had managed to overcome my creative crisis. Alas, the course of the tournament showed that I was wrong. I played inconsistently, alternating wins and losses." (From the book *One Hundred Games*.) In round 11, he would lose to Furman and cede the leadership to Kotov...

Can we say that Smyslov and Kotov had a bad start, since they couldn't avoid defeat either? There's no doubt that the losses of those grandmasters show the high level of the other championship participants rather than a decline of their own talent. But there were other reasons as well.

Kotov's loss in the game with Mikenas, for instance, was a consequence of a badly-chosen compromise opening. The Staunton Gambit has been considered dubious for a long time, and it's especially inappropriate for Kotov's style: he can seize the initiative, but he can also hold a difficult position for hours providing that there are some hidden counterchances available.

I think that Smyslov's and, partially, Boleslavsky's opening strategy is wrong – they're repeatedly using the same lines with black. The Smyslov System in the Grunfeld has brought him a lot of great victories previously and has no principal drawbacks in and of itself, and that is also true of the Boleslavsky System with e7-e5 in the Sicilian. But constant usage of the same line, even a very good one, is a fundamental mistake. Not only because the opponents know exactly what awaits them, but also because the tried-and-tested setups eventually start stifling the imagination and strategic thinking of their creators, forcing them into creative monotony. That's why some fashionable lines used for decades suddenly get mothballed without apparent reason, and then get revived a while later. Chess requires freshness and constant renewal!

We should hope that Smyslov addresses his experience in the games against Levenfish *(see game 207)* and Furman: unlike their predecessors, neither of his opponents tried to refute the Smyslov System in principle but still managed to prove that this line had lost 'the danger of novelty'. *(Losing great games is also a skill. Smyslov lost only those two games – and both received brilliancy prizes!)*

Interestingly, Boleslavsky doesn't use his pet opening system that much now, trying to diversify his repertoire.

Boleslavsky's great start can be explained by his participation in the recent Bolshevik sports society

Thanks to the leader's setback (Smyslov lost in rounds 6 and 8), Paul Keres surged ahead – 6.5/9. Photo by N. Semyonov. From the author's archive.

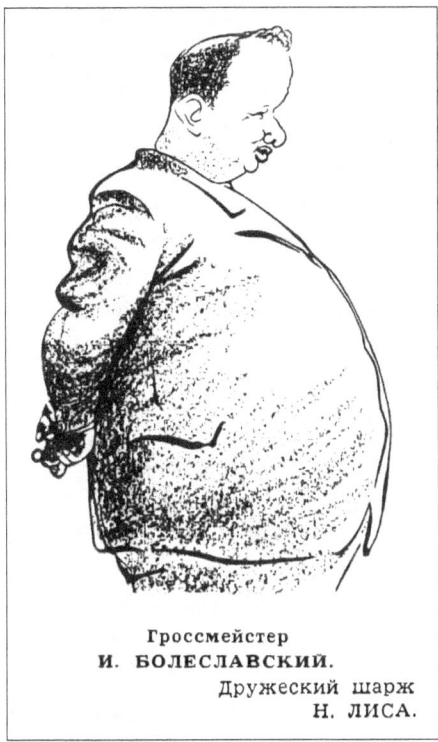

Гроссмейстер
И. БОЛЕСЛАВСКИЙ.
Дружеский шарж
Н. ЛИСА.

Grandmaster Boleslavsky. Cartoon by N. Lis. From the tournament bulletin (20th October 1949).

championship; the grandmaster had enough time to sharpen his chess weapons in games against both experienced masters and young players. We can say the same thing about Levenfish, whose fighting spirit and self-belief have soared after qualifying from the semi-final.

Bondarevsky: "I've been a Soviet Championship regular since 1937, and this is the first time for me to sit among the spectators because of an illness. I'm watching the tournament with pleasure and great interest... Boleslavsky demonstrated the most consistent and logical play in the first half of the championship. This was apparent in all of his games, which he played without obvious mistakes." (Tournament bulletin, 3rd November.)

Romanovsky: "I'm watching the games of Keres and Kotov with great pleasure. But I'm especially impressed with the play of my old comrade and friend Grandmaster Levenfish, who showed everyone how it's done at the start." (Ibid., 28th October.)

In regard to that, I would like to turn to a quote from Kotov that was published in the second issue of the bulletin. 'Too much time passes between our serious competitions,' Kotov writes. 'P. Keres, for instance, hasn't played anywhere since the 16th Soviet Championship. For some grandmasters, the team match against Hungary was the only competition they have taken part in this year. Can't we hold more big tournaments with grandmaster participation in the future?'

It's known that all our grandmasters, except for the world champion, had to and could play in the semi-finals of the Soviet Championship, together with all our masters and the most talented young players. For various reasons, many grandmasters avoid taking part in the semi-finals or other competitions, such as Moscow championships or sports society championships that provide exceptional opportunities for creative improvement.

Bronstein, after surprising Kholmov with 1.e4 e5 2.♘f3 ♘c6 3.♗b5 f5, watches the reaction of his opponent. Have you noticed that he's standing in the same pose as during the game against Smyslov? From D. Bronstein's archive. Published for the first time.

I think that the downside of undervaluing the semi-finals and other tournaments manifested itself in this championship. Those grandmasters who didn't follow the lead of Levenfish, Boleslavsky and Flohr (who took part in the same Bolshevik society championship) hurt their own preparation by not constantly honing their talent in games against opponents of very different styles. Without a doubt, had Smyslov played Furman, had Lilienthal played Petrosian or had Kotov played Sokolsky in the semi-finals, they would've approached their games against those opponents in the final differently, they would have had a clearer understanding of them and wouldn't have lost.

The participation of our best chess players in semi-finals and other, less 'big' and 'serious' competitions would have been beneficial for both the seasoned veterans and the youngsters who play them.

> **Sokolsky:** "Now I'm celebrating two milestones of my chess life – my participation in the 17th Soviet Championship with a very strong lineup, and the publication of my book *Modern Chess Openings* that I have worked on for the last three years.
>
> Now let's discuss the tournament itself. I am sure that **this competition will serve as a turning point for young players as they storm the heights still held by the middle generation** (*emphasis by me – S.V.*). Geller and Taimanov are playing especially well." (Ibid., 30th October.)

And the youth is improving in leaps and bounds! They are learning, but there's also a lot to learn from them. After a bad start, caused in large part by their natural 'awe before great names' and lack of experience in playing such illustrious opponents, the young masters are playing better and better with each round.

Geller, who started the tournament with two losses, has caught up with the leading group. Taimanov and Kholmov are going shoulder to shoulder with him, having already shown their solid, diverse styles in the last championship. Even Petrosian, demoralized by a bad start, showed great play against Lilienthal.

We can say for sure that the youth's onslaught will become even stronger in the second half of the tournament.

Speaking of the youth, we can't help but turn our attention to the perplexing results of its most talented representative – grandmaster Bronstein, the Soviet champion. A series of lifeless draws, sometimes with a board still full of pieces (for example, against Kotov and Flohr), ended with a win against Keres in a good, sharp style, but then he lost a

Рис. Ю. Узбякова

День отдыха на турнире.

"Rest day at the tournament". Participants were accorded only four rest days in the entire championship: after rounds 4, 8, 12 and 16. Cartoon by Y. Uzbyakov. (Sovietsky Sport, 25th October 1949).

theoretically drawn endgame against Smyslov *(a rook and bishop versus a rook)*.

Bronstein's play is inexplicably languid and passive, so uncharacteristic of his spectacular style. Even in the game with Keres, Bronstein quickly got an overwhelming position, but his conversion of the advantage was not perfect.

How can we explain the lack of Bronstein's creative enthusiasm and characteristic willpower and temperament that he showed at the Stockholm Interzonal and 16th Soviet Championship?

Maybe the reason is that he has somewhat undervalued the Soviet Championship in comparison with the upcoming Candidates Tournament in Budapest. Some people still say that the Soviet Championship is a stepping-stone, a training ground for the best Soviet chess players before the battle for the world championship.

In actuality, the Soviet Championship is not just the biggest and most important national competition: it's also the biggest tournament in the world, and any other competition looks second-rate in comparison. In essence, only a Soviet champion has the moral right to challenge for the world championship, because it's hard to imagine that the world champion would play worse than the Soviet champion. Botvinnik's excellent victory in the match tournament of the world's strongest players was the crowning jewel in his long string of wins in international competitions and Soviet Championships. It's no accident that the International Chess Federation ascribed exceptional importance to the Soviet Championships in determining eligibility for international grandmaster and international master titles.

We are sure that Bronstein will not cede his honorable title of Soviet champion without a fight and will show his characteristic creative boldness, diversity and brilliance at the finish." (Tournament bulletin, 3rd November.)

Jostling among the Leaders

The lively, dynamic reports of Boris Galich are indeed sorely missed!.. In all the bulletins, I've only managed to find one sketch by a P. Vensky called "In the Lobby" (you'll find an excerpt below). Thankfully, one of the participants wrote a memoir. As you read his nostalgic writings, you immerse yourself in the unforgettable atmosphere of the post-war championships...

Bronstein: "Back in those years and later, the Soviet Championships were considered the strongest tournaments in the world (this distinction was extended to the semi-finals as well). In addition, the purpose of playing in the championship was different from today's desire to score as many points as possible. At the time, chess was a kind of intellectual spectacle, with fans expecting the players to create brilliant chess artworks. We usually played on stages of theaters and concert halls, with halls full of spectators. The tournaments lasted for a month, with four games a week played (time control was 2.5 hours per 40 moves), two play-off days for adjourned games, and only

The TsDKZh box seats: Gavriil Veresov, Lev Aronin and David Bronstein. From D. Bronstein's archive. Published for the first time.

one rest day. It was exhausting for the players, but very interesting for the fans.

The games started at 5 p.m., and the halls would soon be filled with chess fans who watched the games on big demonstration boards. The spectators took great pleasure in watching the games of the best players in the world. During the rounds, there were simultaneous displays in the lobby, and grandmasters and masters gave lectures.

> **P. Vensky:** "The 'discussion' at the demonstration boards attracts the attention of simultaneous display participants sitting nearby at the chess tables. Some of them run up to the leaders' board and, looking back at Master Averbakh who is giving the simul, write down the latest moves. The daily simultaneous displays in the lobby are immensely popular...
>
> And then, the battle reaches its climax. The time-trouble heat begins. The demonstrators now can't change the position in time – they're moving several pieces at once. One fan aptly described their work: 'They're bringing moves from the hall in bundles.'
>
> There are fewer and fewer people in the lobby – everyone is afraid of missing even a single move. Now, there's no time to argue anymore. The fans rush back to the tournament hall..." (Ibid., 12th November.)

Dedicated bulletins containing all games were printed after each round, and many newspapers published tournament reports. In addition, you could learn the round results from radio news reports, and there was a special chess news section right after midnight. This alone shows how popular chess and chess players were back then!

Even though it was pleasant to bask in all that attention, that didn't make the players' task any easier. Even those Soviet Championship participants whose names weren't widely known were still very strong players, and it wasn't easy to defeat them. There were no computers back then, we could only rely on our own

Kotov led for five rounds in a row (10.5/15), but the loss to Geller in round 16 demoralized him. From D. Bronstein's archive.

resources. I got to play in more than twenty Soviet Championships, and in each of them, I managed to create several beautiful games applauded by the spectators. I must remind you that the prizes in those tournaments were quite small (there were only three money prizes, which were ludicrously low – just 300, 200 and 100 rubles!), and the main reward for taking a high place could be an opportunity to play in a tournament abroad, which was considered a great stroke of luck." (From the book *Sorcerer's Apprentice*.)

Flohr: "After 13 rounds, the situation in the tournament is fascinating: Kotov is the leader, but a big group of players is trailing him, with everyone wanting (and able) to catch up. The finishing stage of the tournament is begining in a very tense environment." (Tournament bulletin, 10th November.)

> "The end is close, but there's no leader!"
> One man said. However, another one Rebuked him fiercely:
> "But there are many combative wins. That's why there's no one leader – Because there are several of them!"
>
> **Yak. Bylanin**

Goglidze: "Not only grandmasters Kotov, Keres, Boleslavsky, Smyslov, Flohr, and Bronstein, but also young masters Kholmov, Taimanov, Furman and even Geller, who's only just received his master's title and is playing in his first Soviet Championship final, still have chances of winning the gold medal." (Ibid.)

Taimanov: "I'm most impressed with Boleslavsky – I like his rich, purposeful play. I think that Boleslavsky, together with Kotov, Smyslov and Bronstein, is a primary candidate for the championship...

I felt uneasy when I went to the tournament. I passed my last postgraduate entry exam for the Leningrad Conservatory on 12th October, and then I played concerts on 14th, 15th and 16th October. That's why, by the way, I couldn't make it to the first round in time.

> Here is an excerpt from an article by the future famous playwright and big chess fan **Emil Braginsky** (according to Beilin, his journalistic debut happened in 1945, in the *Sovetskaya Latvia* newspaper; Koblencs edited the chess column there, but he was playing in the championship and recommended the young Moscow chess player as a replacement):
> "This happened before the first round of the chess championship. The Odessa champion Efim Geller sat at the board and thought sadly that he was going to lose that day. And the next day as well. Such bad luck! He had only just been awarded his master's title, and he had to play two grandmasters in

a row: Keres and Lilienthal. Trying to calm his nerves, Geller grabbed a pawn and moved it two squares ahead.

At the same time, pianist Mark Taimanov played the first chord. He was playing in Leningrad at the Chopin recital in the House of Scientists. On that day, the first move on the Taimanov – Bronstein demonstration board was never made.

There were sounds of applause in the chess championship hall – Keres defeated Geller. There were sounds of applause in the House of Scientists hall as well: Taimanov brilliantly played a Chopin ballad.

No spectators considered the 24 year-old Geller and the 23 year-old Taimanov among potential championship winners in their predictions..." (*Ogonyok*, November 1949.)

Because of that, I had no free time to prepare for the chess. Nevertheless, I've scored more points in the 14 rounds than I did in the entire previous championship, even though I extensively prepared for the latter. This can probably be explained by the fact that I'm not tired of chess this time, and my head is fresh..." (Ibid., 12th November.)

Smyslov: "I have never seen such a sharp and intense finishing struggle before. This can probably be explained by the fact that the players in the leading group can't consistently play at a high level – they have occasionally made mistakes. As a result, nobody has managed to get a clear lead.

I think that such tension will remain until the last round, especially since many leaders are scheduled to play each other." (Ibid., 13th November.)

Before round 16, Kotov was leading the race with 10.5 points, after holding the leader's "yellow jersey" for five rounds. Three players were just a half-wheel behind: Smyslov, Bronstein and Geller (10 points each). They were chased by Keres, Boleslavsky (9.5) and Taimanov (9)... The leader could change in any round.

Последние дни

Рис. Ю. Узбякова

Жарко...

"The last days. It's hot..." Cartoon by Y. Uzbyakov. (Sovietsky Sport, 17th November 1949).

Boleslavsky: "In round 16, all the gazes of spectators, arbiters, demonstrators and even many players were glued to the game of two leaders – Kotov and Geller *(see game 210)*. The young Odessa master, who began the tournament with two losses, picked up at such a great speed that he was participating in the battle for first place by then. The result of this game could affect the standings in a big way: if Kotov won, he could bolster his leadership significantly, but if Geller won, he could overtake his formidable opponent...

They played a well-known line in the King's Indian. After a trade in the center, the usual maneuvering play started and then abruptly stopped on the 15th move when Geller sacrificed a piece. On the surface, this sacrifice didn't look dangerous: black didn't regain the piece, nor did he get an immediate attack on the king. However, it turned out after a few moves that Geller's positional calculation was deep and probably correct... Geller played the last part of the game especially strongly." (Ibid., 15th November.)

> **Geller:** "Nobody except me knows that there was a moment in this game when I'd already 'buried' myself. After quickly playing my favorite King's Indian, I was horrified to see that my opponent had a simple move that either won a pawn and gave me a bad position or forced me to give up a piece. I looked at Kotov; he seemed pretty content. He had probably prepared this whole line at home. Alexander Alexandrovich relished the position for a few minutes and then, of course, made that obvious move... I quickly evaluated the position and sacrificed my knight. This was the only chance to continue the game." (From the book *At the Chessboard*.)
>
> **Goglidze:** "Even the most brutal fights at the chessboard didn't affect the friendly, truly sportsmanlike relationships between the players. Keres shook the hands of his opponents with a friendly smile, regardless of whether he won or lost. Furman, after making a move, went to find his opponent who had walked off the stage, so that his time was not wasted. Kotov said during the game with Geller, 'Now that's a real game!'" (*Shakhmaty v SSSR*, No. 1, 1950.)
>
> At the end of the round, a reporter in the tournament bulletin polled some spectators, asking who was going to become champion. Geller got 4 votes, and Smyslov and Kotov got 3 each. Belief in Bronstein was probably undermined by his quick draw with Boleslavsky. One of the spectators directly said, "Keres and Bronstein have practically lost their chances of winning the championship." It's clear with Keres – he lost, but Bronstein, despite his draw, still retained good chances: Geller, Smyslov – 11; Bronstein, Kotov – 10.5; Taimanov, Boleslavsky – 10; Keres – 9.5... As Yakov Bylanin joked, "they finish as a group, then they all try to come first!"

In round 17, all the "magnificent seven" drew their games. This half-step was especially difficult for the leaders. Their bloody fight was very nervous.

Alatortsev: "Some fights on the board remain in the memory of chess players for years!..

Geller had white. It was clear from the very first moves that a draw was not on the cards. And later, the position became incredibly complicated – even the strongest experts disagreed among themselves...

Smyslov got an initiative and blocked white's kingside pawns. The grandmaster's advantage became clear... What happened next? On move 23, Smyslov suddenly removed the blockade of the f4 pawn. Geller immediately sacrificed it, freeing up his pieces.

The grandmaster's second mistake became the turning point of the game. Now it's white who had the initiative, his pieces came alive incredibly fast. There's a mate threat hanging over the black king's position. To repel the threats, Smyslov sacrifices an exchange. But just a move later, the master sacrifices a knight, and the grandmaster's king is again under a dangerous attack from two white rooks...

The game was adjourned. Will Smyslov be able to create counterplay with his rook and two knights against Geller's king, or will the white king reach a safe haven?" (Ibid., 18th November.)

The Fantastic Finale

Kotov: "You could see that round 18 was critical in the fight for first place even without entering the tournament hall. Crowds of people asking for a 'spare ticket' besieged the Central Railway Workers House of Culture, grabbing any crumb of information from the tournament hall and explaining the course of the battles to the 'novices'.

There's tension and excitement in the hall, and it shouldn't surprise you. All the attention is on two games: Smyslov – Keres and Flohr – Geller. Both leaders have to win to keep their leadership in the tournament, but both have formidable, experienced opponents.

Geller won several complicated, tactical games in this championship. Perhaps that's why Flohr decided that his best chance was to transition into an endgame as soon as possible. In a King's Indian, he traded queens on move 8, hoping for his renowned technique to help him. But Flohr's play in the resulting endgame was unrecognizable...

Smyslov fared worse. The opening didn't bring him any obvious advantage, except for a somewhat better piece position. Keres' defense was strong and inventive. The attack on white's weak queenside pawns gave him an initiative, and he quickly won a pawn. However, there was soon a drawn position on the board: two pawns versus three on the same side, with rooks...

Master Sokolsky didn't play well against Bronstein. Getting a clear advantage out of the opening, he got confused and lost a pawn. It won't be easy to win the adjourned endgame. *(Bronstein did manage to do that!)*

The spectators were baffled at Kotov's play against Lilienthal. They couldn't understand why the well-developed white pieces left their great positions and retreated to their initial squares. Once almost all white pieces had got back to the 1st and 2nd ranks, Kotov also lost a pawn. A quick catastrophe was on the way. But then Lilienthal made a mistake too..." (Ibid., 20th November.)

Before the last round, Efim Geller was half a point ahead of Smyslov and Bronstein.

The standings before the final round: Geller – 12.5; Bronstein, Smyslov – 12; Boleslavsky, Kotov, Taimanov – 11.5; Keres, Furman – 10.5... A sensation was brewing, the kind our championships hadn't seen since 1939: a young master had a real chance of becoming champion in his first outing! Almost nobody doubted that Geller would be able to draw against Kholmov with white, and the only intrigue was whether Bronstein or Smyslov (or both) would manage to win their games and challenge for gold too...

Romanovsky: "The round hasn't even started yet, but the hall is already filled to the brim with fans who have come to support their favorites for one last time. The appearance of Smyslov, Geller, Kotov, and Bronstein on stage was met with applause!

Geller, who took the lead after defeating Flohr in round 18, has a lot of fans among the youth. His bold, active play, 'always for a win', does indeed make fans happy.

Дружеский шарж **Н. Лиса.**

Гроссмейстеры поделили первое место...

"The grandmasters shared first place…" After winning in the last round, Smyslov and Bronstein saw the champion's throne in two as friends. Cartoon by N. Lis. (Sovietsky Sport, 22nd November 1949).

And that's why the role of Geller's opponent in the last round, the young Kholmov *(see game 211)*, was especially important and difficult. The very first moves showed that the Lithuanian master clearly understood the importance of the occasion and had thoroughly prepared for his meeting with the dangerous adversary. In the Ruy Lopez, Kholmov met 3.♗b5 with the old move 3...♘d4. Soon it turned out that the choice was correct. After the game, Geller admitted that he didn't know some lines that suddenly gave black good prospects for a counter-attack...

The fact that Geller didn't want to settle for the 'bird in a hand', which, by the way, he still hadn't caught, and chased for the 'two in the bush' instead, also gave Kholmov good chances. For instance, Geller decided against 18.♗xf6, which, without a doubt, would have made his defense easier, and went for incredible complications with 26.f2-f4. Since that moment, Kholmov's play became very precise and confident. Even the applause that sounded in the hall when Geller left his knight *en prise* didn't perturb him. The Lithuanian master boldly went along with his opponent's dangerous intentions...

Kholmov's win was celebrated so loudly by the spectators that the arbiters had to stop the other games for a while..." (Ibid., 22nd November.)

I hope that the readers won't interpret the following spicy story told by **Kholmov** in his twilight years as any "denigration" of the Soviet chess school:

"Before the last round, I was on 50 percent and had black against Geller. He, sensationally, was in the lead, half a point ahead of Smyslov and Bronstein, and could get clear first place if he won. Mikenas came to me before the game – we were friends back then – and said that Bronstein was offering me money, I don't remember how much, if I didn't lose to Geller. I think that he named a lower amount than Bronstein actually offered, Mikki was quite a sly guy. (Laughs.) But I didn't just 'not lose' to Geller, I actually won!" (From the book *Dialogues with the Chess Nostradamus*.)

Geller: "The admiration of the Moscow chess fans, who always cheer for the lesser-known young masters, the numerous congratulatory telegrams from all corners of the country, especially from Odessa – all that got into my head. I decided to play strictly for a win. No compromises!

I had a real opportunity to draw with Kholmov, but I played too aggressively and lost. Meanwhile, Smyslov and Bronstein won their last-round games and the championship." (From the book *At the Chessboard*.)

Goglidze: "Smyslov and Bronstein played against Lilienthal and Kopylov without hurry – they were probably more interested in how Geller was faring against Kholmov than their own positions. Kholmov's advantage became a sign for them to get more active. Bronstein, combining positional pressure with tactical threats, got an active position and then suddenly sacrificed a knight, creating a strong attack. Kopylov had nothing better to do than give the knight back, losing a pawn in the process. Soon he had to give up a second pawn and then resigned.

Smyslov had to solve a very difficult task, having black against such a seasoned tournament fighter as Lilienthal. His opponent maintained the balance for a long time. However, he couldn't withstand the mounting pressure and sacrificed an exchange, and then lost in the play-off." (*Shakhmaty v SSSR*, No. 1, 1950.)

Botvinnik: "Even though Smyslov and Bronstein only secured their win in the very last round, they fully deserved it." (*Chess*, No. 3, 1950.)

From the press: "The closing ceremony took place in the evening of 21st November. The TsDKZh hall was filled with guests. The participants were greeted with applause.

Chief arbiter V. Goglidze gave a review of the tournament and its sporting results. Smyslov and Bronstein came to their victories in different ways. Smyslov lost two games in the middle of the tournament, but mobilized his will and managed to win. Bronstein mostly played draws in the first half and won because of his brilliant finish.

'The six-game match between the two winners will start on 15th December,' Goglidze said. 'It will determine the sole Soviet champion.'

Applauded by the spectators, Smyslov and Bronstein were presented with first-degree diplomas (they'll receive the gold and silver medals after the match). Geller and Taimanov, who shared 3rd and 4th place, received bronze tokens and third-degree diplomas. Boleslavsky, Kotov and Furman, sharing 5th–7th places, were awarded certificates." (Tournament bulletin, 26th November.)

The result of the battle was postponed.
The lights in the tournament hall
are off.
The championship has already ended,
But... there is still no champion.

Who's going to be the new champion?
No long tirades are necessary.
In the near future, he will be determined
In the match Bronstein – Smyslov.
Yakov Bylanin

Yeah, right. The match never started – neither on 15th December nor on a later date, without any explanation – the 1950 issues of *Shakhmaty v SSSR* never mentioned it. It was as though the match was simply forgotten!.. I only managed to find traces of the matter in the tournament book published in 1952:

"Unfortunately, this match between Smyslov and Bronstein, which would surely have been incredibly interesting, never took place. Right after the 17th national championship, the leading Soviet grandmasters started their preparation for the World Championship Candidates Tournament.

The match was postponed to autumn 1950. However, it didn't take place then either, because Smyslov played in an international tournament in Venice, and Bronstein prepared for the world championship match with M. Botvinnik.

The All-Union Committee for Physical Education and Sport approved the petition of the All-Union Chess Section Presidium to cancel the play-off match between the winners of the 17th Soviet Championship. By the Committee's decree, grandmasters V. Smyslov and D. Bronstein were awarded

ПАРАД ПОБЕДИТЕЛЕЙ...

Дружеский шарж М. КУКАНОВА.

"The winners' parade." Cartoon by M. Kukanov. From the tournament bulletin (26th November 1949).

the titles of 1949 Soviet chess champions, with both of them receiving gold medals."

Such a pity that they didn't play that match! Fate never gave them another chance. And we can only fantasize about how many creative sparks could have flown in the match between two extra-strong chess players with so wildly different styles...

Levenfish on the Winners

Final standings: 1–2. Bronstein, Smyslov – 13/19; 3–4. Geller, Taimanov – 12.5; 5–7. Boleslavsky, Kotov, Furman – 11.5; 8. Keres – 11; 9–10. Aronin, Kholmov – 10; 11. Flohr – 9; 12. Sokolsky – 8.5; 13–15. Kopylov, Lilienthal, Mikenas – 8; 16. Petrosian – 7.5; 17. Ragozin – 6.5; 18–20. Goldberg, Levenfish, Liublinsky – 6.

Levenfish: "The line-up of this championship was especially strong. With the exception of Botvinnik, Bondarevsky and Konstantinopolsky, all the best players of the country took part. And still, five international grandmasters failed to reach the top ten. I doubt anybody would have thought that the fate of the first prize would depend on the result of the last-round game between Geller and Kholmov.

The success of the young masters is only natural. In the Soviet country, the youth have every opportunity to develop their talents in science, technology, art and chess as well. While the USA and England have failed to produce a single strong master in the last 15 years, there are dozens of them in the USSR.

But even with the background of constant improvement of the young

Гроссмейстер
Г. ЛЕВЕНФИШ

Дружеский шарж
С. КУКАНОВА.

This Soviet championship was the last in Grigory Levenfish's glorious career. He took part in three more semi-finals, but alas... Cartoon by M. Kukanov. From the tournament bulletin (26th November 1949).

talent pool, the Odessa student Efim Geller's first outing in the national arena is still exceptionally sudden and brilliant. Such ascents – from candidate master to almost winning the Soviet Championship – are rare in the history of Soviet chess competitions. But points are not the only important thing here. Geller played a number of excellent games – against Boleslavsky, Kotov *(see game 210)*, Levenfish, Ragozin, Flohr, and Furman – where he showed outstanding tactical talent, subtle positional understanding, good endgame technique and unparalleled energy and swiftness. Let's add youthful fervor, self-belief and resilience to that. Without a doubt, Geller has a bright future ahead of him, especially if he does away with the excessive self-confidence that cost him the gold medal.

Geller: "The tournament gave me vast, valuable experience. Now I clearly see my shortcomings. Chief among them is inadequate technique in converting the advantage. I'll now work to eliminate this shortcoming." (Tournament bulletin, 26th November.)

Bronstein: "The Odessa master's play is very active. In every game, he goes for sharp positions, for attacks, not hesitating to sacrifice material. If Geller had more experience, he could have foreseen the incredible tension of the last round. Both Smyslov and I had to play for a win, while he could have calmly settled for a draw. But in the last game against Kholmov, he decided to win at all cost – and lost." (Ibid., 22nd November.)

Now let's talk about the actual championship winners. After the world championship match tournament, Smyslov's chances were rated quite high, and the start of the championship seemed to confirm this: Smyslov only lost half a point in the first five rounds. But the wrong

Incredible progress by Mark Taimanov: from sharing last place in the previous year to winning the bronze token! He never lacked optimism: this photo was taken at the semi-final of the 15th Soviet championship, where he took only 17th place. Photo by M. Volkovysky from his archive. Published for the first time.

training regimen and a standardized opening repertoire led to two losses. Smyslov, however, didn't falter and won five games out of the remaining eight, drawing the other three.

Smyslov's style is deep and diverse. Strategic ideas alternate with bold attacks and skillful defense. Smyslov is an endgame virtuoso.

Bronstein's work rate is exceptional. His opening knowledge is immense, and it's growing every year. Bronstein works a lot on deepening his style as well. Earlier, he was a very aggressive player. Now, he's successful in the purely positional games as well, doesn't fear defending difficult positions, and holds on tenaciously to extra pawns. Unfortunately, Bronstein doesn't pay enough attention to physical exercise and, fearing overexertion, played the first half of the tournament quite sluggishly.

> **Goglidze:** "In the second half of the tournament, it seemed as though Bronstein was reborn. He won four games in a row, and then two more after two draws. Interestingly, the Soviet champion was never in the lead during the tournament, only reaching first place after the last round... This is not the first such tournament in Bronstein's practice. In the Stockholm Interzonal, he only caught up with L. Szabo in the penultimate round and took first place in the last round. In the previous, 16th Soviet Championship, he started with a series of draws and then, step by step, caught up with Kotov, who had a sizable lead, in the second half. Even in the 14th championship, he took third place only in the very last round, when all his rivals lost and he won." (*Shakhmaty v SSSR*, No. 1, 1950.)

Geller's loss in the last round allowed Taimanov to catch him and score his first grandmaster norm. Taimanov owes his success to improvements in defense. He managed to draw in a lot of difficult positions. And when his opponents made mistakes, Taimanov precisely converted that advantage. Taimanov's endgame technique has also got better.

> **Taimanov:** "I managed to play very consistently, losing only one game – to Furman. By the way, Furman is my most 'dreaded' opponent – I've lost every game to him." (Tournament bulletin, 26th November.)
>
> **Bronstein:** "Taimanov possesses great talent. Previously, his play was occasionally too shallow, he underestimated his opponents' plans. Now, he has got rid of this significant shortcoming, and he plays very strongly and consistently." (Ibid., 22nd November.)

Boleslavsky played very evenly for the whole duration of the tournament, and only a loss in the last round deprived him of third prize. Boleslavsky has retained his inventiveness, has become more substantial and solid, but still remains too peaceful.

Many hoped that Kotov would again win the championship, and he was close to the first prize. His bold, forceful play won the approval of many fans. Four rounds before the finish, he was still in the lead. However, Kotov couldn't withstand the intense struggle. After losing to Geller, he couldn't recover and scored only one point in the three last games *(in the last round, he was let down by his desire to defeat Aronin at all cost)*.

Furman had a bad start and was close to the bottom of the table after round 10. However, in the second part, he had a record score, together with Smyslov – 7/9! Furman is a great opening expert who can subtly convert his advantage. His style is rather aggressive. Furman performs worse when he's faced with an unfamiliar opening position.

The "Elders" and the Debutants

While the sturdy Kotov only faltered at the finish, Keres became unrecognizable after 10 rounds, when he had been in the lead. In the last nine rounds, his score was below 50 percent. In such a situation, even eighth place doesn't look too bad.

> **Goglidze:** "The Estonian grandmaster possesses great tactical ability, but often plays in an uncharacteristically dry positional style. In this tournament, Keres won several good games but made some inexplicable blunders. We should wish Keres not to lose heart after a defeat. If he bolsters his willpower and plays for a win more energetically, Keres will be the main contender to win any tournament." (*Shakhmaty v SSSR*, No. 1, 1950.)
>
> The chief arbiter called it perfectly: Keres won the next two Soviet Championships, both of them outright!

The misfortune of the 'elders' helped Aronin, who improved his standing considerably. The talented Kholmov was level with Bronstein and Taimanov after round 12, but three losses at the finish pushed him back to 9th–10th places.

If we look at the lower half of the table, we see a rather fascinating picture. You see three debutants – Kopylov, Liublinsky and Petrosian, whose result was pretty satisfactory for a first outing. The others are 'elders' in their forties and yours truly. They couldn't withstand the long, intense and difficult struggle. In the last 10 rounds, Levenfish and Ragozin scored 2.5 points, Flohr 3, Goldberg 3.5, Sokolsky 4, Mikenas 4.5, and only Lilienthal managed to score 5 points.

Goglidze: "Flohr lost three games in a row for the first time in his tournament career and scored below 50 percent... He was upset by an undeserved loss to Liublinsky *(in round 14)*; at that moment, the grandmaster had gone undefeated and was among the leaders.

For Ragozin and Lilienthal, the creative side is the most important element in every game. But they sometimes forget that chess also has another, sporting side.

Levenfish, the seasoned tournament fighter and a two-time Soviet champion, couldn't withstand the harsh tournament struggle. He played at his full strength for the first 3 or 4 hours, and then made mistakes during the fifth hour...

Sokolsky and Mikenas aren't novices in high-level tournaments. They are players of an attacking style. Even some of the leaders were soundly beaten by them in this championship – Kotov, for instance, lost to both.

Kopylov scored 8 points. Not bad for his first championship appearance. But he can achieve much more if he gets rid of fancifulness in his play... Liublinsky's style is very dry. He constantly plays the same openings, and this is an obstacle for his further development." (Ibid.)

I think that in addition to the obvious growth of the youth, the results were affected by organizational shortcomings. Botvinnik expressed an

Andre Lilienthal's best years were already behind him. The 1950 Candidates Tournament in Budapest (pictured) wouldn't bring him any laurels either. From Y. Averbakh's archive.

opinion that no more than 16 players should take part in the final. But if you do hold longer championships, you have to provide optimal conditions for the players. Just as the Dynamo stadium is responsible for providing a good-quality soccer pitch for the important matches of the national championships, the organizers of all-Union chess championships, especially the chess section of the All-Union Committee, should be responsible for the correct organization of the tournament hall. The popularity of chess is growing every year, the championships attract thousands of spectators. The tournaments should be organized in such a way that provides silence, light, warmth and clean air for the participants.

The tournament was very interesting in regard of chess theory. Some games are examples of the true chess art. But the Soviet chess school, the strongest in the world, can and should create more such games." (*Chess in 1947–1949* compilation book.)

Мастер
В. МИКЕНАС
Дружеский шарж
Н. ЛИСА.

Vladas Mikenas left a mark with his beautiful win against Kotov. Cartoon by N. Lis. From the tournament bulletin (22nd October 1949).

The World Champion's Verdict

Botvinnik provided his review of the championship twice: for *Ogonyok* (No. 48, 1949) and for the English magazine *CHESS* (No. 3, 1950). The articles **"The Growth of Soviet Chess Players"** and **"Notes on the XVIIth USSR Chess Championship"** are quite different: the latter is longer, with subheaders: "Smyslov's Confidence", "Boleslavsky Slips Back", "Keres and Levenfish Disappoint"... There's another difference: the *Ogonyok* review is a purely professional piece, but the text for the Western readers contained some propaganda as well: "The success scored by the talented young players in the XVIIth U.S.S.R. Chess Championship demonstrates the scale and correctness of the training of young chess talent in the Soviet Union. (...) Only in a country where the culture of the people is the special care of the

Communist Party and the Government is such development of young talent possible."

Why do I prefer to cite the *Ogonyok* text here? Because nobody would ever read it otherwise. By contrast, *CHESS* is a specialized magazine, and historians of Russian chess will surely look at it, so I'll only add some excerpts from it in small font (with minor stylistic edits).

Botvinnik: "Ten years ago, the 11th Soviet Championship was held in Leningrad. A. Kotov, a young player who'd just won his master's title, took part. Many experienced players thought of him as 'easy prey'... However, to everyone's amazement, the inexperienced novice overtook a lot of famous masters and almost won the Soviet champion's title.

Sometimes history repeats itself. E. Geller's success in the 17th championship amazed everyone: last year, the humble candidate master Geller played for Ukraine at the USSR republics team championship in Leningrad. Even back then, opponents were wary of him, which didn't stop him from winning six games out of six. Then, Geller won the Tbilisi semi-final tournament and earned his master's title.

Geller's success at the championship was defined by his finish. Showing his best qualities – inventiveness, inexhaustible imagination and good composure – in the decisive games against A. Kotov, V. Smyslov and S. Flohr, he scored 2.5 points in those three games.

> E. Geller, a student of Economics at Odessa University, is twenty-four. In the second half of the tourney he showed up well against the grandmasters. He has his shortcomings. He does not seem to be very strong in the openings and in analysis. However, his rich imagination and his energy brought him excellent results.

Even though last year's winners, D. Bronstein and A. Kotov, put in different performances, they still maintained their prestige. We shouldn't forget that Smyslov, Boleslavsky and Geller didn't take part in the previous championship...

But from the creative point of view, they can't be fully satisfied with their results. Bronstein choked at the start – he had only 6 points after 11 games. The game against Smyslov was especially unpleasant for Grandmaster Bronstein – he managed to lose a theoretically drawn endgame. However, in the second part, he scored 8 points out of 9 (*or, more precisely, 7 out of 8; in* CHESS, *Botvinnik called that "a marvelous finish"*).

Kotov, by contrast, played with great inspiration for a long while and was in the lead before the 16th round. After losing to Geller despite having a winning position at one point, Kotov got demoralized and fell behind the leaders.

V. Smyslov had been playing very well before, but everyone was waiting: when would he start to play even better? It's time to finally win the Soviet Championship! And in this tournament, he lived up to everyone's expectations. Another effort, and Smyslov might have been able to advance even further.

> Since the world championship match-tournament when his excellent play gave him second place, Smyslov has displayed great confidence. (...) Apart from great talent Smyslov possesses an attribute vital to a grandmaster – faultless technique. Still greater achievements may be expected of him.

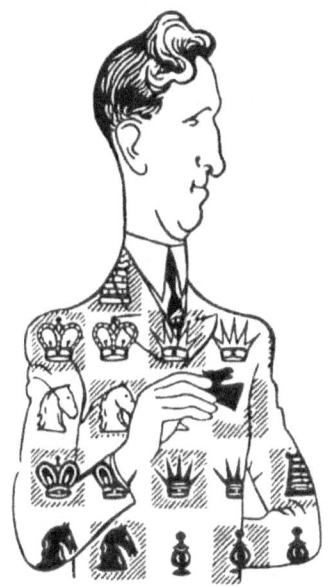

Дружеский шарж **Н. Лиса**

В. СМЫСЛОВ

Vasily Smyslov finally became Soviet Champion at the sixth attempt! He made his debut before the war began, in 1940. Cartoon by N. Lis. (Sovietsky Sport, 12th April 1949).

I. Boleslavsky, unfortunately, is starting to slip back. In previous championships, he consistently took second place. But now, the thirty year-old grandmaster is getting overtaken by the younger players... He should play with his old energy, and the old successes will come back *(in* CHESS, *Botvinnik added: "He should play through some of his old games and see their liveliness and inventiveness").*

The young M. Taimanov also achieved great success. His talent is beyond any doubt, and he's able to achieve even better results.

> M. Taimanov is 23 years of age, but no novice in chess. Before the war he was already playing in tournaments for scholars and has since made good headway. If he had taken chess still more seriously his success would have been more pronounced. There can be little doubt that the grandmasters will more than once have to make room on the score box for these young men, Geller and Taimanov.

After his setback in the M. I. Chigorin Memorial tournament in 1947, Grandmaster P. Keres had been unable to restore his old form. Even though Master Furman couldn't repeat his previous result (3rd place), he can still console himself with the fact that he finished level with such outstanding players as Kotov and Boleslavsky.

And finally there comes Grandmaster G. Levenfish, the "failure" of this contest who became a chess master 38 years ago and is now sixty. G. Levenfish belongs to the pre-revolutionary generation of Russian masters who passed on to the masters of Soviet times the very rich inheritance of Chigorin's school. In the last century, chess fans found delight in Chigorin's brilliant games but at that time his ideas were not understood. His disciples, among them G. Levenfish, adopted his advanced ideas and these have been still further developed in the creative achievements of the Soviet school.

G. Levenfish could not of course stand the pace of such an arduous tourney, but in some games, as against Smyslov, he displayed his old brilliance.

The Soviet Championships haven't attracted such great interest for a long while. It's understandable: the struggle was very intense, there were many inventive and brilliant games played. But there's another factor: the tournament to determine a world championship candidate is starting in Budapest next spring. It was a serious test of strength for the Soviet grandmasters before the important competition. Overall, the 17th championship showed the further growth of Soviet chess mastery, and so Soviet chess players have no reason to worry – the Soviet grandmasters should perform well at the international tournament in Hungary."

A Lot to Look at

Such things happen: you complain how hard it was to choose games, and then, in the very next championship, you get a whole list of brilliant games, a shortlist of candidate games and even a thorough "explanatory note" from Botvinnik himself in *Shakhmaty v SSSR* and the tournament book, telling us why a particular game submitted to the supreme jury, headed by the world champion, did or didn't get an award.

There were 11 candidates for three prizes in honor of "the great Russian chess player M. I. Chigorin", and I thought that I already had 11 examples for my book in the bag. Not so fast! The games Flohr – Kotov and Keres – Levenfish were rejected by Botvinnik himself, I personally didn't like the game Taimanov – Aronin (a 35-move conversion of an extra pawn), and, finally, the computer considered the games Sokolsky – Kotov and Ragozin – Kopylov embarrassing. It's not my fault that these games, in addition to other nice examples (such as the incredibly intense round 17 game between Geller and Smyslov), didn't pass the "computer test": there were too many mistakes both in the games and annotations. I especially feel for Nikolai Kopylov, who submitted three of his games to the jury. Even Mikhail Moiseevich, who criticized them for a lack of "consistency" and other flaws, still admitted that they were "rather interesting", because "in all three games, Kopylov won after sacrificing an exchange", which makes them "partially interesting instructive-wise." So, as compensation, I promise to introduce you to Kopylov's games in my chapter on the 19ᵗʰ championship, where he defeated Botvinnik, Keres and Petrosian!

As you have surely realized by now, my hopes of saving time and effort on the selection stage were ruined, and I again had to delve, grumbling and coughing, into the sources, covered by age-old dust. Out of the 190 games played, I found 55 with annotations in the bulletin, magazine and the *Chess in 1947–1949* compilation. There were even more in the tournament book – 83! Moreover, dozens more games (mostly with variations on the old notes, however) were hidden in the various "selected games" books... To cut a long story short, the selection process was quite long, even though I, as usual, preferred the annotations from the tournament bulletin and *Shakhmaty v SSSR* – they best reflect what the players saw and calculated during the game... And then came a moment when I realized that this process was too similar to home renovations: you never finish them, you just get to a point where you stop. And stop I did.

First Brilliancy Prize

The prizes were officially called "best game prizes", but "brilliancy prize" is both more familiar and preferred by the winners themselves. Levenfish: "The game got the first brilliancy prize." Kotov: "The game received the special Chigorin brilliancy prize..." So, let us call them brilliancy prizes too:

Botvinnik: "The Smyslov system is not to blame for the bad result of its author. It was enough for black to play 17...♛d7!, defusing the tension in the center (after 18.dxc6 bxc6, black always had the move e7-e6, closing off the a2-g8 diagonal), and he would have gotten a satisfactory position. It's more interesting to watch how white created a very strong attack on the black king, exploiting black's somewhat sluggish maneuver ♞b6-d7-f6 (the opening maneuver ♞f6-d7-b6 is obviously not that simple to refute!). Levenfish played this game with brilliance, simplicity and energy."

The cover of a handmade album The Chess Poem by well-known Kazan artist and chess player Galina Satonina (the poetry was also hers), dedicated to the game Levenfish – Smyslov. From A. Zlobovsky's archive.

The game became a classic and was thoroughly annotated in V. Panov and Y. Estrin's *Opening Course* and M. Botvinnik and Y. Estrin's monograph *The Grunfeld Defense.*

And now, a surprise! I was astonished when I read the following in Levenfish's memoir: "The Kazan chess player and artist G. I. Satonina even made an album for me, called *The Chess Poem*. It presents the course of the game in poems and pictures." These pictures would have been such a great addition to the book! But None of Igor Berdichevsky, Murad Amannazarov or Vlad Novikov (our greatest chess bibliophiles) had heard anything about such an album... Thankfully, when I met Murad, I told him that this album depicted the game Levenfish – Smyslov, and he remembered another collector who possessed that handmade album. The thing was, Galina Satonina (a multiple ladies chess champion of Kazan and Tataria) made all these albums with her own hands, and only a handful of them were produced! One such rarity was in the possession of Anatoly Zinovyevich Zlobovsky, who kindly shared the cover and a few pages with me.

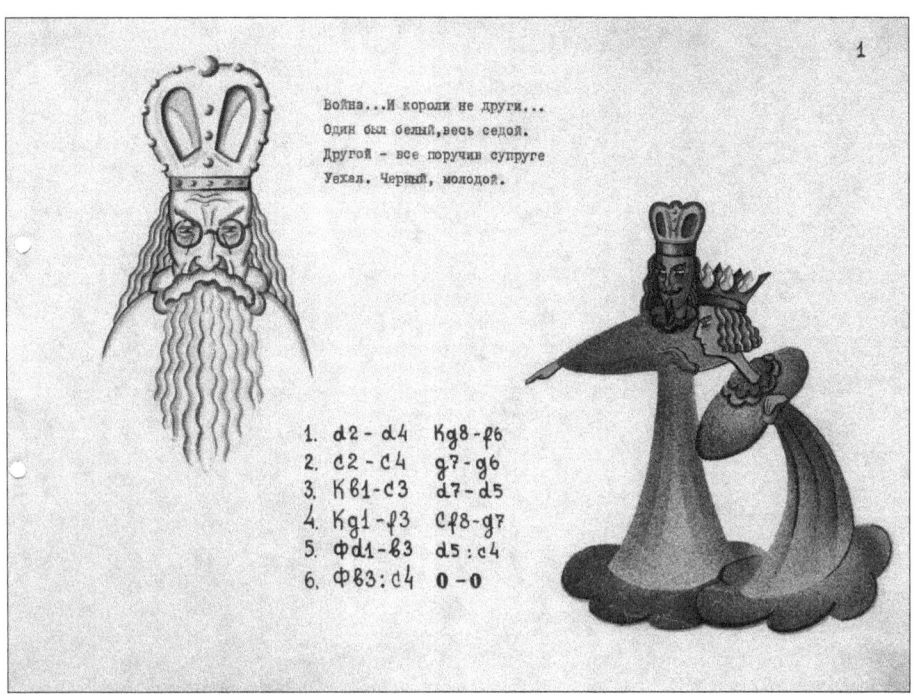

War... and the kings are enemies...
One was white, all bold.
The other delegated everything to his wife
And left. Black. Young.

1.d4   ♘f6
2.c4   g6
3.♘c3   d5
4.♘f3   ♗g7
5.♕b3   dxc4
6.♕xc4   0-0

No. 207. Grunfeld Defense D99
Levenfish – Smyslov
Moscow 1949, round 6
Annotated by G. Levenfish

1.d4 ♘f6 2.c4 g6 3.♘c3 d5 4.♘f3 ♗g7 5.♕b3 dxc4 6.♕xc4 0-0 7.e4 ♘fd7. *"A more correct move order here is 7...♗g4 and only then 8...♘fd7, because in a number of lines, there's no necessity to transfer this knight to b6." (Botvinnik.) The current main lines are 7...a6 or 7...♘a6.*

8.♗e3 ♘b6 9.♕b3 ♘c6 10.♖d1 ♗g4. Black's last four moves form the basis of the Smyslov Variation. Black has already castled and developed all the minor pieces. White, on the other hand, has a pawn center. Will black manage to break it?

11.d5 ♘e5 12.♗e2 ♘xf3+. I think that this trade is too premature and would have preferred the immediate 12...♕c8. *(However, after 13.♘xe5, white's chances are better.)*

13.gxf3 ♗h5. It's worse to play 13...♗h3 14.♖g1 ♕c8 15.f4 ♗d7 16.h4 *(16.f5!?)* 16...e6 17.h5 with a strong attack (Bondarevsky – Ragozin, Saltsjobaden 1948).

Идут у белых пехотинцы,
У черных кони на посту.

У белых ходят на границе,
У черных-все идет в тылу.

7.e2-e4   Кр6-d7
8.Cc1-e3   Кd7-B6
9.Фc4-B3   КB8-c6

The white infantrymen advance,	7.e4 ♞fd7
Black's knights are on duty,	8.♗e3 ♞b6
White's pieces are at the border,	9.♕b3 ♞c6
Black's are all at the rear.	

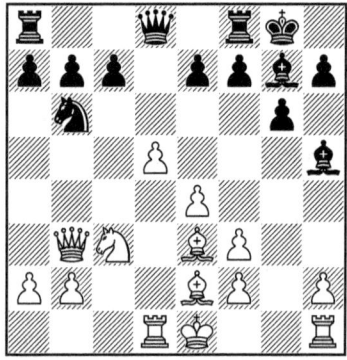

14.f4. *"Now white's strategic idea is clear: leaving his king in the center, he's starting a pawn storm on the kingside, preparing to transfer his major pieces there as well." (Panov, Estrin). Later, 14.♖g1! became the main line.*

14...♗xe2 15.♞xe2 ♕c8. In the game Lilienthal – Bronstein (Saltsjobaden 1948), there followed 15...♕d7 16.h4 c6 17.h5 cxd5 18.hxg6 hxg6 19.♗d4! with strong threats. *(After 19...♗xd4 20.♖xd4 ♔g7, all the threats can be countered.)* The move 15...♕c8, thus, is "state of the art", but, as this game shows, it also has its flaws.

Later, it was found that the simplest reply was the immediate 15... c6!? 16.dxc6 ♕c7(c8) 17.cxb7 ♕xb7, with an initiative for the pawn.

16.♖c1! c6. 16...♕g4 17.♖xc7 ♕f3 18.♞g3 ♖ac8 19.♖xe7 ♞c4 20.♕d1 didn't work – white retained a material advantage.

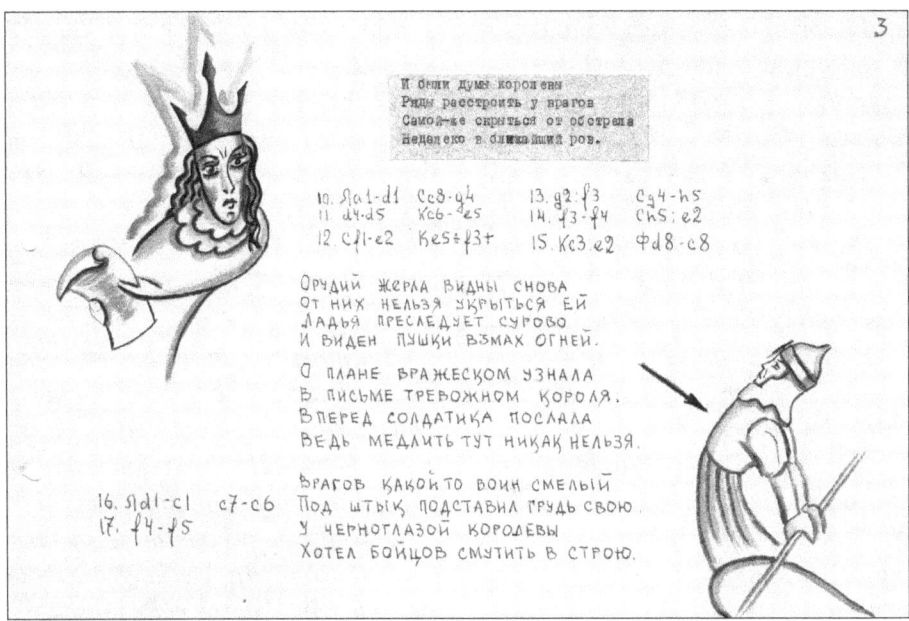

And the queen had thoughts
To interrupt the enemy troops

10.♖d1   ♗g4
11.d5   ♘e5
12.♗e2   ♘xf3+
13.gxf3   ♗h5

The muzzles of the guns are visible once again
She cannot hide from them
The rook chases her ferociously
And a burst of fire is seen from the cannon.
She learnt about the enemy plan
In the king's alarmed letter.
She sent a little soldier forward

While herself hiding from the shelling
Nearby in the next moat.

14.f4   ♗xe2
15.♘xe2   ♕c8
16.♖c1   c6
17.f5

As there is no time to lose.
Some brave warrior
Thrust his chest in front of the enemies'
bayonet.
He wanted to befuddle the black eyed queen's
fighters
Standing in formation.

Levenfish removed this note in his book – he probably noticed that after 20...♕g2! with the idea 21.♕e2 ♗f6 22.♖xb7 ♗h4, white's position was not good. 19.♗xb6! was stronger, but black can improve as well: 17... ♕g2! 18.♘g3 ♖ac8= (19.♗xb6 axb6 20.♕xb6? ♗d4–+).

17.f5! The correct continuation of the attack. h2-h4-h5 is much weaker (17.h4 ♕g4).

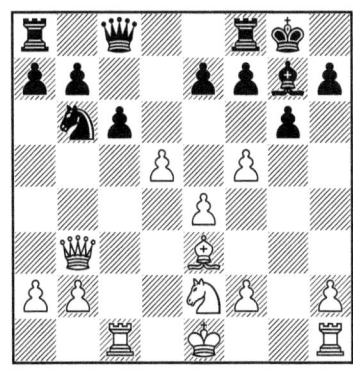

17...♘d7. It's very dangerous to accept the pawn sacrifice. For instance: 17...gxf5 18.♖g1 ♔h8 19.♗d4 ♗xd4 20.♘xd4 ♖g8 21.♔e2 fxe4 22.dxc6 bxc6 23.♕xf7. *But the last move is a fatal mistake: 23...♕a6+! 24.♔e3 (the king can't get to the first rank) 24...♖d3+ 25.♔f4 ♖gf8, and white loses his queen. While after 23.♖xg8+ ♕xg8 24.♕g3, the position is probably better for black.*

"The position on the diagram was thoroughly analyzed," *Levenfish wrote in his book.* "After 17...gxf5, white should play 18.♗d4! For instance: 18...♗xd4 19.♘xd4 fxe4 20.dxc6 bxc6 21.♖xc6 ♕d7 22.♖h6!, and capturing the knight leads to mate, while 22...♔h8 is met with 23.♖g1 (threatening 24.♕g3) 23...♖g8 24.♖xh7+ ♔xh7 25.♕xf7+ ♔h6 26.♖xg8 ♖xg8 27.♘f5+ ♔g5 28.h4+ ♔g4 29.♘e3+ ♔xh4 30.♕xg8, and white should win."

But the computer angrily rails against the move 23...♖g8, insisting on 23...♖ac8, which Levenfish rejected because of 24.♖g5, "and black is defenseless".

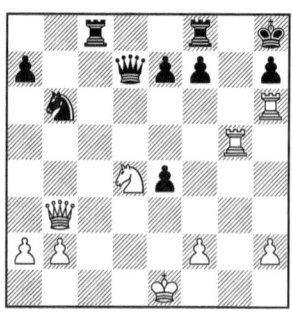

Not so! After 24...♖c1+ 25.♔e2 f6! 26.♖gh5 ♕g4+, there's a draw on the board, even though the path to it is very narrow – any deviation is fatal for both sides: 27.♔d2 e3+ 28.fxe3 ♕g2+ 29.♔xc1 ♖c8+ 30.♔d1 ♕f1+ 31.♔d2 ♘c4+ 32.♕xc4 (there's a mate otherwise) 32...♖xc4 33.♖xh7+ etc.

However, as we already know from the introduction, all these torments weren't necessary: the correct move was 17...♕d7! "Smyslov hadn't noticed that it was a critical moment and, keeping tension in the center, decided to return his knight to the kingside. This was the main reason for his loss." (Botvinnik)

18.♖g1. *"Now white has an obvious advantage, since all his opponent's pieces are passive." (Botvinnik)*

18...♔h8. Trying to avoid the pins along files and diagonals. If 18...♕c7, then 19.fxg6 hxg6 20.♖xg6 fxg6 21.d6+. After 18...♘e5, there's 19.♗d4! ♔h8 20.♕c3 f6 21.♗xe5 etc. *(21.f4! ♘f7 22.fxg6+–).*

19.fxg6 hxg6. 19...fxg6 is obviously bad because it weakens the e6 square. For instance: 20.♘d4 ♘e5 21.f4 ♘g4 22.♘e6 ♘xe3 23.♕xe3 ♖f7 24.f5! gxf5 25.♖xg7 ♖xg7 26.♕d4 ♕g8 27.♔e2 ♖f8 28.♖g1 ♖f7 29.dxc6 bxc6 30.exf5 h6 31.♖g6 ♔h7 32.♖xh6+ ♔xh6 33.♕h4#.

Such long lines without checks are rarely correct: both 23...♖f6!, with the idea 24.f5 ♕b8 25.fxg6 ♖xe6 26.dxe6 ♕xh2=, and 27...♕f7!, with the idea 28.♖g1 ♖ag8, are better.

The greying king calmly
Sits and draws up plans.
Sends a pawn to its death
For whom this role isn't scary.
22.♖g6   fxg6

Black has lots of worried thoughts,
He doesn't know what to do.
He can destroy lots of them at once
But what is better, what to say?

Therefore, 19...fxg6 wasn't bad. It was maybe even better than the other capture!

20.♗d4! White wants to eliminate the only piece that defends the king. He also prepares to transfer the other rook to the kingside.

20...♘f6. A step towards the abyss! But what to play? The situation is looking desperate... The computer found the saving idea: 20...♕c7!! 21.♖c3 c5! For instance: 22.♖h3+ ♔g8 23.♗xg7 ♔xg7 24.♘g3 ♖g8! 25.♘f5+ ♔f8 or 22.♗xg7+ ♔xg7 23.♘d4 ♕xh2! 24.♘f5+♔f6! 25.♖cg3 gxf5 26.♕f3 e6, and black holds.

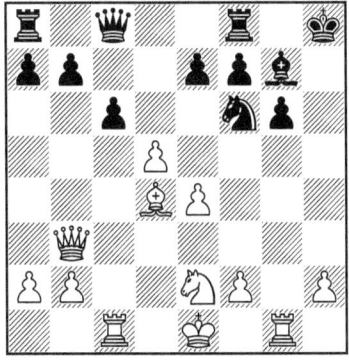

21.♖c3! Beginning a deeply-calculated combination. Black is forced to accept the sacrifice because of the threat 22.♖h3+ ♔g8 23.dxc6 bxc6 24.♖xg6.

21...♘xe4. *"After 21...♘h5 22.♖h3 ♗xd4 23.♕f3! ♕xh3 24.♕xh3, white also won easily."* *(Botvinnik.) That's not exactly so: after 23...♗g7! 24.♖xh5+ ♔g8, only black can win; however, 23.♘xd4! (instead of the flashy 23.♕f3?) actually "won easily".*

22.♖xg6! fxg6 23.♖h3+ ♔g8. After 23...♕xh3 24.♕xh3+ ♔g8 25.♕e6+, the e4 knight is lost.

24.dxc6+ e6. Black couldn't save the game either with 24...♔f7 25.cxb7 ♕d8 26.bxa8=♕ ♕xa8 27.♗xg7 ♔xg7 28.♖h7+ ♔xh7 29.♕xf7+ ♔h8 30.♘f4.

25.cxb7 ♕c6 26.bxa8=♕ ♖xa8. After this operation, white won a pawn. But his attack doesn't subside.

27.♗xg7 ♔xg7 28.♕e3! *"The point. Black can't play 28...♖h8 due to 29.♕d4+. Black's reply is forced."* *(Panov, Estrin)*

28...♘f6 29.♘d4 ♕h1+ 30.♔e2 ♕d5. After 30...♖e8, 31.♘f3! wins immediately, creating the unstoppable threat 32.♕h6+ and 33.♘e5+.

31.♘xe6+.

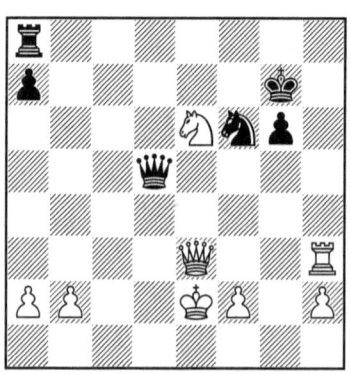

31...♔g8. 31...♔f7 32.♘g5+ ♔g8 33.♕b3! couldn't save black either – white transposes to a "prosaic" endgame with two extra pawns.

Now black seemingly manages to avoid the direct danger, and he even threatens to win a piece with 32...♖e8.

32.♖h8+! New trouble. Black can't capture the rook because of a mate in two.

32...♔f7   33.♘g5+   ♔g7 34.♖xa8. Black resigned. He loses the knight after 34...♕xa8 35.♕e7+.

Second Brilliancy Prize

Botvinnik: "This game leaves a very good impression. Even though the position didn't allow white to force matters, he played very subtly. The maneuver h3-h4-h5xg6 is especially good – it secured a centralized position for his knight. White's combination – which didn't take place in the actual game, since black chose another way to lose – is not fully original, but in this situation, it was spectacular, fresh and well-hidden.

No. 208. Queen's Gambit D36
Kotov – Ragozin
Moscow 1949, round 11
Annotated by A. Kotov

1.d4 d5 2.c4 e6 3.♘c3 c6 4.♘f3. I didn't want to play a sharp combination game against Ragozin. This was the only reason why I decided against the Slav Gambit 4.e4 dxe4 5.♘xe4 ♗b4+ 6.♗d2 ♕xd4 7.♗xb4 ♕xe4+ 8.♗e2, which I consider to be completely sound and, at any rate, no more risky than other gambits.

4...♘f6

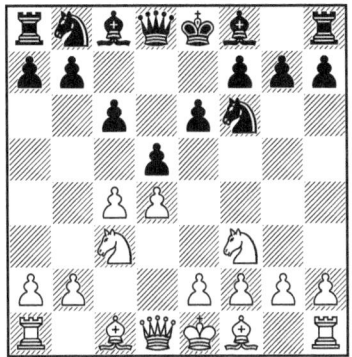

5.cxd5. Botvinnik played this against Euwe in the world championship match tournament. Grandmaster Ragozin, as we know, was Botvinnik's coach at the world championship and, of course, had "something to do" with this line. I couldn't resist the temptation to ask Ragozin to defend against the system with 5.cxd5 himself.

5...exd5 6.♕c2 (preventing 6...♗f5) **6...♘bd7.** Ragozin chooses a common development system, characteristic of the Carlsbad Variation. I think this is correct: Euwe preferred to develop his bishop to g7 in the aforementioned game, but the dark-squared bishop had next to no prospects there.

7.♗g5 ♗e7 8.e3 0-0 9.♗d3 ♖e8 10.0-0 ♘f8 11.♖ab1. Commencing

the "traditional" attack: b2-b4 and a2-a4.

11...♗e6. With this move, Ragozin takes a wrong turn. He only repels white's queenside attack, not creating any kingside activity. As a result, black soon loses all counterplay and has to play a waiting game.

11...♘h5 or 11...♗g4 were better. *These replies haven't taken hold either. 11...♘g6 or 11...♘e4 were played more often, and 11...a5 became the main line.*

12.b4 ♖c8 13.♘a4 ♘e4 14.♗xe7 ♖xe7 (14...♕xe7 is more energetic) **15.♘c5 ♘xc5 16.♕xc5.**

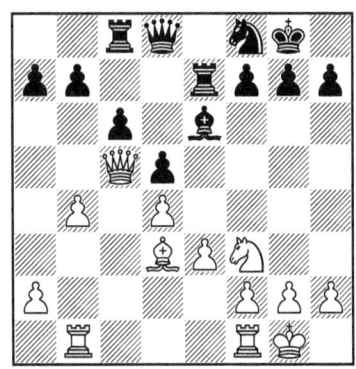

16...b6? Here, Ragozin's combative spirit manifested itself. He suddenly got fed up with passive defense and decided to launch a queenside counter-attack. And still, objectively, this move is a mistake because it creates a perpetual weakness on c6. The correct move was 16...a6.

17.♕c2 ♕d6 18.♖fc1 g6 19.♖b3 ♘d7 20.h3 ♘b8. Very passive. It was necessary to play 20...c5 21.bxc5 bxc5 22.dxc5 ♘xc5 23.♖c3 with an advantage for white, even though black can still successfully defend.

21.a3 ♗d7 22.♖c3 ♗e8. White's advantage is obvious. With the subsequent subtle maneuver, white secures the e5 square for his knight.

23.h4! In accordance with the main positional principle: "After pinning down the opponent's pieces on one flank, strike on the other."

23...a6 24.h5 ♖a7. The rook's position provokes an interesting combination by white. 24...♔g7 was better.

And preventing the pawn from moving at all one move earlier was even better: 23...h5! 24.♘e5 ♖ec7, and if 25.f4 ♔g7 26.f5, then 26...c5, exchanging the rooks.

25.hxg6 hxg6 26.♘e5 a5. Leads to a quick loss. Had black chosen to defend passively, there was still a long and difficult defense ahead, but still, in my opinion, black cannot defend the weakened queenside and prevent the development of a dangerous kingside initiative at the same time: f2-f4-f5 etc.

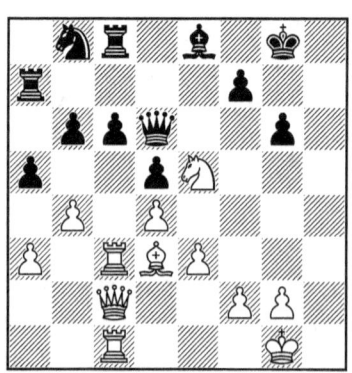

27.b5! Starting the most beautiful combination I'd ever created at the chessboard. The natural 27...c5 was met with the stunning 28.dxc5!! ♕xe5 (28...bxc5 29.♖xc5) 29.cxb6! ♖xc3 30.bxa7!! ♖xc2 31.♖xc2!

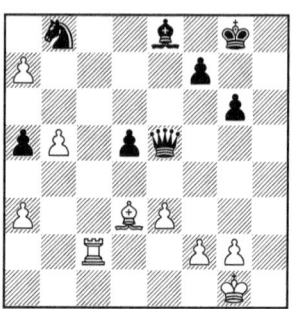

A rare position. The white pawn, after taking the route d4-c5-b6-a7, inevitably promotes, and three black pieces cannot stop it!

In Selected Games, Kotov doesn't say that this combination was the best in his career, but points out proudly: "The game received the special Chigorin brilliancy prize..."

27...♖ac7. The opponents often don't allow spectacular combinations to play out, preferring to just give up a pawn. Still, this game leaves no regrets, because there was a different "combination storm" later on.

28.bxc6 ♔g7. If 28...♘xc6, then 29.♗b5! *(29...♘xd4 30.♖xc7 ♘xc2? 31.♖xc8 ♘xa3 32.♖xe8+)*.

29.♕b1! Preparing the final attack on the f7 square.

29...♘xc6   30.♕xb6   ♖b8 31.♕xb8! In conjunction with the 34th move, this continuation leads to the decisive attack on the black king.

31...♘xb8 32.♖xc7 ♕xa3 33.♗xg6! The maneuver h2-h4-h5 has finally paid off!

33...♘c6. It seems that white is losing – he has several pieces *en prise*. But the logic of events plays out inexorably.

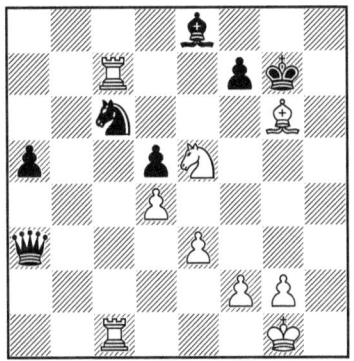

34.♖1xc6! ♗xc6 35.♖xf7+ ♔h6 (if 35...♔h8, then 36.♗h7 and 37.♘g6+) **36.f4! ♕xe3+ 37.♔h2.** There's no good defense against 38.♖h7#.

37...♕xe5 38.fxe5. Black resigned.

Third Brilliancy Prize

Botvinnik: "This game is especially interesting because there was a constant fight for the initiative. With considerable foresight, white exploited black's opening mistake (which led to the black knight being pushed to the edge of the board) and, temporarily sacrificing a pawn, created a strong attack. The unstoppable attack on the black king that was created by white using all his pieces (e6 bishop, f4 knight, c3 rook and b2 queen) was rather spectacular. A deep game."

Later, Botvinnik annotated it for his Grunfeld Defense monograph.

No. 209. Grunfeld Defense D88
Furman – Smyslov
Moscow 1949, round 8
Annotated by S. Furman

1.d4 ♘f6 2.c4 g6 3.♘c3 d5 4.cxd5. This, along with 4.♘f3 ♗g7 5.♕b3, is a good development system. White creates a pawn center, and it's not that simple for black to attack it.

4...♘xd5 5.e4 ♘xc3 6.bxc3 c5 7.♗c4 cxd4. *It's better not to hurry with this trade. Later, 7...♗g7 8.♘e2 ♘c6 9.♗e3 0-0 10.0-0 ♕c7 11.♖c1 ♖d8 became Smyslov's signature line.*

8.cxd4 ♗g7 9.♘e2 ♘c6. After 9...♘d7 10.0-0 0-0 11.♗e3, white controls the center and has an advantage.

10.♗e3 0-0 11.0-0

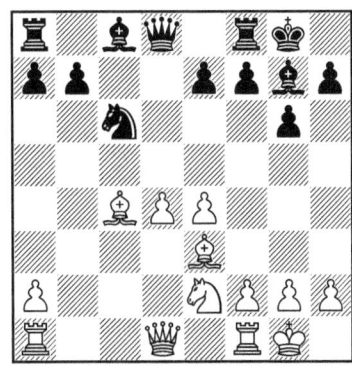

11...b6? Black usually plays 11...♗g4 12.f3 ♘a5 *(the main line)*

or 11...♗d7 *(this move has faded in popularity because of 12.♖b1)*.

In the annotations for the tournament book, Furman changed his evaluation of the move 11...b6: "This move shouldn't be considered a mistake – black's position is difficult after other continuations as well."

However, Botvinnik disagrees: "This move is wrong and leads to white's advantage, because black has no time to stop the move d4-d5 that restricts his light-squared bishop."

12.♖c1 ♗b7. If 12...♘a5, then 13.♗d5 ♗b7 (13...♖b8 14.♗f4 is bad for black) 14.♗xb7 ♘xb7 15.d5, and white is better *(white has also tried 15.♕a4 and even 15.e5)*.

13.♗b5! A strong maneuver. White should quickly make the d4-d5 move before black plays e7-e6. To do this, he has to push the black knight away from the center, because after the immediate 13.d5, there was 13...♘e5.

13...♖c8 *(13...♘a5 14.d5! Spassky – D. Byrne, Palma de Mallorca 1968)* **14.♕a4.**

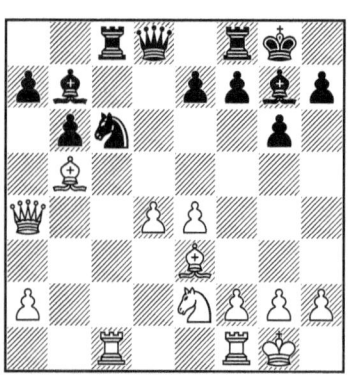

14...♘a5. A forced retreat. 14...♕d6 is bad due to 15.e5 ♕d7 16.d5! ♕xd5 17.♘f4 (but not 17.♖fd1? ♘d4!) 17...♕d7 18.♖fd1 ♕e8 19.♘d5, and there's no defense to the double threat 20.♗xc6 or 20.♘b4.

There actually is a defense: 19...a6 with the idea 20.♗xc6 ♗xc6 21.♖xc6 e6!=. However, 20.♗xa6! ♗xa6 (20...♖a8? 21.♗xb7 ♖xa4 22.♗xc6) 21.♕xa6 leads to an advantage for white.

15.d5 ♕d6. If 15...e6, then 16.dxe6 fxe6 17.♗d7. 15...a6 16.♗d3 is bad as well, because black can't defend the b6 and a5 squares: after 16...b5, there's 17.♕b4, threatening ♗d2.

16.♗d2! ♖xc1 (of course, not 16...e6 due to 17.♗b4) **17.♖xc1 f5.** The best chance for black! Now white has to play very precisely to maintain his positional advantage.

"This move seems logical because it's beneficial for black to break up the opponent's pawn center. However, the main drawback of this move is that it exposes the 7th rank, and this was brilliantly exploited by white in his attack." (Botvinnik.) Incredible positional intuition – here, the computer already gives a long line!

18.♗d7! ♕e5. After 18...fxe4 19.♗e6+ ♔h8 20.♕xe4 ♕e5 21.♕d3, black's position is difficult *(or, more precisely, hopeless)*. For instance, 21...♖d8 is met with 22.♘f4, threatening 23.♘xg6+.

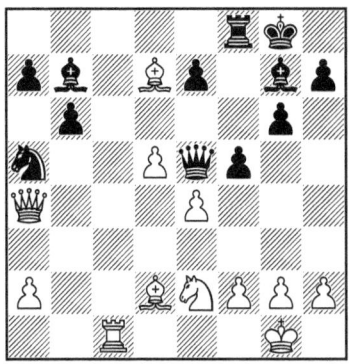

19.♗c3! Starting an interesting combination that ends with a direct attack on the king.

The computer is baffled: why didn't white play 19.♗e6+ ♔h8 20.♕b4, as 21.♗c3 is a deadly threat, and there's

no good counter? For instance: 20... ♕b2 21.♕xb2 ♗xb2 22.♖b1 ♗g7 23.♗xa5 with an extra piece, or after 20...♕xe4 21.♕xe7 ♗xd5 (with a double threat ♗xe6 and ♕xg2#), there's 22.♘f4 ♘c6 23.♕xg7+!! ♔xg7 24.♗xd5 etc.

19...♕xe4   20.♗e6+   ♔h8 21.♗xg7+ ♔xg7 22.♕a3! The point! If now 22...♔f6, then 23.♕c3+ ♕e5 24.♘d4, threatening f2-f4, and after 24...f4, there's 25.♖e1, and white wins. If 22...♖e8, then 23.♕b2+ ♔h6 24.♖c3 etc.

22...♕h4 23.♖c7 ♔h8. If 23... ♖e8

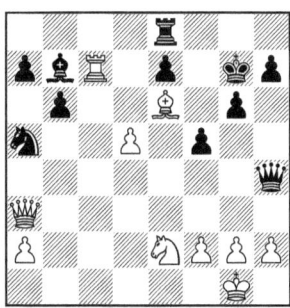

then the simplest continuation is 24.g3 ♕f6 25.♘f4 and h2-h4. 24.d6 was also possible.

The second move nullified all white's efforts after 24...♕e4!. And in the first line, white has to play 25.h4 first, because 25.♘f4? allows a strong reply 25...♕a1+ 26.♔g2 ♗a6! (see the idea? 27.♖xe7+? ♔h6, and black wins!), and the way to victory is not that simple: 27.h4! ♕f1+ 28.♔h2 ♕xf2+ 29.♘g2 ♗f1 30.♕c3+ ♔h6 31.♕c1+! (31.♕e3+ ♕xe3 32.♘xe3 ♗e2!! is a draw) 31...f4 (otherwise

Semyon Furman's win against Smyslov was used as a model example in the book Grunfeld Defense by M. Botvinnik and Y. Estrin. From the author's archive.

32.♖c2) 32.♕xf4+ ♕xf4 33.♘xf4 etc.

24.♖xe7 ♕f6 25.♖c7 ♗a6. 25...f4 doesn't help: 26.♕c3 ♕xc3 27.♘xc3 ♖d8 (defending from d5-d6) 28.♘e4 ♗xd5 29.♘f6 with an inevitable mate.

26.♘f4 ♕a1+ (white threatened 27.♘xg6+ hxg6 28.♕h3+) **27.♖c1 ♕g7 28.♖c3 ♖d8** (or else 29.♘xg6+) **29.♕b2!**

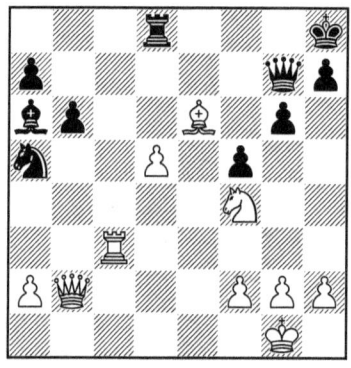

A problem-like idea of ambush! The g6 stronghold now falls, and the black king loses its cover.

29...♘c4 30.♘xg6+ ♕xg6 31.♖xc4+ ♕g7 32.♕xg7+ ♔xg7 33.♖c7+ ♔f6 34.f4! ♗d3 35.♖xa7 ♗e4. Black has managed to avoid a mating attack. However, the endgame with two extra pawns is easily won as well.

36.h3. After 36.♖xh7, there's 36...♖a8 (*this actually immediately lost: 37.♖f7+ ♔g6 38.d6 and d6-d7*).

36...h5 37.♖a6 ♖b8 38.g3 ♔e7 39.a4 ♗d3 40.♖a7+ ♔d6 41.♔f2 ♗e4 42.♔e3 ♗xd5 43.♗xf5 ♔c5. The game was adjourned here.

44.♗g6 h4 45.gxh4 b5 46.axb5 ♖xb5 47.f5 ♖b4 48.h5 ♖e4+. Or 48...♖h4 49.f6 ♖xh3+ 50.♔f4 ♖f3+ 51.♔g5 etc.

49.♔f2 ♔d6 50.h6 ♖h4 51.h7 ♖xh3 52.♖g7 ♔e5 53.♖g8 ♖h2+. If 53...♖xh7, then 54.♖e8+! But not 54.♗xh7? ♗xg8 55.♗xg8 ♔xf5 with a draw.

54.♔g3 ♖g2+ 55.♔h3. Black resigned.

The *Komsomolskaya Pravda* Special Prize

Botvinnik: "The game Kotov – Geller could have been a contender for the highest marks because of its inventiveness, originality and sharpness had it been entirely sound. However, after the opening, Geller could have easily lost had his opponent found the correct plan (f3-f4), and several moves later, he missed a good winning chance himself (b3-b2, pointed out by Bronstein).

Afterwards, there was a struggle with equal chances; after two or three passive moves by white, black played exceptionally energetically and won. So, technically, the game cannot be rewarded as the most beautiful because it features mutual mistakes; moreover, the result could have easily gone either way. However, the game is so unusual, Geller put so much imagination, liveliness and inventiveness into it, that, as an exception, we award him the *Komsomolskaya Pravda* newspaper prize for the most brilliant game of the 17th championship."

Later, this game became one of the gems in Geller's monography *The King's Indian Defense*. Efim Petrovich wasn't known as the biggest expert in this most difficult opening for nothing: he loved it since youth, and he played the King's Indian in six of his nine black games of the 17th championship!

No. 210. King's Indian Defense E68
Kotov – Geller
Moscow 1949, round 16
Annotated by E. Geller

1.d4 ♘f6 2.c4 g6 3.♘c3 ♗g7 4.g3 *(4.e4 – see game 234)* **4...0-0 5.♗g2 d6 6.♘f3 ♘bd7 7.0-0 e5 8.e4 exd4.** 8...c6 leads to a difficult position for black. So, if black wants to execute Bronstein and Boleslavsky's plan with e5xd4, ♘c5, a7-a5, c7-c6, ♘fd7 etc., he should capture on d4 on the 8th move. However, in this case, as we shall see later, black has to contend with certain difficulties.

In Botvinnik's opinion, "a more cautious move here is 8...c6, introduced to tournament practice by D. Bronstein" (this move was played even earlier by Bogatyrchuk, including a game against Kotov himself, Kiev 1938). Geller later also came to the conclusion that 8...c6 was "the most flexible move", and this is indeed the current main line.

9.♘xd4 ♘c5 10.f3. White intends to reinforce the e4 square and then put pressure along the d-file with ♗e3, ♕d2 and ♖ad1.

10...♘fd7 *(or 10...c6 11.♗e3 a5 12.♕d2 a4 Kottnauer – Geller, Szczawno-Zdroj 1950)* **11.♗e3 c6 12.♕d2 a5 13.♖ad1 ♘e5.** Botvinnik's recommendation 13...♘b6 14.b3 ♕e7 led to a loss of a pawn after 15.♘de2.

14.b3 a4. A very similar position occurred in my game with Furman from the same tournament. There, however, ♖e8 was played instead of a5-a4 on move 9, and Furman got a substantial advantage with 15.♘de2.

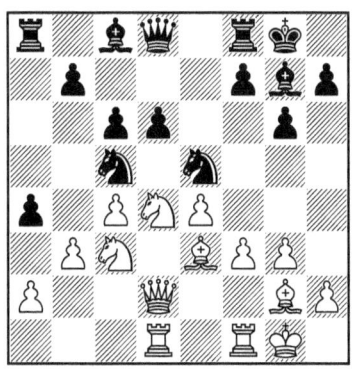

15.♘de2. Kotov repeats Furman's move, which is a serious mistake in this position. The correct move was 15.f4, as pointed out by Botvinnik in his annotations to this game in the tournament bulletin. He proves it with the following line: 15...♘ed3 16.♘xa4 ♘xa4 17.bxa4 ♘c5 18.♘xc6 etc. If we continue this line – 18...bxc6 19.♗xc5 ♗g4! 20.♗xd6 ♖xd1 21.♕xd1 ♖e8 22.e5, then black would have trouble organizing an adequate defense even with an extra exchange.

In the book At the Chessboard, *Geller would change his evaluation:*

"while material is equal, white has a positional advantage, but the position is still double-edged." *And he added:*

"Black has another continuation that would be interesting to test in practice: 15...axb3!? 16.fxe5 bxa2. Now, after 17.♘xc6 bxc6 18.♗xc5 ♗g4 or 17.exd6 ♗g4 18.♖a1 ♕xd6, black's position is quite good. Thus, 17.♘xa2 looks stronger, but after 17...♗g4 18.♘e2 (18.exd6 ♗xd1 19.♖xd1 ♕xd6 20.♘c3 ♖fd8) 18...♗xe5, a very interesting position occurs on the board:

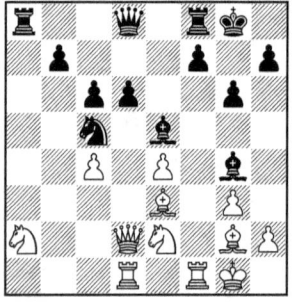

Black already has two pawns for the sacrificed piece. Additionally, the white c4 pawn is very weak. The fact that black pieces have assumed very strong positions, and that it's hard for white to find an active plan, also works in black's favor. All that allows us to evaluate the position as very promising for black.

However, an electronic check allows us to clarify the lines. We won't dwell on small mistakes, going straight for the main novelty, 17.♘xa2. It turns out that instead of 18.♘e2, white has a stronger, paradoxical-looking move 18.♘f3!

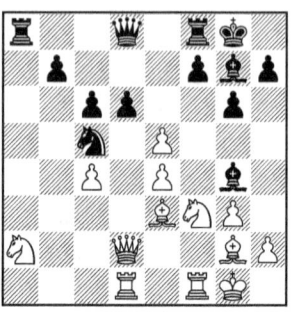

Black's position is quite unenviable: 18...♘xe4 19.♕c2 ♗f5 (19...f5 20.exd6!) 20.g4! ♖a3 21.♕c1 ♖xa2 22.gxf5 gxf5 23.♔h1! or 18...♗xf3 19.♗xf3 ♗xe5 20.♘c1 ♕e7 21.♘d3 ♘xd3 22.♕xd3 etc.

So, was 15...♘ed3 the best defense then? Almost: the same knight, but a different route! As the main counter to 15.f4, Botvinnik showed 15...♘g4 and then refuted it himself: 16.♘xc6! ♕e8! 17.♘d4 axb3 18.axb3 ♗xd4 19.♗xd4 ♘xb3 20.♕d3 with "an advantage that's enough to win".

Geller, probably deferring to the world champion's authority, never even mentioned that move in the magazine, and in the book, he simply wrote, "15...♘g4 is bad due to 16.♘xc6".

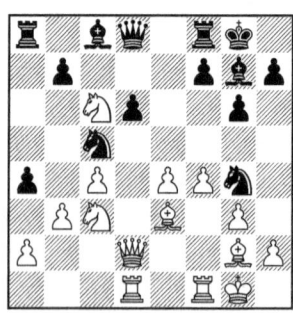

But instead of 16...♕e8?!, black had a counter-strike 16...♘xb3!. Then

17.♘xd8 ♘xd2 18.♗xd2 ♗d4+! and ♖xd8= is quite toothless, while after 17.axb3 bxc6 18.♘xa4 ♘xe3 19.♕xe3 ♕e7, black can hold (20. e5!? dxe5 21.♗xc6 ♖a6 22.♗d5 ♕a3! 23.♘c5 exf4 24.♖xf4 ♖a7, and white is only slightly better)...

Thus, 15...♘g4! seems to be the best reply to 15.f4!.

15...axb3! Black sacrifices a piece, destroying his opponent's queenside and seizing the initiative.

16.♗xc5 ♘xc4 17.♕c1.

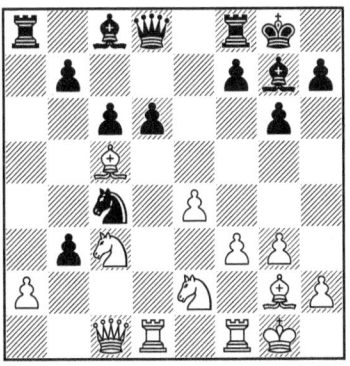

17...bxa2. This gives white a breather. Bronstein's recommended move 17...b2 18.♕c2 dxc5! 19.♖xd8 ♖xd8 was stronger, giving black a big advantage. Botvinnik's continuation 20.♖d1 ♗e6 21.f4 doesn't save white due to 21...♗d4+, and black should win.

But during the game, I was afraid of crossing the line of permitted risk. At any rate, black has an easy and pleasant game after the text move as well.

18.♘xa2 ♕a5 19.♕xc4 ♗e6 20.♕c1 dxc5 21.♘ac3 b5! Black's

plan is simple. He should push the queenside pawns as far as he can. Two long-range bishops can give great support to these efforts. Therefore, white had to limit the range of one of them – without wasting time and perhaps even by giving away some material.

"Kotov, upset by the sudden change in the course of the game (instead of attacking, he was forced to turn to difficult defense), finds the correct plan too late, when one of the black pawns had already reached the 3rd rank." (Botvinnik)

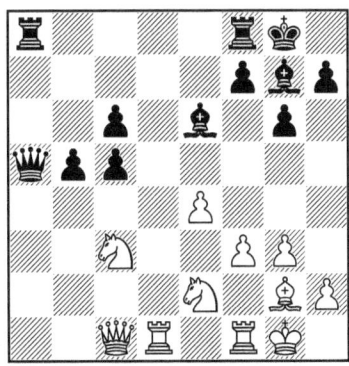

"I saw this position when I started my combination on the 14th move," *Geller would write in* At the Chessboard. "Black has three connected passed pawns on the queenside for the piece. Supported by the long-range bishops, they are pushing forward, and it seems that there's nothing that can stop them."

22.♘b1. It was necessary to play 22.f4 ♗b3 23.♖d6 b4 24.e5!, and the worst is over for white.

Дружеский шарж **Н. Лиса.**

Мастер Е. ГЕЛЛЕР

Geller in a boat named Odessa. Cartoon by N. Lis (Sovietsky Sport, 22ⁿᵈ October 1949).

22...b4 23.♘f4. Here, 23.f4 was also more resilient.

The previous move was just an inaccuracy, but this one is the decisive mistake!

23...♗b3   24.♖d6.   24.♘d2 ♗xd1 25.♖xd1 was better, it wasn't that easy for black to push his pawns *(the computer confidently gives a long line)*. But white sets a trap.

24...c4   25.♖xc6   c3   26.♘d5 ♗xd5 27.exd5 ♕xd5 28.f4 ♕d4+ 29.♔h1. The position has become clearer. White has a piece for two pawns, but his knight is stalemated, and he has almost nothing to move in general. In addition, his exposed king makes it easier for black to exploit his positional advantage.

29...♖a2 30.♗f3 *(preventing 30... ♖xg2)* **30...♖b2.** Threatening 31... b3 32.♖xc3 (32.♘xc3 ♖c2; *after 32.♕xc3, there's only one winning move: 32...♕d7!!)* 32...♖xb1! and preparing ♖f8-a8-a2, just in case.

31.f5 ♗e5 32.♕e1 ♖d8.

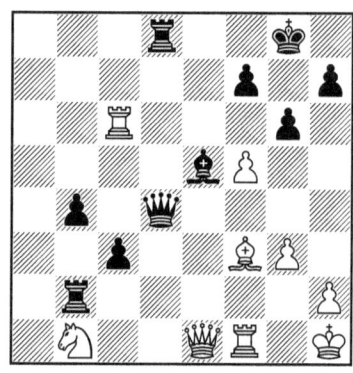

33.♗e4. After 33.♕e4, black won with 33...♕xe4 34.♗xe4 gxf5 35.♗xf5 b3 36.♘xc3 ♖dd2, and there's no defense to mate.

33...♔g7! Provoking 34.f6+. The point is, white is in a zugzwang of sorts. For instance, 34.♖f3 loses to 34...♕xe4!, while after 34.♖g1, there's both 34...♕f2 and 34...♖f2.

"A remarkably elegant idea." (Bronstein)

34.f6+ ♔g8. Now that the g6 square is out of danger, the decisive h7-h5-h4 pawn advance is possible.

35.♖a6 h5 36.♖a5 h4 37.♗xg6 ♖xh2+ 38.♔xh2 ♗xg3+ 39.♕xg3 hxg3+ 40.♔h3 fxg6. White resigned.

"This game is still spiritually close to me," *Geller wrote later.* "Even today, a quarter of a century on, I strive for the same dynamic play in the ideal case. Black's every move in this game is subordinate to one overwhelming idea: attack, attack and attack even more."

Shattered Dreams

Damsky: "A sleety, dank day – 19th November 1949. The last round of the Soviet Championship is played on the TsDKZh stage in Moscow. People are asking for extra tickets at the subway exits. The police are trying in vain to convince the chess fans at least not to crowd the street and be safe. And on the stage, for the second time in the entire history of Soviet chess *(the first time, as you remember, happened in 1939)*, a question is being answered: will a young master win the national championship?..

Geller has white. He gets 'caught' in an opening line in the Ruy Lopez, but still plays with unnecessary, even harmful aggression. And then he loses. The cherished goals, like mirages, float beyond the horizon: he'll become a grandmaster three years later and win the Soviet Championship only six years later...

Many years later, I asked him, 'Efim Petrovich, what were you thinking of before that game? Why didn't you play a Four Knights Opening and make a draw? Did you want clear first place?' Geller shook

his head: 'No... I just played..."" (From the book *Grandmaster Geller*.)

No. 211. Ruy Lopez C61
Geller – Kholmov
Moscow 1949, round 19
Annotated by R. Kholmov
1.e4 e5 2.♘f3 ♘c6 3.♗b5 ♘d4. This move is rarely used in the Ruy Lopez and leads to little-studied lines *(the Bird Defense)*.
4.♘xd4 exd4 5.0-0 c6 6.♗c4 ♘f6 7.♕e2. 7.e5 is not dangerous due to 7...d5!
7...d6 8.e5. *"Geller follows the game Smyslov – Alatortsev (1946 Moscow championship), where, after 8.e5 dxe5 9.♕xe5+ ♗e7 10.♖e1, black found nothing better than to retreat to f8 with his king. Geller probably didn't know that new ideas that neutralize Smyslov's idea were found in the years that passed since that time. A good continuation was 8.c3 dxc3 9.♘xc3 and d2-d4."* *(Romanovsky)*
8...dxe5 9.♕xe5+ ♗e7 10.♖e1 b5! Starting counterplay. Black seizes the initiative. If the bishop retreats to f1, then black plays 11...♗e6 and castles.

This whole system for black was developed by the Leningrad master G. Lisitsin.
11.♗b3 a5 12.a4 ♖a7! The point of black's defensive structure! To speed up his development, he is ready to sacrifice material. White was counting only on 12...b4. Then, after 13.d3 ♖a7 14.♘d2 0-0 15.♘f3

c5 16.♗f4, black's queenside would be weakened.

"Without a doubt, Kholmov knew the game Baturinsky – Lisitsin from the Dynamo society championship that followed this line and was published in the magazine. Yes, to become a grandmaster in our time, you have to watch all chess events closely and study even the games of sports society championships!" (Goglidze)

This game (Shakhmaty v SSSR, No. 7, 1949) was printed in the section "Games for Independent Analysis", without annotations. After 13.axb5 0-0 14.d3?! ♗d6 15.♕g5 ♖e8!, black got an advantage. Geller managed to find the strongest move 14.b6! over the board!

13.axb5 0-0! *It seems that Panov did have a good reason to call Kholmov "an outstanding master of aggressive defense, similar in style to Nikolai Riumin" in the tournament bulletin!*

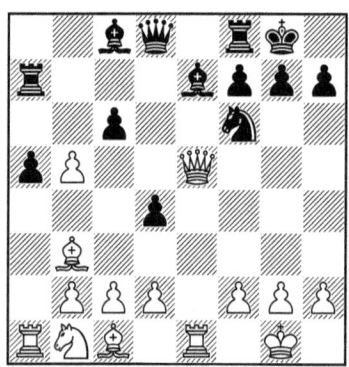

14.b6! Capturing the pawn 14.bxc6 was very dangerous because of 14...♗d6! For instance:

1) 15.♕e2 ♖e8 16.♕d1 ♖xe1+ 17.♕xe1 ♖e7 18.♕d1(f1) ♕e8, and white has to resign;

2) 15.♕b5 ♘g4 16.h3 ♘xf2! 17.♔xf2 ♕h4+ 18.♔f1 ♗a6 or 16.g3 ♘xh2! 17.♔xh2 (*17.♕h5!=, so the correct move is 16...♖e8!*) 17...♕h4+ 18.♔g2 ♕h3+ 19.♔g1 ♗xg3! 20.fxg3 ♕xg3+ 21.♔f1 ♗h3+ 22.♔e2 ♖e8+ etc.

Of course, white may have had a better defense, but at any rate, the sacrifice of two pawns is fully justified because of a huge development advantage. The purpose of the game move is to deflect the queen from the d6 square and prevent the attack on h2, as well as win some tempos to develop his pieces that have got stuck on the queenside.

14...♕xb6. It's necessary to capture the pawn: if the rook retreated, white could play 15.d3 ♗d6 16.♕g5, and there's no pressure on the h2 square because the queen is protected.

15.d3 ♗b4 16.♖f1.

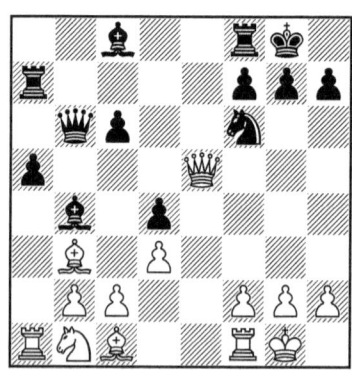

16...♕d8. An irresolute move. Black could maintain the advantage with 16...♖e8 17.♕g3 ♗e6 18.♗h6 ♗f8 19.♘d2 ♗xb3 20.cxb3 ♘d5.

18.♗xe6! ♖xe6 19.♘d2 ♖ae7 20.♘c4= is stronger here. Meanwhile, the "correct attacking plan" presented by Romanovsky and approved by Kholmov in the tournament book – 16...♘d5! 17.♗xd5 ♖e7! 18.♕g5 cxd5 19.♕xd5 ♗b7 – looks too much like a cooperative line: both 18.♗xf7+! ♖fxf7 19.♕h5= and 17.♘d2! ♖e7 18.♕g3 ♖fe8 19.♘c4= are better. So, "irresoluteness" wasn't the problem: the position was actually close to equal!

17.♗g5 ♖e8 18.♕g3. *"It's hard to say why Geller preferred this move to 18.♗xf6 gxf6 19.♕g3+ ♔h8 20.♘a3, after which the exposed black king could become a target for all sorts of attacks, and black couldn't do anything along the open g-file."* (Romanovsky)

18...♗e6 19.♗xe6 ♖xe6 20.♘d2 h6.

dxc3 25.bxc3 ♗xc3 26.♖ac1 *(26. ♗e3! ♖xe3 27.fxe3 ♗xd2! 28.♔f2 is more tenacious)* 26...♗b4 27.♗e3 ♖xe3! 28.fxe3 ♗xd2 gave black the advantage.

21...♖xf6. White has managed to develop normally, but black still has some advantage. The black bishop is clearly stronger than the knight. If white doesn't put the knight on e4, then black seizes the e-file and invades the 2nd rank with the second rook. But white can't hold the knight's position in the center.

22.♘e4　♖e6　23.♕h3　♕d5 24.c3. White has to do something, otherwise there's a very unpleasant move f7-f5. The game move, however, allows black to create an outside passed a-pawn.

Romanovsky is right with the following comment: "The most logical move was 24.g4, and if 24...♖g6, then 25.♔h1".

24...dxc3 25.bxc3 ♗e7.

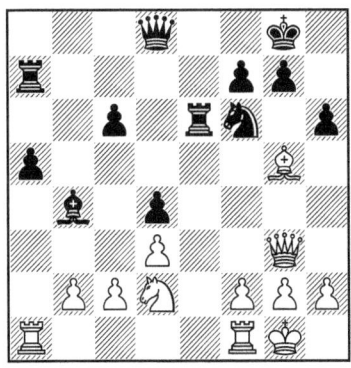

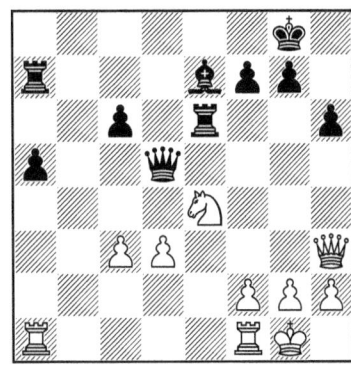

21.♗xf6. 21.♗xh6 ♘h5 22.♕g5 ♕xg5 *(22...♕b8! 23.♕xh5 ♖xh6 – Romanovsky)* 23.♗xg5 f6 24.c3

26.f4? In trying to secure the knight's position on e4, white only worsens his position. But after 26.♖a4

Ratmir Kholmov, taken at a photo studio in Kaunas. From R. Kholmov's archive. Published for the first time.

f5 white is still worse, if not yet lost *(actually, 27.♘g3 ♕xd3 28.♕xf5=).*

"After 26.♖a4 (what else?), there could follow 26...♕b3 27.♖fa1 ♖b7! 28.f4 ♕c2 with the threat ♖b1+." *(Romanovsky.) In the tournament book, Kholmov agreed with the line, but later he wrote:* "Instead of 28.f4?, white has a much stronger move 28.g4!, with very unclear play."

26...f5 27.c4 ♕d4+ 28.♔h1 g6 29.♖ab1. 29.♕xh6 didn't work due to 29...fxe4 (but not 29...♗f8? 30.♕h3 ♖h7 31.♕xh7+! ♔xh7 32.♘g5+ etc.) 30.f5 ♖f6 31.fxg6 ♖xf1+ 32.♖xf1 ♕g7!

29...♗f8 is no worse: instead of 30...♖h7?=, 30...♖ae7! wins (31.♘g5 ♕xa1).

29...h5 30.♖b8+ ♔f7.

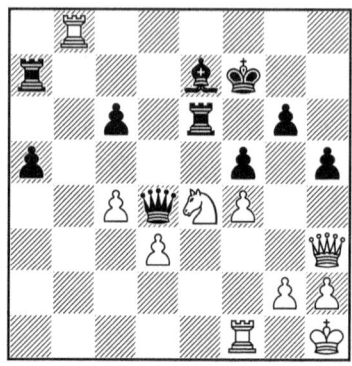

31.♕g3. Seeing that his position is bad, white sacrifices a piece in the hope of sharpening the game. If 31.♘g5+, then 31...♗xg5 32.fxg5 ♖e3!, and there's no 33.♖xf5+ due to 33...♔g7!

31...fxe4 32.f5 ♖f6 33.♖h8 ♕xd3! Black sacrifices an exchange; the resulting endgame is won by force *(there's an even cooler line: 33... ♔g7! 34.♖xh5 ♕xd3 35.♕xd3 exd3 36.♖h3 ♖d7 and d3-d2).*

34.fxg6+ ♔g7 35.♖h7+ ♔g8 36.♕xd3. If 36.♕b8+, then 36... ♗d8, and white can't capture anything. Although black could even get checkmated in the scramble: 36...♖f8? 37.♖xf8+ ♗xf8 38.♖h8+! ♔xh8 39.♕xf8#.

36...exd3 37.♖xf6 ♗xf6 38.♖xa7 ♗d4! *"The finale of black's combination. After 39.♖d7, there's 39...c5, while 39.♖xa5 is met with 39... d2." (Romanovsky)*

39.♖f7 d2 40.♖f1 ♗b2 (40...a4 was simpler) **41.♔g1 a4 42.♔f2 a3 43.♔e2 a2.** White resigned.

The Poisoned Knight

Goglidze: "Grandmaster Smyslov again played an interesting, rich game. Playing his beloved Ruy Lopez, he got a promising position. Liublinsky started a complicated minor piece regrouping, spending seven moves on it. In the meantime, white organized strong pressure on the kingside and in the center. The white knight went to g5 and stood there *en prise* for 13 moves, but black couldn't capture it. On move 21, Smyslov forced an important weakening of the dark squares with the subtle maneuver ♗b3-d5-b3. All that logically led to a beautiful finishing combination."

No. 212
Smyslov – Liublinsky
Moscow 1949, round 13
Annotated by V. Smyslov

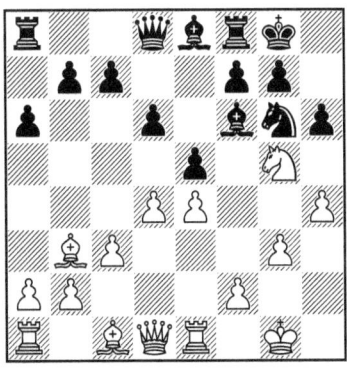

18.♕h5! Intending to meet 18... hxg5 with 19.hxg5 ♗e7 20.♕xg6, regaining the piece *(after 20...♗a4! 21.♕h5 ♗xb3, there's still a lot to play*

for; however, 20.♔g2! forced black to give up his queen). Avoiding the 19.♕xg6 threat, black now puts his knight in a corner, but overprotects the vulnerable f7 square.

18...♘h8 19.dxe5 dxe5 20.♗e3 ♕e7. It's dangerous to accept the knight sacrifice. After 20...hxg5 21.hxg5 g6 22.♕h4 ♗g7 23.♔g2 ♗c6 24.♖h1 ♖e8 25.♕h7+ ♔f8 26.♗c5+ ♖e7 27.♕xh8+! ♗xh8 28.♖xh8+ ♔g7 29.♖xd8 ♖xd8 30.♗xe7, white wins.

After 20...♗d7 with the idea ♕c8, there's 21.f4! and f4-f5, or 20...♕c8 with the idea ♗d7 is met with 21.♘f3! (but not 21.f4? exf4 22.gxf4 c5=) 21...♗d7 22.♘xe5 ♗xe5 23.♕xe5.

21.♗d5! The knight is still indigestible, since 21...hxg5 is met with 22.hxg5 g6 23.gxf6! If black doesn't want to break up his pawn chain, which could happen after 21... ♗c6 22.♗xc6 bxc6, he needs to play 21...c6, taking away this important square from his bishop.

21...c6 22.♗b3 ♗d7 23.♖ad1 ♖ad8 24.♖d2 ♗c8 25.♖ed1 ♖xd2 26.♖xd2.

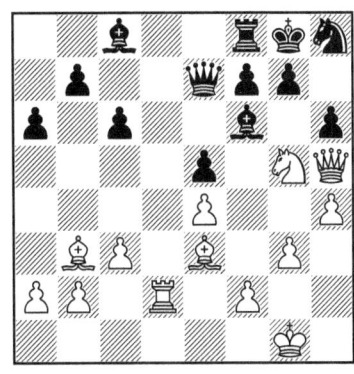

26...♕c7. White has seized the open file and maintained his attacking position. With this move, black wants to drive away the troublesome knight, renewing the threat 27...hxg5 28.hxg5 g6. However, white finds a strong reply.

After 26...b5! with the threat a6-a5-a4, it's unclear how white should continue the attack: 27.a3 (27.a4 bxa4 28.♗xa4 c5=) 27...c5 28.♗d5 ♖d8 and ♗b7 (29.♘f3 g6 30.♕xh6 ♗g7=).

27.♗c5! Now white will meet 27... hxg5 with 28.♗xf8, and after 27... ♗e7 there's 28.♗xe7 ♕xe7 29.♘f3 ♖e8 30.♕xe5! ♕xe5 31.♘xe5 ♖xe5 32.♖d8+ ♔h7 33.♖xc8, when there's no 33...♖xe4 due to 34.♗c2.

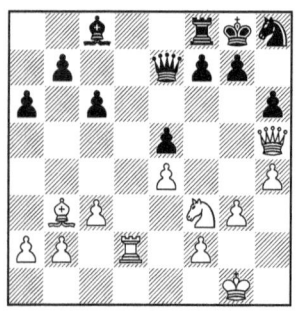

Position after 27...♗e7 28.♗xe7
♕xe7 29.♘f3

The computer doesn't take Smyslov's word for it: 29...♕f6! (instead of 29...♖e8?), and the pawn capture gains nothing (30. ♘xe5 g6!=), while there are no other "serious" threats. So, 27...♗e7! was actually better.

27...♖d8 28.♖xd8+ ♗xd8.

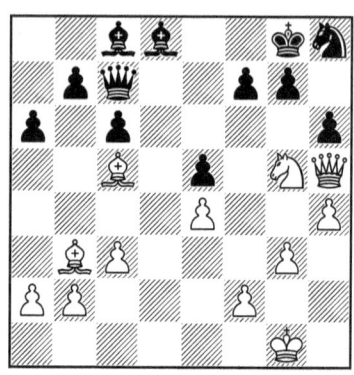

29.♘xf7! ♘xf7 30.♗b6! The point of the combination! White regains the piece, since 30...♕xb6 is met with 31.♕xf7+ ♔h7 32.h5 and a mating net.

30...♕d7 31.♗xd8 ♔h7 32.♗xf7 ♕xd8 33.♗g6+. Black resigned because he loses the second pawn on e5 *(the Megabase erroneously gives the move as 33.♕g6+).*

A Gem of a Draw

From the press: "Mikenas was the hero of the hall for half an hour in round 3 – yesterday he defeated Kotov, and today, he was 'defeating' Smyslov. The grandmaster was a piece down, and there was no obvious way to continue the attack.

Smyslov is unperturbed, as always. He calmly makes a move overlooked by his opponent, putting his second bishop under a double attack! Perpetual check is unavoidable.

Mikenas smiles and shakes Smyslov's hand. Draw! The hall is applauding." *(Tournament Bulletin.)*

No. 213
Smyslov – Mikenas
Moscow 1949, round 3
Annotated by V. Mikenas

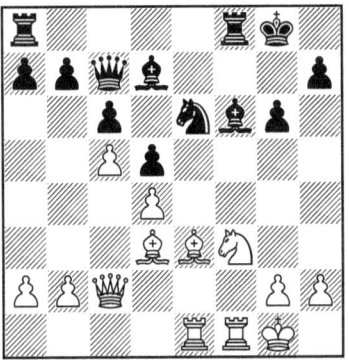

21.♗h6! An interesting pawn sacrifice. I think this is the right decision, since black shouldn't be allowed to reinforce his position with 21...♖ae8. It seems that the grandmaster had already foreseen the combination on move 27!

"Since the continuations 21... ♗g7 22.♗xg7 and 21...♘g7 22.♘e5 weaken the e5 square, and 21...♖f7 can be successfully met with 22.♗xg6! hxg6 23.♕xg6+ ♗g7 24.♘g5, black has nothing more to do than accept the offered pawn sacrifice." (Botvinnik)

21...♘xd4 22.♘xd4 ♗xd4+ 23.♔h1 ♖xf1+ 24.♖xf1 ♕e5! The queen's dominating position in the center limits white's activity. The final combination leads to a spectacular ending.

Smyslov – Mikenas. From D. Bronstein's archive. Published for the first time.

"24...♗g7   25.♗xg7   ♔xg7 26.♕c3+ was dangerous; now white cannot tarry due to the threat 25... ♕h5." (Botvinnik)

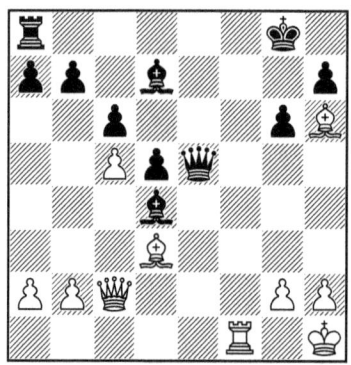

25.♗xg6 hxg6 26.♕xg6+ ♔h8. *"At first sight, the bishop sacrifice was correct... After a 20-minute think Smyslov finds an incredible continuation of the attack." (Botvinnik)*

27.♗e3!! Draw! There could follow 27...♕xe3 28.♕h5+ ♔g8 29.♕f7+, and perpetual check cannot be avoided.

Smyslov couldn't play any other move. For instance, 27.♗g5 ♕g7! or 27.♗f8 ♗e8! *(this is bad due to 28.♕h6+ and ♗d6!; the correct move is 27...♕e4! – Botvinnik)*, and the attack is repelled.

Black couldn't play other moves either. After 27...♗xe3 28.♖f7!, his king gets checkmated (the bishop closed off the e1 square for the queen).

"The beauty of this combination lies in the fact that the black queen is tied to the defense of the d4 bishop and cannot help its king because

of that. Therefore, it's a draw! The final position is spectacular." (Botvinnik)

The Hidden Gem

"In the game against Flohr, Smyslov, who was an exchange and a pawn up, chose an original plan: he sacrificed two pawns, traded queens and then gave up another pawn. Flohr's position became critical. After a sacrifice of yet another, fourth pawn Flohr got checkmated on move 53." (Tournament bulletin)

No. 214
Smyslov – Flohr
Moscow 1949, round 16
Annotated by G. Levenfish

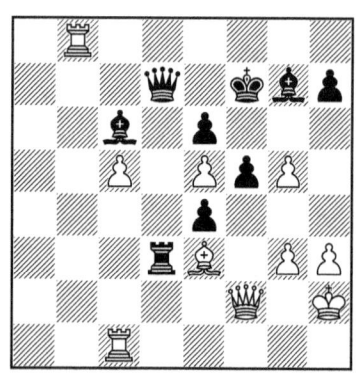

43.♕f4! Starting the spectacular final combination.

43...♕c7. *Levenfish doesn't provide any commentary to this move. However, black had an equally spectacular counter-combination: 43...♕d5! 44.♖cb1 ♗xe5 45.♕h4 ♖d2+!!*

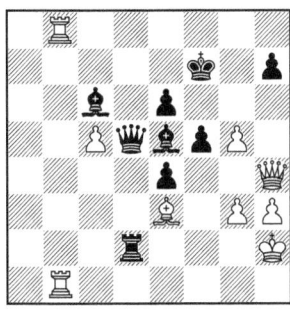

♗d4+ 51.♔e2 (the point) 51...
♗xe3+ 52.♔xe3 ♕b3+ 53.♔f2
♗b5! 54.♕h5 ♗e8 or 54.♕e1 ♕f3+!

44.♖cb1! **♗xe5** (44...♕xe5
45.♖c8!) **45.♕h4 ♗xg3+.** 45...♖xe3
46.♕h5+!, mating.

46.♕xg3 **♕xg3+** **47.♔xg3**
♖xe3+ 48.♔f4! ♖xh3.

*Capturing the rook leads to mate,
while after 46.♔g1 ♖d1+ 47.♔h2
♖d2+, there's a draw on the board!
If white still tries to play for a win,
he'll get punished: 47.♔f2 (47.♔g2?
♕d2+!! 48.♗xd2 e3+, mating) 47...
♕a2+ 48.♖8b2 (48.♖1b2? ♗xb2
49.♕h5+ ♔e7 50.♕xd1 ♗xe5+ with
an extra piece) 48...♗xb2.*

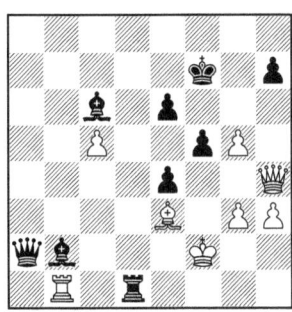

*White has two paths to a draw, and
both require precision:*

*1) 49.♖xd1 ♗d4+, and it's bad
to play 50.♔f1? ♕c4+ 51.♔e1
♕c3+ 52.♗d2 because of 52...
♕f3! The correct move is 50.♔e1!
♕a5+ 51.♔f1 ♕b5+ 52.♔e1 – the
difference is that after 52...♕b4+
53.♗d2!, there's no 53...♕f3;*

*2) 49.♕h5+ ♔g7, and 50.♕h6+?
♔g8 51.♖xd1 is bad due to 51...
♗d4+! The correct move is 50.♖xd1!*

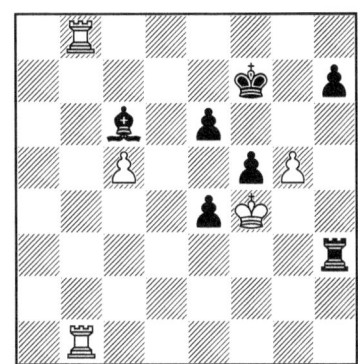

Black has equalized material.
His passed e- and f- pawns look
formidable. But Smyslov has
calculated everything until the end.

49.♖c8! ♗d5 50.c6 ♖f3+. After
the immediate 50...♖c3, there's
51.♖b7+ ♔g6 52.♖g8+ ♔h5
53.♖xh7#.

51.♔e5 ♖c3 52.g6+! hxg6 (or
52...♔xg6 53.♖g8+ ♔f7 54.♖bg1
and ♖1g7#) **53.♖b7#.** A rarity in a
grandmaster game – a natural mate
on the board.

A Psychological Duel

Yudovich: "The game between
tournament leader Keres and
Soviet champion Bronstein was
exceptionally complicated. The

'psychological duel' started right in the opening. Keres threatened to deploy a sharp line in the Ruy Lopez. Bronstein accepted the challenge... The position got so complex that both Bronstein and Keres made mistakes in its handling. Finally, after a break in the center (21.e5), white started to storm the black king's position."

No. 215
Bronstein – Keres
Moscow 1949, round 8[6]

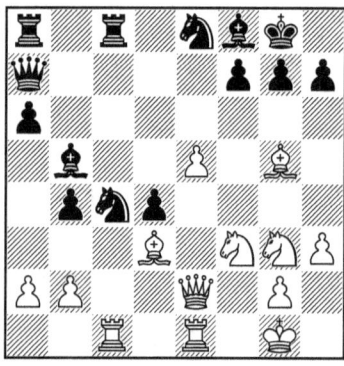

25.e6! Continuing the psychological duel. "The moves e5-e6-e7 were audacious, but they paid off: the position has left the sphere of precise evaluations, and Keres doesn't like this, he believes in his ability to calculate any number of lines, but there's so many of them sometimes! Where, in what section of your brain are you supposed

---

[6]   If the annotation author is not stated, the games were annotated by me (S.V.).

to store the ones you calculated already?" (Bronstein)

25...f6. "Of course, not 25... fxe6 due to 26.♕xe6+ ♚h8 (26... ♕f7? 27.♗xh7+) 27.♗xc4." (Konstantinopolsky)

26.e7!? After 26.♖xc4 (counting on 26...♖xc4? 27.e7! ♕xe7 28.♗xc4+ ♗xc4 29.♕xc4+ ♕f7 30.♕xd4, and the bishop cannot be captured) 26... ♗xc4 27.e7 ♕xe7! 28.♗xc4+ ♚h8 29.♗f4 ♕xe2, white's attack fizzled out.

26...♕xe7. Obviously not 26... ♗xe7? 27.♕e6+. "The position has sharpened considerably, and if we take mutual time trouble into account, we can forgive the grandmasters' subsequent inaccuracies." (Konstantinopolsky)

27.♗xh7+! Complicating things even more! The alternative was 27.♕xe7 ♗xe7 28.♖xe7 fxg5 29.♗f5!, but David Ionovich doesn't like attacking without queens.

The tempting 27.♕c2 was parried by 27...♘e5!

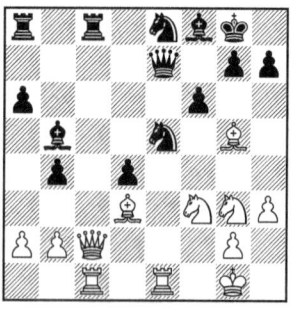

The line looks like a devastating tornado: 28.♗xh7+ ♚h8 29.♘xe5! ♖xc2 30.♗xc2! ♕xe5! (after 30...

♕a7, white gives a perpetual check: 31.♘g6+ ♔h7 32.♘xf8+ ♔g8 33.♘g6 fxg5 34.♗b3+ etc.) 31.♖xe5 fxe5 – black gets an extra pawn, but white no longer has an attack!

27...♔h8 28.♕d1. The queen wants to get to h5, harassing the black king.

28...♘e3. Konstantinopolsky: "After 28...♕a7, white has a rather unpleasant reply 29.♗g6! with mating threats." However, after 29...fxg5 30.♘xg5 ♘f6 31.♖e4, black launches a counter-attack: 31...d3+!! 32.♔h2 (32.♔h1? d2 and the pawn promotes with check) 32...♗d6! 33.♖h4+ ♔g8 34.♕xd3 (34.♘f7? ♗xg3+) 34...♕e3 35.♕xe3 ♘xe3 36.♖xc8+ ♖xc8 37.♗f7+ ♔f8 38.♖h8+ ♔e7 39.♖xc8 ♘f5 with an extra piece. Instead of 29.♗g6?, the correct move is 29.♗f5! fxg5 30.♘e5=.

29.♗xe3 dxe3.

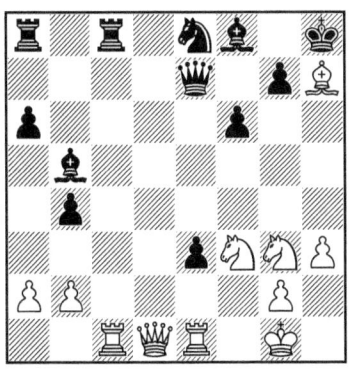

30.♗f5?!! The unusual mark is assigned for the psychological effect! "Instead of 30.♗f5, white could play 30.♖xc8 ♖xc8 31.♕d5 ♔xh7 32.♕f5+!, but who can say

for sure which continuation was the soundest?" (Bronstein.) By the way, the move 32.♕h5+! is erroneously given in the book *200 Open Games* – it loses immediately.

30...e2? Maybe this fatal decision was dictated by a subconscious desire to close off the dangerous d1-h5 diagonal? The simple 30...♖xc1 31.♕xc1 ♕c5 was better for black: 32.♘h4 (32.♕b1 ♘d6!) 32...e2+ 33.♔h2 ♕xc1 34.♘g6+ ♔h7 35.♘xf8+ ♔g8 36.♖xc1 ♔xf8 37.♗g4 ♖d8, and the rook invades the 2nd rank.

31.♕d4! ♖xc1? Blundering a checkmate. "There was still a serious chance: 31...♕c5 32.♗xc8 ♖xc8, and black can still resist."

32.♕h4+ ♔g8 33.♕h7+ ♔f7 34.♕h5+! ("Keres missed this move" – Yudovich) **34...♔g8 35.♗h7+.** Black resigned.

Botvinnik unleashed hell on this game in his red notebook: "'Br' maneuvered cunningly, played ♘g3, ♘h4 and f4 with the initiative – freezing the c1 bishop in the process. He gave up his d4 pawn, but played e5 and put his bishop on g5. He gained nothing, and Keres had a totally won game. But Keres followed his opponent's example, decided to show 'initiative' and blundered a mate. 'Br' sharpened the position well, but got nothing, and the ending is 'cafe-style'. Weak."

A most telling quote! I realize that Mikhail Moiseevich wrote all this for his eyes only, and I'm not going to comment on it. But keep one thing in mind: these notes were created **before** the 1951 match, even though, according to Botvinnik, he "severed all relations" with Bronstein "**after** our match", because of his allegedly "outrageous behavior". He did sever relations only afterwards, but, judging by these notes, he felt animosity long before that – perhaps since that loss in the 1944 championship, where he intuitively felt that this young talent would be a threat to his leadership. And the fact that David was from Kiev actually only made things worse, reminding him of... Bogatyrchuk! And this is not just idle speculation. Botvinnik let it slip in Bronstein's profile written during preparation for the match: "Very cunning, tricky, a true representative of the Kiev school. To get an extra half-point, he's ready to do anything *a la* Bogatyrchuk/Lilienthal." (From the book *Botvinnik – Bronstein Match.*) What was this "anything" and why was Lilienthal mentioned together with Bogatyrchuk, Botvinnik's bitter enemy? We can only guess...

The moral is clear: before blaming David Ionovich for his dislike or even hatred of Botvinnik (as some authors do), remember that this was largely a response to Botvinnik's feelings.

Tactics Lesson From Keres

Romanovsky: "Petrosian got his fifth zero. In the game with Keres,

he chose a difficult opening *(the King's Indian)* and defended without much inspiration. Keres' attack was beautiful and precise, exploiting the depressed mood of the young Yerevan master after a disastrous start."

It's hard to believe that "Iron Tigran" lost five games in a row! However, after this crushing defeat, he managed to break his free fall and, defeating Lilienthal (according to Romanovsky, the latter played "without any temperament and his characteristic tactical inventiveness"), finally started to fight the more famous opponents on equal terms...

No. 216
Keres – Petrosian
Moscow 1949, round 5
Annotated by P. Keres

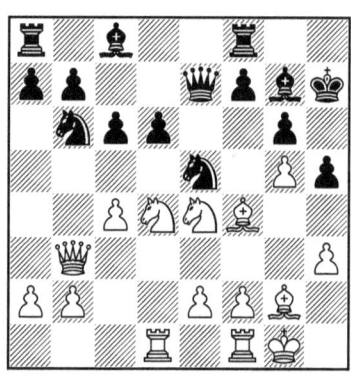

Bronstein was somewhat sarcastic about Keres' ability to "calculate any number of lines", but in terms of depth and precision of his analysis (it almost always matched the computer's first line), Paul Petrovich was superior to everyone else, Botvinnik included.

Only Boleslavsky could rival him in this regard (see the next game)...

19.♕g3! An incredibly powerful move. White threatens both 20.b3 with a big positional advantage and 20.c5! dxc5 21.♘f6+ ♗xf6 22.gxf6 etc. Thus, black is forced to capture on c4.

19...♘exc4 (19...♘bxc4 leads to the same position) **20.b3.** Perhaps Petrosian considered only 20.♘xd6, which he was planning to meet with 20...♘xb2, getting a good position.

20...♘e5.

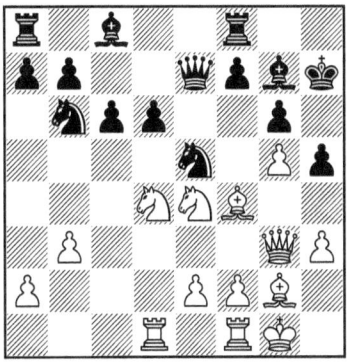

21.♘xd6! The point of the combination that started on move 19. White regains the pawn in a better position, and black can't exploit the position of the g7 knight cut off from the rest of white's army – it's very active there.

21...♕xd6. Almost forced, since after 21...♘d5 22.♘xc8 ♖axc8 23.♗c1, white got an obvious advantage.

The computer disagrees with the "forced" part, insisting on 21...♖d8! For instance: 22.♘f3 (22.♘xc8

♖axc8=) 22...♘xf3+ 23.♗xf3 ♘d5 24.♗xd5 cxd5 25.♖xd5 ♕xe2 26.♖d2 ♕e6=. Instead of 21.♘xd6, it recommends 21.♕h4! with the idea ♗c1, attacking both the d6 pawn (with ♗a3) and the king's position (with f2-f4).

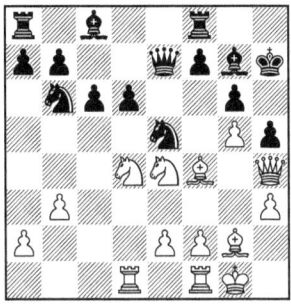

For instance: 21...♘bd7 22.♗c1 d5 23.♘g3 f6 (23...f5? 24.f4 ♘f7 25.♘dxf5! is bad for black) 24.♘xh5! gxh5 25.♕xh5+ ♔g8 26.g6 ♘xg6 27.♕xg6 or 21...♘d5 22.♗c1 ♔g8 (avoiding 23.f4 ♘d7 24.♘f5! gxf5 25.♖xd5! cxd5 26.g6+, winning the queen) 23.♗a3 ♖d8 24.f4 ♘d7 (24...♘e3 25.♘f6+ ♗xf6 26.gxf6 ♕e8 27.fxe5! is worse for black) 25.♗xd6 ♕e8 26.♕g3 with a clear advantage.

22.♘f5.

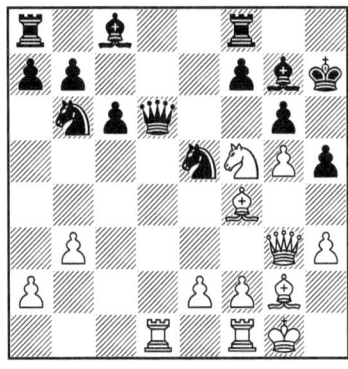

22...♛a3. Black had a wide choice of defensive resources, but none of them were satisfactory:

1) 22...♛xd1 23.♖xd1 ♝xf5 24.♝xe5, and black doesn't have enough compensation for the queen;

2) 22...♛c7 23.♘xg7 ♘bd7 24.♖xd7! ♛xd7 25.♝xe5, and white has two minor pieces for the rook;

3) 22...♛c5 (relatively best) 23.♘xg7 ♘bd7 (or 23...h4 24.♛xh4+ ♚xg7 25.♖d5! ♘xd5 26.♛h6+ ♚g8 27.♝xe5 etc.) 24.♝e3 (24.♖xd7 ♘xd7 25.♝d6 ♛a5 26.♝xf8 ♘xf8 27.♘e8 is also possible) 24...♛e7 25.f4 ♚xg7 26.fxe5 with a substantial advantage for white, since after 26...♘c5, white has a very strong move 27.e6! *(In the bulletin, Keres recommended 25.♝d4, but the simplest was 25.♘xh5! gxh5 26.f4 ♘g6 27.f5).*

Now black has to return the piece and loses an exchange in the process.

23.♘xg7 ♘ed7 *(23...♘ec4 24.♘xh5!)* **24.♝d6 ♛a5.** Not 24...♛xa2, since after 25.♝xf8 ♘xf8 26.♘e8 there's no defense to three threats: 27.♛e5, 27.♛c3 and 27.♘c7. 24...♛b2 was somewhat better, while the game move allowed white to include another strong move, 25.b4!, before capturing on f8.

25.♝xf8 ♘xf8.

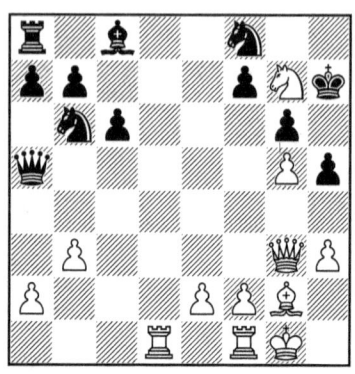

26.♘e8! The knight has got free, and the outcome now becomes clear. 26.b4 ♛xb4 27.♘e8 wasn't as convincing because of 27...♝e6! 28.♘f6+ ♚h8, and if 29.♛e5 then 29...♘c4! *After 30.♛a1!, there's no good defense: 30...♛b2 31.♛xb2 ♘xb2 32.♖b1 ♘a4 33.♖xb7 or 30...♘h7 31.♖b1 ♛f8 32.♖xb7 etc.*

Right after the game, Keres stated that 26.b4 ♛xb4 27.♘e8 "won more quickly", but in the analysis he preferred the text move – and the computer agrees with him!

26...♝e6 27.♘f6+ ♚h8 28.♛f4 ♘h7 29.♛d4 ♘xf6 30.♛xf6+ ♚h7 31.e4. 31.♖d6 won easily, and if 31...♘d5 *(31...♖g8!? is more resilient)*, then 32.♝xd5 cxd5 *(32...♝xd5 33.e4)* 33.♖xe6 fxe6 34.♛f7+ ♚h8 35.♖c1 etc.

With the game move, white sacrifices his queenside pawns to win with a direct attack on the king.

31...♛xa2 32.f4 ♝xb3 33.♖d6 ♖g8 (there was already no defense to the threat 34.f5) **34.f5 ♖g7.** White threatened 35.♖d8 ♖xd8 36.fxg6+ fxg6 37.♛e7+ or e4-e5-e6.

35.♖d8 ♕a5 36.♕d6 f6 37.♕f8 gxf5 (or 37...♗g8 38.gxf6 etc.) 38.♕h8+ ♔g6 39.♕h6+. Black resigned.

Fischer's Favorite Line

Suetin: "The line with 6.♗c4 was introduced to serious practice by the well-known Soviet chess player V. Sozin in the late 1920s. But it attracted truly great interest after this game, which made an incredible impression with its fresh ideas. Of course, safer lines were later found for black. But white's strategic idea, linked to a spectacular piece sacrifice, was truly innovative and drew everyone's attention like a magnet."

Sicilian Defense B88
No. 217
Boleslavsky – Aronin
Moscow 1949, round 12
Annotated by I. Boleslavsky

1.e4 c5 2.♘f3 ♘c6 3.d4 cxd4 4.♘xd4 ♘f6 5.♘c3 d6 6.♗c4 Sozin's continuation had been played quite rarely in the previous twenty years. After the current game, in which white managed to find an interesting exchange sacrifice and demonstrate the attacking chances hidden in this variation, it began to be seen regularly in both Soviet and international tournaments. Soviet players found a bunch of interesting continuations, both in white's attack and in black's defense.

6...e6 7.0-0. *If 7.♗b3 ♗e7 8.f4 0-0 9.♗e3 then a good reply is 9...♘xd4 10.♗xd4 b5 11.e5 dxe5 12.fxe5 ♘d7 13.0-0 ♗c5! (Fischer – Geller, Curaçao 1962). A sharper line is 7.♗e3 ♗e7 8.♕e2 or 8.♗b3 0-0 9.♕e2 and 0-0-0 (the Velimirovic Attack, which Fischer included in his repertoire).*

7...♗e7 Probably the most sensible reply for black, completing development. Practice has shown that attempts at immediate activity on the queenside are highly dangerous for black.

8.♗e3 0-0 9.♗b3 A necessary move. If the immediate 9.f4? then 9...d5! 10.exd5 exd5 11.♗e2 ♖e8 and an advantage for black.

9...a6 Starting a slow action plan, which allows white to launch an attack *(later practice has rehabilitated the move 9...a6)*. Geller demonstrated the most reliable defense in games at the semi-final of the 22nd Soviet championship against Nezhmetdinov and Yudovich: 9...♗d7 10.f4 ♘xd4 11.♗xd4 ♗c6 12.♕e2 b5! and black is doing great.

10.f4 ♘a5 *"The idea of exchanging the menacing bishop on b3 comes at the risk of a dangerous loss of time" (Kasparov). It was safer to play 10...♘xd4 11.♗xd4 b5 (Fischer – Spassky, Reykjavík (m/4) 1972).*

11.♕f3 It was more precise to play 11.g4. The move 11.♕f3 can be made later. *However, after 11.g4 the reply 11...d5!? is unclear (Fischer – Evans, US championship 1958/59).*

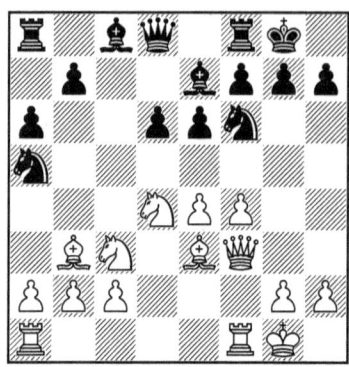

11...♛c7 Black is late with his counterplay: 11...b5! 12.g4 b4 13.♘ce2 ♝b7 14.♘g3 ♘d7! 15.g5 ♘c5 allows him to count on a successful defense. After 11...b5 a more dangerous reply seems to be 12.e5, but after 12...♝b7 13.♛h3 (sacrificing the queen for three pieces – 13.exf6 ♝xf3 14.fxe7 ♛xe7 15.♜xf3 is probably to black's advantage, as he retains a solid center) 13...♘e8 I don't see a way for white to continue the attack.

12.g4 b5 Now this move isn't as powerful as previously, but what then should black have done? After 12...♘xb3 13.axb3 ♝d7 (or 13...♜b8?! 14.g5 ♘d7 15.f5 Ne5 16.♛g3 Fischer – Cardoso, New York (m/2) 1957) 14.g5 ♘e8 15.f5 he is doomed to passive defense. A more natural continuation appears to be 12...♘c4, but white has a strong counter 13.g5! If 13...♘d7, then 14.♘f5! exf5 15.♘d5 ♛d8 16.♝xc4 with a positionally won game. If 13...♘e8 white can pile on the attack with 14.f5 ♘xe3 15.♛xe3.

However, after 13...♘g4! 14.♝c1 ♛c5 15.♜d1 e5 black holds, so it's better

to try *13.♝xc4 ♛xc4 and only then 14.g5 with a slight initiative. Meanwhile, 12...d5!? 13.e5 ♘d7 leads back to the previously mentioned Fischer – Evans game (or if 14.♝xd5, then 14...♘xe5!).*

13.g5 ♘d7? Black overlooks the sacrifice on e6 that decides the game. Of course, he should have retreated the knight to e8, even though after 14.f5 ♘xb3 15.cxb3! black's position is difficult.

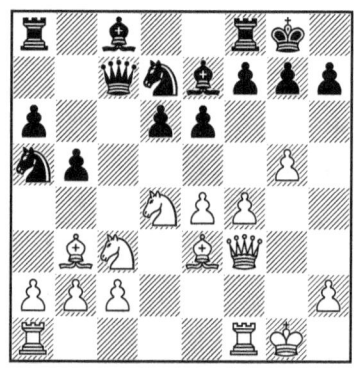

14.♘xe6! fxe6 15.♝xe6+ ♚h8 16.♘d5. *"As though by a wave of some magic wand, the white pieces join the attack against the opposing king." (Suetin)*

16...♛d8 17.♛h5! White does not hurry to regain the sacrificed material with 17.♝xd7, creating a crushing threat on the kingside instead.

17...♘c5. If 17...♘c6, then 18.f5, and black has to give up his bishop due to the threat 19.g6.

After 17...♛e8, there's 18.g6 ♘f6! (not 18...♛xg6+? because of 19.♛xg6 hxg6 20.♘xe7, and black loses by force) 19.♘xf6 ♛xg6+ 20.♛xg6 hxg6 21.♘d5!, and then:

1) 21...♗xe6 22.♘xe7 ♔h7 23.f5 gxf5 24.exf5 ♖ae8 25.♗g5 ♗xf5 26.♖f4! (26.♖xf5 ♖xf5 27.♘xf5 ♖e5 28.♖f1 g6 29.♗d8 ♘b7), and white wins an exchange;

2) 21...♗f6 22.♗xc8 ♖axc8 23.e5! dxe5 24.fxe5 ♗xe5 25.♘e7! ♖xf1+ 26.♖xf1 ♖e8 27.♘xg6+ ♔h7 28.♘xe5, and white should win.

Brilliant lines! But there's a "but": in the first line, instead of 22...♔h7?, black has a stronger reply 22...♖fe8! 23.♘xg6+ ♔g8 24.f5 ♗f7 25.♖f4 ♗xg6 26.fxg6 ♖e6, and white only has an extra pawn.

So, the sacrifice doesn't pay off after 17...♕e8? Yes, it does. However, to find the move 21.♘d7!! (instead 21.♘d5), you have to be a computer... or Mikhail Tal!

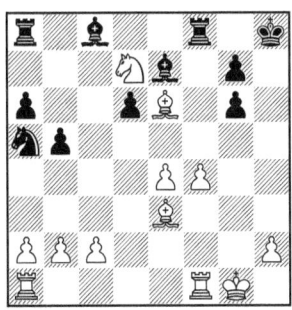

Position after 17...♕e8 18.g6 ♘f6 19.♘xf6 ♕xg6+ 20.♕xg6 hxg6 21.♘d7

The point is that the natural-looking 21...♖d8 leads directly to mate: 22.♖f3! ♗h4 23.♖h3 g5 24.fxg5 ♔h7 25.♗f7 g6 26.♗d4 with the inevitable ♖xh4#!

It's hard to believe, but the game cannot be saved: 21...♗xd7 22.♗xd7 ♘c4 23.♖f3! or 21...♖e8 22.f5 gxf5 23.♖f3! ♗h4 24.exf5 ♗xd7 25.♗xd7 etc.

18.♗xc8 ♖xc8 19.f5 ♗xg5. Necessary. If 19...♔g8, then 20.g6 h6 21.♗xh6 gxh6 22.♕xh6 ♖f7 23.gxf7+ ♔xf7 24.♕g6+ ♔f8 25.f6 with inevitable mate.

20.♗xg5 ♕e8 21.♕xe8 ♖fxe8.

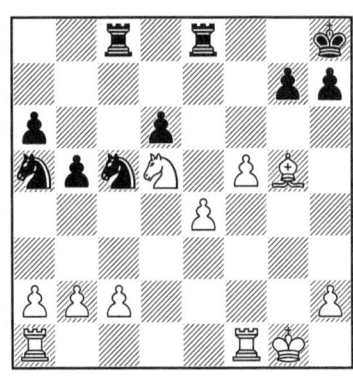

22.f6! Now there's no 22...gxf6 because of 23.♗xf6+ ♔g8 24.b4, winning a piece.

22...♘d7. After 22...♘xe4 23.f7 ♘xg5 24.fxe8=♕+ ♖xe8 25.♘c7 white won easily as well.

23.f7 ♖xe4 24.♘b6! Black might as well resign after this move, but he decided to prolong the struggle.

24...♘f8   25.♘xc8   ♖g4+ 26.♔h1   ♖xg5   27.♘xd6   g6

28.♖ae1 ♖d5 29.♖e8 ♔g7 30.♖d8 ♖e5 31.♘e8+ ♔h6 32.♘f6. Black resigned.

Off-Stage Brilliancies

From the press: "It seems that Kotov, like in the previous championship, decided not to make draws. Bronstein, on the other hand, started with three draws. However, he played his first game *(in round 3)* after an illness. He wasn't allowed to go outside, so the game was played in a room at the Moskva Hotel in the presence of an arbiter.

In round 4, the hall was packed. You can't swing a captured pawn, as they say. After each move in the game between the two champions, there are hushed whispers in the hall:

'Bronstein sacrificed a pawn!'

'And Kotov took it!'"

No. 218
Bronstein – Kotov
Moscow 1949, round 4
*Annotated by D. Bronstein and
A. Kotov*

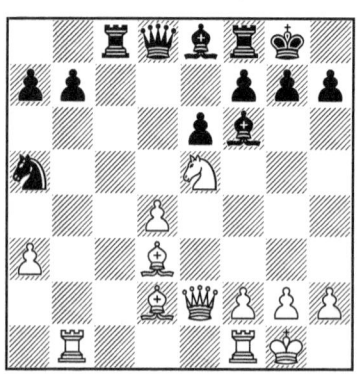

18.♕e4? In his initial calculations, white planned to continue the attack with 18.♗b4 ♗e7 19.d5! and spent a lot of time on the reply 19...exd5 (everything else is bad, for instance: 19...f6? 20.♘f3 e5 21.♗f5! with an overwhelming position). White mostly considered 20.♗f5, but after 20...♖b8, neither 21.♘d7 ♗xd7 22.♗xe7 ♖e8 nor 21.♘g6 ♗xb4! justifies white's material losses.

After 20.♗f5, black can hold with 20...♗xb4! (21.axb4 ♘c4 22.♗xc8 ♕xc8 23.♖bc1 ♗b5); after 20...♖b8, however, white is better: instead of 21.♘d7? (21...♗xb4!) or 21.♘g6?, he gets a strong attack after the same 21.♗xh7+!! blow as below.

Over the board, white couldn't find the strongest continuation of the attack. Meanwhile, instead of 20.♗f5, he could have played 20.♗xh7+!! ♔xh7 21.♘g6!!

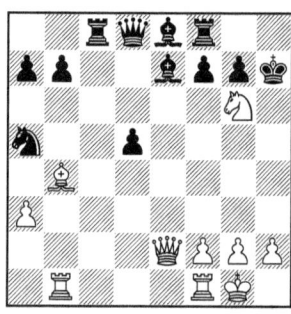

Due to the mating threat 22.♕h5+ and ♕h8#, black is forced to capture the knight: 21...fxg6 22.♗xe7, and his position is difficult because of the threat ♗xf8. For instance: 22...♗b5 23.♖xb5 ♕e8 24.♖xa5 (24.♖b4

♖f7? leads to material losses after 25.♕e6!! and 26.♕h3, but black has to reply 24...♖c4, and the position is roughly equal) 24...♖f7 25.♖xa7, and white retains a small advantage because of his king's safer position. Still, even in this case, the game was most probably drawn, because black's position is solid enough. But this was a logical move. (B.)

In the bracketed line, black even got an advantage after 24...♘c6! 25.♖h4+ ♔g8 26.♕e6+ ♕f7 etc.

18...g6 19.♘g4 ♗g7! White was counting on only 19...♗e7? 20.♕e5! or 19...♘c6? 20.♗xa5! ♗xe4 (20... b6! 21.♕f4 ♗g5 22.♕e5 bxa5=) 21.♗xd8 ♗xd3, and after 22.♗(♘) xf6 he has an advantage. He missed the game move.

White thought that the order of the moves ♕e4 and ♘g4 didn't matter. But it was necessary to play 18.♘g4! first.

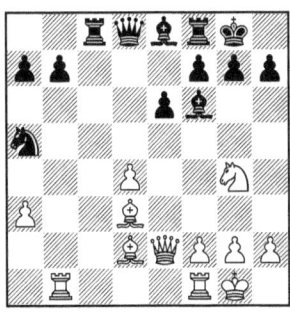

Then, both 18...♗e7? and 18... ♗xd4? are bad due to 19.♕e4, and black has no good defense: 19...f5 20.♕xe6+ etc.

After 18...♗xd4! 19.♕e4 f5 20.♕xe6+, black is fine: 20...♗f7 21.♕xf5 ♗g6 22.♕e6+ ♗f7 23.♕f5=. *However, 18...♗e7? 19.♕e4 f5 20.♕xe6+ ♗f7 21.♕xf5 ♗g6 22.♕e6+ ♗f7 is refuted with 23.♘h6+!! gxh6 24.♕xh6, and there's no 24...♗xf2+ that saves black if the bishop is on d4.*

Therefore, black had to play 18... b6 19.♘xf6+ ♕xf6 20.♗b4 ♕xd4 21.♗xf8 ♔xf8 or 18...♘c6 19.♘xf6+ ♕xf6 20.♖xb7 with a roughly equal position. (B.)

18...♗xd4! is indeed more solid but the above line with 19.♕e4 is not the only one, for instance: 19.♗xa5 ♕xa5 20.♕e4 f5!, and white has to settle for 21.♕xd4 (21.♕xe6+?! ♗f7 22.♕xf5 ♕xf5 23.♗xf5 ♖cd8) 21...fxg4=.

20.♕f4. Now 20.♗b4? lost to 20...f5 21.♕xe6+ ♗f7, and there's no ♕xf5. (B.)

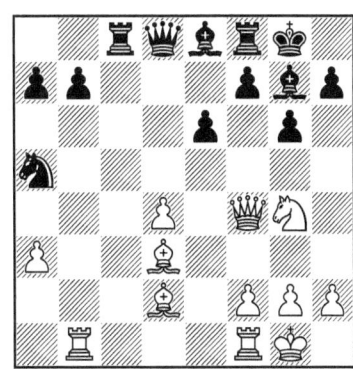

20...♘c6? A mistake! Black had some winning chances after 20...f5!. For instance: 21.♘e3 e5! or 21.♘h6+ ♔h8 22.♗b4 ♗c6! 23.♗xf8 ♕xf8 with the subsequent b7-b6 and ♗xh6, maintaining the material advantage. Or 21.♘e5

♘c6!, forcing 22.♘xc6 ♗xc6 with a clear advantage for black. (K.)

In the first line, it's better to start with 21...♘c6!, not fearing 22.♖xb7, since after 22...♖f7 23.♖xf7 ♗xf7, the threat e6-e5 only grows stronger.

21.♖xb7 e5. If 21...♕xd4, then 22.♕xd4 ♗xd4 23.♗h6 ♗g7

24.♗xg7 ♔xg7 25.♖c1, and white's chances are not worse. (K.)

22.♕g5! The position of the b7 rook is so strong that white may go for a queen trade. (B.) Black underestimated that move. (K.)

22...exd4. In case of 22...♕xd4, there's an unpleasant threat 23.♘f6+. In addition, white can play 23.♗f5!

БОЕВОЕ НАЧАЛО И...

МИРНЫЙ КОНЕЦ

Рис. А. ОРЛОВА и А. КОСТОМОЛОЦКОГО.
(По теме студента В. БОБРИКОВА).

The game between two Soviet champions, Bronstein and Kotov: "A fighting start... and a peaceful finish. A draw." Cartoon by A. Orlov and A. Kostomolotsky ("based on a theme by the student V. Bobrikov"). From the tournament bulletin (13th November 1949). This cartoon then appeared on the front cover of the German magazine Caissa (No. 9, 1950) but with a different annotation: "Enough fooling around. A draw!"

with good opportunities *(alas: 23... ♖d8! 24.♗e3 ♕d6, and black is better)*. The pawn nevertheless had to be captured with the queen. Now black's position worsens.

23.♖e1. 23.♕xd8 ♖xd8 24.♗g5 ♖d6 25.♖e1 is also possible *(the last move is wrong because of 25... h5 26.♗e7 ♘xe7 27.♖bxe7 ♗d7!, so 25.f3 is correct)*. 23...♘xd8!? 24.♖xa7 h5 is fascinating, but the knight escapes with 25.♘h6+ ♔h7 26.♘f5!!. (B.) *After 25...♔h8!, the knight's prospects are grim...*

23...♕xg5 (23...♗d7 24.♘h6+ ♔h8 was worthy of consideration – K.) **24.♗xg5.** Draw.

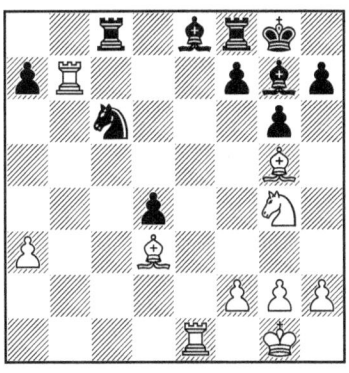

There could have followed 24... f5 25.♗c4+ ♗f7 (25...♔h8 26.♖xg7 ♔xg7 27.♘h6+ is bad; *after 26... fxg4, white checkmates with 27.♗f6!! – B.*) 26.♘f6+ ♗xf6 27.♗xf6 ♗xc4 28.♖g7+ with a perpetual check. (K.)

Bronstein recommended 25.♘h6+! ♔h8 26.♗c4 (After 26.♗a6, he recommended the defense 26...♘b8, but it's not really a defense: 27.♖xg7!

♘xa6? 28.♗f6 and ♖g8#; the correct move is 26...♖b8!), but then found a counter as well – 26...♘d8!*

The strongest move for black is probably 24...♔h8, sticking to the waiting tactic. The continuation could have been very interesting, but white was in severe time trouble and had to stop the struggle. (B.)

"A very short, but exceptionally rich game." (Bondarevsky.) Botvinnik, on the other hand, criticized Bronstein in his notes, as usual: "Used trickery, then baited with a pawn in a difficult position. The advantage changed hands several times in a complicated struggle. Judging by the comments, Bronstein allegedly saw more, but this seems to be bogus, since he came up with all those lines in analysis. Agreeing to a draw on move 24, in an unclear position! Bold, but chaotic – fishing in choppy waters."

Bronstein only dedicated a single sentence to this game in his notebook: "We weren't so much playing as chatting about our our previous game." Did they really? At the board, watched by the crowd and arbiters?

Skirmish of the Champions

Bronstein selected seven games from the 17th championship for subsequent commentary, including three draws and even one loss (as you remember, he unfortunately only wrote short "librettos").

Against Smyslov: "Quite a story. A discussion with Sinyavsky *(see below)*, studying Philidor *(prior to the final session with Smyslov)*, and Vasya's question *(during the game!)*: 'Davy, is that Cheron?'"

Against Geller: "Barely managed to escape. The bishop trap is curious; it seems that I misused my calculation skills."

Against Ragozin: "Bondarevsky thinks that this was my best game in the tournament (a positional achievement)."

Against Petrosian: "Our first game. Tigran played timidly, I wanted to get a win out of nothing and almost lost."

Against Mikenas: "Outwitted Mikki with a simple move order change."

Against Kholmov: "A Ruy Lopez with 3...f5. Ratmir knew nothing and got into trouble immediately. I played sloppily but I got to develop my queenside. Thankfully, I managed to cut the knight off from the king (the bishop again)."

Against Levenfish: "One of my best endgames. Constantly nearly a draw, but only nearly."

I'll tell the "quite a story" with Smyslov below. And now, let's look at the ending of the game where Bronstein "outwitted Mikki" in the opening.

This example shows his incredible ability to create positions where one light push launches a catastrophic "domino effect". Even Botvinnik liked it: "A good game in general."

No. 219
Bronstein – Mikenas
Moscow 1949, round 12
Annotated by G. Levenfish

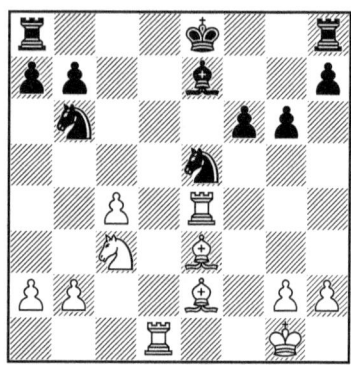

White demolishes black's position with a number of strong tactical blows.

19.c5! ♘bd7 **20.♘d5!** ♔f8. There's nothing better: 20...♘xc5 21.♖xe5 fxe5 22.♘xe7 ♔xe7 23.♗xc5+ or 20...♔f7 21.♗c4! ♗xc5 22.♘b6+ ♔e8 23.♘xd7. *"20...♗d8 21.♗b5 0-0 22.♗xd7 ♘xd7 23.♘e7+ ♗xe7 24.♖xd7 ♗d8 25.♗h6 loses as well." (Bronstein)*

21.♘c7! ♖d8. After any other rook retreat, white forced a mate with 22.♗h6+ ♔f7 23.♖xd7! ♘xd7 24.♗c4#.

22.♘e6+ ♔f7 **23.♖xd8+** ♖xd8 **24.♖ed4!** ♔e6 (of course, not 24...♗xc5 25.♖xd7+ and ♗xc5) **25.b4** ♗f8 **26.♗b5** f5 **27.♗f4.** Black resigned.

The tournament bulletin helped me to decipher the first entry: "The game Smyslov – Bronstein lasted

*The game Smyslov – Bronstein. Still a long time before the question, "Davy, is that Cheron?"...
From D. Bronstein's archive. Published for the first time.*

for six more hours and only ended after 93 moves. Smyslov won a piece by pushing his passed pawn, but Bronstein traded all the pawns, and the game transitioned into a theoretically drawn endgame: rook and bishop versus rook. However, such endings require exceptional precision. Bronstein made a mistake and lost."

OK, it's clear why Philidor and the chess composer Cheron were mentioned – Smyslov was wondering if their ending reflected one of Cheron's positions. But how does the sports radio commentator Vadim Sinyavsky tie into all this? I found a possible explanation in Boris Vainstein's book *Improvisation in the Art of Chess*:

"During the play-off, Bronstein walked around the stage and half-jokingly suggested to the arbiter *(maybe with Sinyavsky as well?)* that the position had already appeared three times, but on different sides of the board. Because of this talk, he overlooked a sequence of moves and resigned just a few moves short *(ten moves, to be precise)* of the necessary fifty. He was upset with Smyslov – why did he play on in a drawn endgame? But when he got older and wiser, he came to realize that a grandmaster, having a material advantage and practical chances to win, is not obliged to immediately agree to a 'theoretical' draw."

Had David Ionovich known then (before round 9) that this game against Smyslov would influence the outcome of first place, he would probably have "walked around the stage" a bit less!

The Chigorinist's Feat

18th Soviet Championship: Moscow, 10th November – 12th December 1950

We're constantly cursing Comrade Stalin,
and, of course, deservedly.
But still, I would like to ask:
who wrote four million denunciations?
S. Dovlatov, The Zone: A Prison Camp Guard's Story

The "Year of Chigorin" didn't quite pan out as planned. It all started with the Candidates Tournament, which, as luck would have it, was won by two Jews – Isaak Boleslavsky and David Bronstein (thankfully, our authorities were proactive and pushed for Budapest as the venue, knowing that the US State Department wouldn't allow Reshevsky to compete in communist Hungary – otherwise, an *American* Jew could have won it!). Then, Bronstein won the play-off match, which bothered both Mikhail Moiseevich and the chess authorities: the world champion had 7–0 (with four draws) against Boleslavsky and 0.5–1.5 against Bronstein (of course, Botvinnik's ethnicity was also "wrong", but he at least was a staunch party member, unlike that son of a former camp convict). And, finally, at the end of the jubilee year, the Soviet Championship wasn't won by some Russian "Chigorinist" such as Kotov or Smyslov, of whom our people could have been proud – the winner was Paul Keres, an Estonian who had barely escaped arrest after the war for playing in German tournaments... And this all happened at the peak of the fight against "rootless cosmopolitans"!

The Sports Committee was headed by state security Colonel-General Arkady Nikolaevich Apollonov, personally appointed by Stalin. The new boss was coarse and inconsiderate; at his old job, deputy minister of the interior, he supervised prisons, and before that, he was the head of the NKVD internal troops. The general didn't know much about sports and talked with his "contingent" in the language of orders. Darkly humorous things happened. The secretary would tell him, "Such-and-such has come to see you". And Apollonov would reply: "Bring him in" using the language normally reserved for calling in a prisoner.

Averbakh: "Apollonov was a typical 'sergeant as a Voltaire' *(a quote from Griboedov's play* The Woes of Wit, *meaning an obscurantist focused on military-style carrying out of orders).* He was feared, and not unreasonably. Brash and categorical, he, like many higher-ups of the time, was on informal 'you' terms with all his subordinates *(Russian 'ty', the equivalent to 'thou' in archaic English, 'tu' in French rather than 'vous', etc.)* and often peppered his sentences with rude soldierly humor and catchphrases.

Igor Bondarevsky, for instance, once said that at one of his first meetings with the general, he complained of hardships. Apollonov interrupted him: 'And what's easy? Only pissing in the bath house is easy!..'

Paradoxically, Apollonov loved chess and understood the game pretty well. I remember how we went to the Szczawno-Zdroj international tournament

Гордится чемпион успехами друзей,
Но и раздумьем он порой охвачен:
— С которым же из двух, хочу я знать скорей,
Мне жаркий поединок предназначен?

Рис. Н. ЛИСА.
Стихи М. АРЦЕВА.

The champion is proud of his friends' success,   "With whom of the two, I want to know now,
But sometimes he's gripped by deep thought: Am I supposed to engage in heated battle?"

The match between the two winners of the Candidates Tournament in Budapest answered this question: David Bronstein earned the right to challenge Botvinnik. Cartoon by N. Lis. Poetry by M. Artsev. From the Budapest Candidates Tournament bulletin (No. 20, 1950).

(June 1950). The plane was scheduled for late at night, and the chess players gathered in the Sports Committee building around midnight. At that time, because of Stalin's habit of working at night, almost all officials followed his example. The general, as usual, was in his office.

Our delegation – Keres, Bondarevsky, Taimanov, Geller, Simagin and I, with Alatortsev (supervisor) and Veresov (coach) – got a firm instruction to win the tournament, and then Apollonov asked Keres to play a game with him. He played quite competently, the game went on for ages. We needed to leave, but the general, engrossed in the game, wasn't in a hurry. The punctual Zubarev didn't dare to intervene and just stood there, anxious, until the game ended. Thankfully, we made it to the airport in time...

Several years later, the higher-ups probably decided that the general had brought enough order to sports. And so they returned him to state security and gave him a promotion – he became the head of the border troops. I remember how he arrived at the Sports Committee in a car with bodyguards to say his goodbyes. And Romanov became the chairman again." (From the book *What the Pieces Don't Mention*.)

The general's relationship with Botvinnik "wasn't exactly rosy" (Averbakh), to the point that in 1954, he told Baturinsky (the future USSR Chess Federation deputy chairman, deputy USSR chief military prosecutor at the time), "You know, I still feel fed up with your Mikhail Moiseevich." On the other hand, judging by the episode with the impromptu game, Apollonov liked Keres, or, at the very least, treated him kindly. And this fact possibly saved Paul Petrovich from the new round of persecution that, as became known recently, threatened him in that "year of Chigorin"!

I thought that the worst was over for Keres in 1947, when he was allowed to take part in the Soviet Championship. And even though a group of players filed a complaint against him, calling Keres "a Nazi", he won the tournament in brilliant style, which seemingly should have protected him from further attacks... But no, the fight against "sycophancy before the West" brought its poisoned fruit to chess as well. Our masters did denounce each other before (see the chapter about the 13th championship in Volume II), but denouncements had never taken the form of an opening book review up until then!

The Estonian State Publishing House has printed the 1st volume of chess grandmaster Keres' theoretical work *Open Games*.

There's no more noble and important task for an author of a theoretical research book than to point out the indisputable authority of both the pre-

In Budapest, Keres was among the leaders, but scored just 1.5/5 at the finish and dropped to 4ᵗʰ place... From Y. Averbakh's archive.

revolutionary Russian and Soviet chess schools, cleverly and convincingly **showing the leading role of the Russian people** *(highlights here and further by me – S.V.)* in such a unique cultural area as chess.

P. Keres did not rise to the task. Worse, he used the platform given to him for rampant glorification of foreign theoreticians, even including **Nazi hirelings and inveterate traitors of the Soviet people**, whose "theoretical" efforts have no value.

(...) The righteous anger and bewilderment of Soviet chess players is caused by systemic, completely unjustified, obtrusive, repeated mention of the **Nazi minion Bogoljubov**, who's now living in the American occupation zone in Germany. Everyone knows that Bogoljubov's theoretical efforts never had any value, and his authority as a chess player, not to mention his heinous political features, have been reduced to zero long ago – if we can even speak of any "authority" of a **Nazi charlatan**.

(...) The phrase "Fine recommends" occurs more than 15 times; "Euwe recommends" and "Tartakower recommends" more than 30 times each. Meanwhile, the name of the genius Russian chess player, the true creator of the majority of modern attacking and defensive systems in the so-called "Ruy Lopez", "Evans Gambit" and other open games that Keres' book purports to describe, is mentioned very rarely. The phrase "Chigorin recommends" is only seen two or three times in this book (...) and his role is disgracefully diminished in Keres' book.

Keres reaches **the limits of nonsense** (...)

This involuntarily poses the question: how to explain such **gross political** and theoretical **blunders**, such sycophancy before any, even the most insignificant foreign name, and such little credit given to the pre-revolutionary Russian and Soviet theoreticians?

The answer is very simple! Keres' work is not an independent, original creative research piece. (...) It's nothing other than a compilation of Euwe and Fine's opening books, published abroad after the war, and the long-known foreign handbooks by Tartakower, Tarrasch and others, condemned by Soviet critics. (...)

A lack of creative independence and originality, together with shoddy work, becomes a fertile soil for **sycophancy before everything foreign, for cosmopolitanism, and for political** and theoretical **mistakes**. (...)

Keres' cosmopolitan, objectivistic book creates a totally wrong impression of the theory and history of national and foreign chess art.

Panov V. N.

Master of Sport in chess, VKP(b) member.

10th May 1950

This colorful document of the "advanced Stalinism" period was referred to in Genna Sosonko's article "Panov's Attack" (*64 – Shakhmatnoe Obozrenie*, No. 7, 2014). The author wrote that the text "was found relatively recently in the Moscow KGB main archive and never published". And explained: "This review of Keres' book was obviously written at the request of the 'competent organs' – the KGB was watching the Estonian grandmaster very closely at the time." Indeed, in 1945–1952, Keres was being actively investigated by

The Soviet delegation at the Budapest tournament was headed by Master Viktor Goglidze (to the left). At the time he headed the Georgian Chess Federation. His elder brother Sergei (right), just like the USSR Sports Committee chairman Arkady Apollonov, was a colonel-general of state security. Painting by I. Sterenberg.

the MGB. But does that mean that Panov was ordered to write his opus by the chekists?

We can't rule out the possibility that the text was first written for *Shakhmaty v SSSR* and then "ideologically refined" (with all those "Nazi hirelings", "minions" and "charlatans" added – you won't see such verbiage in the magazine). Why do I think so? At the time, no book, including brochures such as the *All-Russian Kolkhoz Chess Tournament*, could escape a critical review – the magazine published 10 reviews in 1950, including one by Panov. However, the review of Keres' fundamental work just wasn't there. (Surely we can't call Levenfish's small article in the "Letters from the Readers" column in the December issue, where he calls the book a "compilation", 70% of which consisted of his own *Modern Openings*, a real review?)

Still, this doesn't answer the main question: what was the reason for the attack on Keres?

At first, I wanted to blame the Candidates Tournament: he was in the leading group at the time, but then collapsed, scoring only 1.5 points in the five remaining rounds and dropping to 4th place. Maybe someone didn't want him to play Botvinnik, and the review was used for blackmail: if you don't slow down, we'll publish it? But the dates don't add up: the fatal loss to Kotov happened on 9th May, one day before the date in the review. And, frankly, why go for such complicated schemes if they could just give him a "heart-to-heart" talk? There was even someone to give such a talk: our Budapest delegation was headed by Master Viktor Goglidze, whose brother, like Apollonov, was a state security Colonel-General and Beria's right-hand man... No, there's something more serious here. Maybe even an arrest was planned!

Sosonko called this review "secret". But I've never heard of a "secret" review in all my years of editorial work (internal reviews do exist, but they are ordered by the publisher and written during the manuscript stage, not after publication). And what's the sense in making a review "secret"? To hide the reasons for Keres' potential arrest? No, famous people were treated differently back then: first, they were defamed by the press, and only then arrested. Or, alternatively, just quietly "bumped off", like Mikhoels...

But still, the date of the review turned out to be an important lead! I knew that Keres was saved in 1945 by the Estonian Communist Party first secretary Nikolai Karotamm, who took him under his wing. And when I re-read Heuer's article "The Paul Keres Enigma" (discussed in detail in Volume II), I recalled the statement, "he (Karotamm) continued to support the grandmaster until his downfall in 1950". So, that was it... All the pieces fell into place when I learned the date of the "downfall": 26th March, ten days before the Soviet players went to Budapest!

So, Keres suddenly lost his protector. And someone decided to exploit that – Paul Petrovich had his share of foes, both in Estonia (as Heuer described) and in Moscow (those who branded him a "Nazi" in 1947 hadn't gone anywhere). But there was no suitable occasion: the KGB documents say that the investigation of Keres turned up nothing... And then, possibly, someone had a brilliant idea: use a chess review as a battering ram, turning it into a political denunciation.

The choice of Panov for this hit job wasn't accidental. A party member, exemplary "Soviet patriot", an ethnic Russian. A true "Chigorinist" to boot (he would later write two eulogic books about his idol). Like any neophyte (he'd only joined the party three years earlier), Panov was probably proud of this assignment, relishing the opportunity to kick Bogoljubov, whom he hated with a passion, in the process. And he quickly scribbled down what was asked of him. Why "scribbled down"? Well, it's clear that the text was written quickly, as though in a frenzy. Panov was one of our best chess journalists, but here... The piece is poorly thought-out, with lots of repeats. For instance, he wrote, "whose 'theoretical' efforts have no value". And then, in the next paragraph: "Bogoljubov's theoretical efforts never had any value". Or this: "...is not an independent, original creative research piece", and then: "A lack of creative independence and originality"!

One wonders what excuses Panov would have come up with had this review been published while he was still alive... But does it really matter? A great Russian poet explained everything long ago: "You can explain yourself,/ But they'll never ask, that's what's worst!" (Nikolai Nekrasov.)

Why and when exactly the process was stopped, we can only guess. But the fact that the review was buried in the depths of Lubyanka is telling in itself. It's a pity that we can't ask Apollonov who saved Keres this time – the general himself or somebody else?

Candidates Versus Grandmasters

This year, unlike for the two previous championships, there was no dedicated semi-final bulletin, which is strange, considering that there were five(!) semi-finals, from each of which three people qualified (perhaps the allotted paper was used for publications from the unplanned Bronstein – Boleslavsky match instead?). As compensation, the best semi-final games were published in the *18th Soviet Chess Championship* bulletin. And the best 23 games were included in the *Chess in 1950* compilation book (these books became annual after that year).

 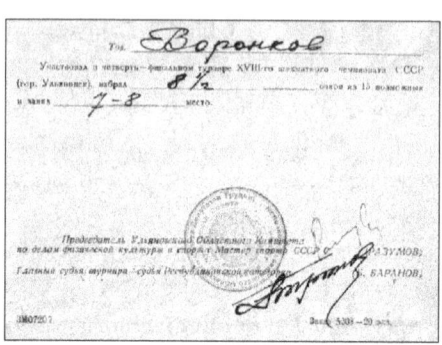

Participant's Ticket of the 18th Soviet championship quarter-final in Ulyanovsk, belonging to my father, Candidate Master Boris Voronkov. It was big and encased in calico – you couldn't put it into your pocket! Published for the first time.

The main novelty of the qualifying tournaments was compulsory, not voluntary, participation of grandmasters. While five of them were exempt from participating, the idea justified itself: out of five others – Bondarevsky, Flohr, Levenfish, Lilienthal and Ragozin – only two managed to qualify for the final!

Ragozin: "The number of masters has been growing year after year, and our chess federation has long since employed a multistage qualifying system for the Soviet Championship finals. About 200 highly-qualified chess players (from first category to grandmasters) are taking part in the battles for the Soviet Championship in the quarter-finals, semi-finals and final.

Before the Great Patriotic War, the championships of the republics, of the biggest chess centers of the country – Moscow and Leningrad – and special masters tournaments held the greatest importance for creative growth of young players and masters. However, the Soviet Championship semi-finals are becoming increasingly important, since they are superior in both chess level and intensity of the struggle to the traditional local tournaments. Now every master prepares for the Soviet Championship semi-final especially thoroughly, as the most important competition." (*Shakhmaty v SSSR*, No. 12, 1950.)

Abramov: "The difficult task of selecting equally-strong groups was not carried out satisfactorily. It's time to use some objective system in such cases, for instance, the system of individual coefficients *(in that same 1950, Lev Abramov was the first to calculate individual coefficients in the USSR)* or some other." (*Chess in 1950* compilation, this or depending on the context *Chess in 1951-1952* referred to as "chess yearbook" later on).

Leningrad semi-final: 1–2. Alatortsev, Tolush – 10.5/15; 3. Bondarevsky – 9.5; 4–5. Kan, Lisitsin – 8.5; 6–9. Klaman, Kondratyev, Taimanov, Khasin – 8; 10. Abramov – 7.5; 11. Zhukhovitsky – 6.5; 12. Koblencs – 6; 13–14. Kopylov, Kuzminykh – 5.5; 15. Matskevich – 5; 16. Ravinsky – 4.5.

The Kiev semi-final. The game Sakharov – Geller is in the foreground. Photo by Y. Begmatov. From the author's archive.

Abramov: "The results were logical: the winners showed great willpower and high class for the whole tournament. The others scored as much as their form allowed. Even Taimanov, whom many hoped to see in the final, couldn't count on a better result this time: he played inconsistently and without his usual confidence." (*Shakhmaty v SSSR*, No. 12, 1950.)

> The outstanding coach and theoretician **Pavel Kondratyev**, a young master back then, never managed to reach the final, even though he regularly appeared in the semi-finals. Already a candidate master, he was conscripted to the navy in 1942, served on the Baltic Sea as a sapper on a minesweeper ship, and was awarded the Ushakov medal. "For almost the whole war, I carried a chess set in my duffle bag," Pavel Evseevich recalled. "Even though I didn't get to play a lot." After the war, he served in the navy until 1950, and Kondratyev (like the runner-up of the Gorky group, junior sergeant Viktor Liublinsky) often wore a striped sailor's jersey to tournaments – to feel a "sailor's recklessness", in his own words.

Kiev semi-final: 1–2. Lipnitsky, Sokolsky – 9.5/15; 3. Geller – 9; 4–5. Ragozin, Saigin – 8.5; 6. Aratovsky – 8; 7–9. Vatnikov, Kopaev, Tarasov – 7.5; 10–11. Sakharov, Chistiakov – 7; 12–13. Pavlov, Panov – 6.5; 14–15. Zagorovsky, E. Kogan – 6; 16. Goldenov – 5.5.

Ragozin: "I hadn't played in semi-final competitions for five years and was very happy to see the growing skills of our young players. Lipnitsky only earned his master's title this year, but he's already a very mature and experienced chess player. He knows theory very well and has a tendency to go for tactical battles. Sokolsky played very inconsistently and made blunders; he played some great games, though. Geller, who played in a very interesting and spectacular style at the last Soviet Championship, was quite indecisive this time around." (Ibid.)

If you have a copy of *Chess in 1950*, open page 104. What, no page 104 in your book? Don't be surprised: it was torn out of most copies. Why? The table of the Kiev semi-final was printed on this page; Yuri Sakharov, the future two-time Ukrainian champion and well-known coach, played in it. The reason for this "vandalism" was Sakharov's arrest in 1951, soon after his win in the Lvov semi-final of the 1951 Soviet Championship. Neither the *Shakhmaty* encyclopedia nor Wikipedia mention this tragic story. I'll tell it in full in the next chapter, I promise...

By the way, pages 185 and 186 were also omitted from this book – there were some tables there as well, since the text seamlessly continues from page 184 to page 187. I couldn't find any copy with these pages intact, so I don't know why were they omitted...

	Киев, сентябрь—октябрь	1	2	3	4	5	6	7	8	9	10	11	12	13	14	15	16	Итого	Место	Номер по жребию
1	Липницкий	●	1	0	½	½	0	1	0	1	½	1	1	1	½	½	1	9½	1—2	15
2	Сокольский	0	●	1	1	1	½	½	½	1	½	1	1	½	0	1	0	9½	1—2	3
3	Геллер	1	0	●	0	½	½	1	½	½	1	½	0	1	1	1	½	9	3	6
4	Рагозин	½	0	1	●	0	½	1	0	0	1	1	½	½	½	1	1	8½	4—5	12
5	Сайгин	½	0	½	1	●	½	0	1	0	1	½	1	1	0	1	½	8½	4—5	16
6	Аратовский	1	½	½	½	½	●	½	1	1	0	0	0	½	1	½	½	8	6	2
7	Ватников	0	½	0	0	1	½	●	0	½	0	1	1	1	1	0	1	7½	7—9	4
8	Копаев	1	½	½	1	0	0	1	●	0	½	1	1	½	½	0	0	7½	7—9	14
9	Тарасов	0	0	½	1	1	0	½	1	●	0	½	1	0	1	0	1	7½	7—9	11
10	Сахаров	½	½	0	0	0	1	1	½	1	●	0	0	1	0	1	½	7	10—11	10
11	Чистяков	0	0	½	0	½	1	0	0	½	1	●	0	½	1	1	1	7	10—11	9
12	Павлов	0	0	1	½	0	1	0	0	0	1	1	●	½	½	½	½	6½	12—13	1
13	Панов	0	½	0	½	0	½	0	½	1	0	½	½	●	1	½	1	6½	12—13	13
14	Загоровский	½	1	0	½	1	0	0	½	0	1	0	½	0	●	1	0	6	14—15	7
15	Коган	½	0	0	0	0	½	1	1	1	0	0	½	½	0	●	1	6	14—15	5
16	Гольденов	0	1	½	0	½	½	0	1	0	½	0	½	0	1	0	●	5½	16	8

The page with the table of the Kiev semi-final that was torn out from almost the entire press run of the Chess in 1950 yearbook. The reason was... the inclusion of Yuri Sakharov (in 10th place)!

Gorky *(now Nizhny Novgorod)* **semi-final:** 1. Aronin – 10.5/15; 2–3. Liublinsky, Petrosian – 10; 4. Furman – 9.5; 5–6. Nezhmetdinov, Ufimtsev – 9; 7. Konstantinov – 8.5; 8. Dubinin – 7.5; 9–10. Levenfish, Soloviev – 7; 11. Byvshev – 6.5; 12–13. Makarov, Ratner – 5.5; 14–15. Sidorov, Estrin – 5; 16. Guldin – 4.5.

Abramov: "The victory of Aronin, who qualified for the final for the fourth time in a row, winning three semi-finals in the process, deserves special praise. Levenfish couldn't withstand the difficult, intense tournament and lost his last four games." (Chess yearbook.)

Aronin: "Petrosian is a growing player. The ease of his play and his sharp tactical vision are remarkable. His strategic interpretation of many different kinds of position is also very high-level.

The strongest sides of Liublinsky's play are maneuvering in complicated positions and tenacity in defense. Nezhmetdinov's play was interesting, as always. Having earned the master's title this year *(he also won the Russian SFSR championship)*, he again exceeded the master's norm." (Ibid.)

His first encounter with Rashid Nezhmetdinov, at the 1948 Russian SFSR championship, left an indelible impression on **Alexei Suetin:**

"Rashid had just been discharged from the army and returned from Berlin, where he had served since 1945 in the Group of the Soviet Occupation Forces in Germany. He wore a frayed military uniform and boots. There were quite a few wrinkles on his tanned face, but there was nothing sedate in his demeanor. Nezhmetdinov was most gregarious, open and friendly. And oh, did he love to talk! He could even engage a boa constrictor in conversation...

But then the tournament started, and Rashid completely transformed. For all five hours, his lively eyes would try to drill a hole in the board. He fought with great gusto, giving his all, completely shutting out the outside world. And during the postmortem analysis, he stunned everyone with his vision of the playing process, with his understanding of the harmony of the pieces.

Both strengths and weaknesses of Rashid's sporting character were obvious by that time. If inspiration hit him, he was incredibly strong, it seemed that he could destroy any, even the most impregnable bastions – but faded away quickly after failures. He played brilliantly in sharp positions, but he loathed maneuvering. He always preferred swashbuckling attacks, especially against the king, to tedious defense. A true chess romantic!" (*Shakhmaty v Rossii*, No. 5–6, 1998.)

Tula semi-final: 1–2. Averbakh, Borisenko – 11.5/15; 3–4. Suetin, Moiseev – 9; 5–7. Ilivitsky, E. Poliak, Simagin – 8; 8. Fridstein – 7.5; 9.

Gusev – 7; 10. Lilienthal – 6.5; 11–13. Goldberg, Kasparyan, Korchnoi – 6; 14–15. Vistaneckis, Pogrebyssky – 5.5; 16. Kaem – 5.

Abramov: "Candidate Master Borisenko played very well in the tournament. He won 9 games – more than all the other 80 semi-final participants!" (Ibid.)

Borisenko: "The tournament winner Averbakh played openings well, persistently fought for the initiative and converted his advantage smartly. The finish was very dramatic for Moiseev. He lost the last two games, and Suetin, who had a better tie-break, caught him...

> **Suetin:** "It so happened that I managed both to become a master and qualify for the final. I must admit that I was inspired by my victory against Lilienthal in round 1 – it was my first win against a grandmaster. His lack of confidence surprised me. He displayed symptoms of a deep crisis, even though he was just 39 years old. The following years showed that the decline was unstoppable. We can only guess the reasons – most probably, this was because of his mental exhaustion and the appearance of the new post-war generation."

(From the book *Chess Through the Prism of Time*.)

The Lvov quarter-final (1949): Rafail Gorenstein, Viktor Korchnoi, Yuri Sakharov and Archil Ebralidze. A fragment of a photo from I. Yaremko's archive (Lvov).

We should pay special attention to Korchnoi's play. It's very inventive and resourceful. Korchnoi would have probably performed better if he hadn't got into severe time trouble so often. The young player also tends to overestimate his position." (*Shakhmaty v SSSR*, No. 12, 1950.) But what a fighter: he only had 1 (one) point after 9 rounds, but then scored 5/6!

Beilin: "1949. Korchnoi and I played in the national championship quarter-final in Lvov. He was 18, the youngest player in the whole tournament. Reserved during the games, active in leisure time. If he has to argue with someone older, he's never at a loss for a witty put-down. We once argued about a position of mine and decided to see who was correct with a blitz game. I was soundly beaten; still, I managed to qualify for the semi-final. Viktor *(who shared 8th – 10th place)* said at the end of our short series of games, 'Don't punch above your weight, maestro'." (From the book *Encounters in the Chess Kingdom*.)

From a letter from Lvov historian and journalist **Ivan Yaremko**: "In May 2000, a supertournament in memory of Leonid Stein was held in Lvov; his old friend and rival Viktor Korchnoi took part. As always, he was accompanied by his wife, Mrs. Petra Leeuwerik. I interviewed her one day. I asked her how she liked Lvov – it was her first time in the city, after all. And she answered, I was there once, but saw nothing. It turns out that in October 1949, she was in a transit prison there, waiting to be transported to Vorkuta! Then I told her that Viktor Lvovich had played in a tournament in Lvov in October 1949. I remember her saying, 'It's incredible what fate deals people...'"

Tartu semi-final: 1. Flohr – 10.5/15; 2–4. Konstantinopolsky, Mikenas, Weltmander – 10; 5. Bannik – 9.5; 6. Kholmov – 9; 7–9. Novotelnov, Chekhover, Scherbakov – 8; 10. Sopkov – 6.5; 11–12. Zagoriansky, Kamyshov – 6; 13. Cherepkov – 5.5; 14. Ebralidze – 5; 15. Rovner – 4.5; 16. Shamkovich – 3.5.

Flohr: "Many, including myself, were surprised by my victory. We're long unaccustomed to such results. I think that I was successful in the semi-final because my play was more enterprising than usual, and I tried to avoid time trouble – as recent years have shown, I'm cable of ruining any kind of position because of it.

Weltmander's play leaves a positive impression. The young player's opening knowledge is a bit shallow. But in worse positions, he plays with exceptional calm, inventiveness and tenacity...

This was the greatest career achievement of Master **Johannes Hugovich Weltmander** (1921– 2014), participant of four Soviet

Johannes Weltmander failed to qualify for the final only because of his Sonneborn-Berger score... From R. Ponyaev's archive.

Izhevsk, 1958. Johannes Weltmander with his mother Enta-Leia Wulfovna, wife Raisa Melchenko, who was also a chess player, and his daughter Irina. From R. Ponyaev's archive.

With his elder brother Hugo (right), a school headmaster in the Estonian town of Kohtla-Jarve. From R. Ponyaev's archive.

Championship semi-finals, many Russian SFSR championships, and two USSR correspondence chess championships, USSR team champion as a member of the Russian SFSR and Iskra sport society teams, multiple-times champion of Izhevsk and Udmurtia. Missing out on the final was most unfortunate (like Moiseev, he was let down by the Berger coefficient). For his success in Tartu, he should have been awarded the master's title... but he only received it in 1953, after Stalin's death.

From a letter to me by **Ruslan Ponyaev**, FIDE master from Izhevsk: "Weltmander was an ethnic Estonian. He became interested in chess in the first grade at school. After his father got arrested (and executed in 1937), his family was exiled from Leningrad to Sarapul... He worked as a coach for most of his life, earning the title of Distinguished Coach of the Russian SFSR. His contribution to chess development in Udmurtia was enormous. He edited a chess column in the *Udmurtskaya Pravda* newspaper for more than 55 years(!)."

Kholmov is a good tactician, but as soon as he gets a worse position, his resistance level decreases. The shallowness of Kholmov's play is also puzzling. Often, despite having a lot of time at his disposal, he quickly makes a move that turns out to be wrong. Unfortunately, Kholmov doesn't prepare well mentally for competition and works too little on developing his chess skills, and this led to his failure." (*Shakhmaty v SSSR*, No. 12, 1950.)

Mikenas: "In early 1950, I started preparing for the next qualifying tournament... In this period, I was counting on the help of Belorussian player Ratmir Kholmov, who caved in under my persistent 'attacks' and agreed to move to Vilnius. I was sure that our joint creative work would benefit us both. I even think that I became a 'co-author' of his later great successes.

But then, disaster struck: an illness in early April left me bedridden for almost three months, and the

A photo of Kholmov taken during the Tartu semi-final.

doctors advised me to stop playing chess for quite a while. Some advice! In late August, together with the new Lithuanian champion R. Kholmov, we traveled to Tartu to play in the national championship semi-final. The tournament was held in the luxurious hall of the Academy of Sciences, which was fitted with radio systems for the spectators' convenience.

I got into the groove. I played freely, at ease, without much regard to the results – the doctors advised me not to worry too much." (From the book *Vladas Mikenas*.)

Levenfish: "The superiority of grandmasters and older masters over the best young masters in the areas of theoretical knowledge, positional understanding and technique, especially noticeable before 1946, is gradually disappearing. This is the main reason for the grandmasters' and international masters' *(Chekhover, Lisitsin, Dubinin, Kan, Kasparyan)* failure to qualify for the final." (Chess yearbook.)

Twice Repressed

The Soviet *Chess Dictionary* (1964) only allotted a few lines to Master Weltmander, and the *Shakhmaty* encyclopedia (1990) never mentions him at all. Thankfully, there are some enthusiasts in the Russian regions who try to preserve the memory of their chess-playing fellow townsmen. The aforementioned Ruslan Ponyaev has been gathering information on Johannes Weltmander for years. The result of his work, an extensive article called "The Patriarch of Udmurt Chess", was published in *64 – Shakhmatnoe Obozrenie* (No. 12, 2021).

But sometimes you delve deeply into someone's fate completely by accident. Which is what happened to a writer called **Ariadna Kornilova**. In spring 2015, she was working as a humble estate agent in the city of Izhevsk. An incidental – but not accidental! – result of this work was her Sosonkoesque essay "Weltmander" that I discovered online (*Rabotnitsa.su*, March 2019). I was stunned by what I read and wanted to contact the author, but how could I do that? Ruslan helped me: he found Ariadna Viktorovna's email for me. "I would like to include your outstanding essay in my book (slightly abridged)," I wrote to her. And explained: "My book is not only about chess – it's about the era the chess players lived and played in." She sent me her text in reply.

***

"...Once, a couple entered my office – a young, slightly overweight woman and a man with darting eyes. They were asking if they needed to carry out extensive presale renovations if the apartment was in poor condition. I assured them that it was not necessary, it was enough to put up some simple new wallpaper and wash the windows – the flat just shouldn't look like it was neglected, that's all.

My visitors glanced at each other, obviously happy with the answer. It was clear that they would never have enough money to do any kind of expensive repairs.

'You see, the building itself is very good, it's considered elite,' and the woman told me the address. 'An elderly man lived there with his daughter, I'm their only heir. Can you tell me how much an apartment in such a building would be worth?'

I reasonably replied that nobody could tell them even an approximate price without seeing the apartment with their own eyes, and, advising them to take out the old owner's junk, I asked to accompany them to their 'inheritance'.

I came to a well-maintained apartment building in a green district on the appointed hour (some workers were carrying out the furniture, followed by mournful gazes of old women sitting on the bench), and I saw a big apartment with a great layout. Of course, the plumbing was very old, and the wallpapers were yellowed and filthy with cockroach droppings, but... I already knew that they were living in a two-room apartment in a panel house with a walk-through room. I couldn't help but ask the heiress' husband: 'Why don't you move in here yourselves?'

'The neighbors hate us,' he waved his hand. 'We want to sell the flat and buy a three-room one in some other building, far from here.'

'Are the neighbors really so horrible? You'll gain six or seven square meters at most. Still, it's up to you to decide.'

I took all the necessary photos. I even photographed the remaining dark polished-wood dresser that looked like the one my grandmother had, who had died fifteen years earlier.

About a month later, Olga, the heiress, paid the notary for the certificate of inheritance and signed the contract with our agency, and I put the apartment up for sale.

The building was indeed attractive; the flat was being offered at a much lower price than usual, and people didn't look much at the photos posted on the site. There were a lot of calls from potential buyers; I took the keys and went there to show the apartment.

I got there earlier than the appointed time and was astonished. During my first visit, I had darted around the rooms, searching for good angles for photos, and hadn't noticed the staggering picture of unattended old age and decay. It seemed that nobody had bothered to wash the floor in the half year that had passed since the owners' death. And half a year before their death, too. There were still traces of old wardrobes in black dirt on the floor. Bits of newspaper at the entrance of the rooms, spread there to postpone cleaning. Dirty traces at arm's level – it seemed that an old man had been walking around the apartment, while leaning on the wall. Grey, smoky windows were wide open. A pile of dusty books and vinyl records in the corner.

The second room, where his daughter seemed to have lived, was cleaner. A pile of black and white photos lay in the middle.

I grabbed some pink leggings, found a bucket and began to wash the flooring. The buyers' reaction was predictably negative: 'Oh, did something burn in there? Such a smell...'

They left, and I immediately called Olga: 'I know you don't have much time because of your baby, but you need to clean everything up and take away the remaining things, especially the books – they smell musty.'

'Of course, of course, we'll come at the weekend, clean everything and throw the rubbish out,' Olga assured me.

The next visit was in an hour, there was no sense in leaving the apartment, and so I decided to restore at least some semblance of order. Documents of a Raisa Ivanovna Melchenko, born in 1920, lay on the windowsill. I opened the wall cabinet to put them away – and found that it was filled to the brim with books, with names like *Theory of Chess Endgames*, *Opening Mistakes*, biographies of great chess players... My God, will all that go in the rubbish bin at the weekend? Chess was beyond me, I didn't know the strategy of the game, and so my respect for those who could play was even greater than otherwise.

There was a chess school in the city, maybe ask them to take this all away? I searched online from my phone, found the number, tried to explain that there were books left after some old man named Melchenko died, it would be such a pity if they are just thrown away...

'Yes, we remember that elderly couple.' The voice in the phone uttered some long German surname that I forgot immediately. 'We will come tomorrow at lunch time, if you like.'

'Bring big boxes. There are a lot of books here.'

The next potential buyers thought that the previous owners kept several dogs in the flat. I didn't try to persuade them otherwise and went back to the office.

Of course, I had visited my share of dirty, neglected homes before, but they obviously belonged to drug addicts or criminals. Yet here was a man of considerable intellect who received a good pension – how could he have died in such awful circumstances? I couldn't help but share my impressions with other agents who were in the office at the time.

'Can you imagine? A whole cabinet full of chess books.'

'What was the name?' asked one of the agents, a middle-aged man.

'Feldman... Waldstein... Something like that, can't remember.'

'Weltmander,' he said clearly. 'The first chess master in our republic. And maybe the only one. I studied under him.'

Two chess players came to take the books away. While one of them sorted through the photos and documents, the other, a younger man, said, 'You should be careful. That heiress – she came out of nowhere. She starved them, his daughter died a week after his funeral. We wrote to the prosecutor's office, asking to open a criminal investigation, collected their neighbors' signatures, but to no avail...'

'Well, he was almost 94 years old when he died,' I objected, leafing through a thick, well-designed book called *Formula of Eternal Youth* on the desk. 'Maybe it was just age?'

'Age, you say? He always rushed around like a horse, I thought he was going to outlive me.'

'That all doesn't matter now – the inheritance was formalized through a notary, she has all the necessary papers.'

After discussing why he didn't emigrate, they took away (in three trips) the boxes with books and diplomas awarded to a Johannes Hugovich Weltmander and said their goodbyes.

I remained sitting on a canvas folding chair among the debris of someone else's life. I was meant to go to other apartments and call other people. But instead, I sat and thought. What if my grandmother, Weltmander's contemporary who died at the age of 79, was still alive? When she died, I also came from another city to register my inheritance, met my future husband and remained here. What if that hadn't happened? How would my life have turned out? Would I still have these children – or others, with different names? It's so strange to penetrate the future – like a radioactive container, blindly, with closed eyes...

I sort through greetings cards of 30 years ago... Weltmander's wife, Raisa Melchenko, also a chess player, had died several years before... A certificate of his father, Hugo Ivanovich, rehabilitation, dated 1956... Guide books for Baltic cities, German culinary books...

A binder made of a reddish, as though oiled, cardboard. An unfilled label in the top corner, with obsolete *yat* letters *(this letter was removed from the Russian alphabet in 1918)*. A pre-war family photo in it: a husband with his wife, two boys and an elderly woman. Another photo on a passepartout, a dark-eyed, sad young Jewish woman, captioned in pencil: 'Friedrich's wife'. Large photos of a building site, with the caption 'Building the House of Soviets of the Narva District, 1931'.

Searches, digging through archives – none of this matters now, when these people are not around anymore, and this small world, which only received news from the outside world through greetings cards on some jubilees, is destroyed. Pencil notes: 'Daddy!..' His daughter Irina was 64 years old, she died of a stroke, she never had children and was never married.

A big notebook, the last item in the binder. 'Weltmander. Poems. 1940–1941.' Its cover made of rough cardboard with wood shavings. Its pages with faded ink:

> Fly to my homeland, my poem,
> Find my house and pass the greetings
> To our dear Neva on your way.
>
> I remember: in the quiet alleys
> We walked together, and nightingales sang to us.
> (24th December 1941)
>
> We will win! It's not the first time
> In the history of our dear homeland
> That our people, like a giant, a hero,
> Fight against the Germans.
>
> *After kiss of belover*[7]... (3rd August 1941)
> I'm slowly walking home,
> The night sky is above me...

The poems showed a restless soul rather than talent, but their value was in the very fact that they survived: how many such notebooks and loves praised in them burned in the flame of the war? Hundreds of thousands? As my grandmother used to say when I looked through her old, intricately cut photos, 'We weren't pretty, but we surely were young!'

Had the exertions of the chess school been successful, who would have inherited that flat? The state? Or a mistress of some bureaucrat? Were there really no other surviving relatives left? I found about five of their namesakes

---

[7]   This single line was written in the archaic English reproduced here, the rest was written in Russian

in social networks, but they never replied to my inquiries. The last thing I wanted was to ask Olga about the Weltmanders.

Instead, I bought the dresser (older than me, but not a single scratch) and a polished table from her, citing my nostalgia as an excuse: we had the same furniture at home when I was small. I asked her to give me the remaining books, too. Then I asked about the neighbors.

'Oh, they'll say a lot of things. They were both sick.'

They gradually cleaned the apartment up and raised the price accordingly. I wasn't interested in it anymore. I quit the agency and left the city; there's still a huge promotional collage on the wall of the chess school. It features a photo of J. H. Weltmander as well. Not that poor old man in a filthy apartment, but a well-respected chess player at the height of his strength, whose achievements can be easily found in Wikipedia.

The difference between happiness and unhappiness is the same as between clean and dirty windows. They both let the sunlight through, but when you wash them... My God, there's so much sun!

I have a house in a taiga village, my 'secret retreat' – a necessary thing when you're flying, and nobody is praying for you. In the winter, I finally got to Weltmander's books – there's no time to read in the city.

I found a petition written by Johannes Hugovich's mother between the pages.

To the Party Commission of the CPSU Leningrad Oblast Committee, from the wife of Weltmander Hugo Ivanovich, private pensioner Weltmander Enta-Leia Wulfovna

Petition

In view of my receipt of a notice concerning the rehabilitation of my husband, Weltmander Hugo Ivanovich, private pensioner, I request to consider the issue of reinstating H. I. Weltmander to the ranks of the CPSU posthumously. 30th May 1957, Weltmander E. W.

Enclosed are the certificate of the Military Board of the USSR Supreme Court dated 20th April 1957, #4n-024067/56, Marriage certificate #131, Housing department certificate (not numbered) for our place of residence in Leningrad, and the details of his arrest.

In 1936 *(on 22nd August)*, in the night, there was a call at the door of our apartment #26 on 6 Roshal Embankment, the old name of Admiralteiskaya Embankment. An NKVD officer entered and asked my husband, Weltmander Hugo Ivanovich, to get dressed and follow him, taking all his documents at the same time. As my husband said goodbye to his sons, boys of 15–16 years old, he told them, 'I'll come back soon, I'm not tarnished with anything nor will I be, listen to your mom.' I often visited the officer to try and learn something about his case, but always got the same answer, 'You do not know and you must not know.' Sometime later (I don't remember exactly, too much time had passed), as I recall someone called me on the phone in the evening and told me to bring warm clothes for my husband, because he was being sent somewhere. I didn't meet him in person. Later, I received a letter from him and sent a package to him, which was returned to me. I never received anything more from him and know nothing more about him. When I asked the officer about his case, I was told that he was sentenced to 8–10 years, according to Article 58. *(Hugo Ivanovich was sentenced to execution on 25ᵗʰ December.)*

In 1937, the janitor informed me that I had to go to the police station with my children and documents. When I arrived at the station, they took away my passport and documents and told me that I had to leave Leningrad in 5–10 days, and that my documents would be sent to my place of internal exile.

Several days later, an NKVD officer showed up, confiscated all our possessions, except for small things, and handed me the tickets for a train, ordering the janitor to help us carry the luggage. Upon my arrival at Sarapul, the NKVD issued a certificate to me, saying that I was in Administrative Exile and that I had to report to the office once per week or per two weeks. They sent us beyond the Kama, to the Motor Transport Base, where I worked as an accountant, my older son as a laborer, and my younger son as a mailman. In 1938, two NKVD officers came to my office and escorted me to a prison, where I spent 2–3 months. After several interrogations, I was freed and told that the reason for my arrest and exile was the fact that I was the wife of Hugo Ivanovich Weltmander.

During the Great Patriotic War, my older son, Hugo Hugovich Weltmander, fought at the front lines, was shell-shocked and wounded; he joined the party and was his company's party organizer, with the rank of sergeant. He earned two medals 'For Battle Merit'. Currently, after graduating from Karelia Institute during his stay at Sarapul, he works in the town of Kotla *(Kohtla-Jarve, to be precise)*, Estonia, as a school headmaster. He graduated from the higher party school in Tallinn. My younger son, Johannes Hugovich, graduated from the Kazan Financial and Economic College; he is a Soviet Master of Sports in chess and works as a coach. He currently resides in Izhevsk, together with me.

Exile saved them from the siege of Leningrad – isn't it disturbing?

I tried to recall why the name Roshal Embankment seemed familiar. Kaverin, *Two Captains*, the house with lions on Roshal Avenue. The Nord-Ost catastrophe and Dr. Roshal.

The wave of publications on repressions in the early 1990s gradually wound down, growing into the endless sugary stylized TV series about that epoch – now, when there's nobody left alive to tell if a movie is honest. My grandmother never read books nor watched movies about the war, saying that they were all lies. In the late 1930s, she was a young judge, on the opposite side of the law from the Weltmanders.

But it seems that we are all hostages of our country."

***

P.S. Thank you to Ariadna Kornilova for her amazing story and agreeing to share it with us. The fate of this talented, hard-working family, like a drop of water, reflects the entire long-suffering fate of Russia in the 20th century. Like Hugo Ivanovich Weltmander, millions of people were executed, and their families exiled... How many lives were destroyed and crippled! It was as though a plague hit the Russian soil. After Stalin's death, the state grudgingly admitted its guilt and rehabilitated those who were innocent. But the children of the repressed continued to carry their cross. And many of them – if not the majority! – died in poverty and obscurity, like Master Weltmander. He was essentially repressed twice...

Glory to the Founder!

From the press: "On 10th November, a ceremony commemorating the 100th birthday of the great Russian chess player Mikhail Ivanovich Chigorin and the opening of the 18th Soviet Championship took place in the Central Railway Workers House of Culture.

Many Moscow fans came to pay their tribute to the great chess player. The great hall was filled to the brim. The stage was drowned in flowers, with a huge portrait of M. I. Chigorin in the middle...

World champion M. Botvinnik read a lecture titled 'The Great Russian Chess Player M. I. Chigorin'. He thoroughly analyzed the chess style and particular traits of Chigorin's legacy, illustrating it with examples from the great Russian chess player's games. Evaluating Chigorin's public activity, the speaker pointed out that Chigorin was a most prominent organizer of Russian chess life, a writer and chess advocate. 'Now, when we celebrate the 100th anniversary of Chigorin's birth, we can say for sure that Chigorin's school was the basis of our Soviet chess school, with its representatives earning a deserved reputation for our socialist fatherland in the area of chess...'

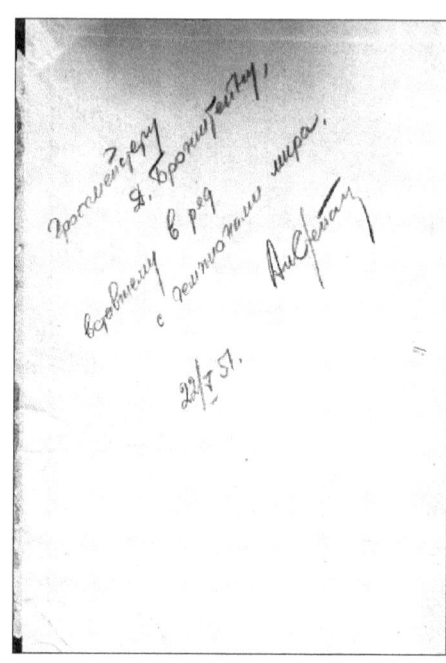

Inscription on the reverse side of the tournament bulletin of the 18th championship: "To Grandmaster D. Bronstein who stands together with the world champions. 22nd May 1951. Al. Stepanov." Who was that? Executive secretary of the Vechernaya Moskva newspaper, Alexander Vasilyevich Stepanov, who organized the first Moscow blitz chess championship in 1947, creating a glorious, near 75-year tradition of Vechernaya Moskva blitz tournaments. From D. Bronstein's archive. Published for the first time.

Nikolai Grekov's monumental work *M. I. Chigorin. His Life and Works* (1939) was reissued for the jubilee, under a new, more patriotic title: *Mikhail Chigorin. The Great Russian Chess Player* (1949). Obviously, Bogatyrchuk's article "The Influence of M. I. Chigorin's Genius On the Development of Chess Art" and all 14 games annotated by him were gone. But why were the articles by Levenfish, Romanovsky and Sokolsky omitted together with Bogatyrchuk's?

I'm sure that it wasn't Grekov himself who initiated that – according to his contemporaries, he was a most dignified man, a true walking chess encyclopedia and educator. Romanovsky called him "the greatest chess historian" in his obituary (Grekov died one month after the championship ended, on 21st January 1951). Do you know in what conditions he lived and worked?

Chistiakov: "Nikolai Ivanovich and his wife Ekaterina Vasilyevna lived in a big block of flats on Malaya Dmitrovka 27, apartment 11. You entered from the courtyard, via a kind of 'back door'. After coming through the kitchen and corridor, I wound up in a long narrow room with one window to the yard, with bookshelves spanning the left wall. There was a big table close to the window; Grekov's hospitable wife treated us to coffee and Swiss cheese sandwiches during our analysis and discussions." (From the unpublished recollections "Nikolai Ivanovich Grekov", kept in my archive.)

Chief arbiter P. Romanovsky reads out the main regulations of the tournament *(time control: 2.5 hours for 40 moves, then 1 hour per every 16 moves)* and invites the players to the draw. The outcome of the draw *(grandmasters in italic)*: 1. A. Konstantinopolsky (Moscow), 2. E. Geller (Odessa), 3. *P. Keres* (Tallinn), 4. *I. Bondarevsky* (Leningrad), 5. A. Suetin (Tula), 6. A. Tolush (Leningrad), 7. V. Mikenas (Vilnius), 8. G. Borisenko (Leningrad), 9. A. Sokolsky (Lvov), 10. L. Aronin (Moscow Oblast), 11. V. Liublinsky (Moscow), 12. *I. Boleslavsky* (Sverdlovsk), 13. *S. Flohr*, 14. T. Petrosian, 15. Y. Averbakh (all Moscow), 16. I. Lipnitsky (Kiev), 17. *V. Smyslov*, 18. V. Alatortsev (both Moscow)." (*18th Soviet Chess Championship* bulletin, 30th November 1950.)

AN UNUSUAL POSITION
The championship is on, but in the final
There's no Levenfish nor Lilienthal.
Ragozin has also remained at the doorstep,
And the youngsters are on the road.
The grandmasters are in such a position
That it is worthy of a pun:
Yes, it so happens in chess that a piece
Sometimes remains beyond the board.
And the pawns, with their stubborn nature,
Are getting ready to promote to queens...
And even the pieces left as "casualties"
Wish them good luck!
Vl. Dykhovichny, M. Slobodskoi (*Sovietsky Sport*, 14th November.)

Panov: "Of course, we should regret the fact that world champion Botvinnik and two outstanding grandmasters, Bronstein and Kotov, declined to take part in the anniversary tournament. Their refusal was deservedly criticized by the Soviet press. Indeed, the fact that the world champion hasn't played in a single competition for almost three years and has missed four national championships in a row is nothing short of baffling." (Ibid., 7th January 1951.)

Botvinnik doesn't mention this championship in his memoirs. However, judging by his request to Apollonov dated 5th September 1950, it's clear that he at first considered playing in the championship as one of the "necessary" stages of his preparation for the match against Bronstein. "Participation, from 15th–20th November, in a strong 16-player tournament – preferably the Soviet Championship. I won't last to the end in a bigger tournament after a 2.5-year absence from chess." The general ignored the world champion's opinion about the number of participants, and, as a result, **Botvinnik** sent a letter to the Sports Committee deputy chairman Nikolai Romanov on 5th November 1950:

> "Dear Nikolai Nikolaevich!
>
> With great satisfaction, I received the Committee's decree on the 18th Soviet Championship with my name in it (decree No. 866, 3rd November 1950) – it seems that I'm almost no worse than other grandmasters...
>
> Still, I'm forced to decline to participate, because of two reasons:
>
> 1) After a 2.5-year absence from chess, I won't last to the end in a 21-round tournament *(it seems that the decree also included Kotov and Bronstein)*. Back in the spring, I asked the All-Union Section and the Committee to decrease the number of participants; I repeated this request on 5th September, but got a negative answer.
>
> 2) My preparation is going rather slowly. I'm still working without my assistant, Grandmaster Ragozin. I haven't started preparing in earnest yet, only looking through old games played in recent years. There are more than 2,000 of them!
>
> Thus, I am not yet ready to play.
>
> With sincere greetings, M. Botvinnik."

The reasons for Kotov and Bronstein's refusal are quite understandable: after an exhausting marathon in Budapest (April – May, 18 rounds), the former played in Venice (October, 15 rounds) and immediately started working on a tournament book, while the latter won his match with Boleslavsky (August, 14 games) and needed a good rest before starting intensive preparations for his match against Botvinnik.

Under the Slogan of Chigorin's Traditions

How else could Panov have named his article about the championship? You couldn't breathe without mentioning the founder. In the past, everyone played as they saw fit, and Chigorin was rarely mentioned in the tournament bulletins. But in the anniversary championship, everything had to be about Chigorin! *Krokodil*'s **Yakov Bylanin** wrote an ode "To the Participants of the Chigorin Tournament", with each verse featuring something like "in Chigorin style", "called Chigorinist", "Chigorin's strength, Chigorin's glory", "Chigorin's banner"...

But you know what I noticed? The stronger the patriotic fervor, the worse the bulletin gets. There was never such a dull championship bulletin before! No reports, no "Our Questions", no "Diary of a Spectator" that filled the previous year's bulletin – that one was already quite "petrified", but it still managed to keep some lively humor... I was saved by the *Sovietsky Sport* tag team of master Lev Abramov and the future famous journalist and writer Viktor Lazarevich Vasiliev (not to be confused with Viktor Andreevich Vasiliev (Vasilyev) who is mentioned in the chapter on the 17th Soviet Championship). He was only taking his first steps then, as was the great cartoonist Igor Sokolov, whose cartoons, together with the works of Yuri Uzbyakov, a master of the satirical genre, graced the round reviews. In comparison with the round reviews in the bulletin, dry as a desert, these newspaper reports resembled water meadows!

They were even a little bit too "watery". It took me some time to "pump" the excess away and leave only the games that were distinctive in some way

In the center: masters Boris Baranov, Ivan Lyskov (wearing a uniform) and Tigran Petrosian in the lobby of the Tchaikovsky Hall during the Botvinnik – Bronstein match. From I. Lyskov's archive. Published for the first time.

or influenced the tournament intrigue. But don't think that I left all the humor out as well. What humor, what are you talking about? Nobody even tried to joke – neither in the newspaper, nor the bulletin, nor the magazine...

Abramov and **Vasiliev:** "Most games in the second round were only picking up pace when applause sounded in the hall: the sign 'White Won' appeared on a demonstration board. Petrosian had forced Tolush to resign. This game has been the shortest one in the tournament.

Tigran Petrosian is just 21 years old. He's not only the youngest championship participant – he's also the youngest chess master in the country... We should point out that Petrosian's play is somewhat one-sided: he's strong in strategy, but not too confident in tactical complications, and in this sense, he needs to learn from the examples of the diverse legacy of the great master M. Chigorin more than anyone else in the championship.

In his book *A Chess Player's Life*, Viktor Vasiliev wrote that Tigran "got to Moscow in late 1949, wearing a light coat, summer shoes and with some chess books under his arm – this was his entire property." But what happened before?

Asriyan: "Vladimir Makogonov was one of the first to notice the exceptional talent of the 19 year-old Yerevan player when he met him at the 1948 Transcaucasian championship. He advised the future world champion to move to Moscow – it offered many more opportunities for rapid growth." (From the book *Vladimir Makogonov.*)

Beilin: "Here's what I was told by Spartak Moscow coach Nikolai Sergeyevich Kolobov, a humble and kind man still remembered fondly by the old Spartak sportspeople:

'I asked my superiors to help Tigran Petrosian move to Moscow. They of course asked about living conditions and salary. I said, he doesn't need much – only soccer tickets and money for... ice cream. We decided to give him a dormitory room in Tarasovka, where soccer players were training.'

That's how the phrase 'Petrosian, Spartak, Moscow' appeared. Such a consistent life philosophy, and loyalty to his hobbies, were part of Petrosian's nature." (From the book *My Encounters in the Chess Kingdom.*)

Traveling from Moscow to Tarasovka (30 km) after the games, especially in winter nights, was rather inconvenient, and Tigran often spent nights in Moscow. "We met in a Moscow chess club," **Lilienthal** recalled according to an interview with Petrosian's son Vartan on the fakty.ua website in 2003. "The last visitors had left around midnight, and I told Tigran: 'Let's go home.' He suddenly got embarrassed and answered sheepishly, 'Well, actually, I'm staying.' It turned out that he lived in the club and slept right on the table."

Of course, this wasn't the best option, and Petrosian shared a flat with his friend, master Ivan Lyskov, for a while. Lyskov's grandson Ilya Lobashov has evidence of that friendship: a photo where Petrosian and Lyskov stand, arm in arm, in the Tchaikovsky Hall lobby during the Botvinnik – Bronstein match (see page 209).

...The play-off of adjourned games is usually something that begins before the opponents actually meet in the tournament hall again: the master often analyzes the position on a pocket chess set on his way back from the round. Then, home analysis in the fullest sense of the word starts.

Sometimes, several games of a player are adjourned at the same time. Then the task becomes more complicated. At last year's Moscow championship, A. Konstantinopolsky once had five play-offs scheduled. The master said that the entire room was filled with chessboards, and he walked between them as though he was giving a simultaneous display.

This time, nobody has had to fear such a prospect: only two rounds have been played. So, the analysis has been very thorough. Two games ended without a play-off: grandmasters Keres and Bondarevsky agreed to draws with Lipnitsky – a worthy result for a player who is taking part in the national championship for the first time.

The article "They Are Playing in the Finals for the First Time" discussed the three debutants. While Georgy Borisenko and Alexei Suetin were introduced by their full names, Lipnitsky's "cosmopolitan" name – Isaak – was cut down to an initial...

A. Glazunov: "Many years ago, an 8 year-old boy was sitting with his father at the Kiev stadium. The soccer field was divided into identical squares, and unusual pieces stood on them. Riders on horses, warriors with halberds, fantasy-land towers... They moved once in a while, and the spectators excitedly discussed every move.

'Daddy, what is this?' the boy asked his father, who was watching the game closely.

'It's chess.'

'What is chess?'

And the father told the boy about that ancient game.

One year later, when the boy finished 2nd grade, his father asked him what gift he would like for his good grades. Without hesitation, the boy answered, 'A chess set.'

That's how Master of Sports I. Lipnitsky started playing chess 18 years ago. He began by studying specialized literature at an early age and signed

Major Isaak Lipnitsky, decorated with two Orders of the Patriotic War and two Orders of the Red Star. Berlin, 1946. From L. Yakir's archive (Kiev).

up for the chess and checkers section of the Young Pioneers House. At the age of 16, he played in his first Ukrainian championship final and took 7th place.

Then the war started. After graduating from artillery school, Lieutenant I. Lipnitsky traversed a rough path from Stalingrad to Berlin. A recipient of four orders and several medals, Major I. Lipnitsky was among the first who entered Berlin... After discharging from the army, he enrolled in Kiev University's philology department and took up chess seriously again. In 1949, he won the Ukrainian championship..." (*Sovietsky Sport*, 25th November.)

After round 3, a clear leader emerged – Master L. Aronin. He had earned the right to take part in the championship final for the fourth time in a row, a feat no other master has achieved in the post-war years. In round 3, Aronin played Liublinsky. This was a real, intense battle... Black's attack was unsound. Aronin broke up his pawn chain, created a dangerous passed pawn and soon won a piece...

The fourth round showed that Smyslov intends to fight hard to retain his title. In his game against Suetin, he energetically attacked in the center and on the kingside. Suetin was resourceful in defense, but still lost a pawn, and the grandmaster has good winning chances in the adjourned position.

From the press: "Suetin won his first game against a chess master 10 years ago. Back then, the 14 year-old Young Pioneer played in a simultaneous against V. Panov. After the war, Suetin met masters over the chess board almost as an equal.

Three years ago, Suetin earned the candidate master's title. Successful chess studies didn't stop him from graduating from the Tula Mechanical Engineering Institute and starting work as a teacher in a municipal construction college.

Last winter, Suetin, as the Trud society champion, played first board for the society's team at the VTsSPS (*All-Union Central Soviet of Trade Unions*) championship... Other successes built up: Alexei Suetin hasn't broken the relationship with his alma mater and gives regular lessons to chess-playing students. This year, the number of category-holding players he has taught has exceeded one hundred, some of them already have first category...

Today, Suetin turns 24. He's playing Grandmaster Smyslov on this day.

'I can't say that I got very lucky on my birthday,' Suetin jokes. 'But still, I'll fight this formidable adversary with all my strength.'" (*Sovietsky Sport*, 16th November.)

I found a curious detail in the book *Chess Through the Prism of Time*: "Our friendship with Petrosian started long before our work together, at the 18th Soviet Championship final. We were the youngest players and quickly felt a liking for each other, which was only strengthened by our interest in opera music and sports."

The spectators eagerly awaited the game Boleslavsky – Aronin. The grandmaster had made three draws before that, and many thought that his dormant strength would finally awaken, especially now that Boleslavsky had white. He rarely loses in general, and has lost only two games with white in recent competitions. However, the grandmaster lost this time...

Дружеский шарж
И. Соколова и И. Рублева

А. СУЭТИН.

The rookie, Alexei Suetin. Cartoon by I. Sokolov and I. Rublev. From the Sovietsky Sport newspaper (16th November 1950).

Panov: "Before the championship started, many thought that it would be a competition between three or four grandmasters, mainly Soviet champion Smyslov and the winner of the Budapest Candidates Tournament Boleslavsky. But the first rounds showed how wrong all such predictions were." (Tournament bulletin, 7th January 1951.)

Keres also won in that round, with black. We get the distinct impression that Geller is unable to get a good start in tournaments. In the previous championship, he only got into his stride after two losses. In

Lev Aronin: a flying start – 5.5/6! All favorites remained behind... Inscription on the reverse of the photo: "A souvenir for my friend Vanya Lyskov, the future USSR chess master. L. Aronin. Moscow, 22nd June 1949." From I. Lyskov's archive. Published for the first time.

this championship, he only had three half-points from the first four games. In the game against Keres, Geller was unrecognizable. Following an interesting pawn sacrifice in the opening, he failed to exploit the hidden opportunities of his position. After a strange trade operation, he blundered an exchange and had to resign...

In each round, the fans are naturally drawn to the demonstration boards with grandmaster games. In round 5, all grandmasters played against masters. And we must admit that this time, the interest was justified in a rather unusual way. Keres and Flohr lost, Smyslov and Bondarevsky adjourned their games in slightly worse positions... On the play-off day, Bondarevsky also joined the list of 'casualties'. Only Smyslov and Boleslavsky managed to save the grandmaster team from a complete disaster. Still, even the score 1–4 looked rather disappointing...

Keres: "The start of the competition didn't bode well for me. After three draws, I defeated Geller who blundered in a complicated position. Then I lost to Alatortsev, playing rather weakly *(see game 225)* and drew with Suetin, against whom I had a lost position." (From the book *One Hundred Games*.)

Round 6 justified the hopes of fans of sharp struggles. Alatortsev and Boleslavsky were the first to deviate from trodden paths. The master, who had white, couldn't get any advantage out of the opening. By contrast, the grandmaster deployed his pet opening, the King's Indian, and got obviously ahead in development... Boleslavsky, who rarely misses an opportunity to finish a game in spectacular fashion, boldly goes for a deeply-calculated queen sacrifice *(the first brilliancy prize! See game 220)*...

Almost every national championship gives us a new name in the group of leaders. This time, Aronin's great start was a pleasant surprise. He had black against Petrosian and quickly equalized. Soon, there was an endgame on the board, somewhat better for black. Still, a draw was probably the most natural result, but then Aronin made a mistake that brought him... victory! And so, avoiding the almost inevitable loss, Aronin both kept his leadership and remained one of the last Mohicans (with Smyslov and Lipnitsky) who are still undefeated." (*Sovietsky Sport*, 14th, 16th, 18th and 21st November.)

Standings after round 6: Aronin – 5.5 (!); Smyslov – 4.5; Tolush – 4; Alatortsev – 3.5; Averbakh, Boleslavsky, Keres, Konstantinopolsky, Lipnitsky, Suetin, Flohr – 3; Bondarevsky, Geller, Mikenas, Petrosian – 2.5; Liublinsky, Sokolsky – 2; Borisenko – 1.5.

A Change of Leader

Abramov and **Vasiliev:** "The round has ended. The spectators leave the TsDKZh, eagerly discussing all the twists and turns of the struggle. But even on Komsomolskaya Square and in the subway car the restless enthusiasts still argue with each other, then agree... and start arguing anew. We know well that there are as many evaluations of any game as there are spectators in the hall... And still, there was one thing that everyone – everyone! – agreed on: Borisenko had an excellent game against Smyslov and deserved his win.

ON THE WAY TO THE FINISH

Everything is as usual in the spacious hall,
We remember the strict-looking stage well.
The experienced Moscow fans
Are watching the chess battle.

The tournament struggle is harsh,
Inaccuracies get punished.
And Borisenko gives V. Smyslov
A spectacular checkmate.

The queens, rooks, bishops and knights
Are hiding cunning and deception.
Aronin won a point,
Petrosian missed a win...

It's quite hard to avoid losses
On the path to an honorable finish.
Lipnitsky, a young fighter,
Earns his laurels on the way.

The staunch advocate of draws,
The master of defense, Salo Flohr,
Has recently changed his style
And left the danger zone.

The excitement is high at the finish,
Time trouble is everywhere...
Towards the victory, near and far,
The sportsmen proceed in a group.
S. Kukanov (tournament bulletin, 19th December).

Дружеский шарж
И. Соколова и И. Рублева

И. ЛИПНИЦКИЙ.

Aronin's victorious march was stopped in round 8 by Lipnitsky, with Smyslov taking the lead. Cartoon of Lipnitsky by I. Sokolov and I. Rublev. From the Sovietsky Sport newspaper (25th November 1950).

The game Tolush – Geller was anticipated especially eagerly. And it did live up to expectations. The game was rife with inventive tactical blows from both sides. There was even a queen sacrifice: Tolush gave it up for a rook, bishop and pawn.

The struggle could have continued for quite some time, but Geller, as always, got into time trouble, and this suddenly upset Tolush's usual calm. He made a common psychological mistake: having seven times more time than his opponent, Tolush got carried away by the high tempo and made a time-trouble mistake himself...

Before round 8, Aronin was 1.5 points ahead of his closest pursuer, Smyslov. Would he be able to maintain this gap, or would the grandmaster get closer to the leader? This question was highly interesting both for spectators and players alike.

> **Romanovsky:** "Aronin's confident play gained him a lot of support, and some fans even expected to see a new national champion – and, therefore, the country's twelfth grandmaster." (Tournament book.)

The game Smyslov – Sokolsky ended first. The black knight's unfortunate incursion led it to its doom, and Sokolsky resigned.

Meanwhile, a storm was brewing in the game Lipnitsky – Aronin. Aronin boldly accepted a pawn sacrifice. White didn't hurry to regain it. Unconcerned at a material disadvantage, he preferred to continue the attack. When the game is sharp, tactical errors are almost inevitable, and he who makes the last mistake usually loses...

> **Lipnitsky:** "Master Aronin had a very strong start at the tournament... In round 8, I managed to win an incredibly complicated game against him *(see game 230)*. This made Aronin stumble, and in the subsequent rounds he had to cede his leadership to others." (*Radyansky Sport*, Kiev, 15th December.)

Дружеский шарж Ю. Узбякова

Round nine like the "Ninth Wave" of the tournament storm. Cartoon by Y. Uzbyakov. From the Sovietsky Sport newspaper (28th November 1950).

And so, before round 9, where Smyslov and Aronin play each other, the gap has decreased to just half a point.

We made this round report together with the artist Yuri Uzbyakov. Look at the picture. There's a furious duel on the top steps of the ladder that leads to the coveted crown. The tournament leader Aronin is doing everything he can to stop Smyslov... Still, the artist couldn't predict the end result: opposite-colored bishops saved a lot of hopeless-looking positions. However, during the play-off, Smyslov, a great master of the endgame, immediately proved that white's efforts to make a draw were futile *(see game 224)*.

Distracted by their duel, Aronin and Smyslov are paying no notice to Boleslavsky. They shouldn't have done that! In the last four rounds, he found his fighting spirit at last, and he scored 3.5 points. In round 9, Boleslavsky crushed Averbakh. The finishing episode, shown by the artist, was preceded by a very energetic attack from the grandmaster and worthy defense by the master...

Levenfish: "The Boleslavsky fans were counting on him to join the battle for the leadership, but the game Boleslavsky – Smyslov *(in round 11 – white* *won on move 83!)* exhausted both the winner and the loser so much that they couldn't compete with the leaders at the finish." (Chess yearbook.)

Lipnitsky is quietly climbing to the top too *(he's in the top right corner of the picture in Sovietsky Sport, holding a "1" in his hands)*. Look how helpful Liublinsky was to him. In the middlegame, Lipnitsky couldn't even dream of such a high place: his position was worsening with every move. However, at the very moment when the time came to reap the fruit of his labors, Liublinsky got afraid of the consequences of winning the queen *(and lost!)*...

You also see Keres and Konstantinopolsky *(wearing a black jacket, with two pawns in his bag)* quickly running up the stairs. The grandmaster had approximately equal chances in his game with Mikenas, but the Lithuanian suddenly tripped over himself and dropped a pawn, deftly caught by his experienced opponent. This accident decided the game.

Konstantinopolsky already has two extra pawns. Look how sad Sokolsky's gaze is – he foresees that he'll have to wear another zero even without a play-off.

Youngsters are bustling around the stairs: in round 9, Borisenko outplayed Geller. The Leningrad player prepared well for the King's Indian structures and never lost his positional advantage, eventually converting it into material.

> **L. Rutitsky:** "About 16 years ago, Mikhail Botvinnik gave a simultaneous display in a Leningrad club. Georgy Borisenko was among the participants. The 11 year-old schoolboy passed the test with flying colors – his game with Botvinnik ended in a draw...
>
> By 1940, Borisenko was already one of the strongest young players in Leningrad. Shortly before the war, he earned his third candidate's norm. Then the war started. Georgy Borisenko fought on the frontlines of the Great Patriotic War *(as a signalman; he was twice wounded, once seriously)*.
>
> Borisenko only returned to chess in 1947, when he got back to Leningrad and enrolled in the Railways Electrical Engineering Institute. Success didn't come easy for the young candidate master. However, he persistently worked to improve his skills..." (*Sovietsky Sport*, 18th November.)

The artist drew Alatortsev and Suetin, looking at their half-points at the side, without much imagination. Still, it's easy to explain: their game was so monotonous that it was only natural that it failed to inspire Uzbyakov.

The inseparable friends, Bondarevsky and Tolush, are talking amicably *(sitting and hugging on the stairs)*. Their game, as all their other ones in

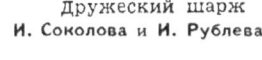

Г. БОРИСЕНКО.

Georgy Borisenko finally managed to breach Geller's King's Indian Defense! Cartoon by I. Sokolov and I. Rublev. From the Sovietsky Sport newspaper (18th November 1950).

recent years, ended without much excitement, in a draw. Friendship, of course, is a good thing, but it would be much better to see a sharp chess fight on their board.

As the reader has probably already guessed, Petrosian was unwell that night *(the artist even drew him lying in bed)*, and the game was postponed. What else could the kindhearted Flohr do? Of course, pay a visit to his ill opponent..." (Ibid., 25th and 28th November.)

Standings after round 9: Smyslov – 6.5; Aronin, Lipnitsky – 6; Alatortsev, Boleslavsky – 5.5; Keres, Konstantinopolsky, Tolush – 5; Averbakh, Petrosian – 4.5; Bondarevsky, Borisenko, Geller, Suetin, Flohr – 4; Mikenas – 3.5; Liublinsky, Sokolsky – 2.

Revenge of the Grandmasters

Abramov and **Vasiliev:** "In round 10, grandmasters again all played masters and took revenge for their losses in round 5. Bondarevsky opened the score. His opponent, Mikenas, is known as an attacking master. In this game, he also prepared for an onslaught. But Bondarevsky managed to force his own tactics upon him and undermined him psychologically *(second brilliancy prize! See game 221)...*

The success was added to by Keres. He had white against Borisenko and went for an early queen trade in the King's Indian *(more of an English)*, obtaining a small positional advantage. It was hard to expect complications in this game. However, they already started on the 11th move. The opponents' pieces constantly attacked each other for 17 moves *(see game 228)...*

Panov: "In our opinion, Keres is a natural, gifted tactician who erroneously thinks of strategy as his main strength. As soon as the circumstances force Keres to forget about this strange self-delusion, he achieves great results." (Tournament bulletin, 7th January 1951.)

After his brilliant performance in the semi-final (in the photo) and two wins at the start of the championship, Salo Flohr was not the same... Beside him, Vladas Mikenas.

The third point for grandmasters was scored by Smyslov. His game against Liublinsky was filled with interesting, if inefficient-looking maneuvering...

When the "Draw" sign appeared on the board where the game Lipnitsky – Boleslavsky was being demonstrated, applause broke out in the hall. One of the spectators even complained: 'What's that? They win – there's applause, they draw – there's applause too...' The spectator wasn't right: this draw is one you can be proud of... An interesting, sharp battle that gave the fans many thrills!

So, the grandmasters now led 3.5–0.5. Flohr almost saved the masters. In his game against Averbakh, he again went for the Caro-Kann Defense. It once brought him many successes. However, after facing the Soviet masters, Flohr's formidable weapon had blunted... But Flohr's tendency to play the Caro-Kann never caused him so much harm as in the first rounds of this championship. Flohr played this defense three times – against Tolush, Aronin and Boleslavsky *(see game 229)* – and lost all three.

This time, black couldn't get a good game either. Averbakh's attack gradually became stronger, and only a pawn sacrifice allowed the grandmaster to simplify... Thus, the grandmasters avenged their loss in round 5 with the same score, 4−1.

> **Botvinnik:** "'Experts' thought that the 1950 Soviet champion was already known: Smyslov only needed to score 4 or 4.5 points out of 7 at the finish to ensure his victory. However, Smyslov showed an inexcusable weakness of character and 'achieved' a truly modest result, scoring just 2.5 points..." (*Ogonyok*, No. 2, 1951.)

The finish was already in sight, which made the 11th round incredibly intense. The game between Boleslavsky and Smyslov was, of course, the

Smyslov had been ahead of Keres for a long time, but faltered at the finish. Their direct encounter in round 2 ended in a draw. From V. Chepizhny's archive. Published for the first time.

main focal point. The young grandmasters had already managed to become old adversaries. They had played twenty games against each other. 12 games ended in a draw, Smyslov had won five and Boleslavsky three *(the latter also won this game)...*

Smyslov's closest competitor, Aronin, lost to Geller. The Odessa master played well for the whole game and won in great style.

The battles in round 12 were even more intense. Tolush won his third game in a row. He's played more than 10 games against Lithuanian master Mikenas. Both opponents play in such a style that none of those games ended in a draw. They continued the tradition in this round, fully justifying their reputation as inventive and imaginative tacticians...

To reinforce his leadership, Smyslov had to win. However, he met fierce resistance from Flohr *(the game was drawn)...*

The other leaders had mixed results. Keres had a small advantage against Aronin during the entire game. However, the master managed to maintain a defensible and even active position. And only towards the end, overestimating his capabilities, did Aronin lose a pawn after an artificial queen maneuver..." (Ibid., 30th November and 2nd December.)

Standings after round 12: Lipnitsky, Smyslov, Tolush – 8; Keres – 7.5; Aronin, Boleslavsky, Geller – 7; Averbakh, Alatortsev, Konstantinopolsky –

6.5; Bondarevsky – 6; Flohr – 5.5; Petrosian, Suetin – 5; Borisenko, Mikenas – 4.5; Sokolsky – 3; Liublinsky – 2.5.

An Equation with Seven Unknowns

Abramov and **Vasiliev:** "Never in all the previous 17 championships was there a situation when almost half of the players were still in contention for the title. Indeed, trying to determine who's the most probable candidate for first place is trying to solve an equation with at least seven unknowns, and no knowledge of advanced mathematics can help you here.

Someone hoped that the 13th round would finally introduce some clarity to the table, but it only poured more fuel on the fire.

> **Levenfish:** "Lipnitsky, who was playing in the final for the first time, took the lead *(he defeated Averbakh)*. Keres, Smyslov and Tolush trailed half a point behind, only because tournament 'luck' shone down on them. Petrosian played a great game against Smyslov, but missed a simple win in time trouble. Keres won a difficult game against Liublinsky, who missed drawing chances during the play-off." (Chess yearbook.) Finally, Tolush saved his game against Borisenko with a perpetual check.

When the game Tolush – Sokolsky ended in round 14, the fight on most other boards was only entering its first stage. Events always unfold very quickly in Tolush's games. In the opening, there was an 'awkward moment' when Sokolsky suddenly offered a draw. We should be grateful to Tolush for his refusal: otherwise, the fans would have missed out on a spectacle *(see game 223)*...

Keres has drawn almost all his games against Boleslavsky. However, this time Boleslavsky launched a risky attack against white's queenside castle position out of the opening. Keres repelled the attack and won the a-pawn, which in the heat of battle had run too deep into the opponent's camp and found itself undefended. Boleslavsky maintained the initiative for a long time and organized a break in the center. There was even a moment when he could have regained the pawn, but he decided against that *(Keres won the play-off)*...

Numerous spectators watched the game Alatortsev – Lipnitsky especially closely. The Kiev player had a real opportunity to keep his lead after round 14. But on that day, Lipnitsky's chances decreased somewhat, and he was the one to blame. He decided against the bold move f5-f4 on move 24, and Alatortsev didn't let go of the initiative after that...

After the incredible tension of the previous rounds, it seemed that nothing more could surprise the spectators. And still, the 15th round managed to astonish even the experienced Moscow fans: out of four games that ended before the break, none were drawn, and the five adjourned ones were unlikely to end in split points either. A drawless round! Such things happen very rarely.

Chess fans have a peculiar instinct for interesting rounds: on that day, there weren't enough tickets to accommodate everyone, and so, two demonstration boards were installed down below, near the ticket offices, showing the two most interesting games of the round – Aronin vs. Tolush and Lipnitsky vs. Smyslov. But let's leave the noisy unlucky fans to argue at the boards and ascend the stairs that lead to the tournament hall.

Дружеский шарж
И. Соколова и И. Рублева

Мастер В. АЛАТОРЦЕВ.

In round 14, Lipnitsky took the lead, but he was stopped by Vladimir Alatortsev, shown here. Cartoon by I. Sokolov and I. Rublev. From the Sovietsky Sport newspaper (7th December 1950).

There's a heated fight at almost every table. Lipnitsky is attacking Smyslov, Alatortsev sacrifices a piece to Borisenko, it's hard to even understand who's attacking and who's defending in the Aronin – Tolush game, and even the peaceful Flohr decides to take a gamble and sacrifices a piece to Keres. A fighting round! And it seems as though the outstanding Russian chess player, the founder of the national chess school, M. I. Chigorin, is watching his worthy pupils with an approving gaze from his huge portrait hanging over the stage...

Even among all the interesting games of round 15, one especially stood out – Smyslov vs. Lipnitsky. We should admit that before this day, Lipnitsky's creative achievements didn't quite match his sporting ones. He scored a lot of points without playing games that would be consistently good from the beginning to the end. In round 15, the Kiev player managed to narrow this gap somewhat...

Aronin had to win – otherwise, he would lose his last chance to get back into the title race. As often happens in tournaments, Tolush desperately needed a win himself – it would have allowed him to reinforce his lead *(however, Aronin won)...*

In conclusion, we have to say something about the playing conditions at the tournament. Round 15 clearly showed that the organization leaves much to be desired. To the ire of the arbiters, the spectators reacted quite loudly after every win. Indeed, conversations and applause hamper the players, but can we really demand that chess fans sit as quietly as the players themselves? Also, the hall is too stuffy, which also negatively affects the creative side of playing. For the all-Union championships, which are more important than the biggest international tournament, we can and should find a bigger venue *(the TsDKZh hall hosted "just" 1,100 spectators!)* that would accommodate everyone who wants to visit the tournament.

It's also absolutely necessary to increase the number of play-off days. Can we really put up with the fact that the players have to finish 26 games before the two last rounds?! Some of them have five adjourned games. This makes it harder to determine the standings and, of course, affects the quality of the games.

...Finally, the dreams of both spectators and players came true: the arbiters changed the schedule and generously assigned three play-off days in a row. This allowed players to finally put the tournament table in order before the penultimate round. For the first time, we didn't have to speculate about the adjourned games – all 26 envelopes with sealed moves were open, and all players knew their results in all their fifteen games." (Ibid., 5th, 7th, 9th December.)

Standings after round 15: Keres – 10.5; Lipnitsky – 10; Aronin, Tolush – 9.5; Smyslov – 9; Alatortsev, Konstantinopolsky – 8.5; Boleslavsky, Bondarevsky, Geller – 8; Mikenas – 7.5; Averbakh, Flohr – 7; Petrosian, Suetin – 6; Borisenko – 5; Liublinsky – 4; Sokolsky – 3.

The Final With an Unimaginable Prognosis

Abramov and **Vasiliev:** "After round 15, we might have thought that Keres' strong finish would finally put an end to the interregnum feel of the last days of the championship. However, this tournament is so unusual that the chess fans don't have a single moment to calm down. Can you believe it? – Aronin and Tolush won in the penultimate round, and Keres and Lipnitsky lost! Again, at least four players have real chances to win the champion's title, and the calculation lovers have got new food for thought.

How did round 16 pan out?

Nobody doubted that Keres, who had white, would do everything possible to defeat Petrosian and virtually secure first place. At first, the game really went like that. Seeing that white's threats were becoming increasingly real, Petrosian tried to create queenside counterplay and even sacrificed a pawn *(his risk ultimately paid off – see game 231)...*

As the dramatic battle between Petrosian and Keres came to a close, the adjacent table hosted an equally interesting game. Lipnitsky (black) fought against his chess mentor Konstantinopolsky... This was something of a final exam for Lipnitsky. The 'examiner' was strict, probably even harsh, and the entire game was so logical and consistent from beginning to end that it really looked like an exemplary lesson *(see game 226)...*

In round 16, the future "Iron Tigran" stood in the way of Keres.

Lipnitsky: "I must admit, I was very sad to resign against him, especially since this game deprived me of clear first place. But I'm thankful to my teacher for showing me, honestly and firmly, how much work I still have ahead of me to improve my play." (*Sovietsky Sport*, 14th December.)

Liublinsky played very well against Tolush. He exploited Tolush's indecisive play, got a more active position and executed a combination with a temporary exchange sacrifice. When the material balance was restored, black's passed pawn should have played the decisive role in the endgame. But... the endgame didn't happen. In severe time trouble, Liublinsky went for a harmless-looking move order. This inaccuracy spelled doom for him... Liublinsky resigned, and Tolush caught up with Keres.

'This is the first time I've played the King's Indian in this tournament; will it fail me?' Aronin asked when he went backstage after the first four moves. However, presumably fearing that it would indeed fail him, he transposed into the Grunfeld Defense on move 5 *(and it didn't fail him!)...*

Before the last round, there was an unprecedented situation that even the most seasoned veterans couldn't remember: three players – Keres, Tolush and

Aronin – had 10.5 points, and Lipnitsky was very close behind (10 points). This made the round incredibly tense.

> **Lipnitsky:** "Who would win the gold medal and the Soviet champion's title? The seventeenth round would provide all the answers. The Moscow fans' incredible interest was fully understandable. All tickets were sold in the morning. Some players came at least 10 minutes late to their games because they had to 'fight' through the throng of chess lovers who couldn't obtain a ticket but still hoped to get into the tournament hall somehow." (*Radyansky Sport*, Kiev, 15th December.)

Naturally, three games attracted the most heated interest of the capacity crowd: Averbakh – Keres, Boleslavsky – Tolush and Aronin – Borisenko... For some time, the games followed well-known lines. But soon, the positions in all games sharpened, and you could guess even without looking at the boards that the calm was disrupted by those who wanted to win the champion's title. The resolute Tolush was the first to do so. In the Ruy Lopez, he deployed a new move 11...d4, prepared together with Keres beforehand. Boleslavsky couldn't cope with the arising complications. Black seized the initiative and soon won an exchange *(see game 232)*.

Tolush's luck spurred his rivals as well. Soon, Keres seized the initiative in his game with Averbakh with a pawn blow in the center. You might have expected the grandmaster to capitalize on this success with some energetic play. However, after losing to Petrosian, he prefers a bird in the hand to two in the bush. And this 'bird in the hand' manifested itself in the guise of white's isolated central pawn *(see game 233)*...

Thus, two leaders got a clear advantage. Then, Aronin's turn came... Borisenko made a bold and unexpected move, 24...g5! The most dramatic moment of the whole round came. The fans intently watched the master gazing at the board, head in his hands.

Indeed, what should white do? Retreat to g3 from h4 with the queen? Then black would play 25...♘h5, and it's necessary to either settle for a draw by repetition or hide the queen in the 'catacombs' with 26.♕h2; it will find a safe haven there, but lose a lot of its strength.

Aronin chose another continuation, bold and risky: he decided to sacrifice a piece, even though this sacrifice only gave him very hazy prospects...

The round was coming to a close. Tolush returned the exchange to his opponent but got an extra passed pawn, which, as everyone thought, gave him good winning chances. Aronin had to do what Geller failed to do to Smyslov in round 1 – prove the superiority of three pawns over a bishop. Keres still maintained that small positional advantage.

> **Lipnitsky:** "The players almost never left their tables, desperately throwing all their energy and skills into obtaining that much-needed point. The five hours of play passed very quickly, and only one game out of nine ended – Smyslov drew with Konstantinopolsky." (Ibid.)

Only 12 hours were left before the play-off. Only 12 hours for everything – the road home and back to the tournament in the morning, for dinner and breakfast, for sleep and analysis. Most players probably didn't sleep well that night...

One of the three leaders' games finished in the hotel: after a long analysis, Tolush came to the conclusion that he couldn't win... The play-off between Averbakh and Keres ended quickly. The adjourned position was unusual – white's isolated d4 pawn was doomed to fall sooner or later. Averbakh decided to create complications with his 42nd move, but that only accelerated the pawn's downfall.

Much in the standings also depended on the game between Lipnitsky and Geller. The complicated, maneuvering struggle on the round day had ended with lightning-fast play by Geller, who had one minute to make 15 moves. He adjourned the game in a worse position, and Lipnitsky confidently converted his advantage and won...

The game tables had already been vacated, and the demonstrators were already packing up the plywood chess pieces in a backstage room, but the hall was still full: Aronin was stubbornly trying to defeat Borisenko. Aronin's desire to win and share first place with Keres was great, but Borisenko's will not to lose was equally strong. The game lasted for more than 80 moves and ended in a draw.

> Were first place to be shared, another exciting show awaited chess fans: "According to the tournament regulations, in case of 1st and 2nd places being shared, a 6-game play-off match between the two winners will take place in ten days to determine the national champion. If more than two players share first place with an equal amount of points, a match tournament will be held in ten days, with each championship contender playing two games against all others." (*Sovietsky Sport*, 21st November.)

In the evening, after the play-off, the closing ceremony took place. The All-Union Committee for Physical Education and Sport deputy chairman,

Чемпион СССР
гроссмейстер
П. КЕРЕС
Дружеский шарж
М. КУКУНОВА.

Paul Keres is the two-times Soviet champion!
Cartoon by M. Kukunov. From the tournament
bulletin (14th January 1950).

I. M. Vereskov, awarded prizes to the players who took the top six places *(Keres got the gold medal, and Aronin, Lipnitsky and Tolush, who shared 2nd–4th places, got silver tokens)*. The special prize for the best result against the prizewinners was awarded to Alatortsev *(3.5/6)*. The prize for best performance in the last five rounds was shared by Keres, Aronin and Mikenas *(4/5)*.

So, the tournament has ended. And there are already messages from all corners of the country, telling us about hundreds of thousands of players taking part in an unprecedented competition – a mass tournament honoring the 100th anniversary of M. I. Chigorin's birth. This mass scale of the chess movement is key to new victories of Soviet chess culture." (Ibid., 12th and 14th December.)

V. Vinogradov, chairman of the All-Union Chess Section (1947–49, 1952–54): "A new talent pool of chess players is getting ready to replace our grandmasters and masters. We have about one million players who have sporting categories in our country. Hundreds of thousands of people are taking part in chess competitions.

For instance, more than 420,000 players played in the 1952 trade union championship. 103,000 players competed in the first all-Russian kolkhoz chess players tournament (1949). More than 300,000 agricultural workers took part in the 1950 USSR kolkhoz chess championship...

1950 was the 100th anniversary of the great Russian chess player M. I. Chigorin's birth. In celebration of this date, the Soviet chess organizations held a mass tournament with more than 730,000 players taking part.

Almost all middle schools and higher education establishments have mass chess sections, the work of which bears decent fruit. Schoolchildren's competitions have become a tradition in all towns and villages." (From the book *Soviet Players in Competition for the World Championship*.)

Incidentally, the first grandmaster of the USSR, **Boris Verlinsky**, died shortly before the start of the tournament, on 30th October, but the tournament bulletin never mentioned that sad loss. The *Shakhmaty v SSSR* magazine, instead of an obituary, published his recollections, calling him "one of the oldest masters"... On the other hand, when **Nikolai Zubarev**, one of the bulletin's editors, died on 1st January the following year, a long obituary was dedicated to him, signed by all the leading chess players, including the "first Soviet grandmaster" Botvinnik.[8]

Averbakh: "In 1929, Verlinsky won the national championship. For this success, he was the first player in the history of Soviet chess to receive the grandmaster's title, moreover, it was specifically awarded 'for life'. However, in the early 1930s, he was quietly stripped of the title – without any official decrees. Boris Markovich, a delicate, very sensitive man, suffered greatly because of this loss; for some reason, he blamed Nikolai Zubarev, who was the head of the highest qualification committee back then. He considered Zubarev his number one enemy. As irony would have it, they both died almost at the same time: Verlinsky – in late October 1950, and Zubarev two months later, it was just about New Year's eve. When I bumped into Verlinsky's widow on Arbat Street the following January and told her that Zubarev had died, she lamented, 'Ah, ah, such a pity that Borya didn't live to see this day. He would have been so glad!'" (Quoted in the book *From Verlinsky to Father Zui* by A. Radchenko and S. Allakhverdian about handicapped chess players in the USSR.)

> The reason for this enmity was deeper than just the "loss" of a title in 1931. From **Beilin's** book *Encounters In the Chess Kingdom* I learned that Verlinsky "lobbied to have his title reinstated. However, Boris Markovich's request fell on the deaf ears of Nikolai Mikhailovich Zubarev, the head honcho of chess back then *(since 1943)*... In the year of Verlinsky's death, FIDE awarded International Master titles. Our Chess Federation filed applications for national masters who played in the Soviet Championship finals at least three times. Verlinsky was one of those masters – he had played in the national championships six times, not entirely unsuccessfully too. So, shortly before his death, he was awarded the International Master title." Sadly, he died before learning that...

---

[8] A detailed biography of Boris Verlinsky by Sergei Tkachenko is forthcoming from Elk and Ruby

The head of the chess department of the Soviet Sports Committee, Master Nikolai Zubarev, died soon after the championship ended, just before New Year... Photo by M. Volkovysky from his archive. Published for the first time.

Averbakh wouldn't be Averbakh if he didn't "balance" (he had the subtlest inner balance!) the episode about Verlinsky's widow with a friendly portrait of Zubarev: "A bulky, bald, always impeccably dressed man, he worked as the chairman of the Sports Committee chess department; as they now say, he was a chess functionary, an official. A taciturn, pedantic man, Zubarev performed his duties with zeal. He was respected in the Sports Committee to the point that they allowed him to distribute additional rations during the war. He was a decent player with a solid positional style, but didn't reach great heights and dedicated himself to organizational work and working as an arbiter. In essence, Zubarev created our qualifications system. And he was an exemplary arbiter – knowledgeable, clear, calm... Nikolai Mikhailovich was protective of young players, gave helpful advice, helped directly if he could." (From the book *A Chess Player's Life in the System.*)

The Winners' Self-Portraits

Final standings: 1. Keres – 11.5/17; 2–4. Aronin, Lipnitsky, Tolush – 11; 5–6. Konstantinopolsky, Smyslov – 10; 7–10. Alatortsev, Boleslavsky, Geller, Flohr – 9; 11. Mikenas – 8.5; 12–13. Bondarevsky, Petrosian – 8; 14. Averbakh – 7; 15–16. Borisenko, Suetin – 6.5; 17–18. Liublinsky, Sokolsky – 4.

Keres: "The participants of the 18th Soviet Championship played in true Chigorin style – sharply, boldly, inventively. 'Grandmaster draws', with only rare exceptions, were absent. And this is the most joyful conclusion I'd like to make.

I was most impressed with the play of Aronin, Tolush and Lipnitsky. The first of these showed great willpower. Having six points after seven rounds,

Aronin then lost several games in a row. Many would have stopped fighting for the leadership after such a disaster. Aronin, however, fought for victory until the very end of the tournament.

Tolush's play was inventive and original as always. He was a title contender up until the last round. Lipnitsky's play was a surprise as pleasant as Geller's performance at the last championship. Lipnitsky is without a doubt a very strong and promising player.

I of course am rather satisfied with my sporting success, but can't say the same about the creative side. I did manage to play several good games – against Boleslavsky and Liublinsky, for instance; however, in a number of games – against Sokolsky, Tolush, and Petrosian (see game 231) – I failed to exploit a fairly clear advantage, and only saved the games against Suetin and Flohr with my opponents' help." (Sovietsky Sport, 14th December.)

"Lipnitsky's result was the biggest surprise of the tournament." (Levenfish.) From V. Chepizhny's archive.

Keres: "After eight rounds, I had only four points and trailed the leader by two points. Nine rounds remained. And then, a winning streak suddenly started... I scored six and a half points in seven rounds. It's hard for me to explain why such winning or losing streaks happen in a tournament, but the fact remains. They happen quite often, even with the strongest lineups." (From the book *One Hundred Games*.)

Botvinnik: "Keres can be satisfied with his performance in 1950. A year earlier, he wasn't too sure of himself at the Soviet Championship. Last year, however, he successfully played at the grandmasters' match tournament in Budapest (4th prize), then at the Szczawno-Zdroj international tournament (1st place), and finally, absolutely deservedly won the Soviet Championship. Subtle understanding of openings and endings, skillful positional maneuvering and inventive tactical blows are characteristic of his game." (*Ogonyok*, No. 2, 1951.)

Paul Keres, his coach Alexander Tolush and Yuri Averbakh (Lilienthal's coach) at the Budapest Candidates Tournament. From Y. Averbakh's archive. Published for the first time.

Aronin: "In the previous championship, I made 12 draws and heard a lot of accusations of lacking enough desire to win. It was upsetting to hear such things, but I had to admit that they were quite deserved.

While preparing for the tournament dedicated to the memory of Chigorin, I promised to myself to play boldly and sharply. As a result, I made only four draws and won nine games – more than any other player. Even though, despite all my efforts, I didn't manage to finish Borisenko off in the last round, I'm still satisfied with my tournament score.

My table neighbors, Lipnitsky and Tolush, played very interesting, distinctive chess. We should point out that Tolush achieved the best result in his entire chess career, and Lipnitsky didn't lose a single game to a grandmaster in his first national championship outing." (Ibid.)

Levenfish: "Aronin's success is fully deserved. This gifted master is diligently working on improving himself and is growing steadily. In the previous championship, he was still a bit afraid of grandmasters and agreed to draws in better positions. In this championship, however, Aronin tried to win every game. Aronin is good in a purely strategic struggle, but, above all, he's a talented tactician, goes for sacrifices eagerly, and deeply and precisely calculates complicated combinations, some of which are very original.

Aronin's weaknesses are still his limited opening repertoire, defense from quick attacks and endgame technique." (Chess yearbook.)

Bronstein: "Aronin's playing style reminded me of Botvinnik and Furman. His style was positional, very solid, but he could play a brilliant combination on occasion." (From the book *Sorcerer's Apprentice*.)

Lipnitsky: "I went to Moscow for the championship with great anxiety. This was my national championship debut, and, naturally, I wanted to play this 'opening' as well as possible. The games against the country's leading players were of most interest for me.

My tournament experience is not great, and taking part in the championship should have helped discover the shortcomings of my play. The tournament clearly showed up my main weaknesses: inadequate opening knowledge and indecisive play in time trouble.

Among my fellow tournament participants, I was most impressed with Keres, Smyslov and Geller. Many of their moves often surprised me with their originality and depth of strategic ideas.

I'm totally satisfied with the tournament results. I would like to specifically point out that I owe this achievement to my chess mentor – Master Konstantinopolsky, with whom I have been friends for years." (Ibid.)

Levenfish: "Lipnitsky's result was the biggest surprise of the tournament. He's a versatile player, evaluates the position well and objectively, and his tactical vision is equally good. Lipnitsky is inventive in attack and tenacious in defense. He possesses valuable sporting qualities – energy, stamina and calm, he plays well in time trouble. Lipnitsky lost only three games in the whole tournament – all of them essentially because of bad openings. Lipnitsky still has to do a lot of work on openings and endgames, but his serious attitude to chess, self-criticism and perseverance give us all reasons to hope that he will achieve even more in the future." (Chess yearbook.)

Teplitsky: "An interesting detail: even after his brilliant championship result, Lipnitsky was still officially... a candidate master! Lyubov Yakir recalled: 'I came to many games of the 18th Soviet Championship, where Lipnitsky, starting off as a candidate master, scored a grandmaster norm. I remember him in the happy days of victories against Smyslov, Geller, Petrosian, Averbakh, and in the sad days of losses to Alatortsev and Konstantinopolsky. Outwardly, he was calm all the time. He never forced his bad mood onto others. He showed the same attitude in the days of illness that gradually and inexorably undermined his health...'" (From the book *Isaak Lipnitsky*.)

Lazarev: "The Kiev player's debut was reminiscent of his mentor's performance at the 1937 Soviet Championship, when Alexander Konstantinopolsky also took second place at his first attempt. Their creative styles were also quite similar. The teacher long outlived his pupil, whose first big success in the national arena remained his greatest." (From the book *Creative Works of Ukrainian Chess Players.*)

Tolush: "The 18th national championship delivered extremely interesting, rich, truly creative battles. An even line-up of the participants helped in that regard.

The masters showed that they were worthy opponents for grandmasters: out of five grandmasters, only Smyslov and Keres challenged for the championship title.

From the creative point of view, I'm fully satisfied with my play. I consider the games with Sokolsky *(see game 223)*, Konstantinopolsky and Mikenas to have been my best ones.

Keres' victory is well-deserved. He was truly the strongest player in this tournament. Of the other participants, I liked Geller's interesting, distinctive play. I think that he could have finished in a higher place." (Ibid.)

Botvinnik: "Tolush has achieved his greatest success in his long chess career. He's skillful in tactical battles and plays confidently in complicated positions. In simple positions, his technique is less perfect, and this is his weak spot – we should think that this flaw can be corrected." (*Ogonyok*, No. 2, 1951.)

Levenfish: "Tolush has long been known as a master of attack, showing a lot of imagination, deep and precise calculation. His opening knowledge is great, and he skillfully chooses openings according to his opponents' tastes and personalities. Tolush was the only player who, despite the difficult conditions of the tournament hall, played without much strain and didn't get into time trouble. He doesn't like cramped positions or long, tenacious defense, but in the double-edged, tactical battles, he's dangerous to any adversary..." (Chess yearbook.)

The "Losers"

Panov: "We should say that almost all the championship participants, from the prizewinners to the 'losers', played in the spirit of the glorious Chigorinist traditions, striving for true, interesting battle...

Konstantinopolsky's result, shared 5th and 6th place with Smyslov, broadly matches the playing strength of this great theoretician who possesses deep understanding of maneuvering play.

Romanovsky: "Konstantinopolsky's five wins, of which his deep strategic attacks against Boleslavsky and Lipnitsky *(see game 226)* are especially impressive, serve as great examples of logic and determination." (Tournament book.)

Bronstein: "I watched with special interest the games of my older comrade and chess mentor Master Konstantinopolsky, one of the strongest Soviet theoreticians and teachers, a man of supreme chess culture (by the way, Master Lipnitsky is also a pupil of his). He relatively rarely takes part in competitions, but always achieves success. It's very hard to defeat Konstantinopolsky. He lost only two games in this tournament, largely because he was trying to win at all cost with white." (*Vechernaya Moskva*, 13ᵗʰ December 1950.)

Of course, much more was expected from last year's champion Smyslov, but his lackluster result had two reasons. First of all, each of his opponents played with special effort and accuracy against him, while Smyslov himself obviously underestimated his opponents, especially the young players such as Borisenko and Lipnitsky. Secondly, as strange as it sounds, we think that Smyslov still hasn't found his creative personality yet. His opening repertoire clearly doesn't suit his style. Smyslov has a strongly pronounced tactical talent and tends to go for Chigorin-style complicated, tricky, double-edged play, while his opening set-ups are essentially designed for some other, positional player who's strong strategically but doesn't like complications and avoids them. As long as this gap between form and substance isn't fully closed, Smyslov won't be able to reach those heights of chess art that he fully deserves.

Botvinnik: "Of course, it's clear to everyone that grandmasters Smyslov and Boleslavsky played below their strength and capabilities. They are both great chess artists. They still played well, but lacked determination." (*Moskovsky Komsomolets*, 13ᵗʰ December 1950.)

Alexander Konstantinopolsky was a tough nut to crack: he lost only three games out of 32 in the semi-final (pictured) and final!

Flohr: "Vasily Smyslov disappointed his numerous fans. His talent is beyond doubt. Unfortunately, Smyslov still can't shake off his old flaw – his inability to handle defeats. As soon as he lost to Boleslavsky in round 11, he lost his way. After this loss, Smyslov played weakly and didn't give his all to catch up with the leaders at the finish...

The biggest surprise is Boleslavsky's result. What's the matter? I think that he has the same flaw as Smyslov. We didn't see it in Boleslavsky earlier – simply because he lost so few games in recent years. In the Budapest tournament, for instance, he remained undefeated. But in the 18th Soviet Championship, Boleslavsky lost four games, three of them at the finish!" (*Komsomolskaya Pravda*, 13th December 1950.)

Alatortsev, Boleslavsky, Geller and Flohr, who scored equal points, might evaluate their results differently; at any rate, in such a strong tournament, it's not a big failure... The reason for Boleslavsky and Flohr not achieving a higher place is that they had got unaccustomed to the intense, combative, 'Chigorinist' character of the battles that prevailed at the championship. The favorite approach of both those grandmasters, representatives of a subtle positional style, is precise exploitation of an advantage in games where they manage to outplay their opponents, and settling for a draw in positions where their opponents haven't made mistakes. That approach didn't work in this championship because the attitude of all participants wasn't at all peaceful, and they managed to correct their mistakes over the board, with incredible tactical inventiveness.

Suetin: "Many were surprised that Boleslavsky took part in the 18th Soviet Championship almost immediately after an exhausting match with Bronstein. I also played in that championship, it was my first one. Three weeks before the start, I was called to a training camp of the Russian SFSR players who had earned their right to play in the final. We (masters Aronin, Liublinsky and I) largely rested, recovering from the intense semi-final battles and admiring the autumn beauty of the Moscow forest.

Isaak Efremovich got to the training camp a bit late and, to my great surprise, started working on analysis all day long. He pulled me in too. In those years, his inclination for coaching work already showed, but back then, it was still more of a 'hobby'.

Nevertheless, he was essentially forcing himself to work. The strain from the match still showed. In the final, he played inconsistently and plain badly at the finish... Still, several of his games were truly magical." (From the book *Grandmaster Boleslavsky*.)

Vasily Smyslov, his coach Vladimir Alatortsev (left) and Alexander Kotov at Margaret Island in Budapest. From the author's archive.

Romanovsky: "Flohr couldn't get to a 50-percent score, but, winning excellent games against Bondarevsky and Suetin in the last two rounds, managed to somewhat improve the dull picture he 'artistically' painted with six draws in a row in rounds 8–13." (Tournament book.)

Geller was hypnotized by his previous year's success and took unjustified, unhealthy risks even in games against the strongest opponents, often suffering from time trouble and getting caught in traps of his own making. If this talented master was more objective, he would have probably achieved a better result. Geller's limited opening repertoire allowed his opponents to prepare thoroughly for every game against him. Geller and some other young masters lack self-criticism and the ability to work diligently on self-improvement, with more accent needed on eradicating weaknesses than improving their strengths.

Lipnitsky: "One of the three representatives of Ukraine, Master Geller, again showed that he was a very gifted player. I think I won't make a mistake if I call him the most talented young master of our country.

However, he lacked the necessary restraint in this championship, and very often, he would throw brilliantly-played games away with one gross blunder.

Isaak Boleslavsky's play was affected by overexertion in his match against Bronstein. From Y. Averbakh's archive. Published for the first time.

This happened in the games with Smyslov and Keres, where Geller had winning positions, but only scored half a point instead of the two he deserved. Geller very often got into time trouble, where, as we all know, unfortunate mistakes are inevitable. For instance, he blundered his queen in one move against Suetin in a clearly better position." (*Radyansky Sport*, Kiev, 15th December.)

Bronstein: "This master is characterized by rich imagination and exceptional tenacity in attack. He's one of the adherents and experts of the Ukrainian Defense (which is called the 'Old Indian'[9] for some reason). This defense, or rather counter-attack, brought him a lot of brilliant victories in the last championship. I think that he would have agreed to play black in every game if he was allowed to use his favorite Ukrainian Defense. But in this championship, his opponents were already aware of his strengths and prepared beforehand. Had Geller diversified his opening repertoire, he might have been able to repeat last year's success and earn the grandmaster title. At any rate, he can still achieve this." (*Vechernaya Moskva*, 13th December 1950.)

Levenfish: "Of all the masters who have come to prominence in recent years, **Geller possesses the greatest tactical talent** (*emphasis by me – S.V.*). His imagination and swift attacks are reminiscent of Chigorin and Alekhine." (Chess yearbook.)

Alatortsev clearly stumbled at the finish; for almost the whole tournament he played in his old, heavy, strategic style, but he overestimated his resources in the games against Mikenas and Sokolsky and lost at least a point in those games, which prevented him from reaching a higher place.

Distinguished Master of Sports Mikenas and young Master Petrosian played inconsistently, but still, their places approximately match their playing strength.

---

[9]   The Old Indian Defense is the Russian name for the King's Indian Defense

Mikenas: "It was nice to take part in such a strong tournament. And even though, frankly, my health was still affected by the aftermath of a severe illness, I played with enthusiasm, and I still sometimes play through all the games – the wins, the losses (6 of both) and the draws with equal pleasure. I can't understand where I got such energy from on the home stretch: I scored 4 points in the last five rounds, defeating Alatortsev, Borisenko, Sokolsky and Liublinsky, and losing to Aronin." (From the book *Vladas Mikenas*.)

Дружеский шарж Ю. Узбякова

Гроссмейстер С. ФЛОР.

A brilliant finishing spurt – 3/4! – brightened up the impression made by Flohr's flaccid play. Cartoon by Y. Uzbyakov. From the Sovietsky Sport newspaper (2nd December 1950).

We think that the explanation for Bondarevsky's bad result lies beyond sporting reasons: like Keres, Bondarevsky, who is a sharp, interesting tactician by nature, artificially forced himself to switch to a dry positional style, trying to boil down the essence of the struggle to technical maneuvering. However, when the position gets complicated, either naturally or by his opponent's choice, Bondarevsky uses tactical opportunities most excellently. This is the style he should be playing in.

Averbakh's setback is explained not only by the fact that he plays in serious tournaments too frequently but also because he, like many other young players, overestimates the importance of theoretical preparation while according too little freedom to his creative fantasy and experimental initiative. In such strong tournaments as the Soviet Championship, you need more than just technique and knowledge of scientific principles of the game – you also need creative boldness and the ability to fight in any environment, not only in the positions you're accustomed to.

There was also another reason. Averbakh wrote that Verlinsky ("my loyal fan") told him, "It's bad that you have a second profession. If you

Vladas Mikenas shared the prize for the best result in the last five rounds with Keres and Aronin. Photo taken during the semi-final in Tartu.

The two-times Moscow champion (1949 and 1950) and newly-baked chess professional Yuri Averbakh. From Y. Averbakh's archive. Published for the first time.

were hungry, you'd surely have become a grandmaster long ago!" Someone might wonder: how could Verlinsky utter such a long statement if he could barely talk? Yuri Lvovich explains: "He frequently came to visit, since he lived close by. He would sometimes sit down at the piano in our apartment and play, his deafness didn't hinder him in the slightest. We got along very well, and I understood him easily despite his speech impairment."

In early 1950, **Averbakh** got tired of "sitting on two chairs" and left his scientific institute, where he'd already started his candidate's thesis, to take up chess full-time:

"After I became a professional, I started playing in tournaments without worrying about whether I would get leave from my job. I won a prize in Szczawno-Zdroj, became Moscow champion for the second time in a row, and shared first place in the national semi-final. But the finals didn't go too well. For most of the tournament I played fine, staying in the top 10, but played with too much strain, tried too hard – and after the play-off with Alatortsev, a game which lasted for 90 moves, I got completely exhausted and lost my last three games, only taking 14th place. This result was almost identical to my first outing in the national championship finals, but there was a difference: now I was a professional!" (From the book *Centre-Stage and Behind the Scenes.*)

Borisenko and Suetin's performance in their first

tournament with such a strong line-up was not bad, they played some excellent games.

Of the remaining players, Sokolsky's clearly bad result is of note – he was out of form because of ill health. Liublinsky's lack of success, repeating last year's result, should not be considered unusual – most probably, he can't withstand the strain of a long tournament." (Tournament bulletin, 7th January 1951.)

Some Stats

Do you remember how disappointed I was when I tried to look at the trends in draw percentages in the post-war championships? 17th and 16th – both 45%, 15th – 49%, 14th – 35%! "It's unlikely we will ever see such an 'anti-draw' championship again..." I wrote then. And I was proven wrong: this championship was almost as "anti-draw" as the 14th: 38%!

Abramov: "If we also consider that most draws were made in sharp, tense games, we should come to the conclusion that the participants played boldly and aggressively, in other words, the Chigorin way. This impulse swept up even the most peaceful players. Flohr, who drew two-thirds of his games in the 15th, 16th and 17th championships, had less than half *(8)* of his games drawn this time. The contrast is even sharper in Aronin's games – 12 draws in the last championship and only 4 this time, and what draws they were! More than 80 moves against Borisenko, 61 moves against Bondarevsky, a sharp and complicated fight against Alatortsev, and mutual caution only shown against Averbakh."

Igor Bondarevsky's performance in the next championship would be exactly the same. He would share 12th–13th place again, even with the same score: +4–5=8!

Afterwards, the author of the **"At the Tournament Table"** series of articles compared the last four championships from the "grandmasters versus masters" point of view:

"In all the championships, masters lost their 'team matches' against grandmasters, but they only managed to score 34% of points in the 15th championship versus 42% now. But this calculation is not too representative. We should compare the results of grandmasters against the same number of the best masters. In this 'team match', grandmasters scored on average 6.3 points out of each 10 games in the 15th championship, 5.3 points in the 16th, 5.2 points in the 17th, and only 4.2 points in the 18th. This means that for the first time, the five grandmasters who took part in the championship lost their match against the top five masters – Aronin, Lipnitsky, Tolush, Konstantinopolsky and Alatortsev – with a score of 10.5–14.5.

> **Lipnitsky:** "What was the most characteristic feature of this championship? I think that it was the onslaught of the young, who counteracted the grandmasters' great experience and high playing class with their boldness, novelty and originality of ideas, and great willpower." (*Radyansky Sport*, Kiev, 15th December.)

What conclusions should we draw? Have the grandmasters grown weaker? Or have the masters become stronger?

The first suggestion is easily refuted. This same year, Boleslavsky brilliantly won the Budapest tournament. Smyslov and Keres also performed well and then confirmed their high class in Szczawno-Zdroj and Venice. Concerning Bondarevsky and Flohr – the results of the semi-finals, at the very least, showed their good sporting form.

Thus, we can say that the masters' playing level is steadily growing, and the line between the best masters and grandmasters is getting increasingly blurred. It's also worth pointing out that in the last four championships, the number of masters in the top ten was 2–5–5–6, and in the top four 0–1–2–3, respectively. These numbers show the steady growth of Soviet chess players' mastery." (Ibid., 14th January.)

The Ordeals of Abundance

It's now rather funny to recall how I complained about the lack of surviving games, then the lack of annotated games, then the lack of players' annotations to their own best games... I now face a different problem: what should I do with the ever-growing mass of "masterpieces and dramas"? See for yourself. There were two fewer participants in this championship than in the previous one, but the number of annotated games in the bulletin, *Shakhmaty v SSSR* magazine and yearbook was considerably greater: 78 instead of 55. The tournament book raised the bar further: 96 annotated games out of 153 (versus 89 out of 190). Also, almost all participants published their own books with selected games...

The selection of examples was also made difficult by the fact that the candidate list for three "prizes in honor of the great Russian chess player M. I. Chigorin for the best games" was not published this time. Even though the jury, consisting of Romanovsky and Abramov, surely had some kind of short-list to select the top games... Thankfully, Panov gave his own list of "brilliant games worthy of M. I. Chigorin's memory" in his review article, which, together with "Levenfish's list" (games he selected for the yearbook), made my choice considerably easier.

One fact upsets me: many worthy games were left out. This happened before, but only now did I get the idea to give you the list of "eliminated" games, so that you can play through them as well. Here it is (winners in italic): *Keres* – Boleslavsky, *Lipnitsky* – Geller, Boleslavsky – *Aronin*, Aronin – *Geller*, *Tolush* – Mikenas, Bondarevsky – *Smyslov*, Borisenko – *Alatortsev*, *Lipnitsky* – Smyslov and a very sharp duel between Petrosian and Smyslov that ended in a draw.

First Brilliancy Prize

Suetin: "Boleslavsky was once asked to name his favorite game in the *Shakhmaty v SSSR* editor's office. After thinking for a while, he named this one. Why? I think that its content will explain." I'll add that Isaak Efremovich called this game "the best in his whole life" in an interview.

No. 220. King's Indian Defense A53
Alatortsev – Boleslavsky
Moscow 1950, round 6
Annotated by I. Boleslavsky
1.d4 ♘f6 2.c4 d6 3.♘c3 (*3.♘f3 – see game 250*) **3...e5 4.e4.** A problematic continuation. White is trying to prove that a solid center prevents the opponent from exploiting his development advantage. But from the practical point of view, this move gives black good counterchances and is thus used very rarely.

Black does not fear either 4.dxe5 dxe5 5.♕xd8+ ♔xd8= or 4.d5 ♗e7 (Makogonov – Boleslavsky, Sverdlovsk 1943), but the move 4.♘f3 is more popular (see game 155 in volume 2). "Alatortsev's move is the start of the development plan recommended by him." (Levenfish.) "Currently, this move, fashionable in the 1940s, has almost disappeared from practice. And this game played a major role in that." (Suetin)

4...exd4 5.♕xd4 ♘c6 6.♕d2. *6.♕d1 was already unsuccessfully tried in a game between the same opponents (Alatortsev – Boleslavsky, 1942 Moscow championship).*

6...g6 7.b3 ♗g7 8.♗b2 0-0 9.♗d3. A bad move. White's plan involving kingside castling didn't work. He had to castle long instead *(after 9.0-0-0, 9...a5 is a good reply; or 9.♘ge2 a5! Kan – Boleslavsky, Sverdlovsk 1943).*

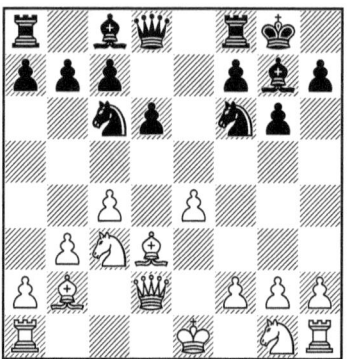

9...♘g4! Now, after 10.♘ge2, there's 10...♘ce5 *(or the immediate 10...♕h4!, as in the "immortal" game Polugaevsky – Nezhmetdinov, Sochi 1958)* 11.♗c2 ♕h4 12.♘g3 *(12. ♕f4 and ♕g3 is better)* 12...♘xh2 with strong threats. If 10.0-0-0, then 10...f5 11.exf5 ♖xf5! 12.♗xf5 ♗xf5 with an attack. White is forced to develop the knight to f3, even though it goes against the spirit of the position.

Annotating the game for the tournament book, Boleslavsky corrected the second line: 11...♘b4 12.♗e4, and only now 12...♖xf5! 13.♗xf5 ♗xf5 "with a very strong attack". Both he and Suetin (in the book Grandmaster Boleslavsky*) missed that instead of 13.♗xf5?, white can stop the attack with 13.♘h3! – here, after 13...♗h6? 14.f4, black can even lose! At any rate, it's not that*

important, because after 11.f4!, black has nothing.

10.♘f3 ♘ge5 11.♗e2. 11.♘xe5 dxe5 12.♘e2 was more prudent, with only a minimal advantage for black. White only worsens his position by trying to keep his advantage in the center.

11...♘xf3+　12.♗xf3　♘d4 13.♗d1 f5 14.exf5 ♗xf5.

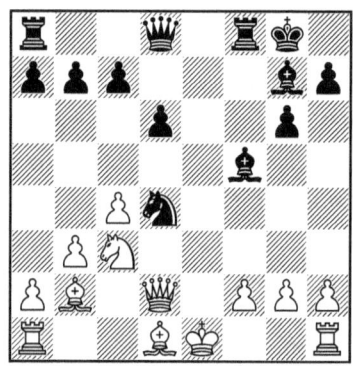

15.♘e2? White doesn't sense the danger. He had to castle immediately, and black would have played 15...c5, strengthening the d4 knight.

15...♘xe2 16.♗xe2. Leads to a quick defeat. 16.♗xg7 was the lesser evil; black planned to meet this with 16...♘f4! Now, after 17.♗xf8, there's 17...♕f6! 18.f3 (best; if 18.0-0, then 18...♕g5) 18...♖e8+ 19.♔f2 ♘d3+ *(19...♕g5! wins immediately)* 20.♔g3 g5!, and there's no defense to the killer queen check on e5.

The best continuation for white is 17.♕xf4 ♕e7+ 18.♗e5 (after 18.♗e2 ♔xg7, black has a strong attack; *18... ♕xg7! with the idea 19.0-0 ♗b1! 20.♕c1 ♕xa1 is much stronger)* 18...

dxe5 *(18...♖ae8, recommended by Boleslavsky in the tournament book, is weaker)* 19.♕e3 ♕b4+ 20.♕d2 a5 21.a3 ♕xd2+ 22.♔xd2 ♖ad8+ 23.♔e1 ♖d4, even though black's advantage is still undeniable in this case.

16...♗xb2 17.♕xb2 ♕g5! Now, castling will be met with 18...♗h3.

"Boleslavsky is in his element. A series of brilliant moves follows, deciding the game." (Levenfish)

18.g3 ♖ae8! *"18...♗h3 was tempting, but after 19.f4 and 0-0-0, white is out of danger." (Levenfish)*

Дружеский шарж Ю. Узбякова

Гроссмейстер
И. БОЛЕСЛАВСКИЙ.

Boleslavsky armed and dangerous. Cartoon by Y. Uzbyakov. From the Sovietsky Sport newspaper (23rd November 1950).

19.0-0 ♗h3 20.f4. Had the rook retreated, black would have won with a sacrifice on f2, for instance: 20.♖fc1 ♖xf2! 21.♔xf2 ♕e3+ 22.♔e1 ♗g4 23.♖c2 ♕g1+, and black wins.

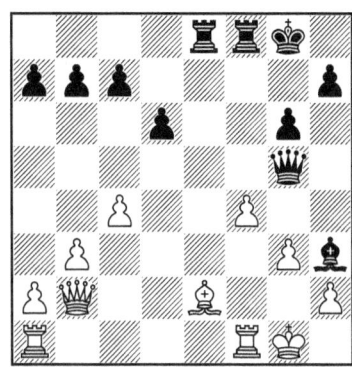

20...♗xf1! The queen sacrifice is the strongest continuation of the attack. After 20...♕c5+ 21.♖f2, white could still hold.

"An unexpected and spectacular queen sacrifice. Black gets a rook and bishop for the queen, but the interaction of these pieces works wonders." (Levenfish)

21.fxg5 ♖xe2 22.♕c3. Black's task would have been somewhat more difficult after 22.♕d4. But even here, after 22...♗h3 23.♕h4 ♗g2 24.♖e1 ♖xa2 25.♕g4 ♗f3 26.♕e6+ ♖f7 27.♕h3 ♗c6 28.b4 ♖f5 29.b5 ♖g2+ 30.♕xg2 ♗xg2 31.♔xg2 ♖xg5, black got a won endgame.

Suetin repeated this line in his book, again not noticing that the correct move was 25...♖f5!, since after 25...♗f3?, there's a draw on the board: instead of 26.♕e6+ ♖f7 27.♕h3?, white has 27.♕e8+ ♖f8 (but not 27...♔g7? 28.♖e7, winning) 28.♕e6+ etc.

22...♗g2! *With a crushing "windmill" threat: 23...♗c6 and ♖g2+.*

23.♕d3. After 23.♖e1, black won with 23...♗h3 and ♖ef2, exchanging everything. *According to Levenfish, "Boleslavsky calculated beforehand that the pawn ending was easily won for black."*

23...♗f3 24.♖f1. After 24.♔f1, there's 24...♖xh2 25.♕d4 c5 26.♕c3 (26.♕xd6 ♗c6+ 27.♔e1 ♖h1+ and ♖xa1) 26...♗c6+ *(there's a beautiful mate after 26...♗e2+! 27.♔e1 ♖f1+ 28.♔d2 ♗xc4+ 29.♔e3 ♖e2#)* 27.♔e1 ♖f3 28.♕a5 ♖h1+ etc.

24...♖g2+ 25.♔h1 ♗c6! 26.♖xf8+ ♔xf8 27.♕f1+ ♖f2+. White resigned.

Second Brilliancy Prize

Panov: "Bondarevsky's attack was brilliant. He chose an original line with white in the Albin Countergambit against Mikenas. After opposite-side castling, white created a strong piece attack on the queenside, where the black king was hiding, with an unexpected, deeply planned exchange sacrifice..."

No. 221. Albin Countergambit D09
Bondarevsky – Mikenas
Moscow 1950, round 10
Annotated by I. Bondarevsky
1.d4 d5 2.c4 e5. This gambit move rarely occurs in practice and is little developed in modern theory.

3.dxe5 d4 4.♘f3 ♘c6 5.g3. Fianchettoing the king's bishop when the central squares d5 and e4 are weakened is the most logical continuation.

5...♗g4. Black wants to develop his queenside quickly and start some activity before white finishes his development.

6.♘bd2 ♕d7 7.♗g2 0-0-0 8.h3. A useful move *(though 8.0-0 was played more often).* Now black should determine his bishop's position. If 8...♗h5, white had a solid position after castling.

While after 8...♗e6 9.a3 ♘ge7 10.b4 ♘g6 (Podolny – Mikenas, Vilnius 1949), the improvement 11.♕a4! was probably planned.

8...♗f5 9.a3 f6. Black, in accordance with the gambit spirit, hurries to open the central files for his pieces, but this gets refuted in an unexpected way. 9...♘ge7 10.b4 ♘g6 was better.

"White's threat to deploy his queenside forces with b2-b4, ♗b2 and b4-b5 forces black to forego the quiet maneuver ♘ge7-g6. For instance: 9...♘ge7 10.b4 ♘g6 11.♗b2 d3 (or 11...♘gxe5 12.b5 ♘xf3+ 13.♘xf3 ♘a5 14.♕a4, with a clear advantage for white) 12.e3 ♖e8 13.♕a4 ♔b8 14.b5, and white's attack quickly grows." (Konstantinopolsky)

10.exf6 ♘xf6 11.b4 ♖e8. *"A very tempting move, creating a strong threat ♗d3. Bondarevsky's counter-combination is so original and bold that it's hard to blame black for making his*

11ᵗʰ move and going for the line that begins with 9...f6." (Konstantinopolsky)

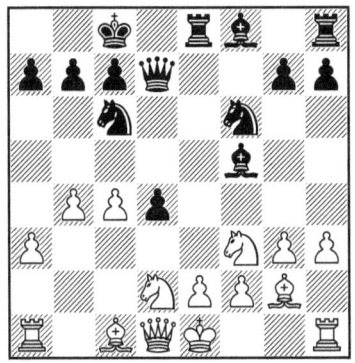

12.♗b2‼ *"A deep idea! White gives up the e2 pawn and the*

Гроссмейстер
И. БОНДАРЕВСКИЙ
Дружеский шарж
М. КУКУНОВА.

It's hard to surprise Bondarevsky with a gambit. Cartoon by M. Kukunov. From the tournament bulletin (27ᵗʰ December 1950).

exchange, completes the development of his pieces and organizes a quick attack on the black king with his incredibly strong bishops. Black still could have averted the catastrophe with 12...d3, but probably considered his calculations to be more correct." (Konstantinopolsky)

It's hard to believe, but it's already impossible to avoid a catastrophe: 13.e3 ♔b8 14.b5 ♘d8 15.g4! ♗g6 16.♘e5, and after 17.♘xg6 and ♘f3, black loses the d3 pawn.

12...♗d3 13.0-0! White is forced to give up an exchange, but he intended exactly that when he made his previous move.

13...♗xe2 14.♕a4   ♗xf1 15.♖xf1. Even though black is an exchange up, white has everything ready for an attack on the king, which is developing with great force.

15...♔b8 16.b5 ♘d8 17.♘xd4.

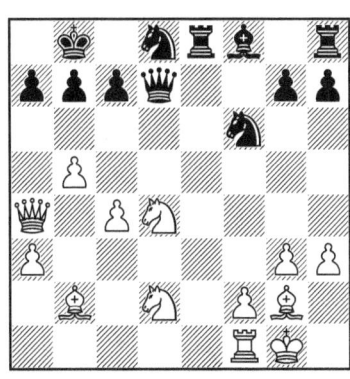

17...♗c5. *"Black has no better move."* (Konstantinopolsky)

Now the attack plays itself. However, with 17...♘e6!?, black could have tempted his opponent to make the fancy move 18.♗c6 which is actually pointless: 18...♘c5 19.♗xd7 ♘xa4 20.♗xe8 ♘xb2 etc. While after 18.♘xe6 ♖xe6, white had to find the only move 19.♖d1! (preventing the black knight from going to c5) that leads to the goal: 19...♖d6 20.♕c2 ♖d3 (c4-c5 was a threat) 21.♗f1 ♖d6 22.♗e5! ♖e6 23.♘f3 and c4-c5, or 19...♕e8 20.♗d4! ♖a6 21.♕c2 ♖e6 22.♘f3 ♘e4 23.c5, or, finally, 19...♗d6 20.♗d4! b6 21.♘b3 and ♘a5.

18.♘2b3 ♗xd4 19.♗xd4 b6 *(19...a6 20.♕a5!)* **20.c5 ♖e7.** This loses quickly, but after 20...♖e6 21.cxb6 cxb6 22.♗e3 ♘d5 23.♖d1, black couldn't save the game either.

"Black could prolong the struggle only by returning the exchange: 20...♖e4 21.♗xe4 ♘xe4 22.cxb6 axb6 23.♗xb6 cxb6 24.♕xe4 ♕xb5 or 20...♖e6 21.cxb6 cxb6 22.♗e3 ♖xe3 23.fxe3 ♖e8, still remaining a pawn down in a worse position." (Konstantinopolsky)

The computer considers all three moves – ♖e7, ♖e6, ♖e4 – equally bad...

21.cxb6 cxb6 22.♗xb6! axb6 23.♕a8+ ♔c7 24.♕a7+ ♔d6 25.♖d1+ ♔e5 26.♖xd7 ♘xd7 27.♕c7+ ♔e6 28.♘d4+ ♔f7 29.♘f5 ♖e1+ 30.♔h2 ♖d1 31.♕c2. Black resigned.

Third Brilliancy Prize

Geller: "Black had to overcome a huge temptation – white's unprotected central e5 pawn – but it was too unbearable for him. All in all, this game has the character and some traits of a miniature, which cannot be played without 'help' from the opponent."

Funnily enough, neither Geller nor other analysts managed to find the move that served as that "help". Only a computer finally managed to do that! You may ask why I didn't use Efim Petrovich's own annotations from Yakov Damsky's book *Grandmaster Geller*. The reason is simple: they are not original; in essence, these are "artistically processed" notes from the tournament book (probably by the book's author, not by Geller himself). And if that's really so, it's better to go to the original source.

No. 222. French Defense C18
Geller – Sokolsky
Moscow 1950, round 10
Annotated by M. Bonch-Osmolovsky
1.e4 e6 2.d4 d5 3.♘c3 ♗b4 4.e5 c5 5.a3 ♗xc3+ 6.bxc3 ♘e7 7.♕g4. *Much more aggressive than 7.♘f3 (see game 167 in volume 2) and 7.a4 (see ibid., games 139 and 150).*

7...cxd4. Since the game Ragozin – Botvinnik (Moscow 1935), this continuation has been considered the strongest for black.

Later, the preferred move order for black was 7...♕c7 8.♕xg7 ♖g8 9.♕xh7 cxd4, to meet 8.♗d3 with 8...c4.

8.♗d3! This move first occurred in the game Bonch-Osmolovsky –

Khasin (Moscow 1949). While after the usual 8.♕xg7 ♖g8 9.♕xh7 ♕c7 10.♘e2 ♘bc6 11.f4 white retains the pawn at the cost of being somewhat behind in development, the game move sacrifices a pawn to maintain the initiative.

8...♕c7. Another possible move is 8...♕a5 9.♘e2 0-0, and it's hard for white to create an attack.

9.♘e2 dxc3. In a later game (Lvov 1951), Rovner tried 9...♕xe5 against Bonch-Osmolovsky. There followed 10.♗f4! (Panov's recommendation 10.cxd4 is weaker due to 10...h5! 11.♕h4 ♕c7, and white can't break down his opponent's pawn set-up)

Efim Geller. From the author's archive.

10...h5 11.♕h4 ♘f5 12.♕g5 ♕f6 13.♕xf6 gxf6 14.♗xf5 exf5, and after 15.♗xb8 white got an advantage in the endgame, despite his opponent's extra pawn.

"He also has a better endgame after 10...♕f6 11.cxd4 h5 12.♕g3 ♘bc6 13.♗g5 ♘f5 14.♗xf6 ♘xg3 15.♗xg7 ♖g8 16.hxg3 ♖xg7 17.♖xh5." (Geller)

10.♕xg7 ♖g8 11.♕xh7 ♕xe5? Winning a central pawn is tempting, but after that, white's dark-squared bishop enters the game with decisive strength. By playing 11...♘bc6, black forced 12.f4 *(12.♗f4!, Unzicker – Uhlmann, Varna 1962, is sharper and more principled)*, restricting the c1 bishop, and could choose between 12...♖xg2 and 12...♗d7! with the subsequent 0-0-0!.

12.♗f4 ♕f6. Another move is 12...♕h8 13.♕xh8 ♖xh8 14.♗e5 ♖f8 15.♗xc3 ♘bc6 16.f4 etc.

The correct move is 16.♗f6! and h2-h4. But this cramped position could be avoided with 15...f6!, holding. So, 14.♘xc3, with a somewhat better endgame, is more promising.

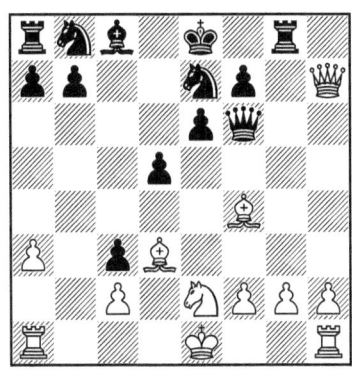

13.h4! The idea of this pawn push is not new, but in this situation, because of the dark-squared bishop's support, it becomes much stronger.

Levenfish assigned two exclamation marks to this move: "This is the essence of Geller's whole novelty. After 13...♖h8, there's 14.♗g5 ♖xh7 15.♗xf6, and the pawn advances."

13...♘bc6. If 13...e5, then 14.♗g5 ♕g7 15.♕xg7 ♖xg7 16.♗f6 (16.♘xc3!?) or 14...♕b6 15.♗xe7 ♖xg2 16.♗g5 ♕xf2+ 17.♔d1 with an extra piece.

By prolonging the line by one move – 17...♗g4! (Geller missed it too),

we see that the attempt to save the piece – 18.♖e1? – fails spectacularly: 18...♔d7! 19.♕h8 (19.♕g8 ♘c6! 20.♕xa8 ♗xe2+ 21.♗xe2 ♖xg5 is even worse) 19...♘c6! 20.♕f6 ♕xf6 21.♗xf6 ♖f2! 22.♗g5 e4 23.♗b5 a6, and after this bishop gets traded away the pin on e2 wins the game. Thankfully, white has a perpetual check: 18.♕h8+ ♔d7 19.♕d8+ ♔c6 20.♔c1!! (the only move) 20...♗xe2 21.♕c8+ ♔d6 (not 21...♔b6? 22.♗d8#) 22.♕f8+ etc.

However, after the simple 15.0-0! (instead of 15.♗xe7), threatening ♗xe7, black's position is rather difficult: 15...♘bc6 16.♖ab1 or 15...e4 16.♗xe4 dxe4 17.♗xe7 ♕g6 18.♕xg6 ♖xg6 19.♗g5 etc. So, the move 13...e5? is incorrect, but other moves were tested later: 13...♖xg2 14.♔f1 ♖g8 or, most often, 13...♘d7 14.♗g5 ♕h8.

14.♗g5 ♕e5 15.♕h6. White plays consistently: the queen is transferred to f6 to give way to the h-pawn.

However, subsequent practice showed that the immediate 15.f4! poses much more trouble.

15...♗d7 16.♕f6 ♖c8. White's threats are so strong that such developing moves are inappropriate. Black could complicate the game with 16...♕xf6 17.♗xf6 e5, for instance: 18.h5 e4 19.♗b5 ♗f5.

But after 20.♖b1!, it's unlikely he can hold. Instead of 17...e5?, 17...d4 is better, with the idea ♘d5, and the immediate 16...d4! is even stronger, with the whole struggle still ahead.

17.f4! ♕e3. *The key moment that went unnoticed by all commentators. After 17...♕xf6 18.♗xf6 d4!, the game could have gotten a prize... for best defense!*

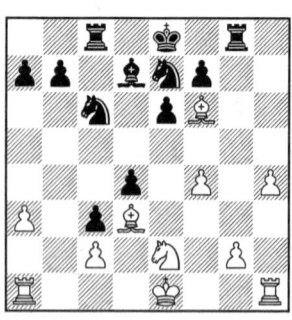

White has to trade one of the bishops, and the attack fizzles out: 19.♗xd4?! (19.♘xd4? ♘d5 is better for black) 19...♘xd4 20.♘xd4 ♘d5 21.♘e2 ♖xg2 or 19.♗e4 ♘d5 20.♗xd5 exd5 21.h5 ♗f5 22.h6 ♗xc2! 23.h7 ♗xh7 (the bishop sacrifice is forced but sufficient) 24.♖xh7♖xg2 etc.

After 17...♕e3?, however, there's no salvation...

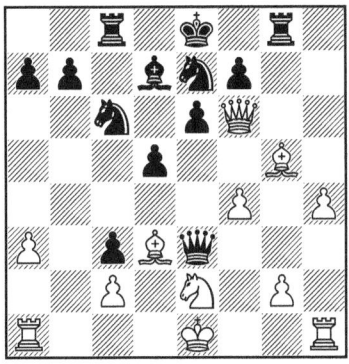

18.h5 e5 19.h6 e4 20.♗b5 ♖xg5. Hoping for 21.♕xg5? ♘d4 (in fact, 22.h7! still wins), but...

21.h7! ♗g4 (if 21...♖xg2, then 22.♕h8+) **22.♕xg5 ♕d2+ 23.♔f1 ♗xe2+ 24.♗xe2 ♘d4 25.h8=♕+.** The white pawn's victory march has ended, and black resigned.

"A theoretically valuable game, very well-played by white." (Panov)

"Come On, Kazimirych!"

Taimanov: "Tolush had his signature attacking techniques. Alexander Kazimirovich was incredibly adept at destroying the pawn covers of castling positions.

Tolush was especially celebrated as a g7 square specialist! He was ready to give up everything to get the opponent's king under the fire of his pieces."

No. 223
Tolush – Sokolsky
Moscow 1950, round 14
Annotated by A. Tolush

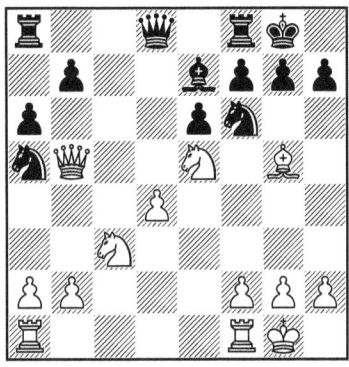

15.♕e2! ♘d5. Of course, not 15...♕xd4 due to 16.♖ad1, and white gets a decisive advantage: 16...♕b4 17.a3 ♕b3 18.♖d3! *(18.♘d7!?)* or 16...♕a7 17.♘d7 *(17.♘e4!)* 17... ♖fd8 *(17...♘xd7 18.♗xe7 b5 is more stubborn)* 18.♘xf6+ ♗xf6 19.♗xf6 gxf6 20.♕g4+ ♔h8 21.♕h4 etc.

16.♗d2 ♖c8 17.♖ad1 ♘c6. 17... b5 was worse, since after 18.♘xd5 black is forced to recapture with the pawn.

18.♗c1 ♘xc3. The starting stage of the struggle was clearly in black's favor, since white is constantly facing trouble in the center, so the most logical move here was 18... ♗f6, increasing the pressure on the d4 pawn and threatening the

Дружеский шарж
И. Соколова и И. Рублева

Мастер А. ТОЛУШ.

Alexander Tolush, the attacking genius. Cartoon by I. Sokolov and I. Rublev. From the Sovietsky Sport newspaper (30th November 1950).

unexpected 19...♘xd4 20.♖xd4 ♖xc3 21.bxc3 (21.♖xd5 ♕xd5 22.bxc3 ♕xe5) 21...♘xc3 etc. with an extra pawn *(more precisely, two extra pawns, but this threat is illusory – 21.♘xf7! maintains the balance).*

Black's continuation gives white the necessary respite in defense of the d4 pawn, and now he can organize a kingside attack.

19.bxc3 b5 *(black could still keep the advantage with 19...♘xe5! 20.dxe5 ♕a5)* **20.♖d3 ♕d5** *(20...♘xe5!)* **21.♘g4.** *"Now white avoids simplifications." (Panov)*

21...♖fd8 *(the immediate 21...b4 or 21...♗d6 taking away the g3 square*

from the rook was better) **22.♖g3 b4?** Black is too careless. He had to play 22...g6. The game move gets refuted spectacularly.

23.♘h6+ ♔f8.

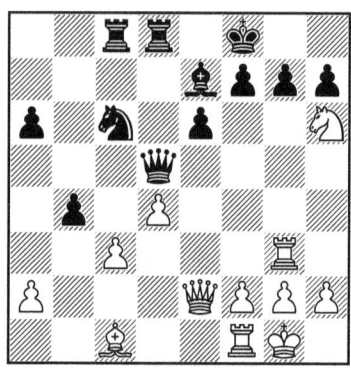

24.♖xg7! The rook sacrifice that black is forced to accept gives white a strong attack.

Panov (and Romanovsky) gave two exclamation marks to the move: "White wins the game with a brilliant Chigorin-like combination."

24...♔xg7 25.♕g4+ ♗g5. The only move that prevents an immediate loss. 25...♔f8 or 25...♔h8 doesn't work because of the mate in one, and after the last remaining move, 25...♔f6, white wins easily with the following line: 26.c4 ♕a5 27.d5! *("A purely problem-like idea!" – Panov)* 27...♖xd5 (27...exd5 28.♗g5+ ♔g7 29.♗xe7+, mating) 28.cxd5 ♕xd5 29.♕f4+ ♔g7 30.♕xf7+ ♔h8 31.♗b2+.

26.c4 ♕xd4. After 26...♕a5, the simplest is 27.d5!, and black can't defend the lonely king; 27.♗xg5 ♖xd4 28.♕g3 ♔f8 29.♗f6 is also possible.

27.♕xg5+ ♔f8 28.♗e3. The

most simple and logical finishing touch here was 28.♕g8+ ♔e7 29.♕xf7+ ♔d6 30.♗f4+ ♘e5 (not 30...e5 31.♘f5+ or 30...♔c5 31.♗e3) 31.♘g4, winning.

28...♕h8. The only move. If the queen retreated somewhere else, there would follow 29.♗c5+ ♔e8 30.♕g8+ and ♕xf7+.

29.♗c5+ ♔e8 30.♘g4 ♔d7. *30...♖d3!? 31.♘f6+ ♔d8 could prolong the struggle.*

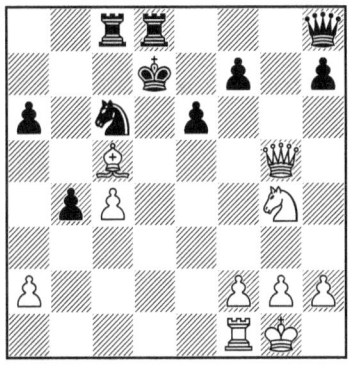

31.♗b6. As Panov correctly stated in the bulletin, white should have played 31.♕f4!, winning immediately because of the double threat of 32.♘f6+ and 32.♕xf7+. The only reply 31...♖c7 is met with 32.♗b6, and after 32...♖b7, white wins with 33.♕xf7+ ♔c8 34.♕xe6+ ♔b8 35.♕xc6.

31...♖b8 *(31...f5 32.♘h6!)* **32.♖d1+ ♔e8 33.♗xd8.** 33.♘f6+! ♕xf6 34.♕g8+ and ♗c5+ wins immediately.

33...♖xd8 34.♖xd8+ ♘xd8 35.♘f6+ ♔f8. Loses by force, so black had to play 35...♔e7 36.♘d5+

♔d6 37.♕e7+ ♔e5 38.♘xb4 *(38. ♕c5! is stronger)* 38...♔f5. Black still can't save the game, because his pieces are placed very badly, but it was the best practical chance.

36.♕c5+ ♔g7 37.♘h5+ ♔h6 (37...♔g8 38.♕g5+ and ♕xd8#) **38.h4 ♕a1+** *(38...f6 39.g4!)* **39.♔h2 f6 40.♘f4.** Black resigned. After 40... ♔g7 41.♕e7+ ♘f7 42.♘xe6+ ♔g6 43.h5+ he loses a piece.

"This is probably the most beautiful game of the tournament." (Panov)

Time-Trouble Mistakes

Panov: "The first leadership change happened in this round. In the tense game Aronin – Smyslov, white kept the initiative for a while, but after 19.♕d6 (19.cxb5 was better), the grandmaster gradually built up his activity. Smyslov won two pawns and then the whole game in the play-off, taking the lead."

No. 224
Aronin – Smyslov
Moscow 1950, round 9
Annotated by V. Smyslov

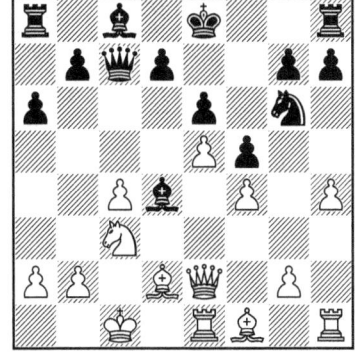

15...b5! Black's counter-attack involves opening lines on the queenside. After 16.cxb5 axb5 17.♕xb5 black can play 17...♗xc3 18.♗xc3 ♘xf4, regaining the pawn *(with a clear advantage)*.

16.h5 ♘e7 17.♕d3 ♗f2 *(17...♕xc4!?)* **18.♖d1 ♗b7 19.♕d6.** *The computer (and Panov in the bulletin) recommends 19.cxb5, while after 19.♕d6, there's 19...♕xd6!? 20.exd6 ♘c8 with a roughly equal game.*

19...♕c8. Avoiding the queen sacrifice, black is planning to meet 20.cxb5 with 20...♗c5 21.♕d3 axb5 or 21...♘d5, with good attacking chances.

Later, in the book Selected Games, *Smyslov noticed that after 20.cxb5, there was a much stronger reply 20...♘d5! 21.bxa6 ♗xa6, "threatening to trap the opponent's queen with ♗c5." While after 21.♕a3 axb5 22.♕b3 b4, white loses a knight without any compensation.*

20.♖h3! A strong defensive maneuver. After 20...bxc4, white eliminates black's dangerous bishop with 21.♗e3 ♗xe3+ 22.♖xe3.

20...♗c5 21.♕d3 bxc4 22.♕xc4 ♘d5 23.♘xd5 *(23.♔b1!)* **23...♗xd5 24.♕c2 ♕b7! 25.♔b1.** After 25.♖c3, there could follow 25...♗d4 26.♖c7 ♗xb2+ 27.♔b1 ♕b8.

25...♖c8 26.♖c3. *26.♗c3!? was worthy of consideration.*

Дружеский шарж
И. Соколова и И. Рублева

Гроссмейстер В. СМЫСЛОВ.

Vasily Smyslov played this game in his best style. Cartoon by I. Sokolov and I. Rublev. From the Sovietsky Sport newspaper (5th December 1950).

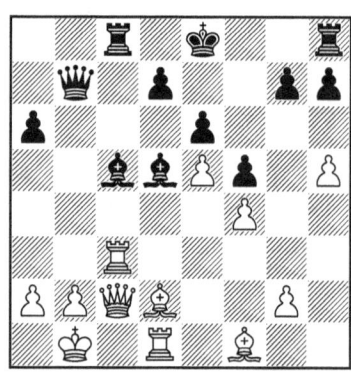

26...♔f7! Successfully completing development. After 26...0-0, there could follow 27.♖c1 ♗e4 28.♗d3 ♗xd3 29.♕xd3 ♗e7 with simplifications. Now, 27.♖c1 can be met with 27...♗d4 28.♖xc8 ♖xc8 with unstoppable threats.

The computer insists on 26...0-0! with an attack, since 27.♖c1? is bad due to 27...♗d4!! 28.♖xc8 ♗e4 29.♖xf8+ ♔xf8 30.b3 (the point of the combination is that the b2 square is not protected: 30.♗d3? ♗xd3 31.♕xd3 ♕xb2#) 30...♗xc2+ 31.♖xc2 g5, etc.

27.♗c1. After this natural-looking move, white gets into trouble. Of course, he couldn't play 27.♖xc5 due to 27...♗e4. He had to play 27.♗c4, and if 27...♗e4, then 28.♗d3 ♗d4 29.♗xe4 fxe4 30.♖b3! So, black would have met 27.♗c4 with 27...♗xc4 28.♖xc4 ♗e7.

27...♗b4 28.♖xc8. *It was time to sharpen the game with 28.♖c4!, exploiting the king's exposed position on f7.*

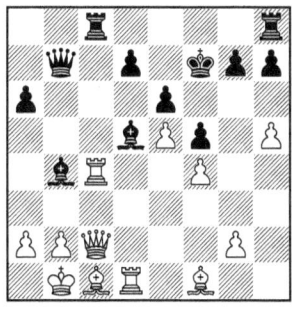

For instance: 1) 28...♗xc4 29.♗xc4 ♔e7 (white threatened 30.♕xf5+) 30.g4!, and black can't play 30...fxg4? due to 31.f5 with a strong attack; 2) 28...♔e7 29.g4! ♖hf8 30.gxf5 ♗xc4 31.♗xc4 ♖xf5 32.♕e2=; 3) 28...♗e4 29.♗d3 ♖xc4 30.♕xc4 ♗xg2 31.♕xa6=.

28...♖xc8 29.♕a4 a5 30.♗b5. Defending from the threat 30...♗c6 31.♕b3 a4, white tries to save the game with tactical complications.

Too late! The computer already gives a long line here...

30...♖c5! 31.♗xd7 ♔e7? Both opponents were already in time trouble. 31...♗e4+ 32.♔a1 ♗c2 33.♗xe6+ ♔e7! 34.♖d7+ ♔xe6! was stronger, keeping the extra piece. By missing this opportunity, black makes his task more difficult *(even though the game move is winning too!).*

32.♗e3! After 32.♗e8, black planned 32...♗e4+ 33.♔a1 ♗c2 34.♖d7+ ♔xe8.

32...♕xd7. *Strangely, Smyslov missed the obvious move 32...♖c7! even in his analysis.*

It's all over: 33.a3 ♗e4+ 34.♔a2 ♗c2, winning the rook, or 33.♗b5 ♗e4+ 34.♗d3 ♖d7 35.♕c2 ♖xd3 36.♖xd3 ♕b5 with an extra piece.

33.♕xd7+ ♔xd7 34.a3! A subtle move *(34.♗xc5 ♗xc5 is hopeless)*. Still, even though white regains the piece, black's piece activity gives him a clear advantage.

34...♗xa3 35.bxa3 ♖c3 36.♗c1 ♖g3. Despite the opposite-colored bishops, black still has very real chances. It's hard for white to hold the g2 and h5 pawns, so he decides to double his opponent's pawns along the h-file.

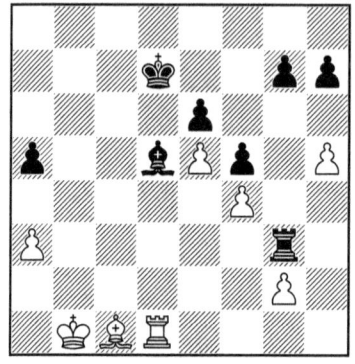

37.h6 gxh6 38.♖h1 ♖g6 39.♖h2 ♗xg2 40.♗d2 a4 41.♗b4 ♗f3. The sealed move. 41...♔c6! 42.♗f8 ♔d5 43.♖xh6 ♖g4 44.♖xh7 ♖xf4 was even stronger.

42.♔c2 h5 43.♖h3 ♖g2+ 44.♔c3 ♖f2 45.♔d4 ♗g4 46.♖d3 ♔c6! Not letting the white king get to c5. After 47.♖c3+, there's 47...♔b7 48.♔c5 ♖d2 49.♔b5 h4!

47.♔c3 ♔b5 (*47...h4!*) **48.♖d6 ♖f3+ 49.♔d2 ♖xf4 50.♖xe6 ♖e4!** Black saddles the white rook with the defense of the e5 pawn, and the black passed pawns quickly decide matters.

51.♔d3 h4 52.♖e7 h3 53.♗d6 h5 54.e6 ♗e2+ 55.♔d2 ♗c4 56.♖h7 ♖d4+. White resigned.

Gambit Passions

V. Vasiliev: "As we know, Keres is a recognized King's Gambit expert. He regularly uses this opening in actual games and dedicated a lot of pages to it in his opening handbook. They say that Keres gave Alatortsev a signed copy of the book with a friendly inscription suggesting to try this promising opening. And while Alatortsev hasn't become a King's Gambit fighter yet, he did take advantage of the gift: his defensive system is indeed one of the strongest 'antidotes' to this opening..."

A nice story, but untrue: Alatortsev couldn't possibly have "taken advantage" of that gift, because the second volume of *Theory of Chess Openings: Open Games* with the chapter on the King's Gambit was only published in 1952! From where then did Vasiliev get the "lot of pages" allegedly dedicated to that gambit? He just made it up. Or, more accurately, this was a conjecture: there was no volume number on the cover of what proved to be the first volume (1949), and he decided that the book encompassed all open games.

No. 225. King's Gambit C35
Keres – Alatortsev
Moscow 1950, round 5
Annotated by V. Alatortsev

1.e4 e5 2.f4. The King's Gambit was M. I. Chigorin's favorite opening; he played it with equal skill both for white and black. In our days, the King's Gambit is successfully used by Bronstein, Keres and Tolush.

2...exf4 3.♘f3 ♗e7. Black uses the defensive system recommended by his opponent – Grandmaster P. Keres.

"Earlier, this move was linked solely with the continuation 4.♗c4 ♗h4+, which is better for white." (Konstantinopolsky)

4.♗c4 ♘f6! Black is trying to castle as soon as possible – it's usually difficult to achieve that in the King's Gambit.

5.e5 ♘g4. *"This line first occurred in the all-Union championships in the game Bronstein – Koblencs (14th Soviet Championship, 1945)." (Romanovsky)*

6.0-0. 6.h3 is bad due to 6...♗h4+ 7.♔f1 ♘f2 8.♕e1 ♘xh1 9.♕xh4 ♘g3+.

6...♘c6! A necessary move, since after 6...d5 there's 7.exd6 ♗xd6 8.♖e1+. Black is preparing the move d7-d5, attacking the e5 pawn with tempo.

7.d4 d5 8.exd6 ♗xd6. Now, after 9.♖e1+ there's 9...♘e7. Black hasn't castled yet, but now it's clear that white isn't able to prevent that.

9.♘c3. *"9.h3 was worthy of serious consideration." (Romanovsky.) For instance: 9...♘e3 10.♗xe3 fxe3 11.♕d3!, eventually capturing the e3 pawn.*

9...0-0 10.♘e2. The black king is safe, and white is trying to at least regain the sacrificed pawn. After 10.♘d5, black has 10...♗e6 (*11.♗b3 g5! – Konstantinopolsky*).

Thus, the correct move was 10.♘e4!

10...♘e3 11.♗xe3 fxe3 12.a3. Seemingly forced. After 12.♕d3, there could follow 12...♘b4! and ♗f5. White still hasn't regained the pawn. Black has two active bishops, and his advantage is obvious.

After 12...♘b4, there's 13.♕e4! ♗d7 (13...♖e8? 14.♗xf7+!) 14.♘e5=. Konstantinopolsky insists on 12.♕d3! ♘a5 13.♗b3 ♘xb3 14.axb3, but after 14...♖e8!, white has no compensation for the pawn.

12...♕f6. Black threatens to transfer the queen to h6 and start a dangerous attack on the white king. 12...♗f5 was also possible (*"but then 13.♗d3, and white's queenside pawns are on the move" – Konstantinopolsky*).

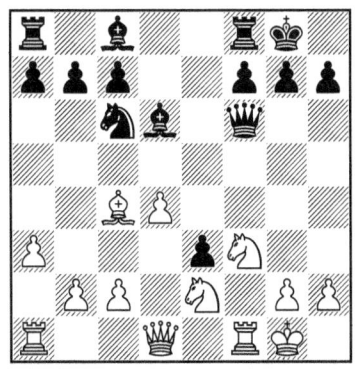

13.♕d3. Only the move 13.♘e5! could lead to some counterplay, even though after 13...♕h6 14.♖xf7! ♖xf7! (*14...♗e6, recommended by Keres in* Theory of Chess Openings, *was weaker due to 15.♗xe6! ♕xe6 16.♘f4 ♕e8 17.♖xf8+ ♕xf8*

18.♕f3!=), black still retained his advantage: 15.♘xf7 ♕xh2+ 16.♔f1 ♗e6 *(16...♔f8! 17.♘xd6 ♗h3! 18.♗d5 ♔e7! wins spectacularly)* 17.♗xe6 (if 17.♘xd6, then 17... ♖f8+) 17...♖f8 with the threat ♘d8 or 15.♗xf7+ ♔h8 16.♗b3 *(16. ♘g3 ♕f4!)* 16...♗xe5 17.dxe5 ♗g4 18.h3 ♘xe5 19.hxg4 ♘xg4 with an unstoppable attack.

In the last line, 19.♕d4(f1) prolongs the struggle, and Konstantinopolsky corrected the line: instead of 18...♘xe5, "black gets a decisive advantage" with 18...♖d8! 19.♕e1 ♗xe2 20.♕xe2 ♘d4! and e3-e2.

13...♕h6 14.♖ae1 ♗g4 15.h3. White should have played 15.♘g3.

15...♗h5! 16.♘c3 ♖ae8 *(with a lethal threat 17...♗g3, ♗f2+ and ♗xf3)* **17.♘d5.** Missing black's next move.

Incredibly, it was at this moment that white could have repelled the attack and got some practical chances to save the game: 17.♘e4! ♗f4 (17... ♔h8? 18.♘fg5!) 18.♘h4!!

The idea that came to the electronic brain is impressive: 18...

e2? 19.♘f5 exf1=♕+ 20.♔xf1. *White is a rook down, but how can black keep the extra material? After 20...♕g6 (20...♗e3+ 21.♖xe3 ♕xe3+ 22.♘xe3 ♖xe4 23.♘f5 is worse) 21.♕xf4 there's a new threat: 22.♘h4 ♕h6 23.♕xh6 and ♘f6+. Black has to settle for 21... ♘xd4 22.♘xd4 ♕b6 23.c3 ♕xb2 with double-edged play.*

Its main line is good too – 18... ♗g4! 19.g3! (the only move) 19... ♗xg3 20.♘xg3 ♕xh4 21.♖xe3 ♖xe3 22.♕xe3 ♗d7!! (the only move too: 22...♕(♗)xh3? 23.♖xf7!) 23.c3 ♕xh3 24.♕f4! or 23.♖f4 ♕xh3 24.♖e4! with some compensation for the lack of material.

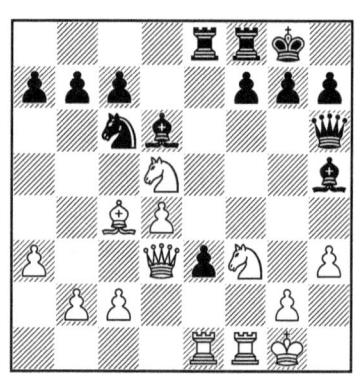

17...e2! The winning move. If 18.♖xe2, then 18...♖xe2 19.♕xe2 ♘xd4! So white decides to give up the exchange.

18.♖f2 ♗g3 19.c3 ♘a5. Threatening to meet 20.♗a2 with 20...c6 21.♘b4 ♖e3!

20.♖exe2 ♗xf2+ 21.♖xf2 ♘xc4 22.♕xc4 c6 23.♘b4 ♗xf3 24.♖xf3 ♕c1+ 25.♔h2 ♕xb2. Now white loses a pawn as well. His position is hopeless.

26.d5 a5 27.♘d3 ♕xa3 28.♖g3 ♕d6 29.♕d4 g6 30.c4 cxd5 31.cxd5 f5 32.♘c5 b6 33.♘b7 ♕c7. White resigned.

Tactics as Strategic Support

In the tournament book, Alexander Markovich Konstantinopolsky – probably out of modesty – assigned only one exclamation mark to his moves. In his best games compilation (1985), he gave out five. But I decided to follow the lead of the "independent expert" Levenfish, who generously awarded six exclams (after combining the two annotations, I got seven overall) and finished his annotation in the yearbook with "An outstanding creative achievement by Konstantinopolsky."

No. 226. Reti Opening A13
Konstantinopolsky – Lipnitsky
Moscow 1950, round 16
Annotated by A. Konstantinopolsky
1.♘f3 ♘f6 2.c4 e6 3.g3 d5 4.b3 c5 5.♗g2 d4. A double-edged move *(5...♘c6 is quieter)*. Black gets solid pawns in the center and good piece development, but white's g2 bishop gets stronger, and after opening the e-file, he manages to seize it with the rooks.

6.0-0 ♘c6 7.e3! *"This position was usually interpreted differently:*

7.d3, 8.e4, 9.♘e1, 10.f4, and black equalized." (Levenfish)

7...e5 8.exd4 exd4 9.a3. To hide his intention to double rooks on the e-file from his opponent, white doesn't immediately play 9.♖e1+.

9...a5. It seems that black would have been better off without this move, immediately developing the bishop to e7 instead.

Levenfish agrees, but later we'll see that the lunge a5-a4 could have become a good "antidote" to white's strategy in the center...

10.d3 ♗e7 11.♖e1 0-0.

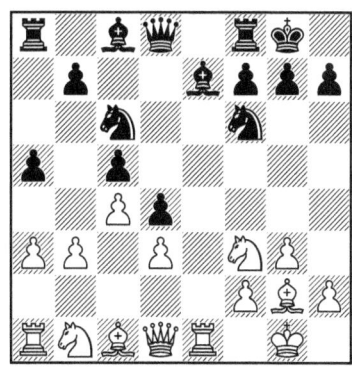

12.♖a2! *"An original and strategically beautiful solution by white – he uses the free artery that leads to the center in the shape of five free squares on the second rank. Konstantinopolsky's maneuver deepens the meaningful, strategic essence of Czech grandmaster Reti's ideas." (Romanovsky)*

12...h6. 12...♗f5 was stronger, to complete development with ♕d7 and ♖fe8 afterwards. Black prevents

♗g5, intending to get his e7 bishop to d6, but it was not necessary.

13.♖ae2 ♗d6 14.♘bd2 ♗e6. Black had to play 14...♗f5 and then meet 15.♘e4 with 15...♘xe4 16.dxe4 ♗e6, or 15.♘f1 with 15...♕d7 and a comfortable position. Also, after 15.♕c2 ♕d7 16.♘h4 ♗g4, black retained his freedom of activity; however, after his 14th and especially 15th move, white manages to seize the initiative.

In his book of selected games, Konstantinopolsky added a comment in brackets after 16...♗e6 in the above note: "White would have played 17.♖f1! and ♘e1-d3 with the idea f2-f4", missing the move 17...a4! (18. bxa4? ♗xc4) that drastically changes the situation on the board.

15.♘h4 ♕d7. White's goal is to trade off the f6 knight with ♘e4 and get his rooks and queen into play. Therefore, black had to play 15... ♗g4, forcing white to play 16.f3 or 16.♗f3 and deviate from his plan.

16.♘e4! ♗e7. Black's position becomes difficult: after 16...♘xe4 there follows 17.♖xe4, then ♕h5 and a bishop sacrifice on h6. If 17...♖fe8 (to meet 18.♕h5 with 18...♗f8), then 18.♕e2, with an unpleasant pin along the e-file.

After 16...♗e7, white trades away the dark-squared bishop (using the weakness of the g6 square) and gets a certain positional advantage.

"A spectacular combination follows. It doesn't gain any material, but increases white's positional advantage." (Levenfish)

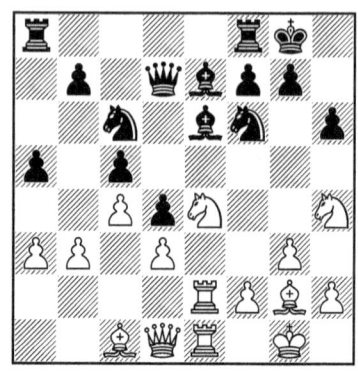

17.♘g6! ♖fe8. The lines 17... fxg6 18.♘xf6+ ♖xf6 19.♖xe6! ♖xe6 20.♖xe6 and 17...♘xe4 18.♘xf8 ♘c3 19.♘xd7 ♘xd1 20.♖xd1 ♗xd7 21.♗xc6 were detrimental for black.

However, the f8 rook should have been put on d8 or c8, because it's X-rayed by the white rooks on e8.

18.♘xe7+ ♕xe7 19.♗f4. 19.♗h3! (19...♖xh3? 20.♘xf6+ ♕xf6 21.♖xe8+ etc.) was stronger – it would be hard for black to untangle.

This is not that clear because of 19...♖f8, but 19.♘xf6+!? ♕xf6 20.♗f4 was worthy of consideration.

19...♖ed8. *Black couldn't ease the pressure with 19...♘xe4 20.♖xe4 ♕f8 21.♕e2 ♗d7 22.♕h5, and after 22... ♖ed8 the bishop breaks through to b6: 23.♗c7 ♖dc8 24.♗b6! f5 25.♖4e2 ♖a6 26.♗d5+ ♔h7 27.♗xc5! ♕xc5 28.♕f7 with a quick win.*

20.♘xf6+ ♕xf6 21.♗e5. White wants to exploit the weakness of the c5 pawn by putting the bishop on b6, but first, he wants to drive the queen away from f6. Since black can now reply 21...♕e7, preventing the bishop from getting to c7, 21.♗c7 was more precise (21...♗g4 22.f3!).

21...♕g6? Black underestimated the strength of the subsequent maneuver (♗c7-b6).

22.♗c7 ♖d7. After 22...♖dc8 23.♗b6 ♗f5 24.♗xc5 ♗xd3 25.♖d2, black lost the d4 pawn (25...♕g5 26.♗d5).

In the bracketed line, white has a much stronger move 26.♗xc6! (26...♕xc5 27.♗xb7 or 26...bxc6 27.♗e7 and ♖xd3). But black needs to play 23...♗g4!, and after 24.f3 holds the position with 24...♗f5 25.♗xc5 ♗xd3 26.♖d2 ♗f5.

23.♗b6 ♗f5. 23...♕h5 24.♖e4 (not 24.♗d5 due to 24...♖xd5! 25.cxd5 ♕xd5) 24...♕g5 25.h4 ♕f5 26.♖f4 is no better. *But 24... ♕xd1 25.♖xd1 a4 is more resilient. Therefore, the correct move is 24.h3!*

And after 23...♗g4, white now has a cunning reply 24.♗f3! ♗xf3 25.♖e8+ ♖xe8 26.♖xe8+ ♔h7 27.♕xf3 f6 28.♖e4! and ♗xc5, with an extra pawn and winning chances.

24.♖e8+ ♖xe8 25.♖xe8+ ♔h7 26.♗e4! *This is actually not the best move. White could keep the advantage with 26.♗f3! (26...♗xd3? 27.♗h5).*

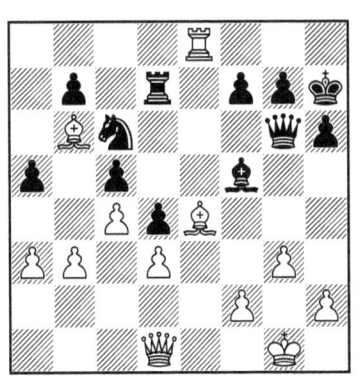

26...♗xe4. *The decisive mistake that was not noticed by anyone! 26... ♘e5! led to drawing simplifications, for instance: 27.♗xc5 ♗xe4 28.♖xe5 ♗xd3 or 27.♖xe5 ♗xe4 28.♖xe4 ♕xb6 etc.*

27.♖xe4 f5. If 27...♕d6, then 28.♕h5, while after 27...♕f5 28.g4 ♕g5 29.f4 ♕h4 (29...♕g6 30.f5) 30.♗xc5 f5 31.gxf5 ♖f7 32.♗xd4, black has no compensation for the lost pawns.

The bracketed move 29...♕g6! 30.f5 ♕d6 is actually correct, while if 30.♗xc5 then 30...f5! 31.♖e1 fxg4. But instead of 28.g4, the right move is 28.♕e2 (Levenfish), and after f2-f4, ♖e8 and ♕e4, the c5 pawn falls.

28.♖e1 ♕d6 29.♕f3 g6 (after 29...♖f7 white wins with 30.♕d5) **30.♕f4 ♕f8 31.h4 ♖e7.** After 31... ♖f7, white improves his position by playing 32.♖e6 and then, when the right moment comes, ♖(♕)d6 or h4-h5.

Now white trades the major pieces and finally captures the c5 pawn.

32.♖xe7+ ♕xe7 33.♕c7 ♕xc7 34.♗xc7 ♔g8 35.♗d6. 35.♗b6 ♘e5 36.♗xc5 ♘xd3 37.♗xd4 ♘c1! was worse.

35...b6. 35...♔f7 36.♗xc5 ♔e6 was relatively better.

36.♗c7 ♔f7 37.♗xb6 ♘e5 38.♗xc5 ♘xd3 39.♗xd4 ♘c1 40.♗e3! ♘xb3 41.a4! Now the knight is cut off, and the white king threatens to approach it (for instance, after 41...h5).

41...♔e6. Black sealed this move

and then resigned without resuming the game because he will end up minus two pawns.

Blow for Blow!

Levenfish: "A game of great magnitude, worthy of the Chigorin tournament because of the depth of ideas created by both opponents."

No. 227. Ruy Lopez C99
Aronin – Tolush
Moscow 1950, round 15
Annotated by L. Aronin
1.e4 e5 2.♘f3 ♘c6 3.♗b5 a6 4.♗a4 ♘f6 5.0-0 ♗e7 6.♖e1 b5 7.♗b3 0-0 8.c3 d6 9.h3 ♘a5 *(9...♗e6 – see game 165 in volume 2)* **10.♗c2 c5 11.d4 ♕c7 12.♘bd2 cxd4 13.cxd4 ♗b7.**

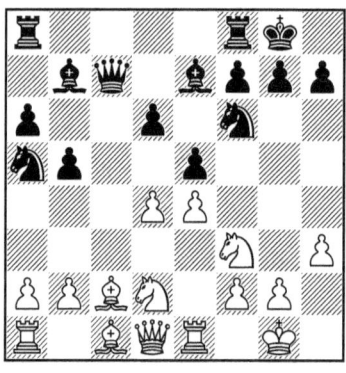

This line of the Chigorin Defense was introduced into practice by master V. Panov. The idea of this continuation is to meet 14.♘f1 with a counter-strike in the center: 14...d5 *(14...♖ac8 – see game 237)* with the possible continuations: 15.dxe5

♘xe4 16.♘g3 f5 17.exf6 ♗xf6 or 15.exd5 e4! *(15...exd4!?)* 16.♗xe4 *(16.♘g5!)* 16...♘xe4 17.♖xe4 ♗xd5.

14.d5. White made this move to avoid the aforementioned lines. Even though it loses a bit of time, this move more importantly grabs space in the center and restricts the black bishops.

14...♖fc8 *(14...♗c8 – see game 238)* **15.♗d3 ♘d7 16.♘f1 ♘c5** *(16...♘c4!)* **17.♘e3.** White has nothing against trading away the d3 bishop. The course of the game showed that the white knights became very active.

Boleslavsky and Konstantinopolsky, the authors of the opening review in the tournament book, called the bishop trade "a strategic error", because it "makes the queen invasion along the c-file possible. White should have retreated 17.♗b1, threatening 18.b4. If 17...b4, then after 18.b3 the b4 pawn is weak, and the black pieces are stuck on the queenside, while their kingside is not adequately defended." So, the correct move is 17...♘c4! 18.b3 ♘b6 with an acceptable position. On the other hand, the immediate 17.b3! is stronger, cutting off the a5 knight.

17...♘xd3 18.♕xd3 ♘c4 19.♘f5 ♗f8 20.b3 ♘b6 21.♗d2. White forces the reply with the threat 22.♗a5.

21...♘d7. Most of the black pieces are concentrated on the queenside, and, naturally, white is trying to attack the kingside. But this is far from simple in the absence of any weaknesses of the black king's pawn cover. White's next move causes such a weakness to appear.

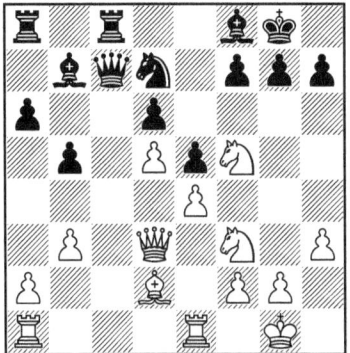

22.♘g5 h6 *(22...g6!?)* **23.♘f3 ♔h7** (intending to kick away the second knight as well with g7-g6) **24.♘3h4!** Now after 24...g6 there's 25.♕f3, and, as it's simple to verify, white gets a crushing attack if the knight is captured.

But black isn't forced to capture the knight (25...♘c5=), so the best move was 24...g6 or the immediate 24...♘c5. On the other hand, the queen's excursion that black chooses instead is very risky, as it leaves the f7 square unguarded.

24...♕c2 25.♕e3 ♘c5. Again threatening to trade queens (26... ♕d3).

26.♗b4! *"A subtle move!"* *(Levenfish)* Now 26...♕d3 is impossible due to 27.♗xc5, while if 26...♘d3 there follows 27.♖e2 ♘xb4 28.♖xc2 ♘xc2 29.♕b6! ♘xa1 30.♕xb7 ♔g8 31.♘e7+ ♗xe7 32.♕xe7, and white is better.

26...g6! The only move! After 27.♖e2 black has 27...♕xe4.

But 26...a5! 27.♖e2 ♕xe4 28.♗xc5 ♕xe3 29.♗xe3 g5 30.♘f3 ♗g6 31.g4 ♗xd5 with some compensation for the piece was more resilient.

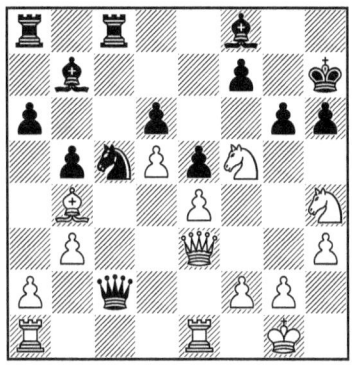

Дружеский шарж
И. Соколова и И. Рублева

Л. Аронин атакует крепость
С. Флора.

"L. Aronin attacks S. Flohr's fortress." He brought down Tolush's fortress as well. Cartoon by I. Sokolov and I. Rublev. From the Sovietsky Sport newspaper (21st November 1950).

27.♕f3! This move makes black face difficult problems *(27.♘xd6! ♗xd6 28.♕f3! ♔g7 29.♖e2 ♕d3 30.♕xd3 ♘xd3 31.♗xd6 with a healthy extra pawn was even better).*

Accepting the sacrifice loses: 27... gxf5 28.♕xf5+ ♔g8 29.♖e3 ♗g7 30.♗xc5 ♖xc5 31.♖g3 ♔h8 (31... ♔f8 32.♕h7) 32.♕xf7 ♖c7 33.♘g6+ ♔h7 34.♘e7!

If black doesn't capture the knight, he has to defend against a number of threats, primarily 28.♘e3 with a blow on f7. All in all, the weakness of the f7 square is the main motif for the subsequent combinations. After 27...♔g8, there can follow 28.♖e2 ♕d3 29.♖e3 ♕c2 30.♕g4 with a subsequent sacrifice on g6 *(30...♘xe4 is unclear here, so the most precise way is 30.♗xc5! ♖xc5 31.♕g4 and ♘xg6).* Trying to protect the f7 square with 27...♖c7 loses to 28.♖e2 ♕d3 29.♖e3 ♕c2 30.♖c3 ♕b2 31.♖ac1 gxf5 (white threatened 32.♖3c2 or 32.♘xd6) 32.♘xf5 *(32.♕xf5+ ♔h8 33.♖3c2 or 33.♗xc5 is the simplest)* 32...♕xa2 33.♕g4 ♕b2 34.♖1c2 ♕b1+ 35.♔h2 with an unstoppable threat ♖g3.

In this difficult position, Tolush finds the only possible, but sufficient move.

27...♘xe4! 28.♖xe4 *(28.♘xd6!? ♘g5 29.♕e3)* **28...♗xd5 29.♖ae1** *(29. ♘g3!=).* The position has sharpened. Black has got some counterchances after his piece sacrifice. He can already restore the material balance, but the position is less defined by the material

and more by whether black can stop white's attack.

29...♖c6. Black had to play 29... ♗xe4 30.♖xe4 d5, and white has three pieces *en prise.*

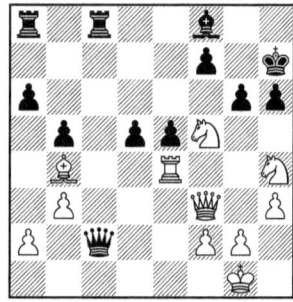

After the game, Tolush said that he looked at this move, but, erroneously thinking that he had an advantage, decided against it because 31.♘d6 could force a draw. Indeed, after 31... dxe4 32.♕xf7+ ♗g7 33.♕xg6+ ♔g8 34.♕e6+ ♔h7 white has nothing but a perpetual check.

But after 31...♖c7! black wins! For instance: 32.♖e3 a5 33.♘xb5 axb4 34.♘xc7 ♕xc7 35.♕xd5 ♖xa2, and there's no 36.♕xe5? due to 36...♕xe5 37.♖xe5 ♖a1+ 38.♔h2 ♗d6.

Does white, however, have any way to play for a win? It seems that the solution is 31.♖e2 ♕d1+ 32.♔h2, and black can't capture on b4 because of 33.♘e3, attacking the queen and f7 square. However, black has a strong Zwischenzug 31...e4!, and white has nothing better than 32.♖xc2 exf3 33.♖xc8 ♖xc8 34.♗xf8 ♖xf8.

Why check on d1, exposing the queen to the threat ♘e3? After 31... ♕c1+, white can't save the game:

32.♖e1 e4 33.♕g3 ♕g5 or 32.♗e1 e4 33.♕g4 (33.♕g3 ♕d1) 33...♕a1! and ♖c1 with a deadly pin.

So, if white did want to continue the fight, he had to go for the following: 31.♖e1 gxf5 (31...♗xb4 is bad due to 32.♘e3! ♕c7 33.♘xd5 and ♘xb4) 32.♕xd5 or even 32.♕h5, sacrificing an exchange to keep up the threats. For instance: 32.♕h5 ♕c7 33.♘xf5 ♗g7 34.♗d6 (32...♖c7 is probably better). Obviously, playing for a win with 31.♖e1 required risk. So black had to go for that continuation.

The bracketed line is drawn after 33...e4!: 34.♖xe4 ♕c1+ and ♗d6+ (but not 34.♕xe4? ♕d6!). On the other hand, the main line is won for white: 34...♕d8 35.♗xe5, 34...♕c2 35.♘xg7 or 34...♕c6 35.♕xf7 ♖g8 36.♘e7! So, 32...♖c7 is indeed "better" – it leads to a draw, but 32...♖a7! 33.♘xf5 ♕c6! is even better, with good winning chances. However, after 32.♘xf5, white can draw easily (32...♕c6 33.♘d6!).

And still, Tolush's intuition didn't let him down: the position after 29.♖ae1 is indeed better for black. Instead of 29...♗xe4, the unassuming 29...a5!! won.

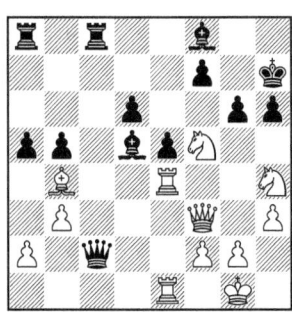

White doesn't have much choice. He can't retreat with the bishop, while capturing on d6 with the knight is bad too, so only 30.♗xd6 remains, but then 30...♖c3! forces the queen trade: 31.♕g4 (31.♘e3 ♕xe4 or 31.♖1e3 ♗xe4) 31...♕xe4 32.♖xe4 h5! 33.♕e2 ♕xe2 34.♖xe2. Now we finally capture the knight – 34...gxf5 35.♗xf8 ♖xf8 36.♖xe5 ♖b8 or 36...♖fc8 37.♖xb5(f5) ♖8c5, and black should convert his extra exchange: white is let down by his weak queenside pawns.

30.♘g3. A temporary retreat to regroup the forces.

The position after 30.♘xg6! fxg6 (30...♗xe4? 31.♘xf8+) 31.♘d4!! hides a treasure trove of combination ideas:

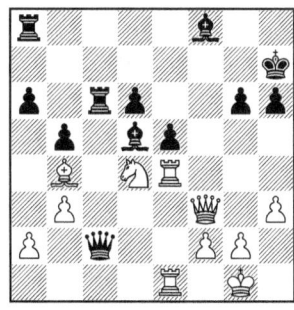

31...exd4? loses to 32.♖e7+ ♔h8 33.♕xd5, while it's not that easy to find the line 31...♕xe4! 32.♖xe4 exd4 33.♖e7+ ♗xe7 34.♕xd5 ♖c1+ 35.♔h2 ♖f8...

30...♗e7. Black was tempted by the opportunity to target the h4 knight, which looks difficult to defend. However, this move gets emphatically refuted. 30...♗g7 was better.

31.♖d1!

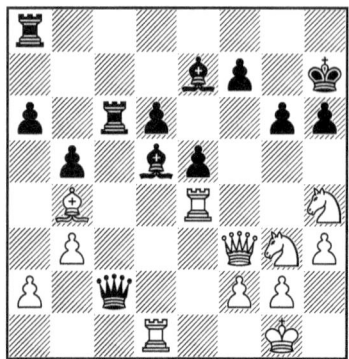

31...♗e6. *Here's the decisive mistake! After the suicidal-looking 31...♗xe4!, it turns out that the black king isn't under threat: 32.♕xf7+ ♔h8 33.♕xe7 ♕xd1+ 34.♔h2 ♕d4, and white has to give perpetual check.*

32.♖ee1! That's the point. Because of the threat 33.♖d2, white had enough time to regroup.

32...♖cc8 33.♖d2 ♕c7 34.♘hf5! Again offering a knight sacrifice, and this time, black couldn't refuse it.

34...gxf5 35.♘xf5 ♗g5 (35... ♖g8 gave more chances to save the game) **36.♖xd6 ♗f4.** After this move, white also sacrifices an exchange, and his queen invades the black king's position, forcing victory.

37.♖xe6! *(a dual – 37.♘d4! a5 38.♕d3+ ♔g8 39.♘xe6 and ♖d7)* **37...fxe6 38.♘e7 ♖f8 39.♕e4+ ♔g7 40.♕g6+ ♔h8 41.♕xe6 ♔h7 42.♕g6+ ♔h8 43.♗d6 ♕c3 44.♗xe5+.** Black resigned.

A "Long" Combination

Romanovsky: "The Soviet champion Keres played a very strong, consistent and subtle attack against Borisenko. This game is one of the best in the tournament."

No. 228. English Opening A20
Keres – Borisenko
Moscow 1950, round 10
Annotated by P. Keres

1.c4 e5 2.g3 g6 3.d4 d6. A good reply. White doesn't gain any advantage with the capture 4.dxe5 and subsequent queen trade, but black has to consider this possibility constantly for the next few moves.

4.♗g2 ♘c6 5.♘f3 ♗g7 6.e3. White wants to maintain the tension in the center and fortify the important central d4 square.

6...f5. This only weakens black's position on the kingside and gives white an opportunity to create positional threats with the trade on e5. The correct move was 6...♘ge7 or 6...♘f6.

7.♘c3 ♘h6? After this, black's position becomes rather difficult, because his knight on h6 is positioned very badly. The right move was, of course, 7...♘f6.

8.dxe5! dxe5 (8...♘xe5!?) **9.♕xd8+ ♘xd8.** After 9...♔xd8, there would still have followed 10.e4.

10.e4 ♘hf7. White threatened 11.♘xe5. Black chooses the most natural defense, but after 10...fxe4 or 10...♘df7 white's advantage is still considerable.

After the game move, white gets a decisive advantage with a deeply calculated combination.

11.♘d5 ♘e6. In case of 11...fxe4 12.♘xc7+ ♔d7 13.♘xa8 exf3 14.♗h3+ ♘e6 15.♗xe6+ and ♘c7+ black loses the exchange.

12.exf5 gxf5 13.♘h4 c6. After 13...♘d6, white will, of course, play 14.c5. *However, 13...f4 14.♘f5 ♗f8 was not that clear.*

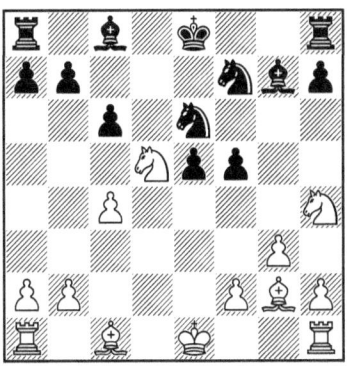

14.♘xf5! Black counted on 14.♘e3 ♘d4 with a successful defense, because the capture 14.♘xf5 seems to drop a piece. But white's calculation was deeper.

14...cxd5   15.cxd5   ♘d4 16.♘xg7+   ♔f8. Now black threatens both 17...♔xg7 and 17...♘c2+, and material losses seem inevitable for white. But he still has a good way out.

17.♘e6+!   ♗xe6   18.dxe6 ♘c2+   19.♔d1   ♘xa1   20.exf7 ♖d8+. When white went for this

"long" combination on move 11, he considered the position to be good and was mostly expecting 20...♔xf7 21.♗d2 ♖ac8 22.♗c3 *(22.♖e1!)* 22...b5 23.♗xe5 ♖hd8+ 24.♔e2, with an advantage. However, he has an even stronger continuation 21.♗g5! h6 22.♗h4 ♖ac8 23.♗e4, after which there's no satisfactory defense to 24.♔d2, winning the knight.

After the game move, the endgame is also lost for black.

21.♗d2   ♔xf7   22.♔c1. "Not 22.♗xb7 because of 22...♖d7, 22.♗e4 is also bad due to 22...♖d4!

Georgy Borisenko was a co-author of one of the best games of the tournament. Photo from the Leningrad championship of 1948 by M. Volkovysky from his archive. Published for the first time.

But the king move is unpleasant enough for black." *(From the book One Hundred Games.) And the most energetic continuation here is 22.f4! ♖he8 (22...exf4 23.♗f1) 23.♗f3 and then ♔c1.*

22...♖c8+ 23.♗c3 b5 24.♔b1 ♘c2. Black has managed to save his knight, but the white bishops now become rather strong.

25.♗xe5 ♖he8. 25...♖hd8 26.♗e4 is better; even though the h7 pawn drops, this allows black to activate his rooks. Now white wins easily.

26.♗d5+ ♔f8 27.♗f4!

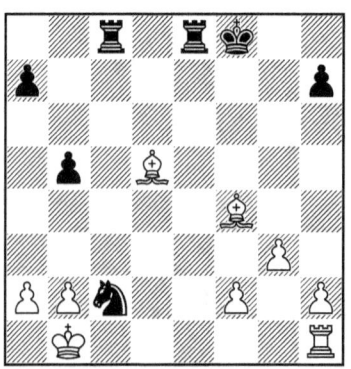

27...♘d4. The move 27...♖e2 is clearly bad for black. *For instance: 28.♖c1 ♖e1 29.♗b7! ♖c4 30.♖xe1 ♘xe1 31.♗a6 ♖d4 32.♗xb5 ♖d1+ 33.♗c1 ♘d3 34.♗xd3 ♖xd3 35.♔c2 etc.*

However, black had a much better move than 27...♘d4?: 27...♖e1+ 28.♖xe1 ♘xe1.

28.♗h6+ ♔e7 29.♗e3 ♘c6. "The immediate 29...♖ed8 doesn't work of course due to 30.♗g5+,

while after 29...♔d6 there's 30.♗b7, and 30...♖b8 is bad due to 31.♗f4+." *(From* One Hundred Games.)

30.♖d1 (30.♗e4! and ♗xh7) **30...♔f6 31.h4.** "Of course, white isn't going to part with his bishop pair just to win a pawn – 31.♗xc6 ♖xc6 32.♗xa7." *(From* One Hundred Games.)

31...a6 32.♗g2! Now the rook invades through the d-file, and black's resistance quickly ends.

32...♘e5 33.♖d6+ ♔f7 34.♗d5+ ♔e7 35.♖xa6 ♘c4 36.♗f4 ♔d7? A mistake in time trouble. Black could have still tried 36...♖ed8, since the straightforward 37.♗g5+ ♔f8 38.♗xd8? leads to mate after 38...♘d2+!. But white wins with 37.♖e6+ ♔f7 38.♖c6+! or 37...♔d7 38.♖h6 etc.

37.♖a7+. Black resigns.

Just Like the Old Masters

"For the golden treasure trove of combination masterpieces" – that's how Suetin called this game in the book *Grandmaster Boleslavsky*, prefacing it with the words: "It seemed that there were no portents of danger, and the blow 15.♗xe6! followed out of the blue. The beauty of this combination was reinforced by deep calculation of complicated lines."

No. 229
Boleslavsky – Flohr
Moscow 1950, round 7
Annotated by I. Boleslavsky

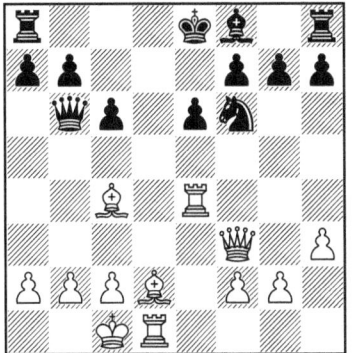

15.♗xe6!! *"A brilliant sacrifice! If the rook retreated, black could castle long and maintain a defensible position."* (Sokolsky)

15...fxe6   16.♖xe6+   ♗e7. After 16...♔f7, there would follow 17.♖xf6+!! *(Romanovsky's exclams)* 17...gxf6 18.♕h5+, and white wins, as the following lines show:

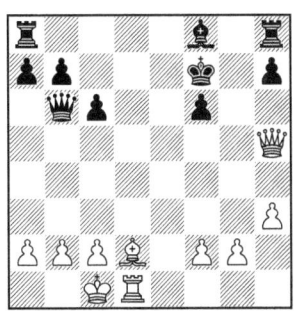

1)   18...♗e7   19.♖e1+   ♔d6 20.♗f4+♔d7 21.♕f7+;

2)   18...♔g7   19.♗h6+   ♔g8 20.♕g4+   *(20.♖d7!)*   20...♔f7 21.♖d7+♗e7 22.♕g7+;

3)   18...♔g8   19.♕g4+   ♔f7 *(19...♗g7   20.♕e6+   ♔f8   21.♗f4)* 20.♕c4+, for instance:

a)   20...♔g7 21.♗e3 ♕b4 *(21...♕c7   22.♕g4+   ♔f7   23.♖d7+)* 22.♖d7+ ♔g6 23.♕f7+ ♔f5 24.c3 ♕b5 25.g4+ ♔e4 26.♕xf6 with a quick mate;

b)   20...♔g6   21.♕e4+!   ♔f7 22.♗a5! ♗h6+ *(22...♕c5 23.♖d7+ ♗e7 24.♗b4)* 23.♔b1 ♖ad8 *(23... ♖hd8   24.♕xh7+   ♗g7   25.♕h5+)* 24.♕c4+ ♔g7 25.♕g4+, winning.

17.♖de1 ♘d5. At first sight, it seems that black could win an exchange with 17...0-0 18.♖xe7 ♘d5; actually, though, after 19.♖xg7+! ♔xg7 20.♗c3+ ♘xc3 21.♖e7+ ♔h6 22.♕xc3! he gets checkmated in a few moves.

18.♗g5 *(18.♕h5+ g6 19.♖xe7+! ♘xe7 20.♕e5 is stronger)* **18...0-0-0 19.♗xe7   ♘xe7   20.♖xe7   ♖hf8 21.♕g4+ ♔b8 22.♕xg7.**

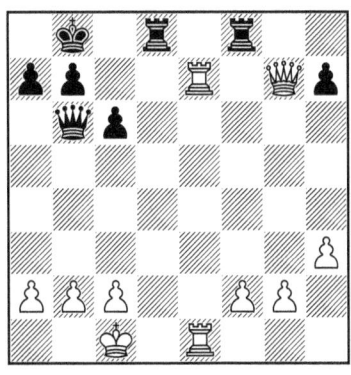

22...♕xf2. After   22...♖xf2, white has 23.♖e8 *(or, even better, 23.♖xb7+! ♕xb7 24.♕g3+)*. With the game move, black sets a trap:

if 23.♖xb7+? then white loses after 23...♔a8, since the e1 rook is hanging, and there's a mate threat (24.♖be7 ♕d2+ and ♕d1+). However, white's next move removes all the dangers.

23.b3 ♖g8 24.♕xh7 ♖xg2 25.♖xb7+ ♔a8 26.♖be7 ♕c5 27.h4 a5 28.♖e8 ♕d4 29.♔b1 ♖d2 30.♖xd8+ ♕xd8 31.♕e4 ♕f6 32.h5. Black resigned.

A Session of Mutual Blindness

Panov: "In round 8, the game between tournament leader Aronin and Kiev master Lipnitsky was at the center of attention... At one point, luck smiled on Aronin: Lipnitsky played an erroneous bishop sacrifice, and had Aronin accepted it and replied with a spectacular queen counter-sacrifice, he would have probably won easily..."

No. 230
Lipnitsky – Aronin
Moscow 1950, round 8
Annotated by I. Lipnitsky

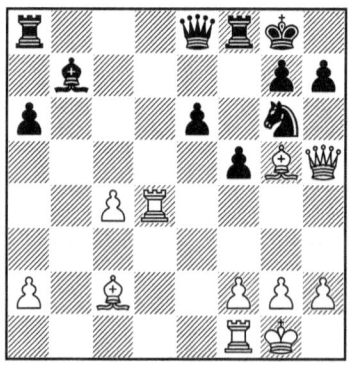

24.♖d6. Both opponents show incredible blindness, missing the counter-strike 24...♗xg2! *(25. ♔xg2? ♘f4+, so white has nothing better than 25.♖fd1 ♗e4 26.♗xe4 fxe4 27.♗e3=).* White had to play 24.♕d1! ♕c6 25.f3, maintaining the advantage.

24...h6 25.♖e1?? A gross blunder: black could now play 25... hxg5! 26.♖dxe6 ♕xe6! 27.♖xe6 ♘f4 28.♕xg5 ♘xe6.

And after 29.♕e7, white only fights for a draw. However, after 25.♗xh6! ♗xg2 (25...gxh6 26.♗a4! is even worse) 26.♗a4! ♕f7 27.♗d7!, he could get an advantage again.

25...♗e4?? Loses immediately.

26.♗xe4 fxe4 27.♗e3 ♘f4 28.♕xe8 ♖axe8 29.♖xa6 ♘d3 30.♖b1, *and black resigned on move 52.*

He Who Doesn't Risk Doesn't Get to Drink Champagne

Panov: "In round 16, Petrosian, who was playing rather badly against Keres from the abstract analysis point of view, chose a perfectly valid approach from the tournament psychology point of view: with a probably incorrect piece sacrifice, he created incredible complications that confused his opponent, leading him into time trouble..."

No. 231
Keres – Petrosian
Moscow 1950, round 16
Annotated by T. Petrosian

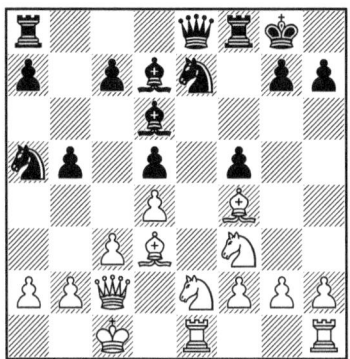

Дружеский шарж Ю. Узбякова

Т. ПЕТРОСЯН.

Tigran Petrosian proved to be a subtle psychologist. Cartoon by Y. Uzbyakov. From the Sovietsky Sport newspaper (16th November 1950).

13...b4!? Black starts a risky combination with a piece sacrifice that should have led to a loss with the correct defense. However, other continuations were also better for white.

14.♗xd6 cxd6 15.cxb4 ♘ac6 16.a3 a5 17.b5 ♘b4 18.axb4 ♖c8 19.♘c3 axb4.

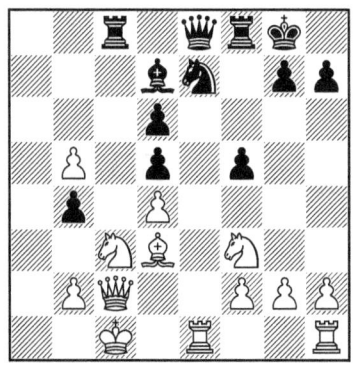

20.♔d2. White shouldn't have returned the sacrificed piece. A stronger move was 20.♕e2! ♕d8

(20...♖f7 21.♘g5 bxc3 22.♘xf7 cxb2+ 23.♔xb2 ♔xf7 24.♕h5+ and white wins) 21.♕xe7 ♕a5 22.♕xd7 bxc3 23.♔d1!, and it's unclear how black can continue the attack.

There is one way to continue the attack, but it leads to a loss: 23...♕a1+ 24.♔e2 ♕xb2+ 25.♔f1 c2 26.♗xc2! ♖xc2 27.♖e8!, and black might as well resign (27...♖xf2+ 28.♔e1).

20...♕f7 21.♕b3 bxc3+ 22.bxc3 ♖b8 23.♖e3. After the earlier mistake, white fails to find the correct plan in time trouble. He should have played 23.♖b1 ♘c8

24.♖hc1 ♘b6 25.♔e2, getting the king to safety.

"White had two good moves: 1) 23.♘g5 ♕f6 24.f4, radically preventing the possibility of f5-f4 and freeing up the f2 square for the king; and 2) 23.♖a1, starting an operation along the a-file. In both cases, white's win was only a matter of time." (Boleslavsky)

23...h6 24.♖he1 ♘c8 25.c4 *(25. ♘h4!?)* **25...♘b6! 26.cxd5 ♖fc8.**

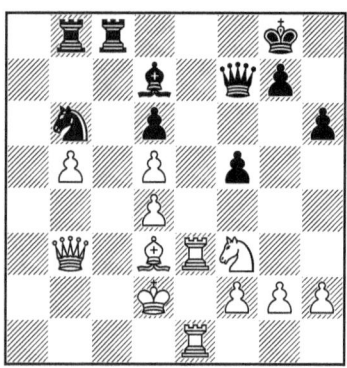

27.♖e7. White's position had become dangerous, and he had to try and simplify the position with 27.♖c1 ♖xc1 28.♔xc1 ♕xd5, after which chances are roughly equal *(they are after 29.♕xd5+ ♘xd5, but after 29.♗e2(f1), white keeps a small plus).*

27...♕f6 28.h4 ♖a8 29.♖7e2 f4 30.♘e5? A miscalculation in time trouble. White should have played 30.♖e4 *(and if 30...♗g4, then 31.♔e2= ♗xf3+? 32.gxf3 ♕xh4 33.♖e6).*

30...dxe5 31.dxe5 ♕e7 *(31... ♕xh4!)* **32.♖e4** *(32.d6+!? ♗(♕)*

e6) 32...♖a3 33.♕b2 ♗f5! 34.♕d4. 34.♖d4 ♖xd3+ 35.♖xd3 ♘c4+ and 34.d6 ♕a7 changed nothing.

34...♖a2+ 35.♔d1 ♕a3. White resigned.

A Trap for the Analysts

Strangely enough, when speaking of Tolush, everyone (including his widow who compiled the book *Alexander Tolush*) only regrets one missed chance to win the Soviet Championship – in 1957. But had he defeated Boleslavsky in the last round here, he could have caught up with Keres and become the champion in 1950! In the two previous championships, the play-off match didn't take place, and both winners were awarded gold medals... However, had they played a match, Tolush would have probably suffered – Keres was on the ascent at the time!

No. 232
Boleslavsky – Tolush
Moscow 1950, round 17
Annotated by A. Tolush

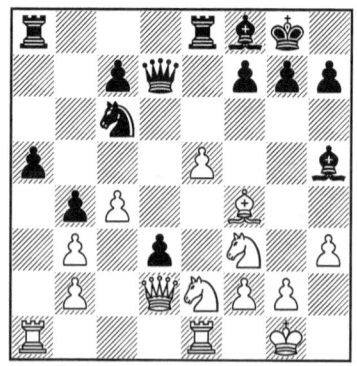

Положение после 24-го хода черных.

The position after 24...♘d4! As you can see, such "3D" diagrams didn't appear yesterday. Moreover, they occurred even before the war! From the Ogonyok magazine (No. 2, 1951).

23.♘h2. Not 23.g4 due to 23... ♗xg4, while after 23.♘c1 there would have followed 23...♗xf3 24.gxf3 ♕xh3 25.♕xd3 ♖ad8 26.♕e4 ♘d4!

Even the best try 23.♘g3 ♗xf3 24.gxf3 a4! 25.♖xa4 ♖xa4 26.bxa4 ♘a5 didn't save white. But the retreat to h2 is a losing move.

23...♗xe2. Black's position is so strong that he had an alternative: 23...a4! 24.♘g3 (24.bxa4 ♘a5 or 24.♘c1 a3 were even worse) 24...♗g6 25.♖xa4 ♖xa4 26.bxa4 ♘d4! etc.

24.♖xe2 ♘d4! 25.♖e3.

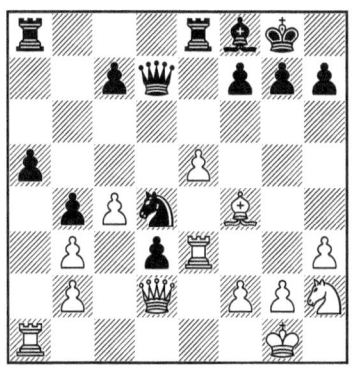

"His position was completely lost after move 25. Tolush was beaming. And then, Boleslavsky's energy and inventiveness returned to him. With each move, his resistance, almost meek just a short while later, was growing..." (Suetin)

25...♖ad8. The first mistake that doesn't miss the win yet. It was better to play 25...♖ed8!, but it seems that there was an even stronger move 25...♘xb3 (! – *Botvinnik*) 26.♖xd3 ♘xd2 27.♖xd7 ♘xc4 28.♖xc7 ♘xb2 etc.

Botvinnik stops the "winning" line after 27...♘xc4. Boleslavsky also thought that after 28.b3 (instead of 28.♖xc7?) 28...♘b6 (still, 28...♘xe5! is better) 29.♖xc7 ♘d5 30.♖c4 ♘xf4 31.♖xf4 ♖xe5, there was an "ending with the extra pawn with a technically simple win", but my computer almost locked up trying to prove this with concrete lines.

So, Boleslavsky was right when he said that "the simplest was 25...♖ed8! After 26.♕xd3 (there's nothing better) 26...♘f3+ 27.♘xf3 ♕xd3 28.♖xd3 ♖xd3 29.♘d2 ♖ad8, black wins easily."

26.♕xd3. Of course white could have kept the queens on the board with 26.♖xd3, but this only simplified matters for black: 26... ♘e2+ 27.♕xe2 ♕xd3 28.♕g4 ♕xb3, winning easily.

26...♘f3+ 27.♘xf3 ♕xd3 28.♖xd3 ♖xd3 29.♖xa5 ♖xb3 30.♖a2. 30.♗c1 was stronger, and if 30...♖d8 then 31.♔h2 ♖d1 32.♗e3!, and now 32...♖xb2 is impossible due to 33.♖a8!

But after 31...h6! (32.♖a7? ♗c5) with the subsequent ♔h7, the b2 pawn falls.

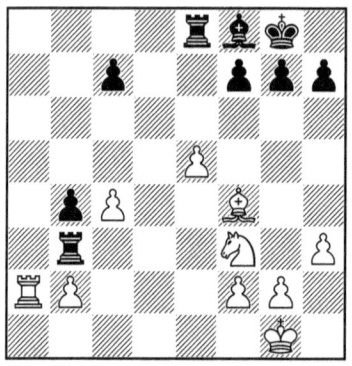

30...♖d8. *"The beginning of a wrong plan. Black shouldn't have weakened the 8th rank. The correct move was 30...♖d3!, threatening to win the b2 pawn with 31...b3 and the subsequent transfer of the rook to b1. If 31.♖a1 then 31...♖ed8, and black either wins the b2 pawn or trades rooks. In either case, he should win easily." (Boleslavsky)*

31.♔f1. *A mistake! 31.♗e3! was much more tenacious, neutralizing 31...♖d1+ 32.♔h2 ♖b1 due to 33.♖a8, and the threat ♗c5 forces 33...♖xe3=.*

31...♖d1+ 32.♔e2 ♖b1 33.♖a8 *(! – Botvinnik).* White's last hope! Pinning the black bishop, he tries to create some counterplay that unexpectedly succeeds.

33...♖1xb2+ 34.♘d2 h6. *The spectacular pendulum 34...♖c3! 35.♗g5 ♖a3! (35...♖xc4? 36.♗e7=) with the idea 36.♖c8 ♖a5 37.f4 (37.*

♖xc7 ♖xe5+ 38.♗e3 ♖e8 is worse) *37...♖ba2 38.♗d8 ♖a6! can only be found by a machine...*

35.♗e3. *"Perhaps white should have immediately played 35.♖c8, not leaving the e5 pawn undefended." (Botvinnik.) After this, black wins with 35...♖c3! 36.♖xc7 (best) 36...g5! 37.♗e3 ♖a2 38.♖c8 b3 etc. The game move was the strongest one.*

35...♖a3 *(! – Botvinnik)* **36.♖c8.** *Boleslavsky thought that this move was a "serious mistake", recommending 36.♖b8 ♖a5 37.c5 ♖ba2 38.♔d3, "and black had to give up the b-pawn to get rid of the pin." However, black had a stronger continuation: 36...♖ba2! 37.c5 ♖c3, etc.*

36...♖a5 37.c5. *"37.f4 was necessary" (Botvinnik), but this is bad due to 37...c5, ♖ba2 and ♖a8.*

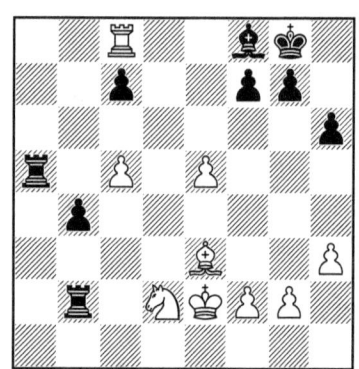

37...♖c2? The decisive mistake that misses the win. Black had to play 37...♖b5! with a terrible threat 38...b3 and ♖xd2+, and the b-pawn promotes.

"With 37...♖b5! (it's almost always beneficial to support a passed pawn

from behind) 38.♔d1 b3 39.♔c1 *(otherwise 39...♖xd2+! and b3-b2)* 39...♖a2, *black could have posed white a very difficult problem"* (Botvinnik). *Or, more precisely, an unsolvable problem:* 40.♔b1 ♖a4 41.♔b2 *(41. ♖xc7? b2 42.♔c2 ♖c4+!) 41...g5!, and the b-pawn pushes ahead (42. ♖xc7 ♗xc5).*

Boleslavsky also agreed that 37...♖b5, shown by Tolush, "won immediately". And this means that he wouldn't likely have found the line 38.♔d3! (or 38.♗d4! ♖a2 39.♔d3) 38...b3 39.♘c4 ♖a2 40.♗d4 over the board, neutralizing the dangerous passed pawn: 40...b2 41.♗xb2 ♖axb2 42.♘xb2 ♖xb2 43.♖xc7 ♖xf2 44.c6 ♖f1 45.♔c2=. Therefore, 37...♖c2! is objectively the best move.

38.♔d1 ♖cxc5. *Only this move was the decisive mistake. 38...♖c3! still retained some winning chances.*

39.♗xc5 ♖xc5 40.f4. When black made his 37th move, he erroneously thought that he could now play 40... g5 and ♔g7, but failed to notice that white could meet that with 41.♘e4!

40...♖c3. Analysis showed that black could not bring his king and bishop into the fight, because white can push his pawns (f4-f5 and e5-e6), securing equality. And so, the opponents agreed to a draw. The sealed move was **41.♔e2.**

Without a Hitch

As we know, Keres lost to Petrosian one round before the finish, and now only a win could guarantee him a championship medal. "I had black against Averbakh," he wrote in *One Hundred Games*, "and it's easy to imagine my disappointment when my opponent played the Four Knights Opening. Still, we didn't play a boring draw – the middlegame was rather interesting. I managed to gain a small positional advantage, and the game was adjourned in a slightly better endgame for me."

No. 233
Averbakh – Keres
Moscow 1950, round 17
Annotated by P. Keres

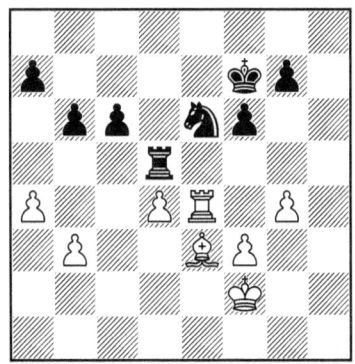

The white pieces are tied to defending the d4 pawn, and he can only move his king. So, black has time to regroup his forces for the decisive queenside action.

The main threat is the b6-b5 break, which wins a pawn by force. But the execution requires some preparation – the king must be centralized, for one thing. After

41.♔e2, for instance, the immediate 41...b5 was too premature, since after 42.a5 b4 (42...a6 is better) 43.a6! white gets some counterplay both after 43...♘c7 44.♔d3 ♘xa6 45.♔c4 and 43...♖a5 44.d5 cxd5 45.♖xb4 etc.

41.♔g3 ♔e7. After 41...b5, white would have played 42.♔f2 and gotten counterplay after 42...bxa4 43.bxa4 ♖a5 with 44.d5! cxd5 45.♖b4. To avoid that, black wants to put his king on d7 first.

42.g5? An error that gets white in big trouble. Even though this move contains an interesting trap, the passive waiting move 42.♔f2 was better, with black still having great technical difficulties to overcome.

42...f5! After 42...fxg5 43.♔g4!, white could get some counterplay for the pawn.

43.♖e5 ♔d6 44.♖xd5+ ♔xd5 45.g6! Relatively better. White creates a counter-chance in the form of an attack on the g7 pawn and sets a cunning trap.

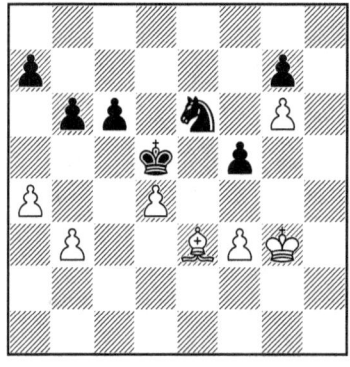

45...a5! If black immediately took on d4, then the pawn endgame

after 45...♘xd4 46.♗xd4 ♔xd4 47.♔f4 would have probably been drawn. The thing is, after the best moves 47...b5 48.axb5 cxb5 49.b4! ♔c4 50.♔xf5 ♔xb4, white saves the game with the only move 51.f4! If now 51...♔c5, then 52.♔e6! b4 53.f5 b3 54.f6 b2? 55.f7 and 56.f8=♕+, while if 51...♔c3, then 52.♔g5! b4 53.f5 b3 54.f6 gxf6+ 55.♔xf6 b2 56.g7 with a likely draw.

Black is thus forced to play 51...a5, which looks enough for a win at first sight, since the queen endgame after 52.♔e6? a4 53.f5 a3 54.f6 gxf6 55.g7 a2 56.g8=♕ a1=♕ 57.♕f8+ ♔b3 is easily won.

White, however, achieves a study-like draw by playing 52.♔g4! a4 53.f5 a3 54.f6 gxf6 55.g7 a2 56.g8=♕ a1=♕ 57.♕f8+ ♔b3 58.♕f7+ ♔c2 59.♕g6+ ♔d2 60.♕h6+ ♔e2 61.♕h2+ ♔d3 62.♕g3+, and black has to give up the b5 pawn to avoid perpetual check. The pawn endgame is very interesting.

In One Hundred Games, *Keres showed a simpler path to the draw: 52.♔e4! a4 53.♔d3! "and the king makes it to the battlefield just in time."*

46.♔h4. Black had threatened 46...♘xd4 47.♗xd4 ♔xd4 48.♔f4 b5 with an easy win.

46...♘xd4. Black shouldn't have hurried to capture this pawn that only restricted the bishop's range. It was simpler to play 46...b5 first and only capture on d4 after b5-b4.

47.♗h6! ♘e6. Obviously not 47...gxh6? 48.g7 etc. The continuation 47...♘xf3+ 48.♔h5 ♘e5 49.♗xg7 ♘xg6 50.♔xg6 f4 51.♗f6 also gave white enough defensive resources.

48.♗e3 c5. Black is playing very indecisively, seriously hampering his winning chances. With the game move, he devalues his own queenside pawns: now two white pawns hold the three black ones and make it harder to create a passer there. It was better to play 48...b5 49.♗b6 b4! 50.♗xa5 c5 with an advantage that would quickly decide the game.

49.♔h5. 49.♗c1 didn't save the game either due to 49...c4! 50.bxc4+ ♔xc4 51.♗b2 b5 52.axb5 ♔xb5 53.♗xg7 ♘xg7 54.♔g5 a4 55.♔f6 a3 etc.

49...♔e5. Black is trying to convert his advantage in the most surefire way, but he overlooks the hidden defensive resource on move 53. The simplest way to win was 49...c4 50.bxc4+ ♔xc4 51.♗xb6 ♔b4, and the passed a-pawn quickly decides matters. By the way, 49...♔c6 with the subsequent 50...b5 also won.

50.♗c1.

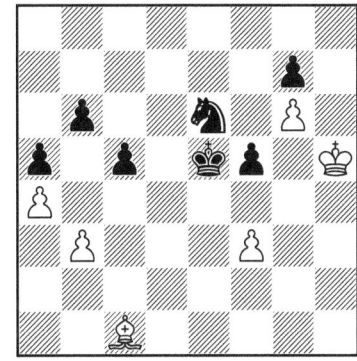

50...♘d4. Now black has to calculate long lines very precisely to achieve victory. The natural-looking 50...♔d4 51.♗b2+ ♔e3? was an error, since after 52.♗xg7! ♘xg7+ 53.♔g5! there's no win in sight: 53...♔xf3 54.♔f6 ♘h5+ 55.♔xf5 ♔e3 56.♔e5 ♔d3 57.♔f5! or 53...♘e8 54.♔xf5 ♔xf3 55.♔e6 ♔e4 56.♔d7 etc. White also had sufficient defense after 50...f4 51.♔g4 ♔f6 52.♗b2+ ♔xg6 53.♗e5! – he has compensation for the two pawns in the form of the weakness on f4 and the attacking possibility ♗b8-a7.

Black achieves nothing with the game move; if the defense was correct, he would have soon had to return the knight to e6. The right way to win was to create a passed pawn on the queenside: 50...♔d5! 51.♗b2 c4 52.bxc4+ ♔xc4 53.♗xg7 (or else 53...b5) 53...♘xg7+ 54.♔g5 ♘e8! 55.♔xf5 ♔d5!, and white is defenseless against the threat 56...b5.

51.♗h6 (obviously 51.♗b2? ♔f4 is bad) **51...♔f6.** Continuing with the wrong plan. Black had to play 51...♘e6 immediately.

52.♗g5+ ♔e6.

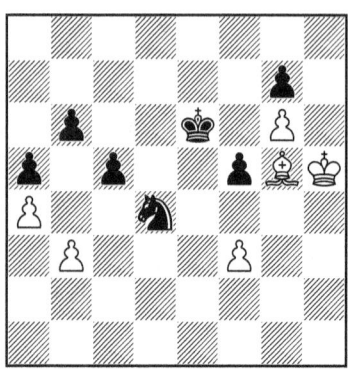

53.♗h6? A blunder in time trouble. White could have posed another difficult problem for his opponent with 53.♗d8! During the game, black intended to meet this move with 53...♘xb3 54.♗xb6? c4, but white has a stronger continuation – 54.♔g5!, threatening 55.♗f6! Now there's nothing better for black than 54...♘d4 55.♗xb6 ♘xf3+ 56.♔h5! ♔d5 57.♗xa5 ♘d4 with some winning chances.

But even after 53.♗d8! black has a clear way to win with 53...♔d7! If now 54.♗xb6 then black can play 54...♘xb3 55.♔g5 c4, and the c-pawn will cost white the bishop. If 54.♗f6 ♘e6 55.♗e5 ♔c6 56.♗xg7 ♘xg7+ 57.♔g5 then black wins with 57...♘e8! 58.♔xf5 ♔d6!, for instance: 59.f4 ♔d5 60.♔g5 ♔e6 61.f5+ ♔e5 or 59.♔f4 ♔e6 60.♔e4 ♘d6+ 61.♔f4 ♔f6 62.g7 ♔xg7 63.♔e5 c4! etc.

53...gxh6 54.♔xh6 ♘c6! Now the pawn is stopped *(a dual – 54... f4!).*

55.g7 ♘e7 56.♔h7 ♔f7 57.♔h6 ♔g8 58.f4 ♔f7. White resigned.

An intense, combative game. The endgame inaccuracies are explained solely by the nervous conditions of the last round.

Believe it or not, the poor computer, failing to find even a single mistake in this analysis, asked me to take my hat off to Keres and... not to make it do superfluous work again!

The Wooden Man's Gibberish

19th Soviet Championship: Moscow, 11th November – 14th December 1951

> "...all kinds of scum are leeching on patriotism,
> because it's hard to force worthy people to write what they don't want to,
> but for scum, it doesn't matter what they write, and nothing is sacred for them."
> *V. Astafiev, from a letter to A. Makarov*

Have you noticed that there are fewer and fewer quotes from *Shakhmaty v SSSR* in each championship chapter? It's not because I'm purposefully avoiding the magazine. It was just so... I can't even find the right word... diluted, emasculated, pretentious and servile, that there was almost nothing to quote from except for the purely professional articles. I even worried because of that, fearing accusations of being too prejudiced towards the magazine (I did work for it myself, even if much later), until I found Peter Romanovsky's letters to Vladimir Zak, published in the early 2000s.

I'll say one thing immediately: I think that letters are the best "witnesses" of their time, no memoirs can ever come close (even diaries can be edited). And the letters to a close friend are invaluable for any historian. Where else can you find what a person thought for real, especially in Stalin's times, when people were afraid of their own shadow?

I'll save Romanovsky's frank assessment of the championship for the chapter finale, but for now let's read his opinion about the *Shakhmaty v SSSR* magazine. Peter Arsenyevich worked closely with the magazine and knew the inner workings of the editorial office very well.

"The magazine was audited by a committee led by Panov," he wrote on 20th January 1952. "An awful mess. There was a lot of stupid drivel, but very serious shortcomings went unnoticed. A reprimand is planned for Ragozin, but I think that nothing will come out of that. The All-Union committee had already delayed the hearings twice – 'we don't have time!' There are many disagreements within the magazine as well. Take note of the writer Safonov's article in the first issue. This piece was largely organized by yours truly. The magazine is bad, it has become too official, toothless on principal questions, lacks self-criticism ..." (*Shakhmatny Peterburg*, No. 5, 2002. The letters were provided to the magazine by Zak's daughter Irina.)

The "hearings" in the Sports Committee mentioned by Romanovsky did eventually take place. I read about the proceedings in the memoirs of Yuri Averbakh who replaced Ragozin as the chief editor. The story tells us about the incredible ideological pressure the magazine was under at the time and the possible repercussions of any careless word.

Averbakh: "My deputy Yudovich liked to tell the story how in 1952, in Stalin's times, the *Shakhmaty v SSSR* magazine was discussed at the Sports Committee panel hearings.

Those were troubled times. *Pravda* had written about the 'murderer doctors plot' just the other day *(see the chapter "Between Heaven and Earth")*. There was a purge, Jews were removed from managerial positions everywhere. According to Yudovich, he was going to be kicked out of his job, too.

But Mikhail Mikhailovich was an old gun. During the war, when the chess newspaper and magazine closed, he worked as the executive editor of a newspaper with a ridiculous tautological name *Patriot Rodiny (Patriot of the Homeland)*, then in the *Sovetskaya Militsiya* magazine and on the radio. He alluded to his powerful protectors many times. To cut a long story short, Yudovich got proactive, used his connections and managed to keep his job.

But I'm getting ahead of myself. Now I'll provide an excerpt from his tale that he liked to act out. This episode vividly shows the atmosphere of the times.

'At first, the floor was given to the reviewer A. Iglitsky, candidate master, a professional journalist who worked for *Novy Mir*. A thorough, meticulous man, he knew the contents of the magazine very well and methodically picked apart all of its flaws. Iglitsky finished his critical speech in what he thought was a very spectacular fashion:

'And lastly. Why didn't the magazine respond to the publication of Comrade Stalin's work "Marxism and the Problems of Linguistics"?'

As soon as he closed his mouth, there was an ear-piercing scream:

'What do you mean by 'didn't respond'?'

Sports Committee panel member Alexander Shelepin, then VLKSM *(Young Communist)* Central Committee third secretary *(and later, under Khrushchev, chairman of the KGB)*, even got up from his chair.

'Do you understand what are you talking about?' he chewed the poor Iglitsky out. 'What do you mean by 'respond'? They should have dedicated an entire issue to Comrade Stalin's work!'

There was a special resolution issued about the magazine. However, despite *Shakhmaty v SSSR* indeed not having responded to the leader of the people's publication, there were no adverse consequences. Yudovich indeed had very powerful protectors!" (From the book *What the Pieces Don't Mention*.)

Almost three years passed, Stalin died, but nothing changed (from a letter dated 15th November 1954): "Our magazine (I have to call it that because

The "Year of Chigorin" had passed, and the photos of the founder disappeared from the chess stages, giving way to other heroes. This Soviet team championship game between Boleslavsky (left) and Bondarevsky (right) in Tbilisi (autumn 1951), featuring many participants of the individual championship (Aronin is behind Bondarevsky), was hallowed by the faces of the Soviet "holy trinity": Stalin, Beria and Molotov. From I. Boleslavsky's archive. Published for the first time.

I'm still a member of the editorial board) still pretty much remains a boring official record, the abode of Yudovich and Abramov. It looks like that same record of 1947, or 1950, or any other year. Even the 'Reader Criticizes' column is too official, let alone the games section and everything else. I quit the education department one year ago, because I couldn't ensure non-interference from Ragozin and Yudovich. My income took a hit because of that, and I am quite short of money right now, but you know well that I'm not one of those people who sell their views to the highest bidder." (*Shakhmatny Peterburg*, No. 1, 2003.)

I also took note of Vadim Safonov's article "The Beauty of Chess Creativity" (No. 1, 1952). It stuck out too much, and the magazine was criticized very harshly by the author. But it seems that chief editor Vyacheslav Ragozin didn't have a choice: how could he refuse to publish an article by a Stalin Prize winner and the favorite of academician Lysenko, the very same one who persecuted Vavilov and destroyed Soviet genetics? But we definitely can't accuse Safonov of harboring a lack of love for chess (as you remember, this was also an excuse for the NKVD general Apollonov who was "transferred to sport"). The article is big, so I'll only provide some excerpts:

Safonov: "A dull man enters a hall where people are playing chess. He's frowning. Joys, sorrows, difficult winding paths, iron grips? No, he sees only wooden pieces with small wooden circles glued to their bottoms to prevent loud thuds.

My god, a huge capacity crowd in the world-famous hall *(the championship was held in the Column Hall of the House of the Unions)*, the pieces on huge demonstration boards are moving noiselessly; but what's that rumble, first anxious then joyous, that appears in the hall like a hushed breath of some giant, and then suddenly a rush of applause: they can't be stopped by any lighted signs! Because of noiseless plywood pieces? No, because of incredible creativity of the world's best chess masters, because of ideas of such beauty and depth that they'll be remembered for decades to come, because of the heated battles where attack and defense are equally valuable and skillful.

What does the frowning man make of that? He only believes his own, very shortsighted and almost unseeing eyes. (...)

I must admit that I do not know this dull frowning man. But when I read chess commentary, I sometimes can't help but think that this is the fruit of the wooden man's wooden labors.

There are, of course, different ways to become a chess player or chess fan. (...) I found chess columns in old magazines. They spoke of a captivating world of fantastic combinations, fearless attacks, heroic defenses and of people who were masters of this world. And I remember very well the passionate desire to enter that world burning inside me.

These were old chess columns by Chigorin.

Of course, nobody ever held such a poll, but there's no doubt that thousands upon thousands of youngsters were attracted to chess by the passionate **stories** of great masters about this game – not just the dry sequences of moves and opening lines, but the inner essence of it, the **human competition** behind the chess board.

Why then are we drying out the chess stories so often? Why are we listening to the boring wooden man's gibberish? Chess is, above all, a very **interesting** game (otherwise, who would ever play it?) – why then don't we tell why and **how** it's interesting? Why are there so few **human** materials on the pages of the chess magazine?

I think that *Shakhmaty v SSSR* is drier than Chigorin's chess columns, and it's very unfortunate. There's no need to deny the necessity of the purely technical research and annotations for moves and lines in a specialized magazine. But we shouldn't forget that there's also a wider reality: the human competition, the clash of will, boldness, self-discipline and mind, the beauty of creativity that overcomes the obstacles – that's what attracts people to chess.

And we need to find other words to talk about that. Not dry ones, but passionate ones, as passionate as the creativity of any great masters, as passionate as the fight; as imaginative as real art..."

...Yes, I almost forgot. The magazine did finally publish a review of Keres's book *Open Games*! It was two years late (No. 1 and 2, 1952), but huge: seven pages. Unfortunately, the author was not Vasily Panov (oh, it would have been so interesting to compare the two versions!): it was written by master Nikolai Kopylov, another familiar figure – and, by the way, one of the heroes of the 19th championship. Of course, there are no "Nazi minions and hirelings" in the text. Everything was very smooth: mistakes, omissions, wrong evaluations pointed out, sometimes grudging – very grudging – praise... But all this gibberish wasn't as harmless as you might have thought. "Keres used extensive materials in his work on the book, but he made a big principal mistake by not showing the leading role of Soviet players in developing all (*!!* – *S.V.*) main parts of opening theory." I don't know who wrote this "blindly patriotic" passage – Kopylov himself or Ragozin and Yudovich, but it stinks. Like a denunciation.

P.S. In that same 1952, the second volume of *Theory of Open Games* was published. In the foreword, the author wrote that he "took the criticism of the first part into account", and that "Soviet theoreticians and masters brought numerous new ideas into all the most important openings described in the book." Name frequency analysis showed that Keres did draw conclusions from the review – and it seems that Panov's review (the one mentioned at the start of the chapter on the 18th Soviet Championship) influenced him much more than Kopylov's one (if I'm correct in my assumption that Panov first wrote his unpublished review for *Shakhmaty v SSSR* and that it was "ideologically refined" later, meaning that an original draft would have been retained by the magazine that Keres might have been shown). Judge for yourself. In the first volume, Bogoljubov was mentioned 65 times, and Chigorin just 62; in the second one, there's not a single mention of Bogoljubov, while Chigorin is the most frequently mentioned player. The numbers for other names that attracted Panov's criticism were quite telling as well: Tartakower – 90 in the first book vs. 22 in the second, Euwe – 92 vs. 14, Tarrasch – 119 vs. 14, and Fine – 40 vs. 0!

The Qualifying Campaign

No semi-final bulletin was again published, and their selected games were, like the previous year, crammed into the main bulletin, which again led to its "dilution". But that's not even the main complaint. The overwhelming majority of the semi-final games simply never made it to circulation, never seen by theoreticians or players. *The Four Semi-Finals* bulletin (1949) published all 612 games played, but out of the almost 740 games played in the semi-finals of the 19th championship, less than one third were printed – only 218!

A. Prorvich (caretaker chairman of the Sports Committee chess section): "Out of 111 quarter-final players, representing all the Soviet republics, there were 5 masters, 83 candidate masters and 23 first-category players. Three winners of each group progressed to the semi-final tournaments where they met grandmasters and the strongest masters. 79 players took part in the four semi-finals of the 19th championship, held in May – June 1951: 7 grandmasters, 53 masters and 19 candidate masters." (*19th Soviet Chess Championship* tournament book.) Four players qualified from each semi-final.

Baku group: 1. Novotelnov – 13.5/19; 2–4. Lipnitsky, Taimanov, Kholmov – 12.5; 5. Furman – 11.5; 6. Shamkovich – 11; 7. Makogonov – 10.5; 8–10. Kasparyan, Kotlerman, Nezhmetdinov – 10; 11. Goldberg – 9.5; 12–14. Zhukhovitsky, Lilienthal, Estrin – 9; 15–16. Levenfish, Tarasov – 8.5; 17. Klaman – 7.5; 18–19. Zak, Prokhorovich – 6.5; 20. Velibekov – 2.

Goldberg and Zak: "Novotelnov's play was strong and consistent during the whole tournament; he was exceptionally inventive and showed great energy and will to win... Taimanov's greatest qualities are quick and precise calculation and deep opening knowledge. He's playing with ease and able to preserve his strength until the end of the tournament... Kholmov's good health is one of the main factors behind his success. One of his flaws is a relative lack of opening theory knowledge... The Russian SFSR champion Nezhmetdinov is very skillful in attacking the king, without regard for material sacrifices, but he's much weaker in games that take the course of quiet positional struggle." (*Shakhmaty v SSSR*, No. 8, 1951.)

Sverdlovsk group: 1. Petrosian – 13.5/19; 2. Geller – 13; 3–4. Averbakh, Boleslavsky – 12.5; 5–7. Weltmander, Konstantinov, Shaposhnikov – 11; 8. Kondratiev – 10.5; 9. Cherepkov – 10; 10–14. Bannik, Ilivitsky, Kirillov, Ravinsky, Ufimtsev – 9.5; 15–16. Dubinin, Liublinsky – 8; 17. A. Kofman – 7.5; 18. Antoshin – 6.5; 19. Saigin – 5; 20. Grechkin – 2.5 (Saigin dropped out after round 15 and Grechkin dropped out after round 11.)

Boleslavsky: "Petrosian and Geller were unrecognizable in this tournament. It's as though they switched styles. Petrosian won eight games, with a direct attack on the king in six of them. Geller, on the other hand, showed great positional mastery and good advantage conversion technique... Averbakh is very precise in the opening and converts his positional advantage with good skill and patience. He's less confident in complicated positions." (*Shakhmaty v SSSR*, No. 9, 1951.)

Averbakh: "Four rounds before the finish, Geller, Petrosian and I had 12 points out of 15. Boleslavsky (I beat him in our game, by the way), was one point behind... And you had to finish in the top four to qualify for the final.

Before the next round, Geller came to my room.

'Do you want to win this tournament?' he asked.

'No,' I said, 'it's enough for me to make it to the final.'

'Same here,' Geller continued. 'Let's help Petrosian win the tournament. He's just moved to Moscow, and he needs a win to strengthen his reputation.'

I agreed. To fulfill the promise, I had to draw all my remaining games, and my opponents had long lost all chances of qualifying for the final.

Participants and arbiters of the Sverdlovsk semi-final, May to June 1951. Sitting (left to right): ?, A. Ufimtsev, A. Kozlov (arbiter), I. Boleslavsky, Y. Averbakh, J. Weltmander, A. Cherepkov. Standing: V. Antoshin, G. Ravinsky, T. Petrosian, E. Geller, V. Kirillov, ?, G. Ilivitsky, I. Berezin (arbiter), Y. Shaposhnikov, P. Kondratiev, A. Bannik. From R. Ponyaev's archive.

Leningrad semi-final. Korchnoi versus Smyslov. From the cover of Shakhmaty v SSSR (no. 9, 1951).

I made draws in rounds 16 and 17, and in round 18 I played against the Moscow master V. Liublinsky, whom I've known since childhood. In the morning of the playing day, he called me and asked, 'Do you agree to a draw?'

'I do.'

'Of course, a draw is enough for you,' he said. 'Okay, let's meet at lunch.'

When we sat down at the table, he suggested ordering vodka. I usually adhered to a strict regimen during tournaments, never touching any alcohol.

'But we have already agreed to a draw,' I thought, 'and there would be no real competition.' So I accepted.

We went to the game in a rather buoyant mood. My opponent, who had white, played the sharp Evans Gambit.

'Is this now called playing for a draw?' I thought.

An hour before the end of the round, I decided to offer a draw, even though, the truth be told, white had a somewhat better position. My opponent took a drag on his cigarette, puffed a cloud of smoke over the board, right under my nose, and said, 'Let's play!'

Only then did I realize that I had been conned.

It wasn't easy to get back into fighting mood: I was too upset and angry. The game was adjourned, but I couldn't save it in the play-off. When I resigned, my opponent smiled sheepishly and said, 'Sorry, my nerves are all over the place, and I had too few points!'

Participants and arbiters of the Lvov semi-final. Sitting (left to right): L. Garkunov (arbiter), Y. Sakharov, V. Mikenas, V. Ragozin, S. Flohr, A. Konstantinopolsky, Y. Gusev, an arbiter. Standing: V. Simagin, M. Beilin, E. Zagoriansky, E. Poliak, A. Sokolsky, I. Vistaneckis, D. Rovner, L. Aronin, an arbiter. From the author's archive.

Thankfully, even the unexpected loss didn't hurt my chances of progressing to the final." *(*From the book *What the Pieces Don't Mention.*)

Yuri Lvovich's memory played a trick on him. Boleslavsky: "Averbakh's defeat in round 16 deprived him of any chances of first place, and the battle in the last three rounds was waged between Petrosian and Geller." Given that Averbakh only lost two games in the entire tournament, Boleslavsky was referring to his zero against Kondratiev. Round 17 was a draw, and he qualified for the final thanks to "a plus in the last round from Saigin, who had withdrawn ill." (Boleslavsky). Averbakh knew about this earlier, which is why he was willing to agree a draw with Liublinsky. Moreover, as Averbakh finished with 12.5 points, he must have had 11 at the time of his conversation with Geller and not 12.

Leningrad group: 1. Smyslov – 13.5/18; 2. Terpugov – 11.5; 3. Moiseev – 11; 4. Kopylov – 10.5; 5–8. Bondarevsky, Kan, Korchnoi, Suetin – 10; 9–10. Tolush, Chekhover – 9; 11. Lisitsin – 8.5; 12–14. Krogius, Ratner, Reshko – 8; 15. Panov – 7.5; 16–18. Aratovsky, Kuzminykh, Chistiakov – 7; 19. Lutikov – 5.5.

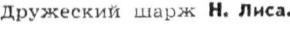

Мастер В. ЛЮБЛИНСКИЙ

Master Viktor Liublinsky later became a distinguished trainer of the RSFSR and edited popular chess columns in the Smena magazine and Moskovskaya Pravda newspaper. Cartoon by N. Lis. From the Sovietsky Sport newspaper (20th October 1949).

Kan: "Three and a half points in the first ten games – such a result could have discouraged even a more experienced player. But Terpugov didn't lose heart, didn't crumble. Showing the will to win, so characteristic of a member of the Soviet chess school, the Moscow candidate master didn't just catch up – he won eight games in a row!.. The success of the young master Moiseev is totally natural. In the last few years, he has achieved significant success... Kopylov is a talented player. However, two factors stop him from achieving greater and more consistent success: his penchant for fanciful play and excessive fascination with a psychological approach...

Leningrad player Korchnoi, who scored a master's norm, belongs to the ranks of our most talented chess youth. Creative-wise, he's largely on the right path, even though he sometimes engages in calculating fantastic lines and combinations too much." (*Shakhmaty v SSSR*, No. 9, 1951.)

Korchnoi: "To succeed, I had to win almost all the games at the finish. I did win three in a row. And in the last round, I had white against Grandmaster Smyslov. He breezed through the tournament and easily got first place. I was told that Smyslov wasn't inclined to play that evening. Counting on a quick draw, he bought theater tickets. A draw was enough for me to score the master's norm. But if I won, I could qualify for the Soviet Championship final! Of course, I decided to play and ruined Smyslov's evening. After five hours of play, the game was adjourned in an unclear position. Then there was a night of analysis together with Tolush and the play-off. I barely managed to save the game." (From the book *Chess Without Mercy.*)

Lvov group: 1. Sakharov – 12.5/19; 2–3. Aronin, Simagin – 12; 4–6. Gusev, Mikenas, Flohr – 11.5; 7–8. Bonch-Osmolovsky, Zagoriansky – 11;

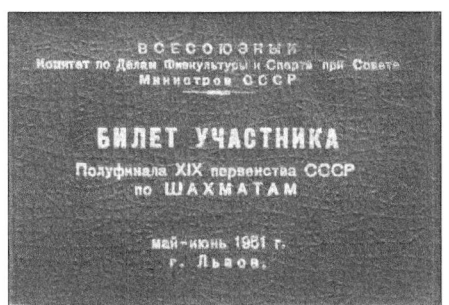

A Participant's Ticket of the Lvov semi-final. An impressive document: bound in calico, with the arbiter's signature and stamp. From I. Lyskov's archive. Published for the first time.

9–10. Borisenko, Vistaneckis – 10.5; 11–12. E. Poliak, Sokolsky – 9.5; 13–14. Beilin, Byvshev – 8.5; 15. Lyskov – 8; 16. Rovner – 7; 17–18. Konstantinopolsky, Ragozin – 6.5; 19–20. Kopaev, Makarov – 6.

Sokolsky: "The victory of Kiev candidate master Sakharov was a big surprise. He was among the leaders for the whole tournament. Aronin is a regular championship final participant, and he proved his reputation as one of the strongest masters in the country... Simagin, as always, played originally in the openings and skillfully created complications in the middlegame... Ragozin and Konstantinopolsky were most likely exhausted after the Botvinnik – Bronstein match *(the first FIDE-run world championship match in history was played in Moscow in spring 1951; it ended in a draw, +5–5=14, and Botvinnik retained his title).* This tiredness obviously affected their results." (*Shakhmaty v SSSR*, No. 9, 1951.)

Prorvich: "Grandmasters M. Botvinnik, P. Keres, D. Bronstein, A. Kotov and I. Bondarevsky were personally invited to the final. Grandmaster I. Boleslavsky could not take part in the final due to illness." (Tournament book.)

A strange "illness". Right under Alatortsev's first round play-off report in *Vechernaya Moskva*, there's a news item about Boleslavsky... winning the Minsk championship! He moved there in autumn 1951 – perhaps he decided to sit out the national competition and play in the city championship to thank the hosts for their welcome and the great apartment in the center of the city he received from them?

The Forge of Talents

Smyslov: "The honorable place that chess holds in the life of the Soviet people can be explained first and foremost by the general growth of culture in our country. Chess has become one of the most popular sports. As of 1st January 1951, there were more than one million organized chess players in the USSR.

Mikhail Ivanovich Kalinin said, 'Millions take part in our physical education movement. And, of course, it's easier to find talents among the

Участники XIX шахматного первенства СССР

Гроссмейстер П. Керес (Таллин).

Гроссмейстер С. Флор (Москва).

Мастер Ю. Авербах (Москва).

Гроссмейстер И. Бондаревский (Ленинград).

Photo portraits were published of the players in advance of the final. Clockwise: Keres (top left), Flohr, Bondarevsky and Averbakh. From Y. Averbakh's archive.

millions than thousands, and it's easier to find talents among the thousands than hundreds.'

> **From the same newspaper issue:** "As of 1ˢᵗ October 1951, 11 players held the grandmaster title, and 80 players had the master's title, 25 international masters among them. There are 330 candidate masters and more than 3,000 first-category players in the USSR."

The popularity of Soviet chess among the common people is a strong, inexhaustible source that helps more and more new masters, new young talents grow... Building upon the best traditions of the national Chigorin school, the chess players of the Soviet Union have gained the glory of the strongest players in the world.

The mere list of the 19ᵗʰ Soviet Championship participants speaks for itself: world champion M. Botvinnik *(he hadn't played in the national championships for six years!)*, grandmasters I. Bondarevsky, D. Bronstein, P. Keres, A. Kotov, V. Smyslov and S. Flohr, masters Y. Averbakh (Moscow), L. Aronin (Moscow Oblast), E. Geller (Odessa), N. Kopylov (Leningrad), I. Lipnitsky (Kiev), O. Moiseev (Moscow), N. Novotelnov (Grozny), T. Petrosian, V. Simagin (both Moscow), M. Taimanov (Leningrad), and the young candidate master E. Terpugov (Moscow). This tournament is going to be an outstanding chess competition, the greatest in recent years." (*Sovietsky Sport*, 10ᵗʰ November 1951.)

> An attentive leader might ask: where are the Lvov group winner Sakharov and one of the Baku group qualifiers Kholmov? You'll read Sakharov's story below, while Ratmir Dmitrievich told the story of why he didn't play many years later.
>
> **Kholmov:** "In 1951, I got disqualified. Why? It happened at the national championship semi-final. So, there we were, Tarasov, Nezhmetdinov and I, sitting and drinking, and then two girls showed up. And Rashid was a sort of extra man, he was about fifteen years older than me and Tarasov. 'Turn off your tape recorder, turn it off, can you imagine what will happen if my wife sees this?'
>
> All in all, Nezhmetdinov got angry (he was drunk, of course), went to the balcony and started throwing things down – vases, dishes. When Nezhmetdinov drank, he did all sorts of crazy stuff – lying down on the tram rails, all that. Perhaps they would've swept everything under the rug, all those broken dishes, but Kotov took a special interest in the incident. He started gathering info on what happened – disorderly conduct, the police, all

that, and the tournament was quite important – qualification for the national championship. So, all three of us were summoned to Moscow, to Rodionov – the Sports Committee chairman. Rashid groveled at his feet, and, as a party member, he was spared, but they banned me and Tarasov for a year. They also stripped me of the stipend that I received as a member of the national chess team." (From the book *Dialogues with the Chess Nostradamus*.)

Memory failed Kholmov here. The editorial "Moral Character of a Soviet Master" in *Shakhmaty v SSSR* (No. 12, 1951) stated that "For moral corruption, the All-Union Committee for Physical Education and Sport stripped V. Tarasov (Kishinev) of his master's title and disqualified him for 2 years, and masters R. Nezhmetdinov (Kazan) and R. Kholmov (Vilnius) were banned from taking part in chess competition for one year."

An unfortunate story. Kholmov was on the rise back then and would have probably performed very well in the final. In a training match with Bronstein (before his championship clash with Botvinnik), he won one and drew three games out of four!

Zagoriansky: "The first time in the final... It's somewhat strange to hear this phrase applied to such talented international masters as Novotelnov and Simagin.

Master Vladimir Simagin, 1947 Moscow champion. Postcard from the author's archive.

Chess is not always fair. Vladimir Simagin, deep, original and highly educated in chess regards, failed to qualify from the Soviet Championship semi-finals for several years in a row. In between, he regularly achieved great success in the Moscow championships and sometimes in international competitions...

Nikolai Novotelnov. Who doesn't remember his play in the pan-Slavic tournament in memory of Chigorin *(1947)*? Who doesn't remember his last round game against Keres? For 40 moves, the Soviet champion struggled to fend off the master's attacks. He managed to adjourn the game in a position that was called 'unclear' by the press.

However, Novotelnov sealed a move that took the grandmaster by complete surprise. Keres had to resign just four moves after the game resumed...

In the 1942 tournament of Moscow masters and candidates, I shared 1st–2nd place with Panov. I suffered my only loss to a tall, quiet young man whose name – Oleg Moiseev – didn't ring any bells. I remember the game as well. My opponent had black, and in a worse position caught me in a cunning trap with a well-hidden piece sacrifice... If Moiseev manages to eliminate his main flaw – his timidity – then he should perform well. His understanding of the game is very good.

I think that the creative style of Evgeny Terpugov has not yet been fully formed. He occasionally suffers from a somewhat fanciful, contrived interpretation of the position, and his propensity for difficult, laborious lines. In general, this readiness to solve difficult problems instead of easier ones is very commendable, but this can't but affect the results. On the other hand, Terpugov's fighting qualities are very strong." (Ibid., 17th November.)

Prorvich: "The opening ceremony of the 19th Soviet Championship took place on 10th November in the conference room of the USSR Council of Ministers Committee for Physical Education and Sport. Caretaker Committee chairman N. N. Romanov wished all the participants creative success.

The tournament chief arbiter, Distinguished Master of Sports P. A. Romanovsky, read out the tournament regulations *(2.5 hours for 40 moves, then 1 hour for each subsequent 16 moves)*...

Thorough reports on the tournament appeared both in the central and local press. There was a specialized radio program with the latest chess news from the tournament hall." (Tournament book.)

Secrets of a Crippled Future

But still: where is Yuri Sakharov? You won't find anything about him in the press of the time: its ability to cover the tracks was unsurpassed. The bulletin *19th Soviet Chess Championship* (edited by V. Ragozin) did a very simple thing: it printed the tables of the other three semi-finals before the games, but not the Lvov one (and make of that what you will: either they just "forgot", or the printers "made a mistake"). Alexander Prorvich, the editor of the tournament book, was also no fool: he just gave the list of everyone who qualified from the semi-finals – without places and points. Abramov, the editor of the *Chess in 1951–1952* yearbook, had a harder time, but he also managed to elegantly avoid the standings; omitting Sakharov, he wrote, "In Lvov, Aronin, Simagin (12/19) and Flohr (11.5) qualified for the championship."

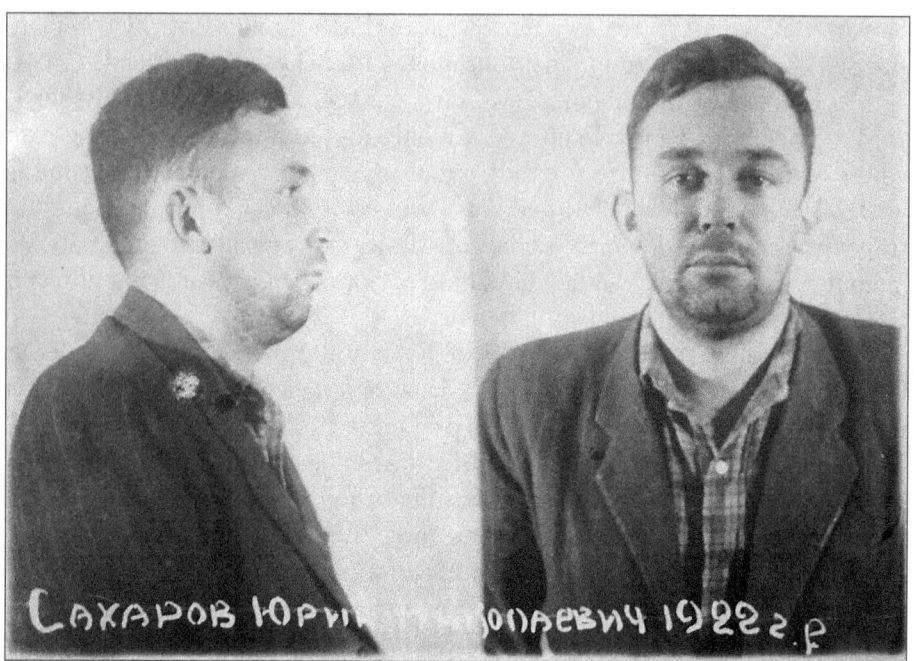

Photo from Yuri Sakharov's dossier. This document was found in the declassified SBU archive by Mykola Fuzik (Kiev).

And only a very thorough reader, counting the number of players – 19, could have asked: *why 12 points out of 19, not 18? Probably a misprint...*

What did Sakharov do to get unpersoned in such a way? The famous Ukrainian chess historian **Efim Lazarev** answered that question in his essay **"Pan Inspector, or the Secrets of a Crippled Future"** in Yuri Semenko's book (1993), which I quote from below (the original text is in Ukrainian). However, recently, Kiev journalist and historian **Mykola Fuzik**, who is working on a book about Sakharov, found his declassified two-volume case file No. 149819 in the SBU archives, which was preserved in the KGB Record and Archive department. He summarized his research in the article **"Yuri Sakharov: Twists of Fate"** (Chesspro site, 2020), which clarifies some points in Sakharov's biography and the circumstances of his arrest. I asked Nikolai to write a short version of his findings for this work – they're given as small-font insertions.

Lazarev: "In 1937 Yuri Sakharov's father, a supervisor of the Donbass coal industry, was repressed (and later, as expected, rehabilitated).

> **Fuzik:** "His father was born in Chernigov, in a colonel's family, and graduated from cadet school and the St. Petersburg Mining Institute. Even though he joined the Bolshevik Party after the October Revolution

and worked in the same field he studied in, his aristocratic lineage came to haunt him. In 1935, Nikolai Matveevich Sakharov, deputy director of the Makeevka Research Institute at that point, was expelled from the party, and he was arrested in 1938 as a 'member of a counter-revolutionary Ukrainian nationalist organization' and sentenced to execution with confiscation of property. A standard (but false) verdict was given to the family members, ten years without the right of correspondence, so they only learned the truth much later."

When the war with Hitler started, Yuri wasn't conscripted into the Red Army (probably as a son of an 'enemy of the people'). He wound up in occupied territory and, together with many others, was captured by the Nazis and used for slave labor. The lad worked in occupied Belgium in coal mines. When Belgium was liberated by the allies, Sakharov, as he told me later, joined the US army and reached Elba with a weapon in his hands, and then returned to Ukraine. He settled in Kiev, married and enrolled in a Romance-Germanic language correspondence course at university (he didn't graduate), working in the Ukrainian Sports Committee as an inspector – he supervised chess and four more sports. Since that time, he got a funny nickname – 'Pan Inspector'. Why 'pan' *('Mr' in Polish and Ukrainian)*? Sakharov mostly spoke Ukrainian and never hid his liking for the Polish people (his mother, according to him,

1956. Front right (with a suitcase), rehabilitated political prisoner Yuri Sakharov. He spent five years behind barbed wire... From E. Lazarev's archive (Kiev).

belonged to a noble Ukrainian-Polish family, the Levitskis), he knew the Polish language, history and literature very well.

> **Fuzik:** "The *Shakhmaty* encyclopedia says that Sakharov was born on 18th September 1922 in Yuzovka (later Stalino, now Donetsk). This information is posted in the Russian, Ukrainian and English Wikipedia. The date is correct, but the declassified case file says that he was born in Vlasovka, Rostov Oblast...
>
> When the war started, Sakharov was not conscripted into the standing army (possibly as the son of an 'enemy of the people'), but was twice called for trench digging. Both times, because of the Germans' swift attacks and general chaos on the front lines, the mobilized personnel were left to their own devices, and Sakharov returned to Stalino. After his second return, he learned that the enlistment office was already evacuated. And, frankly, Yuri probably wasn't too eager to give up his life for the Soviet state after everything they did to his father...
>
> He remained on occupied lands together with his mother. To survive, they had to sell their belongings or exchange them for food. In spring 1942, their situation became desperate, and Sakharov decided to enlist as an 'Ostarbeiter' and go to work in Germany. He wound up in the town of Alsdorf, at a camp that served the Anna-3 mine; in addition to his main duties, he was assigned as the translator for the camp superintendent because he knew German well. This later served as one of the pretexts for 'treachery' and 'collaboration' accusations.
>
> When the Americans arrived in 1944, he, together with other Soviet citizens, was transferred to another camp, in Belgium. As Yuri Nikolaevich said at the interrogations, he never served in the U.S. army, never held a weapon in his hands, but was used for some support work... Despite the offer to remain, Sakharov preferred to return to Ukraine, which he loved with all his heart."

In spring 1951, he performed brilliantly in Lvov at the Soviet Championship semi-final. The young candidate master, who defeated famous masters, wore a *vyshivanka* and spoke good Ukrainian, got a lot of sympathy in the city. And then someone ratted him out – wrote something to you-know-where.

But what exactly was written?

Those who knew the exact answers back then kept silent. And so, the wide chess community had to contend with, as Vladimir Vysotsky sang, 'gossip in the guise of versions'. The most popular claim was that he worked as a... translator in the Gestapo. But it turned out to be false. Actually, as he said later, he was never accused of anything of the sort. In Lvov, he was recognized by another former Nazi slave who worked together with him in Belgium. Even back then, she suspected him of collaboration with the occupiers, because he would occasionally bring and share food that was not given to anyone else. She didn't know that the young Ukrainian was a strong chess player who found his way into the local chess club where he played with the Belgians for money (according to him, he even met the future well-known grandmaster O'Kelly there) and then bought food for his compatriots. I don't know for sure if this really happened – I only say what I myself heard.

> **Fuzik:** "Thanks to Lazarev, it was thought that Sakharov was enjoying a good life after the war, and that his life was only ruined by a random denunciation. No! They had been trying to get him for years. The renowned coach Mikhail Trosman wrote, from the words of Sakharov himself, that 'his ascent was stopped by our 'valiant' security services, who had been investigating him for a long time.' The case materials fully corroborated that story: many witnesses were interrogated long before his arrest; the earliest protocol was dated 1946, and even back then, there was already talk of 'treasonous and collaborationist activity' by Sakharov. Concerning the denunciation – it may have been simply used as a trigger. The organs' own digging could have lasted indefinitely, but when you get a signal from outside, you have to actually do something."

Then, in Lvov, the 29 year-old Kiev player took first place and got a master's norm. But he didn't get to play in the Soviet Championship final or to be bestowed that honorable title: he was arrested in autumn 1951. He was tried by a tribunal behind closed doors and given 25 years – according to him, for fighting the Nazis in the US army for several months *(as a reminder 1951 was the peak of the Korean War, where the USSR and United States confronted each other)*. 'If this is a crime,' he said in court after hearing his verdict, 'then I refuse to understand Russian language and will only speak Ukrainian until my sentence is overturned.' Of course, such a statement didn't exactly make things easier.

Then he was sent to the notorious Vladimir Central prison, and from there to participate in the construction of the Bratsk hydroelectric plant...

> Let's digress here. So it turns out that Yuri Nikolaevich also described his ordeals, both during the war and after the arrest, to the coach **Mikhail Trosman:**

"I was delicate enough and didn't bother Sakharov with too many questions. I can only retell what he told me himself.

During the war, Sakharov, on the recommendation of the Donetsk master Selezniev, went to visit Bogoljubov who lived in Germany. He helped Sakharov get a job. I suspect that he was working as a translator, especially since Sakharov knew Polish and German in addition to Russian and Ukrainian.

After his arrest, during the investigation, Sakharov shared a cell with the Kiev Operetta Theater artist Blashchuk and a young, completely uneducated, 'dim', as Sakharov said, young lad from Transcarpathia. The story of Blashchuk's arrest is typical and telling for the times. During a tour of Odessa, Blashchuk met an American journalist and was soon arrested for suspected espionage. Was he going to divulge some top secret theater information to the journalist? The Transcarpathia lad was arrested because

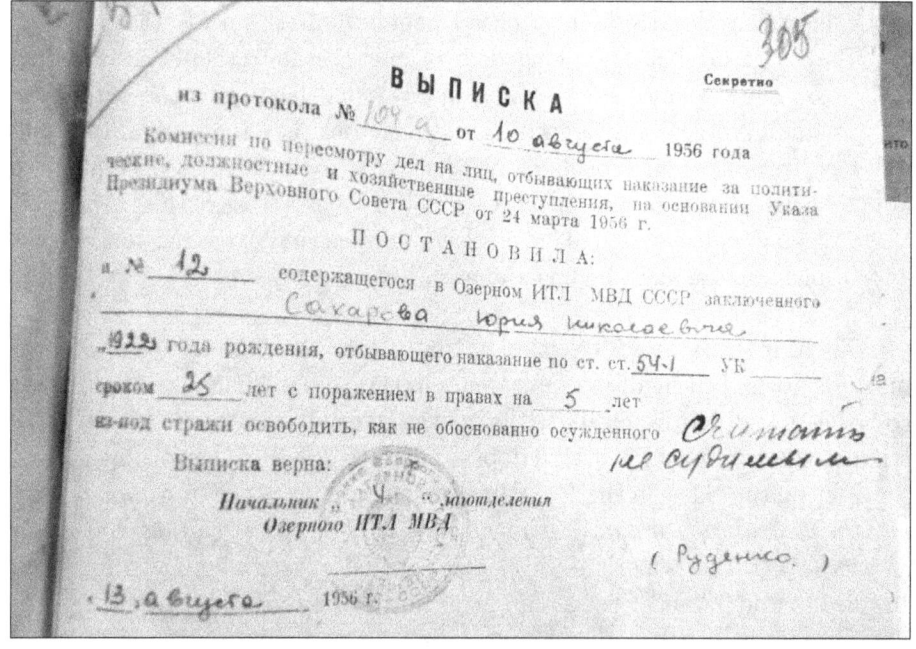

"Secret. Extract from Protocol No. 104a dated 10 August 1956. The commission for reviewing cases of persons imprisoned for political, workplace and economic crimes, on the basis of Decree of the Presidium of the USSR Supreme Soviet dated 24 March 1956, hereby resolves: point 12, to free prisoner Sakharov Yuri Nikolaevich born 1922 imprisoned at Ozerny correctional labor camp of the Interior Ministry of the USSR, being punished under article 54-1 of the criminal code with a sentence of 25 years with denial of rights for 5 years, as having been convicted without a basis. To be considered as having no criminal record. Head of Camp Department No. 4 of Ozerny correctional labor camp of the Interior Ministry Rudenko. 13 August 1956." This document was also found in the declassified SBU archive by Mykola Fuzik.

when some unknown man was shot while trying to cross the border, a piece of paper with the lad's address was found in his pocket. The investigators were quite insistent in their interrogation, but the poor lad couldn't even understand what was wanted of him. And then Sakharov and Blashchuk told him, 'Do you want them to stop beating you and start feeding you normally?' Of course, he agreed. The two came up with a legend for the lad, which he told at the next interrogation. The beatings indeed stopped, and he was fed normally. But the investigators realized very soon that there were a lot of inconsistencies in the legend, and they determined who the authors were even more quickly. The two 'authors' were sent to a disciplinary cell.

Sakharov told me about their two-month summer journey on a steamship along the Lena river to their place of imprisonment. The guards took in a set number of prisoners and had to deliver the same number to the destination. Therefore, the living continued their way together with the dead. It was stuffy in the ship's hold, which only increased the death toll. Prisoners from the Baltics had it especially tough." (From Adrian Mikhalchishin's article "The Post-War Quarter-Final", Chesspro site, 2016.)

In 1955, he was offered an amnesty, but he refused resolutely, demanding rehabilitation. In 1956, he was fully rehabilitated, returned to Kiev, finally got awarded his master's title, and got a job – not in the Sports Committee though, but as a head instructor at the Young Pioneers Palace chess club.

Fuzik: "Throughout his time behind bars, he wrote complaints and petitions asking for a retrial. Yuri Nikolaevich's tone grew increasingly confident and demanding in his later letters. Here is an excerpt from his complaint dated 28th October 1955: 'The amnesty order of 17th September, for reasons unknown to me, did not extend to me at all, even though at least half of my case is a product of the investigative organs' literary creativity.'

As you see, Sakharov didn't refuse any amnesty offer – moreover, he demanded an amnesty! In 1956, he was freed by one of the many local retrial commissions as 'wrongly convicted', with an added note: 'to be considered as having no criminal record'."

Soon, there was a suggestion to elect him to the Ukrainian Chess Federation presidium. One of the delegates argued that Sakharov had served time, that there were rumors that he had done certain things... Then Peter Didenko, a chess enthusiast and police colonel back then, answered: 'I personally looked through his case in the competent organs – he's totally innocent.' Sakharov was elected.

In 1963, he was awarded the title of Distinguished Coach of Ukraine – the republic's youth team won several Soviet youth championships. We should also point out that 'Pan Inspector' had discovered and gave the first chess lessons to many young talents, including well-known masters such as Alexei Kosikov and Elena Sedina, Dmitry Komarov and Vladimir Peresypkin, he helped Vladimir Savon, Gennady Kuzmin and Lidia Semenova grow into grandmasters... This list can be continued.

So, was the 1951 case finally closed? Technically – yes. In practice, however, no. When Sakharov visited the 'corridors of power' for whatever reason, he still felt the politicians' distrust. He was 'shut down' at any possible opportunity, especially when there were invitations to play abroad.

And there were quite a few. Even though Sakharov was not exactly young when he returned to tournament play, even though five years of undeserved, difficult detention caused irreparable damage to his sporting form and psychological state, his great chess talent still brought him success for many more years. Paradoxically, Sakharov reached his peak when he was in his forties..." (From Semenko's book *Chess in Ukraine*.)

> **Fuzik:** "Sakharov was watched for many years afterwards. There are enquiries dated to the mid-1960s in his case, asking to clarify whether there were any compromising materials on him. It turns out that Sakharov was a person of interest in a case that was destroyed in 1992, but three index cards survived. So: 'Form of investigation: Surveillance. Nickname: Chess Player. Essence of the investigation: Ukrainian nationalist.' Here's a record dated 21st April 1967: 'While serving time, he came into close contact with a number of Ukrainian nationalists, took part in organized anti-Soviet activity in the camps. After release, he continued to maintain criminal links with them.'
>
> Unfortunately, it's likely impossible to learn any details or even clarify whether it's true. I must say that none of Sakharov's friends or acquaintances remember him telling them anything of that sort. Knowing Yuri Nikolaevich's love for Ukraine, I can only surmise that he befriended some nationalists during his time in the camp, and after his release, he kept in touch with them..."

P.S. He won the Ukrainian championship outright twice (1966, 1968, and also shared 1st–2nd place in 1960), and took part in five Soviet Championship finals (1961, 1964/65, 1965, 1967, and 1968/69). His best performances were 7th place in 1965, where Sakharov was the only player to defeat the champion, Stein, and finished ahead of Bronstein and Korchnoi, and 6th place in 1967 (a Swiss tournament with 126 players), ahead of a number of grandmasters and international masters. But he only earned the international master's title in correspondence play, since Sakharov was essentially banned from traveling abroad (his only tournament outside the USSR was Varna 1968, which he won). And the small, 10-line article in the *Shakhmaty* encyclopedia doesn't even mention that he won two gold medals in the team correspondence championship as a member of the Soviet team (1968–1972 and 1972–1977)!

Yuri Nikolaevich Sakharov tragically died in 1981, before his 60th birthday in unclear circumstances. His bloodied body was found by rail tracks at dawn on 26th September in Bucha, where he had a dacha and to where he had set off by train from Kiev the previous evening... Lazarev: "The father was executed for nothing, the son was imprisoned for nothing. And when he was rehabilitated, they only stopped belittling him after his death. Or did they?.."

Yuri Sakharov achieved his greatest successes after turning 40. Photo by S. Titov. From the author's archive.

King For a Day

The bulletin made me happy this time: the degree of "patriotism" was lowered, which immediately improved the actual content. The game descriptions became even too verbose; they only managed to find some balance towards the middle of the tournament. So, this time, we'll use both *Sovietsky Sport* and the bulletin to watch the tournament unfold. Especially since the newspaper reports lacked the previous year's sheen, and the descriptions of games were occasionally supplanted by simple move-by-move commentaries. Of course, this is a matter of taste, and some might prefer the style of Alexander Tolush and Nikolai Tarasov (poet and journalist, he would later become the chief editor of *Sovietsky Sport*; he knew chess well enough and was friends with Petrosian). But why was the previous year's decent tag team dissolved – did Lev Abramov and Viktor Vasiliev perform too poorly?

After a considerable break (since 1944), the Soviet championship again took place in the Column Hall of the House of the Unions. From the Chess Review magazine (No. 2, 1952). Courtesy of US Chess.

It turns out that Viktor was also let down by his "fifth point" – the place in the Soviet "internal passport" (as the ID document is known) where the holder's race was recorded. Vasiliev was his stepfather's surname, and his biological father, pharmacist Lazar Arkus, was a Jew and an "enemy of the people" to boot (he was executed in 1938). Even though Viktor had been a frontline soldier and worked at *Sovietsky Sport* for two years as a reporter, he was fired in 1951, during the anti-cosmopolitan (essentially, anti-Semitic) campaign. He was reinstated only in 1958 and worked at his beloved newspaper for another quarter of a century...

Panov: "The 19th Soviet chess championship is being held in the Column Hall of the House of the Unions. This clearly shows the admiration and respect that the ancient wise game commands in our country.

The Moscow fans of chess art filled the Column Hall on 11th November. The chess tables are placed on a nicely decorated stage. Above, on the backdrop of the wavy, dark red velvet draped curtain, 'XIX Soviet Chess Championship' is written in golden letters. Nine big demonstration boards are ready to relay the upcoming fights to the spectators.

The tournament participants arrive on stage, bathed in applause. The arbiters start the clocks. The battle for the Soviet Championship gold medal has started." (*19th Soviet Chess Championship* bulletin, 23rd November 1951.)

There's almost no poetry in the bulletin this time – only one poem, which is more fitting for some factory newspaper. I'll quote the beginning and the end, because everything else is a sad attempt to find rhymes for the participants' surnames:

WHO WILL WIN?

Who will win? Who'll be first?	Who will win?.. We will find out,
Who will keep the most strength?	But the answer is clear even now:
Are the veterans' nerves stronger?	There are no players in the world
Is the youngsters' fervor hotter?	Stronger than those in the Soviet land!
[... ... ...]	**Mikh. Artsev** (Ibid., 25th November.)

Tolush and **Tarasov**: "The first round and the subsequent play-off day have immediately clarified the standings at the start. The leaders are: world champion M. Botvinnik, Soviet champion P. Keres, grandmasters V. Smyslov, A. Kotov and I. Bondarevsky, masters I. Lipnitsky and N. Kopylov... Seven decisive games out of nine! Isn't it the best evidence of the indomitable fighting spirit of the best representatives of the Soviet chess school!

Botvinnik again demonstrated his exceptional ability to exploit a barely noticeable weakness in his opponent's *(Moiseev's)* position. Keres again showed his brilliant tactical talent *(against Terpugov)*.

Moscow is the universally recognized center of world chess culture. It's not easy to become the Moscow chess champion. And in the first round, the Leningrad master Kopylov boldly and energetically storms the position of the capital city's champion (and the youngest player of the tournament, by the way) Petrosian with a cascade of sacrifices and wins a very good game *(see game 249)*.

Kotov and Bronstein are playing. Both of them are, without a doubt, among the main contenders for the championship. Why should they take a risk in the first round? Isn't it better to go down well-trodden paths and play out a so-called 'grandmaster draw' to save their energy for the finish? No. Such an outcome isn't acceptable for Soviet grandmasters. Both of them go for a sharp continuation. Both are fighting with the full strength of their talent, using their entire arsenal of technical and tactical mastery *(see game 247)*.

After this loss, Bronstein temporarily falls to the bottom of the table and lets one of his main rivals get ahead. Well, a fight is a fight! There are more rounds of the battle ahead, and he who wins the most games will become champion.

This is the only way of thinking for Soviet sportsmen.

There's a rule in this championship that states that the opponents cannot agree to a draw before the 30th move without the chief arbiter's approval. Until all the main resources are exhausted, while there are still opportunities to fight for a win, the battle must go on. This is the law of the Soviet chess school.

> The anti-draw campaign was started back in the quarter-finals, but... From **Romanovsky**'s letter to Zak (20th January 1952): "The new tie-break method, number of wins, seems not to have worked. It may not be worse than the Berger coefficient, but it's clearly not better. It did lower the draw percentage, but not too significantly, and the cries of unhappiness were heard from everywhere." (*Shakhmatny Peterburg,* No. 5, 2002.) In the semi-finals, Berger tables were used as the main tie-break...

Seven decisive games out of nine is also a blow to the reactionary ideas of some players from capitalist countries, to apologists of the silly bourgeois theory of the so-called 'death by draws' of chess. A draw, as a rule, occurs only in games where the players avoid struggle, where lively, inspired

Like a year earlier, Smyslov and Geller met in the first round. Back then, they drew, but now Smyslov managed to win. From D. Bronstein's archive. Published for the first time.

Leningrad's Nikolai Kopylov playing Levenfish, while Furman stands watching. Photo of their game from the semi-final of the 15th Soviet Championship by M. Volkovysky from his archive. Published for the first time.

creativity is replaced by purely technical calculations, where the principle of 'economizing on mental strength', which is so alien to the Soviet people, prevails...

Round 2. When Keres has black, he usually replies 1...e5 to white's 1.e4. In the game against Kopylov, he went against that tradition and chose a line in the Sicilian Defense that was rejected by theory. Early complications arose. After move 7, the queens were already gone from the board, and black got weak queenside pawns.

Kopylov skillfully used the advantages of his position and, getting his rooks to the queenside through the 3rd rank, improved his position considerably. Keres defended persistently, but still had to give up a pawn *(and ultimately lost – see game 242)*.

Even though Kopylov turned out to be a king for just a day (he only scored half a point in the subsequent four rounds), his play made a great impression again, especially his sensational win against Botvinnik in round 12. The master's moves were so original that his colleagues actually... tried to guess his moves and placed bets on them!

Nikolai Georgievich Kopylov was a pupil of Romanovsky. A war veteran, holder of a candidate's degree in engineering, and an ICCF international master. By coincidence, he won gold medals for the USSR in the same correspondence chess world team championships as Yuri Sakharov (1968–1972 and 1972–1977)... Why didn't he achieve more success in over-the-board play? One of the possible reasons was his gentle disposition: "Having good time management skills, Kopylov was always sympathetic towards his opponents suffering from time trouble: after making a move, he didn't hurry to press his clock, allowing his opponent to think at the cost of his own time!" (From the book *People and Chess* by Dlugolensky and Zak.)

Round 3. In 1939, a group of young chess players were studying in the Leningrad Young Pioneers Palace under the tutelage of Botvinnik. Among them was the 13 year-old sixth-grade student of the Conservatory musical school Mark Taimanov. It was Botvinnik who revealed the laws of the ancient and wise game to him, who laid the basis for his creative growth...

In winter 1941, Mark defeated his mentor in a clock simul in the Young Pioneers Palace, and Botvinnik annotated his loss for a newspaper – a unique occurrence! At the end, he chided his pupil for "not watching the latest games and literature closely enough" and gave the following summation: "Unfortunately, Taimanov is still not objective enough: as a rule, he overestimates his position. Mark Taimanov is now growing as a chess player, and we should hope that in the future he will continue to grow, paying no heed to the excessive praise that corrupts our youth too often." (*64*, 26th February). Botvinnik was indeed an incredible diagnostician: Mark Evgenyevich never managed to eliminate that excessive optimism in evaluating his chances!

And now, they face each other at the board. Botvinnik has white... Soon it turns out that they have chosen the Nimzo-Indian Defense, an opening favored by both. Botvinnik has won many great games in that opening. The 25 year-old Taimanov is also considered an expert on the Nimzo-Indian Defense. He recently finished a manuscript of his book on this opening *(the book was published only in 1956)*.

The young master played the opening in a very original way. His pawn had already reached h3 on the 7th move. Still, Botvinnik castled kingside: it was clear that Taimanov would not be able to create an attack on the king... Botvinnik didn't choose the best plan for the middlegame. Taimanov skillfully used his resources and stopped his opponent's plans with tactical blows. On move 38, the world champion agreed to a draw and congratulated his pupil warmly...

> It wasn't for nothing that Botvinnik turned to Taimanov on the eve of the world championship match tournament. Here's a fragment from his confidential letter ("Please don't tell anybody about this letter or its contents!") dated 27th September 1947, which Taimanov only published in his book *Remembering the Greatest*...:
>
> "I'm now beginning to prepare for the match tournament, or to be more accurate, I'm putting together a preparation plan and decided to ask you, Mark, for help.
>
> First, I would ask you, Mark, if it's not a secret, to inform me of all the interesting opening novelties to be found in games in Leningrad. Secondly, I'm looking for opponents for closed training games that are provisionally planned for January. The training will probably take place at a hotel in the Moscow region. (...) I think that this endeavor will also be useful for you – you really need to take up chess seriously one day.
>
> I'm asking you, Mark, because I don't have that many friends appropriate for closed training games, i.e. who know when to keep their lips sealed. But I'm relying on you in this respect."
>
> Taimanov couldn't recall what prevented their collaboration – or didn't want to...

The fourth round was one of the most exciting. Geller is known as a player who can organize and execute a brilliant attack on the king. The Odessa master is especially dangerous when he has the initiative. But this time, Geller himself fell victim to the formidable power of a sudden but well-prepared attack *(see game 237)*...

> **Romanovsky:** "The quiet rumble of hundreds of whispers fills the Column Hall. The sign 'Observe the silence!' – a silent order from the arbiters' board – frequently lights up on the stage. The tension on the boards, especially in the games Geller – Keres and Averbakh – Smyslov, excites the numerous spectators. And when Keres sacrifices a knight, some applause is heard in the hall. Geller thinks deeply on his 32nd move and then suddenly stops his clock. There's an ovation in the hall." (Tournament bulletin, 30th November.)

Sometime later, applause sounds. The sign "White won" appears on the Averbakh – Smyslov game demonstration board.

After a badly-played opening, Smyslov fell under a very strong attack by the master. After the 32nd move, both opponents had only a rook, bishop and an equal amount of pawns. But the material equality didn't matter here. Averbakh's king and other pieces actively supported his passed pawn...

There was an interesting maneuvering game between Kotov and Simagin. The opponents know their mutual strengths and weaknesses well: Simagin worked as Kotov's coach for a time. Interestingly, they had never drawn against each other before. Kotov won four games, and Simagin four *(and here it is, their first draw!)*.

> **Beilin:** "After playing in his first Soviet Championship final, Volodya *(Simagin)* told me that it's easier to play in the final than in an ordinary tournament. If someone sacrifices material to you in an ordinary tournament, you search for some refutation of the sacrifice. While in the final, you can believe your opponent and save valuable time." (From the book *My Encounters in the Chess Kingdom.*)

> Petrosian scored his first win in this round. **Flohr** recounted a little anecdote: "In 1951, after Petrosian lost his first two games in the 19th Soviet Championship, he once answered the phone to hear an unknown voice, which asked him in Armenian: 'Who gave you the right to lose?' This question struck him so hard that he no longer disappointed his fans." (From the book authored by Petrosian and actually compiled by Eduard Shekhtman *Reliability Strategy.*)

Round 5. On 19th November, deep in the Column Hall stage, one of the most important games of the whole tournament was played on a table in the second row. The world champion Botvinnik and the most recent challenger Bronstein again fought for a win. Millions of chess players eagerly awaited this encounter. It's clear why. Bronstein made an honorable draw in the world championship match and was the only participant to have a plus score against Botvinnik: out of 26 games, Botvinnik had won five, Bronstein six, and fifteen ended in draws.

The complicated and sharp Botvinnik System in the Queen's Gambit was played. By the way, Botvinnik showed his intentions to play this opening line numerous times during the match, but Bronstein never went for it, and now, finally, he accepted the challenge *(see game 239)*...

> **Yudovich:** "The game is relayed by phone to many chess clubs of the capital city and other cities too. For instance, many fans have gathered in the Riga chess club *(a first-category lad called Misha Tal may have been among them;*

Half a year before the championship, Botvinnik and Bronstein tortured each other in the world championship match that ended with a 12–12 score. From the author's archive. Published for the first time.

according to Vasiliev, he would "often visit the basement on Weidenbaum Street, where the Riga chess club was located"). The phone rings. The tournament press bureau speaks. Bronstein played 12.♕e2. 'How do the masters evaluate this maneuver?' Riga asks. 'This seems to be a new continuation...' Yes, indeed, the development of the queen to e2 was unexpected for everyone who watched the game and maybe even for Botvinnik himself...

The crisis in the intense struggle happened on the 22nd move, when Bronstein launched a tempting kingside attack. Instead of 22.♕g4, white had to play 22.d7, which would have led to a sharp position with mutual chances. Without a doubt, Bronstein missed Botvinnik's brilliant counterblow 23...c5. He immediately got into trouble, but found interesting tactical opportunities and cunning traps with his characteristic inventiveness." (Tournament bulletin, 2nd December.)

Both grandmasters were in severe time trouble for the last 15 moves. This explains all the mistakes they made. Still, even in the adjourned position, Bronstein has no chances to save the game." (*Sovietsky Sport*, 15th, 17th, 20th and 22nd November.)

The Art of Home Analysis

In our time, this is a lost art... because it's not needed anymore! For years, chess players have been free of the necessity to analyze adjourned positions for hours, sometimes until the morning, after an intense game. Not many remember that David Bronstein was the first player to lobby to abolish the adjournment, back in the 1970s. He would later write, "I think that adjourning the game and continuing it the next day is contraindicated for chess. All the opening, middlegame and endgame problems should be solved over the board, without thorough home analysis which – why hide that? – is conducted with the help of seconds or even solely by them. And it's often unclear who really won the game." (From the 2nd Russian edition of *The Modern Chess Self-Tutor*, 1986.)

By the way, the participants lived near the House of the Unions – in the Moskva hotel, one of the best in the whole city. This was good for the Moscow players also, most of whom lived in communal apartments – freed of domestic issues, they could fully concentrate on chess. In their comfortable rooms, they prepared for games, analyzed the adjourned positions and played the games postponed due to illness (with the course of the game demonstrated in the tournament hall.)

Evaluating his adjourned position against Botvinnik in round 4 as hopeless, Lipnitsky resigned without resuming the game. Photo by A. Vochinin. From M. Botvinnik's archive.

Tolush and **Tarasov:** "The play-off day... Let's try to look into a master's lab one day before that. Looking into the position on the board that has his full attention, it's almost impossible to recognize a game that was stopped at the height of struggle. The number of pawns has decreased, the knights have been traded away, and the king has taken a breathtaking walk from h8 to a2.

So what's that about? Why is the master so interested in this seemingly unfamiliar position? It turns out that if one of the many, but most likely lines is played, this position will be the hardest for the master to win.

But what should he do if his opponent seals the weakest move? What if there's some study-like draw, too?

And the master is working. Hour after hour, he analyzes one line after another. Nothing should be overlooked. He needs to study the greatest number of possible continuations.

The third play-off day at the tournament was held the day before yesterday.

The low stage of the October Hall of the House of the Unions. Five chess tables and the yellow and black squares of the demonstration boards over them. The pieces are still in their starting positions. Silence...

The arbiters and demonstrators arrive first. Before the play-off starts *(at 4:30 p.m.)*, it's necessary to restore the exact position of the stopped fights in the five games...

The participants enter the hall through the lively corridor of spectators. Here goes the world champion, confident, fit and energetic. The position in the game with Bronstein raises no doubts: he sealed the best move, and his opponent should stop resisting quite quickly.

> **Romanovsky:** "Since the first days, it was clear that Botvinnik was very nervous, that some things weren't working out for him, that, like in the Bronstein match, he was unable to avoid severe time trouble. Still, he manages to win the grudge game against Bronstein in round 5. He poured all his strength and inspiration into this game." (Tournament book.)

Kopylov slowly ascends the steps. It's hard to hide his bad mood. Home analysis didn't bring the master any joy. He has to fight both against Taimanov's white pawns and Aronin's black pawns in clearly worse positions. He needs to fight for a draw, and it's not in the Leningrad player's character.

Simagin is stern and concentrated. Kotov has an extra pawn and the bishop pair in their adjourned position. The master reaches the stage and sits down at the table first. He looks at the position for the last time. The arbiters come and open the envelope with the grandmaster's sealed move. The game continues. *(Simagin managed to hold!)*

> **Kotov:** "Since 1948, I've been working with my coach – a man of exceptionally original talent, the author of numerous discoveries in the opening, strong over-the-board player Vladimir Simagin. (...) We have worked together quite productively, I became a Soviet champion with his help, but it was clear that the coaching role didn't quite fit his 'freedom-loving' character.
>
> 'I'm not your servant!' Simagin would often exclaim, looking at me crossly from behind his thick glasses. And I realized that he wouldn't be helping me for long. That's exactly what happened: after the 1950 Candidates Tournament, Volodya and I alas parted ways." (From Kotov's book *Mastery*.)

The sealed move often determines the outcome of an adjourned game. That's exactly what happened in the game Smyslov – Moiseev. The arbiters played Smyslov's sealed move, and the opponents agreed to a draw." (Ibid., 22nd November.)

Standings after round 5: Botvinnik, Taimanov – 4; Keres – 3.5; Aronin, Kotov – 3; Averbakh, Bondarevsky, Geller, Kopylov, Moiseev, Petrosian, Smyslov – 2.5; Bronstein, Lipnitsky, Simagin, Flohr – 2; Novotelnov, Terpugov – 1.

Nobody Is Invincible!

Tolush and **Tarasov:** "In round 6, the games Kotov – Keres and Flohr – Smyslov attracted the greatest attention from spectators. Both were sharp since the very beginning.

The Nimzo-Indian Defense usually occurs after 1.d4 ♞f6, but in this game, Keres played ♞f6 only on the fifth move. On his ninth move, he pushed the h7 pawn two squares ahead. This turned the game very sharp. It became even sharper when the national champion castled long... In the middlegame, Keres didn't play too well and ceded the initiative to Kotov. Both players were in time trouble. Kotov managed to create a strong attack and won on the 40th move.

> **Flohr:** "The chess world remembers well the last game between Alekhine and Capablanca on 21st November 1938 *(actually on the 19th, but Flohr was born on the 21st and so exercised his artistic license)* at the tournament in the Netherlands. It was Capablanca's 50th birthday *(which was true, his birthday was on the 19th)*. The 'impolite' Alekhine won the game in a crushing style, completely ruining Capablanca's festive mood.

М. Ботвинник (слева) и В. Смыслов, одержавший в этой партии победу над чемпионом мира.

The central game of round 7, Smyslov versus Botvinnik, which ended in a win for the former. From the Sovietsky Soyuz magazine (No. 12, 1951).

In today's game Flohr – Smyslov, Flohr had a better position. But then Flohr blundered, and Smyslov won the game. He consoled me, 'Don't be upset. I knew that it was your birthday today, and you can't help but lose on that day.'" (*Ogonyok*, No. 49, 1951.)

Strangely, the game that was ultimately awarded the first brilliancy prize *(see game 234)* got only a single sentence in the newspaper. **Suetin** was also quite stingy in the tournament bulletin (6th December):

"Moiseev and Simagin played with great inspiration. The latter played the King's Indian Defense. The opponents castled in opposite directions. Simagin energetically attacked the white king's position and boldly sacrificed a piece on move 20. At the critical moment, Moiseev failed to find the defense. Simagin's attack was successful."

Round 7. At every round, spectators hurriedly climb the stairs when the ticket collectors, in accordance with the strict rules of the chess championships, are already closing the hall doors. Nervously pacing up and down the lobby, the latecomers, listening to the thousand-strong choir of voices and short flashes of applause, are trying to guess what is happening on the nine chessboards in the most intense minutes of struggle.

The day before yesterday, international master I. Kan was one of those latecomers.

'As I was removing my coat, I already realized that something unusual had happened!' he said.

'Smyslov won!'

'How did it happen?'

...In the last 30 minutes of the games, the flags of many players are already hanging, and time, tangible as the beating of a tired heart, imperiously invades the unhurried, wise course of the game. The tempo sharply increases. Moves follow moves with such speed that the demonstrators cannot keep up with the players, and the spectators learn the result even before the actual sign is put on the demonstration board.

It happened this time as well. Botvinnik shook Smyslov's hand, got up and looked at the board. The black knight slowly lifted off the d8 square. Now it's going to be put on c6, and *(after the move 39.♖xa6)* the sign "White won" will appear in the middle of the board.

> **Romanovsky:** "The intense battle had to end in a draw, but then something inexplicable happened. Half an hour before time control, in an endgame with equal material, Botvinnik makes three mistakes, one after the other. With the last one, he blunders a knight and immediately resigns."

Those who were in the hall will remember the finale of this interesting game for a long time. There was a flurry of applause. The signs 'Observe the silence' lighted up on the stage, and the players had to stop their clocks for several seconds...

Another leader couldn't avoid defeat in round 7 either. The game Bronstein – Taimanov was interesting from the very beginning. White chose a sharp line with 4.a3 in the Nimzo-Indian Defense. The grandmaster sacrificed a pawn on move 12 and got a very promising position due to the threat of pushing the f-pawn. Not willing to settle for a difficult defense after castling short, Taimanov sent his king to the other flank.

Bronstein continued to develop the initiative on the kingside... Taimanov's position became difficult. He opened up the g-file in search of counterplay. For the last 10

The world champion watching Simagin play at the Moscow – Budapest match (1949). From the author's archive.

moves, Taimanov was in severe time trouble, fully ceding the initiative to the grandmaster.

...And so, after the play-off day, there are now no players left who haven't suffered at least one loss. Nobody is invincible. And this again shows the high playing class of our best grandmasters and masters." (*Sovietsky Sport*, 22nd and 24th November.)

Rokhlin: "During the tournament, an exhibition of the Soviet chess art's achievements opened in the Column Hall's lobby. We see different sections there: 'Chess is the favorite game of the peoples of the USSR', 'Chess in the village', 'Woman chess players', and others.

A special place is allotted to photo documents that show the successes of Soviet chess players at international tournaments... There's also a lot of public work in the lobby. Grandmaster A. Lilienthal, masters V. Panov, V. Liublinsky and others have already given simultaneous displays. There were also lectures by Distinguished Master of Sports F. Duz-Khotimirsky 'Remembering Chigorin and Alekhine' and Master E. Zagoriansky 'Russian Chess Players Competing for the World Championship', etc." (Ibid., 24th November.)

Chistiakov: "Round 8 ended with victory for the grandmasters: masters only managed to avoid defeat in two games out of seven *(the overall result was also in the grandmasters' favor – 46.5–30.5; however, if we count only the results of the seven masters from the top of the table, the score is almost even: 26–23).*

Eight years ago *(at the 1943 Moscow championship)*, the young candidate master Simagin played the King's Indian Defense and lost to Botvinnik in a sharp struggle. Today, he used the [Semi-]Slav Defense. Botvinnik is an expert in the Meran Variation. But Simagin tried an interesting novelty: instead of the popular move 12...♛b6, he played

Isaak Lipnitsky failed to reproduce his previous year's success... From L. Yakir's archive (Kiev).

12...♗b7. The first impression was that black was worse due to his broken pawn structure. But on the 16th move, Simagin managed to create threats to the white king with an inventive exchange sacrifice. Botvinnik had to return the gained material. The subsequent struggle was double-edged. In the final position Botvinnik thought for 45 minutes and decided not to risk playing for a win. *(In the 1950s and 1960s, the two met at the board three more times and drew all the games!)*

Smyslov played Lipnitsky. Everyone remembers the Kiev player's win over the grandmaster in the previous championship. This time, Smyslov played confidently and energetically. In the opening (a Nimzo-Indian Defense), he played an interesting move 7...♘a5!, posing difficult problems for his opponent due to the weakness of his light squares. In his search for counterchances, Lipnitsky launched a kingside attack, but unsuccessfully. With some instructive maneuvers, Smyslov obtained a positional advantage and developed an unstoppable attack...

After a good start (2/3), Lipnitsky scored only 1.5 points in the next eight rounds! What was the reason? In the opinion of his biographer **Vadim Teplitsky**, this could have been an early symptom of polycythemia – a blood disease that eventually killed the master: "Lipnitsky made many mistakes and got tired quickly, which was noticeable from the outside as well. Sometimes he felt a little dizzy during the games, writing it off as a consequence of his

На шахматном чемпионате СССР в концертном зале Центрального Дома Советской Армии.

Some rounds were played in the concert hall of the Central House of Officers of the Soviet Army. From the Sovietsky Soyuz magazine (No. 12, 1951).

pre-tournament preparation." (From the book *Isaak Lipnitsky*.) On the other hand, these mistakes could have been caused by the stress he suffered in the aftermath of his fiasco (6.5/15, 12th place!) at the Tbilisi tournament, one month before the championship:

"The behavior of I. Lipnitsky (Kiev) during the masters and candidate masters tournament in Tbilisi was unacceptable. The young master forgot his duty to share his experience with other chess players, to demonstrate exemplary sporting behavior. Chasing easy money during the tournament, slipshod play and even a failure to show up to one of the games showed that Lipnitsky didn't understand what a Soviet master should be like. We must hope that the penalty imposed on him (a strict reprimand) shall serve as a serious warning for him." (*Shakhmaty v SSSR*, No. 12, 1951.)

Geller again chose the King's Indian Defense *(more of a Queen's Pawn Game)* against Taimanov. At the VTsSPS championship, Taimanov managed to defeat Geller in brilliant style. The opening was the same as today. But that defeat didn't demoralize the Odessa master. Avoiding well-known lines, Taimanov developed his bishop to b2. Meanwhile, black played actively and quickly organized pressure on the queenside, pinning down the white pieces. Geller was active on the kingside as well. With combined play on both flanks, he won two pawns *(Geller was awarded the second brilliancy prize! – see*

In round 10, tournament leader Smyslov unexpectedly lost to Nikolai Novotelnov. Photo by N. Smirnov. From V. Smyslov's archive.

game 235)... Winning an important point, Geller joined the group of leaders."
(Tournament bulletin, 12th December.)

Standings after round 8: Botvinnik, Geller, Smyslov – 5.5; Keres, Kotov
– 5; Averbakh, Bondarevsky, Bronstein, Taimanov – 4.5; Petrosian, Simagin
– 4; Aronin, Kopylov – 3.5; Lipnitsky, Moiseev, Flohr – 3; Terpugov – 2;
Novotelnov – 1.5.

The Plot Thickens...

Alatortsev: "Round 9 was played in the TsDSA *(Central House of
the Soviet Army)* concert hall. A demonstration board was installed in the
spacious lobby to show the central game, Smyslov – Bronstein *(see game
246)*, to the fans who couldn't get into the tournament hall.

Bronstein met 1.e4 with the Sicilian Defense, which he uses quite rarely.
It seems that he specifically prepared for this game, anticipating the line *(the
Closed Sicilian)* that Smyslov would choose. This made the battle all the
more interesting... On the 11th move, Bronstein sacrificed a knight, then a
queen, and then, several moves later, another knight and bishop for a rook.
He regained the queen; as for the other 'material', this was the end result:
Smyslov got a bishop and a knight pair, and Bronstein had a rook and four
connected passed pawns.

What's more favorable? This question fascinated all the spectators. But
the doubts dissolved soon. Smyslov confidently refuted his opponent's idea
and launched a strong attack." (Ibid., 14th December.)

> **Flohr:** "Botvinnik said after the Bronstein match: 'We also have
> Boleslavsky, Keres and Smyslov, whose strength is equal to the participants
> of the match.'
>
> Smyslov defeated both the strongest and second-strongest player in the
> world in this championship, proving that Botvinnik's comment wasn't just a
> show of politeness." (*Ogonyok*, No. 50, 1951.)

Tolush and **Tarasov:** "The Moscow champion Petrosian played against
the world champion. In a Queen's Pawn Opening, Botvinnik played a very
risky-looking move 4...g5. When Petrosian castled long, Botvinnik launched
queenside activity, but then castled long as well. An interesting struggle began...
(The game lasted for more than 11 hours, but "Iron Tigran" managed to hold!)

Round 10. Smyslov is the tournament leader. His opponent, Master
Novotelnov, hasn't performed very well. But it was this game that brought big
surprises. The grandmaster thought for long on unexpected complications...

«Молодые перетягивают».　　　Дружеский шарж Н. Лиса.

"The Youth are Winning the Tug of War." An illustration to Flohr's article "Onslaught of the Youth". To the left: Botvinnik, Kotov, Smyslov and Bondarevsky; to the right: Geller, Taimanov, Petrosian, Averbakh and Lipnitsky. From the Ogonyok magazine (No. 50, 1951).

Panov: "The experts were mainly surprised by Smyslov's psychological mistake: he went for a double-edged line *(1.d4 ♘f6 2.c4 e6 3.♘c3 ♗b4 4.e3 d5 5.♘f3 0-0 6.♗d3 c5 7.0-0 ♘c6 8.a3 ♗a5 9.cxd5 exd5 10.dxc5 ♗xc3 11.bxc3 ♕a5 12.c4!)* that Novotelnov had already tried against Tolush in the autumn in Tbilisi.

White deliberately provokes black into playing 12...♕c3 with a double attack on the rook and c4 pawn... It was obviously some kind of trap. Tolush avoided this tempting move, playing 12...dxc4 13.♗xc4 ♕xc5. Smyslov, on the other hand, played too riskily, failing to see through his opponent's plan. After 12...♕c3? 13.cxd5 ♕xa1, Novotelnov played 14.♕c2!, and it quickly became clear that the position of the trapped black queen was hopeless, and white had great attacking prospects... Smyslov gave the rook back, managed to trade queens and transitioned into an endgame a pawn down. Still, Novotelnov converted his advantage into a win." (Tournament bulletin, 16th December.)

The game between Botvinnik and Keres attracted a lot of attention. These outstanding players faced each other for the first time since the 1948 world championship match tournament.

Botvinnik selected his signature 4.e3 move in the Nimzo-Indian... Keres hesitated with committing the position of his king. Once the center closed, he castled short. Botvinnik regrouped his pieces on the kingside and started creating threats. But the world champion had too few forces for a serious attack, since both his bishops were behind their own pawns and couldn't join the fight. Trading the white knight on f5, Keres eliminated all the attacking prospects for Botvinnik and executed a pawn breakthrough on the queenside shortly before the break *(Botvinnik found a study-like draw in the play-off! – see game 243).*

Efim Geller played this game against Averbakh wearing the proverbial "leader's yellow jersey". From D. Bronstein's archive. Published for the first time.

Even though Tolush thought that the game Geller – Averbakh clearly disappointed the spectators, Ragozin, Botvinnik and Suetin took part in the postmortem. Photo by N. Kireev (Russian State Film and Photo Archive (RGAKFD), Moscow). First published in Chess Review (No. 2, 1952). Courtesy of US Chess.

Flohr: "Today Geller got a valuable point off Kotov, and Taimanov got one from Bondarevsky. When I saw that the masters were 'beating up' my grandmaster colleagues, I finally 'took a swing' and won my first game *(against Terpugov)...*

Ten rounds have passed. This is a solid distance already. The final is close. Who's the leader? Not the world champion, not the Soviet champion. Not Smyslov either. Bronstein and Kotov are 'offside' now. The young Odessa master Geller is in first place! This great tactician won a lot of support from the spectators at the 1949 championship. Only his loss to Master Kholmov in the last round allowed Bronstein and Smyslov to overtake him and share first place.

I won't be guessing how the championship is going to end. But it's fully possible that Odessa will get its own grandmaster – E. Geller. I asked him today, 'Would you agree to finish the tournament with today's standings?' The Odessa master replied modestly, 'I agree to third place.' But Botvinnik, Keres, Smyslov, Bronstein, Kotov do not agree to finish the tournament like that. They say, 'Let's play on, let's see how dangerous Geller, Taimanov, Averbakh, and Petrosian really are...'

And I would like to say: see what great young players are growing!" (*Ogonyok*, No. 50, 1951.)

In round 11, Geller played Averbakh. This game clearly disappointed the spectators, who expected to see sharp, aggressive play from the Odessa man. Geller went for simplifications from the outset, and his opponent gladly helped him in that regard...

The tournament hall emptied, but Petrosian and Bronstein remained at the rightmost table on the stage for a long time, analyzing their game that stopped in the heat of the battle. Both made their last 15 moves in severe time trouble, and only now did they look through the various possible continuations they didn't risk going for in the actual game..." (*Sovietsky Sport*, 29th November, 1st and 4th December.)

Bonch-Osmolovsky: "Bronstein sacrificed three pawns in a row, creating dangerous threats. Despite severe time trouble, Petrosian managed to find some strong defensive moves. With his sealed move, he sacrificed one of the pawns, forcing a trade of the active black pieces. Bronstein soon managed to regain a second pawn and drew the resulting rook endgame." (Tournament bulletin, 19th December.)

Standings after round 11: Botvinnik, Geller, Smyslov – 7.5; Keres – 7; Averbakh, Taimanov – 6.5; Kotov, Simagin, Petrosian – 6; Bondarevsky, Bronstein, Moiseev – 5.5; Flohr – 5; Aronin, Kopylov – 4.5; Lipnitsky – 3.5; Novotelnov – 2.5; Terpugov – 2.

The World Champion's Collapse

Abramov: "Round 12. Our fans have become highly-qualified players and strict judges. They approved of the world champion's opening play, appreciated Kopylov's tactical counterplans, and rightfully thought that Botvinnik had to win the exchange and shouldn't have gone for the rook endgame. Then, the spectators anxiously pointed out the grandmaster's time-trouble mistakes and, even though they saw clearly that Kopylov's success wasn't entirely flawless, they still rapturously applauded the young master for inventive active defense, for resourcefulness and boldness, and for his will to win *(see game 241)*. Thus, one of the leaders lost, while the other two scored valuable whole points.

In the game Smyslov – Simagin, the opponents maneuvered, executed pawn breakthroughs on flanks, and traded pieces, but every step brought them closer to one purpose – preparing operations in the center. Simagin tried especially hard to improve the configuration of his central pawns, but, even though he solved this difficult problem correctly at first, he went for simplifications too hurriedly in the endgame. Smyslov seized the open file, he tied down his opponent's pieces, broke through the demarcation line with his king and swiftly and precisely won the play-off *(the third brilliancy prize! – see game 236)...*

And so, Geller and Smyslov have moved one point ahead of Botvinnik. But the world champion isn't alone in third place. Both Keres, who drew with Bronstein, and Averbakh have scored the same amount of points. The young master is playing in his third final, but only this time, despite a rough start (two losses), has his great creative talent brought him good results. Petrosian has also joined the leading group." (Ibid., 21st December.)

Zagoriansky: "In round 13, the spectators witnessed a rare occurrence of two games being played out in exactly the same way. Geller had white against Flohr, and Petrosian against Smyslov. Both played a sharp Queen's Gambit line with a pawn sacrifice for white *(the Tolush-Geller Gambit – see game 188 in volume 2)*. The grandmasters defended in exactly the same way, choosing a plan to create dangerous passed pawns on the queenside...

> **V. Vasiliev:** "Back then, Tigran was friends with Efim Geller. Even though the young masters were rivals at tournaments, they often prepared for games

together and had no secrets from each other. In round 13, the friends decided to use the same sharp, risky line against their opponents... Strictly speaking, this was Geller's idea, but it didn't take too much time to convince Tigran: sharp? OK, let's play sharply!" (From the book *A Chess Player's Life.*)

On the 17th move, Geller and Petrosian thought for long and went separate strategic ways. Geller played the passive 17.♖b1, not stopping the b5-b4 breakthrough. Flohr immediately went for it *(and eventually won)...* Petrosian was more 'cunning'. Correctly evaluating the position as lost for white, he boldly sacrificed another pawn, trying to create chances along the opened d-file *(see game 240).*

Гроссмейстер В. СМЫСЛОВ.
Дружеский шарж
И. Соколова и И. Рублева

After a lucky catch of several "butterfly-ones", Smyslov caught two zeroes in rounds 13 and 14... Cartoon by I. Sokolov and I. Rublev. From the tournament bulletin (19th December 1951).

Мастера Т. Петросян и Е. Геллер. Фото Н. Киреева

Back then, Geller and Petrosian were inseparable and often prepared for games together. Photo by N. Kireev. From the Smena magazine (No. 1, 1952).

Smyslov couldn't find the best reply and had to face many more difficulties than Flohr, fending off Petrosian's dangerous piece attack. Soon the white knight invaded on d6, and black had to give up a rook for it..." (Ibid., 23rd December.)

Geller and Smyslov's setbacks allowed their competitors to catch up: Botvinnik defeated Aronin, and Keres defeated Novotelnov. Four players had 8.5 points, and three more (Averbakh, Petrosian and Taimanov) were just behind – it was clear that the finish would be as bloody as the previous year!

Flohr: "No other Soviet Championship was filled with such incredible 'sporting fervor'. The end is near, and the players in their forties – Botvinnik, Flohr, Bondarevsky, Kotov – are starting to get tired. However, the youngest master Tigran Petrosian is on fire at the finish – 4.5 points out of 5 games!

Today, Petrosian played Simagin and easily repelled white's attacking efforts. And these unsuccessful attacks took their toll in the rook ending. Petrosian won the game on the 55th move and became one of the championship leaders, a candidate for first place. Not a bad trajectory, especially if we remember that Tigran started with two zeroes!

The main roles in round 14 were played by Botvinnik, Geller, Smyslov and Keres.

The world champion obviously didn't want to swim in the treacherous 'King's Indian' waters of the Black Sea master Geller. Botvinnik played 2.g3, 3.c4, and Geller took on c4. There followed: 4.♘f3 ♘c6 5.♘c3 e5. What opening did Botvinnik and Geller play? It's hard to say. It's a curious mixture of the Catalan, Queen's Gambit Accepted, Ruy Lopez and Albin Countergambit! Is it any wonder that after five or six moves, the opponents thought for a long time and fell behind the other players...

> **Petrosian:** "Geller is well-versed in endgames and can create energetic counterplay even in worse positions. It's enough to recall his win against Botvinnik. In the middle of that game, the world champion could have made a draw, but decided against it. Then he offered the young master a draw twice, but both offers were refused. Soon, Botvinnik had to resign. Even home analysis couldn't help him this time." (*Radyansky Sport*, Kiev, 18th December.)

Smyslov and Keres have known each other for a long time. Their game was initially quiet. The bishop pair gave white a small advantage, but the

Round 14 spelled doom for Botvinnik. In the playing hall: Isaak Boleslavsky, arbiter Boris Baranov, and chess federation official Boris Ravkin. From I. Boleslavsky's archive. Published for the first time.

bishops are only good when they can play. Smyslov's bishops just stood in place, and he didn't go for an exchange sacrifice, even though he didn't risk anything – he had a guaranteed draw. Keres skillfully maneuvered his knight in the center of the board and went for simplifications that benefited him. The bishop endgame was very difficult for Smyslov. With light-squared bishops on the board, all Keres' pawns were placed on dark squares, and Smyslov's ones on light squares. During the play-off, Keres put all his opponent's pieces into zugzwang in just a few moves...

Bronstein seems to have launched his famous finishing spurt. Alas, he's a bit too late this time!.. He quickly got a sharp position against Kopylov. On the other hand, there are no quiet positions in Kopylov's games. The vanquisher of Botvinnik, Keres and

The losses in rounds 12 and 14 knocked the world champion out of the leading group. Photo taken during Botvinnik's preparation at the dacha for his match with Bronstein. From the author's archive.

Petrosian intended to defeat the world 'vice-champion' as well. In a sharp rook endgame, Bronstein started to look for ways to win, despite his opponent being a pawn up. Kopylov sealed a bad move, then played carelessly and lost...

Three rounds remain. Our chess 'stars' are in quite bad shape. New stars are emerging on the horizon. Only one grandmaster is in the top three – Keres. The grandmaster candidate Geller clearly intends to repeat his success of 1949!" (Ibid., 26th December.)

Standings after round 14: Geller, Keres – 9.5; Petrosian – 9; Botvinnik, Smyslov, Taimanov – 8.5; Averbakh, Bronstein – 8; Kotov – 7.5; Bondarevsky – 7; Aronin, Kopylov, Simagin, Flohr – 6.5; Moiseev – 6; Lipnitsky – 4.5; Novotelnov – 3; Terpugov – 2.5.

Onslaught of the Youth

Yudovich: "What can secure success in competitions? Above all – the relentless will to win, the originality of chess thought, creative boldness. All these qualities are characteristic of the championship participants.

The 15th round confirms these thoughts.

In the game Keres – Simagin, the Moscow master chose the Ilyin-Zhenevsky system in the Dutch Defense, which leads to very sharp positions. Keres didn't play too well in the opening... After a long think, Simagin sacrificed a central pawn, planning to organize an attack on the white king. Evaluating the sharp position deeply, Keres, in his turn, sacrificed an exchange, opening up the black king's position. White's advantage grew with every move. Keres attacked persistently, with great will to win, and the spectators greeted the grandmaster's well-deserved victory with applause on the 40th move.

Annotating the sixth game of the Botvinnik – Bronstein match, Bondarevsky voiced a number of interesting thoughts about the methods of playing with white in one of the complicated lines of the Sicilian used by the world champion *(1.e4 c5 2.♘f3 ♘c6 3.d4 cxd4 4.♘xd4 ♘f6 5.♘c3 d6 6.♗g5 e6 7.♕d2 h6)...*

Today, he had an opportunity to test his point of view in practice. By putting the bishop on h5, Bondarevsky created pressure on the f7 square and limited his opponent's mobility. On move 18, Botvinnik sacrificed a pawn without good reason. However, Bondarevsky subtly parried black's efforts to seize the initiative. During the play-off, he chose a tempting, but wrong plan. White managed to win a second pawn, but opposite-colored bishops remained on the board, and Bondarevsky ultimately failed to win the game...

Lipnitsky defended passively with black. Geller slowly prepared a decisive attack on his opponent's position and, sacrificing first a bishop and then a rook, swept away the black king's pawn cover. Lipnitsky resigned on the 34th move.

Smyslov got a difficult position against Terpugov. The young master had all the initiative. But Smyslov didn't lose heart. He fought tenaciously and created counterchances with exceptional tactical inventiveness. Shortly before the break, Terpugov got tempted by an opportunity to win two pawns, but didn't take into account the fact that his king's position would be bad,

Round 16. The Column Hall is packed! Spectators are focused on the main battles: Petrosian against Keres and Bronstein against Geller. Averbakh is at the bottom right. Two photos combined by N. Kireev (RGAKFD, Moscow). Published for the first time.

and the black pieces would get into strong attacking positions... *(Another leader to win was Petrosian, who defeated Taimanov.)*

In his game against Bronstein, Aronin got a positional advantage out of the opening, and then, after strengthening his center, traded the dark-squared bishops, and white seized the initiative. Aronin's finishing onslaught was very powerful. White's attack ended with a beautiful queen sacrifice..." (Tournament bulletin, 28th December.)

A. Kazantsev and **V. Safonov:** "The standings before the penultimate round looked quite unusual. The leaders were tightly packed. Five players were just one and a half point apart. Many things could change. Almost everything could be decided as well. Thousands of Moscow fans tried to enter the Column Hall after the doors were closed. Demonstration boards were installed in the lobby. The masters went downstairs to describe the course of the battles...

No international tournament, even such exceptional ones as the 1925, 1935 and 1936 Moscow Internationals, with Lasker and Capablanca taking part, can be compared with the 19th Soviet Championship. World champion Botvinnik, his recent challenger Bronstein, national champion Keres, 'the world's second board' Smyslov and the whole glorious cohort of Soviet grandmasters and masters are competing for the Soviet Championship gold medal.

The young-looking but battle-hardened Keres is playing as he perhaps hasn't played for many years, combining his old fervor with exceptional technique, faultless calculations, composure and distinctive elegance in his play.

And the onslaught of the youth is so brilliant! Geller, outwardly calm, with an ironic smile, waddling around the tables and bringing down the whole power of his temperament upon his opponents, is in the lead again! Two years ago, he almost took first place. Today, nobody can say that he just 'got lucky': even the most seasoned grandmasters should be afraid of his improved strength.

The 22 year-old Petrosian has quietly caught up with the leaders. His play is amazingly simple and confident.

Мастер Е. ГЕЛЛЕР

Дружеский шарж
И. Соколова и И. Рублева

The guard of honor of victorious points salutes Geller. Cartoon by I. Sokolov and I. Rublev. From the tournament bulletin (14th December 1951).

Everything will be decided in this round. Or, more correctly, it could be decided. Keres is playing Petrosian, and Geller faces Bronstein.

A win against Bronstein almost definitely secures first place for Geller. And for Bronstein, who sacrificed too many pawns and pieces in this tournament, this game could serve as proof that he's 'still got it', that the strength of the world champion's formidable challenger wasn't exhausted.

And so, there's the 'evergreen opening' – the Ruy Lopez. Many are surprised: Bronstein follows his recent game against Keres and Geller's game against Keres too! White got worse positions in both of those games! But events took a sharp turn from trodden paths on move 15: ♖b1! The black pieces have huddled on the 7th and 8th ranks *(see game 238)*. It did seem though that Geller had seized the open a- and c-files. But Bronstein moved the 'fire' of the threats to the other flank. And Geller, whose position became increasingly cramped, had to give up his queen for a rook and knight. He tried to resist and even adjourned the game, but...

The events in the game Petrosian – Keres unfolded differently *(a year earlier, they also played in round 16, and Keres lost!)*. The 14th move. Petrosian proves logically to Keres, who chose the Queen's Indian, that the movement of the d-pawn is too premature. Keres thought for 40 minutes. Petrosian's knights invade the opponent's camp. The a7 pawn falls. But will the knights make it out alive? Petrosian is calm. The knights came back without giving up their loot. Keres is already two pawns down. And he's very low on time. But Keres managed to extricate himself from the difficult situation with incredible skill." (Ibid., 3rd January 1952.)

In the penultimate round, Bronstein destroyed Geller, and Keres surged ahead. From Y. Averbakh's archive. Published for the first time.

Flohr: "Smyslov improved his standing with the win over Kopylov and still retains some practical chances to win the championship. Botvinnik says that the tournament is already over for him after the loss to Kopylov. The world champion makes a quick draw today *(with Kotov, in 21 moves; in the last round, he drew with Averbakh in 16 moves)*. Only first place would satisfy him. And if it's not first, does it really matter whether it's third, fourth or fifth?.." (*Ogonyok*, No. 52, 1951.)

This passage angered some **K. Mitin** from Chita (*Shakhmaty v SSSR*, No. 3, 1952): "We are sure that the world champion never said anything of the sort. And, of course, such arguments have no place on the pages of our newspapers and magazines. The duty of our grandmasters is to nurture the young players, teach them to persevere and give their all even in bad patches."

Behind the criticism of Flohr, it's easy to see an accusation against Botvinnik. Why did the magazine editor Ragozin, his old friend and second, allow it to print such a letter? It turns out that they had a "complete falling-out" after the championship (see the subchapter *Summary. The Unpublished Version*).

Standings after round 16: Keres – 11; Geller, Petrosian, Smyslov – 10.5; Botvinnik, Taimanov – 9.5; Averbakh, Bronstein – 9; Aronin – 8.5; Kotov, Flohr – 8; Bondarevsky, Kopylov, Simagin – 7.5; Moiseev – 6.5; Lipnitsky – 5.5; Novotelnov – 3; Terpugov – 2.5.

The Triple Champion!

Ragozin and **Abramov:** "The last round!.. How important these words are for every chess player. They hide an anxious crowd of fans at the entrance, the festive excitement in the entrance hall, on the stairs and in the lobby, the incessant noise in the spectators' hall, filled to the brim...

Geller, Petrosian and Smyslov had to win on demand. This was their only hope of catching or even overtaking Keres if he failed to win, or to guarantee a shared second place. Each of them approached this task differently.

Geller chose a relatively quiet opening... Novotelnov protected his position solidly, and it looked impregnable. The inventive Geller came up with an interesting maneuver and got his rook to the 7th rank. Even though the rook was surrounded, the idea was correct. The subtle 34.♕a3! would have taken the attack to its logical conclusion. However, after 34.♕d1?, Novotelnov won a piece. Nevertheless, in chess, he who makes the last mistake

Last Round Thrill! Paul Keres (left) clinches title against Master M. Taimanov.

The decisive game of the last round. From the Chess Review magazine (No. 2, 1952). Courtesy of US Chess.

usually loses. In this game, Novotelnov blundered last, and Geller executed a spectacular mating combination.

Petrosian tried to sharpen the game from the very first moves, but Terpugov at first found his way in the complicated position and launched an attack on the black king. Petrosian's queenside counterplay developed more slowly. But then Terpugov failed to find the right continuation and allowed Petrosian to execute a decisive counter-attack...

The Pirc Defense chosen by Smyslov is not easy for black. In addition, the grandmaster, instead of complicating the game, tried to simplify it and got no counterchances... With each subsequent move, Smyslov's position became increasingly unpleasant, and Aronin's victory seemed to be beyond doubt. However, Aronin made a gross blunder in the play-off, going for a drawn pawn endgame without a good reason.

Who would have thought that this play-off would destroy Lev Aronin's life! And even though he played in three more Soviet Championships and lived to 62, this wound was mortal, fatally affecting his health...

Taimanov: "The 1951 Soviet Championship determined both the champion and the five participants of the Interzonal tournament in Stockholm, an important stage in the world championship system. (...) The competition was ruthless, but before the last round, four qualifying places were already taken. Efim Geller, Tigran Petrosian, Yuri Averbakh and I had virtually guaranteed ourselves tickets for the Interzonal 'ship'. The last place remained, and the talented, smart master Lev Aronin was one of the contenders. But his task certainly wasn't easy – he had to defeat none other than Smyslov on demand. *(The actual players to be sent to the Interzonal would be drawn from a list of candidates to be published by the Sports Committee later. The higher the players finished in the national championship, the better their chances were of getting selected. But it wasn't simply a matter of finishing in the top five (excluding Botvinnik). Yet beating Smyslov here would have vastly improved Aronin's chances of being selected.)* During the game, it seemed that the brave fighter was close to his goal: the adjourned position was winning for Aronin. The general evaluation and preliminary analysis pointed to his undoubted win. His friends heartily congratulated him. Aronin was jubilant and, in his joy, even threw a small banquet in the restaurant for his friends. Everything looked rosy. The only thing that remained was to identify the most decisive way to the desired goal with concrete lines. He had enough time for that.

The next day, Aronin confidently – way too confidently, as it turned out – sat at the board. He expected his opponent to resign quickly. But

Мечта юного «болельщика»...   Рис. Н. ЛИСА

"The fan's dream." The idea is not new – see the cartoon from the Pionerskaya Pravda newspaper about the Spassky vs Nikitin game later. Cartoon by N. Lis. From the tournament bulletin (6th December 1951).

something incredible happened: on the way that seemed the simplest and safest for Aronin, he encountered a 'time bomb' prepared by the endgame wizard Smyslov, and this bomb exploded at the exact moment when it seemed that the game was already won. A draw suddenly became inevitable. You can only imagine Aronin's shock: he lost the deserved victory, all his hopes, plans and prospects got ruined. Fate had failed him. And he couldn't live with that. The critical position in the game became a negative dominant idea of his existence. He showed it to everyone he met – chess players and friends who didn't know a thing about chess alike. Lyova constantly returned to this story – he took what happened tragically... and his mental health collapsed. Aronin got very ill. And even though medicine did help him recover some of his health, his entire life went downhill – Aronin couldn't fully return to chess..." (From the book *Remembering the Greatest*...)

The renowned coach **Chapai Sultanov** recalled: "He had deep knowledge of everything – literature, chess, music. Talking to him would make anybody happy – all participants of the tournament *(the 1956 Azerbaijan championship)* wanted to hang out with him.

The well-known incident in the game against Smyslov had a horrible effect on his health, he was essentially crippled – his elderly mother accompanied him, a grown man, to all tournaments. 'That's what chess did to my Lyovushka – turned an exemplary Young Pioneer, a top student, into a cripple,' she told me. Lev Solomonovich was firmly convinced of one thing: to be a great chess player, you should possess diverse knowledge. 'How can I improve my skill?' Polugaevsky once asked Aronin. 'Read more classical literature, Lyova,' Aronin told him." (From the book *Chess... And Not Only Chess*.)

The game Keres – Taimanov was the most tense of all. Taimanov also had a stake in the result: if he won, he would finish in a high place. Keres felt the competitors breathing down his neck, so his play was very energetic." (Tournament bulletin, 5th January 1952.)

Petrosian: "However, the young Leningrad champion resisted tenaciously. His move 27...♕c1, in turn, threatened Keres with checkmate. There were flashes of applause in the hall. Some spectators thought, not entirely without reason, that the queen sacrifice would help the Leningrad player to avoid the danger. In addition, the Soviet Champion was in severe time trouble. The flag on his clock was already rising. He needed great composure to find his bearings quickly in the complicated situation, evaluate the position correctly and identify the best continuation. Keres did it and became the champion for the third time." (*Radyansky Sport*, Kiev, 18th December.)

Flohr: "The usual 'winners' problems' started: they were besieged by the reporters, cameramen, and spectators. Keres is a very experienced grandmaster in that regard. He smiles at the photographers and knows what to say to the correspondents. Geller and Petrosian are still young. They become rather shy when asked to give interviews. But they'll learn this art – it's not harder than finishing in a high place in the Soviet Championship.

Keres: "If I say that I'm satisfied with my result, the reader will, of course, believe me. But I mean not only the sporting result, but the creative side of the championship as well. Still, I'll say frankly that this victory didn't come easy to me... This championship featured a strong and successful onslaught by young players. The future belongs to them. But I'm sure that Botvinnik, Bronstein, and Smyslov will try to take revenge at the next tournament."

Geller: "I had chances for 1st place, but also had chances to end in 4th. I got a fine average – sharing 2nd and 3rd places. This was my dream before the tournament... I think that in the next tournament, in addition to the renowned grandmasters, I'll have to compete against the new young 'upstarts' as well."

Petrosian: "My friends joke that I 'almost' became the champion. But this would have been 'indecent' on my part. I'm the youngest participant, and I think that I've already 'hurt' our grandmasters enough. I'm more than satisfied with my result, and I'll be glad to perform at least as well in the next championship."

The big crowds of spectators don't disperse immediately. The fans of Keres, Geller, Petrosian, and Smyslov are standing on a street near the House of the Unions. They'll calm down only after walking the winners home, to the Moskva Hotel." (*Ogonyok*, No. 52, 1951.)

The Stockholm Bonus

From the press: "The closing ceremony of the 19th championship took place on 15th December in the Column Hall of the House of the Unions. The All-Union Chess Section chairman M. Kharlamov gave the floor to the tournament chief arbiter P. Romanovsky.

'There were lots of combative, interesting games at the tournament,' he said. 'The fact that there were few draws made at this championship *(36% – two percent lower than the previous year)* is especially valuable...'

The tournament winner is invited on stage. On behalf of the All-Union Committee for Physical Education and Sport and the chess section, Comrade Kharlamov congratulates P. Keres and awards him a gold medal and first-degree diploma.

Masters E. Geller and T. Petrosian are awarded silver tokens and second-degree diplomas... P. Keres and T. Petrosian are granted awards for the best results in the last five rounds *(both scored 4.5/5)*, A. Kotov and S. Flohr are granted awards for the best results against the prizewinners *(both scored 4/8)*. A special prize *(a cup)* is awarded to N. Kopylov who defeated the world champion M. Botvinnik and Soviet champion P. Keres.

ЧЕТЫРЕ БОГАТЫРЯ...

Новый вариант картины В. Васнецова.
Дружеский шарж Н. ЛИСОГОРСКОГО.

"The Four Bogatyrs... a new version of V. Vasnetsov's painting." Petrosian and Geller share the same horse: one prize for the two and one horse for the two! Cartoon by N. Lisogorsky (Lis). From the tournament bulletin (9th February 1952).

The youngest tournament participant, Petrosian (22), is also awarded the All-Union Committee certificate for the best result in games against grandmasters *(5/7!)*." (*Sovietsky Sport*, 18th December.)

Prorvich: "The 19th Soviet Championship also served as a qualifying *(zonal)* competition for the Interzonal tournament to be held in Stockholm in late 1952. Five Soviet chess players are sent there: grandmasters A. Kotov, E. Geller *(promoted to grandmaster in spring 1952 for gaining 2nd place at the Budapest tournament)* and masters Y. Averbakh, T. Petrosian and M. Taimanov." (Tournament book.)

Strangely, neither the bulletin nor the magazine mentioned the "zonal" nature of the tournament, even though **Averbakh** told me that there was such an article in the championship regulations. "The Sports Committee weren't exactly thrilled by the youngsters' success and thought that it would be safer to send grandmasters to Stockholm. Therefore, in addition to the five of us

Taimanov against Aronin. Lev Aronin was included in the candidates list for the Stockholm Interzonal, but... got replaced by Kotov. From D. Bronstein's archive. Published for the first time.

(Geller, Petrosian, Taimanov, Averbakh and Aronin) as well as Flohr, the published candidate list also contained Kotov, Bondarevsky and two players who didn't play in the final at all – Lilienthal and Tolush. Three of them ultimately preferred to go to the Interzonal as coaches (Flohr worked with Taimanov, Bondarevsky with Geller, and Lilienthal with Petrosian), and I was preferred instead of Tolush at the last moment. As a result, the only one of the 'young five' who suffered was Aronin – he was pushed out by Kotov *(who was Russian)*."

When I later looked into the book *What the Pieces Don't Mention*, I also learned a plausible reason for that: "It's possible that another factor was at work as well: among the five of us, there was an Armenian, two half-Jews *(one of which was Averbakh, the other was presumably Taimanov)* and two full Jews. And not a single member of the titular nation. But Aronin did do enough to qualify, and Kotov didn't! This replacement tragically affected Aronin's life. He developed schizophrenia. First, he started fearing heart attacks, then cancer. He wound up in a psychiatric clinic. He was never the same after this blow..."

But, as we know, a win is a win. Kotov brilliantly won the Interzonal, fully justifying his participation!

Averbakh: "Later, there were numerous discussions in our press: should the national championship final serve as a zonal tournament as well? There were arguments both for and against. For instance, some said that participation of players who have no interest in the qualification process might affect the results of those who are competing for the Interzonal places. But this argument is not convincing: as a rule, only the strongest players don't have to qualify, and this means that playing them only increases the quality of the selection. There were two main arguments for combining the two tournaments: firstly, a lot of money was saved this way, and, secondly, this made the championships more important.

In the 1950s and 1960s, these competitions were combined *(the only exception was the 1964 Zonal, criticized by Bondarevsky on the pages of Shakhmaty v SSSR).* For instance, I played in the zonal tournaments five times, and these tournaments also served as national championships. In the 1970s, however, separate zonal tournaments became the norm, basically forcing the players to qualify twice." (From the book *A Chess Player's Life in the System*.)

Summary. The Published Version

The final standings: 1. Keres – 12/17; 2–3. Geller, Petrosian – 11.5; 4. Smyslov – 11; 5. Botvinnik – 10; 6–8. Averbakh, Bronstein, Taimanov – 9.5; 9–10. Aronin, Flohr – 9; 11. Kopylov – 8.5; 12–13. Bondarevsky, Kotov – 8; 14. Simagin – 7.5; 15–16. Lipnitsky, Moiseev – 6.5; 17. Novotelnov – 3; 18. Terpugov – 2.5.

Romanovsky: "Before the competition started, many thought that the participation of the world champion M. Botvinnik and the recent challenger D. Bronstein would make it easier to predict the probable winner. However, the struggle became more and more intense with every round, and it soon became clear that the experts' predictions were being proven wrong one after another, breaking on the sharp angles of the players' creative efforts.

In round 2, Master N. Kopylov defeats P. Keres in excellent style. Botvinnik used that to get ahead, and after round 6, he was clear first. Some thought that the battle was already over. However, in round 7 Botvinnik had black against V. Smyslov and seemed to underestimate the subtle maneuvers of his formidable opponent. He got into time trouble. Catastrophe seemed to occur suddenly. One mistake, then another, and Botvinnik resigned... After this loss, he made several draws in a row. Before round 12 Botvinnik was still in the lead, but together with Smyslov and Ukrainian master E. Geller, who quietly caught up with them. Keres was half a point behind. And the subsequent events mixed up all the cards. Botvinnik lost to Kopylov and then to Geller shortly afterwards. After drawing his last three games, the world champion only took 5th place.

>   **Ragozin:** "The coolness and composure that he showed after individual setbacks in earlier times had abandoned him. These qualities of his were always enviable for any sportsman. Botvinnik had got unaccustomed to the tournament atmosphere with its intense sporting struggle (which was especially intense in this competition!) and completely collapsed at the finish." (*Shakhmaty v SSSR*, No. 1, 1952.)
>
>   **Petrosian:** "But we shouldn't forget that the world champion belongs to the category of people who are able to draw the right conclusions both from their successes and failures." (*Radyansky Sport*, Kiev, 18th December.)

Smyslov, who played very well in the middle part of the competition, also lost games at the finish, to his closest competitors to boot – T. Petrosian and P. Keres. Both of them, probably inspired by this success, started winning one game after another. And when, in the decisive round 16 game against Keres, Petrosian failed to exploit his extra pawn that he won in the opening, the balance tipped in Keres's favor... His last-round win against Taimanov was greeted with a loud ovation in the Column Hall.

>   **Keres:** "I managed to win the Soviet Championship for the third time. This tournament showed that I was somewhat more successful in the crucial games. And that is a very important skill." (From the book *One Hundred Games*.)
>
>   **Petrosian:** "Speaking of the tournament results, everyone points out the unprecedented success of the young players. This is completely justified. But I

The three-times Soviet champion Paul Keres (when he won for the first time, in 1947, champions weren't yet awarded gold medals). From P. Kivine's archive (Tallinn).

would like to say that the winner, the 36 year-old grandmaster Keres, was almost the youngest and freshest one because of his playing style, brilliant tactical talent, and originality of his chess thinking." (Ibid.)

This win by Keres is probably the greatest and most convincing one in his entire chess career. He won nine games, and the style and manner of these wins were appreciated by the Soviet fans. Spectacular, determined attacks in the games against Terpugov, Moiseev, Geller, Simagin, Novotelnov and Lipnitsky, and the subtlest patterns of thought in his battles against Taimanov, Smyslov and Aronin, tell us that we are witnessing a great artist who confidently walks towards his goal with the help of deep ideas, and elegant and bold solutions...

Alexander Kotov – the winner of the Venice tournament (pictured). The triumph in Stockholm awaited. From A. Kotov's archive. Published for the first time.

Not all grandmasters endured trials as confidently as the Soviet champion. Bronstein, whose numerous fans had placed high hopes in him, couldn't reinforce the attractive side of his thinking with the necessary dose of prudence and composure. Only by defeating the tournament leader Geller in the penultimate round did he manage to stay in the top half of the table.

Smyslov lost to Novotelnov, Averbakh, Petrosian and Keres. Three losses against youngsters caused major harm to such an outstanding chess player. Smyslov needs to focus more on improving his sporting qualities.

In the tournament book, **Romanovsky** was more forgiving about the grandmaster's performance: "The numerous fans of the interesting, distinctive style of Smyslov were somewhat disappointed with his result – 4th place. It's unnecessary! Smyslov played boldly and enterprisingly, a bit riskily, as always, and lost four games. But we should say that he overestimated his defensive resources too much in all those games. Smyslov's nine wins are the result of his originality, and his energetic, logically executed attacks and counter-attacks."

Out of seven games with grandmasters, Tigran Petrosian lost none and won three! He gifted this photo to Vladimir Alatortsev with an inscription on the back "To the Old Strategist from the Young Petrosian. 26.07.1952. Moscow." From V. Alatortsev's archive. Published for the first time.

What are the reasons for Bondarevsky and Kotov sharing 12th–13th places? The reasons for Bondarevsky's failure can be largely found in his poor performance in the Leningrad semi-final, where he finished outside the top three. Kotov hadn't played a single serious game since the Venice tournament and, therefore, wasn't prepared for the championship... *(Peter Arsenyevich "forgot" another grandmaster – Flohr, and Master Aronin as well, even though they performed better than Kotov and Bondarevsky.)*

There were many deep games, captivating in their sharpness and complexity. Geller, Petrosian, Simagin, Kopylov, Taimanov – this is the main group that created the greatest tension in the tournament and engaged the other participants in a very sharp and intense struggle...

Don't our young masters Geller and Petrosian, and then Averbakh and Taimanov deserve grandmaster titles? Petrosian, for instance, didn't lose a single game to grandmasters – he won three and drew four. Averbakh also performed well against grandmasters, losing only to Bronstein and defeating Smyslov and Bondarevsky *(see game 245)*.

In the tournament book, **Romanovsky** provided detailed descriptions of the styles of Petrosian and Geller; the creative portraits drawn by him were fascinating:

"We can say that Petrosian doesn't have a pronounced style yet. He doesn't go for anything definite in his games as much as seeks out, persistently and industriously, beneficial opportunities in the constantly changing situation on the board. He always considers the particular traits of the position, creatively approaching evaluation.

Petrosian is very dangerous both in attack, which he executes with initiative and boldness, and defense, where he, quite stubbornly, uses any available opportunity to obtain counterplay. He likes sharp positions, is not averse to risk, but in general, he likes double-edged positions where he can calculate concrete lines. The technical side of the struggle is less interesting to Petrosian, as well as the ending stage, where he makes most of his mistakes...

Geller's chess personality is different. Like Petrosian, he possesses a sharp tactical vision, but he always follows a strict logical line and can be very determined in its execution. Geller's attacks are well-founded and prepared, full of tactical thoughts as the struggle sharpens. Geller is somewhat weaker in defense, where it's harder to plan ahead and you have to subordinate your play to the opponent's will...

Geller doesn't like draws *(he made only three!)*, and the sharp, attacking style characteristic of his play fits this sporting quality very well."

I would also like to point out the excellent achievements of the Leningrad master Kopylov – despite taking only 11th place, he brilliantly defeated Botvinnik, Keres and Bondarevsky. Kopylov's play is very distinctive, full of risk and tactical complications. He committed a lot of inaccuracies in his games, as we say in chess, but these inaccuracies, always dangerous for opponents by the way, are compensated for by the uniqueness and boldness of his ideas.

Curiously, there are two distinct trends of chess thought among the young masters who played at the 19th Soviet Championship. The most outstanding representatives of those trends are Geller, Kopylov and Simagin on one side, and Averbakh, Taimanov and Moiseev on the other... We think that the first three stand closer to the traditions of the Russian chess school, boldly going down the path of daring creative search.

Averbakh: "Chess reflects in the most sacred way a thing that happens covertly in real life: the battle of the generations.

We can easily prove that by looking at the national championship tables. This battle was not always obvious, but there were tournaments in our chess history when generations were literally pitted against each other. For instance, the 7th Soviet Championship in 1931, when the young generation, spearheaded by Botvinnik, loudly declared their presence. The 19th championship served a similar purpose." (From the book *What the Pieces Don't Mention*.)

On the backdrop of the great creative success that was the showcase of Soviet chess mastery, we can't help but point out the very poor results of Novotelnov and Terpugov. The history of Soviet Championships has never seen such clearly substandard results before. Each of them lost 13 games out of 17! Combined, they both scored fewer points than Lipnitsky and Moiseev each, who shared 15th–16th places." (*Sovietsky Sport*, 18th December 1951, and tournament bulletin, 18th January 1952).

Summary. The Unpublished Version

Romanovsky (from his letter to Vladimir Zak dated 20th January 1952): "The post-tournament meeting in Romanov's office was a disgrace for the 'cream' of our chess society. At first, it was impossible to make anyone talk. Nikolai Nikolaevich's appeals were futile. They were answered with yawns, people covering their mouths with their hands, and deathly silence. Then I spoke, expressing my astonishment. Don't even Novotelnov and Terpugov, whose performances at the championship were unprecedentedly bad, have anything to say, I asked (Botvinnik and Bronstein were conspicuous by their absence!)? Their tongues finally loosened. The first to speak was Novotelnov, with a pathetic statement!

> **Ragozin:** "Novotelnov showed a total inability to control his nerves. At his first Soviet Championship outing, this clearly talented master suffered so much after every loss that he couldn't play even a single game to the best of his abilities." (*Shakhmaty v SSSR*, No. 1, 1952.)

Terpugov spoke, got nervous and began to cry. Romanov gradually steered the discussion towards helping the youth. There was talk (same old, same old!) about assigning masters and grandmasters as mentors to the young talents.

Then, Alexander Kazimirovich *(Tolush)* and Igor Zakharovich *(Bondarevsky)* came out with their Leningrad grievances. They complained that they were 'away from where it was happening' in Leningrad, that the methodological jobs were occupied by poorly-qualified players such as Zak in the Young Pioneers Palace among others. Coaching questions also came

Кандидат в мастера Е. ТЕРПУГОВ
(«Наука»).
Дружеский шарж Н. ЛИСА.

The two biggest disappointments of the championship – Candidate Master Evgeny Terpugov (left) and Master Nikolai Novotelnov. Cartoon by N. Lis from the Moscow championship bulletin (25th January 1949), and photo from Y. Averbakh's archive. Published for the first time.

up. The speakers criticized the Committee, the voluntary sports societies and other culprits for their failures. A bad workman always blames his tools, you know...

I gave a big speech at the end of the meeting. First of all, I provided a thorough description of what a 'coach' and 'coaching' are, as well as of educational work and its supervisor, and the lead methodologist. I drew a parallel between chess and other sports and came to the conclusion that some second- or first-category players may be better as methodologists than some grandmasters. Only one person in the USSR combines great pedagogical and playing skills, I said – it's Levenfish. I harshly criticized the grandmasters' coaches, pointing out that Smyslov's regress was partly caused by his former coach Alatortsev. There's no doubt, I said, that Ragozin hadn't given Botvinnik much either. (By the way, they had a complete fallout – they're enemies now!)

Then I moved to the question of chess education; in particular, I pointed out that I never made so many methodical and pedagogical mistakes as when I was Soviet champion. The majority of our literature, educational included

The arbiters board. Front (left to right): M. Kamyshov, Chief Arbiter P. Romanovsky, A. Khachaturov, G. Ravinsky, M. Bonch-Osmolovsky. Back: B. Baranov, A. Bogatin. From A. Bogatin's archive. Published for the first time.

(Sokolsky, Maizelis, Yudovich, Panov, etc.), is rife with gross methodical mistakes and pedagogical flaws. (...) I, for instance, have wide teaching experience, I love this job, I have given all my heart to it, but there are still lots of issues that I haven't managed to resolve. Levenfish is also struggling with a lot of matters, clearly realizing the difficulty of chess education and great prospects for its further development. However, I said that many veritable authorities don't realize that, including, obviously, Bondarevsky and Tolush, who are trying to associate chess mastery with pedagogical mastery. This is a deep fallacy; while both Bondarevsky and Tolush are, without a doubt, better chess players than candidate master Zak, the reverse, I think, is true in regard of educational skills. (...)

The results of the 19th Soviet Championship are quite scandalous. When we meet in person, I'll tell you the story of my arbiter's work at the tournament, which I initially refused – Alatortsev was already appointed. Everything changed afterwards. During the tournament, I was granted leave from all my jobs (at least formally). Nevertheless (I knew it!), the job was so intense that I had to interfere with the work of Romanov himself six times, and many Sports Committee staff members (including Prorvich, accountants and the finance department) likely won't remember me with kind words

The tournament participants were reprimanded dozens of times (mostly for talking). With the help of the police, who did an excellent job, more than 20 noisy spectators were expelled from the hall at various times. The public was occasionally very rowdy, regardless of their overall cultural level. Once, in the middle of a round, I had to address (in the Column Hall's middle aisle) the famous violinist David Oistrakh with the following words: 'Dear David Fyodorovich, when you play in concerts, you think of any noise, even coughs, as a sign of disrespect to you, and the chess players sit quietly at your performances. I think that they have the right to demand the same of you. If your emotions take such a noisy form again, I'll have to ask you to leave the hall.'

David Fyodorovich immediately and profusely apologized in the presence of pianists, Zak and Flier, and promised to keep absolute silence. Both on that day and during all subsequent rounds, he stayed true to his word.

> It seems that the musicians were an emotional bunch. I immediately remembered **Botvinnik's** story about the 12th Soviet Championship (1940) that I recounted in the previous volume: "They said that, after a win by Keres, Sergei Prokofiev applauded loudly. His neighbors in the box reprimanded him. 'I have a right to express my feelings,' the composer retorted." (From the book *Achieving the Aim*.)

The results of the tournament are remarkable, but not too reassuring. I read some lectures and semi-official reports in several places, based on the standard talking points. Great creative achievements, the triumph of youth, the further progress of art, the development of Chigorin's traditions, the necessity of constant practice (Kotov, Botvinnik), the demoralization of Novotelnov and Terpugov.

However, I gave two lectures in light of dialectic analysis of the results. One of them, in the House of Scientists, was fully dedicated to psychological and historical analysis of sporting and creative results. The lecture lasted for 3.5 hours, and I only showed... one game: Botvinnik – Kopylov. The world champion's fifth place was the central piece of the lecture. It took 1.5 hours to uncover Botvinnik's deep internal psychological conflict, its gradual creation (1949) and development, its striking reflection in the match against Bronstein, the 'backstage' of the 19th championship – as facts that serve as evidence of the peak of this conflict, and the game against Kopylov was used as a striking example of this conflict.

We can talk about this championship at great length. We'll discuss it more when we meet. (...) The tournament has undermined my health, especially my heart and back. I've been taking medication for months – various remedies." (*Shakhmatny Peterburg*, No. 5, 2002.)

It's due time to remember **Peter Arsenyevich Romanovsky** with a kind word. His role in shaping Russian chess culture and education cannot be overstated.

Averbakh: "One of our chess luminaries, a teacher of several generations of Leningrad and Moscow players. He was the arbiter of the Moscow championship where I earned my master's norm. After the tournament, Romanovsky invited me to his home, and I became a frequent guest. Peter Arsenyevich was a very hospitable man. Many young chess players visited him – Dima Ter-Pogosov, Misha Bonch-Osmolovsky, Yura Steinsapir, who studied under

Peter Romanovsky. Photo by N. Volkov. From Y. Neishtadt's archive. Published for the first time.

him back in Leningrad. We played chess, solved studies, discussed various problems of chess. Sometimes Peter Arsenyevich would read us lectures on chess history, the development of chess ideas, chess schools and great masters of the past. Romanovsky helped me to broaden my perspective in the area of chess that was my main weakness – combination play and tactics. We once held a training tournament at his home, but it was unfinished. Among Peter Arsenyevich's frequent guests were the historian and Chigorin's biographer Nikolai Ivanovich Grekov, playwright and theater critic Volkenstein, and chess historian Isaak Maksovich Linder.

I remember Romanovsky once holding a concert for us: it turned out that he was a skilled balalaika player and knew a lot of classical music. He also read his poems. One of his poems, *The Old Wolf*, was deeply autobiographical – in 1942, he was evacuated from the besieged Leningrad, half-dead, and his entire family perished ..." (From the book *A Chess Player's Life in the System.*)

Max Euwe: "The Soviet Championship usually enlists the efforts of almost half the holders of the title of FIDE Grandmaster. So the tournament attracts the attention of the whole chess world. And, when the World Champion, his recent challenger and quite a few other prominent players get tossed around like tickets in a lottery wheel, quite a few questions arise.

There are questions, for example, as to the relation of age to playing strength and the ability to maintain one's prestige. We begin also to wonder once more about the relative playing strength of West and East.

Botvinnik and Bronstein were disappointments. Petrosian and Geller came through as pleasant surprises. Yet there is still no reason to turn the world's rating list upside-down. A single tournament does not carry too much conviction. And, besides that, the styles of Botvinnik and Bronstein are so enterprising – not to say, downright provocative – that one must really wonder that their failures were not even more resounding.

Even a World Champion is not absolutely free from blunders, as we have seen in the recent title match. In this Soviet Championship, Botvinnik's fallibility was again demonstrated: in a drawn position, against Smyslov, he left a piece *en prise*, and he needlessly dropped a point against Geller.

In contrast to the collapse of the greatest of the greats, we have the splendid showing of Keres, who not only won the title but finished with a whole point to spare ahead of Smyslov, who came fourth. Keres has the perfect style for this type of mixed tournament: always on the lookout for combinations and never afraid of complications. From the showing made by Keres and the actual play, one is more than ever convinced that Keres is just the man to stop the young Russian masters; he knows how to fight fire with fire. When it comes to the established grandmasters, Keres is much more peacefully inclined. See, for example, the details of the Candidates Tournament at Budapest, 1950. They reveal that, of his 18 games in that event, Keres drew no less than 13!

The style of the newer Russian masters is something out of the ordinary. Particularly noticeable is the nonchalance with which they make long-term sacrifices. Older players avoid such lines for purely practical reasons: chess is so rich in surprises that one cannot calculate everything in advance; some hidden finesse may turn up, transforming a temporary sacrifice into a permanent one! It may well be that this readiness for long-term sacrifices may give us a hint of the trend in the years to come. Masters of the future may differ from the older ones in paying less attention to material advantages. In this connection, Saemisch has made one of the most telling comments I have ever encountered on the subject: he remarks that he finds it easier to sacrifice in a blindfold game than in a regular game – because, in a blindfold game, he finds it easier to ignore purely material considerations.

A final point: are Petrosian, Kopylov and Geller stronger than Evans, Unzicker and Matanovic? The future, that is to say the Interzonal Tournament at Stockholm, will supply the answer. One thing is certain: these young Russians, who were anything but easy prey for Botvinnik, Bronstein and Smyslov, are just as unlikely to be bowled over by Gligoric, Stahlberg and Szabo. Anyone who thinks otherwise should take a look at the following game from the recent Soviet Championship *(see game 249 between Petrosian and Kopylov)*." (*Chess Review,* No. 3, 1952.)

The Masterpieces Come in Droves

I still can't get used to this "pendulum": I was complaining about the lack of a candidate list for the brilliancy prizes, and here I get a stunningly thorough shortlist. Thankfully the committee, chaired by Romanovsky, bore the brunt of the selection efforts. Do you know how many games they had to study to choose the three winners? 40 (read it again: forty)!! Peter Arsenyevich even wrote in his report (tournament bulletin, 9th February 1952) that the committee's task "was rather hard".

Here was their verdict: "The special M. I. Chigorin prizes are awarded to: V. Simagin for the win against Moiseev, E. Geller for the win against Taimanov, and V. Smyslov for the win against Simagin." Unlike the previous championships, there were no gradations (first, second and third prize), but the order of the list presumably implies that.

I must admit that I was surprised at the winners list. Where is Keres' brilliant victory over Geller? Where's Bronstein win against the same Geller, which was called "perhaps the best game of the tournament" by Romanovsky in the foreword of the tournament book? By the way, it heads the list of games praised by the committee as "victories deep in their ideas and execution", and Keres' game is among the top ones, too.

The other games that made the list (winners in italic): *Averbakh* – Smyslov, *Kopylov* – Bondarevsky, Moiseev – *Geller*, *Botvinnik* – Lipnitsky, Aronin – *Botvinnik*, *Aronin* – Bronstein, *Taimanov* – Averbakh, *Petrosian* – Smyslov, *Smyslov* – Botvinnik, *Keres* – Taimanov, *Simagin* – Terpugov, *Bronstein* – Taimanov and Geller – *Flohr*. Add the "games won in great style", Petrosian – *Kopylov*, *Lipnitsky* – Terpugov and *Keres* – Simagin, and you'll get the full list of "masterpieces".

I did include some of them here, but not all. Not solely because I had to leave some space for the "dramas". I'm choosing my examples mainly by their aesthetic and emotional power, not the refined correctness that's good for text books but doesn't feed the soul that much. There are already too many "mechanical" devices in the modern world, so at least let the old games remind us that mistakes are the factor that makes chess a spectacular and beautiful game…

First Brilliancy Prize

Romanovsky: "There was no shortage of beautiful, fresh and sharp attacks, often with sacrifices. Here, of course, we should highlight the game Moiseev – Simagin above all: the consistently executed combinational attack with knight and exchange sacrifices and the spectacular move f4-f3! that brought black's king's bishop into play, finishing with the white king completely surrounded."

No. 234. King's Indian Defense E90
Moiseev – Simagin
Moscow 1951, round 6
Annotated by V. Simagin
1.d4 ♘f6 2.c4 g6 3.♘c3 ♗g7.
"The number of adherents of this opening grows every year. In the
19th *championship, for instance, in addition to the old King's Indian fans such as Geller, Aronin and Petrosian, it was also used by Kotov, Moiseev, Simagin, and Bondarevsky." (Bronstein)*

4.e4 0-0 5.♘f3 *(5.♘ge2 – see game 125 in the second volume)* **5… d6 6.h3 e5.** Immediately fixing the position in the center, black intends to play f7-f5 as quickly as possible. It's now not threatening to play 7.dxe5 dxe5 8.♕xd8 ♖xd8 9.♘xe5 ♘xe4!, and black has an advantage.

7.d5. *"A cunning system, used by Makogonov in his time." (Kasparov)*

7…♘h5. The most active continuation. Black planned to meet 8.g4 with 8…♘f4.

The moves 7…a5 and 7…♘a6 are now more popular, and instead of 8.g4 white usually plays 8.g3 or 8.♘h2 – one of the main ideas of this set-up.

8.♗e3 f5 9.exf5 gxf5 10.♗e2! 10.♘xe5? doesn't work due to 10...♕e8! 11.♘d3 f4 12.♗e2 fxe3 13.♗xh5 exf2+ and black is better *(as the game Dzindzichashvili – Hebert, Lone Pine 1981, showed).*

10...♘f6 11.♕c2 ♘a6 *(11...f4!? and a7-a5)* **12.g3.** White still has to prevent the move f5-f4.

12...♘b4! An interesting idea (the knight is usually developed to c5): if white kicks the knight away with a2-a3, the weakness of the b3 square might tell later.

Played in Simagin's distinct "crooked gun" style! The computer proposes the typical pawn break 12...c6! and considers the knight move dubious.

13.♕b3 a5 14.0-0-0. Black's initiative has fizzled out, and he has a number of weaknesses in his position, while white is well-developed. The effort to make the game even more complicated now is, therefore, completely reasonable.

14...f4! *(14...♘d7 is much safer)* **15.gxf4.**

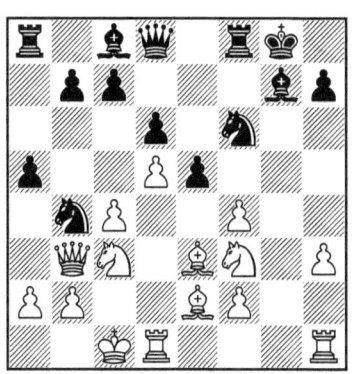

15...♗f5! The best continuation! Master Ufimtsev, annotating the game for the bulletin, considers this move a mistake. But we cannot agree with this assessment. The move 15...exf4 led to white's advantage after 16.♗d2!. It was then bad to continue 16...♗f5 17.♘d4! and it's unclear how black is supposed to continue the attack, while white already has the open g-file.

Indeed, after 17...♘d7 18.♘xf5 ♘c5 white has a spectacular queen sacrifice: 19.♘xg7! ♘xb3+ 20.axb3 ♔xg7 21.♖hg1+ with dangerous threats. However, after 16...♕e8! with the idea ♘d7-c5 it's now white who is in trouble. Thus, after 15...exf4 it's better to play 16.♗d4! ♗f5 17.♖d2 and ♖g1 with a clear advantage.

In the compilation Best Games, Simagin removed the exclamation marks for 14...f4(?) and 15...♗f5. He also evaluated 16.♘e1? much more objectively: "since this moment, white's position gradually worsens."

16.♘e1? A mistake that immediately leads to a lost position for white. There was no reason to go on the defensive here. He had to sacrifice an exchange: 16.fxe5 ♗c2 17.♕a3 ♗xd1 18.♖xd1 dxe5 *(18...♘h5 19.♘e4 is better)*, and white's chances are no worse in the subsequent double-edged struggle.

If Moiseev had gone for this line and played 19.♘g5!, it was black who could have got "a lost position"!

For instance: *19...♕d7 20.♘e6 ♖f7 21.♕b3! b6 22.c5! (22...♘bxd5 23.♘xg7 etc.).*

16...exf4 17.♗d4. It's even worse to play 17.♗xf4 ♘e4, with a number of unstoppable threats.

Here's one example: 18.♗e3? ♘xf2! 19.♗xf2 ♗h6+ 20.♖d2 ♗g6 21.♖f1 ♕g5 22.♕d1 ♕f5 with a problem-like idea 23...♕b1+! 24.♘xb1 ♘xa2#. 18.♘xe4 ♗xe4

19.♖g1 ♘xa2+ 20.♔d2! is more resilient, but black also has a better move: 17...♘d7!

17...♔h8 18.a3. *18.♖g1!? was more consistent.*

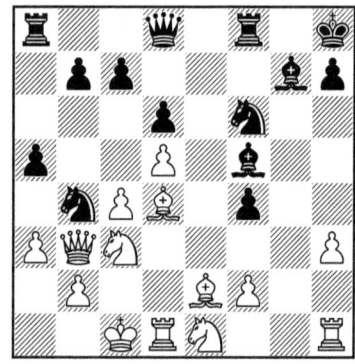

18...c5! If the knight retreated, white would get an advantage with 19.♗d3. Sacrificing a piece, black

The game Simagin versus Averbakh. Nikolai Kopylov can be seen to the right. From D. Bronstein's archive. Published for the first time.

unleashes all his remaining forces against the white king's position.

19.♗xf6. 19.dxc6 ♘xc6 is completely joyless for white: black trades off the d4 bishop and gets a strong attack with equal material.

The en passant capture allowed white to maintain some counterchances. But do you know how the computer evaluates the trade on f6? "–+"!

19...♕xf6 20.axb4 axb4.

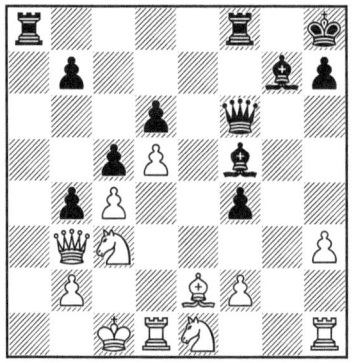

21.♘b5. The best retreat. Other moves led to a quicker loss: 21.♘a4 ♖xa4, or 21.♘a2 ♖a7 22.♔d2 ♕d4+, or, finally, 21.♘b1 f3! 22.♗d3 b5 *(22...♗d7!)* 23.♗xf5 *(23.♘d2!? bxc4 24.♘xc4)* 23...bxc4 24.♕c2 b3 25.♕c3 ♕xf5 etc.

Ufimtsev showed a beautiful line: 21.♘b1 b5 22.♘c2 f3 23.♗d3 bxc4 24.♗xc4 ♗h6+ 25.♘e3 ♖a1 26.♔d2 ♕d4+ 27.♗d3 ♖a2!

The move 27...♖a2?? is spellbinding... but not for long: 28.♔c2! and black is lost. Black had to play more simply: 27...c4! 28.♕xc4 ♕xb2+ 29.♕c2 ♖a2 etc.

21...♖a1+. Black could also win with 21...f3 *(the simplest!)* 22.♗d3 ♖a1+ 23.♔c2 ♖xd1 24.♔xd1 ♖a8 25.♔c2 ♖a1. However, he chooses a more spectacular way to win.

22.♔d2 f3!!

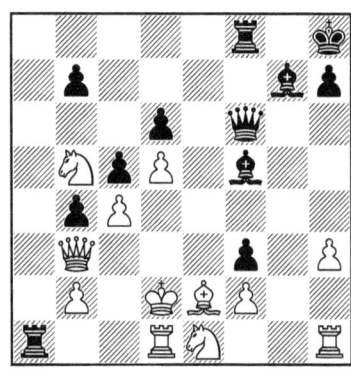

23.♘c2. White's position is hopeless in all lines:

1) 23.♖xa1 ♗h6+ 24.♔d1 fxe2+ 25.♔xe2 ♗g6!! (25...♗g4+ 26.f3 achieves nothing) 26.f3 (both 26.♔d1 ♕f4 and 26.♖h2 ♕e5+ are bad; after 26.♖f1 there's 26...♗e8+ 27.♔d1 ♕f4) 26...♗e8+ 27.♔f1 ♕e5 28.♕d1 ♕g3! 29.♘g2 (otherwise 29...♖xe1+!) 29...♖f8 30.♘e1 ♗e3 31.♕e2 ♗d3!!;

2) 23.♗d3 ♗h6+ 24.♔c2 ♖xd1 25.♔xd1 ♕g5 26.♕c2 ♖a8!;

3) 23.♗xf3 ♖e8 24.♖xa1 (24.♘c2 ♗xc2 25.♔xc2 ♕f5+ 26.♕d3 b3+ 27.♔d2 ♕f4+) 24...♗h6+ 25.♔d1 ♕g5 26.♕e3 ♖xe3 27.fxe3 ♕xe3 28.♖h2 ♕b3+!;

In the bracketed line, the winning move is 24...♖xd1+! (24...♗xc2=), and 26...b3+ is an error too: after 27.♔xb3 white wins (26...♕f6=)...

However, as Boleslavsky liked to say, "it's all empty words": after 23.♗xf3, there's a crushing blow 23...♗b1!

4) 23.♘xf3 ♗h6+ 24.♔e1 ♗c1! (after that, white gets an amusing position where he has no good moves; the threat 25...♖b1 decides matters) 25.♖g1 (or 25.♘d2 ♗d3!; *25...♗c2! is stronger, while if 25.♗d3, then 25...♗d7!)* 25...♖b1 26.♕a4 ♕xb2 *(26...♖xb2!)* 27.♘xd6 ♕c3+ 28.♔f1 ♗xh3+ etc.

Taimanov: "It is hard to believe that Simagin saw all this, or even the majority of the variations, but in view of the powerful cooperation of black's forces he would have felt he was correct in his assessment." (B. Cafferty, M. Taimanov The Soviet Championships, 1998.)

23...♗xc2! (thwarting the attempt to block the e3 square with the knight) **24.♔xc2.** 24.♕xc2 fxe2 25.♖xa1 ♕xf2 is bad.

24...fxe2 25.♖xa1 ♕g6+! An important subtlety. After 25...♕f5+ white could still defend: 26.♕d3! b3+ 27.♔d2 ♗h6+ 28.♔c3 *(after 28...♕xf2 29.♔xb3 ♖f3, he's still lost).* Now, 26.♕d3 is met with 26...e1=♘+ 27.♖hxe1 ♖xf2+ or 26...b3+ 27.♔d2 ♗h6+ 28.♔c3 ♖f3! 29.♕xf3 ♕c2#.

26.♔d2 ♗h6+ 27.♕e3. White gives up his queen out of desperation. If 27.♔xe2, then 27...♕e4+, winning both rooks; or 27.♔e1 ♕g2!

27...♖xf2 28.♖he1 ♗xe3+ 29.♔xe3 ♕g3+ 30.♔d2 ♕f4+. White resigned.

Second Brilliancy Prize

Romanovsky: "As a bit of self-criticism, we should point out that in awarding a special prize to the game Taimanov – Geller for a deeply thought-out and fascinatingly executed attack on both flanks by Geller, the committee, unfortunately, overlooked an interesting chance to save the game that Taimanov had at the very end of the game because of an inaccuracy by Geller."

Thankfully, the committee didn't have a computer, which is rather prone to put flies in any ointment!

No. 235. Queen's Pawn Game D04
Taimanov – Geller
Moscow 1951, round 8
Annotated by A. Lilienthal

1.d4 ♘f6 2.♘f3 g6 3.b3. As in a number of other games, Taimanov wants to avoid well-trodden paths and chooses a rare move.

3...♗g7 4.♗b2 0-0 5.e3 d5! Exactly! It's now disadvantageous to play 5...d6 due to 6.♘bd2 ♘bd7 7.♘c4, and it's hard for black to push the pawn to e5 *(but 6...c5! is quite safe).*

6.♗e2. White plays very passively in the opening. It was necessary to play 6.c4, without giving up the central e4 square so easily *(the most popular move is 6.♗d3).*

6...♘e4 7.0-0 c5 8.♕c1. Now, 8.c4 *(8.♘bd2 is more popular)* could be met with 8...dxc4 9.bxc4 ♘c6 with pressure on the d4 square.

8...cxd4 9.♗xd4. Intending to weaken black's kingside with the dark-squared bishop trade. However, this severely weakens the c3 square in white's camp.

9...♗xd4 10.exd4. If 10.♘xd4 then 10...e5 11.♘f3 ♕f6 12.♕b2 ♘c6 13.♖d1 ♗e6 *(13...d4!?)* with a good position for black.

10...♘c6 11.♕e3. White got nothing out of the opening. I think that he had to play 11.♕h6, maintaining the balance: 11...♗g4 12.♘bd2 (threatening ♘xe4 and ♘g5) 12...♗xf3 13.♘xf3 e6 14.♗d3 ♕f6 15.♗xe4 dxe4 16.♘g5 ♕g7 17.♕xg7+ ♔xg7 18.♘xe4 ♘xd4 19.c4.

After 18.c3!, white is even somewhat better, but black can play 14...f5 or 14...♕e7.

11...♗g4 12.♘bd2 ♘xd2 13.♕xd2 e6 14.♖fd1 ♕f6 15.♘e5 ♗xe2 16.♕xe2 ♖fc8. Black's position is more promising because of the open c-file. White has no opportunities to attack the black king.

17.♘g4 ♕f4 18.c3. There's no other way to protect the d4 pawn. Of course, white can't play 18.g3 due to 18...♘xd4.

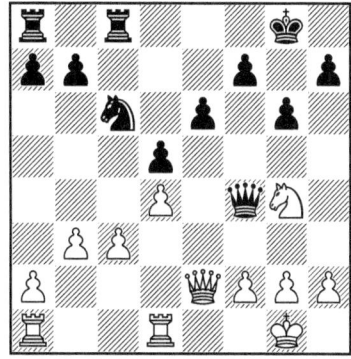

Grandmaster Bronstein took an interest in Geller's opening plan against Taimanov. From D. Bronstein's archive. Published for the first time.

18...h5! A good move. The immediate 18...♖c7 could be met with 19.g3 ♕d6 20.c4 dxc4 21.d5 exd5 (21...♘a5 22.b4 ♕xb4 23.♕e5, winning; or 21...♘e7 22.bxc4 ♖ac8 23.♕e5!, and white is better) 22.♖xd5 ♕e6 (22...♕e7 23.♕b2!) 23.♕xc4.

And after 23...h5 24.♘e3 ♖e8, the position is roughly equal. However, in the second bracketed line, instead of 23.♕e5? (23...♕xe5 24.♘xe5 ♖c5!=), white can win, as well as one move before, with 23.♘f6+ ♔f8 24.♘e4.

19.♘e3 ♖c7. *Or 19...♖ab8 and b7-b5 with a classical pawn minority attack.*

20.g3? The decisive mistake *(not exactly!).* It was necessary to play 20.c4!, since 20...♘xd4 is not possible due to 21.♕d3, and it's hard for black to improve the position.

But 20...♖d8! gives him a stable advantage. Therefore, 20.♖ac1 was better.

20...♕f6 21.♖d3 ♖ac8 22.♖e1 b5!

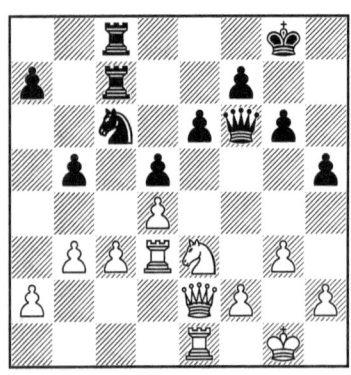

Permanently fixing the weakness on c3. White's position is difficult.

23.♘c2 ♘e7 24.♖f3. *Losing an important tempo. The immediate 24.♕d2! was better, with the idea ♘b4-a6-c5 and regrouping the rooks to defend the c3 square.*

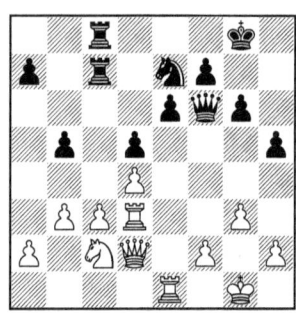

For instance: 24...♘f5 (24...a5 25.♘e3, again taking the f5 square under control) 25.♘b4 ♘d6 26.f3 (26.♘a6? ♘e4) 26...a5 27.♘a6 ♖e7 28.♘c5 ♘b7 29.♕e3 ♖ec7, and only now 30.♘xb7 ♖xb7 31.♖d2 ♖bc7 32.♖c2 and ♖ec1.

24...♘f5   25.♕d2   ♕g7. Geller shows subtle positional understanding. He doesn't hurry with the move a7-a5 – first, he retreats his queen, maintaining the pressure along the h8-a1 diagonal. The immediate 25...a5 is weaker, since after 26.♘e3 there's no 26...♖xc3? due to 27.♘xd5 etc.

But 26...♕g5! decides matters. White would have had to suffer after 26.b4 axb4 27.♘xb4 ♕d8.

26.♖d3. Taimanov can't find a good plan. Trying to transfer the knight to the queenside would have been unsuccessful: 26.♘b4 ♘d6 *(26... a5! 27.♘a6 ♖c6 28.♘c5 b4!, crushing)* 27.♘a6 ♘e4, and black wins.

26...a5 27.♘e3 ♘d6 28.f3.
Tempting black to play 28...
♘e4. White's position is joyless:
black threatened 28...b4 with the
subsequent ♘e4.

28...♛f6. Geller decides against
winning the exchange. He probably
thought that after 28...♘e4 29.fxe4
dxe4 30.c4 exd3 31.♛xd3 bxc4
32.bxc4 ♖d8 33.d5, white improved
his position.

*But after 32...♖b8! he is doomed.
After 28...♛f6?!, however, the
situation gets more complicated.*

29.♔g2 ♘f5 *(29...g5!?)* **30.♖e2
♛g5.**

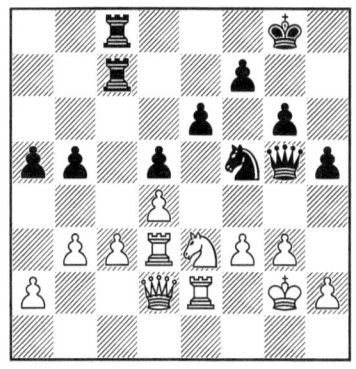

31.a3. Transitioning into a rook
ending wouldn't save white: 31.♘xf5
♛xd2 32.♖exd2 gxf5 33.♖c2 b4, and
black wins.

*It might sound strange, but he
doesn't! After 34.♔f2 ♖xc3 35.♖dxc3
♖xc3 36.♖xc3 bxc3 37.♔e3 e5
38.dxe5 d4+ 39.♔d3 ♔f8! 40.a4
♔e7 41.♔c2!, white saves the game by
creating passed pawns on both flanks:
41...♔e6 42.b4! ♔xe5 43.b5 or 41...
♔d7 42.h3! ♔c6 43.e6! fxe6 44.g4=.*

31...h4. After tying up all the
white pieces to the defense of the
c3 pawn, Geller starts storming the
opposing king's position.

32.f4 ♛h5 33.♘xf5. This loses
more quickly, since black gets a
decisive attack along the open g-file.

33...gxf5 34.gxh4. 34.♖f2 was
met with 34...h3+ 35.♔g1 b4 36.axb4
axb4 37.cxb4 ♖c1+ 38.♖f1 ♖1c2
39.♛d1 ♖g2+ 40.♔h1 ♖cc2 etc.

34...♖xc3 35.♖g3+. The line
35.♖xc3 ♖xc3 36.♛xc3 *(after 36.♖e3
♖xe3 37.♛xe3, black wins with 37...
♛d1!)* 36...♛xe2+ 37.♔g1 ♛g4+
38.♛g3 ♔h7 is better for black, since
the pawn ending is hopeless for white.

*Alas, this is an illusion: 39.♛xg4
fxg4 40.h3!=. Therefore, instead of
37...♛g4+?, the correct move is 37...
♛e4!−+.*

**35...♔h7 36.♖f2 b4 37.axb4
axb4 38.♛e1 ♛xh4 39.♛e5 ♖g8
40.♖ff3 ♖c2+ 41.♔f1.**

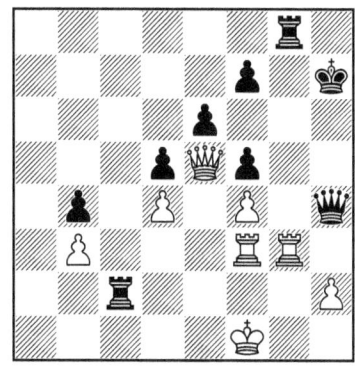

41...♖xh2? This allows white to
get a study-like draw: 42.♖xg8 ♔xg8
(42...♖h1+? 43.♖g1) 43.♖g3+!!
♛xg3 44.♛b8+ ♔g7 45.♛g8+! ♔xg8

– stalemate (the line was shown by K. Korabelnikov from Lyubertsy).

The move 41...♖g4, with the threat to capture on h2, won. If now 42.♖h3, then 42...♖c1+ 43.♔e2 ♖e1+ *(43...♖g2+ 44.♖f2 ♖xf2+ 45.♔e3 ♖c3# is simpler)* 44.♔d3 ♖xe5 45.dxe5 ♖xf4 etc.

42.♕e3 ♖a8 43.♖g7+ ♔h6. White resigned.

"The game clearly demonstrates the future grandmaster's energy and great talent." (Petrosian)

Third Brilliancy Prize

Romanovsky: "The game Smyslov – Simagin was an intense struggle across the entire board that ended with a beautifully trapped black knight, the little remaining forces being completely equal."

No. 236. English Opening A35
Smyslov – Simagin
Moscow 1951, round 12
Annotated by V. Smyslov
1.c4 c5 2.♘c3 ♘c6 3.♘f3 g6 4.e3. White is preparing the push d2-d4 to have an opportunity to meet cxd4 with exd4, creating a pawn center. If white immediately plays 4.d4, then after 4...cxd4 5.♘xd4 ♗g7, the bishop would exert a lot of pressure along the a1-h8 diagonal.

4...d6 *(4...♗g7 or 4...♘f6 5.d4 cxd4 6.exd4 d5 are more popular)* **5.d4 ♗g4 6.♗e2 ♗g7 7.d5.** Pushing the pawn with tempo, white gains a space advantage.

7...♘b8. Not 7...♘e5 due to 8.♘xe5 ♗xe2 9.♕a4+ *(but 7...♗xf3 8.♗xf3 ♗xc3+ 9.bxc3 ♘e5 or 8...♘e5 9.♗e2 ♘f6 were played more often).*

8.h3 ♗xf3 9.♗xf3 ♘f6 10.0-0 0-0 11.♕d2. The purpose of this maneuver is to prepare the flank development of the dark-squared bishop. 11.b3 could be met with 11...♘xd5 12.♗xd5 *(12. ♕xd5! is more precise)* 12...♗xc3 13.♗xb7 ♗xa1 14.♗xa8 ♘d7 *(14... ♕a5!)*, and black's opening troubles are left behind.

11...a6. Black planned a queenside pawn breakthrough. He intended to meet 12.b3 with the line 12...b5 13.cxb5 axb5, and white can't play 14.♘xb5 due to 14...♘e4.

12.♖b1. It's good to get the rook away from the dangerous diagonal. If now 12...b5 13.cxb5 axb5, then 14.b4 ♘a6 15.a3, which is better for white.

12...♘bd7 13.♗e2 *(preventing b7-b5)* **13...♘e8 14.b3 e5 15.dxe6.** This trade is consistent with the strategic principles of the struggle, since it's known that opening up the game increases the strength of the long-range bishops. Further, it now creates a target for attack on the d-file – the d6 pawn.

15...fxe6 16.♗b2 ♕e7 17.♖bd1 ♖d8 18.f4. Intending to put the bishop on f3 and complete the most sensible set-up of the white pieces. This structure allows white to take control over the central squares and creates the necessary preconditions for kingside activity.

18...♘df6 19.♗f3 ♘c7.

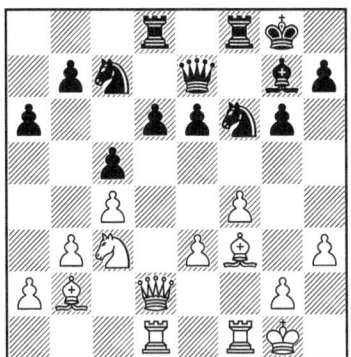

Black gives up a pawn to change the unfavorable course of the game with tactical complications. After 20.♗xb7 d5 he gets some counterchances because of the white bishop's isolated position.

Strangely, the computer sees no such chances after 21.♕c1(e2)...

20.g4! Deciding against the problematic lines involving winning a pawn, white prefers to launch a kingside attack.

20...b5 21.g5 ♘fe8 22.h4. 22.♘e4 is safer, hampering black's counterplay in the center.

22...b4. Black could reply 22...d5, and if 23.cxd5 then 23...b4 24.♘a4 exd5, attacking the e3 pawn. White would have most probably had to play 23.a3, and now 23...b4 24.axb4 cxb4 25.♘a4 gave him better prospects.

The move 23.a3? is clearly beneficial for black due to 23...bxc4! 24.bxc4 ♘d6, while 23.cxd5 ♘d6! 24.♖fe1 (24.dxe6 ♘c4!) 24...♘f5 25.h5 gxh5 leads to a sharp struggle.

So, 22...d5!? was a chance to escape the grip.

23.♘e4 ♗xb2 24.♕xb2 d5 25.♘f2 ♕g7. There was a dangerous attack brewing if the knight got to g4, so black's intention to trade queens is natural.

26.♕xg7+ ♔xg7 27.♘g4 ♘f5 28.♔f2. White has an advantage in the endgame because his pieces and pawns are more active. He now threatens 29.♘f6+, which forces his opponent to make his mind up in the center. He cannot capture the white pawn, because after 28...♘xh4 29.♘f6+ ♔g7 30.♖h1 there are threats along the h-file.

28...dxc4. By opening up the central file, black gets a pawn advantage on the queenside. Another plan, with the move 28...d4, led after 29.e4 ♘d6 30.♔g3 to a position where white could prepare an attack by doubling rooks along the h-file and the subsequent h4-h5 *(the immediate 30.♘f6+! is even better).*

29.bxc4 a5. *After 29...♔g7 there's a strong reply 30.♘e5! ♘xh4 31.♘d7 ♖f7 32.♗c6.*

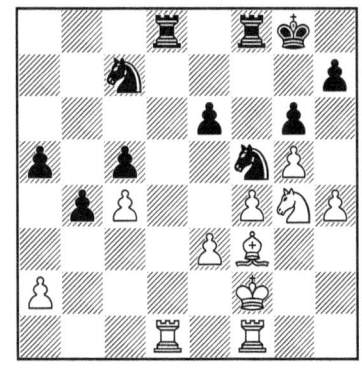

30.♘f6+. The beginning of a forcing maneuver that wins the c5 pawn.

30...♔g7 31.♘d7 ♖f7. Black is forced to give up his fight for the open file, because it's difficult to keep the material balance otherwise. If, for instance, 31...♖fe8, then white can play 32.h5 h6 33.♖g1 *(33.gxh6+! and ♖g1 is stronger)*, creating a direct attack on the king.

32.♘xc5 ♖xd1 33.♖xd1 ♘xh4 34.♘d7. This maneuver prevents black from liquidating his backward pawn through e6-e5.

34...♘xf3 35.♔xf3 ♘d5. A futile attempt to steer the game towards a rook ending; after 36.cxd5 ♖xd7 37.d6 ♔f7 38.♔e4 ♖d8 39.♔e5 ♖b8, threatening ♖b5+, black got some counterchances *(after 40.e4! ♖b5+ 41.♔d4 ♔e8 42.♔c4! there's very few of them).*

36.♘c5 ♘c7 37.♔e4. Following well-known endgame principles: the king has occupied a strong position in the center, and the rook controls the open file. Despite the material equality, black can't prevent white from activating his pieces. 37...♖f5 is bad due to 38.♖d7+ ♔f7 39.♖xc7 ♖xc7 40.♘xe6+ and ♘xc7.

Black tries to make his position somewhat less cramped with the h-pawn push.

37...h6 38.♖d6 hxg5 39.fxg5 ♔f8 40.♖c6 ♔e8 41.♔e5! White consistently executes his plan to invade his opponent's camp with his pieces. Now the king goes to d6, and

it's better than the prosaic 41.♘xe6 ♖e7 42.♖xc7 ♖xe6+, when black gets rid of his "bad" c7 knight at the cost of a pawn.

41...♔d8.

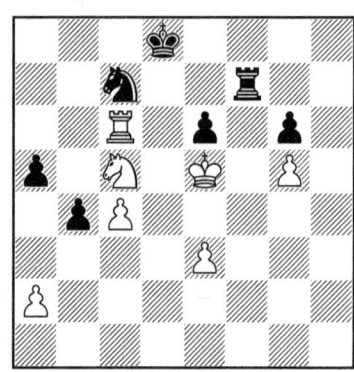

42.♖b6! Freeing the way to the 6th rank for the king. The immediate 42.♔d6 was too premature because of 42...♘e8+ 43.♔xe6 ♖e7+ and ♖xe3. The game move makes white's finishing attack much stronger.

42...♔c8. After 42...♖f5+ there's 43.♔d6 ♘e8+ 44.♔c6 ♔e7 45.♖b7+ ♔f8 46.♘xe6+ ♔g8 47.♖e7 etc. If 42...♔e7 then 43.e4 ♖f2 44.♖b7 ♔d8 45.♔d6 ♖d2+ 46.♔c6, and black still can't save the game.

43.♔d6 ♖f2. Searching for counterplay. If 43...♘e8+ then 44.♔c6 ♖c7+ 45.♔b5, and the black pawns are vulnerable.

44.♔c6! (Of course, not 44.♖b7 ♘a6) **44...♖c2 45.♖b7 ♘e8.** 45...♘d5 doesn't help either due to 46.cxd5 ♖xc5+ 47.♔xc5 ♔xb7 48.dxe6 etc.

46.♖a7 ♔b8 47.♖e7. Black resigned.

Counter-Strike!

Tolush: "Until the 14th move, events in the game Geller – Keres unfolded exactly as in the game Boleslavsky – Keres at the 1950 Budapest tournament. Keres got an advantage quite quickly there. We should assume that the memories of that game left him more confident about the result of this encounter as well..."

No. 237. Ruy Lopez C99
Geller – Keres
Moscow 1951, round 4
Annotated by P. Keres

1.e4 e5 2.♘f3 ♘c6 3.♗b5 a6 4.♗a4 ♘f6 5.0-0 ♗e7 6.♖e1 b5 7.♗b3 d6 8.c3 0-0 9.h3 ♘a5 10.♗c2 c5 11.d4 ♕c7 12.♘bd2 cxd4. The defensive system chosen by black, developed and analyzed by Chigorin, is still *(in the 1950s)* the most popular line of the Ruy Lopez. It usually leads to a complicated and interesting struggle. With the game move, black launches an immediate attack on white's center.

13.cxd4 ♗b7. *Fashion of the times. Later, 13...♘c6 with the subsequent ♗d7 became more popular.*

14.♘f1. Now black manages to execute the important advance d6-d5 and open the files.

Many theoreticians recommend closing off the center with 14.d5, but black probably still gets enough counterplay by immediately playing 14...♗c8. Bronstein's move 15.♖b1 in the game against Geller *(see game*

238) brought him success, but with correct defense, black shouldn't face much trouble.

In the next championship, Keres went for this line against Byvshev, but after 15...♗d7 16.♘f1 ♘c4 17.b3, he eventually lost...

14...♖ac8 15.♗b1. This is the novelty prepared by Geller. After 15...d5 16.exd5, white intends to prevent the possible pawn sacrifice 16...e4, which is now met with the simple 17.♘g5 and an advantage for white.

White usually played 15.♗d3 or 15.♖e2, after which black got a sustained initiative after a pawn sacrifice – 15...d5 16.exd5 *(16.dxe5 ♘xe4=)* 16...e4 *(after 15.♖e2, the correct move is 16...exd4!).* 15.♘e3 is an error; in the game Boleslavsky – Keres (Budapest 1950), black got a very good position after 15...♘xe4! 16.♘f5 ♕xc2 17.♘xe7+ ♔h8 (18.♘xc8 ♕xf2+! with an overwhelming attack).

15...d5 16.exd5 (16.dxe5 ♘xe4 17.♘g3 f5 18.exf6 ♗xf6! with a good position; *if the bishop is on b1, 17...♗b4! is also strong*) **16...exd4!** Black equalizes with this simple trade.

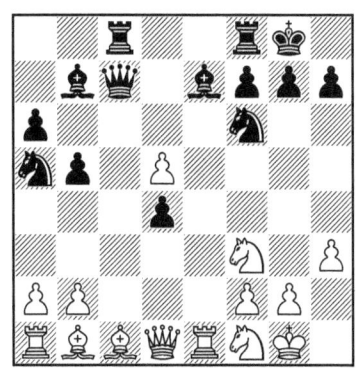

17.♗g5! h6. The immediate 17...♘xd5 could be met with 18.♗xe7 ♘xe7 19.♗xh7+ ♚xh7 20.♘g5+ with a dangerous attack. However, the game move is not the best either, since now white could offer an interesting piece sacrifice: 18.♗xh6! gxh6 19.♕d2, and it's very hard for black to defend. After 19...♖fd8 20.♕xh6 ♖xd5 white has a strong reply 21.♖e4!, pointed out by Konstantinopolsky. Thus, black would probably have had to decline the sacrifice with 18...♘xd5 19.♕d3 f5, with an unclear position.

Let's start from the beginning. In the book One Hundred Games, *instead of 17...h6? Keres proposed 17...♖fe8, but white has an unpleasant 18.♕d3!, and the attempt to defuse the tension with 18...♕c4? doesn't work due to 19.♖xe7! ♖xe7 20.♕a3. Because of that, the computer recommends 17...♖ce8! (18.♕d3 ♕c4=).*

Next, in the same book, Keres continued the 21.♖e4 line above with 21...♖h5 22.♖g4+ ♘xg4 23.♕xh5 ♘f6 24.♕g5+ ♚f8 25.♕h6+ ♚e8 26.♗f5, missing the reply 26...♘d7!, after which the attack fizzles out.

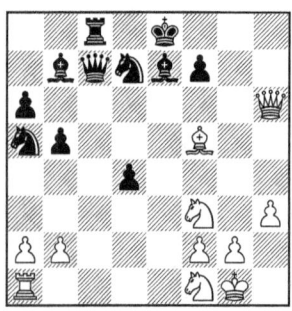

For instance: 27.♕h8+ ♘f8 28.♗xc8 ♗xf3! 29.♗xa6 ♕b6 30.♗xb5+ ♕xb5 31.gxf3 ♕xb2, and black has two pieces for a rook and two pawns, with equal chances.

So, does the piece sacrifice ultimately gain nothing?

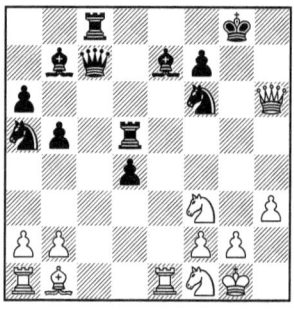

Position after 18.♗xh6 gxh6
19.♕d2 ♖fd8 20.♕xh6 ♖xd5

After 21.♖e4, it indeed gains nothing. However, the seemingly unassuming move 21.♘g3!! with the threats ♘f5 and ♘g5 leads to a win! Each subsequent chain of moves is even prettier than the last one: 21...♗f8! 22.♕xf6 ♗g7 23.♕h4! d3 24.♗xd3 ♖xd3 25.♘f5! ♗xf3 (otherwise 26.♘g5) 26.♘e7+ ♚f8 27.♕h7 ♗e5! (an elegant defense to mate) 28.♘xc8!! ♖d8 29.♖ac1 ♗c6 30.♖c5!! (30.♖c3? ♖xc8!, but not 30...♗xc3? 31.bxc3, mating) 30...♖d5 31.♖c3! ♗d4! 32.♖d3 (with the threat 33.♖xd4 and ♕h8#! – white's key threat; 32.♖g3?? ♕xg3) 32...♗g7 33.♖g3 – curtains!

And lastly, black can't decline the sacrifice with 18...♘xd5: after 19.♗xg7!! white wins! However,

Бойцы вспоминают
минувшие дни...
Дружеский шарж Н. ЛИСА.

"The fighters remember the bygone days..." (A quote from a poem by Alexander Pushkin.) When Geller stopped the clock in his game against Keres, an ovation erupted in the hall! Cartoon by N. Lis. From the tournament bulletin (5th January 1952).

only a machine can see through all the subtleties over the board. Here's one line: 19...♔xg7 20.♕xd4+ ♘f6 21.♘e3!! (the only move!) 21...♗xf3 22.♘f5+ etc. Later, Keres found the correct defense – 18...♖fd8!.

18.♗h4? ♘xd5 19.♕d3. White is going to attack, even though he lacks a positional foundation and

is unlikely to succeed. The queen is placed badly on d3, which was the reason for his subsequent difficulties. The correct move was 19.♗xe7 ♘xe7 20.♘xd4 ♖fd8 21.♕g4.

19...g6 20.♗g3. But now, 20.♗xe7 ♘xe7 21.♘xd4 ♖fd8 is better for black, for instance: 22.♕e3 ♘c4! 23.♕xe7 ♖xd4 etc.

20...♗d6. *And now the whole advantage slips through Keres' fingers, even though he could have kept it with 20...♕b6!*

21.♗xd6. The attempt to create an attack with 21.♘e5 is repelled with 21...♘c4!, for instance: 22.♘xg6 fxg6 23.♖e6 ♖f6 24.♖xf6 ♘xf6 25.♕xg6+ ♕g7 or 23.♕xg6+ ♕g7 24.♕e6+ ♔h8 25.♗xd6 ♘f4!

But for some reason, Geller missed the simple 21.♕xd4! ♖fd8 22.♗e4=.

21...♕xd6 22.♕d2? 22.♕xd4 was necessary.

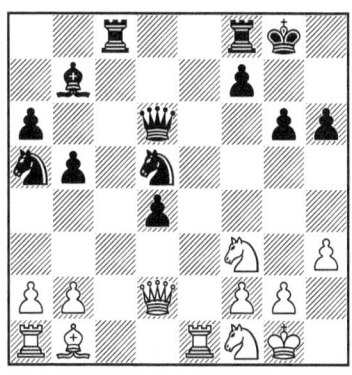

22...♘f4! With a piece sacrifice, black destroys the white king's position and creates a very strong attack.

23.♕xa5. 23.♗e4 was relatively best, even though it's probably not enough to fully equalize. Black can continue with 23...♘c6 24.♘e5 ♘xe5 25.♕xf4 g5 and ♗xe4, retaining the extra pawn, but even the simple 23...♖fe8 gives him some advantage in the endgame after 24.♗xb7 ♘xb7 25.♘xd4 ♖xe1 26.♖xe1 ♘c5.

In the second line, the immediate 25...♘c5! is stronger, winning a pawn: 26.♘f3 ♕xd2 27.♘1xd2 ♘cd3 or 26.♖ad1 ♖xe1 27.♖xe1 ♕f6. 25.♘g3! (with idea 25...d3? 26.♘e4) was more resilient, meeting 25...♘c5 with 26.♖xe8+ ♖xe8 27.♕xd4 and simplifying the position while keeping material equal.

23...♗xf3   24.gxf3   ♘xh3+ 25.♔g2. After 25.♔h1 ♕f4! white does not have sufficient defense to the multiple threats, for instance: 26.♔g2 ♕h4 27.♕d2 (or 27.♘h2 ♘f4+ 28.♔h1 ♕xf2) 27...♘f4+ 28.♔g1 ♕g5+, winning the queen, or 26.♗e4 ♘xf2+ 27.♔g2 ♘xe4 and ♖c2+, or, finally, 26.♘h2 ♘xf2+ 27.♔g2 ♖c5! with an unstoppable attack.

25...♘f4+   26.♔g1   ♘h3+ 27.♔g2 ♘f4+ (repeating moves to buy some time) **28.♔g1 ♕d5.** After 28...♕d7, white has the defense 29.♕d2 g5 30.♖e4 and ♖xf4.

Even this doesn't save him due to 29...♘h3+! 30.♔g2 ♘g5 31.♗e4 ♕h3+ 32.♔g1 ♕h4! and ♘h3-f4.

29.♘g3. 29.♗e4 ♕g5+ 30.♘g3 h5 is hopeless.

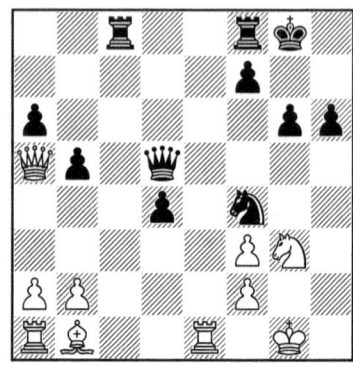

29...d3! Cutting off white's entire queenside. 29...♕xf3 was of course weaker due to 30.♗e4.

30.♘e4   ♕f5   31.♕b4. Loses immediately. 31.♕d2 was necessary, to meet 31...♖c4 *(the simplest is 31...♖fd8!)* with 32.♗xd3. Black can't play 32...♖xe4? due to 33.♖xe4 ♕g5+ 34.♔f1 ♕g2+ 35.♔e1 ♕g1+ 36.♗f1, but after 32...♖d4 33.♗e3 ♖fd8, he would have regained the piece while maintaining a strong attack.

31...♖fe8! White resigned. After 32.♘g3 black wins with 32...♕h3!, while after 32.♗xd3 ♖xe4 33.♖xe4 ♕g5+ 34.♔f1 ♕g2+ 35.♔e1 ♘xd3+ he loses the queen.

The Unpretentious Beauty of Strategy

Romanovsky: "In the penultimate round, Bronstein played perhaps the best game in the whole tournament, defeating Geller, who had led the tournament together with Keres, in a subtle strategic style and clearing the way for Keres at the decisive moment."

The winner's annotations are dissonant with Peter Arsenyevich's evaluation, but there's a good reason for that. Disappointed with his championship performance, Bronstein annotated only two games from it, and he was too self-critical in the second game as well: he assigned six exclamation marks to Taimanov's moves and only four to his own!

No. 238. Ruy Lopez C99
Bronstein – Geller
Moscow 1951, round 16
Annotated by D. Bronstein

1.e4 e5 2.♘f3 ♘c6 3.♗b5 a6 4.♗a4 ♘f6 5.0-0 ♗e7 6.♖e1 b5 7.♗b3 0-0 8.c3 d6 9.h3 ♘a5 10.♗c2 c5 11.d4 ♕c7 12.♘bd2 cxd4. Up until now, the game had followed well-known lines. Black's defense until 11...♕c7, developed by Chigorin, is still considered one of his safest systems in the Ruy Lopez.

With his last move, black avoids the widely-used 12...♘c6, but even now the game is far from original. The line with the pawn trade on d4 has occurred rather often in tournaments in the last few years. Let's remember, for instance, the games Geller – Keres *(round 4)* and Bronstein – Keres *(round 12)* in this very championship.

The purpose of the pawn trade is to create counterplay on the queenside.

13.cxd4 ♗b7 14.d5. After 14.♘f1 ♖ac8 15.♗b1 d5 16.exd5, white also retains a small advantage,

but the game gets greatly simplified *(see game 237)*. Now, black's bishop is positioned rather awkwardly.

14...♗c8. *Later, black developed a plan with 14...♖ac8 (14...♖fc8 – see game 227) 15.♗d3 ♘d7 16.♘f1 f5 (Matanovic – Geller, Zagreb 1958).*

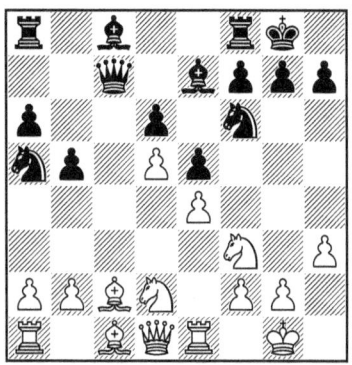

15.♖b1! The purpose of this move is to be able to capture on b4 with a pawn, restricting the b7 knight's range after 15...♘b7 16.b4 a5 17.a3 axb4 (in the game Bronstein – Keres, white played the weaker 15.♘f1 ♗d7 16.♘3h2 ♖fc8 17.♗d3 ♘b7 18.b4 a5! 19.♗d2 axb4 20.♗xb4 ♘c5, with a great position for black).

Therefore, the whole line that starts with 12...cxd4, weakening a number of squares on the queenside, looks too risky for me. Chigorin's main line 12...♘c6 is much safer *(as well as what became the most popular continuation 12...cxd4 13.cxd4 ♘c6).*

15...♗d7 16.♗d3 ♖fc8 17.♘f1 ♗d8 18.♘g3 ♕a7. Both sides are maneuvering slowly. White's pieces have more freedom of action, and this defines his advantage. Black can't find any vulnerabilities in white's position.

19.♖f1. Preventing 19...♗b6, which is now met with 20.♘h4 and a strong attack *(even though after 20...g6, white needs to be very inventive in its execution)*.

19...♘e8 20.♔h1. *A great move! With the idea 20...♗b6 21.♘h4 g6 (21...♗xf2? 22.♕f3) 22.f4!*

20...♘b7 21.b4 a5. Black's last two moves weren't the best. The knight's position on b7 is bad, and the b5 pawn is under attack. The correct moves were 20...g6 and ♘g7.

22.a3 axb4 23.axb4.

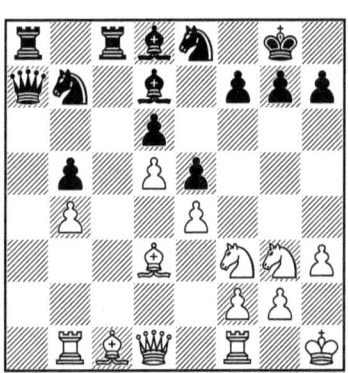

23...♗e7. The decisive mistake – more from a psychological than from a playing point of view. Having no good strategic plan, black decided to assume a waiting position. He had to play 23...♗b6, which he did only two moves later. Still, the game was very difficult and probably even lost for black here too.

24.♘e2! In opening the a-file, black has gained nothing – he has only created a new weakness, the b-pawn, in his own camp.

24...♗d8 *(24...♘d8!? 25.♗d2 g6 with the idea f7-f5)* **25.♗d2 ♗b6 26.♘c3.** The b5 pawn falls. As consolation, black takes on f2, but it's more than obvious that opening the f-file only aggravates his troubles.

26...♗xf2 27.♘xb5 ♕b6 28.♕e2 ♗g3 29.♗e3. White pieces control the entire board. Black now can't avoid great material losses.

29...♕d8 30.♘a7 ♖c3 31.♕d2 ♖a3 *(31...♕c7 32.♖a1!)* **32.♘c6 ♕f6.** 32...♕c7 33.♖fc1 was even worse.

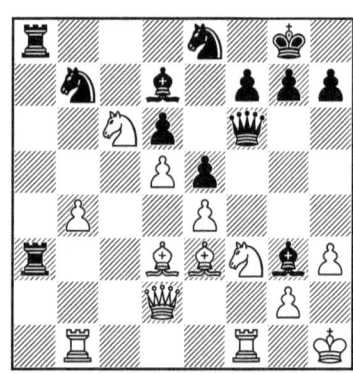

33.♘fxe5 ♗xe5 34.♖xf6 ♗xf6 35.♗c4? Starting to show off. White could have won by simply pushing his b4 pawn to b6.

This is too self-critical: the computer doesn't consider this move to be any worse; at any rate, it surely doesn't deserve a question mark!

35...♖c3 36.e5 ♖xc4 37.exf6 ♘xf6 38.♗d4 ♗xc6 *(38...♘xd5 39.♕g5!)* **39.dxc6 ♖xc6 40.♕g5 d5.** White missed this simple reply. After

40.♗xf6 gxf6, the win was still easy *(41.♖b3)*. Now black suddenly gets good drawing chances.

41.♖f1 *(white won more quickly with 41.b5 ♖d6 42.♗xf6 ♖xf6 43.♕xd5 etc.)* **41...h6 42.♕g3** (the game was adjourned here**) 42...♘e8 43.♕e5** *(43.♕f3!?)* **43...♖d8 44.♕h5!** The strongest continuation.

44...♘f6? Black shouldn't have given up so soon. Any other defense (such as 44...♖g6 or 44...♘bd6) was much better. White *(after 45.b5)* would still need to do a lot of work to convert his advantage, and any inaccuracy could spell doom for his efforts. But now it's all over.

45.♗xf6 ♖xf6 46.♖xf6 gxf6 47.♕f3. Stopping the d5 pawn in its tracks.

47...♖d6. If black could give up his knight for the b4 pawn, he would have some drawing chances. But he can't do that. Passive defense 47...♔g7 loses immediately to 48.♕g3+ ♔f8 49.♕c7.

48.♕g4+ ♔h7 (or 48...♔f8 49.♕c8+ ♘d8 50.♕c7) **49.♕c8 ♖b6 50.♕c7.** Black resigned.

Black had a bad game. This can be explained by the fact that a win would have secured Geller first place. He chose a bad opening line, got more nervous than usual and couldn't create proper counterplay.

"Have At!"

Flohr: "This game was played with great 'sporting fervor' by both grandmasters. The struggle was so intense and captivating that the spectators weren't the only ones watching it with bated breath. The championship participants were at times more engaged with the Bronstein – Botvinnik game than their own."

Boleslavsky: "After the world championship match ended in a draw, chess fans eagerly awaited the game between Botvinnik and Bronstein in this tournament. The interest in this game was further increased by the fact that it featured the sharp, complicated Botvinnik System that Bronstein avoided during the match."

No. 239. Semi-Slav Defense D44
Bronstein – Botvinnik
Moscow 1951, round 5
Annotated by E. Zagoriansky

1.d4 d5 2.c4 c6 3.♘c3 ♘f6 4.♘f3 e6 5.♗g5 dxc4 6.e4 b5 7.e5 h6 8.♗h4 g5 9.exf6. *"After 9.♘xg5 black loses a pawn, but gets pressure in the center and on the queenside; in this line, on the other hand, white sacrifices one or two pawns himself, getting a significant positional advantage in exchange." (Boleslavsky)*

9...gxh4 10.♘e5 ♕xf6 11.g3 *(11. a4!? became more fashionable later)* **11...♘d7 12.♕e2!** An interesting idea! White reinforces the e5 square and prepares queenside castling at the same time. Bronstein's move is probably stronger than L. Pachman's continuation 12.f4, which weakens the g3 square.

12...♞xe5. Without this trade, black cannot defend his queenside. After 12...♝b7 there's 13.♝g2 with the threat ♞xc6 or ♞xb5 *(but here, both 13...♞xe5 and 13...♝b4 are good)*.

13.dxe5 ♛e7. More or less forced – the queen should protect the b7 square.

Actually, it shouldn't: 13...♛g5! is bolder, and if 14.f4 then 14...♛d8, not fearing 15.♝g2 ♝b7 16.♞xb5?! due to 16...♛b6!

14.♝g2 ♝b7 15.0-0-0.

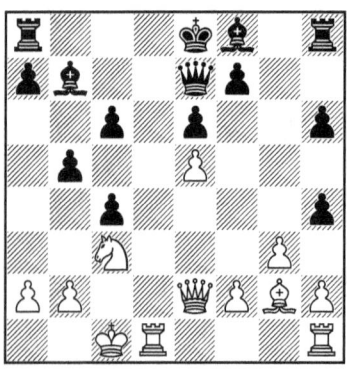

"Black's position looks exceptionally dangerous. After 15...♖d8, white wouldn't have traded, since the black king would have found safety on the queenside; instead, he would have played 16.♞e4 ♖d5 17.♞d6+ ♚d8 18.♝xd5 with a powerful advantage. These considerations force the black king to seek safety on his own flank." (Botvinnik)

15...♝g7 16.f4 0-0 17.♖d6. *The tempting 17.♞e4 gains nothing because of 17...h3! (17...c5? 18.♞f6+*

with an extra piece) 18.♝f3, then for instance: 18...c5 19.♞f6+ ♝xf6 20.exf6 ♝xf3 21.fxe7 ♝xe2 22.exf8=♛+ ♚xf8 23.♖d7 a6 etc.

17...♖ad8 18.♖hd1 ♖xd6 19.exd6 ♛d8 20.♞e4 ♛a5!

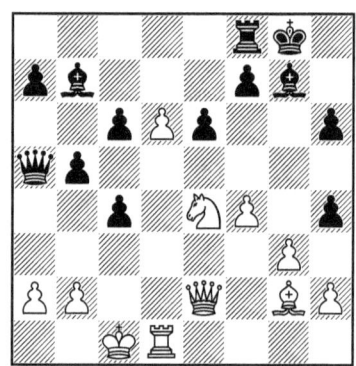

Facing complications, the world champion starts playing very inventively. It wasn't easy to foresee that the king would be positioned worse on b1 than c1. In addition, this move sets a cunning trap: 21.♞c5 ♛xa2 22.♞xb7 ♛a1+ 23.♚d2 ♛a6! (but not 23...♛xb2+ 24.♚e1 with the subsequent ♚f1 and d6-d7), and the white knight is trapped, since after 24.♞c5 there's 24...♛a5+ 25.♚e3 (if 25.♚c2 then 25...♛b4!) 25...♛b6 26.b4 cxb3 27.♖c1 b2.

26.♛h5! e5 27.d7 ♛xc5+ 28.♚e2 is much more tenacious. Therefore, the right way is 22...c3! 23.♛c2 ♛a6! 24.bxc3 (both 24.d7 cxb2+ and 24.♞c5 ♛a1+ are worse) 24...♛xb7.

21.♚b1 ♛b6. *If Bronstein had black, he might have played 21...b4!? 22.♛xc4 c5, posing his opponent difficult problems.*

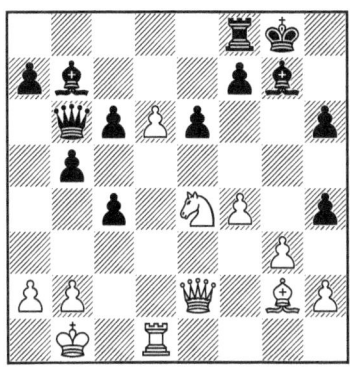

22.♕g4? This miscalculation loses the game for white. He should have played 22.d7! ♖d8 23.f5! c5! *(23...exf5? 24.♘d6)* 24.♘d6 ♗xg2 25.fxe6 fxe6 26.♕xe6+ ♔h7 27.♖e1! ♖f8! 28.♘e8 ♖f1! (but not 28... ♕d8? due to 29.♕e7) 29.♕xb6 ♖xe1+ 30.♔c2 axb6.

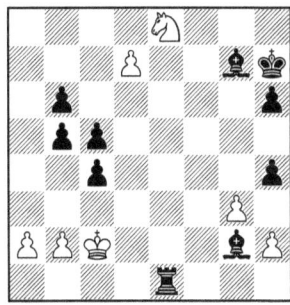

31.d8=♕ ♖e2+ 32.♔d1 ♗f3!, and black has at least perpetual check.

Botvinnik corrects this evaluation: "even the extra queen cannot save white". But there's another baffling thing; in Analytical and Critical Works he showed this line, forgetting the fact that Boleslavsky found a draw for white back in 1952: 31.♘xg7! ♖e2+ 32.♔c1 (not 32.♔d1? ♖e5 or 32...♗f3) 32...♖e1+ etc.

Grandmaster Bronstein, the author of the above line, said that he didn't see 27.♖e1! over the board and thought that he'd have to settle for a perpetual check with 27.♕f5+ and 28.♕e6+. Thus, wanting to avoid the draw, he decided against 22.d7 and played 22.♕g4.

In Bronstein's notebook, we read, "I felt awful and couldn't play. Still, I played with pleasure prior to f5, made all the proper moves. Found nothing but the move repetition, played ♕g4? and was punished – I missed the threat f7-f5."

22...f5 23.♕g6 c5! This is the move that white missed! Immediately accepting the piece sacrifice 23... fxe4 24.♕xe6+ *(24.♗xe4!)* was very dangerous for black.

24.g4. Not 24.♘xc5 ♕xc5 (24... ♗xg2?? 25.♘xe6!) 25.♗xb7 ♕f2!, and white has no defense to mate. Bronstein is trying to complicate the game in any way possible.

24...♗xe4+ 25.♗xe4 fxe4 26.g5 hxg5 27.fxg5.

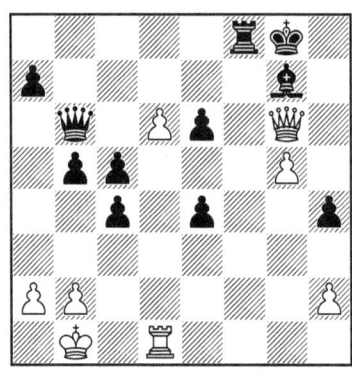

27...♕d8. *"Black played several only moves in a row, but they were enough for a successful defense."*

(Botvinnik.) *27...♕c6!* *28.♕xe6+ ♔h8 was even more convincing.*

28.♕xe6+ ♔h8 29.♕g4 ♕e8. Threatening 30...♕e5. This puzzling position forced both players to expend most of their time, and the ending part was played in mutual time trouble.

30.g6 ♗h6 31.♕xh4 ♔g7 32.d7 ♕d8 33.♕xe4 ♗g5. Now black's position is solid enough, and white has only random tactical chances.

34.a4 ♕e7 35.♕g4 ♕f6 36.♔a2 b4 37.♖g1. *"White could have prolonged the struggle with 37.♕xc4"* (Boleslavsky), *which Botvinnik planned to meet with 37...♕f2.*

37...b3+ *(37...c3!)* **38.♔a3** *(38. ♔a1? ♕f1+)* **38...♗e3 39.♕h5!**

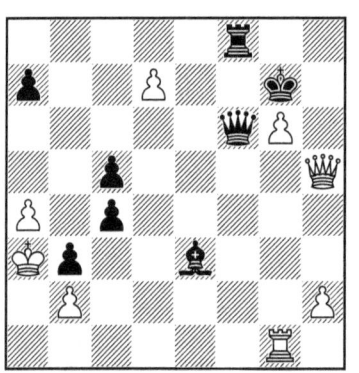

In the last seconds, white sets a cunning trap for his opponent: 39... ♖h8? 40.d8=♕!, and now, after 40... ♖xd8, there's 41.♕h7+ ♔f8 42.g7+, while after 40...♕xd8, white regains the piece with 41.♕e5+ *(40...♖xh5 41.♕xf6+ ♔xf6 42.g7 is no better)*.

39...♗h6 *(with the mortal threat c4-c3)* **40.♕xc5? ♖d8?** Mutual errors in time trouble. 40...♗e3! won immediately.

41.♖d1? The last mistake. The struggle could have been prolonged with 41.♕xc4 *(41...♖xd7 etc.)*.

41...♔xg6. The sealed move. White's position is hopeless, since he can't play 42.♕xc4 because of 42... ♗f8+ 43.♔xb3 ♖b8+.

42.♕g1+ ♔h7 43.♔b4 ♖b8+ 44.♔c5 ♗e3+ 45.♕xe3 ♕b6+ 46.♔xc4 ♕xe3 47.d8=♕ ♖xd8 48.♖xd8 ♕e6+ 49.♖d5 a5 50.h4, and white resigned without waiting for his opponent's reply.

One of the most interesting games of the tournament!

A Psychic Attack

Romanovsky: "The ability to find unexpected resources in a difficult and complex situation is a characteristic trait of Petrosian's play. The psychological aspect of such play is so dangerous that even Smyslov couldn't solve the problems facing him in this case."

No. 240
Petrosian – Smyslov
Moscow 1951, round 13
Annotated by T. Petrosian

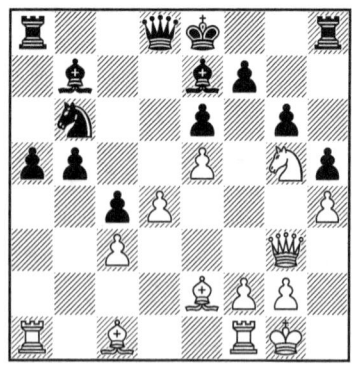

"Interestingly, the same position occurred on the same day in the game Geller – Flohr. Geller chose 17.♖b1, and after 17...b4 18.f4 ♕d7 19.♖a1 b3 quickly got a completely hopeless position and resigned on the 34ᵗʰ move.

Petrosian approached the position differently. The decision he made can be considered brilliant in its boldness and depth of understanding of the position's features." (Romanovsky)

17.d5?! White sacrifices a pawn to complicate the game as much as possible. However, if black found the right reply, even this sacrifice wouldn't have worked.

Petrosian's "dubious" mark is an objective evaluation of the move, not taking psychology into account. Yet Romanovsky (and Kasparov many years later!) gives it two exclamation marks: "This move was deservedly greeted with the spectators' applause." Maybe the applause confused Smyslov?

17...♘xd5? An unexpected mistake. Black should have played 17...♗xd5!. Now, the white knight occupies the great e4 square without much hindrance.

"However, I think that after 17...♗xd5 18.♖d1 ♕c7 19.♗e3! (19.♗f3 ♗xf3 20.♕xf3 0-0 is worse) white has strong pressure, and black faces the same problem – what should he do with his king?" (Kasparov)

18.♖d1 ♕c7 19.♘e4 0-0-0. Not 19...0-0 due to 20.♗xh5. On the other hand, queenside castling is also quite dangerous. Now it's hard to find a satisfactory defense for black.

"Perhaps 19...♔f8 and ♔g7 with chances to defend was best," Simagin wrote in the tournament book, and the computer, after thinking for some time, agreed with him:

20.♗g5 ♗xg5 21.♕xg5 ♔g7 (the h5 pawn is not hanging) 22.♗f3 ♕e7!, and black shouldn't fear 23.♕xe7 ♘xe7 24.♖d7 due to 24...♗xe4 25.♗xe4 ♘d5 26.♗xd5 exd5 27.♖xd5 ♖hb8 or 27.e6 b4!, winning.

20.♗g5! A strong move that forces the trade of dark-squared bishops, which creates a number of weaknesses in black's camp.

20...♗xg5 21.♕xg5.

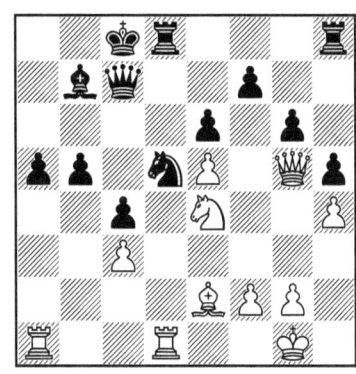

21...a4. *Missing the chance to tear out the thorn on e5: 21...f6!!* "This fantastic resource that I found in the late 1990s destroys white's entire plan: after 22.exf6 ♘f4 23.♖xd8+ ♖xd8 24.♗f3 ♗d5! he loses his main trump – the knight on d6. The position is very sharp, but the unpleasant threat b5-b4 allows us to evaluate it in black's favor." (Kasparov)

22.♕g3 f5. *Pointless weakening (22...♕a5!?, and 23.♘d6+? ♖xd6 24.exd6 ♖d8 is bad for white).*

23.♘d6+ ♖xd6. The exchange sacrifice is the best defensive chance, since otherwise, after 24.♘xb5, black immediately gets a hopeless position.

24.exd6 f4? The decisive mistake. 24...♕g7! gave better chances to save the game, and if 25.♗f3, then 25...♖d8 (but not 25... ♘xc3, which would have been met with 26.d7+!).

After 24...♕g7, white has the dangerous 25.♗xc4! bxc4 26.♖xa4 ♗c6! (26...♘b6? 27.d7+; 26...♔d7? 27.♖b1) 27.♖xc4 etc. 24...♕d7! 25.♗f3 (25.♕xg6? ♘f4) 25...♖d8 is much safer.

25.♕xg6 ♕xd6 26.♗f3 ♗c6 27.♖e1 ♖e8 28.♗xd5. *"This trade is very impressive. 28.♖ad1!? is also possible, but Petrosian goes for the endgame." (Kasparov)*

28...♕xd5.

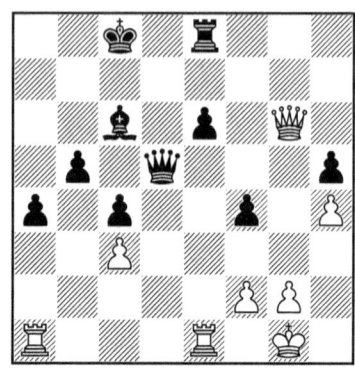

29.♖ad1! White forces black to transition into a lost endgame.

29...♕f5 30.♕xf5 exf5 31.♖xe8+ ♗xe8 32.f3 ♔c7 33.♔f2 ♔b6 34.♔e2 ♔a5 35.♖b1 a3 36.♔d2 b4. If 36...♔a4, then 37.♖xb4+ ♔a5 38.♔c2 with the subsequent ♔b1-a2 and ♖b1-e1.

37.cxb4+ ♔a4 38.♔c3 a2 39.♖a1 ♔a3 40.♔xc4! This move wins immediately.

40...♔b2. The game was adjourned here in a completely hopeless position for black.

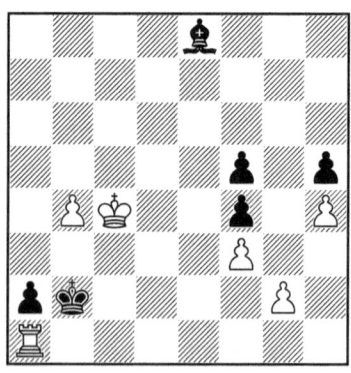

41.♖e1. *Oh, that pesky Megabase! It gives a different move, 41.♖d1, which led to a draw: 41...♗a4! 42.♖e1*

♗c2 43.b5 ♗b1 44.♖e2+ ♗c2 etc. *After 41.♖e1, black is one tempo down...*

41...a1=♛   42.♖xa1   ♚xa1. Despite the extra bishop, black's position is lost because his king is too far away from the kingside pawns, and white has a dangerous passed pawn.

43.b5 ♗d7 44.b6 ♗c8 45.♚d4 ♚b2 46.♚e5 ♚c3 47.♚xf4 ♚d4 48.♚g5 ♚e5 49.♚xh5 ♚f6 50.g4 ♗b7 51.♚h6. Black resigned.

"The Scourge of Champions"

Remember the 1909 St. Petersburg tournament, where Duz-Khotimirsky was the only player who managed to defeat both the world champion Lasker and Russian champion Rubinstein, getting the nickname "The Scourge of Champions" for that? In this championship, Nikolai Kopylov repeated his feat: he was the only player who managed to defeat both the world champion and Soviet champion in the same tournament!

No. 241. Dutch Defense A81
Botvinnik – Kopylov
Moscow 1951, round 12
Annotated by N. Kopylov
1.d4 f5 2.g3 ♘f6 3.♗g2 g6. This flank development of the bishop was used many times by the Leningrad chess players Kuzminykh and Vinogradov. There's no clear way to

refute black's opening structure, and this game clearly shows it.

4.♘c3 *(the system with c2-c4 is much more popular)* **4...♗g7 5.♗g5.** White's threat to trade the dark-square bishops forces black to take decisive, but careful action. After 5...h6, there's 6.♗xf6 ♗xf6 7.e4 with an advantage for black.

5...♘c6 *(! – Bronstein)* **6.♛d2 d5.** *The computer doesn't approve of this move (Bronstein preferred 6...d6). And Kopylov deleted his note from the tournament book:* "A move that gives black a good game."

7.♗xf6. The continuation 7.♗h6 ♗xh6 8.♛xh6 is interesting. By playing 8...♗e6, preparing long castling, black gets a very good position. More dangerous is 8...♘xd4 9.0-0-0 c5 *(9...e5! solves all the problems)* 10.e3 e5 11.exd4 cxd4 12.♘f3 *(12.♘b5!)*, and white has a strong attack.

7...♗xf6   8.♘xd5   ♗xd4 9.♘xc7+! After 9.c3 ♗g7 10.♖d1 e6 black's position is better.

But 9.0-0-0! 0-0 10.c3 or 10.♘c3 was even stronger.

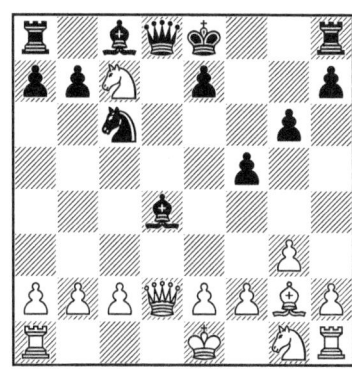

9...♘f7! The knight is untouchable – the line 9...♕xc7 10.♗xc6+ ♕xc6 11.♕xd4 leads to a victory for white *(after 11...0-0 12.♘f3 ♕xc2 13.♕d5+ e6 14.♕e5 ♕e4 a win is rather far away)*.

10.♘f3. Capturing the rook leads to a position where black both restores the material balance and gets a decisive attack: 10.♘xa8 ♗xf2+ 11.♔d1 ♕xd2+ 12.♔xd2 ♖d8+ 13.♔c3 ♗d4+ 14.♔b3 ♗e6+ 15.c4 ♘a5+ 16.♔c2 ♘xc4.

However, 16.♔b4! ♘xc4 17.♘c7 gives white the advantage! But black could equalize with 11...♗e3! 12.♕xd8 ♖xd8+ 13.♔e1 ♘d4.

The game move allows white to obtain a material advantage that should be enough for a win.

10...♗xb2!? The stronger continuation 10...♗xf2+ 11.♔xf2 ♕xc7 *(in reality only slightly better)* allowed black to complete his development, for instance: 12.♖hf1 *(12.♖hd1!)* 12...♕b6+ 13.e3 h6 14.♔g1 ♗e6, but gave the game a quiet character.

Trying to refute the erroneous move *(as the annotator thought)* 10...♗xb2 with the least risk, white spends too much time on thinking and eventually gets into time trouble.

11.♖b1 *(11.♘g5+ ♔f6!)* **11... ♕xd2+.** *An error! Black is fine after 11...♕xc7 12.♖xb2 ♖d8.*

12.♘xd2 ♗c3 13.♖b3. Maintains the advantage. However, more resolute moves were also worthy of consideration:

1) 13.♗xc6 bxc6 14.♘xa8 *(14.♖b3! ♗xd2+ 15.♔xd2)* 14...♖d8 15.♖d1;

2) 13.♘xa8 ♖d8 14.0-0 ♖xd2 15.♘c7 ♖xe2 16.♘d5 or 14.♖d1 ♗e6 15.♘c7 *(with an easy win)*.

13...♗xd2+ 14.♔xd2 ♗e6. *The only move!*

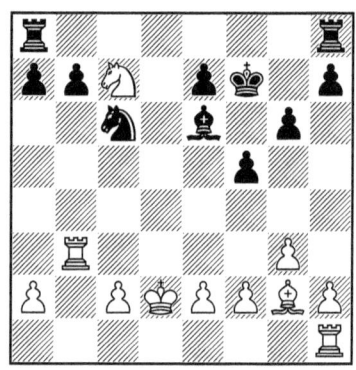

15.♘xe6? It was better to play 15.♘xa8 ♗xb3 16.axb3 ♖xa8 17.♗xc6, keeping chances to win the rook endgame.

And 15.♖xb7! ♖ad8+ 16.♔c1 was even better, for instance: 16... ♗c8 17.♗xc6 ♗xb7 18.♗xb7 ♖d7 19.♗d5+! ♔f6 (19...♔g7? 20.♘e6+) 20.♘e8+ ♖xe8 (20...♔e5? 21.♗c6) 21.♗c6, with an extra passed pawn.

Now black manages to activate the rooks.

15...♔xe6 16.♖xb7 ♖hd8+ 17.♔c1 ♘d4 18.♖e1 ♖ac8 19.♖b2 ♖c5! Intending to double rooks along the c-file and transfer the knight through b5 to c3.

20.e3 ♘b5 21.♖d1 ♖dc8 22.♖d5! It's dangerous to let the knight get to c3. White forces the transition to a rook ending.

In the tournament bulletin, Kopylov assigned a question-mark to this move, but a more thorough analysis of the position probably changed his opinion.

22...♖xd5 23.♗xd5+   ♚xd5 24.♖xb5+ ♚e4.

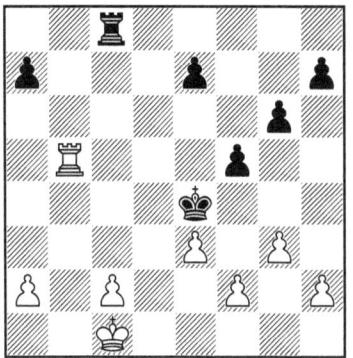

25.♖b7 ♖e8 26.♖xa7? The black king's active position fully compensates for the material loss.

A cartoon by the famous cartoonist Boris Efimov marking Botvinnik's victory in the 1948 world championship. But in this championship Botvinnik's tank received 3 hits, including from the debutant Kopylov.

White had to go for the line 26.♚d2 ♚f3 27.♚e1 ♖c8 28.♖xe7 ♖xc2 29.♖xa7 ♖xf2 30.♖xh7 ♖xa2 31.h4 ♚xe3 *(it's impossible to capture the g3 pawn: 31...♚e2+ 32.♚d1 ♖xe3 33.♖g7 ♖e6 34.♚d2 ♚xg3 35.h5=)* 32.♖e7+ ♚f3 33.♖e6 with a draw.

White's attempt to play for a win leads to his defeat, because black forces the movement of his own passed pawns, supporting them with his king.

26...♚f3 27.a4. *Only this is the decisive mistake! White could still have saved the game by pushing the c-pawn: 27.♚d2 ♚xf2 28.c4! e5 29.♖xh7 ♖d8+ 30.♚c3 ♚xe3 31.♖g7! ♖d6 32.c5 ♖a6 33.♚c4 ♖xa2 34.h4=.*

27...♚xf2 28.a5 g5 *(28...♚xe3!)* **29.a6 ♚xe3** *(and here, 29...♚g2! was correct)* **30.♖b7 e5 31.a7.** *The final mistake (31.♖b5=).*

31...♖a8! 32.♖xh7. 32.♖b5 e4 33.♖xf5 ♖xa7 34.♖xg5 ♚e2 was more tenacious. However, even in this line black still won by promoting his passed pawn.

32...f4 33.gxf4 gxf4 34.♚d1 f3 35.c4. 35.♚e1 doesn't save the game either due to 35...♖g8 36.♚f1 ♖d8.

35...♖d8+ 36.♚c2 f2 37.♖f7 ♖a8. White resigned, because 38...♖xa7 is inevitable.

Boris Spassky said (and he was possibly told this story by Kopylov himself – they lived in the same city) that Botvinnik was incredibly angry with his loss. But the next day, he approached Kopylov and said, "Your idea was very interesting."

No. 242
Kopylov – Keres
Moscow 1951, round 2
Annotated by N. Kopylov

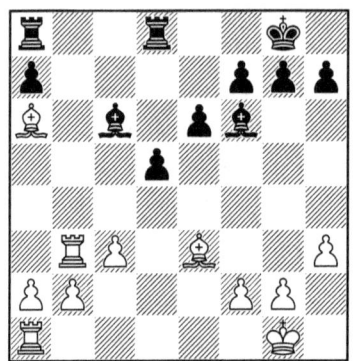

20...e5 21.♖c1. White prevents 21...d4. The position should be evaluated as roughly equal.

21...♖d7 22.♗e2. White planned to meet 22...♖ad8 with 23.♗g4 ♖c7 24.♖a3 ♖a8 25.♖a5, seizing the initiative.

The immediate 23.♖a3! was even better. Even in the actual game, this move was worthy of consideration on move 22.

22...♗e7. Black threatens to win an exchange with 23...♗a4. White has to trade the light-squared bishops.

23.♗b5 ♖c8? A mistake that leads to a pawn loss. It was better to play 23...♗xb5 24.♖xb5 f6, and black's position is slightly better.

24.♗xc6 ♖xc6 25.♖b8+ ♗f8. 25...♖d8 26.♖xd8+ ♗xd8 27.♖d1 or 25...♗d8 26.♖d1 *(26...a6!, so the correct move is 26.♗xa7!)* are even more unfortunate for black.

26.♖d1 f6 27.♖b5 d4 28.cxd4.

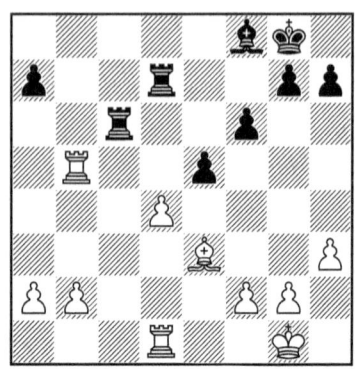

28...a6? This loses. Only 28...♗c5 gave black chances to save the game. The moves 29.d5 ♗xe3 and 29.♖c1 exd4 30.♗xd4 ♖xd4 31.♖cxc5 ♖xc5 32.♖xc5 ♖d1+ 33.♔h2 ♖d2 involved swapping the bishops. In the rook ending, white's advantage is not as significant, and it would likely not be enough to win.

30.♖bxc5!? ♖xc5 31.♖xc5 dxe3 32.fxe3 ♖d2 33.♖b5 gave better chances in the second line.

29.♖b8 ♔f7 30.d5 ♖c2 31.♖b6 a5 32.♖b5 a4 33.♖c1. White is trying to force the movement of the passed a- and d-pawns, but first he trades rooks.

33...♖xc1+ 34.♗xc1 ♗d6 *(34... ♖c7 35.♗e3 f5 was better)* **35.♗e3 ♖c7 36.♖a5 ♖c2 37.♖a7+ ♔g6 38.♖a6** *(38.♖xa4! ♖xb2 39.♖a6)* **38...♗b4 39.d6.** *Too rash! 39.♖xa4 ♖xb2 40.♔f1 kept the advantage.*

39...♖xb2 40.d7. This humble pawn gets an exceptionally honorable mission. For ten moves it locks down the black pieces and only falls when the game is completely decided in white's favor.

40...♖b1+ 41.♔h2.

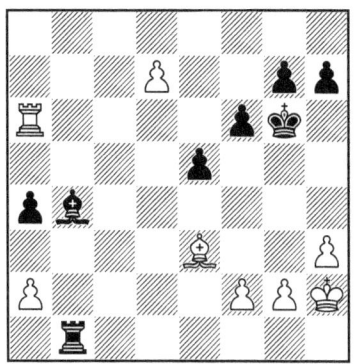

41...♖d1. *Only this is the decisive mistake! After 41...♗e7! there's no win: 42.♖d6 ♗d8= or 42.♖xa4 ♖b7 43.♖a7 ♖xa7 44.♗xa7 ♗d8=.*

42.♖xa4 ♗e7 43.♖a7 ♗d8. *If 43...♔f7 44.a4 ♔e6 45.a5 ♖xd7, then 46.♖a8 ♔d5 47.♖b8 ♗d6 (47... ♗c5? 48.♖b5 ♖c7 49.a6) 48.♖b5+ ♔c4 49.♖b1 or 48...♔c6 49.♖b6+, and the a-pawn is ready to run.*

44.a4 ♖d5 45.g4! The sealed move *(the straightforward 45.♖a8 ♖xd7 46.a5 also won).*

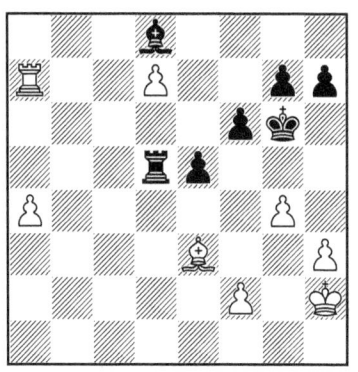

Analysis showed that black was rather limited in his choice of moves. For instance: 45...♔f7 46.♖a8 ♖xd7 47.a5 ♖d6 48.a6 ♗b6 49.a7 ♗xe3 50.♖f8+ and white wins. 46...♔e7 47.a5 ♖xa5 (47... ♗xa5 48.♖xa5) 48.♖xd8 doesn't save black either.

King, rook and bishop moves are impossible. Thus, black has only pawn moves, and he will eventually run out of them.

45...h5 46.♔g2. 46.♔g3 is weaker; there could follow 46...hxg4 47.hxg4 f5 48.♖a6+ ♗f6 49.gxf5+ ♔xf5 50.a5 ♖xd7 51.♖a8 ♗g5 52.♖f8+ ♔g6 53.♗b6 ♖d3+ 54.♖f3 ♖d6 with drawing chances.

After 55.♖a3! with the threat 56.a6, there are no chances: 55...♗e7 56.♖a4 or 55...♗d8 56.♗xd8 ♖xd8 57.a6 ♖a8 58.a7 etc.

46...hxg4 47.hxg4 e4 48.♔h3! Black is in zugzwang and forced to make his last remaining pawn move.

48...f5 49.♖a6+ ♔f7 50.gxf5 ♖xd7 51.♔g4 ♗f6 52.♖a7 (after the rook exchange, the black pawns are defenseless) **52...♖xa7 53.♗xa7 ♗e5 54.a5 ♔e8 55.a6 ♔d7 56.♗e3 ♔c6 57.♔g5 ♗c7 58.♗d4 ♗d6 59.♔g6.** Black resigned.

The Study-Like Draw

Tolush: "During the play-off, the Soviet champion didn't pay due care to the subtle plans of his formidable opponent, even though he quickly managed to reach a winning position."

No. 243
Botvinnik – Keres
Moscow 1951, round 10
Annotated by P. Keres

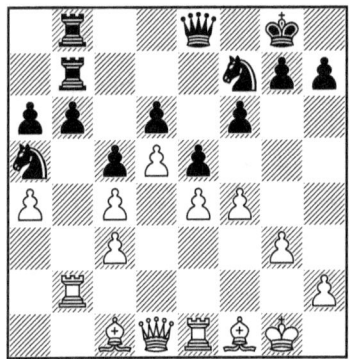

31.♗d3? White could have immediately launched a kingside attack with 31.f5, intending g3-g4 and h2-h4. In this case, black would have had to settle for passive defense and to try to get his king to the queenside, but it's unlikely that he could fully equalize.

31...b5! Black uses the first opportunity to free up his position a bit and create active counterplay on the queenside. The pawn sacrifice gives him good chances for full equality, especially if we take mutual time trouble into account.

32.axb5 axb5 33.cxb5 c4. *"I completely overlooked such an obvious move." (Botvinnik.) Perhaps that's why the world champion didn't play 34.♗f1! ♖xb5 35.♖a2, which was less pleasant for black.*

34.♗c2 ♕c8. Of course, not 34... ♖xb5 35.♗a4. Now it was better for white to return the pawn immediately with 35.♗e3 ♖xb5 36.♖a2, retaining a

minimal positional advantage *(that slips away after 36...♘b7)*. Trying to hold onto the pawn is unsuccessful, because the position of the white pieces is poor.

35.♗a4 ♘b3! 36.♗e3. The line 36.♗xb3 ♖xb5 37.♗xc4 ♖xb2 is not good for white.

36...♖a8 37.♖a2. After this, it's white who should struggle to equalize. The correct move was 37.♗xb3 ♖xb5 38.♖b1 cxb3 39.♖xb3 ♖xb3 40.♕xb3, even though 40... exf4 41.♗xf4 ♖b8 still gives black enough counterplay for the pawn.

37...♖xb5 38.♗xb3? A decisive mistake. It was necessary to play 38.♖ee2, after which black either had to play the simple 38...♖bb8 or else launch a dangerous attack by sacrificing a pawn with 38... ♖ba5 39.♗xb3 cxb3 40.♖xa5 ♖xa5 41.♕xb3 exf4 42.♗xf4 g5!.

"There were no strong threats yet, and white could have adopted a waiting game (for instance, with 38.♔h1)." (Botvinnik)

38...cxb3. This strong passed pawn should have decided the game.

39.♖xa8 ♕xa8 40.c4 ♖b4. White sealed his move here.

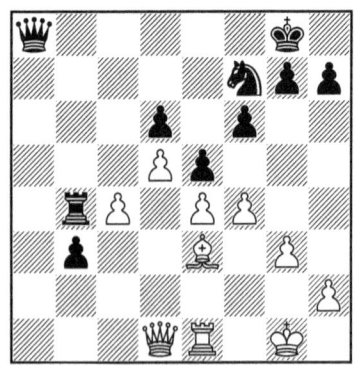

41.♗d2. The objectively better move was, without a doubt, 41.♕d3, which black would have met with 41...♕c8! 42.♖b1 exf4 43.gxf4 ♕g4+ 44.♔f2 g5! 45.♖xb3 ♖xb3 46.♕xb3 gxf4 47.♗d2 ♘g5!, getting a strong attack that's sufficient to win. After the game move, black's task is easier.

Instead of 45.♖xb3?, white had a safer continuation 45.♗d2! ♖b8 and only then 46.♖xb3 ♖xb3 47.♕xb3 gxf4 48.♕f3, with enough time to capture the f4 pawn. Thus, the immediate 43...g5! (44.fxg5? ♕g4+) was better. However, this is all moot, because after 41.♕d3 white is completely paralyzed by 41...♕a2!

41...♕a7+ 42.♔h1. After 42.♗e3 or 42.♔g2, 42...♕a2 is very strong.

42...♖b8 43.♕f3. *"Just three moves had passed since the play-off started, but black had already been thinking for ages. The simple 43...♕a2 44.♕d3 b2 45.♖b1 ♖b3 46.♕c2 led to a win for black after the maneuver ♘d8-b7-c5."* (Botvinnik)

43...♕d4 44.♕c3 ♕f2. The simple 44...b2 45.♕xd4 exd4 46.♖b1 ♖b3 with the subsequent ♘d8-b7 etc. won as well.

45.♕e3. *"White forces a queen trade, after which he... loses a piece. But then it turns out that he has gained some hope of saving the game."* (Botvinnik)

45...♕xe3 46.♗xe3 b2 47.♖b1 ♖b3.

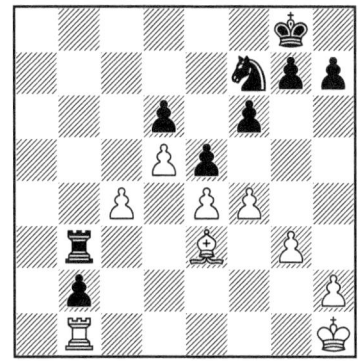

48.c5! White's only chance, since after the bishop retreat the maneuver ♘d8-b7 won easily.

48...♖xe3. 48...dxc5 49.♗xc5 made it harder for black, since 49...♘d8 gives nothing because of 50.fxe5 fxe5 51.♗d6!, and the knight must return to f7. After 49... g5 black still has winning chances, but white had good defensive resources.

48...exf4! is more spectacular, for instance: 49.gxf4 (49.♗xf4? dxc5) 49...♖xe3 50.♖xb2 g5! 51.c6 ♖c3 or 49.♗d4 dxc5 50.♖xb2 ♖xb2 51.♗xb2 fxg3 and ♘g5.

49.♖xb2.

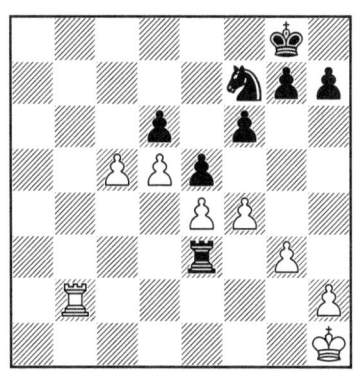

49...g6? A time-trouble mistake, after which it's very hard for black to win, if it's still possible at all. The winning move was 49...h5!, for instance: 50.c6 ♖c3 51.♖b7 ♘h6, and the knight enters the game in earnest, while after 50.♖b8+ ♔h7 51.♖f8 black wins with a piece sacrifice: 51...dxc5! 52.♖xf7 exf4 53.gxf4 ♖xe4.

In the first line, white can play 52.fxe5 fxe5 53.h3!, preventing the knight from reaching g4, but after 53...♔h7! (53...♖xg3? 54.♖b8+ and c6-c7) 54.♔g2 ♘g8 55.♖d7 ♘f6 56.♖xd6 ♘xe4 57.♖e6 ♖xg3+ black still wins with precise play.

50.c6 ♖c3 51.♖b7 ♔g7? After this, an interesting drawn position occurs: the extra knight doesn't give black chances to win. The last chance to win was 51...♔f8, to meet 52.c7 *(Botvinnik's move 52.♖b8+ is weaker due to 52...♔g7! 53.♖b7 f5)* with 52...♔e8.

Both Keres and Botvinnik stop the line here, even though after the calm 53.♔g2!! there's no win in sight (53...♔d7? 54.c8=♕+ ♔xc8 55.♖xf7).

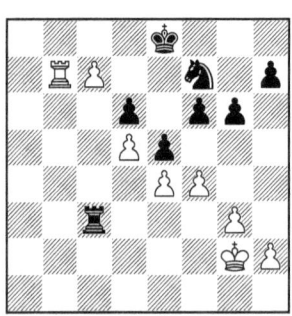

For instance: 53...h5 54.h3! h4 55.♖b8+! ♔d7 56.♖f8 ♘h6 57.gxh4!! (the knight is untouchable: 57.♖h8? ♖xg3+ 58.♔f2 ♔xc7 59.♖xh6 exf4 60.♖xh4 g5 etc.) 57...♖xc7 58.♖xf6 ♖c2+ 59.♔f1! exf4 60.h5! (but not 60.♖xf4? ♔e7), and you can check this on your computers – there is no win! Here's just one of the "study-like draws": 60...♖c4 61.hxg6 ♖xe4 62.g7! ♘g8 63.♖f8 ♖e8 64.h4!! ♔e7 65.♖xf4 ♘f6 66.h5! ♔f7 (66...♘xh5 67.♖e4+) 67.h6 ♔g6 68.♔g2, and black can't save his last pawn.

52.c7 ♖c2 53.♔g1 h5. Now black can't win because he can't unpin his knight. The attempt 53...exf4 54.gxf4 g5, to meet 55.f5 with 55...g4 and the subsequent h7-h5-h4, doesn't work due to 55.e5! fxe5 56.fxe5.

54.h4 ♖c4 55.♔g2 ♖c2+ 56.♔f1 ♖c4 57.♔g2 ♖c2+ 58.♔f1 ♖c4. Draw.

Capablanca's Templates

Flohr: "Capablanca would be proud if he saw how clearly and skillfully white exploited the weakness in black's camp. White seizes the c-file, his bishop is stronger than the knight – a typical Capablanca position. Long ago, only a few people understood that. Now a dozen of our masters possess exceptional technique to convert a positional advantage... I think that this was one of the best games of the championship."

No. 244
Taimanov – Averbakh
Moscow 1951, round 14
Annotated by M. Taimanov

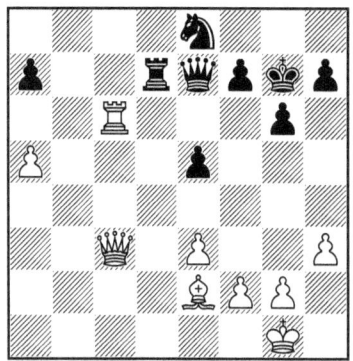

Black is planning to simplify the position with 31...鹭c7, but white manages to prevent this.

31.f4! f6. After 31...鹭c7 32.鹭xc7 鹭xc7 33.鹭xc7 公xc7 34.fxe5, black is unlikely to save the endgame.

32.fxe5 fxe5 33.鹭c5 當f6 34.鹭c6+ 當g7 35.鹭c8! The signal for a forceful attack. White threatens 36.兽b5.

35...公d6. Of course not 35...鹭c7 36.鹭xe8! And if 35...公f6 36.兽b5 鹭d1+ 37.當h2 公g4+, then 38.當g3! and white wins. *But the knight check is a mistake!*

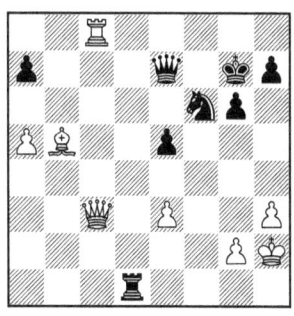

Position after 35...公f6 36.兽b5
鹭d1+ 37.當h2

37...公d5! maintains the balance. For instance: 38.鹭b3 (38.鹭c2 公xe3=) 38...鹭d2! or 38.鹭c5 鹭xc5 39.鹭xc5 公xe3 40.鹭c7+ 當h6 41.鹭xa7 鹭d2! with a draw.

After 35...公d6?, however, white got a sizable advantage.

36.鹭c5 當f6 (36...公f7 is bad due to 37.兽g4) **37.鹭c6.** The only move. 37.兽g4 gains nothing because of 37...公e4 38.鹭c6+ 鹭d6!

37...當g7. Perhaps black should have played 37...h5, even though this created new weaknesses.

38.兽g4 公f5. The only move. After 38...鹭b7 there's 39.a6, while 38...公e4 loses to 39.鹭c2 *(this is a mistake due to 39...鹭b4!=; the right move is 39.鹭c1!).*

39.當h2! Of course not 39.e4 because of 39...公d4! But now, black can only prevent the threat 40.e4 by severely weakening his position.

39...h5 40.兽xf5 gxf5.

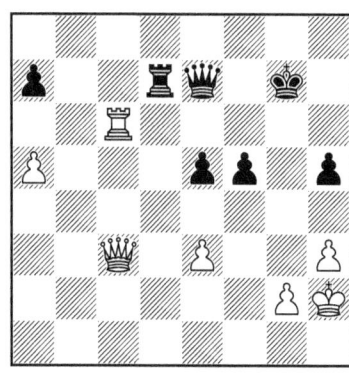

41.鹭c5. Hoping that after 41... 當f6 42.鹭c6+ 當g7 (42...鹭d6? 43.鹭c7 鹭d7 44.鹭c6+), the same position as after move 40 will occur, and that white will find a win in home analysis. However, he was disappointed.

It was necessary to play 41.♖a6! immediately with the threat 42.♕c6 *(and if 41...♖c7, then 42.♕d3!)*. This won quickly.

41...h4! An inventive defense. After 42.♖xe5 there's 42...♕d6!, while after 42.♕xe5+ ♕xe5+ 43.♖xe5 ♔f6 44.♖c5, black saves the game with 44...♖e7.

42.♔g1! The best reply. Now 43.♖xe5 is a threat, and after 42...♔f6 there's a very strong move 43.♕c4! *(this is met with 43...e4!=; the immediate 43.♖c8! is stronger)* 43...♔g7 44.♖c8.

42...♕d6. *42...♖d1+! 43.♔f2 ♔f6 left good drawing chances.*

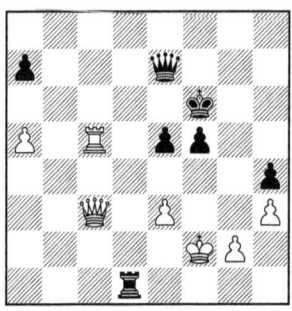

For instance 44.♕c4 (44.♖c6+ ♔g5!) 44...♔g7 45.♖c8 ♖d8 or 45.a6 ♖d6.

43.♖c6. White also won with 43.♕xe5+ ♕xe5 44.♖xe5 ♔f6 45.♖c5, since after 45...♖e7 there's 46.♔f2. But before going for this line, white sets a trap.

43...♕d5? Black steps right into the trap. After 43...♕e7 44.♖c5 *(44.*

e4!?) 44...♕d6 45.♕xe5+, the game transitioned to the rook ending from the previous note. Now, white has an even simpler win.

44.♖c4! The h4 pawn is suddenly defenseless.

44...♔g6   45.♖xh4   ♕d2 46.♕c6+. Of course, not 46.♕xe5 ♕e1+ 47.♔h2 ♕xh4 48.♕e6+ ♕f6 49.♕xd7 ♕e5+ 50.♔h1 ♕xe3 with a draw.

46...♕d6 47.♕a8 ♕f6. If 47...♖d8 then simply 48.♕xa7.

White's task was somewhat harder after 47...e4!? 48.♕h8! ♕d1+ 49.♔h2 ♕d6+ 50.♖f4 ♖h7 51.♕g8+ ♖g7 52.♕e8+ ♖f7 53.g4 ♔g7 54.♔g3 etc.

48.♕g8+ ♖g7 49.♕e8+ ♖f7 50.♖h8! ♔g5. White threatened 51.♖f8, while after 50...♕e7 there would have followed 51.♕g8+ ♖g7 52.♖h7!, winning a second pawn.

51.a6! Now black has no useful moves and loses.

51...e4 52.♕g8+ ♖g7 53.♕b8! ♔g6 54.♕e8+ ♕f7 55.♕c6+. Black resigned.

Half a Set for... an Extra Pawn!

Abramov: "Averbakh defeated Bondarevsky in a complicated and intense struggle. In the King's Indian Defense, white closed off the center, didn't castle and launched a pawn storm on the kingside. The grandmaster defended against direct threats and started preparing queenside activity... But while

Averbakh increased the pressure on the black king's position with every move, Bondarevsky, for some reason, decided against creating counterplay and went for all-out defense..."

No. 245
Averbakh – Bondarevsky
Moscow 1951, round 12
Annotated by Y. Averbakh

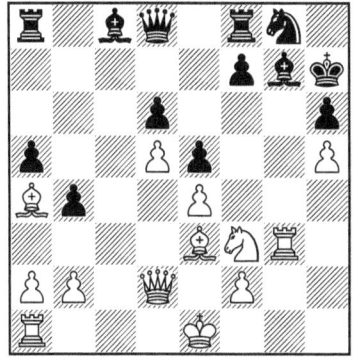

21...f5! Black uses the opportunity to activate. Now white has to play very precisely to avoid getting a lost position.

22.exf5 ♗xf5 23.♔e2! The correct decision. It's necessary to connect the rooks.

23...♖c8. Black got nothing after 23...e4 24.♘d4 ♕h4 25.♖ag1 ♕xh5+ 26.♔e1 ♗e5 27.♘xf5 ♖xf5 28.♖g4.

28.♗d1! ♕f7 29.♖g4 is much stronger. After 27.♗d1! or 27.♗f4! black is on the verge of losing as well. Instead of 25...♕xh5+? it's necessary to play 25...♗e5, while the immediate 24...♗e5! is even better.

24.♖ag1 ♖f7 25.♔e1 ♗e4. 25... ♘f6 lost to 26.♖xg7+! ♖xg7 27.♖xg7+

♔xg7 28.♗xh6+ and 29.♘g5! *(an obvious misprint: 29.♕g5!).*

26.♗d1.

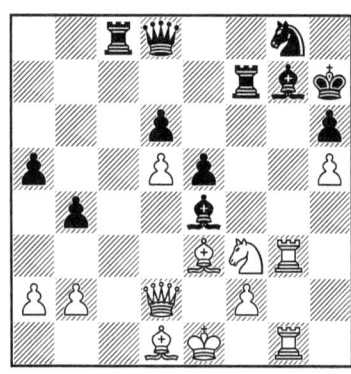

26...♕e7. Black saw through white's cunning plan just in time. After the natural 26...♘f6, a spectacular combination would have followed: 27.♗xh6!! ♗xh6 28.♕xh6+!! ♔xh6 29.♖g6+! ♗xg6 30.♖xg6+ ♔xh5 (30...♔h7? 31.♘g5+ ♔h8 32.♘xf7+ and ♘xd8) 31.♘xe5+ ♘g4 (31... ♔h4 32.♖h6+ ♔g5 33.♘xf7+ ♔f5 34.♘xd8 ♖xd8 35.♗c2+ ♔e5 36.f4+) 32.♗xg4+ ♔h4 33.♖h6+ ♔g5 34.♘xf7+ ♔xg4 35.♘xd8 with good winning chances.

However, the best defense was 26... ♗f5!

27.♕e2 ♗f5. After 27...♘f6 I intended to play 28.♗g5! ♗xd5 (28... ♗xf3 29.♕xf3 hxg5 30.♕f5+ and ♕xc8+; 29...♔h8 30.♗e3!) 29.♗xf6 ♗xf6 30.♕d3+ e4 31.♕xd5 exf3+ 32.♔f1 with a sharp position where black's small material advantage plays no role.

28.♖g6 ♔h8 29.♖6g3 ♗h7? After 29...♘f6 there's 30.♘h4 with strong threats, so black withdraws the bishop from a potential attack. However, the move is bad. Black probably needed to play 29...♚h7 and it's unclear what white does next.

30.♕a6!

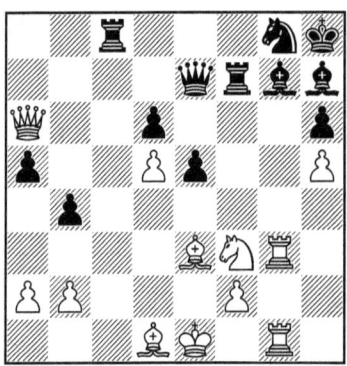

30...♕d8. *Only this loses! In the book* Centre-Stage and Behind the Scenes, *Averbakh "rehabilitated" the move 29...♝h7:* "In mutual time trouble, Bondarevsky loses his way. He had to abandon the queenside pawns and play 30...♖cf8 31.♕xa5 ♘f6, trying to launch kingside activity. For instance: 32.♘h4 ♘e4 33.♘g6+ ♝xg6 34.hxg6 (34. ♖xg6 ♘xf2) 34...♘xg3 35.gxf7 ♘f5 36.♕xb4 ♘xe3 37.fxe3 ♕xf7, and the opposite-colored bishops give black good chances of saving the game."

32.♕b5!? is stronger and more effective, with the idea 32...♘xh5 33.♘g5!, seizing the initiative. Therefore, 31...♕b7! (with the idea 32.♘h4 ♖a8) is safer, and even earlier – 30...♕c7! and ♘e7.

31.♘h4. That's the point. The knight enters the game with great

force, while the black pieces are positioned poorly.

31...♖a8 32.♕c4 ♘f6. After 32...♖c8, there's 33.♕g4.

And if 33...♘f6 34.♕e6 ♖e7, then 35.♝xh6!! ♖cc7 (35...♖xe6 36.♝xg7+) 36.♘g6+ ♝xg6 37.♝xg7+!, crushing.

33.♘g6+.

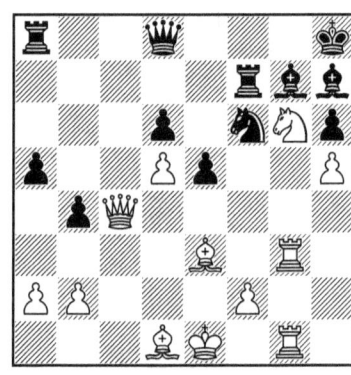

33...♝xg6. Black has to capture on g6. If 33...♚g8 then 34.♘xe5! dxe5 35.d6!, and black is defenseless: 35...♚f8 36.d7! ♕xd7 (36...♘xd7 37.♖xg7 ♖xg7 38.♝xh6 etc.) 37.♝c5+ ♚e8 38.♖xg7! (38.♝a4!! with an inevitable mate) 38...♖xg7 39.♖xg7 ♕xg7 40.♕e6+ ♚d8 41.♝b6+ or 35...♘e8 36.♝b3 ♕d7 37.♝xh6 (37.♕xf7+! ♕xf7 38.d7 is even more spectacular) 37...♚f8 (37... ♚h8 38.♕xf7 ♕xf7 39.♝xf7 ♝xh6 40.♖g8+) 38.♝xg7+ ♖xg7 39.♖f3+ ♝f5 40.♕g8+ ♖xg8 41.♖xg8#.

34.♖xg6 ♖c8 35.♕d3 e4. This loses immediately, but white's attack should still have been enough to win after other continuations *(for example, 35...♕f8 36.♝g4 ♘xg4 37.♖1xg4).*

36.♕d2 ♘g8 37.♗g4! It's fascinating how both the knight and now the bishop join the attack on the black king.

37...♖c4 38.♗e6 ♖e7 39.♗xg8 ♕xg8 40.♖xh6+ ♗xh6 41.♖xg8+ ♔xg8 42.♗xh6. Black resigned.

Dramas Instead of Masterpieces

Alatortsev: "Smyslov started the game with 1.e4. Bronstein replied with the Sicilian Defense, which he doesn't use very often. Evidently, the grandmaster specifically prepared for the game, anticipating the opening Smyslov would choose. And indeed, the spectators saw the Closed Variation, which Smyslov played with white numerous times in that tournament..."

No. 246
Smyslov – Bronstein
Moscow 1951, round 9
Annotated by V. Smyslov

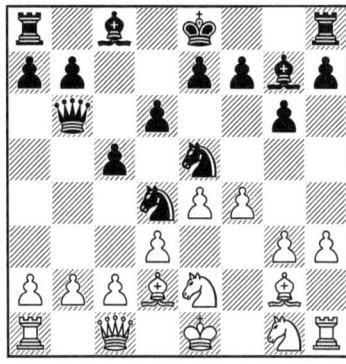

11...♘xc2+!? A tempting, but not entirely correct move. The purpose of this piece sacrifice is to create a queenside pawn majority. Still, it was better to go for the line 11...♘ec6

Bronstein versus Smyslov. From V. Smyslov's archive. Published for the first time.

12.c3 ♘xe2 13.♘xe2, where white got an easy position to play.

From Bronstein's notebook: "Childish. Prepared everything up until the moment of the sacrifice... and went for a bogus line. I knew that it was bogus, (but) I wanted to sacrifice a queen and knight to Smyslov, and I was plagued by the thought that there would never be such an opportunity again ('never' is such a horrible word)."

12.♕xc2 ♕xb2 13.♕xb2 ♘xd3+ 14.♔f1! The correct retreat. The position was better for black after 14.♔d1 ♘xb2+ 15.♔c2 ♘c4, and the c4 knight stands well.

14...♗xb2. After 14...♘xb2 there was 15.♗c3, trading the dark-squared bishops.

However, black's three pawns fully compensated for the sacrificed piece: 15...0-0 16.♗xg7 (16.a4 ♗d7) 16...♔xg7 17.♘f3 ♘a4 18.♔f2 b5.

15.♖b1 ♗e6. This leads to further complications *(15...♗g7! is safer).*

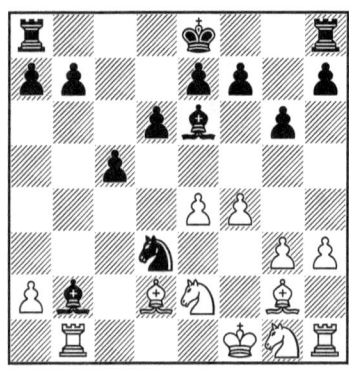

16.♗c3! Defuses the tension. White could have gained more material with 16.♖xb2 ♘xb2 17.♗c3. But after 17...♘d1 *(17...0-0!?)* 18.♗xh8 f6 19.♗g7 ♗xa2, black's passed pawns could become dangerous.

And still, white's extra pieces should have been enough for a win: 20.♔e1 ♘e3 21.♗f3 etc.

16...♗xa2. Black is trying to create a big pawn majority on the queenside. However, he fails to prove the correctness of this decision.

After 16...♗xc3 17.♘xc3 ♗c4 18.♘ge2 0-0-0 19.♗f3 and ♔g2, white has finished development and kept a better position, but black, with three pawns for the piece, could mount a defense *(19...e6! 20.♔g2 d5).*

17.♖xb2 ♘xb2 18.♗xb2. An original position, with white's two knights and bishop confronting black's rook and four pawns. Of course, white could have captured the rook as well, but after 18.♗xh8 f6 the dark-squared bishop was out of play.

18...♖g8 *(18...0-0 is better)* **19.♔f2.** *Black eventually resigned on the 39th move under the threat of inevitable mate.*

And rightly so: even the most tempting gambles don't do any good. However, the spectators love such fights, and I can only imagine their range of emotions when they saw this cascade of sacrifices!

A similar thing happened in Bronstein's game against Kotov. He wrote in the same notebook: "Came up with a new plan over the board, but, alas, again didn't take the exchange, and it was wrong. Now, I have eradicated this malady. Or you just value material more as you age?"

No. 247
Bronstein – Kotov
Moscow 1951, round 1
Annotated by A. Kotov

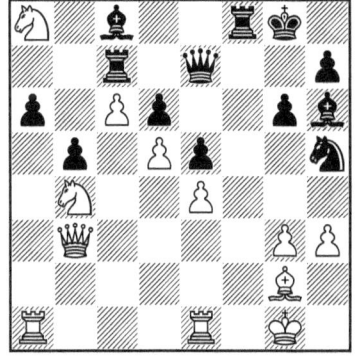

Black had just played b7-b5, freeing the trapped rook...

33.♘xa6? In mutual time trouble, the opponents thought that it was bad to capture the rook due to a pretty sacrifice – 33.♘xc7 ♕xc7 34.♔h2 ♘xg3! The evaluation of this move was probably right, for after 35.♔xg3 ♗f4+ 36.♔f3 ♕b6 with the subsequent a6-a5, b5-b4 and ♗a6, black got a formidable attack on the white king stuck in the center.

A hallucination! After 37.♘d3! ♗d2+ (37...a5? 38.♘xf4) 38.♔g3! ♗xe1+ 39.♖xe1, there's no "formidable attack" – the computer confidently provides a long line...

However, by playing 33.♘xc7 ♕xc7 34.♖f1!, white kept the advantage. Now his position is lost.

33...♖a7! 34.♘c5. Other moves, such as 34.♘b8, couldn't save the game because of 34...♗d2.

No, it was this move that turned out to be the decisive mistake! White got better chances after 34.♘8c7! with the idea 34...♖xc7 35.♘xc7 ♕xc7 36.♖f1!

34...dxc5. The simple 34...♗d2! would have forced white to resign immediately because of the unstoppable threat ♕g5.

35.d6+ ♕f7 36.♕xf7+ ♖axf7 37.♘b6 ♗e6 38.d7.

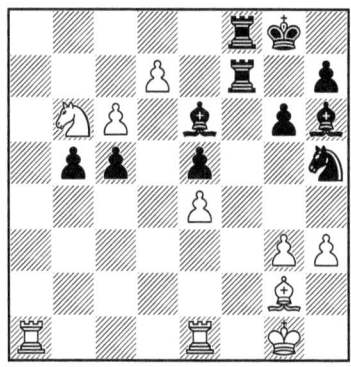

38...♘f6. Black is playing imprecisely in time trouble. Transferring the bishop to d4 decided the game immediately: 38...♗d2! 39.♖e2 ♗c3 and ♗d4+. White's passed pawns lost their threats due to the unstoppable c5-c4.

39.♖f1 is more resilient. However, black indeed had a quick win: 38...♗g5!

39.♖ad1 ♘xd7 40.cxd7 ♖d8

41.♗f1. 41.♖d6 ♗xd7 *(41....♖e7! with the threat c5-c4)* 42.♖ed1 ♗e3+ and ♗d4.

41...c4! The sealed move. Analysis showed that this position was lost for white, but that black should play cautiously...

White resigned on move 67. This disappointing loss at the start affected Bronstein's performance in the championship as a whole...

The Chinese Box

There's no denying it: the computer usually only ruins the beauty of a "masterpiece's" combinations, finding hidden flaws and devaluing the chess player's creative efforts. Thankfully, there are occasions when the "flaw" found by the computer is itself worthy of the collection of chess beauties. This is one such case.

No. 248
Lipnitsky – Terpugov
Moscow 1951, round 12
Annotated by I. Lipnitsky

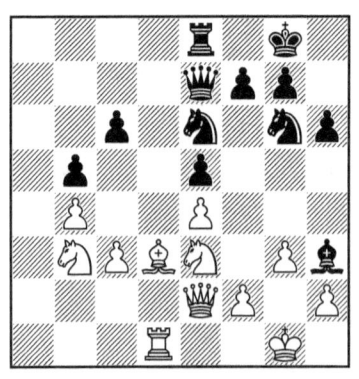

28.♕h5! Preventing 28...♕g5 and restricting the mobility of the black pieces.

28...♘g5 29.♘c5 ♕f6 30.♘f5. White's second knight has also secured a key square for itself. Black is very cramped.

30...♔h7. 30...♘e7 is bad due to 31.f4, winning a piece. The other knight, which is defending the bishop, also has no moves. Obviously, 30...♗xf5 leads to a difficult position as well. Black could prolong the struggle with 30...♖d8 31.♗c2 ♖xd1+ 32.♕xd1 ♘xe4 33.♘xh6+ gxh6 34.♗xe4, but even in this case white, controlling all the key squares, should still win because of the weak b5 and c6 pawns.

In the first line, after 31...exf4 32.gxf4 ♗xf5 33.fxg5 ♗g6! black saves the piece: 34.gxf6 ♗xh5 35.♖f1 ♘g6 36.fxg7 ♔xg7=. And in the second line, the correct move is 32...♘f8!=. He should have chosen one of these continuations (or even immediately played 30...♘f8), but then... we wouldn't have got this study within a study!

31.♗c2 (now black has no defense to ♖d6) **31...♖d8.** After 31...♗xf5 white won with 32.exf5 ♘f8 33.♘d7 *(this is bad due to 33...♘xd7 34.♖xd7? e4!; the winning move is 33.h4!).*

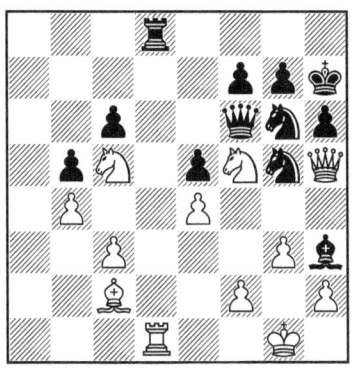

32.♘d7 ♛e6 33.♗b3! The queen is trapped! After 33...♛xb3 white would have played the same move as in the game. After 33...♛xd7 34.♖xd7 ♖xd7 35.♛e2, the win is also technically easy.

Not so! Black has a fantastic resource 35...♖d2!! that completely changes the position's evaluation.

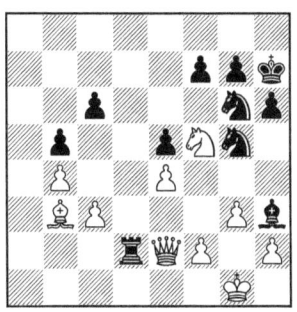

The players have seemingly switched sides – it's now the white queen that has only two available squares, and both of them are mined:

1) 36.♛h5 ♖b2 37.♗d1 (the line 37.♛d1 ♘xe4! 38.♗c2 ♗xf5 saves the queen, but not the game) 37...♘e7! and now white has to give up the queen – 38.♘xe7 g6 39.♛e2 (39.♛h4 ♘f3+, mating) 39...♖xe2 40.♗xe2,

but after 40...♘xe4 41.♘xc6 ♘xc3 42.♗f1 ♗xf1 43.♔xf1 f6 the knight endgame is won;

2) 36.♛e3 ♘f4!! (36...♗g4 37.h4 ♘h3+ 38.♔f1 ♖xf2+ 39.♔e1 ♖b2! 40.♗xf7 ♘gf4!! 41.gxf4 ♘xf4= leads only to a draw) 37.gxf4 exf4 38.♛xf4 ♖e2!!

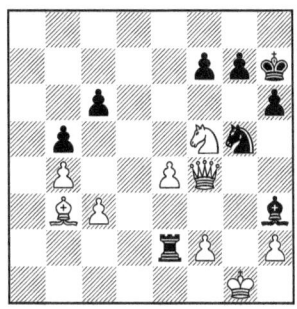

The mating threat (39.f3 ♗g2 and ♘h3#) again forces white to sacrifice the queen: 39.♛e3 ♘f3+! 40.♔h1 ♖xe3 41.fxe3 (41.♘xe3 ♔g6) 41...♘e5, and chances are obviously in black's favor. How real are they? We can find the answer if we get the computer to work... But there's no need, because instead of 35.♛e2? the correct move is 35.♗d1, even though after 35...♖d3 (35...♘xe4? 36.♗c2) 36.♛e2 ♖xc3 37.♛b2 ♖d3 (37...♘xe4? 38.f3) 38.♛c2 ♖d7 it's very hard for white to crack black's defenses.

33...♛e8 34.♘f6+. Checkmate or the loss of the queen are inevitable. Black resigned.

Long-Term Sacrifice

And finally, here's a surprise for you: a Soviet Championship game annotated by Max Euwe. These annotations were written by the ex-world champion for the "Game of the Month" rubric in *Chess Review* (No. 3, 1952, reproduced here with stylistic edits). The game was prefaced with the short review of the 19th Soviet Championship that we quoted from earlier. Analyzing the playing style of "the newer Russian masters," Euwe foresaw the future changes in chess trends: "Masters of the future may differ from the older ones in paying less attention to material advantages." He essentially foretold the appearance of Tal when the latter had recently graduated from high school!

No. 249 Nimzo-Indian Defense E43
Petrosian – Kopylov
Moscow 1951, round 1
Annotated by M. Euwe
and used with permission of US Chess

1.d4 ♘f6 2.c4 e6 3.♘c3 ♗b4 4.e3 b6 5.♘f3. The alternative, 5.♘ge2, has been somewhat discredited since the 17th game of the Botvinnik – Bronstein match *(spring 1951)* because of the reply 5...♗a6. Perhaps this judgment is too harsh, as white has a good move in 6.♘g3 (rather than 6.a3, *as in the game mentioned above*).

5...♗b7 6.♗d3 c5 7.0-0 0-0 8.a3 cxd4 9.♘a4. White avoids a doubled c-pawn and also initiates a queenside advance. With a slight transposition, the game is now following the 5th game of the Botvinnik – Bronstein match.

9...♗e7 10.exd4 ♕c7 *(the current popular line is 10...d6 11.b4 ♘bd7)* **11.b4.** White follows his plan consistently.

11...♘g4. Here we see a drawback to the system adopted by white. Due to the decentralization of his queen's knight, he is not in a position to block the diagonal of black's queen's bishop. The consequence is that black can force a painful weakness in white's camp, with far-reaching consequences.

12.g3. This is the best that white has against the threat of 12...♗xf3 and 13...♕xh2#. Thus, if 12.d5, then 12...b5! 13.cxb5 ♗xd5. Or 12.♖e1 *(?)* ♗xf3 13.♕xf3 ♕xh2+ 14.♔f1 f5!, and, if 15.♕xa8 ♘c6 16.♕b7, then 16...♘xd4! and mate is unavoidable.

Instead of 15.♕xa8??, white can hold with 15.b5! However, after 14...♕h4! (threatening ♘h2+) 15.♔e2 ♘c6 16.♗b2 f5!, white's position is tough.

12...f5. Always a valuable move when the queen's bishop has been fianchettoed *(though 12...d6 or 12...a5 were better here)*.

13.♖e1. In the 5th game of the Botvinnik – Bronstein match, white played a stronger move, 13.♘c3, in order to be able to block the long diagonal.

"In the game Alatortsev – Lisitsin (1937 Soviet Championship, where this line occurred for the first time – S. V.), white played 13.♘e1,

which allowed black to solve all his troubles in defense. In the Soviet Championship (autumn 1951), white played 13.♖e1, and N. Kopylov, a very creative 1950s player, launched a counter-attack against Petrosian with 13...f4! 14.♗xf4 ♖xf4" (Bronstein).

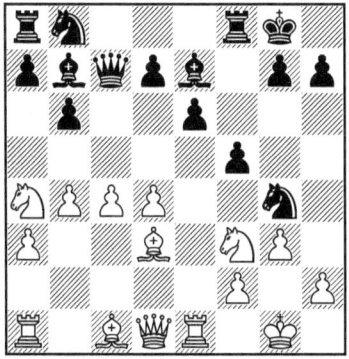

13...f4! Black prepares a sacrifice which is obvious, yet very deeply calculated. Curiously enough, one's first impression that the attack is irresistible is soon dispelled by a whole series of resourceful defensive moves, and the considerable power of black's sacrifice is established only after 15 moves or so.

The computer evaluates this move as losing, recommending instead 13...♗xf3 14.♕xf3 ♘c6=. The tournament book is not as categorical: "The exchange sacrifice is incorrect, but leads to great complications."

14.♗xf4 ♖xf4 15.gxf4 ♕xf4 16.d5. Thus black's attacking bishop is neutralized. So white apparently gains time for the comfortable defensive maneuver ♗f1-g2 or ♗e4.

There is also a little threat of ♖e4, winning a piece.

16...exd5! To keep the bishop's line open, black offers a piece in addition to the previous sacrifice of the exchange. One of the risks that black runs is that white will very likely have opportunities to beat back the attack by returning some of his extra material.

17.♖xe7. White hopes to crush his opponent, but he only deceives himself. The right way is 17.cxd5 and, if 17...♘xf2, 18.♔xf2 ♗h4+ 19.♔g2 ♕g4+ 20.♔h1 ♗xe1 – whereupon white saves himself *(actually, he wins)* with 21.♕e2!

Hence, on 17.cxd5, black has nothing better than 17...♕f7. And, after 18.♘c3 or 18.♕e2, black gets far less compensation for the exchange than he does in the actual play *(17...♕f7 is as hopeless as any other move).*

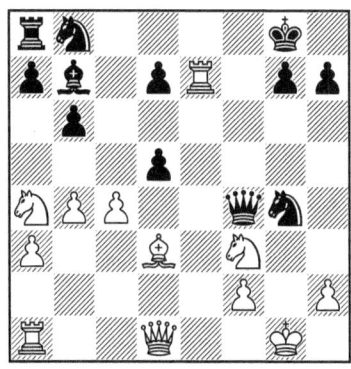

Black's position would still look quite good if 17...dxc4 were feasible. But, in that case, white has 18.♗xc4+! ♕xc4 19.♕d4 *(19.*

♘g5!, *threatening* ♖e8#, *is even stronger*), not to mention 18.♗xh7+ ♔xh7 19.♕d4 *(and here, 19.♕c2+! is the correct move).* One can imagine with what confidence white looked forward to the coming play.

The computer, however, evaluates the position after 17.♖xe7? as 0.00, and after that the game almost exactly follows the first line until move 31.

17...♘c6! Now the rook must retreat. 18.♖xd7, for example, is refuted by 18...♘ce5! and its threats of quick mates: 1) 19.♘xe5 ♕xf2+ and ♕xh2#; 2) 19.♖xb7 ♘xf3+ 20.♔g2 ♘h4+ 21.♔h3 ♘xf2#! or 20.♔f1 ♘d2+ 21.♔g2 ♕xh2#.

18.♖e1. At first sight, 18...♘d4 seems to be a killer; but white extricates himself, returning material by 19.♗xh7+ ♔xh7 20.♕xd4 ♕xf3 21.♖e7 *(21...♖g8 22.c5! with an extra exchange).* And 18...♘ce5 likewise encounters simplification by 19.♖xe5 ♘xe5 20.♘xe5.

18...♖f8. Now 19...♘ce5 is again a threat. For example: 19.h3? ♘ce5 20.♖xe5 ♘xe5 21.♘xe5 ♕xf2+ 22.♔h1 dxc4+ with ruin for white.

19.♗e4! A very ingenious idea, yet not conclusive.

It's actually the only saving move. "A very difficult move to find over the board, very problem-like. Now white repels the attack." (Tournament book)
19...dxe4 20.♕d5+ ♔h8 21.♕xe4. White's last seems to force the exchange of queens. For retreat by black's queen costs a piece, and

21...♕xf3?? 22.♕xf3 ♖xf3 23.♖e8+ is fatal.

21...♕f6! Black plays this, anyway.

There was an alternative: 21...♘xf2! 22.♕xf4 ♘h3+, since there's no 22.♔xf2? due to 22...♕xh2+ 23.♔e3 ♕h6+ 24.♔e2 ♘d8!

22.♕xg4.

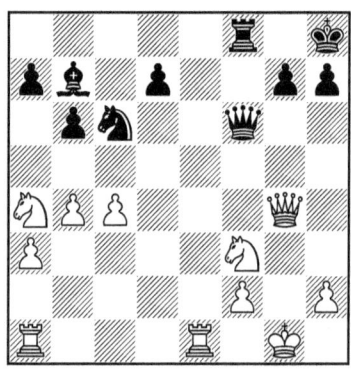

22...♘d8! Another turning point. White's knight at f3 is lost, as a move by it allows direct mate. And, if 23.♖e3, the other white rook falls by the wayside.

A valuable hint to the student: note how much black's onslaught gains by the offside position of white's knight on a4: valuable center squares are unprotected and the long diagonal remains open.

Incidentally, 22...♘d4 (instead of the text) is not good enough: 23.♕xd4 ♕xf3 24.♔f1, etc.

23.♕g3 ♗xf3. Black has ample compensation for the exchange: so long as his bishop can be maintained at f3, white's king is in mortal danger.

24.♖ac1. Beginning a maneuver to get the knight into effective play.

24...♘e6 25.♘c3 ♘d4. White's knight has returned in time to take the sting out of ♘e2+.

26.♖e3. Beginning the new liberating maneuver: white threatens 27.♖ce1 and 28.♘d5 with counterplay and gradual realization of the advantage of the exchange. What is black to do?

26...♗c6. He finds an exceptionally subtle means to continue the attack.

27.♘d5 ♕f7. Now 28.♖e7 is a mistake because of 28...♗xd5! 29.♖xf7 ♘e2+, capturing white's queen *with check*!

By playing 28.♖d1, however, white leaves his opponent nothing better than 28...♘f5 29.♕f4 ♘xe3 30.♕xf7 ♖xf7 31.fxe3 etc. Thus white can return the exchange to get an even ending.

28.♖ce1.

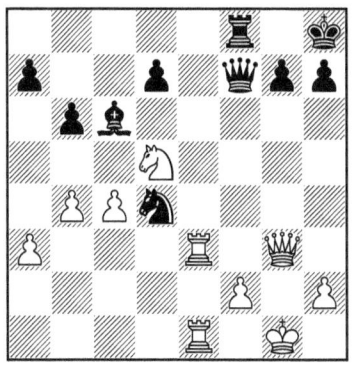

Black can now play 28...♘f5; but, after 29.♖e7 *(29.♖f3! ♗xd5 30.cxd5 ♕xd5 31.♕f4 wins)* 29...♘xe7 *(29...*♕g8=) 30.♖xe7, white has the better of it.

So black hits on a better plan: he undermines the position of white's knight.

28...b5! 29.♖e7 ♕g8. There is nothing in 29...♘f3+ 30.♔f1 etc. *(this is better for white)*. But who would dream that this position offers any winning prospects for black?

30.♔f1 bxc4. *30...♘f5 31.♕g4 ♘xe7 32.♘xe7 ♕f7 33.♕h4 ♗f3 or 33...bxc4 also leads to equality, but this move is trickier.*

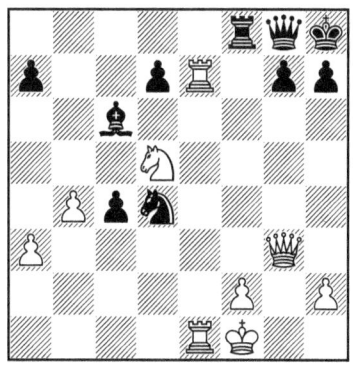

31.♘e3. This knight is just as useful here as it was at d5 – with this exception: the bishop's diagonal is open again!

This seemingly natural move is a blunder! It was necessary to play 31.♖1e5! ♘f5 32.♕g5, for instance: 32...♘xe7 33.♘xe7 ♕f7 34.♖f5= or 32...♘h6 33.♘f6! gxf6 (33... ♖xf6? 34.♖e8, and there's no 34... ♖f8 because of 35.♕d8) 34.♕xh6 fxe5 35.♖xh7+! ♕xh7 36.♕xf8+ ♕g8 37.♕h6+ with a perpetual check.

31...c3. Another unexpected resource *(31...♗b5 prolonged the struggle: 32.a4! ♗xa4 33.♖c1 c3 34.♖xc3 ♗b5+ 35.♔e1 ♘e2 36.♕e5 ♘xc3 37.♕xc3 etc.).*

32.♖c1 c2. *A mistake in return. "In time trouble, black overlooked the opportunity to regain the exchange: 32...♗b5+! 33.♔e1 ♘e2."* (Tournament book)

33.♘xc2. This move brings the game to an untimely end. Best is 33.♖xc2! after which black has the better of it without having a forced win. For example: 1) 33...♖f3 34.♕e5 ♖xe3? 35.fxe3 ♘xc2 36.♖e8, and white wins *(the correct move is 34...♘xc2=);* 2) 33...♘xc2 34.♘xc2 ♕c4+ 35.♔g1 ♖g8 36.♘e1 ♗b5 37.h3 ♕f1+ 38.♔h2 ♗c6 39.♘g2, and white can still hope. He threatens 40.♖xg7 with perpetual check.

Or 33...♗b5+ 34.♔g1 ♘xc2 35.♘xc2 ♖f6 36.♖e5 ♗c6 37.♕d3, and white holds.

33...♕c4+ 34.♔e1 (on 34.♔g1, the quickest winning move is 34...♘f5!) **34...♘f3+.** White resigned: 35.♔d1 ♕d3#.

The End of an Era

20th Soviet Championship: Moscow, 29th November – 29th December 1952

"Tell me, will there be war?"
"No. There won't be war.
But there will be a fight for peace,
so fierce that no stone will be left standing."
Soviet joke

The participants of the 20th championship probably weren't aware that it would be the last one during Stalin's lifetime and – strange coincidences do happen – the last one to be won by Botvinnik. And while Botvinnik's era continued much longer, and he would fit neatly into Khrushchev's times, the first Soviet world champion was and always will be an embodiment of Stalin's epoch.

And the sunset of that epoch was gloomy, bloody and very dangerous – as was the decrepit Kremlin dictator who still dreamed of world domination. The Korean War, where Soviet pilots almost openly fought with American ones, cast ominous glares around and threatened to grow into a new global slaughter. The anti-American hysteria in the country turned monstrous in its scope. The recent allies in the fight against Nazism were now called "fascists" themselves! Thankfully, there was no mass television back then, but newspapers and magazines became a collective "combat broadsheet". Even in *Sovietsky Sport*, I found a cartoon with an American general portrayed as Hitler.

(There were comparisons with fascism even before that. Back in 1947, a *Shakhmaty v SSSR* editorial ended with the Party Central Committee's appeals on the eve of 1st May: "Without fighting fascism, there's no democracy! Away with the false democrats who support fascists! Here's to the full victory of democracy over fascists and their patrons!")

The help of the "imperialists" during the "Great Patriotic War" was forgotten. Lend-Lease? What Lend-Lease? *Shakhmaty v SSSR* (No. 11, 1952) dotted all the i's: "The treacherous attack of Hitler's invaders on the USSR was prepared and launched by the imperialist camp. American and English warmongers, encouraging Hitler in his expansion to the East, were counting on the Soviet Union's defeat in this war, on the destruction of the first socialist state in the world. But they grossly miscalculated." (So they supplied the USSR with weapons, technology and food for the entire war, while counting on their defeat – and yet the USSR still won?!)

"The Executioners". To the right (with Hitler's portrait under his arm), General Dwight Eisenhower, the future U.S. president. Before him (right to left): Bradley, Ridgeway, Montgomery, de Lattre de Tassigny, Juin, Guderian, Halder, Fraser and Collins, and at the bottom Yugoslav leader Tito. Drawing by Kukryniksys. From the Krokodil magazine (No. 9, 1952).

Those same warmongers were accused by "the great standard-bearer of peace, Comrade Stalin" of trying "to entangle the masses with lies, deceive them and draw them into a new world war", but the simple-hearted Molotov, speaking at the 19th party congress in October 1952, blabbed out the true plans of the "dove of peace": "We should always take past factors into consideration. And these facts tell us that Russia got away from the capitalist system after the first world war, and a sizable number of European and Asian countries got away from the capitalist system after the second world war. There is every reason to think that the third world war will cause the world's capitalist system to collapse." (In essence, this was almost a paraphrase of text from the 1938 film *A Great Citizen*: "Yeah, in about twenty years' time, after a decent war, we'll emerge and witness a Soviet Union of thirty or forty republics. Dammit, how nice that will be!" The scene with these words was later deleted. The sole full copy of the film is preserved in the Krasnogorsk archive.)

In the meantime, the Soviet Union tried to destroy the hated West with propaganda. Sportspeople and chess players, who, unlike all other builders of the bright future, were allowed to travel abroad, played an important role in it – with their successes, they had to "vividly demonstrate the advantages of the Soviet system of physical education and socialist culture as a whole, and expose the lies and slander about the Soviet system by the numerous agents of Wall Street." (*Shakhmaty v SSSR*, No. 5, 1952.)

Now you understand just how important the performance of our grandmasters was at the Helsinki Chess Olympiad – the first in Soviet chess history.

Mutiny on Board

However, preparation was marred by an unprecedented scandal: the leading players unanimously voted to exclude the world champion from the national team! Yet nobody knew anything about that for a long time: both *Shakhmaty v SSSR* and the chess yearbook just listed the team's line-up, failing to point out Mikhail Botvinnik's absence.

So what happened? The first to pull back the curtain on this mystery was Isaak Boleslavsky in *At Home and Abroad* (1968), a book on the performance of Belorussian chess players in 1952-1966, for which he wrote a chapter "Foreign Battles".

> **Boleslavsky:** "The All-Union Chess Section decided to hold two training camps: a theoretical one in the winter and a practical one in the summer...
>
> The new *(second)* training camp was held in July, at the Voronovo hotel complex... They decided to hold a training match tournament with the same regulations as the Olympiad: four boards, playing two games each. It was decided beforehand that the results of this tournament wouldn't affect the team selection, and to make things more exciting, the 'veterans' were pitted against the younger players. The 'veterans' team comprised M. Botvinnik, P. Keres, A. Kotov and – because of his success rather than his age – V. Smyslov. I. Boleslavsky, D. Bronstein, E. Geller and T. Petrosian played for the 'youth' team...
>
> In the first two rounds, the 'veterans' lost 1–3, and only in the second half of the tournament did they manage to put up some resistance.
>
> The start of the match tournament was rather promising for me: I defeated Keres, Botvinnik and Kotov... Later, I failed to capitalize on that success. I lost both games to Smyslov and made two draws. Bronstein performed the best, scoring 1.5/2 against each of Smyslov, Keres and Kotov.
>
> The team was fully settled by the end of the training camp. The starting line-up (by boards) was 1. Keres, 2. Smyslov, 3. Bronstein, 4. Geller. Substitutes: 1. Boleslavsky, 2. Kotov."

So that's a possible reason: Botvinnik didn't play well in the match tournament! But wait: wasn't it "decided beforehand that the results of this tournament wouldn't affect the team selection"? Why then wasn't Mikhail Moiseevich included? The author was obviously hiding something...

Ten years later, Botvinnik himself clarified the situation in his book *Achieving the Aim*. The other participants of those dramatic events still kept silent or, at most, only gave vague hints. As though the law of omerta kept their mouths shut.

Botvinnik: "I usually prepared at my dacha, but this time, I thought: it's a team tournament, my comrades will probably be unhappy if I don't come. Training games were scheduled. I lost the first two games, then evened the score. I was playing a game with Bronstein, and then suddenly someone touched my shoulder. 'You have to stop the game and go to Moscow immediately,' the training camp deputy administrator L. Abramov said.

We got to Moscow, to Skatertny Lane *(where the Sports Committee building was located)*, and sat in the waiting room. First, the deputy chairman Ivanov (Romanov was in Helsinki) called in only Keres. Then Keres came out. I was called in; training camp administrators and Committee chess staff entered together with me.

In my presence, they reported to the deputy chairman that everything was going well, but the team members thought that Botvinnik was playing badly...

'Do you guarantee that you will take first place on first board?' the deputy chairman asked.

'Invite Keres here, please,' I asked. It was clear to me that Keres had just given such a guarantee in case he replaced me... After some embarrassing wait, they did invite Keres. He came in, pale and embarrassed. I realized then that Keres wouldn't be able to play in Helsinki after this 'confrontation' – he's too fragile psychologically. Playing is different from giving guarantees!

'I request we discuss this matter at a team meeting,' I said. We finished at that.

I couldn't sleep that night. In the morning, I went to the bathroom and saw Smyslov there, cleaning his teeth.

'Vasily Vasilyevich, I was told that you think I can't play chess?'

Smyslov continued to clean his teeth for a very long time, then answered quietly, 'I didn't think that this would get out.'

Only Smyslov could answer with such sincerity!

Ivanov soon arrived and assembled the whole team. Keres said that Botvinnik was in bad form, and it's hard to improve form quickly (he forgot to add that it's easy to lose form very quickly!). Bronstein said that if Botvinnik loses a pawn, he will lose the game, while if Keres loses a pawn, he'll manage to make a draw somehow (a wise thought!). Smyslov and Kotov simply demanded to remove me from the team. Only I. Boleslavsky stood up for the world champion... E. Geller was my replacement in the team.

They said in Helsinki that Botvinnik was ill..."

The discussion in the bathroom didn't go exactly as Botvinnik described. I learned that from an interview given by Smyslov *in June 1993 in Vienna to the* New in Chess *magazine editor Dirk Jan ten Geuzendam (the text was sent to me by Smyslov's biographer Andrei Terekhov):*

"I read this book *(Achieving the Aim)* and must say that Botvinnik describes this situation as he experienced it himself. In fact I can tell you that all through my life I have tried to stay out of such matters. Such intrigues. I can explain what really happened. I was most surprised that Botvinnik, who was World Champion and who held the highest position in our chess hierarchy, did not know about this and asked him, 'Why, you didn't know? You didn't know that such measures were going to be taken against you? How can that be? You are the World Champion. You are a top person in our chess life. You should know everything. And you didn't know that all this had been prepared? You, as a member of the communist party?'

At the Budapest tournament in March 1952, where Mikhail Botvinnik finished behind Keres and Geller. On the photo: Botvinnik, Smyslov, Tolush, Alatortsev, Keres, Geller and Petrosian.

Botvinnik erroneously deduced that this answer meant that I had been involved in this matter. There had been a team meeting that Botvinnik also attended. When I was asked my opinion about Botvinnik's participation in Finland I said that it was not up to me to decide. That Botvinnik had to decide by himself whether he wanted to play or not. It was not my job to decide. He was the World Champion.

Then fate was very favourable to me. At the Olympiad in Helsinki I showed the best result of the Russian team. Therefore I can say that I was right and not Botvinnik (laughs slightly triumphantly)." (From the book *Finding Bobby Fischer. Chess Interviews by Dirk Jan ten Geuzendam*, Netherlands, 1994.)

Years passed... And nobody knew that David Bronstein possessed the minutes of that team meeting where Botvinnik's participation was discussed! The grandmaster himself didn't want to publicize it, but when the *64 – Shakhmatnoe Obozrenie* editor Alexander Roshal asked him to share his memories of the Helsinki Olympiad, he thought that the story wouldn't be full without the minutes.

Bronstein didn't want to write an article himself, and he asked me to conduct an interview. It's rather long (see *64*, No. 1, 2003), so I'll cite only a few excerpts here.

David Ionovich, why, even though we joined FIDE in 1947, did we only take part in the Chess Olympiad for the first time in 1952?

Because the first post-war Olympiad (1950) was held in Dubrovnik, and our relationship with Yugoslavia was awful at the time. In addition, the Cold War was already upon us, and the "iron curtain" was pulled down. There was a war on cosmopolitanism in the country, all discoveries were ascribed to our scientists. I remember it as it were yesterday: someone came and said, "Oh, you wouldn't believe what happened in the university today! The

Paul Keres won four tournaments in a row, including two Soviet championships. From the Sovietsky Soyuz magazine (No. 4, 1952).

professor read a physics lecture, everything went well. And at the very end, he suddenly blurted out, 'Well, now you know how Mikhail Vasilyevich Lomonosov discovered the Boyle-Mariotte law.'" It seems that he knew that he had to mention Lomonosov and finally cracked... This was a horrible time, many decent people suffered.

Chess was indirectly affected too. Back then, it was thought that if Soviet sportspeople competed abroad, they necessarily had to win. In 1949, one of our prominent sprinters stumbled and failed to win the gold at the skating world championship, and the Sports Committee chairman lost his job as a result!

But who could have come up with the idea not to include the world champion in the team?!

It was Botvinnik's own fault. After he failed to defeat me in the match, he started saying that he hadn't played chess for three years, that he was in bad form, and all that. Then he finished behind Keres, Geller, Petrosian and Smyslov at the Soviet Championship. Then he failed again in Budapest, letting Keres and Geller overtake him. That was scandalous! And it seems that even back then, there were doubts as to whether he should play first board. What if he loses to Najdorf, Gligoric or Reshevsky? He wouldn't be a "true" world champion if he lost to Reshevsky! In the heated political environment of the time, Botvinnik just had no right to lose to an American or a Yugoslav...

Whose idea was it to remove Botvinnik from first board?

You know, only a few days ago, when I, advised by Fred Malkin, looked into his book Alexander Kotov, I discovered that the idea belonged to Kotov! I always suspected that, but there was no proof. The Sports Committee likely played a role, too. Kotov was a close friend of Postnikov, the Sports Committee deputy chairman who accompanied us in all our foreign travels. Postnikov also adored Keres, calling him "Petrovich"...

In the training match tournament, Botvinnik produced only an average result, which "gave Kotov, as the team captain, a reason to speak against the world champion playing on first board" (a quote from that book)... Our team selection was based on our real strength at that moment in time. And Keres, who had won two Soviet Championships in a row, of course had the right to lead our team. Therefore, when Botvinnik pulled me aside after the meeting and asked, "Why are you against me being in the team?" I answered, "I'm only against you playing on first board."

Still, what was the original reason for this "mutiny on board"? Did you fear that Botvinnik would perform badly, and this would affect everyone?

Yes, we feared repercussions in case of failure. That if we didn't win gold medals, it would be a catastrophe. You'll be surprised, but this wasn't

Alexander Kotov and deputy chairman of the USSR Sports Committee Dmitry Postnikov. Photo taken during the Zurich Candidates Tournament (1953). From A. Kotov's archive. Published for the first time.

even a personal attack on Botvinnik. That's why the team's decision was so unanimous!

David Ionovich, did this story affect Botvinnik's relationship with all of you?

Since he wasn't exactly friendly even before that, we couldn't really tell if his attitude worsened. There was no contact before, there was no contact later. Did it teach him anything? I think he became vengeful. He was very proud of the fact that he beat almost all of his "offenders" in subsequent tournaments...

The icing on the cake was, of course, the record of the team meeting that then took place on 15th July at the Voronovo hotel complex. You can find the full text of the minutes in the magazine, I'll only quote – removing insignificant details and official verbiage – the opinions of grandmasters and Lieutenant General Vinogradov, who returned as chairman of the All-Union Chess Section in 1952 (he was previously the chairman in 1947–1949). But first, I'll share an almost accidental finding with you.

I had thought that, back then, all the important questions in chess, especially those directly linked to the prestige of the Soviet state, were decided by the party higher-ups. And so, as I read the minutes, I was shocked by the "rampant democracy" in the discussion of the world champion's candidacy.

Did that mean that the chess elite wasn't completely voiceless and could insist on their opinion if needed? Especially if they sensed danger? Remember Bronstein's admission: "Yes, we feared repercussions in case of failure. That if we didn't win gold medals, it would be a catastrophe"? I thought that these words were the key to understanding that "mutiny".

But no! It turns out that even this time, the higher-ups still had a hand in the events. I would probably have never learned about that if I hadn't read the book *Yuri Razuvaev. Essays* by Genna Sosonko and Boris Gulko. According to Sosonko, Yuri Sergeevich "told [him] how he once asked Smyslov about the 1952 Helsinki Olympiad and Botvinnik's removal from the team. '*Yuri, are you serious? There was a party group working among us...* – this explanation by Vasily Vasilyevich said it all. Can you imagine? That's exactly what he said: *a party group working*'..."

Now it's much clearer why Smyslov addressed Botvinnik as "a member of the communist party" and why "the idea belonged to Kotov": both of them, unlike Keres, Smyslov, Bronstein, Boleslavsky and Geller, were party members! It reminded me of the story of Boris Vainstein's removal from the highest chess post in 1945 (see the chapter "The Palace Coup" in the second volume). Back then, he spoke against the match with Alekhine that Botvinnik insisted on: "The vote was open, and I remember well that both Kotov and Ragozin (Botvinnik's future coach) voted against Botvinnik! And then someone present (I think it was Abramov) said to Kotov, 'Sasha, there was a meeting of the party bureau *(chess players who were party members)*, and we decided that the match should take place.' Kotov muttered, 'I didn't know about that... We should re-vote.' We re-voted, and this time, all the party members voted 'as needed'."

The only difference was that the party bureau's position coincided with Botvinnik's opinion the previous time, but didn't this time... But let's get back to the minutes.

> **Vinogradov:** "I reported to the Committee directors about the lack of trust in Botvinnik's form among the team members and their proposal to replace him with the young grandmaster Geller. My own opinion is based on Botvinnik's bad results in the 1951 Soviet Championship and the Budapest international tournament."

> **Kotov:** "Bronstein and Smyslov are saying one thing behind his back, but they're afraid to speak the truth to Botvinnik himself. We should speak straightforwardly, the party way: we all value the world champion's prestige, and at the present time, all team members, me included, have great doubts about the world champion's form."

Keres: "Compared with 1948, Botvinnik's performances have declined considerably. I'm sure that this is a temporary effect... Botvinnik should say himself what he thinks about his abilities. At any rate, Botvinnik's play in the last two years raises serious doubts."

Smyslov: "It would be better if Botvinnik didn't play for the team, I said that before, and I won't hide it. But if he is sure of his ability and he wants to play, it's hard for me to express my opinion."

Boleslavsky: "Botvinnik has suffered setbacks, but it's hard to say whether they would lead to his failure in a team championship. Form tends to change... A team without the world champion, I think, will not look good."

Bronstein: "Botvinnik's bad form is causing concern among all the team members. Botvinnik often gets into time trouble. In the most important games, he can easily get mixed up, make a mistake and lose. Compensating for Botvinnik's losses on other boards is hard, and we wouldn't like to do that."

Flohr: "Botvinnik has an ironclad personality, we don't have another player like him. It's hard for him to play against our chess players, the strongest in the world, but he's always inspired when he plays against foreigners."

Vinogradov: "Boleslavsky didn't say all he wanted to say, but he told me in a private conversation that Botvinnik might not perform worse than others, however, he's difficult for the team to be around. Why doesn't anyone speak about that side of the matter? There should be unity in the team. This is

At the Helsinki Olympiad, the Soviet grandmasters, despite the world champion's absence, managed to win golden medals! Left, Keres and Bronstein. From D. Bronstein's archive.

Back to Moscow. The whole country knew these faces: Alexander Kotov, Paul Keres, Vasily Smyslov, Efim Geller, David Bronstein and Isaak Boleslavsky. The mood of the Olympic champions is not too cheerful, which is only logical: the win came very hard for them. From D. Bronstein's archive.

the only way to achieve success. If Botvinnik changes his behavior, the team might become more united."

Can you imagine how curiously Geller, Petrosian and the team coaches, Alatortsev, Tolush and Sokolsky (as you see, the circle of "initiates" was rather wide), must have been watching the proceedings? Of those five, only Alatortsev spoke out, saying that "Botvinnik, as a communist, should clearly answer all the questions posed before him." However, the world champion refused and asked to "allow him to ask questions to the team members himself." Ultimately, the Sports Committee deputy chairman Ivanov announced, "Due to Botvinnik's unwillingness to answer the questions asked of him, the meeting is over."

The training camp deputy administrator Lev Abramov would go on to help Mikhail Moiseevich write ten books. But then they had a fallout. His memories of the camp were printed in the same issue.

> **Abramov:** "The fact that Botvinnik wasn't playing at the peak of his creative and sporting potential was clear. And the training games proved that. And, at any rate, I never took part in any 'conspiracies', as Botvinnik

later wrote. It was all incredibly simple. During a round of the training tournament, we got a sudden call from Moscow and were told to get to the Sports Committee in Skatertny Lane immediately. When we arrived, everyone was asked to state their opinions. I personally confirmed my point of view that Botvinnik hadn't regained his strong sporting and creative form yet, and because of that, we could not guarantee his success on first board. Others said the same thing. Since Botvinnik, as world champion, couldn't play any board other than first, it was decided to exclude him from the team altogether."

That's the whole story. And I wouldn't have tried to stoke the old coals if this exclusion scandal hadn't directly affected the tournament. Botvinnik's passionate desire to take revenge on his detractors made the games especially fierce, creating ever growing intrigue at the finish... By the way, it's known that Botvinnik started playing better if he disliked his opponent. So, who knows – perhaps that decision by his colleagues only helped him win the championship medal!

An Exam for Grandmasters

The games filtering process was quicker this time. Because there were fewer issues of the bulletin (15 instead of 20), even fewer semi-final games featured in them: only 84 out of 612! And this was despite the fact that these tournaments were the strongest in the country, second only to the Soviet Championship finals. A telling detail: none of the five grandmasters who took part in them – Bondarevsky, Levenfish, Lilienthal, Ragozin and Flohr – managed to qualify for the final!

Yudovich: "The 20th championship was preceded by nine quarter-finals, held in Moscow, Leningrad *(two tournaments in each)*, Riga, Kishinev, Kiev, Rostov-on-Don and Yaroslavl. Five winners of each tournament progressed to the semi-finals." (*20th Soviet Chess Championship* tournament book.)

> **Ragozin:** "In 1951, the All-Union Committee for Physical Education and Sport made an important decision that masters would participate in the quarter-finals (earlier, the majority of masters were personally invited to the semi-finals). Grandmasters are now admitted straight to the semi-finals, while only two players – the world champion and last year's Soviet champion – are admitted straight to the final...
>
> I'm happy to point out that two quarter-finals – Riga and Rostov – were won by Chaplinsky and Kots, who only recently played in youth competitions.

One of the youngest participants, Alexander Nikitin, a 9ᵗʰ grade student of one of the Moscow schools, also achieved great success. The 15 year-old Borya Spassky, a pupil of the Leningrad Young Pioneers Palace, finished just half a point behind the winners." (*Shakhmaty v SSSR*, No. 3, 1952.)

This was the only time that the future master **Efim Aronovich Korchmar** (1914–1978) made it to the semi-final. He was the author of the "eternal Ukrainian game" played in the 1937 Ukrainian final when he mated Evsei Poliak after sacrificing a knight, queen and rook! A three-time champion of Odessa who joined the army in June 1941 and became a lieutenant and commander of a telephone division. A Companion of the Order of the Red Star, with medals "for capturing Berlin" and "for liberating Prague". He lived in Saratov after the war, where he twice won the city championship. His son became a chess coach and his grandson became an International Master. Korchmar was famous for his humor (an Odessite, after all!), and composed witty verses. I remember Yuri Averbakh no less reciting this autoepitaph:

Pedestrian, stop! Cars, step aside!
I report a terrible cauchemar:
A great genius has died,
We have lost Efim Korchmar.
In the Central Committee at a mourning session,
Dedicated to the death of a genius,
Steps up Iosif Stalin,
The pupil of Vladimir Lenin:
"Comrades, it's time to wipe away those tears!
Let's stop our weepin'!
The best wreath on Korchmar's coffin –
Is a socialist competition!"

Abramov: "Because of the new system, a lot of young players took part in the semi-finals. There were 19 candidate masters alongside the 45 winners of the quarter-final tournaments *(only 26 masters out of 51 qualified!)*. The battles for the right to take part in the final took place in May – June 1952 in Minsk, Riga, Leningrad and Sochi. This time, only three winners of each group progressed to the finals, because the grandmasters who played for the USSR national team *(Smyslov, Bronstein, Geller and Boleslavsky)* were personally invited to the final." (*Chess in 1951–1952* yearbook.)

Sochi group: 1. Simagin – 11/17; 2–4. Aronin, Kasparyan, Konstantinopolsky – 10.5; 5–6. Lilienthal, Shaposhnikov – 10; 7. Bonch-Osmolovsky – 9.5; 8–9. Goldberg, Novotelnov – 9; 10–11. Levenfish, Ratner

Boris Spassky and Alexander Nikitin debuted in the quarter-finals. Three years earlier, they performed successfully in the Soviet youth team championship (1949). Standing, Anatoly Bykhovsky. Photo by B. Utkin. From A. Nikitin's archive.

The three protagonists recreated the scene in 2003 at the Central Chess Club in Moscow. The original is also in my possession from A. Nikitin's archive.

– 8.5; 12–14. Baranov, Katalymov, Liublinsky – 8; 15. Zak – 7; 16. Chistiakov – 5.5; 17. Soloviev – 5; 18. Knyshenko – 4.5.

Lilienthal and **Zak:** "Simagin's victory is very convincing. Rich imagination, bold, original play, exceptional inventiveness in defense, a diverse opening repertoire and great technique were demonstrated by him throughout the tournament. The success of Kasparyan, a very deep and interesting player, is also a delight. We think that his sporting results are hurt by his propensity for unusual, sometimes fanciful opening set-ups." (*Shakhmaty v SSSR*, No. 8, 1952.)

As in the previous year, **Mikhail Alexandrovich Bonch-Osmolovsky** (1919–1975) fell one point short of qualifying for the final! He was awarded the master's title in 1951 for drawing a match with Aronin – this result tells much. However, he soon quit over-the-board play,

Пионеры Шура Никитин (Москва) и Боря Спасский (Ленинград) получили звание шахматистов 1-й категории.

9. Рад и Ботвинник, рад и Смыслов
Партии юных двух мастеров.
Пока что ребята — не мастера,
Но очень упорная эта игра.

"Pioneers Shura (Alexander) Nikitin (Moscow) and Borya Spassky (Leningrad) gained their 1ˢᵗ category titles.
Both Botvinnik and Smyslov
Are glad to see the game of two young masters.
The lads aren't masters as of yet,
But this game is very tenacious."
The game Spassky – Nikitin through the eyes of the Pionerskaya Pravda artist (4ᵗʰ November 1949).

devoting himself to academia in the Moscow Power Engineering Institute. Later, he gained a doctorate in technical sciences. According to Averbakh, who became friends with Bonch-Osmolovsky when they were both students at the Bauman Institute, the master's retirement was forced. The secret police tried to recruit him and force him to report on his colleagues. He couldn't refuse that offer, but Mikhail Alexandrovich didn't want to become an informer either...

Why couldn't he refuse? Because his father, a professor of Japanese economics, was imprisoned in Bamlag for 18 years (1937–1955). After release, he was ordered to live 101 kilometers from the capital in the city of Alexandrov, but for the most part he actually lived in Moscow at his son's place, in a wing of a two-story building on Vosstaniya Square (now Kudrinskaya

Кандидат в мастера
М. БОНЧ-ОСМОЛОВСКИЙ.
Дружеский шарж Н. ЛИСА.

Mikhail Bonch-Osmolovsky became a master in 1951. Cartoon by N. Lis. From the Moscow championship bulletin (4th February 1949).

Square) right in the center of Moscow that currently hosts the Tchaikovsky museum. Averbakh recalled that he had to knock on the door in a special manner, so that the hosts knew that a trusted person was there...

Minsk group: 1. Lipnitsky – 11/17; 2–4. Goldenov, Korchnoi, Suetin – 10.5; 5–6. Averbakh, Flohr – 10; 7–8. Antoshin, Kholmov – 9.5; 9–11. Borisenko, Saigin, Solntsev – 9; 12. Zagorovsky – 8.5; 13–14. Zurakhov, Kopaev – 8; 15. Korchmar – 6; 16. Stolyar – 5.5; 17. Lutikov – 5; 18. Bastrikov – 3.5.

Suetin: "Lipnitsky showed exceptional tenacity in defense of difficult positions. Goldenov's success also pleases us. He has good technique. Now he no longer avoids sharp positions. When you look through Korchnoi's games, you come to the conclusion that his achievement in the tournament isn't too convincing. However, we should admit that Korchnoi possesses great skill and positive sporting qualities.

The main reason for Averbakh's relative failure is his lack of confidence in complicated, tactical struggle... In addition, Averbakh has started to get into severe time trouble regularly." (Ibid.)

Averbakh: "One round before the finish *(actually two)*, the situation was like this: if I win the game, I qualify for the final and win the tournament. However, my opponent, the strong master Isaak Lipnitsky, was in the same situation.

Before the game, he made me an unexpected offer: 'Let's play on the following conditions: the loser, since he doesn't progress to the final, gets the winner's prize as compensation.'

I agreed without thinking too much.

On the morning of the game, I was invited to train with the local Dynamo volleyball team, and I played a few sets. It was an inexcusable mistake: before important games, you should avoid unnecessary expense of nervous and even physical energy.

The game started after lunch. I quickly got a much better position, but... got horribly sleepy. I also started to regret my rash decision to accept my competitor's offer. Ultimately, I blundered, and my position became hopeless." (From the book *Centre-Stage and Behind the Scenes*.)

When I spoke to Yuri Lvovich years later, he remembered that incident and said, "It was a good lesson, and I swore to myself never to make such deals again."

Leningrad group: 1–2. Byvshev, Moiseev – 11/17; 3. Taimanov – 10.5; 4. Lisitsin – 10; 5–7. Kopylov, Kots, Rovner – 9.5; 8–9. Alatortsev, Panov – 9; 10–13. Bondarevsky, Klaman, Sopkov, Khasin – 8.5; 14. Zamikhovsky – 7.5; 15. Furman – 7; 16. Kondratyev – 6; 17. Kuzminykh – 5.5; 18. Noakh – 4.

Bondarevsky: "A remarkable success for the young Leningrad master Byvshev. He played the whole tournament very consistently, skillfully punished his opponents for mistakes and didn't lose heart after defeats... Moiseev is playing with great ease and is not plagued by time trouble. On the other hand, Byvshev, in my opinion, is better in positional evaluation.

Minsk semi-final. Neither Averbakh nor Kholmov managed to qualify. From R. Kholmov's archive.

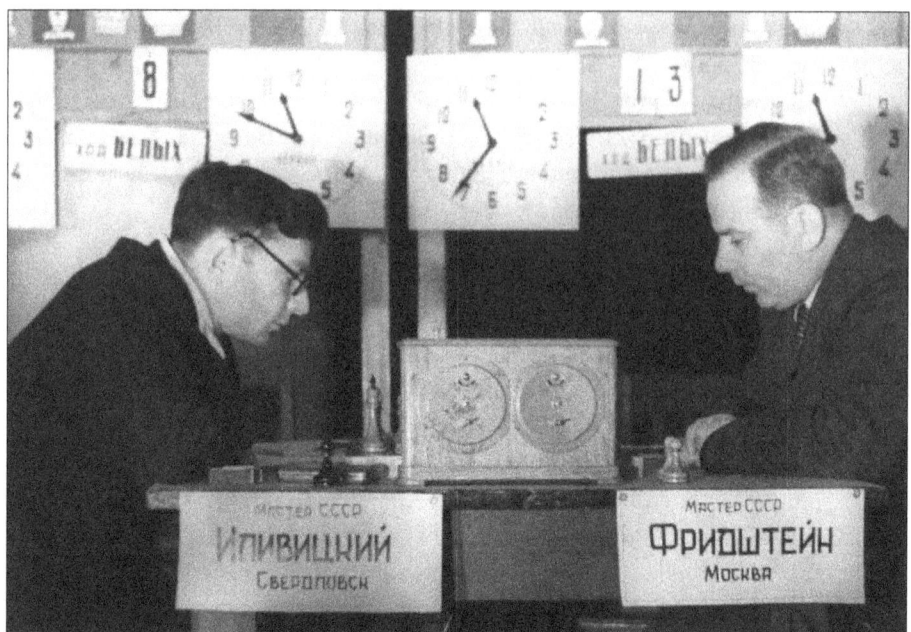

Riga semi-final. After a four-year break, Georgy Ilivitsky (left) managed to reach the final again! From his opponent G. Fridstein's archive. Published for the first time.

Taimanov prepared well for the tournament; he was one of the few players to use carefully prepared lines rarely seen in tournament practice." (*Shakhmaty v SSSR*, No. 9, 1952.)

Riga group: 1. Kan – 12.5/17; 2. Tolush – 11.5; 3. Ilivitsky – 11; 4–5. Nikitin, Ravinsky – 10; 6. Ragozin – 9.5; 7. Terpugov – 9; 8–10. Weltmander, Mikenas, Chaplinsky – 8.5; 11. Chekhover – 8; 12–13. Bannik, Klavins – 7.5; 14–15. Koblencs, Fridstein – 7; 16–17. Nei, Cherepkov – 6; 18. Pasman – 5.

Mikenas: "Kan's victory is fully logical. He played a number of outstanding games... Tolush didn't play like his usual self. Instead of breathtaking complications characteristic of his style, this time he would try to get an advantage out of the opening... Ilivitsky was equally good in defense and positional attacks.

We should take especial note of the young Nikitin. He is working with an experienced coach (G. Ravinsky), and he is on the correct creative path. Without a doubt, we have a great, promising chess talent in him." (Ibid.)

However, Nikitin only managed to make it to the Soviet Championship final in 1959 – together with another talented Moscow player. "Evgeny Vasiukov didn't waste his free time: he constantly worked on improving his chess skills, often meeting with the great chess teacher and strong master

Grigory Ionovich Ravinsky, who imparted him with a fanatical love of chess and a work ethic, which are both necessary to climb the chess Everest. Grigory Ionovich worked with me a little as well, but in 1952, I started to prepare in earnest to obtain a golden medal at school and enroll into college, so our lessons became less and less frequent. In the same year 1952, however, I put in a good performance in the Soviet championship semi-final and was awarded the master's title. The Pionerskaya Pravda newspaper even printed a cartoon with our trio in their New Year issue, with the following caption: 'His inspiration helped him nurture Vasiukov and Nikitin. Let's hope that Ravinsky trains a true chess giant.' I decided that Evgeny was the one who should become that giant, though, as I was already planning to take a different path. I was preparing to quit full-time chess for a while." (From Nikitin's book *Evgeny Vasiukov, Chess Champion of Moscow*, Elk and Ruby, 2020.)

Scandal in the Noble Family

As per tradition, each round was described by a different author in the bulletin, which occasionally (when Flohr or Panov took the pen) colored the dull picture a bit. With the exception of round reports and "player profiles", there's literally nothing more to read: no reports from the tournament hall, no essays, no amusing verses. Photos and five or so cartoons – that was the whole "entertainment program". At least the cartoons were drawn by a great artist: Iosif Igin, *Krokodil* staffer and a friend of the poet Mikhail Svetlov. He created a whole portrait gallery of chess players, and, as it turned out, even received his first ever fee as an artist (in 1935) for a cartoon of Capablanca!

The creative duo in *Sovietsky Sport* changed again, but not as radically as last time: the master was replaced by a young grandmaster. This switch was more or less forced: Alexander Tolush took his place on the stage this time, while his replacement in the newspaper Tigran Petrosian preferred to watch the championship from the hall. According to **Karolyi** and **Gyozalyan** in *Petrosian Year by Year: Volume I (1942–1962)* (Elk and Ruby, 2020), "The Soviet Chess Federation offered Petrosian the choice between participating in the Soviet championship or the following year's Bucharest tournament; he opted for the latter."

Alas, the comparison with the previous year was clearly not in chess' favor. The round reports in the newspaper became totally "faceless" (not a single photo for the whole tournament) and decreased in size. In the previous years, they could take up a full page, but this time, they weren't always given even half a page, and sometimes the reports included two rounds at once. As a result, there's a detailed report on the main game, with several lines, but all the other games get only brief mentions...

From the press: "The final tournament will be held in the Great Hall of the Central Railway Workers Culture Center from 29th November to 28th December. Korchnoi and Byvshev will play in the final for the first time. Leningrad University student Korchnoi is 21 years old. He's the youngest participant of the 20th Soviet Championship. Goldenov, Ilivitsky, Moiseev and Suetin *(and Simagin)* are taking part in their second finals.

As we know, there are now 15 grandmasters among the ranks of Soviet players. Seven of them take part in the tournament now starting...

According to the new All-Union Sporting Classification, to obtain the USSR grandmaster title a player should take first place in the national championship final, or take 2nd or 3rd place two times in three years (each of those successes equals one grandmaster norm), or win a 14-game qualifying match against a USSR grandmaster, or achieve strong results in international competitions. In case of sharing 3rd–4th place in the Soviet Championship final, a grandmaster norm is counted if the player finishes ahead of three grandmasters. It's interesting to note that masters Tolush, Lipnitsky and Aronin already have one grandmaster norm." (*Sovietsky Sport*, 25th November 1952.)

From the press: "The opening ceremony of the 20th Soviet Championship took place on 28th November in the conference room of the USSR Council of Ministers' Committee for Physical Education and Sport. Chief arbiter I. Bondarevsky read out the championship regulations. Then, lots were drawn *(grandmasters in italic)*: 1. *M. Botvinnik* (Moscow), 2. B. Goldenov (Minsk), 3. A. Tolush, 4. *M. Taimanov* (both Leningrad), 5. L. Aronin (Moscow Oblast), 6. V. Simagin, 7. *D. Bronstein* (both Moscow), 8. *P. Keres* (Tallinn), 9. I. Lipnitsky (Kiev), 10. *V. Smyslov* (Moscow), 11. V. Korchnoi (Leningrad), 12. *I. Boleslavsky* (Minsk), 13. G. Kasparyan (Yerevan), 14. I. Kan (Moscow), 15. G. Ilivitsky (Sverdlovsk), 16. *E. Geller* (Odessa), 17. O. Moiseev (Moscow), 18. V. Byvshev (Leningrad), 19. A. Suetin (Tula), 20. A. Konstantinopolsky (Moscow)." (*20th Soviet Chess Championship* bulletin, 8th December 1952.)

Petrosian and **Tarasov:** "Even before the start of the round *(5:30 p.m.)*, the hall is already packed. You can see renowned scientists, famous Stakhanovite workers from Moscow factories, writers, artists, college students, schoolchildren. The tournament excites everyone – not only in Moscow, not only in the Soviet Union. People from all corners of the world are watching the tournament.

There's silence in the hall. The first steps towards victory are made on the ten chessboards. Specially-cut pieces slowly move on the big demonstration boards. The participants play cautiously, thinking over the opening lines for ages...

The fans' attention was attracted to the games Botvinnik – Konstantinopolsky, Smyslov – Korchnoi, Keres – Kasparyan and Bronstein – Kan. While there was a complicated, maneuvering struggle in the first two games, the other two were quite sharp. Bronstein sacrificed two pawns in a Queen's Gambit. Kan took one, but prudently declined the other, since white's attack along the open g- and h-files would likely be unstoppable. Combining defensive measures with tactical threats, Kan managed to create a solid position...

Kasparyan deployed his favorite Caro-Kann Defense. Keres didn't position his minor pieces too well and got into serious trouble. Trying to sharpen the struggle, he sacrificed two pawns, and black replied with a queen sacrifice for a rook and knight. When the position stabilized, and chances got roughly equal, this game also ended in a draw *(on the 19th move!)*.

> **Bondarevsky:** "The youngest tournament participant, Korchnoi, played well for the whole game *(see game 258)*. Smyslov didn't get any advantage out of the opening or in the middlegame, and then lost a pawn in the endgame. The Leningrad player transitioned to a rook ending and adjourned the game with good winning chances. On the play-off day, Korchnoi needed just a few moves to convert his advantage." (Tournament bulletin, 8th December.)
>
> **Edgar Chaplinsky** later described their night-time analysis:
>
> "Korchnoi and I played for the Nauka sports society, as we were both students: he was studying at the history faculty in Leningrad, while I was at the physics faculty in Moscow. At the time I was a candidate master and clearly inferior to him, but he asked me to become his coach. I hope that Viktor Lvovich won't take offense if I tell you his terms. As his coach, the society was meant to pay me 800 rubles under a contract, a rather decent amount in those times (the monthly salary of a worker or engineer). But Korchnoi's terms were that we would split this sum in two, and, naturally, I eagerly agreed.
>
> My duties included analyzing his adjourned games and collecting information about upcoming opponents. And so, we were to analyze the adjourned game with Smyslov. I spent all night analyzing and, I thought, found a sure way to win. However, Korchnoi immediately found a 'hole' in my analysis in the morning, as early as on the fifth move. I was awfully down and also surprised a lot, as he hadn't analyzed the position given that he was due to play it only after the next round. When I asked him how he had found it, he replied with his customary smile that he had carried out all the analysis in his sleep. Chess players know that this is actually plausible, and you do often find the right solution in your sleep that you're unable to find during sleepless analysis." (From an unpublished article in my archive dated 1991 which Chaplinsky submitted to the *Shakhmaty v SSSR* editorial board.)

With a bold kingside pawn advance, Botvinnik created strong pressure on Konstantinopolsky's position. In the adjourned position, he has an extra piece for two pawns and can count on victory..." (*Sovietsky Sport*, 2nd December.)

Flohr: "The last day of November. Sunday. Evening comes. Where to go? People in Moscow have a wide choice of cultural events. But the soul of a chess fan can be best warmed at the tournament where our strongest grandmasters and masters battle it out. Many of them have performed successfully at tournaments this year, but abroad, and so the Moscow fans have been missing them somewhat.

There are many masters in the hall, as well as on stage. Grandmasters are among the spectators, too. Of course, a grandmaster would be much happier to be sitting among the participants, but what can you do if youth pushes out us 'elders?'...

In the second round, the world champion's game with Goldenov was very instructive. In the opening, Botvinnik surprised everyone with 8.♗xc6. Usually, such a bishop for knight trade tears the soul of a bishop pair fan into pieces. But in this case, Botvinnik's strategy was correct: with doubled pawns, the

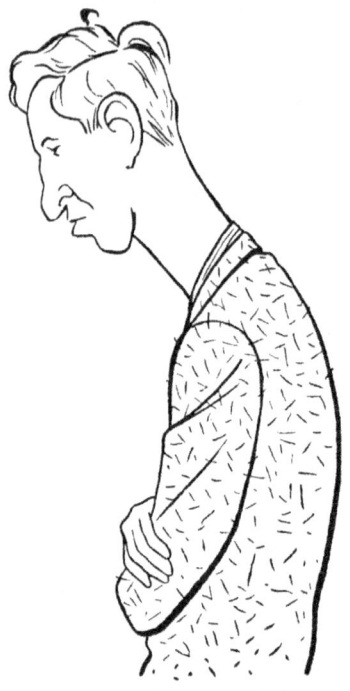

Старт, как и прежде, неудачен,
Болельщик снова озадачен.
Надеемся, что будет в силе
На финише Смыслов Василий.

С. ВЛАДИМИРОВ.

Дружеский шарж
И. ИГИНА.

The start is poor, as before,
The fan is baffled again.
We hope that the finish
Will be stronger for Smyslov Vasily.

The hopes of Smyslov's fans didn't come true.
Cartoon by I. Igin. Poetry by S. Vladimirov.
From the tournament bulletin (17th December 1952).

black bishops aren't particularly strong. One white knight got entrenched on c4, and the other one went on a journey f3-e1-g2-f4 and struck a blow on g6... With all my due respect for the bishops, I should admit that they were utterly crushed in this game. Botvinnik convincingly demonstrated the 'knight pair advantage'!

Smyslov deployed his signature a7-a5 line in the Slav Defense. Boleslavsky used up 10 minutes for 13 moves, while Smyslov spent a full hour. It seems that it wasn't Boleslavsky who was surprised by the new idea *(see game 253, note to black's 10th move)*. Smyslov managed to extricate himself gradually from a cramped position and he opened the g-file, but this suddenly spelled doom for him. White unleashed all his major pieces on the black king along the g-file...

Smyslov's numerous fans are unhappy with his bad start. But everything is still to play for. In Budapest, Smyslov didn't start much better, but the tournament didn't end too badly for him *(shared 3rd – 5th places with Botvinnik and Stahlberg)*.

Only at the very end of the evening did Keres manage to outplay Kan. The endgame was reminiscent of two Keres games – against Mikenas and Smyslov. It probably wasn't too pleasant for Kan to recall that Keres won them both. The Soviet champion won easily on the play-off day.

Byvshev clearly intended to crush Taimanov. In the Sicilian, he played f2-f4, h2-h4 and even g2-g4. How can you not attack after that?

It wasn't by coincidence that Byvshev thought for almost two hours. It would be simpler if he'd just read Taimanov's articles on that topic in the *Shakhmaty v SSSR* magazine. The attack didn't materialize, and Taimanov

The only draw in encounters between Tolush and Botvinnik. But what a draw it was! From the author's archive. Published for the first time.

launched a strong counter-offensive. Only one thing was not clear: why Byvshev adjourned the game and then resigned without resuming the next day? *(Nevertheless, in round 10 Byvshev launched a similar pawn storm against Boleslavsky's king... and won!)*

It's equally unclear why Simagin adjourned the game against Geller. The Odessa player executed his attack in a classical way and proved that he's quite adept at fighting his own weapon – the King's Indian Defense – with white. It's possible that Simagin has some doubts about our grandmasters' advantage conversion technique. But still, doubting that Geller would win with four extra pawns was overdoing things!

Now, with the tournament just started, I would like to repeat what we have stated many times: you should not adjourn hopeless games. This is disrespectful towards your opponent and our outstanding chess fans. Do not fear the applause for your opponents! A master should be able to win, but he should also be able to lose gracefully, too." (Tournament bulletin, 12th December.)

Alatortsev: "Round 3. The game Tolush – Botvinnik was the center of attention. They played the French Defense. The light-squared bishops were already traded on move 8, which is better for black – it's easier for him to protect the kingside. But Tolush managed to create dangerous threats even without a light-squared bishop. The black king didn't castle until move 25, and then it hastily ran to the queenside to hide from the white pieces. Botvinnik prepared a pawn break b5-b4 there. The struggle got complicated again...

> **Petrosian** and **Tarasov:** "Time trouble disrupted the natural flow of events. The world champion had only a few minutes before time control. He didn't go for active operations and started repeating moves, trying to force his opponent to trade queens, which was beneficial for him. Tolush couldn't count on a successful attack, and a three-fold repetition occurred on the 41st move of this exciting game." (*Sovietsky Sport*, 4th December.)

Suetin sacrificed a pawn to Taimanov in the opening. However, the complications ended in white's favor. In the subsequent struggle, the grandmaster won a second pawn, and it seemed that the game was already decided. However, Taimanov was not careful enough, made a mistake and lost an exchange. Suetin skillfully converted his advantage during the play-off...

The game Korchnoi – Boleslavsky ended in 16 moves. This was not a dull, or, as they say, 'grandmaster' draw. But chess fans were rather baffled as to why the opponents stopped such an interesting and intense game.

Yudovich: "Unfortunately, in some draws, we are seeing a harmful tendency of avoiding the struggle in unclear and sharp positions. Such an approach to chess creativity, when getting a result is now considered all-important, was resolutely criticized by our chess society." (Tournament book.) Getting ahead of myself, I'll say that the draw percentage in this championship was much higher than in the previous one: 42% versus 36%.

Smyslov couldn't convert his advantage in the game against Kasparyan. He was doing better at various points. And there was a moment when Kasparyan outplayed the grandmaster as well. The position equalized before the break and the opponents agreed to a draw." (Ibid.)

Petrosian and Tarasov: "Round 4. Last year, Taimanov – a young master – met Botvinnik in a tournament game for the first time. That game ended in a draw. And now, grandmaster Taimanov plays Botvinnik again.

Just like last time, they played the Nimzo-Indian Defense – it's the favorite opening for both... Botvinnik's efforts to complicate the game led to the black knight, obviously badly positioned on b7, rejoining the game with unexpected great force. Taimanov, probably underestimating his capabilities, offered the world champion a draw, and he agreed. However, I. Bondarevsky, after looking at the position, rightfully forbade them from stopping *(see game 251)*...

> Actually, it was Botvinnik who offered the draw when the chief arbiter approached the board. He wrote about that in *Achieving the Aim*: "During the game, I offered a draw," but then adds: "My opponent accepted it (we only had to make the 30 moves necessitated by the regulations), but then started playing for a win." And gives a footnote: "Even though, by unwritten but traditional rules of chess ethics, you could only renounce the draw agreement if the opponent agreed to that too."

> A serious accusation, but there's a "but": his opponent did not accept the draw!

> **Taimanov:** "A game against the world champion is always remarkable, and, frankly, I just wanted to make an honorable draw. That's why, after getting a good position with black out of the opening, I deemed it possible to offer the Teacher a draw. But Mikhail Moiseevich seemed to have a different goal. At any rate, he, referring to the tournament rule that banned agreeing to a draw before the 30th move without the chief arbiter's approval, coldly declined my offer and... immediately made a bad move. My strong reply was quite unexpected for him, and Botvinnik took a long think.

> I was very surprised and, I must admit, disappointed when Mikhail Moiseevich suddenly... offered a draw on his own. Knowing Botvinnik's

The game Botvinnik – Taimanov, marred by an unfortunate incident between the players, served as the prologue for their Soviet championship play-off match. Cover of the Shakhmaty v SSSR magazine (No. 2, 1953).

principled approach, I couldn't quite understand why he chided me for offering a draw on the 22nd move, and then, just a move later, made a U-turn. I could only delicately reply that the question of a draw agreement before move 30, as the maestro himself rightfully pointed out before, couldn't be resolved without the arbiters' board's approval. Chief arbiter Igor Zakharovich Bondarevsky was invited to our table, and, upon objectively evaluating the position on the board, refused to approve a draw. He officially suggested that we continue playing, and we complied. *(Taimanov revealed the underlying reason for the arbiter's decision in a later interview: Bondarevsky* "wasn't Botvinnik's biggest fan. When he saw that his position was dangerous, he was rather happy to say that he objected to the peace.") The game continued, and after some tactical complications, I managed to win.

Late at night, Botvinnik called Flohr – he was my second at that point – and expressed unhappiness about his trainee's actions. Flohr himself had a reputation of a very impartial man, and colleagues respected his opinion. He, of course, knew about the incident, but he took my side:

'Misha, Markusha wasn't planning to defeat you. He was the first to offer a draw, which you declined.'

'If he wasn't planning to win, why then did he win?' Botvinnik parried.

'The arbiter demanded that you adhere to the regulations. Wasn't that fair?'

'Of course it was,' Mikhail Moiseevich agreed, but he held a grudge for a while afterwards." (From the book *Remembering the Greatest...*)

Keres had played Master Geller five times in tournaments, with a score of 4.5–0.5, but it was the first time that he had faced Grandmaster Geller. Unlike all previous encounters, Geller started the game with 1.d4. Keres used a rare line in

Гроссмейстер
Е. ГЕЛЛЕР

Дружеский шарж
И. ИГИНА.

In round 4, Geller's tank ran over the Soviet champion. The shock was so strong that Keres lost two games out of the next four. Cartoon by I. Igin. From the tournament bulletin (22nd December 1952).

the Nimzo-Indian Defense, immediately putting his bishop onto the a8-h1 diagonal. The opponents quickly left the well-trodden path...

> **Sokolsky:** "Black was unable to fully mobilize his forces. His knight stood on its starting square until move 24... Despite an early queen trade, Geller inventively developed an initiative, creating various threats and preventing the development of black pieces. With 20.♗xh7, the young grandmaster sacrificed an exchange for two pawns, correctly evaluating the position. With precise play, Geller won the resulting endgame. The spectators met the talented player's achievement with applause *(see game 252)*...
>
> Interesting events unfolded in the game Moiseev – Bronstein. In the Old Indian Defense, black pushed his pawn to e4 on the sixth move, cramping white's position. Moiseev played passively and made several positional mistakes, weakening the light squares. As a result, black put his knight on d5 and launched an unopposed attack on the kingside. Bronstein was quite skillful in attack... The game can be used as teaching material." (Tournament bulletin, 17th December.)

Tolush, one of the tournament leaders, has again got the spectators excited; he's showing the youngest and most sparkling play in this championship.

Summer 1952. Isaak Lipnitsky playing a casual game against Efim Geller at the Chkalov hotel complex in Odessa. From L. Yakir's archive (Kiev).

Goldenov's queen, after getting to h6 on move 11, voluntarily entombed itself there, making no further moves until the end of the game. Meanwhile, Tolush, easily securing his king, invaded the second rank with his rook, won a pawn and started pushing his two connected passers... In the search for counterchances, Goldenov got into time trouble, and Tolush checkmated him on move 38.

Round 5. There was no real struggle in the game Aronin – Botvinnik. After 15 moves, most pieces had already left the board, and the draw was a natural consequence of the trades.

Lipnitsky and Geller also drew their game. The fight was short, but furious. When Geller went for the perpetual check, the white king was on h5, and the black one on d7. The queens showed a lot of energy. Black's kingside and white's queenside looked like they had been swept by a hurricane.

Smyslov scored his first win. Against Ilivitsky's Sicilian, the grandmaster employed the Closed System, which he has studied thoroughly and which was readily and successfully used by the great Russian chess player M. I. Chigorin. This system, enriched with Smyslov's ideas, is a formidable weapon in his hands.

Tolush won again *(he defeated Konstantinopolsky)*. Boleslavsky defeated Kasparyan in 39 moves; the latter failed to obtain the usual kingside counterplay in the King's Indian as black and was doomed to losing out of the opening." (*Sovietsky Sport*, 7th December.)

Standings after round 5: Boleslavsky, Tolush – 4; Bronstein, Geller, Korchnoi, Taimanov – 3.5; Botvinnik, Suetin – 3; Aronin, Ilivitsky, Keres, Lipnitsky, Moiseev – 2.5; Konstantinopolsky, Smyslov – 2; Kasparyan, Simagin – 1.5; Goldenov, Kan – 1; Byvshev – 0.5.

Heating Up

Petrosian and **Tarasov:** "In the first rounds, about 50 percent of all games ended in draws, but after round 6, the games on all boards became much sharper. The spectators now realized that reconnaissance was over, and the true battle had begun.

The play of Viktor Korchnoi and Vasily Byvshev is especially interesting. Both are young, both are debuting in the final, and both show outstanding skill. They still lack composure, the ability to manage their time effectively, distribute their energy, and evaluate both their own position and the opponent's chances correctly, but their play is bold, imaginative and persistent. The points scored by Korchnoi speak for themselves. It's harder to speak of Byvshev's merits – he's currently occupying one of the last places.

V. Ivanov, championship arbiter: "Viktor Korchnoi was born in Leningrad in 1931. Everyone in his family played chess, so he took an interest since he was seven. At the age of thirteen, Korchnoi started studying in the chess section of the Young Pioneers Palace and got first category two years later.

In 1947, Korchnoi won the Soviet youth championship. This was his first major success. The next year, he also won the youth championship, jointly with the Estonian schoolboy Nei... In 1951, the final of the All-Russian Chigorin Memorial tournament was held in Leningrad. After losing to Lutikov in the first round, Korchnoi scored 7.5 points in the next 12 games and was awarded the master's title, which he confirmed in the 19th Soviet Championship semi-final. (...)

Vasily Mikhailovich Byvshev was born in 1922 in the Kalinin *(now Tver)* Oblast, in a peasant's family. In 1931, he moved to Leningrad together with his parents. He picked up chess in 1935 *(almost by chance: he was hospitalized with a broken leg and a friend brought him a chess set and Alekhine's book* My Best Games). In 1937, he joined the Young Pioneers Palace chess section and progressed from a non-category to a first-category player in just a year *(8th grader Vasya Byvshev defeated Botvinnik in a simul in 1937!)*.

In 1940–1947, he served in the Soviet Army. After decommissioning, he enrolled in the A. A. Zhdanov Leningrad University law school. Byvshev shared 2nd–3rd places in the All-Union Candidate Masters tournament (1948), earning his master's norm and qualifying for the 17th Soviet Championship semi-final." (Tournament bulletin, 22nd and 28th December.)

Master Vasily Byvshev. His performance was a huge surprise: after a 0.5/5 start, he scored 7 points in the next 8 games – an incredible achievement! Photo taken at the Leningrad Chigorin memorial in 1951 by M. Volkovysky from his archive. Published for the first time.

In round 6, Byvshev played Keres. When he made his 29th move, g4-g5, attacking the bishop, the spectators filling the TsDKZh Great Hall on Sunday concentrated their attention on that exciting game.

What will Keres do? Will he find a satisfactory defense? At that moment, Keres' position was already hard to defend. And after his mistake on move 35, white won a second pawn, and black's position became hopeless. The young master's convincing victory was warmly greeted by the fans.

> **Suetin:** "Keres' big flaw is his long depression after a failure, which severely affects his creative inventiveness and therefore his form. For instance, after the world team championship in Helsinki, Keres had no creative achievements in the 20th championship that were worthy of his talent. He had to defend often (for example, against Botvinnik, Smyslov, and Geller), and defense is one of his weaker skills, especially if he can't find counterplay." (Chess yearbook.)

Korchnoi had black against Ilivitsky. He got a promising position in a sharp line of the Grunfeld Defense. To simplify the game, white forced a queen trade. However, the black rook invaded the 2nd rank, and white's position worsened even more. With a simple but elegant combination, Korchnoi won two pawns...

> **Korchnoi:** "Taking part in my third national championship semi-final, I, to the surprise of many and even myself, achieved the goal – I qualified for the Soviet Championship final! My chess was quite poor back then. A limited opening repertoire targeted mostly against weaker opponents. But I prepared for the championship in earnest. I remember a fascinating thought once expressed by I. Bondarevsky: 'When a chess player tries to expand his opening repertoire, change the opening, it's a sign of their growth.' I did prepare a new opening for the championship – the Grunfeld Defense." (From the book *Chess Without Mercy*.)

Botvinnik and Simagin played the last 15 moves in mutual time trouble. Botvinnik got a more promising position and, creating pressure on the weak c7 pawn, launched queenside activity. Simagin subtly sacrificed a pawn and seized the initiative... Both made their moves very quickly: the flags were hanging and they had only seconds to make their moves. After the 40th move, it turned out that Simagin had lost a bit of his advantage...

> The draw with the world champion had an encouraging effect on Simagin, who had started the tournament with three zeroes, and he now won two games in a row, including one against Tolush.
> **Botvinnik:** "Before becoming a professional chess player, Simagin worked as a factory mechanic. He looked sickly, somewhat gloomy, non-talkative,

but quite intelligent. However, he had a resolute personality and a great, distinctive chess talent." (From the book *Vladimir Simagin*.)

Beilin: "One well-known master, an engineer by education, wanted to praise Simagin and our way of life and wrote (and said) that Simagin was a worker, a mechanic. Indeed, Vladimir did work as a mechanic at a defense plant during the Great Patriotic War. The funny thing was that this engineer master's speech was somewhat clumsy, showing gaps in his schooling. And Volodya himself told me that he wasn't from the working class. His father was a grammar school headmaster and an astronomer. Before the revolution, of course." (From the book *My Encounters in the Chess Kingdom*.)

The game Geller – Smyslov exactly followed Boleslavsky – Smyslov *(round 2)* until the 12th move. Smyslov was the first to deviate. Soon, the game transitioned into a complicated endgame, where Geller's chances were probably better. But he couldn't find the right continuation and seemingly overestimated his resources... Smyslov won the game in the play-off." (*Sovietsky Sport*, 9th December.)

The second half of this game (moves 34–58) earned detailed commentary by none other than Max Euwe – on three whole magazine pages! (*Chess Review* No. 7, 1953). The analysis is deep and quite original: five "hypotheses" with one "instructive diversion". I could have included it in this book, but... it wasn't a masterpiece (despite symmetry in variations like in a nice study) and it wasn't a drama either. It was more study material for a textbook. Yet it would be a sin not to quote the final sentence: "An endgame worthy of two of the greatest masters of modern times!"

Panov: "Bronstein – Botvinnik was the central game of round 7. The

В. СИМАГИН.
Дружеский шарж
И. Соколова и И. Рублева

Vladimir Simagin. After their first game in 1943 Botvinnik never again managed to defeat him: all four remaining games were drawn. Cartoon by I. Sokolov and I. Rublev. From the 19th Soviet Championship bulletin (28th December 1951).

opening stirred up the spectators' interest: white offered the King's Gambit. Botvinnik boldly accepted the pawn sacrifice. And, as is known, Bronstein won all 10 games in which he played the King's Gambit in recent years...

> **Bronstein:** "During preparation for the 1951 world championship match, I couldn't solve the mystery of Botvinnik, the secret of his constant victories. However, I was lucky to find a more important thing: the algorithm of my own play in the upcoming match. After studying a few hundred of the world champion's games, I made an important decision: to improvise at the board at all cost, despite the obvious risks.
>
> Why? It's perfectly clear! Botvinnik is at the cutting edge of chess theory, and what we know today, he already knew yesterday. And, therefore, what we'll only know tomorrow, Botvinnik already knows today...
>
> But just a year later, I forgot my own golden rule and, rather naively, offered the world champion a King's Gambit. Of course, he was prepared for the opening." (From the book *200 Open Games*.)
>
> And in his notebook, he wrote, "It's all fine, but why did I have to play for a win to the point of insanity? It was an equal position, I didn't want to do it."

Botvinnik played the opening with classical recipes, immediately returning the gambit pawn and creating a solid position in the center. Bronstein played 13.g3?! Then made a positional mistake that's inexcusable for a world-class chess player, locking his own light-squared bishop out of play with 15.c4?... As a result, black essentially had an extra piece in the middlegame, the decisive stage of the game!

The fans watching the game were rather disappointed. Losing to a world champion in 25 moves is not something to be ashamed of, but playing in such a careless style that

Гроссмейстер Д. БРОНШТЕЙН.
Дружеский шарж
И. СОКОЛОВА и И. ФРОЛОВА.

Bronstein's choice of King's Gambit against Botvinnik hardly surprised the knowledgeable fans: he'd tried to taunt his formidable opponent even in the world championship match. Cartoon by I. Sokolov and I. Frolov. From the 19ᵗʰ Soviet championship bulletin (3ʳᵈ March 1952).

you rarely see even in simultaneous displays, such obvious underestimation of such a formidable opponent, deserves severe reprehension.

> What does underestimation have to do with anything? He'd already tried to "yank the lion's tail" before. I remember asking him in an interview, "David Ionovich, admit it: did you deliberately taunt Botvinnik in your match?" He said with a smile, "Yes, of course. Unfortunately, I did taunt him. Unfortunately..." And then, talking about that 22nd game, he repeated, "You said that I taunted him. Yes, I taunted him! You solved the mystery. I made five very stupid moves – and he didn't know how to attack."
>
> And when Bronstein went for the Botvinnik System in the previous tournament, didn't he taunt the "formidable opponent"? Of course he did. With the King's Gambit, he again challenged the champion: losing in a "cafe" opening would be humiliating for him... But, as we know, revenge is best served cold.

The chess of Smyslov, another Moscow fan favorite, is also unrecognizable. It seems at times that he's not using all the resources of his great talent to the full and isn't developing it. The reason for the principal flaw of Smyslov's play recently is his narrow opening repertoire.

In reply to the Sicilian Defense deployed by Moiseev, he went for the Closed Variation, as usual. And, even though Smyslov managed to create a dangerous-looking threat to the opponent's king, the activated black pieces, led by a talented master, put up stiff resistance, and after a spectacular skirmish, the game ended in a draw.

Simagin won a brilliant game. Goldenov played poorly in the Nimzo-Indian Defense and created an irreparable weakness in his camp – the e6 square. The struggle to claim this key to black's position started immediately. The kingside attack grew with every move, and the white rook soon invaded on e6. The final stage of the attack was executed very cleanly by Simagin *(see game 255)*.

Taimanov is playing boldly and confidently in this championship, with enviable ease – he wasn't afraid to put his recently earned grandmaster title to a new test. A great example for some players!

The King's Indian Defense was played in the game Taimanov – Konstantinopolsky. Soon black misevaluated his prospects and forced simplifications, but the position changed in his opponent's favor. White went for an endgame; his bishop was clearly stronger than the knight, the rook got into his opponent's camp, and the king marched inexorably towards the weak black queenside pawns." (Tournament bulletin, 22nd December.)

Petrosian and **Tarasov:** "The struggle in round 8 was even more intense. For the first time, everything had already been clarified on almost all boards before 10 p.m., and several minutes later, only one table was left occupied in the first row: Smyslov was thinking on his last time-control move in the game against Byvshev.

On move 37, despite severe time trouble, the young master evaluated the position correctly and, totally sure of his success, decided to give up a rook for knight... The game is adjourned. Even though Smyslov hasn't yet exhausted all his attacking moves, he's unlikely to stop the victorious advance of white's passed pawns *(see game 257)*...

The game between Botvinnik and Keres attracted exceptional interest. A well-known line of the Queen's Gambit was played, and white started to prepare a pawn advance in the center. Keres maneuvered poorly with his minor pieces and allowed the world champion to exert strong pressure along the f-file after advancing his pawns. Black's position deteriorated with every move. On the 30th move, Botvinnik transferred the knight to h6 and created unstoppable threats to the black king... This game was played very well by the world champion *(see game 254)*.

Geller is always ready to play the King's Indian as black. This time, he had to fight against his favorite weapon with the white pieces. In the middle of the game, Geller seized the initiative and steered the game towards a won ending. On the 44th move, tournament leader Boleslavsky suffered his first defeat." (*Sovietsky Sport*, 11th December.)

Aronin also lost his first game, unable to cope with Taimanov in the King's Indian. Now all 20 players had suffered at least one defeat!

Standings after round 8: Taimanov – 6; Boleslavsky, Botvinnik, Korchnoi – 5.5; Geller – 5; Bronstein, Moiseev, Tolush – 4.5; Aronin, Ilivitsky, Simagin – 4; Byvshev, Keres, Lipnitsky, Smyslov, Suetin – 3.5; Konstantinopolsky – 3; Kan – 2.5; Goldenov, Kasparyan – 2.

Taimanov Breaks Away

Ravinsky: "Each round turns into a kind of match between grandmasters and masters. In round 9, there was a 7-board match like that. The grandmasters scored an impressive victory, winning four games and drawing three...

Moiseev had black against Boleslavsky, and used a system recommended by his opponent. In recent years, the Boleslavsky system in the Sicilian Defense has become widely popular. Black uses it quite successfully, and no wonder that it's under close attention from theoreticians. In this game, Boleslavsky failed to refute his own system...

Petrosian and **Tarasov:** "Botvinnik went for an idiosyncratic line in the Chigorin System, deploying a new piece structure *(14...♗d6 – see game 257, note to move 12)*. Lipnitsky opened the a-file and then transferred his knights to the center, where they assumed important positions. Botvinnik had to trade his dark-squared bishop for one of the knights, and white obtained the bishop pair... Not long before time control, Lipnitsky could have gone for a threefold repetition, but decided against it. The game was agreed a draw without play resuming." (*Sovietsky Sport*, 13th December.)

In the game Simagin – Taimanov, the Nimzowitsch Attack, where white tries to invade the central e5 square with pieces (this opening is successfully used by the young Moscow master Antoshin), occurred with a different move order *(1.b3 d5 2.♗b2 c5 3.e3 ♘c6 etc.)*. Simagin played somewhat recklessly in the middlegame. Trying to create a direct attack on the king, he decided to sacrifice an exchange, but Taimanov sacrificed an exchange of his own and gained a decisive advantage... He reinforced his lead with this win.

Panov: "Simagin sometimes ignores the necessity of positional preparation and tries to create sharp skirmishes at the cost of a pawn or piece sacrifice (and sometimes at **any** cost!). Thus, despite Simagin's immense talent and a number of beautiful combination attacks executed by him, there have been too few strategically consistent, seamless games in his career – ones where the breadth of ideas is combined with the logically following mastery of maneuvers and the clarity of the finishing tactical blow." (Tournament bulletin, 12th January 1953.)

Korchnoi likes to use structures where he has to fight against his opponent's strong pawn center. In the game against Byvshev, his task was made easier by the black queen's poor maneuvering in the opening...

Bronstein deployed the rare move 10.d5 in the Meran System and got a better position. Tolush sacrificed an exchange to ease up the position a bit. Bronstein could have accepted the sacrifice, which would have given him a clear advantage. However, he went for a sharp continuation involving a piece sacrifice. In the resulting complications, both opponents played far from their best... Black ultimately blundered and resigned on move 36." (Tournament bulletin, 26th December.)

Petrosian: "In round 10, the games of young Leningrad players Taimanov and Byvshev attracted the most attention.

The tournament leader played against Bronstein, who chose his favorite King's Indian... When white closed off the center with 8.d5, the strategic structure of the battle was settled. Taimanov launched a queenside operation, while Bronstein intended to harass the opponent's king, transferring the rook to h6.

White's position on the kingside looked impregnable. And when the c-file opened, black's pieces were positioned rather awkwardly for defense. To stop white's invasion, Bronstein had to push his a- and b-pawns. Soon, the entire queenside was controlled by white... Taimanov won on move 41 *(see game 250)*.

The game between Byvshev and Boleslavsky was enthralling *(see game 256)*. The Richter-Rauzer Attack is known for its sharpness. Opposite-sides castling led to mutual attacks on the kings' positions... Byvshev's position became quite difficult towards the 22nd move, and he made the only correct decision: despite the losses, to try to open up the black king's position... They got into mutual time trouble, and Boleslavsky chose the wrong continuation. Instead of going on the defensive, which would have led to a win, he tried to create a counter-attack and made a decisive mistake." (Ibid.)

Petrosian and **Tarasov:** "One of the main merits of this tournament is the attacking onslaught of the young generation. It's no accident that such

Viktor Korchnoi's first game against Botvinnik. The young master managed to survive in terrible time trouble. From M. Botvinnik's archive.

luminaries as Keres, Smyslov and Boleslavsky have succumbed to Vasily Byvshev's attacks *(I can't help but remember Kopylov's exploits the previous year)*. Viktor Korchnoi showed his great talent. The 26 year-old Mark Taimanov had a great start: 8 points in 10 rounds. It's been a long time since someone achieved such a result in our championships!.. *(In 1944 and 1945, Botvinnik's start was even stronger – 8.5/10!)*

In round 11, Korchnoi played his first game against the world champion. Botvinnik strategically outplayed his young opponent with black. He had several opportunities to decide matters quickly, but preferred to transition to a won endgame.

> **Suetin:** "Korchnoi is similar to Tolush in his creative outlook. He strives for a tactical battle, finding unexpected possibilities even in the simplest positions." (Chess yearbook.)

The game Keres – Taimanov promised to become very sharp. In the Sicilian Defense, after opposite-sides castling, they reached a complicated position. With his 15th move, Taimanov sacrificed an exchange, but it turned out that the sacrifice didn't give him much chance to win. However, the young grandmaster still had an opportunity to force perpetual check, which he did immediately.

Byvshev won his fifth game. Kasparyan didn't get any advantage out of the opening with white, made a number of mistakes later and lost." (*Sovietsky Sport*, 16th and 18th December.)

Alatortsev: "Round 12. The fans were pleased with the great creative battle in the game between Botvinnik and Boleslavsky, who chose the King's Indian Defense. On the 14th move, Botvinnik put his knight under attack by a pawn. Several moves later, the world champion won a pawn, then, soon, an exchange *(not exactly "soon": the black rook was en prise for eight moves!)*, but returned the pawn, and then, in the subsequent struggle, the exchange as well. We can say that there was a period of temporary mutual sacrifices from the 14th to 30th moves.

The material balance didn't last for long. The world champion again got an extra pawn. However, Boleslavsky almost forced the white king into perpetual check along the 1st and 2nd ranks. Botvinnik evaded the checks but returned the pawn. On move 42, the grandmaster battle ended in a draw.

> **Yudovich:** "The term 'grandmaster draw' appeared in the early 20th century as a direct consequence of the impoverishment of chess thought in foreign competitions. The reactionary theories of chess' 'draw by death'

assigned a 'theoretical' basis to the businesslike approach to chess creativity, providing excuses to top players who avoided real fights.

The Soviet chess school, developing the traditions of Chigorin and Alekhine, dealt a crushing blow to the 'draw by death' apologists, and brought new, incredibly rich content to the art of chess. The term 'grandmaster draw' now sounds like an anachronism. The games between grandmasters can and should be highly sharp, combative and interesting. The games between the strongest players should teach the art of battle to the young.

The game between grandmasters Botvinnik and Boleslavsky was one such game." (Tournament book.)

There was a substitution in our championship: 'Byvshev' *(whose surname approximately translates as 'the Former')* was replaced by 'Nastoyaschev' *('the Present')* or even 'Buduschev' *('the Future')*, as people were saying in the tournament hall. The talented Leningrad player passed his maturity exam with flying colors. His wins against Keres, Boleslavsky and Smyslov will be remembered by all spectators for a long time to come.

Today, Byvshev played boldly against Kan, temporarily sacrificing an exchange. When the game was adjourned, he had two extra pawns that brought him a full point during the play-off." (Tournament bulletin, 28th December.)

Standings after round 12: Taimanov – 9.5; Geller, Korchnoi – 8; Boleslavsky, Botvinnik – 7.5; Bronstein, Moiseev, Tolush – 7; Byvshev – 6.5; Aronin, Ilivitsky, Keres, Simagin, Smyslov – 6; Suetin – 5.5; Lipnitsky – 4; Kan, Konstantinopolsky – 3.5; Goldenov – 3; Kasparyan – 2.5.

Chasing the Leader

Bondarevsky: "Round 13. The game Smyslov – Taimanov attracted special attention from the numerous spectators. Smyslov deployed the most principled set-up in the Nimzo-Indian Defense – he got the bishop pair in exchange for weakened queenside pawns. The game immediately sharpened. White was the first to go for resolute action. Both opponents made the moves after 18.♘g5 very quickly – apparently, they had calculated the subsequent complications beforehand... Smyslov went for a very comfortable endgame, but failed to convert his chances in time trouble.

Petrosian and **Tarasov:** "Kasparyan started the game with 1.e4. After the early c2-c4-c5 *(in the French Defense line 1...e6 2.d4 d5 3.exd5 exd5 4.♘f3 ♗d6)* it became clear that events would be very interesting.

Botvinnik seized the e4 square with his knight and played f7-f5, and then launched kingside activity... There was a moment when it seemed that Kasparyan wouldn't be able to avoid defeat: black threatened to destroy the white king's defenses with a piece sacrifice. But white's position remained impregnable." (*Sovietsky Sport*, 20th December.)

By the 15th round, Taimanov had a 2-point lead over his closest pursuers! A photo taken during the championship.

Geller suffered a setback. Moiseev used a solid, but somewhat passive defensive system in the Queen's Gambit. Geller had a small positional advantage for about 30 moves... Then time trouble set in. Trying to confuse his opponent, the grandmaster went for complications, which, however, ended quite miserably for him.

The game Ilivitsky – Byvshev was adjourned in a slightly better endgame for black. In the play-off, white failed to create counterplay, and the game was adjourned again in a won position for Byvshev." (Tournament bulletin, 2nd January 1953.)

Indeed, such a thing had never happened in the championship before: scoring 7 points out of 8 after 0.5/5 at the start was a phenomenal achievement by Vasily Byvshev! However, the nervous strain eventually did take its toll: a bad streak began in the very next round...

Zagoriansky: "Round 14. Another brilliant game by Tolush – one of the chess fans' favorites *(in round 12, he had already destroyed Smyslov – see game 253)*. On move 11, Boleslavsky, after a long think, decided to sacrifice his queen for a rook and knight, hoping to exploit the poor development of white's pieces on the kingside. However, white completed his development without much hindrance, his pieces got space, and soon black lost more material. Tolush scored an important victory on move 29.

Taimanov played one of his closest pursuers... As usual, Korchnoi got into severe time trouble and inventively sought out tactical chances. However, with the last move before time control he lost any chance to save the game, dropping a piece and then the point...

The game Byvshev – Geller was quite interesting. White's position was better for a long time, but on the 34th move Geller, deeply and subtly evaluating the position, sacrificed an exchange for a pawn. Byvshev accepted the sacrifice, and... black seized the advantage. Soon, Geller won another pawn and adjourned the game with good winning chances... Byvshev resigned on move 85." (Ibid., 5th January.)

Lilienthal: "We can argue over what exactly should be considered the final leg of a big tournament, but the last five rounds are definitely a final leg, a 'home stretch'.

Before round 15, Taimanov had 11 points – a brilliant score! The gap between him and Botvinnik, Geller and Moiseev was quite substantial – two points. Would any of them manage to close the gap in the last five rounds and challenge for the esteemed title of Soviet champion?..

The leader, of course, realized that in case of a favorable result in the game against Boleslavsky, his lead would be reinforced so much that nobody would be likely to catch him up, let alone overtake him. Perhaps that's why Taimanov, who had black, went for early trades and simplifications, hoping to reach a draw safe haven quickly. However, it's long known that such a strategy is bad for tournament struggle.

The game reached the endgame stage on move 20. The advantage of white, who had two active bishops in an open position and a queenside initiative, was beyond doubt. Boleslavsky's endgame technique was outstanding...

The leader's loss sharpened the tournament standings. All three of his pursuers energetically strove for a win.

Botvinnik, who had black against Ilivitsky, quickly equalized in a Catalan. After a mass trade on the c-file, the world champion's forward-thinking idea became obvious. With subtle maneuvers, he won an important pawn. All of Ilivitsky's efforts to give perpetual check proved to be unsuccessful, and the game was adjourned. But this only delayed the inevitable loss for a short while.

Probably not everyone knows that the young Moscow master Moiseev was Kotov's coach at the Stockholm tournament. We can say for sure that Moiseev maintained his reputation – he's playing temperamentally and powerfully in this championship. The battle between Moiseev and Byvshev was sharp and intense. Both opponents eagerly went for complications. The position was unclear, and Byvshev was in time trouble as well. The Moscow player won, elegantly cutting off the paths to retreat for the opposing queen...

> **Kotov:** "At the 1952 Interzonal tournament, I was helped by master Oleg Leonidovich Moiseev, a chess player with great positional understanding. I think that Moiseev's over-the-board results were well below his knowledge and chess understanding. Moiseev was indispensable as a coach and assistant. In Saltsjobaden, he undertook heroic efforts to ensure my victory.
>
> I especially remember our walks before the game. Even though it often rained outside, the northern wind howled, and Oleg quietly, innocently grumbled, he would always accompany me for an hour-long walk before every game. He quoted Mayakovsky's entire poems by heart to me, read lyrical verses, interspersing them with humorous 'homebrewed' quatrains. Time passed very quickly during these walks, and, what's more important, my coach distracted me from thoughts about the upcoming fights, and this was the most important thing in these times of great nervous strain." (From the book *Mastery*.)

Thus, Botvinnik and Moiseev were just one point behind Taimanov after round 15. It seemed that Geller would join them as well. But this didn't happen – and he can only blame himself.

At the early stage of the game, Suetin missed a tactical blow and lost his queen and a pawn for a rook and bishop. Still, he decided to resist further, and his efforts were suddenly rewarded. Geller, probably sure of an easy win, played shallowly and allowed Suetin to create a closed position, similar to an impregnable fortress. At any rate, Geller failed to break through...

Bronstein's interpretation of the opening in the game against Lipnitsky was quite fresh. After 1.d4 e6 2.e4 d5 3.♘d2 ♘c6 4. ♘gf3

he played 4...g6 5.c3 ♗g7 6.♗d3 ♘h6 7.e5 f6 8.exf6 ♛xf6, then castled long, played the break e6-e5 and seized the initiative. Bronstein's idea deserves serious consideration *(still, 4...♘f6 remains the main line)*. Incredibly puzzling complications ensued, with almost all 'main' pieces being *en prise* at one point or another, but they ended in a rook and bishop ending with an equal amount of pawns... A draw." (Ibid.)

Standings after round 15: Taimanov – 11; Botvinnik, Moiseev – 10; Boleslavsky, Geller, Korchnoi, Tolush – 9.5; Bronstein – 8.5; Keres, Smyslov – 8; Byvshev, Suetin – 7.5; Aronin, Simagin – 7; Ilivitsky – 6.5; Lipnitsky – 5.5; Kan – 4.5; Konstantinopolsky – 4; Goldenov, Kasparyan – 3.5.

Steps of the Commander

Petrosian and **Tarasov:** "Round 16. Botvinnik had played Geller twice and had ceded a whole point to him both times. In the previous championship, Geller, still a master, won in an intense struggle. He defeated Botvinnik for the second time at the Budapest tournament.

The world champion, like in the previous two encounters, had white and played 1.d4. Geller chose the King's Indian Defense – but a line that he usually doesn't employ *(6... ♘c6 instead of 6... ♘bd7)*.

> **Panov:** "Black's entire system did not fit Geller's style, since the white king was totally safe. Geller's efforts to create a queenside counter-attack were easily and fundamentally stopped by Botvinnik, who was probably only glad that his opponent moved all his forces to the queenside, weakening the kingside. At the right moment, Botvinnik launched an attack along the e-file. The pawn reached the e6 square (something unheard of in this opening), and white's pawn chain essentially cut black's position in half..." (Tournament bulletin, 7ᵗʰ January.)

In a difficult position, Geller lost a piece and resigned after a few moves. *(This was Botvinnik's only win over Geller in his entire career, with four losses and three draws; the Odessa player won all his games with black!)*

Taimanov took another important step towards winning the championship. He played the whole game against Kasparyan very well; the latter played a very fanciful opening and got into serious trouble because of his queen's poor position. Kasparyan's attempt to free himself from the growing pressure with 19... f5 led to unfortunate consequences...

> This championship was the fourth one for the future chess composition grandmaster **Genrikh Moiseevich Kasparyan**. What other great study composer can boast of such achievements in over-the-board play?!

Ragozin: "Kasparyan, a master in over-the-board play, is also a master of composition. He is currently rightfully considered the strongest chess composer both in the Soviet Union and the entire world. As a player, he likes complicated struggle and always strives to create new, original positions. Alas, he often underestimates the importance of laws of chess strategy and loses as a result. The limitations of the game are too tight for the flight of his creative fantasy, and this explains Kasparyan's relatively poor sporting achievements. However, he's an unsurpassed master of analysis." (Ibid., 12th January.)

This championship was the last for Genrikh Kasparyan. From Y. Neishtadt's archive. Published for the first time.

Byvshev, after a great performance in the middle of the tournament, again lost the required balance and, losing three games in a row *(the third loss was to Konstantinopolsky)*, worsened his standing considerably.

To earn the right to become a grandmaster, Tolush has to finish in the top three. This compels him to play only for a win. In the game with Kan, he took a gamble and sacrificed two pawns in the opening, trying to attack the king immediately. However, Kan easily countered the threats and seized the initiative with an exchange sacrifice. Correctly evaluating the position, Tolush sacrificed an exchange of his own and steered the game towards an ending where black's extra pawn would mean nothing because of the opposite-colored bishops...

Aronin caused Boleslavsky a lot of trouble and will probably take an important point off him; if Boleslavsky won, he would have still competed for one of the top places *(the grandmaster resigned without resuming the game)*...

Zagoriansky: "Aronin has managed to get rid of his shyness before the big names, but there are still other flaws in his play. The most important of them is his shallowness of evaluation, the element of superficiality. This defect costs him a lot...

Aronin is 32 years old, he loves chess and works on it. There's no doubt that the greatest successes are still ahead for this gifted master." (Ibid., 9th January.)

The battle between Keres and Lipnitsky was sharp. The national champion has been performing quite poorly in this tournament. In trying to improve his standing, he launched a tempestuous attack on Lipnitsky, but it was ultimately unsuccessful, and he lost.

Round 17. Moiseev has white against Botvinnik. The young master has the same chances to win the Soviet Championship as the world's strongest chess player, and their game is central to the entire round.

The position from this game is being analyzed on pocket chess sets by many spectators. The demonstration boards are watched both in the hall and the lobby. The moves are relayed by phone to the Moscow clubs. There are calls from other cities as well. Even fans who failed to get tickets have gathered around the demonstration board installed at the TsDKZh entrance.

Levenfish: "The previous round went badly for three championship contenders. Boleslavsky, Geller and Moiseev lost. It became obvious that only Botvinnik and Taimanov would compete for first place at the finish.

Taimanov is a point ahead, and to catch him, Botvinnik has to play for a win in all the remaining three games. For this reason, Botvinnik returned to the Grunfeld Defense in his game against Moiseev – an opening that was part of his arsenal for years, but occurred only once in his match with Bronstein." (Ibid.)

After losing to Botvinnik in round 17, Oleg Moiseev also lost all hope for first place. From Y. Neishtadt's archive. Published for the first time.

The spectators were also interested in the game Kan –

Taimanov. However, the leader, who is one point ahead, does not want to take risks. Cautiously playing the Queen's Indian, he goes for simplifications. Kan sacrifices a pawn. It seems like the position has sharpened. But all of the master's attempts to seize the initiative are futile... A draw on move 25.

> **Levenfish:** "Moiseev solved the opening problem very well, and on the 16th move white's pressure in the center, reinforced by two active bishops, became significant.. The crisis came on the 26th move. White had several strong continuations, but he played 26.f4 too hastily, and black managed to push back the bishops... Botvinnik sacrificed a pawn and created a dangerous passer on c3. In his turn, Moiseev skillfully activated his bishops, and had he interposed with his bishop on the 39th move, he would have been able to save the game. After the erroneous 39.♔h2, Botvinnik won an exchange with a simple combination." (Ibid.)

The play-off day before the last rounds always attracts special interest from chess fans. Almost all demonstration boards are used, and the battle rages on everywhere... Taking a 15-minute rest *(after losing a 112-move game to Suetin, the longest in the whole tournament)*, Moiseev continued his fight with Botvinnik. The world champion is not only a formidable opponent over the board – he's also an outstanding master of home analysis. He proved this reputation once again in the game against Moiseev...

Smyslov had white against Keres. In the middle of the game, Keres had to give up a pawn. During the play-off, Smyslov first won another pawn in the endgame, then created two connected passed pawns and forced the national champion to resign on move 56." (*Sovietsky Sport*, 25th and 27th December.)

Alatortsev: "The penultimate round. Today Botvinnik tried to catch up with the leader, but... unsuccessfully.

Taimanov confidently advanced towards his goal. Ilivitsky equalized the position, but then got tempted to win a pawn. His light-squared bishop got stuck on the queenside, and black got a difficult position. Taimanov seized the long diagonal, creating unstoppable threats to the black king...

In the game between Botvinnik and Byvshev, the world champion had an advantage, but it got suddenly complicated before the break. Botvinnik won an exchange for two pawns and invaded the 7th rank with his rook. But he underestimated his opponent's tactical ability. The resourceful Leningrad player put up great resistance and brilliantly used his chance to save the game. Botvinnik missed the cunning reply 40...♗d7 that drastically changed the situation on the board (had Byvshev played 40...♗c6!, he would have probably achieved even more). The adjourned position was thoroughly analyzed. The chances were equal, and so the opponents agreed to a draw without resuming the game *(see game 261)*.

Korchnoi has shown himself to be an inventive player. But today he played too carelessly against Keres. On move 16, the master lost a bishop and knight for a rook and had to resign on move 22 under threat of further material losses.

> **Korchnoi:** "My first game with Keres. The very first encounter always plays an important role, greatly influences the subsequent relationship at the chessboard. And so, when Keres played against young opponents, he was always no-nonsense. Exploiting my poor opening play, he sacrificed a pawn, got a great initiative and won in 22 moves. Afterwards, I treated Keres with reverence and even some fear. He became my most difficult opponent. I couldn't even get a better position against him, let alone defeat him *(he won his only game against Keres in 1975)*. More than twenty years later, in a difficult situation for me, when supporting me was basically tantamount to disobeying the authorities, Keres was one of the few who wasn't afraid to offer his help (before the 1974 match with Karpov). I had to decline the offer – his authority was too great for me, I felt overwhelmed." (From the book *Chess Without Mercy*.)

Tolush played Geller, who chose the King's Indian Defense... With 12... d5, Geller exploded white's pawn center, and then, accepting a pawn sacrifice, suddenly gave away his queen for two minor pieces. Geller's overly bold play soon justified itself – he managed to restore the material balance, gaining a rook, a bishop and two pawns for his queen. But the position remained double-edged...

Geller repeated moves, seemingly ready to agree to a draw. Tolush declined, and it was a mistake; he overestimated his resources, sacrificed a bishop for two pawns and tried to use his active queen in vain. In the subsequent struggle, Geller proved the strength of his pieces and won." (Tournament bulletin, 9th January.)

Standings after round 18: Taimanov – 13.5; Botvinnik – 12.5; Boleslavsky, Geller – 11; Bronstein, Moseev, Tolush – 10.5; Korchnoi, Smyslov – 10; Suetin – 9.5; Aronin, Keres – 9; Byvshev, Ilivitsky – 8; Simagin – 7.5; Konstantinopolsky, Lipnitsky – 7; Kan – 6; Goldenov – 5; Kasparyan – 4.5.

Who Asked for a Happy Ending?

Yudovich: "Will Botvinnik be able to catch up with Taimanov? This is the question that torments all the tournament participants, all the spectators who filled the Great Hall of the TsDKZh and all the chess fans anxiously waiting for the special chess radio program today.

Will he or won't he? Botvinnik's task is made even more difficult by the fact that it's not enough for him to win. Taimanov is one point ahead, and so only his losing would give Botvinnik chances for first place. Both have black.

Taimanov chose the Nimzo-Indian Defense. However, Geller deviated from the well-known lines and chose a new continuation *(he improved upon the game Matanovic – Taimanov from the Stockholm Interzonal – 8.c5 instead of 8.cxd5)*. The game quickly sharpened, and Geller seized the initiative, even though it weakened his queenside pawn chain *(see game 262)*.

Meanwhile, the game Suetin – Botvinnik was played without many complications. The world champion chose a difficult line in the Sicilian that he used earlier against Bronstein and Bondarevsky. It seemed as though the world champion had peaceful intentions. He didn't avoid simplifications, and queens were traded by the 15th move.

'Can you really play for a win like that? Or has Botvinnik already accepted second place?' many spectators wondered.

Yes, that's exactly how you should play for a win. You shouldn't avoid simplifications if your position otherwise gets weakened. You shouldn't rush headlong into an attack – such playing for a win is deservedly called 'playing for a loss' – but you should rather create difficult problems for your opponent in the endgame as well. You should remember that even in so-called 'simple' positions, resources in chess are inexhaustible.

> **Botvinnik:** "I approached Geller during the round.
> 'So, how's it going?'
> 'Go and work, go and work...' the Odessa player replied." (From the book *Achieving the Aim.*)

At the same time that Geller skillfully launched an attack on Taimanov's position, Botvinnik, defending against Suetin's threats along the f-file, made a sudden positional pawn sacrifice that led to more piece trades *(see game 263)*.

White's onslaught in the game Geller – Taimanov was so swift that the leader didn't have time to create a counter-attack, his pieces were pushed back to their initial positions, and Geller won a pawn. It seemed that the game was over. But Geller made some inaccuracies in time trouble and gave Taimanov an opportunity to get some counterchances. The game was adjourned, and Taimanov had to seal a move. It seems that he was too agitated to find the correct move 42...♖f8!. After the bad move 42...♖b8, Geller deservedly won.

The result of the Suetin versus Botvinnik game was very important for Mark Taimanov. From M. Botvinnik's archive.

And in the game Suetin – Botvinnik, white, a pawn up in a 'simple' endgame, got into trouble...

Botvinnik: "During the play-off, Geller won quickly, and I made some bad moves, and, despite black having an extra pawn, the endgame was drawn. And then a miracle happened – Suetin carelessly pushed his king into the center, and, even though only nine pieces remained on the board, the white king got caught in a mating net!" (Ibid.)

Suetin: "I only played one game with Botvinnik. This happened in the last round of the 20th Soviet Championship. Botvinnik had to win on demand. My tournament standing was good as well, and I certainly wasn't intending to lose. But it all started when I played badly in his signature opening line and got a difficult position. I defended tenaciously and almost managed to equalize, but then made a mistake right before the time control and lost a pawn.

I was very upset. Forgoing rest and food, I analyzed the game late into the night. The play-off took place early next morning. I went to the game tired and hungry, but in a fighting mood.

To my surprise, Botvinnik didn't play too well. A draw seemed realistic. I saw that my mighty opponent looked confused and unsure. And then I let my guard down, made a bad move and lost in a very simple position. Hiding my bitterness, I congratulated the world champion on his win.

I've never seen such a kind and charming Botvinnik as during the analysis of that game. *(In the book* Outstanding Soviet Chess Players, *there were two more sentences:* "And in the evening, showing the endgame, he was generous with compliments. Such a pity that cassette recorders didn't exist back then!")

Now I think sometimes that this ill-fated game became the reason for our good relationship in the 1950s. In the middle of that decade, the champion agreed to give me a consultation, and I even got to visit his home...

His attitude towards me changed drastically in 1963, when I became Petrosian's coach during their battle for the world crown. This continued for a long time. By Botvinnik's logic, I 'stood in his way', and he never forgave that... For a time, he didn't do anything actively. But then, in 1967, I was 'nominated' by the Sports Committee to play at the prestigious Palma de Mallorca tournament. Shortly before the start, I learned that I was going together with Botvinnik... I was crestfallen: everything looked very shaky, even though my friend Petrosian assured me that Botvinnik didn't object, and everything would be OK. But then, a week before traveling, I suddenly learned that I was removed from the line-up. Later, the chess section chairman of the day (Beilin) confidentially explained the reason for my removal to me. Yes, Botvinnik didn't object with the Sports Committee, but immediately filed a petition to the higher-ups that he couldn't stay abroad together with me.

About 20 years later, I was commissioned by Sportverlag to write a book about Botvinnik; the Verlag management gave it the title *Das Schachgenie Botwinnik (The Chess Genius Botvinnik)*. I must point out that Botvinnik, unlike, say, Morphy and Alekhine, had never got such a flattering 'label' before (so, Sportverlag probably played a historical role in that). I didn't present the book to Botvinnik myself. But, judging by the fact that he warmed up to me considerably, I realized that he had held it in his hands. Still, such 'sympathies' are very fragile.

Perhaps this 'clash' with me was something exceptional, not characteristic of him? Unfortunately, I think that it was a rather typical case. Isn't it telling that in 1952, in his heyday, the USSR team members unanimously voted against him playing at the Olympiad, citing his bad form at the pre-tournament training camp?" (From the book *Chess Through the Prism of Time*.)

So, first and second places were shared by Taimanov, who played brilliantly in the first half of the tournament, and Botvinnik, who had a great finish.

All the other encounters were overshadowed by the leaders' games, even though many of them were also important for determining the standings..." (Tournament bulletin, 12th January.)

From the press: "On 29th December, the closing ceremony of the 20th Soviet Championship took place in TsDKZh. Chief arbiter I. Bondarevsky reported on the results of the tournament.

To determine the 1952 Soviet champion, it was decided to hold a six-game match between grandmasters Botvinnik and Taimanov, who shared 1st and 2nd place, in January.

Grandmaster Geller, who took 3rd place, was rewarded with a bronze token and a third-degree diploma. Grandmaster Boleslavsky and masters Tolush and Korchnoi were awarded certificates of the USSR Council of Ministers' Committee for Physical Education and Sport." (Ibid., 14th January.)

Significant Results

This was the title of Peter Arsenyevich Romanovsky's article, and it's hard to disagree with him. For the second championship in a row, the young generation had forcefully announced themselves, and again, the reputation of the chess elders was only saved in the very last round by the hand of fate that allowed Keres to overtake Geller the previous time and Botvinnik to catch up with Taimanov this time.

Final standings: 1–2. Botvinnik, Taimanov – 13.5/19; 3. Geller – 12; 4–5. Boleslavsky, Tolush – 11.5; 6. Korchnoi – 11; 7–9. Bronstein, Moiseev, Smyslov – 10.5; 10–11. Keres, Suetin – 9.5; 12–13. Aronin, Byvshev – 9; 14–15. Ilivitsky, Simagin – 8.5; 16. Konstantinopolsky – 7.5; 17. Lipnitsky – 7; 18. Kan – 6.5; 19. Kasparyan – 5.5; 20. Goldenov – 5.

Romanovsky: "The creative thought of the leading Soviet chess players is shining brightly – this is the first significant and joyous result of the championship. Unfortunately, not all players equally managed to show their boldness and daring, aspiration for something new, or their creative growth.

The creative atmosphere of the tournament was mainly set by the Leningrad participants – Taimanov, Tolush, Korchnoi, Byvshev, and also by world champion Botvinnik and Grandmaster Geller.

The tremendous sporting result achieved by Taimanov might seem unexpected to many, but if we look into the content of his games at the

The closing ceremony. The championship was held "under a huge, overwhelming portrait of Stalin" (Korchnoi). The first page of the tournament bulletin (No. 14, 1953).

Stockholm Interzonal, we can easily say that his championship win was well-deserved.

There's little gloss in Taimanov's games, but he doesn't specifically strive for it. His games are sometimes dogmatic, technically dry, and creative interests are occasionally subordinated to sporting calculations. But this is not the main feature of the young grandmaster's creativity. Taimanov possesses great theoretical knowledge that has become an integral part of his deep plans. Taimanov links his openings with middlegame strategy and is able to execute his plans with consistency and tenacity...

Taimanov can easily find his way in difficult positions and he is particularly adept at refuting attacks launched without due preparation. Bronstein, Simagin, Korchnoi, and Byvshev fell victims to such premature attacks. It's hard to defeat Taimanov. Out of his three defeats in the tournament, only the game against Boleslavsky was lost as a result of a proper, intense struggle.

Taimanov is the only player who managed to defeat the world champion in this tournament.

> **Zagoriansky:** "Taimanov's playing style has deepened, solidified, become more polished. He isn't afraid of complications, he calculates deeply and precisely, almost never making a mistake. He has a healthy, logical positional understanding, great composure, enviable tenacity... Let's add that Taimanov plays with incredible ease, that he's not prone to time trouble – and you'll see a chess player of great playing strength with a wonderful future." (Tournament bulletin, 2nd January.)

Because of the relative setbacks suffered by Botvinnik in 1951 (the 19th Soviet Championship) and 1952 (the Budapest tournament), our chess community watched his latest outing with special interest.

After six rounds, Botvinnik had 3.5 points, and his chess was still as uncertain as during the previous year. Then he played Bronstein and Keres. Both grandmasters were destroyed in their games. It seemed that everything was going well, but... five draws in a row followed, and the distance between the leader, Taimanov, and the world champion increased to 2 points.

Six rounds were left until the end of the tournament – a very short distance to close such a gap. In round 14, both won, but in round 15, Taimanov lost and Botvinnik won again. The gap decreased to one point and remained as such until the last round, when Taimanov lost to Geller, and Botvinnik defeated Suetin. 5.5 points out of 6! – an exceptional finish from the world champion.

This is, of course, a great victory for Botvinnik – not as much against Taimanov as in the struggle against himself. The tournament didn't go too well, and to steer the events in such a strong fashion, when battling numerous competitors, you have to be at least a world champion!..

> **Flohr:** "In the last two or three years, many 'experts' thought that Botvinnik was not the same, that he had grown old, that he was too nervous. Only people who didn't know Botvinnik's great willpower, his great work rate, his ironclad composure. It's not in Botvinnik's nature to give up the high

ground at the age of 41! The tournament showed that Botvinnik had started to regain his good form (even though it's still not at its best), and Botvinnik's numerous fans are glad that the doctor of technical sciences is still playing very good chess.

If we consider the Soviet championship as a kind of mini world championship, then Botvinnik confirmed his world championship title. Sharing first place with his own pupil Taimanov is also a moral success for Botvinnik. In four years, Taimanov has grown significantly, his play is stable, without setbacks. Taimanov's brilliant win is the best achievement in his short career. But I'm sure that Taimanov will 'harass' his chess teacher many more times." (*Ogonyok*, No. 2, 1953.)

Let's say a few words about the youngest participant of the tournament – Viktor Korchnoi. The creative tendencies of this chess player are very interesting. Despite his youth, he possesses relatively big experience and good technique. Korchnoi's chess is far from matching established patterns, his thinking is bold and original, he prepares and executes combinations very well. Nevertheless, all this happens somewhat shapelessly in Korchnoi's play, it looks unfinished.

This game was played in the last round. Had Boleslavsky (left) won against Keres, he would have caught up with Geller, but alas... From I. Boleslavsky's archive. Published for the first time.

Often, when clear and simple solutions are needed, he goes for needless complications without good reason. Sometimes this leads to fanciful play. Korchnoi obviously disregards the classics. That's the main reason for the disasters he suffered in the games against Suetin and Keres. Korchnoi's wins deserve attention because of the ideas he manages to implement, but there are too few games that look consistent.

> **Korchnoi:** "The 20th Soviet Championship was held on the stage of the Railway Workers House of Culture in Moscow, under a huge, overwhelming portrait of Stalin. Several months later, Stalin died. On that day, I had to go to a clinic for bandaging in the morning. The radio in the procedure room screamed away, repeating the news of the great man's death again and again. The nurse, an elderly Estonian woman, was almost hysterical. Only many years later did I realize that she was weeping for joy!
>
> But let's get back to the tournament. A difficult test for a novice, but a lot of memories, invaluable experience. My first game against Bronstein. I couldn't equalize with white in the Giuoco Piano. I basically stopped playing 1.e2-e4 after that game. My first game against Botvinnik. In a closed position, he gradually outplayed me. I couldn't understand the meaning behind his moves. Only about eight years later did I manage to comprehend the subtlety of his strategic ideas. When I got into time trouble, he became visibly agitated and let me out of his strategic grip. A draw...
>
> I took 6th place in the tournament, ahead of Smyslov, Bronstein, Keres and almost another dozen great players – a tremendous result!" (From the book *Chess Without Mercy*.)

Tolush's creativity speaks of eternal youth. 'You have to play, not offer draws,' he exclaimed angrily when one of his opponents in the 1943 Moscow championship offered him a draw in a winning position.

Tolush played a number of exciting games and, as always, showed examples of bold attacks executed with great creative inspiration. His games against Goldenov, Konstantinopolsky, Byvshev and especially Moiseev and Smyslov serve as a bright illustration of the domestic school's traditions.

> **Panov:** "Tolush is an optimist. He always believes that, even in the most adverse circumstances, he'll find some hidden tactical resource. Without a doubt, Tolush's creative journey is far from over, and great new successes await him." (Tournament bulletin, 24th December.) The prediction was incredibly spot on: just two months later, Tolush won an international tournament in

Bucharest, ahead of Petrosian, Smyslov, Boleslavsky and Spassky, and was awarded the Soviet grandmaster title!

Geller played well in the tournament. His thinking has become stricter and deeper, but hasn't lost its sharpness or inventiveness... Like Taimanov, Geller lost three games, but his losses to Smyslov and Moiseev speak more of his carelessness. Geller complained about his tiredness. Alas, it's not an explanation and surely not an excuse.

> **Kan:** "His style has got deeper and more versatile lately. Geller is now skillfully combining subtle positional understanding with active intentions. Bold combinations are interspersed with deeply planned simplifications that lead to a good endgame...
>
> We should point out that the punishing schedule, with the first rest day being the 8th in the tournament, exhausted many players." (*Shakhmaty v SSSR*, No. 4, 1953.)

Boleslavsky had a good start, winning four games and drawing two in the first six rounds. At that point he was the sole leader, but both of his draws – with Korchnoi (after 15 moves in a sharp position) and a dull 25-move one with Konstantinopolsky – were somewhat symptomatic. They spoke of his declining fighting spirit...

Boleslavsky decorated the tournament with several 'colorful' games in the 'good old' manner of his youth. He played decent attacks against Kan and Kasparyan, made a very interesting draw against Botvinnik and had a very strong game against Taimanov *(see game 260)*.

We should look differently at the failures, both sporting and creative, of several of the country's leading players. We chiefly mean our 'Olympians' – Bronstein, Keres and Smyslov. The chess community was baffled not so much by the results

The very next year, Vasily Smyslov would win the Candidates Tournament and challenge for the world championship. From V. Chepizhny's archive. Published for the first time.

themselves, but by the factors that led this outstanding trio to these frankly modest results.

What really hides behind Keres' 50-percent result? We would like him to answer this difficult question himself.

> **Keres:** "The successes in the last few years allowed me to hope for a good result at the Helsinki Olympiad. I was going to face strong opponents on first board. And, to my great disappointment, I had to admit that my form was very bad. I couldn't improve my play and only got a 50-percent result in the final group. The 20th national championship experience was similar. I stayed in the middle of the table for the most part and only managed to improve my standings somewhat in the last few rounds. However, I was still plagued by setbacks. I lost two games in a row, and only my win against Korchnoi got me back to 50 percent...
>
> This was my worst result both in the Soviet Championships and in the last ten years. The quality of games wasn't too high either. I obviously suffered from a creative decline." (From the book *One Hundred Games*.)

The aggressive, sharp, enterprising players Bronstein (games with Moiseev and Aronin) and Smyslov (game with Ilivitsky) mostly 'maneuvered' at the tournament. Let's take, for instance, the game Taimanov – Bronstein and try to trace the routes of black pieces led by the 'sharp' thinking of Bronstein. Here they are: ♛d8-e8-h5-f7-e8, ♞g8-f6-d7-f8-d7-f6, ♜h8-f8-f6-h6-f6-f8, ♝c8-d7-c8 *(see game 250).* This 'maneuvering' caused so much strain for Bronstein that he even got into time trouble. The same can be said about the game Boleslavsky – Smyslov, where the black queen followed the route d8-h4-h6-h5-h6-f8, and the bishop – c8-f5-g6-h5-e8-b5.

Some grandmasters, it seems, think that it's below their dignity to take part in the semi-finals, and in the finals, resting on the heights of their splendor, they 'maneuver', confidently make draws and slowly, but surely... forget how to play. Otherwise, Smyslov would have won the game against Taimanov, and Bronstein wouldn't have sacrificed a rook to Aronin, who missed the refutation at the right moment and still got checkmated. Bronstein maneuvered so much in the last-round game against Kasparyan that he eventually lost *(this was Kasparyan's only win in the tournament!)*. His chess was vastly different and attracted everyone's sympathies when he was only on his way to grandmastership...

> **Suetin:** "Smyslov's relative setbacks in the 19th and especially the 20th championships can be mostly explained by the fact that he underestimates

the transitional stage of the middlegame. He's especially monotonous, and therefore vulnerable, when he has black... Smyslov started restricting his creative outlook; counting on his endgame skills and great intuition, he sometimes avoids concrete decisions even in his favorite positions.

Bronstein, who achieved exceptional success beforehand, performed even worse in both tournaments. He played without his usual creativity and energy, sometimes fancifully and antipositionally, getting into severe time trouble to boot... It seems that Bronstein's beautiful and original chess thinking cannot find the necessary forms to achieve its potential." (Chess yearbook.)

Гроссмейстер Д. Бронштейн.

Bronstein couldn't prepare – he had been fighting to save his father's life for almost the whole year and buried him three weeks before the tournament started... Photo portrait published in advance of the championship. From D. Bronstein's archive.

A lack of "creativity and energy"? I think that chess was the last thing on **Bronstein's** mind – for the whole year, he fought for the life of his father, who died three weeks before the tournament started:

"In December 1951, soon after my match with Botvinnik, he had a stroke. He lay in one hospital, then in another... Then the head doctor called me and asked me to take my father home: 'You know, he says strange things in his delirium at nights.' I didn't ask for details, but I understood that it had something to do with the camp... The doctor told me that there was a good ward for psychoneurotic people in the Kaschenko psychiatric hospital, and we put him there...

When he died, I brought him from the hospital to my mom's flat, where he never got to live. Then I went to the Dynamo office and asked them to place an announcement in the newspaper about my father's death – and they printed my notice in Moskovskaya Pravda. Not in *Vechernaya Moskva*, but in the party-aligned Moskovskaya Pravda! I rehabilitated him myself in 1952, I'm a madman... But I did rehabilitate him! I notified the whole of Moscow,

Мастер Г. ИЛИВИЦКИЙ.

Дружеский шарж
М. КУКУНОВА.

Georgy Ilivitsky's stellar hour was still to come – in the 22nd championship he would share 3rd–6th place with Botvinnik, Petrosian and Spassky. Cartoon by M. Kukunov. From the tournament bulletin (9th January 1953).

'The Moscow office of the Dynamo sports society reports the death of Ion Borisovich Bronstein that occurred on 7th November after a long illness and expresses condolences to the deceased's son and relatives.' I added where he was going to start his final journey: 4/10 Sadovaya-Triumfalnaya, the KGB building! My father was driven through Red Square on the way to the graveyard, it wasn't closed back then...

In 1955 there were rumors about possible rehabilitation, and my mother sent a letter to the Kiev prosecutor's office. In December, we received an answer: 'We inform you that your husband's case has been reviewed and dismissed for lack of evidence.' Reviewed? When, by whom?.." (*Shakhmaty v Rossii*, No. 5–6, 1996.)

The chess of seasoned masters Konstantinopolsky, Kan, Kasparyan, Ilivitsky, Lipnitsky, Simagin, Aronin and Goldenov deserves strict criticism.

And, of course, the reason is not their sporting results – someone is bound to finish in the bottom half of the table – but the meager creative content provided by these renowned chess players in many of their games. This stood out especially against the achievements of the young who both brought sporting ardor to their fights and shone with rich creative ideas. Masters Korchnoi, Moiseev, Byvshev and Suetin showed that they were already mature players and dangerous even for international grandmasters.

Kan: "Moiseev showed himself as a strong, growing player. His best features are good positional understanding and the ability to sustain a tenacious, maneuvering struggle. Moiseev isn't completely averse to complications, but he mostly tends to play in a positional style. He's behind many masters in knowledge of theory, but Moiseev can compensate for this shortcoming with well thought-out and determined middlegame play...

Byvshev is slightly inferior to Korchnoi from the stylistic diversity point of view. He's not as strong in positional play as in tactics... Byvshev and Korchnoi have similar flaws – poor fitness and frequent time trouble. When both of them came together, we often saw the sad picture of young masters making lightning-fast moves with trembling hands – and, alas, those moves weren't always the best." (*Shakhmaty v SSSR*, No. 4, 1953.)

Of his seven games against grandmasters, Byvshev won three (against Keres, Smyslov and Boleslavsky) and drew with Botvinnik. The arithmetic considerations are not the main thing, however – the style and character of those wins are much more important. The Leningrad player scored 9 points in the tournament (half a point behind Keres), but the components of this are rather telling: eight wins and two draws. Byvshev won more games than Bronstein, Keres or Smyslov and the same amount as Boleslavsky and Geller.

What characterizes Byvshev's play? Great vividness, sharpness, active thinking. His opponents always have a hard time. They're constantly harassed with big and small blows, threats of sudden combinations, impetuous attacks, inventive counter-attack ideas. Having said that, Byvshev's play is not lightweight, he doesn't count on random chances. His plans are mostly deep and 'stylish', imbued with the living spirit of initiative. Such play is hard, and Byvshev constantly gets into time trouble, but his opponents can't boast of having excessive time to solve the problems posed before them either. We remember his game against Boleslavsky: the grandmaster wasn't able to figure out the position that occurred at the board." (Tournament bulletin, 14th January.)

Interestingly, Botvinnik ended his conversation with a reporter from *Pravda* – the main newspaper in the country – on Byvshev as well (unfortunately, he only spoke some general words about the championship, so there's nothing to quote). However, Byvshev didn't live up to expectations as a player. He played in two more finals, but finished mid-table (1954 – 10th–11th, 1956 – 11th–12th), and never even made it to the top three of Leningrad championships. Byvshev's true calling was coaching! He taught chess in the Leningrad/St. Petersburg Young Pioneers Palace, became a Distinguished Coach of Russia, and trained many pupils. Among the best-known are Alexander Khalifman, Evgeny Solozhenkin, Lyudmila Rudenko and Irina Levitina...

Some Exclusive Treats

This time, the "best game problem" was solved quite radically by the organizers: no prizes at all! For brilliancy, for best result against the prizewinners, for best finish – all were abolished... That's a pity. Especially the lack of prizes for beautiful play. Without them, the sporting results dominate, pushing the aesthetic component to the background.

On the other hand, nothing limited my freedom of choice! And there was a lot to choose from: the bulletin (19 games), *Shakhmaty v SSSR* (20), the tournament book (190 – the first one with all the games annotated!), the yearbook (6), and game collections (30)... The list was long. But it was dominated by well-known games. Of course, it's impossible not to include them (masterpieces are masterpieces), but let's not forget about dramas as well; in addition, I wanted to share some exclusive treats, too, such as Vasily Byvshev's games – where else will you find them? And he played very well! The comparisons with Korchnoi were well-deserved.

Due to space constraints, some masterpieces were omitted. But you'll easily find them in the game collections (winners in italic): *Botvinnik* – Goldenov, Bronstein – *Botvinnik*, *Botvinnik* – Geller, *Bronstein* – Moiseev, *Tolush* – Boleslavsky, *Geller* – Boleslavsky, *Smyslov* – Ilivitsky, *Keres* – Korchnoi, and the mind-boggling draw between Botvinnik and Boleslavsky.

Knockout in the King's Indian

Zagoriansky: "In this championship, Taimanov played a number of games using a single formula: he builds a solid defensive position on the kingside and then calmly launches queenside operations. The opponent rushes to 'explode the bastions' on the kingside, but the bastions refuse to be exploded, and the game is already won by Taimanov on the queenside. He managed to defeat such attacking masters as Bronstein, Aronin, Korchnoi and others in this way."

No. 250. King's Indian Defense E99
Taimanov – Bronstein
Moscow 1952, round 10
Annotated by D. Bronstein
1.d4 ♘f6 2.c4 d6 3.♘f3 g6 4.♘c3 ♗g7 5.e4 *(5.♗f4 – see game 190 in the second volume)* **5...0-0 6.♗e2.** *"The King's Indian Defense has brought black many successes. Naturally, white has had to search for various ways to turn the tide in this interesting and complicated opening. The move 6.♗e2 has become fashionable lately. Taimanov readily uses it instead of developing the bishop to g2." (Lilienthal)*

6...e5 7.0-0 ♘c6. In this game, both opponents go for a line they specifically prepared.

8.d5 ♘e7 9.♘e1. White is too slow to launch a pawn attack on the queenside *(however, this became the main line!)*. The moves 9.a3, 9.♖b1 or even 9.♗d2, and then b2-b4 and c4-c5 are much more dangerous for black. In this case, it's harder for him to reply with f7-f5 due to the constant threat ♘f3-g5-e6. To protect the g5 square, black will have to lose a tempo on h7-h6, which is not always beneficial to him. Thus, by launching an immediate queenside attack, white has better chances.

9...♘d7 10.♗e3 *(10.♘d3 is an alternative)* **10...f5 11.f3.** Watching the game Taimanov – Aronin in round 8, I was quite surprised by white allowing the f5-f4 advance, since in such positions it always affords black a productive attack against the white king. I thought then and still think now that white's strategic plan is a mistake.

Since Taimanov was sure that his defensive line was impregnable, and I had black against him, I decided to repeat this entire line.

11...f4 *(in the game Taimanov – Aronin, black played 11...h5)* **12.♗f2 g5 13.♘d3.** As I prepared for the game, I analyzed this position and found some promising possibilities. Some of them were later used in practice, and others are still waiting for their time. Concerning the next move, it's not bad in and of itself,

but black combined it with a poor forcing line.

Later, white tried 13.b4 and even 13.♘b5 (Korchnoi – Hulak, Zagreb 1987), and in the 1990s, 13.a4 or 13.♖c1 became popular.

13...♘f6. *13...♘f6! 14.c5 ♘g6! is stronger (Taimanov – Najdorf, Zurich 1953).*

14.c5 ♖h6. Of course, black could simply play 14...♘g6, then ♘f6 and g5-g4 *(after 15.cxd6 cxd6 16.♘b5, the correct move is 16...g4 17.fxg4 ♘f6, while the immediate 16...♘f6? is bad due to 17.♖c1!)*, but black overestimated his position and tried to get too much out of it. He didn't consider all the defensive and counter-attacking resources, hoping to force white to play ♖e1, ♗f1 and h2-h3. Then the attack ♖g6 and g5-g4 would have been much stronger of course.

15.cxd6 cxd6 16.♘b5.

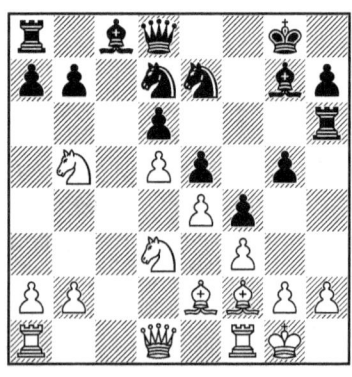

This position was also on my board in home analysis. I thought that white can't play this because of 16...♘f6, after which there's no satisfactory defense to the threat

♕e8-h5. The loss of the a8 rook in some lines (♘xa8) wasn't significant in the subsequent complications, which were beneficial for black. However, unfortunately for myself, I saw the strong reply 17.♖c1 at the board, to meet the tempting 17... ♕e8 with 18.♖xc8!, eliminating black's most important attacking piece and all hopes for a successful game. I'm saying "unfortunately for myself" because persistent execution of a plan, even if it's not fully correct, is more likely to lead to success than a sharp U-turn halfway through.

After thinking for almost an hour, black ultimately didn't go for 16... ♘f6 due to 17.♖c1 ♕e8 18.♖xc8 ♘xc8 19.♘c7 ♕h5 20.h3 ♖b8, and it's now quite difficult for him to revive his attack. I regretted not playing a different move before and lost faith in my plan. At this point, the result was predetermined, since psychological defeat almost always entails sporting defeat as well.

Black was correct in making that "sharp U-turn halfway through"! White had the even stronger reply, 18.♘xd6! with the idea 18...♕h5 19.h4 gxh4 20.♔h2, and the king is safe (20...♖g6 21.♖g1 ♖g3 22.♘xc8 ♘xc8 23.♖h1 etc.).

16...♘f8. Protecting the e6 square and still hoping for the maneuver ♕e8-h5.

17.♗e1! A great move that solves two problems at once: it intensifies the queenside attack (threatening ♗a5 and ♗b4) and frees up the f2

square for the knight, strengthening the h3 and g4 squares. Now white's advantage is obvious. I should point out, however, that if the black knight was on f6, the move 17.♗e1 wouldn't be too useful because of the possible 17...g4!

17...a6? The psychological mistake is followed by a purely chess one, which turns out to be decisive. It was necessary to give a check on b6, abandoning hopes for an attack.

18.♘a3 b5 19.♘c2 ♘d7 (a desperate effort to catch up) **20.a4!** Opening new lines for the attack.

20...bxa4 21.♖xa4 ♘f6 22.♘f2 ♗d7 23.♗a5 ♕e8 24.♖b4.

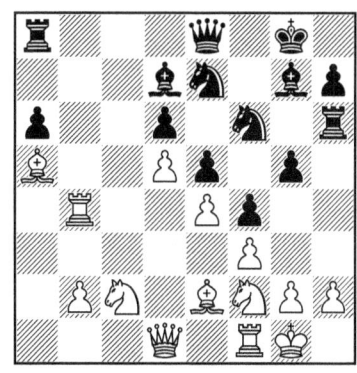

24...♕h5. Of course, now that the king is well-defended, this lunge is of only symbolic significance.

Only this is the decisive mistake! 24...♘g6! gave some counterchances, for instance: 25.♘a3 ♘h4 26.♘g4! (the only way: 26.h3? ♕h5 27.♘g4 ♘xg2; 26.♘c4? ♕h5 27.♘g4 ♘xf3+) 26...♘xg4 27.fxg4 ♖f6 or 25.h3 ♘h4 26.♖e1 (26.♘g4 ♖g6 and h7-h5) 26...♘h5 27.♗f1 ♘g3 etc.

25.h3 ♕f7. *Now, 25...♘g6? is already bad: 26.♘g4 ♘xg4 27.fxg4 ♕h4 28.♖b7 and ♗e1, trapping the queen.*

26.♘a3 ♘h5 27.♖b7 ♗c8 28.♖c7 ♘g3. Black can't create any real threats, and white's attack basically plays itself.

29.♖e1 ♖b8 30.♘c4 ♕e8 31.♘b6 ♖f6 32.♕c2.

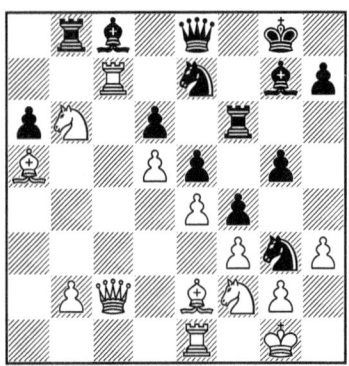

32...♖f8. *"White threatened 33.♖xe7 and 34.♘xc8." (Lilienthal.) And there could have been quite a trap, in true Bronstein style! He was probably too demoralized at that point, otherwise he would surely have spotted the continuation of the line 32...h5 33.♖xe7? ♕xe7 34.♘xc8 that was found by the computer: 34...♘xe2+! 35.♖xe2 ♕d7, attacking two pieces (36.♘b6 ♕b5 37.♘c4 ♖c8 38.b3 ♖xc4 39.bxc4 ♕xa5).*

33.♖c1 ♗f5. To give at least some freedom to the g7 bishop, black is now ready to part with the c8 bishop. Oh, how times change!

34.♗d3. *"If 34.exf5 then 34...e4, allowing black to prolong the*

resistance." (Lilienthal.) Not so: 35.f6! (not the immediate 35.♘d7? ♖xb2=) 35...♗xf6 36.♘d7 etc.

34...♗g6 35.♘d7 ♘xd5 36.♗c4 ♖b5 37.♘xf8 ♗xf8 38.♗xd5+ ♖xd5 39.♕c4 ♘e2+ 40.♔h2 g4 41.♘xg4. Time trouble ended, and black immediately resigned.

We should give credit to Taimanov, who played the whole game very clearly and confidently. His wins in the two games of the 20th championship where this King's Indian line occurred were quite impressive and even led to a wrong evaluation of the entire line as beneficial for white. However, the subsequent games Najdorf – Gligoric, Eliskases – Gligoric (Mar del Plata 1953) and Taimanov – Najdorf (Zurich 1953) were won by black, which restored the balance somewhat and proved the viability of this system in the King's Indian.

The Champion's Double Whammy

For the next win, Mark Evgenyevich had to pay a heavy price – the suspension of his relationship with the Teacher (that was how he called Botvinnik in his memoirs, with a capital "T"): "Thankfully, Botvinnik clearly set the duration of his 'sentences' and didn't speak with his 'offenders' for a long, long time. My 'sentence' ended about two years later... At first, the Patriarch softened a bit when he defeated me in the Soviet Championship match, and then there was a full amnesty."

No. 251. Nimzo-Indian Defense E40
Botvinnik – Taimanov
Moscow 1952, round 4
Annotated by M. Taimanov and S. Flohr

1.d4 ♘f6 2.c4 e6 3.♘c3 ♗b4 4.e3 ♘c6 *(a relatively rare line now)* **5.♘ge2 d5 6.a3 ♗e7 7.cxd5.** In the previous game with Taimanov (19th Soviet Championship), Botvinnik played 7.♘g3, but after 7...h5! 8.cxd5 exd5 9.♗d3 h4 10.♘f1 h3 11.g3 0-0 black got a promising position. In this game, the champion is searching for new ways.

7...exd5 8.g3. A bad move. Botvinnik found the right plan, to exert piece pressure on the d5 pawn, but his execution is not precise. There was a much stronger move in the fourth game of the Soviet Championship play-off match Botvinnik – Taimanov: 8.♘f4 0-0 9.♗e2! ♗f5 (to meet 10.♗f3 with 10...♗e4) 10.g4!, and white seized the initiative *(see game 267)*.

8...0-0 9.♗g2 ♘a5! Black is preparing to protect the pawn with c7-c6 and also takes control over the b3 and c4 squares, which were weakened after the white bishop left the f1-a6 diagonal.

10.0-0 c6. Black has got a better position out of the opening. He has developed without hindrance and now threatens to play ♕b6-b3 and then ♗f5, with strong pressure along the light squares.

11.♘a4 b6 12.♘ac3 ♗a6 13.♖b1. After getting a cramped position, Botvinnik defends very carefully. After the natural 13.♖e1, black could play 13...♗c4 with strong pressure. Now white has a reply 14.b3.

13...♖c8. An unexciting move made out of "general considerations". Such moves are appropriate for positions that aren't yet clarified, but this position required a concrete approach. White is clearly worse: he's behind in development, and it's hard to get the c1 bishop into the game. It's clear that the only acceptable plan for him is to prepare the liberating advance e3-e4. Black had to prevent this plan first and foremost, so he had to play 13...♖e8 14.♖e1 ♗d6, with growing pressure.

Leaving the a7 pawn undefended, he allows the opponent to create counterplay on the queenside with 14.b4 ♘b7 (the knight has to go to this bad square because after 14...♘c4 15.♕a4 ♗b7 16.♕xa7 ♕c7 17.♕a4, black loses a pawn) 15.b5! cxb5 16.♘xb5, and white's pieces come alive.

14.♕c2. Botvinnik makes a mistake by not going for that plan.

14...♗d6. After this new inaccuracy, the world champion manages to eliminate all troubles. Black still had to play 14...♖e8, and 15.b4 ♘b7 16.e4 (16.♕a4 ♗d3) would not work due to 16...dxe4 17.♘xe4 ♘d6, and black is better.

15.b4! ♘b7. 15...♘c4 is bad due to 16.♕a4. *Why? Let's continue the line: 16...♗b7 17.♕xa7 ♕e7! 18.♕a4 ♖a8 19.♕c2 b5 with a roughly equal game.*

16.e4! dxe4 17.♘xe4 ♖e8 18.♗g5 ♗e7 19.♗xf6 ♗xf6 20.♖fd1 ♘d6 21.♘xf6+ ♕xf6 22.♘c3. White has managed to simplify the position. Chances are now equal, since the weakness of the d4 pawn is balanced by the weak c6 pawn.

22...♗c4.

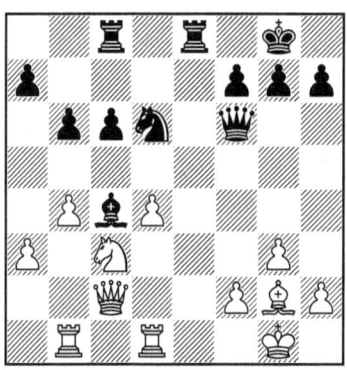

In this position Taimanov offered a draw, but Botvinnik declined it and... immediately made a serious mistake.

23.♕d2? After that, white suddenly gets a clearly worse position. 23.♘e4 ♘xe4 24.♗xe4 ♗d5 25.f3 etc. led to a simple draw.

After 25...♖cd8! black is obviously better: 26.♗xh7+ (26.♕d3 c5!) 26... ♔f8 27.♗e4 ♗xe4 28.fxe4 ♖xd4, so the correct move is 25.♗xd5.

23...♘b5! Botvinnik probably underestimated the strength of

this move. Now white no longer objected to a peaceful ending, but the arbiters, citing tournament regulations, asked the players to continue the game.

24.♘e4. Black threatened both 24...♘xa3 and, in case of 24.a4, the blow 24...♘xd4! 25.♕xd4 ♖e1+. After 24.♘xb5, there was 24... ♖e2! 25.♕f4 ♕xf4 26.gxf4 cxb5, with a better endgame for black. Still, Botvinnik had to go for this continuation, because the game move loses a pawn.

24...♕g6 25.a4. Neither 25.♕f4 ♗d5 nor 25.♕c1 ♗e2! help white.

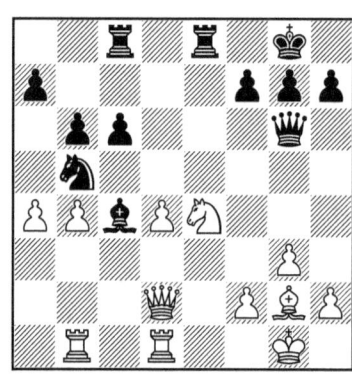

25...♖xe4! 26.axb5. Necessary, since after 26.♗xe4 ♕xe4 27.axb5 (27.♖e1? ♘xd4!) black gets an unstoppable attack with 27...♗d5.

26...♖e2 27.♕f4 ♗xb5 28.♗f3. 28.♗f1 gave nothing because of 28... ♖e4. The immediate 28.d5!? was worthy of consideration.

28...♖e7 29.h4 ♖d8 30.♖bc1 ♖ed7 31.d5. Necessary. Otherwise, black will play h7-h6, preventing this move.

Гроссмейстер
М. ТАЙМАНОВ

Дружеский шарж
И. ИГИНА.

Mark Taimanov – the servant of two muses. Cartoon by I. Igin. From the tournament bulletin (28th December 1952).

31...cxd5 32.♖xd5 ♖xd5 33.♗xd5. It seems that white has managed to create counterplay due to the threat 34.♖c7. But black finds a way to eliminate his opponent's initiative.

33...♕f6!

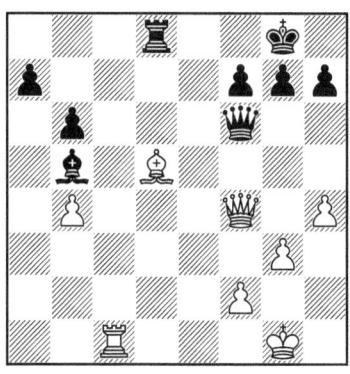

34.♖c7? A tempting but erroneous move that makes black's task simpler. 34.♕xf6 gxf6 was bad as well, since the endgame probably can't be saved, but with 34.♕c7! ♗e8 (not 34...♖xd5? 35.♕b8+ ♖d8 36.♖c8) 35.♗e1 ♔f8 36.♖e5 white still had some chances.

This is bad due to 36...♖d6! 37.♖f5 ♕e7. 34.♕xf6 gxf6 35.♗c4 was the most resilient.

34...♕xf4 35.gxf4 ♗e8. That's the entire point. Black retains his material advantage, and all white pawns are broken up. The rest is simple.

36.♗c4 ♔f8 37.b5 (or 37.♖xa7 ♖d4 38.♖c7 b5 etc.) **37...♖d4 38.♔g2 ♖xf4 39.♔g3 ♖f5 40.♖xa7 ♗xb5 41.♖a8+ ♔e7 42.♖a7+ ♗d7 43.♖b7 b5 44.♗d3 ♖c5 45.♗xh7 g6 46.♗g8 ♖d5 47.h5 ♖g5+ 48.♔f4 ♖xh5 49.♔e4 ♖f5 50.f4 ♔d6.** White resigned.

Catching the Moment

This name was given by the winner himself when he annotated the game for the book *Grandmaster Geller*, and he explained why: "White had a positional advantage since he was better developed. In such cases, it's enough to miss one moment, and everything is lost... Here, I managed to maintain the advantage with an exchange sacrifice.

No. 252. Nimzo-Indian Defense E52
Geller – Keres
Moscow 1952, round 4
Annotated by E. Geller

1.d4 ♘f6 2.c4 e6 3.♘c3 ♗b4 4.e3 b6 5.♗d3 *(5.♘ge2 – see game 168 in volume 2)* **5...0-0 6.♘f3 d5 7.0-0 ♗b7.** The opponents played the Rubinstein System, which was popular, especially at that time. It gives both sides rich possibilities in choice of plans.

8.♗d2. White intends to develop all his pieces first and only then make his intentions public. The move is quite modest, but back then, together with 8.♕e2, it was considered one of the main lines. *(The current fashions are 8.cxd5 and 8.a3.)*

8...dxc4 (giving up the center looks too premature) **9.♗xc4 c5.** In the game against Taimanov (19th Soviet Championship), Averbakh played 9...♘bd7 10.♕e2 c5 11.a3 ♗xc3 12.♗xc3 ♘e4 13.♖ac1 ♖c8 with a satisfactory position.

10.a3   cxd4. This is the downside to the two previous moves. Black has to part with his dark-squared bishop, because 10...♗a5 11.dxc5 bxc5 12.♕e2! gives white a better position. 10...♗xc3!? 11.♗xc3 ♘e4 *(later, this became the most popular reply)* 12.♗e1 was worthy of consideration, even though white got the bishop pair advantage.

11.axb4 dxc3 12.♗xc3.

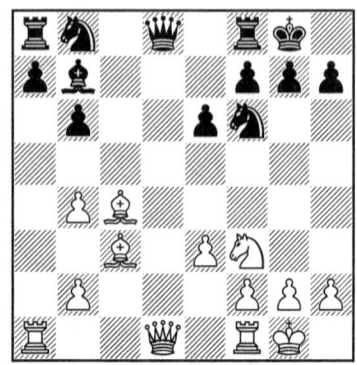

12...♘e4? Black had to play 12...♘c6 *(12...♕e7!?)* 13.b5 ♘e7 14.♗b4 ♗d5, even though white is still better in this line. The attempt to equalize immediately leads to trouble.

13.♕xd8 ♖xd8 14.♖fd1! That's it! The simplifications are beneficial for white, and the mating threat on d8 allows him to keep the bishop. In the resulting open position, the bishop pair advantage will eventually tell.

It's now bad to play 14...♖xd1+ 15.♖xd1 ♘c6 *(15...♔f8!?)* due to 16.b5 ♘xc3 17.bxc6 ♘xd1 18.cxb7 ♖b8 19.♗a6, and the maneuver ♘e5(d4)-c6 cannot be prevented.

14...♖c8   15.♗e1   ♔f8. Fundamentally preventing the mating threats that could occur, for instance, after 15...♘c6 16.b5 ♘b4 *(16...♘e7 17.♖d7)* 17.♗xb4 ♖xc4 18.♖xa7.

16.♖d4. Winning an important tempo to double rooks (black can't play 16...♘c6).

16...♔e7 17.♖ad1 ♖c7 18.♘e5!

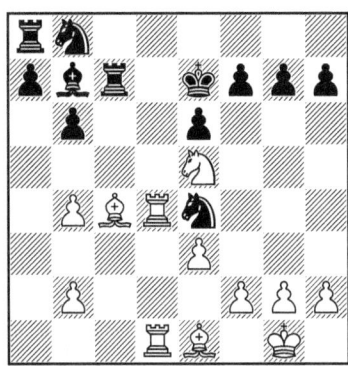

The tangle of black pieces on the queenside looks quite sad, and it's hard to disentangle it. With 19.f3 ♘f6 20.♗h4, white wants to improve his position even more, intending to sacrifice an exchange. Otherwise, black could finish his development unopposed and count on a good result.

18...f6. This natural move suddenly leads black to a hopeless endgame by force. 18...♘f6 was better, but after 19.f3 ♘bd7 the white bishop would still get to g3 with great effect.

19.♗d3 ♘d6. The main variation was 19...fxe5 20.♖xe4 ♗xe4 21.♗xe4 ♘c6 22.b5 ♖d8 23.♖c1, and white gains a material advantage that's enough for a win. The attempt to sharpen play with 19...♘xf2 is refuted: 20.♗xf2 fxe5 21.♗h4+ g5 (otherwise 22.♖f1+) 22.♗xg5+ ♔f7 23.♖h4.

Master Saigin recommended 19... ♘g5 20.♖g4 ♘d7 21.♘xd7 ♖xd7 22.f4 ♖ad8 in the bulletin, "retaining the defensive resources", but after

20.♖c4! ♖xc4 21.♘xc4 the position is still unpleasant for black. For instance: 21...♘d7 22.h4 ♘f7 23.♗xh7 (23... ♖h8 24.♗g6 ♖xh4? 25.f4!).

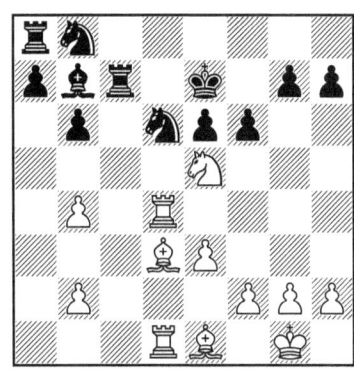

20.♗xh7! This was a bit difficult – not because of calculations, but because it was necessary to thoroughly evaluate the position after the intended exchange sacrifice. Black couldn't avoid it (20...♘b5) due to the Zwischenschach on g6.

20...fxe5   21.♖xd6   ♗d5 22.♖6xd5   exd5   23.♖xd5   ♖c1 24.♔f1   ♘c6   25.♔e2. 25.b5 ♔e6! was too premature.

25...♖d8. Chasing the pawn with 25...♖h8 led to dangerous activation of white's pieces: 26.♗e4 ♖xh2 27.b5, and the black king is still uncomfortable even in the endgame. It's clear why Keres is trying to trade rooks.

26.♖xd8 ♘xd8 27.♗c3 ♔e6. Now white's task is to create passed pawns on the kingside. And here's the solution:

28.♗g8+   ♔d6   29.f4   exf4 30.exf4. It turns out that it's impossible to defend the g7 pawn.

30...♘e6 31.♗e5+.

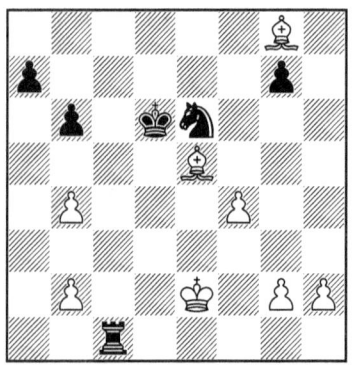

31...♔d5. Or 31...♔d7(e7) 32.f5. *The position is full of nuances. After 31...♔d7 black's position is bad, but 31...♔e7! gave some chances to save the game: 32.f5 ♘g5 33.♗d5! (33.♗xg7? ♖c2+) 33...♘h7 34.♗xg7 ♘f6! (black wouldn't have this move if the king were on d7) 35.♗e6 ♖c2+ with a draw. So in this case, capturing the pawn is a mistake, and white retained the advantage with 34.♗c3!*

32.♗xg7 ♖c8 33.♗xe6+. White can't keep the bishop pair – 33.♗f7 ♖c7, but it's not necessary now.

33...♔xe6 34.♔f3 ♖c4 35.♗c3 ♔d5 36.h4 a5 37.bxa5 ♖xc3+. White's pawns are still unstoppable.

38.bxc3 bxa5 39.h5. It was enough to get into the square of the last remaining black pawn – 39.♔e2, but white shows another way to win. If now (after the game move) 39... a4 then 40.h6 a3 41.h7 a2 42.h8=♕ a1=♕ 43.c4+.

39...♔e6 40.♔e3. Black resigned.

In Signature Style

Sokolsky: "Tolush is known for his sharp and enterprising play. His games are usually quite tempestuous and often end in unexpected ways."

No. 253. Slav Defense D18
Tolush – Smyslov
Moscow 1952, round 12
Annotated by A. Tolush

1.d4 d5 2.c4 c6 3.♘f3 ♘f6 4.♘c3 dxc4 5.a4. *Tolush avoids his gambit 5.e4 b5 6.e5 ♘d5 7.a4, in which he lost to Smyslov in the 15th championship (see game 188 in the second volume).*

5...♗f5 6.e3 e6 7.♗xc4 ♗b4 8.0-0 a5. *8...0-0 or 8...♘bd7 are much more popular.*

9.♕e2 ♘e4 10.♘a2. *An improvement. In the training tournament game Boleslavsky – Smyslov (May 1952), white played 10.♘xe4 ♗xe4 11.♗d3 ♗xd3 12.♕xd3 0-0 13.e4 ♘a6 with a roughly equal game.*

10...♗e7. All this had already occurred in Smyslov's games. Against Boleslavsky *(round 2)* he replied 10... ♗d6, and after 11.♗d3 ♗g6 12.♘c3 he played 12...♘xc3, which led to difficulties. Against Geller *(round 6)* he played 12...♘g5 and also failed to equalize *(the computer recommends 13.♘e1!).*

But the development plan used by Smyslov in this game also gives white a big advantage, and so the entire line *(with 8...a5 and 9...♘e4)* should be considered unsatisfactory for black *(Smyslov never played it again after this game)*.

11.♗d3 ♘f6 12.e4 ♗g4 13.♗e3 0-0 14.♘c3 ♘a6 15.♖ad1 ♘b4 16.♗b1 ♕c7 17.h3 ♗xf3. 17... ♗h5 is dangerous due to 18.g4 ♗g6 19.♘e5 with the subsequent f2-f4.

18.♕xf3 ♖fd8 19.♖c1 ♖d7 20.♕e2 g6. After 20...e5 white got a big advantage by playing 21.dxe5 ♕xe5 22.f4. Now the only acceptable reply for black is 22...♕h5, but after 23.♕xh5 ♘xh5 his pieces will be out of play for a long time.

With the game move, Smyslov planned the eventual f7-f5 advance.

"20...♖ad8 was more consistent. Black's continuation noticeably weakens the kingside." (Chistiakov.) The computer agrees.

21.f4 ♕d8 22.♕f2 ♘e8 23.g4 ♘g7. Black is threatening to play 24...f5, so white's next move is necessary.

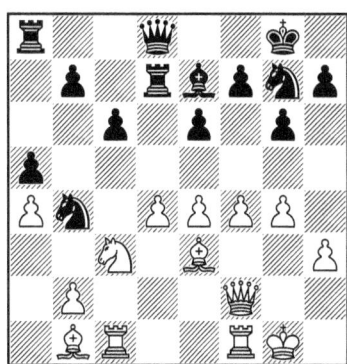

24.f5! exf5 25.gxf5 ♗g5. If 25... gxf5 then the simple 26.♔h1, with an attack along the g-file, is very strong.

26.♗xg5 ♕xg5+ 27.♔h2. Now white can set up his attack on the king unhindered, since his opponent doesn't have enough counterplay. It's obvious that the pressure on the d4 pawn is easily countered by white.

27...♖ad8 28.♖g1 ♕h6 29.♖cd1 ♔h8 30.♖g4.

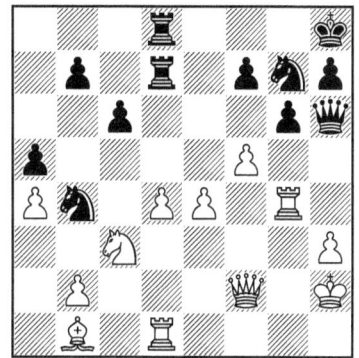

A year later, in Hastings (pictured), Tolush already played as a grandmaster! From the author's archive.

30...gxf5. After 30...♞h5 there was 31.e5, threatening to eventually play e5-e6 or 32.♞e4, strengthening the attack. After Smyslov's move, white gets an opportunity to sacrifice a pawn and launch a decisive attack.

31.♖h4   ♛d6+   32.e5   ♛e6 33.♞e2? A mistake that gave black an opportunity to avoid defeat. The correct move was 33.♛f4!, threatening 34.♖h6 and 35.♛h4 *(33...♛g6 34.♖h6 ♞e6 35.♛h4 ♖xd4 doesn't work because of 36.♖xg6 ♖xh4 37.♖xe6, with an extra piece for white).*

33...c5 34.♛g3 ♛g6 35.♛f2.

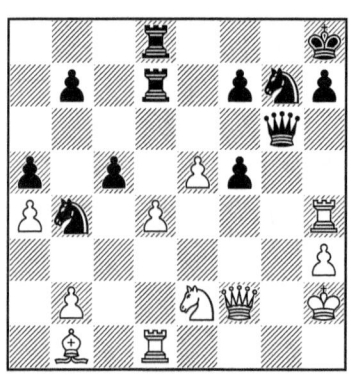

35...cxd4? Smyslov, probably because of his time trouble, misses the correct continuation – 35...♛e6!, and it's unclear how to improve the attack in a decisive way: 36.♖g1 cxd4 37.♞f4 ♛xe5 38.♛g3 ♞e6!, or if 37.♛g3 then 37...♛g6 38.♖g4 fxg4 39.♗xg6, and even though white gets a queen for rook and knight, the strong passed d-pawn equalizes chances.

You have probably spotted that the positions after 33...c5 and 35...

♛e6 were the same (in other words, Smyslov decided against repeating moves). But it's not drawn!

Position after 35...♛e6 36.♖g1 cxd4 37.♛g3 ♛g6

Instead of 38.♖g4, after which it's indeed "unclear how to improve the attack in a decisive way", white should play 38.♛e1!! A beautiful idea! Even though it's obvious: by defending the e5 pawn, white deprives black of the move 38...♛e6 (due to 39.♞f4 ♛e7 40.♛g3 ♛f8 41.♖xh7+ or 40... ♖g8 41.♞g6+, mating). The game can't be saved: 38...♛b6 39.♖xg7! ♚xg7 40.♗xf5 or 38...d3 39.♖xg6 fxg6 40.♞f4 ♚g8 41.e6 d2 42.♛d1 ♖e7 43.♞d3!! (an elegant finishing stroke) 43...♖xe6 44.♛xd2 ♞xd3 45.♗xd3, and 45...♖ed6 gives nothing due to 46.♗c4+.

For a fuller picture, I'll add that instead of 36...cxd4 in Tolush's line black can play 36...♖xd4!, but even here, after 37.♛g3 ♛g6 38.♞xd4 ♛xg3+ 39.♚xg3 cxd4 40.♖h6! ♞c6 41.♖d6, white should gradually win.

After the game move, white gets a won position by force.

36.♘f4 ♕c6 37.♖g1 d3 38.♕g3. Now black is defenseless. White threatens checkmate on g7.

38...♖g8 39.e6! Black lost on time, but there was no defense against the rook sacrifice on h7 with immediate mate.

Completely One-Sided

Yudovich: "It's known that some grandmasters and masters play rather badly against certain opponents. Botvinnik was just such a 'nemesis' opponent for Keres for a number of years. The Estonian grandmaster suffered many heavy losses in games against the world champion. In this championship, Keres played quite uncertainly and was brilliantly crushed by a direct kingside attack."

No. 254
Botvinnik – Keres
Moscow 1952, round 8
Annotated by A. Lilienthal

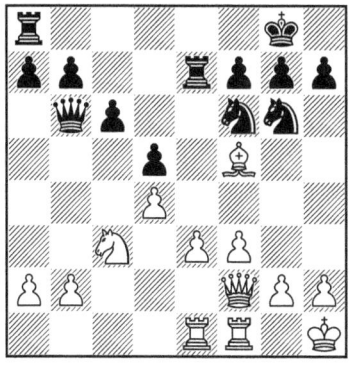

20.e4 dxe4. *"By opening up the game, black is hoping to get* some counterchances, but white's activity also increases as a result!" *(Botvinnik)*

21.fxe4 ♖d8 22.e5 ♘d5 23.♘e4! Now the white knight forcefully invades the opponent's camp, increasing the threats to the f7 pawn.

23...♘f8 24.♘d6 ♕c7. Black has no other defense to the threat 25.♘c8. 24...♖c7 25.♘xf7! lost immediately: if 25...♖xf7, then 26.♗e6.

25.♗e4 ♘e6 26.♕h4! Botvinnik doesn't hurry with the trade on d5, forcing black to weaken the kingside first.

26...g6. If 26...h6, then 27.♘f5 with a double threat: 28.♘xe7+ or 28.♘xh6+.

27.♗xd5. *"Everything in this brilliant game is simple, natural and very subtle at the same time. By trading the d5 knight, white eliminates black's only active piece." (Yudovich)*

27...cxd5 28.♖c1 ♕d7 29.♖c3 ♖f8. The last chance to complicate the game – hoping for 30.♖h3 f5 31.exf6? ♕xd6.

30.♘f5!

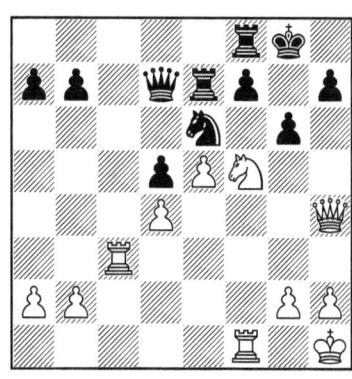

The finishing blow that immediately forces the win. The knight can't be captured due to mate in three, while after 30...♖ee8 white wins with 31.♘h6+ ♔h8 32.♕f6+ ♘g7 33.♘xf7+.

30...♖fe8 31.♘h6+ ♔f8 32.♕f6 ♘g7 33.♖cf3. *"A picturesque position! White threatens 34.♕xf7+ ♖xf7 35.♖xf7+ ♕xf7 36.♖xf7#."* (Botvinnik)

33...♖c8 34.♘xf7 ♖e6 35.♕g5 ♘f5 36.♘h6 ♕g7 37.g4. Black resigned.

Praise for the Bold Pawn

Simagin: "Of course, white couldn't calculate all the consequences of h2-h4 on the 25ᵗʰ move, but he followed the well-known rule: when you attack, all your pieces should be moving towards the opponent's king."

No. 255
Simagin – Goldenov
Moscow 1952, round 7
Annotated by V. Simagin

25.h4! ♖e8. The only way to prevent the rook invasion on e7. However, black weakens the e6 square and removes the attack on the d5 pawn.

26.♖xe8+ ♘xe8 27.♕f4 ♕d7. Other lines: 27...h6 28.♕xf5 hxg5 29.♘xg5; 27...♖a4 28.♕e3; 27...♗c8 28.♗d3.

28.♖e6 ♕a4! The best chance. Black has prepared a cunning trap that will show up on the 32ⁿᵈ move.

29.♕e3 ♘c7.

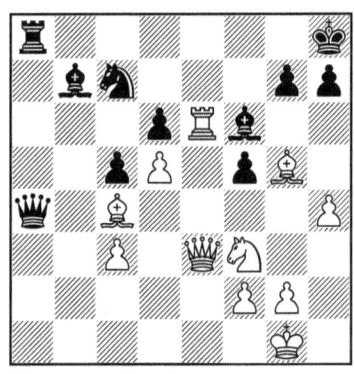

30.♖xf6! ♕xc4. Of course, not 30...gxf6 because of 31.♗xf6+ ♔g8 32.♕g5+.

31.♕e7 ♗xd5 (31...♕xd5 32.♕xc7) **32.♗h6!** Destroying black's idea: 32.♕xc7 ♗xf3 33.gxf3 (and definitely not 33.♖xd6 ♖a1+ 34.♔h2 ♖h1+! 35.♔xh1 ♕f1+ and ♕xg2#) 33...♖a1+ 34.♔h2 ♖h1+! 35.♔xh1 ♕f1+ with perpetual check.

32...♕g8. *An awkward moment! Neither Goldenov over the board nor Simagin in his analysis noticed* *a spectacular refutation of white's combination: 32...gxh6 33.♖xh6*

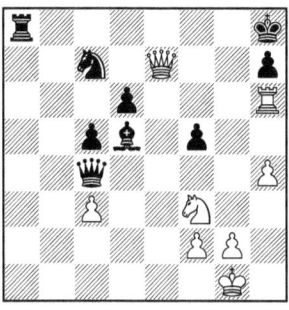

33...♗f7!! (Simagin only showed 33...♗g8 34.♕f6#) 34.♕f6+ ♔g8 35.♕g5+ ♔f8! (35...♔h8? 36.♕xf5 etc.) 36.♖xh7 ♔e8 37.♕f6 ♕e6 38.♕g7 ♕c4 39.♕f6 with a draw!

33.♘g5! All the white pieces are looming over the black king. After 33...♕xh4 white forces mate: 34.♗xg7+ ♖xg7 35.♖f8+ ♗g8 36.♖xg8+ ♔xg8 37.♕d8+ and ♕xe8#.

33...♘e8 34.♖xf5! There's no defense to the threat 35.♖xd5 and ♘f7+.

34...♕xc3 35.♖xd5 ♕c1+ 36.♔h2 ♕f4+ 37.♔h3. Black resigned. Had white opted for the modest h2-h3 on move 25, black would now have perpetual check!

The Sicilian Phalanx

Yudovich: "For many moves, the grandmaster successfully fended off the young master's tactical blows, but then got befuddled in time trouble – he's unaccustomed to it..."

Golovko: "Even such a master of chess as Boleslavsky had a hard time finding the right way in the maze of complications created by Byvshev."

No. 256. Sicilian Defense B63
Byvshev – Boleslavsky
Moscow 1952, round 10
Annotated by A. Sokolsky
1.e4 c5 2.♘f3 ♘c6 3.d4 cxd4 4.♘xd4 ♘f6 5.♘c3 d6 6.♗g5 e6 7.♕d2 ♗e7 8.0-0-0 0-0. This Rauzer line has become popular lately. In the game Byvshev – Taimanov (round 2), black decided to trade on d4 first: **8...♘xd4 9.♕xd4 0-0.** There followed **10.f4 ♕a5 11.♔b1 h6 12.h4 ♖d8 13.g4 e5 14.♕g1.** White is attacking on the kingside, but black has counterplay in the center.

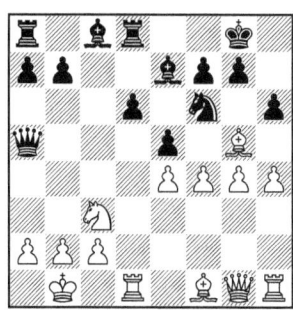

You'll see the same formidable pawn phalanx e4-f4-g4-h4 in this game as well!

9.♔b1. This continuation is probably not better than the usual 9.f4, since it leads to a forced dark-squared bishop trade.

9...h6 10.♗xf6 ♗xf6 11.♘b3 ♕b6 12.f4 a5! 13.♘a4 ♕c7 14.g4.

The move 14.♕xd6 had a beautiful refutation: 14...♖d8! 15.♕xc7 ♖xd1+ 16.♘c1 ♗d8, and, regaining the queen, black wins an exchange.

14...♖d8. The pawn sacrifice 14...b5, intending to open the b-file, was worthy of consideration, but black prepares counterplay in the center.

15.h4! *This line can probably be called the "Byvshev Attack".*

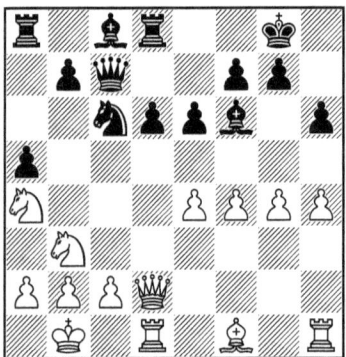

Byvshev goes boldly into attack. The straightforward plan of a pawn storm, shown in the games against Taimanov and Boleslavsky, is, at any rate, interesting and leads to great complications.

15...d5 16.e5 ♗e7 17.♖h3. Giving black an important tempo to create a counter-attack. 17.g5! looked stronger, and if 17...h5 then 18.g6!, launching an immediate attack.

17...♗d7 18.♘c3 *(18.g5 ♘xe5=)* **18...a4 19.♘b5 ♕b6 20.♘3d4 ♘a5!** By transferring the knight to c4, black manages to create dangerous threats faster than his opponent.

21.f5 ♘c4 22.♗xc4 dxc4.

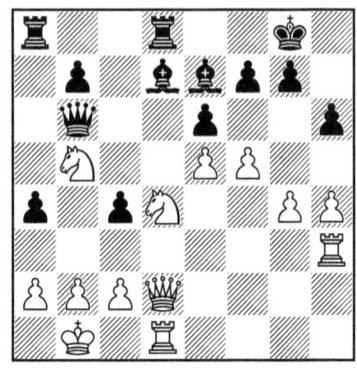

23.f6! Sacrificing material without hesitation, Byvshev finds an interesting opportunity to complicate the game. 23.♘c3 was clearly bad due to 23...♗a3.

To be fair, the computer already shows an "–+" evaluation here. This makes Byvshev's inventive efforts to muddle the famous grandmaster's brain even more interesting!

23...gxf6 24.g5 fxg5. Of course not 24...♗xb5 25.gxf6 ♗f8 26.♕g2+ ♔h7 27.♖g1, mating.

25.hxg5 ♗xb5 26.c3. After 26.gxh6 black has the simple 26...♔h8. Now white threatens 27.g6! *(which didn't work immediately due to 26...♖xd4).*

26...♗c6. Here, by playing 26...♗xg5 27.♖g3 (or 27.♖g1 ♔f8!) 27...♖xd4! 28.♖xg5+ ♔f8! 29.cxd4 hxg5 30.♕xg5 c3!, black could have won *(the game move was winning too).*

27.♕f4. 27.g6 didn't work: after 27...♗e4+ 28.♔a1 ♗g5 29.gxf7+ ♔xf7 30.♖f1+ ♔e7 the black king escapes to the queenside, maintaining black's material advantage.

27...a3 28.♖h2 ♖xd4. Boleslavsky pointed out that he could have defended with 28...h5!, for instance: 29.♖f1 ♖f8 30.♕h4 ♔g7 31.♕xh5 ♗e4+ 32.♔a1 axb2+ 33.♖xb2 ♕a5, and white can't transfer either of his rooks to the h-file.

Incredible! Even in home analysis, Boleslavsky failed to notice that both the game move and the line with 28... h5 (even though many moves in it aren't the strongest) should have led to black's victory!

Position after 28...h5 29.♖f1 ♖f8 30.♕h4 ♔g7 31.♕xh5 ♗e4+ 32.♔a1 axb2 33.♖xb2

Instead of 33...♕a5, black had a beautiful knockout blow: 33... ♕xb2+!! 34.♔xb2 ♖xa2+ 35.♔xa2 (35.♔c1 ♗a3+ 36.♔d1 ♖a1+ 37.♔e2 ♗d3+ doesn't save the game either) 35...♖a8+ 36.♔b2 ♗a3+ 37.♔a2 ♗c1#!

29.cxd4 ♗xg5 30.♖g1 ♔f8. The last opportunity to keep the material advantage was 30...f6! 31.exf6 ♕b5, and black should win because of the threat 32...♕f5+.

31.♕xf6 led to another spectacular finish: 31...♗e4+ 32.♔a1 axb2+ 33.♖xb2 ♖xa2+! 34.♖xa2 ♕xd4+ 35.♖b2 ♕xg1+ 36.♔a2 ♕a7#.

But now the position is drawn!

31.♖xg5 ♗e4+ *(the only move)* **32.♕xe4 hxg5 33.♕f3!** *"In mutual time trouble, Byvshev inventively creates serious threats to the opposing king." (Golovko)*

33...♖d8! The only move: 33... ♕xd4? 34.♖h8+ ♔e7 35.♕xb7+ ♕d7 36.♕b4+ led to mate.

34.♕xa3+ ♔e8 35.♕a4+. It was necessary to return the queen to f3; the game could have been drawn after that.

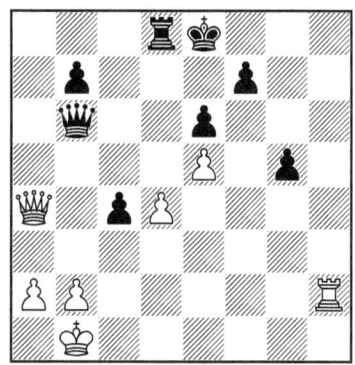

35...♔e7? A mistake in return. After 35...♕c6, black gains an advantage. The pawn ending after 36.♕xc6+ bxc6 37.♖h8+ ♔e7 38.♖xd8 ♔xd8 is lost for white.

The rook endgame is lost as well: 37.♖g2 ♖d5! 38.♖xg5 f5 39.♖g6 ♔f7 40.♖f6+ ♔e7 41.♖h6 ♖xd4 42.♖h7+ ♔e8 43.♔c2 ♖e4 44.♔c3 ♖xe5 45.♔xc4 ♖d5 etc.

36.♕a3+ ♔e8 (36...♔d7 is better; this maintained the advantage) **37.♕f3 ♖xd4?** The decisive mistake. After 37...♔d7 38.♕xf7+ ♔c8 black drew the game easily.

38.♖h8+ ♔d7 39.♕xf7+ ♔c6 40.♕xe6+ ♔b5 41.a4+! Black resigned.

The Eye-Catching Classic

I couldn't choose between providing Byvshev's wins against Keres and Smyslov at first, but when I failed to find the second game in the Megabase (the only one missing from the entire championship!), I had no more doubts.

Liublinsky: "The master executed the complicated positional struggle characteristic of the Chigorin System very well. Smyslov is considered an expert in this opening, but he couldn't outplay his less experienced opponent with black... Byvshev's technique during the play-off phase was exceptional."

No. 257. Ruy Lopez C97
Byvshev – Smyslov
Moscow 1952, round 8
Annotated by V. Byvshev
1.e4 e5 2.♘f3 ♘c6 3.♗b5 a6 4.♗a4 ♘f6 5.0-0 ♗e7 6.♖e1 b5 7.♗b3 d6 8.c3 0-0 9.h3 ♘a5 10.♗c2 c5 11.d4 ♕c7 12.♘bd2

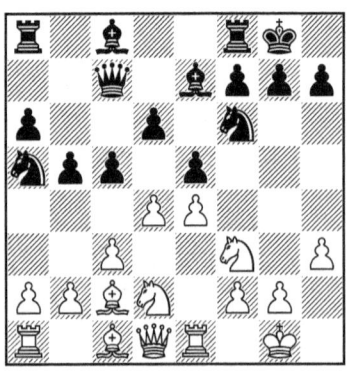

12...♗d7. *Another possibility is 12...cxd4 (see games 237 and 238), while in the game Lipnitsky – Botvinnik (round 9) white got an advantage after 12...♘c6 13.dxc5 dxc5 14.♘f1 ♗d6?! (14...♗e6) 15.a4 ♖b8 16.♗g5 ♘e8 17.axb5 axb5 18.♘e3.*

13.dxc5 dxc5 14.♘f1 ♖fe8 15.♘3h2. The purpose of this maneuver is to trade one of the black pieces that control the d5 square and free up the f3 square for the queen.

15...♖ad8 16.♕f3 ♗e6 17.♘g4. *In round 14, Aronin, after 17.♘e3 ♘c4, "went for very risky complications": 18.♘f5 ♗xf5 19.exf5, but Smyslov, "with a subtle positional pawn sacrifice" – 19...e4! – secured a "long-term initiative" for himself (Aronin).*

17...♘xg4 18.hxg4 h6? A serious mistake. Black unnecessarily weakens the king's position, which then gets exploited by white. It was necessary to seize the d-file with the rooks to prevent the knight from reaching d5.

19.♘e3 ♗g5 20.♘d5 ♗xd5 21.♗xg5 hxg5 22.exd5. As a result of black's imprecise play, white has got a great position: he has a passed pawn in the center and great attacking opportunities on both flanks.

22...♕e7. Losing a tempo. Black had to play 22...g6.

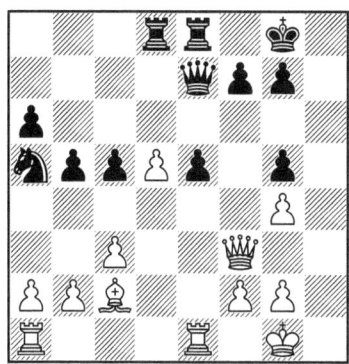

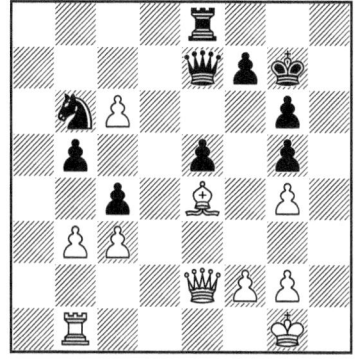

23.a4! Now 23...b4 24.♕d3 is bad, so black is forced to give up the a-file.

23...♘c4 24.axb5 axb5 25.♖a6 d6. White threatened 26.♕h3. 25...g6 is bad due to 26.♗xg6 fxg6 27.♖xg6+ ♔h7 28.♕f5, and white wins. 25...♘d6 was probably the most resilient move.

26.♖c6 g6. If 26...♘xb2 then 27.♕e4 g6 28.♖xc5 ♖b6 29.♕b4 etc.

But the game move is also a mistake! Black could get a roughly equal position with 26...♖h6! 27.♖xh6 gxh6, and meet the seemingly dangerous 28.♕e4 with 28...♕f6.

27.b3 ♖xc6 28.dxc6 ♘b6. After 28...♘d6, white could play 29.♕d5! ♘c8 30.♗xg6 ♘b6 31.♗xf7+, getting four pawns for the piece.

After 31...♔g7! (not 31...♕xf7 32.♕xc5 ♕c7 33.♕xb5), he got only three pawns: 32.♕d3 ♔xf7 33.♕xb5 ♘d5. The most precise continuation is 31.♕e4! fxg6 32.♕xg6+ ♔f8 33.♖e3 e4 34.c7!, winning.

29.♗e4 ♔g7. If 29...♘a8 then 30.♖d1 ♖d8 31.♖xd8+ ♕xd8 32.♗d5 ♕e7 33.♕d3!

30.♕e2 c4 31.♖b1.

31...♕c5. After 31...♖b8, there could follow 32.bxc4 bxc4 (32...♘xc4 33.♗d5 ♘a3 34.♖a1) 33.♖b4, threatening 34.♕e3.

After 33...♕d6, this is not a threat: 34.♕e3 ♕d1+ 35.♔h2 ♘d5! (cutting through the Gordian knot of problems) 36.♗xd5 ♖h8+ 37.♔g3 ♕xd5=. Therefore, the preparatory move 34.g3! was necessary.

32.b4 ♕e7 33.♖a1 ♖d8. 33...♖a8 didn't save the game due to 34.♖a5 ♖xa5 35.bxa5 etc.

34.♕e3 ♘a8. After 34...♘d5, white also won with 35.♖a7!.

Only he didn't! After 35...♕d6! he loses the c6 pawn: 36.♗xd5 ♕xd5 37.♕xg5 ♖h8 38.♖d7 ♕e4 etc. The correct move is the immediate 35.♗xd5 ♖xd5 36.♕a7! (not 36.♖a7 ♕d8=) 36...♕xa7 37.♖xa7 ♖d8 38.♖b7 ♖c8 39.♖xb5 ♖xc6 40.♖xe5, and the c4 pawn also falls.

35.♖a7 ♘c7. If 35...♖d1+ then 36.♔h2 ♕d8 37.♕c5 ♕h8+ 38.♔g3 ♕h4+ 39.♔f3 ♕h2 40.♕e3 ♘b6 41.♕xg5 etc.

36.♕b6 ♖c8. After 36...♖d1+ the following line is possible: 37.♔h2

♕f6 38.♕xc7 ♕f4+ 39.g3 ♕xf2+ 40.♗g2 ♖d2 41.♕xf7+ ♕xf7 42.♖xf7+ ♔xf7 43.c7.

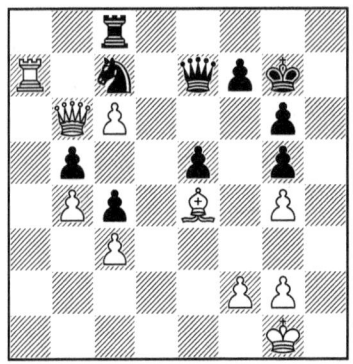

37.♖xc7! The exchange sacrifice is the simplest way to win.

37...♕xc7 38.♕xb5 ♖a8. *The decisive mistake! With 38...♕a7! black could still save the game.*

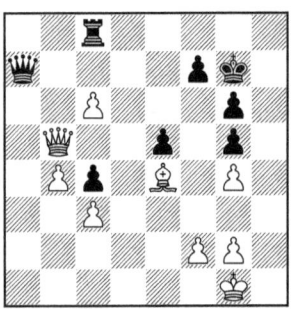

After 39.♕xc4 ♕a1+, white has to play 40.♕f1, giving up the c3 pawn, because 40.♔h2? loses: 40...♖h8+ 41.♔g3 ♕c1! 42.♗d3 f5! 43.c7 ♕f4+ 44.♕xf4 gxf4+ 45.♔f3 e4+ etc.

39.♕xe5+ is better (counting on 39...♔g8 40.♗xg6! fxg6? 41.♕e6+ and ♕xc8), but after 39...f6! the computer confidently delivers a 0.00 evaluation...

39.♕xc4 ♕d8 40.♕d5 ♖a1+ 41.♔h2 ♕h8+ 42.♔g3 ♕h4+ 43.♔f3 ♕h2. The game was adjourned here. Analysis showed that black's attack is not dangerous.

44.♕d2 ♖g1 45.♔e2 ♕h4 46.♗f3 ♕h8 47.♕d6! Winning another pawn, since 47...♕e8 is met with 48.♕d7, threatening ♗d5.

47...♕h1 48.♕xe5+ ♔h7 49.♔d2 ♖a1 50.♔d3 ♕f1+. The move 50...♖e1 would have given white more trouble *(after 51.♗e2! it's curtains: 51...♕xg2 52.f3 ♖a1 53.c7 ♖a8 54.♕d5 etc.).*

51.♕e2 ♕b1+ 52.♔d4 ♕c1 53.♕e3 ♕a3 54.♕xg5 ♕a7+ 55.♕c5 ♕c7 56.♕e5 ♕a7+ 57.♕c5 ♕c7 58.♔c4 ♖a3 59.♗d5 ♕e5 60.♕d4 ♕e2+ 61.♔c5 ♕e1. Or 61...♕e7+ 62.♔b5 ♕e2+ 63.♗c4 ♕e7 64.♕d7 ♕e5+ 65.♗d5 ♖xc3 66.♕xf7+ ♔h6 67.f4 etc. *(67.♕f8+! ♔g5 68.f4+ was simpler).*

62.♕f6 ♖xc3+ 63.♔d6 ♖d3 64.♕xf7+ ♔h6 65.♕f4+ ♔g7 66.♕e5+. Black resigned.

Right off the Bat

Korchnoi: "In 1952, I earned the right to play in the Soviet Championship for the first time – a competition that was on the level of the best grandmaster tournament and surpassed any international tournament in its intensity. And this is my very first game in that championship." (From the book *My 55 Wins With Black.*)

No. 258
Smyslov – Korchnoi
Moscow 1952, round 1
Annotated by M. Taimanov and S. Flohr

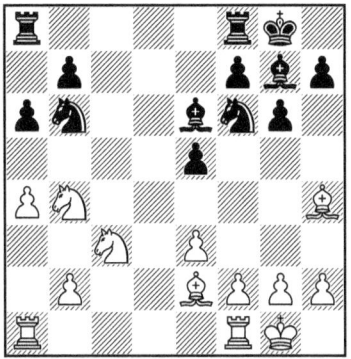

Photo portrait of Korchnoi published in advance of the championship. From D. Bronstein's archive.

"At this moment, thinking that the position had equalized, I offered a draw. But the grandmaster, probably thinking that he had no right to draw with a novice, declined the offer." (Korchnoi)

16...♖ac8. White's queenside is weakened, and black's advantage is clear. However, to convert such a small advantage you need great positional maneuvering technique. Not so long ago, only famous grandmasters possessed such a skill. In our time, Soviet players' technique has improved so much that even many young masters have learned to get a win out of a minimal advantage.

17.♖fc1. We think that 17.♗xf6 ♗xf6 18.♖fd1 ♖fd8 19.e4, creating a stronghold for the knight on d5, gave more chances to defend.

"The declined draw leaves a psychological mark on the subsequent course of the game: the 'pacifist' is thrown off balance, but probably gets an additional stimulus to play better than he did before, while the 'hawk' obliges himself to play for a win..." (Korchnoi)

17...a5! (fixing the weak a4 pawn) **18.♘d3 ♘fd5 19.♘xd5.** *In Korchnoi's opinion, this is the "decisive mistake", while after 19.♘e4! ♖xc1+ 20.♘xc1! "the position is equal" (he advises against 20.♖xc1 due to 20... ♘xa4 21.♖a1 ♗d7 22.♘ec5 ♘xc5 23.♘xc5 ♗c6 24.♖xa5 b6 25.♖a6 ♖c8 26.♘b3 e4 etc., but after 22.♗d1! or 26.♘e4!, the game is equal as well).*

19...♗xd5! Now the a4 pawn is doomed, since after 20.♘c5 black has an unpleasant reply 20...e4.

20.♗e7   ♖xc1+   21.♖xc1. 21.♘xc1 ♖c8 is not too appealing either.

21...♖e8 22.♗a3 ♘xa4. Black has an extra pawn in a good position. The game is already decided.

23.♗d1 ♘b6 24.♖c5 ♖d8!

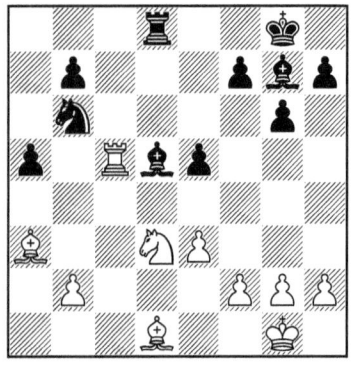

25.f3. 25.♖xa5 is bad due to 25...♗c4. Now, after 25...♗c4 white can play 26.♘f2.

25...♗f8! 26.♖c1. After 26.♖xa5 ♘c4 27.♖a7 (no other moves are better) 27...♘xa3 28.bxa3 ♗c4 29.♘f2 ♗a6, black wins *(26.♖c3!? Korchnoi)*.

26...♗xa3   27.bxa3   ♗xf3 28.♗xf3   ♖xd3   29.♖b1   ♘c4 30.♖xb7 ♘xe3 31.a4 ♖d4 32.♗c6 ♘g4 33.♖b1. Otherwise, white might lose another pawn, and he doesn't have many of them.

33...e4 34.h3 ♘e5 35.♗b5 f5 36.♖c1 f4. 36...♔f7 37.♖c7+ ♔f6 was simpler.

37.♖c5 ♖d1+ 38.♔f2.

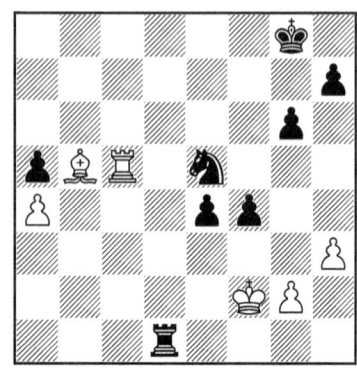

38...♘d3+. *"Incredible things happen in time trouble! After 38...e3+ 39.♔e2 ♖d2+ 40.♔e1 f3, the game would have ended there and then."* (Korchnoi)

39.♗xd3 ♖xd3 40.♖xa5 ♖d2+ *(40...e3+!)* **41.♔f1 ♔f7 42.♖a7+ ♔f6 43.♖xh7.** Smyslov has managed to restore the material balance, but piece activity is the decisive factor in such positions.

43...e3 44.♖h8 ♖d1+ 45.♔e2 ♖g1 46.a5 *(46.♔f3 ♖f1+)* **46... ♖xg2+ 47.♔f3 ♖f2+ 48.♔g4 ♔e7!** Korchnoi transfers his king to the queenside with tempo (threatening 49...e2) to neutralize white's passed pawn *(48...e2? 49.♖e8 f3 50.a6=).*

49.♖h7+ ♔d6 50.♖h8 e2 51.♖e8 ♔c6. White resigned.

The Cooked Study

Alatortsev: "This game can be compared to a dramatic miskick in soccer that puts the ball into your own net. Kasparyan prepared a mate in a few moves for his opponent... and lost."

No. 259
Suetin – Kasparyan
Moscow 1952, round 12
Annotated by V. Alatortsev

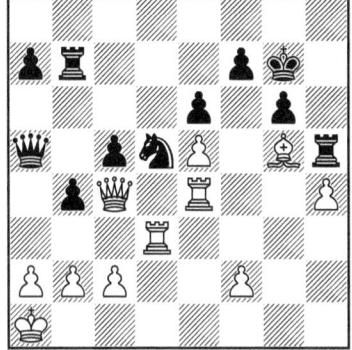

Here, black played **31...♘b6??** and immediately resigned after the obvious reply **32.♗f6+**, since there's no defense against the maneuver ♖d8-h8. For instance: 32...♔h7 33.♖d8 g5 34.♕e2 etc.

Nevertheless, Kasparyan clearly saw the win after 31...♖xg5! 32.hxg5 ♘b6 33.♕b3 c4 34.♖xc4 ♘xc4 35.♕xc4 b3!, and it's white who gets checkmated on a2 or e1!

He excitedly explained all of that to the journalists surrounding him in the players' room. But why did the talented master make that fatal mistake? It's a mystery to the reporters and, it seems, to Kasparyan himself as well.

The Leader's Loss

Yudovich: "Only yesterday, it seemed that Taimanov had almost secured first place, but now it's clear that there'll still be an intense fight for the national championship title. Taimanov made a mistake in the opening in his favorite Nimzo-Indian Defense, and Boleslavsky steered the game towards a favorable endgame. Showing great endgame technique, he defeated the tournament leader."

No. 260
Boleslavsky – Taimanov
Moscow 1952, round 15
Annotated by I. Boleslavsky

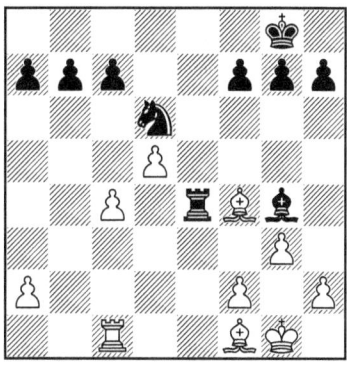

24.h3! The most precise move order. Before advancing the c-pawn, white forces the bishop to commit.

24...♗f3. If 24...♗d7 then 25.f3 ♖e7 26.c5 ♘e8 27.♗xc7! ♘xc7 28.d6 ♖e8 29.dxc7 ♖c8 30.♖d1 ♖xc7 31.♗b5, and white wins.

25.c5 ♘e8 26.♖c3 g5. Desperation! After 26...♗d1 there's 27.d6 cxd6 28.cxd6 ♗a4 29.♗g2 ♖e1+ 30.♔h2 b6 31.♖a3 with an easy win. The continuation 26...♖xf4 27.gxf4 ♗xd5 28.♗g2!

♗xa2 29.♖a3 also left black no chances.

27.♗xg5 ♗d1 28.♔g2 ♖e1+ 29.♔h2 ♖e2 30.♗e3 b6. Black misses the following tactical blow. 30...♖xe3 was more resilient.

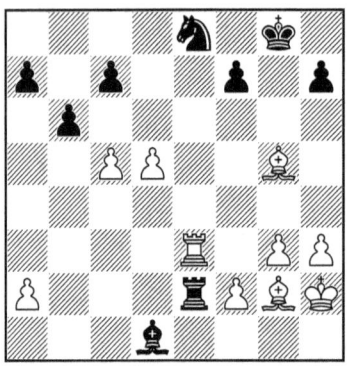

31.d6! *White wins a piece with this simple but elegant combination.*

31...cxd6 32.cxd6 ♘xd6 (if 32...♖xe3 then 33.d7) **33.♖d3 ♗a4 34.♖xd6 ♖xa2 35.♗h6 ♖e2 36.♖d4 ♗b5 37.♖g4+ ♔h8 38.♗e3.** Black resigns.

Spots on the Sun

Kan: "...we should also seriously criticize the world champion – precisely because he's the Soviet world champion, the deserved and recognized leader of the Soviet chess school. We have to acknowledge that not everything in Botvinnik's play is satisfactory for Soviet chess players. In some games, Botvinnik got into time trouble, made mistakes, couldn't always clearly convert his advantage into a win. This happened, for instance, in the games against Korchnoi and Byvshev..."

No. 261
Botvinnik – Byvshev
Moscow 1952, round 18
Annotated by G. Goldberg and D. Rovner

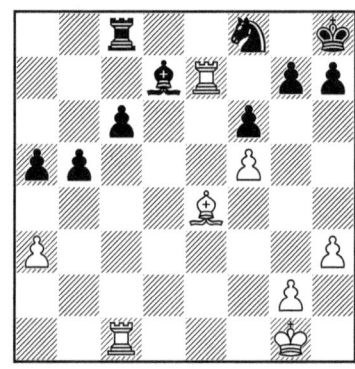

33.♖d1? A completely inexplicable move that squanders almost all the advantage. The natural 33.♖c5 with the subsequent king march into the center gave white a simple win. For instance: 33...b4 34.axb4 axb4 35.♗c2, and the pawns are stopped.

33...♗e8 34.♔f2 a4 35.♔e3 c5. Now it's very hard for white to hold the black pawns.

36.♗b7 ♖b8 37.♖d5. Another mistake that misses the win. White could still play for a win after 37.♔d2! b4 38.♔c2 bxa3 39.♖d6, intending ♔b1-a2.

Here, after 39...♗b5! (with the idea 40.♔b1 ♗c4 41.♔a1 ♗b3=), white still had his work cut out for him: 40.♗d5 c4, and if 41.♖b7 then

41...♖c8! (such moves are quite unpleasant in time trouble: 42.♖xb5? a2 43.♔b2 c3+ 44.♔xa2 c2=) 42.♗e4 a2 43.♖d1 ♗d7 etc.

White had a much stronger move: 37.♖c7! b4 38.axb4 cxb4

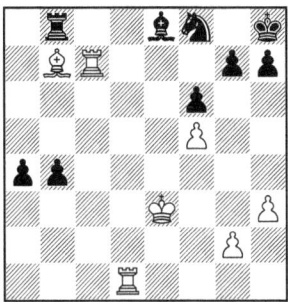

39.♗c8!, and 39...b3(a3) doesn't help due to 40.♖d8! b2 41.♖xe8 h5 42.♖f7 b1=♕ 43.♖fxf8+ ♔h7 44.♖h8#. The straightforward 39.♖c8 ♖xc8 40.♗xc8, on the other hand, squandered all the advantage: 40... b3 41.♔d2 (41.♖d8?? b2 42.♖xe8 h5 etc.) 41...a3=.

37...b4 38.♖xc5 bxa3 39.♖c3? The third mistake that should have led to white's loss. It was necessary to play 39.♗d5.

39...a2 40.♖a3.

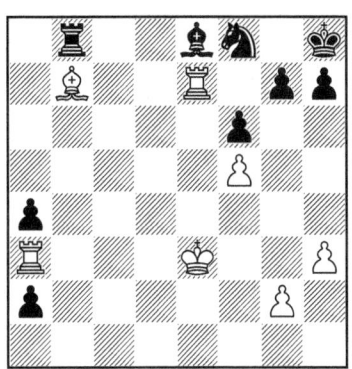

40...♗d7? Black misses the move 40...♗c6!. After 41.♗xc6 there's 41...♖b3+ 42.♖xb3 axb3 43.♖e8 g6, and the black pawn inevitably promotes. Or 41.♖xa2 ♖xb7 42.♖xb7 ♗xb7, and black gets two minor pieces and a pawn for the rook.

41.♗d5. Botvinnik sealed this move, and the opponents agreed to a draw without resuming the game. Home analysis showed the drawish nature of the position after 41...♖b3+ 42.♗xb3 axb3 43.♖xd7 b2 44.♖a8 ♔g8 45.♖dd8 ♔f7 46.♖a7+.

Can you imagine Botvinnik's disappointment? The game was played in the penultimate round, and he would have almost caught up with the leader had he won...

A Drama in Two Acts

Petrosian and **Tarasov:** "The last round. It's clear that Taimanov will be in the lead, but Botvinnik could still catch him up. Everything depends on the results of the leaders' games. The world champion had black against Suetin, and Taimanov, who also played black, battled against Geller." As a reminder, for Botvinnik to "catch up" he had to win and Taimanov had to lose!

Act One

No. 262
Geller – Taimanov
Moscow 1952, round 19
Annotated by P. Romanovsky

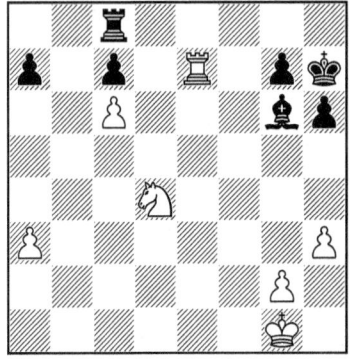

36...♗e8! Great play! In the endgame after 37.♘e6 ♗xc6

38.♖xg7+ ♔h8 39.♖xc7 ♖xc7 40.♘xc7, black has a chance to draw.

On the other hand, 37.♘b5! a6 38.♘a7 dispelled any illusions: 38... ♖d8 39.♖xc7 ♖d1+ 40.♔h2 ♖c1 41.♖e7 ♗xc6 42.♖c7, winning.

Black should have attacked the c-pawn from behind with 36...♗d3!, targeting the b5 square and forcing the transition to the very endgame where "black has a chance to draw": 37.♘e6 (or 37.♖d7 ♔g6 38.♘e6 ♗e4) 37... ♗e4 38.♖xg7+ ♔h8 39.♖xc7 ♖xc7 40.♘xc7 ♗xc6.

37.♘f5 ♔g6 38.g4. *The computer shows 0.00 here, insisting on the rook ending after 38.♘xg7 ♗xc6 39.♖e6+ ♔xg7 40.♖xc6. Analysis showed that it's also drawn with best play!*

The game against Geller was fatal for Taimanov. Photo by N. Volkov. From V. Chepizhny's archive. Published for the first time.

38...♔f6. 38...♗f7 was better, and if 39.♖d7 then 39...♔f6 40.♘e7 ♖e8.

39.♖xg7   ♗xc6   (39...h5!=) **40.♖h7 ♗e4 41.♖xh6+ ♔g5.** *The losing move! However, after 41...♔e5 black is still in serious trouble.*

42.♔f2? A mistake that should have led to a draw. It was necessary to play 42.♖h5+ ♔f4 43.♔f2 ♖b8 44.♘d4 or 43...♖d8 44.♘g3.

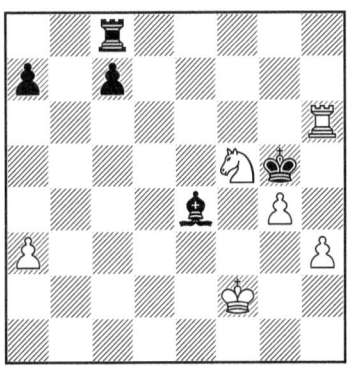

The game was adjourned in this position, and Taimanov sealed his move. Analysis showed that white couldn't win after the correct move.

42...♖b8? Black should have played 42...♖f8. The main line: 43.♖h5+ ♔g6 44.♔e3 ♗xf5 45.♖xf5 ♖xf5 46.gxf5+ ♔xf5 47.♔d4 ♔g5 (exhausted by great nervous strain, Taimanov thought that this position was lost for black) 48.♔c5 ♔h4 49.♔c6 (the preliminary 49.a4 changes nothing: instead of 49...a5? black of course plays 49...♔xh3 50.a5 ♔g4 51.♔c6 ♔f5 52.♔xc7 ♔e6 etc.) 49...♔xh3 50.♔xc7 ♔g4

51.♔b7 a5! 52.a4 ♔f5 53.♔b6 ♔e6 54.♔xa5 ♔d7 55.♔b6 ♔c8, and black makes it just in time.

43.♖h5+   ♔f4   44.♘d4   ♗g6 **45.♘e6+♔e4 46.♖h6♖g8 47.♔g3.** The capture 47.♘xc7 would have led to unexpected trouble after 47...♔f4 48.♘e6+ ♔e5.

Let's check: 49.♘g5 ♔f6 50.♘f3 ♔g7 51.g5, and black can't save the game.

47...c6   48.♘f4   ♗e8   49.♖e6+ **♔d4.**

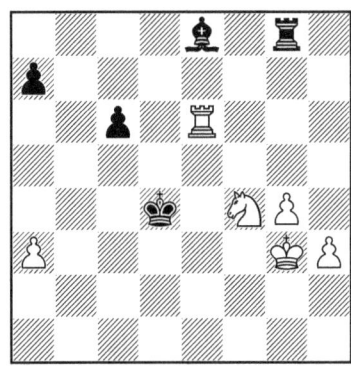

50.♖e1! A pretty move: black can't play 50...c5 due to 51.♘e6+ ♔c4 (51...♔d5 52.♘c7+) 52.♖c1+. The game is lost for black, since the h- and g-pawns are ready to march ahead at any minute.

50...♗f7 51.♖e7 ♗b3 52.♖d7+ **♔c4 53.h4 c5 54.g5 a5 55.g6 ♗c2** **56.h5   ♔b3 57.g7 c4 58.h6 ♗h7** **59.♘d5 c3 60.♖b7+ ♔xa3 61.♖c7** **♔b2 62.♘f6.** The idea is obvious: 62...c2 63.♘xh7 c1=♕ 64.♖xc1 ♔xc1 65.♘f6.

62...a4 63.♘xh7 a3 64.♘f6 a2 **65.♖b7+ ♔a1.** Or 65...♔c2 66.♖a7

♔b2 67.♘d5 c2 68.♖xa2+ ♔xa2 69.♘b4+ and ♘xc2.

66.♘d5 (preparing for 66...c2 67.♖c7 ♔b2 68.♖xc2+ etc.) **66... ♖c8 67.♘b4 c2 68.♘xc2+ ♖xc2 69.♖a7 ♖c1 70.♖xa2+.** Black resigned.

Act Two

"We were both exhausted in the last round. After the game, Botvinnik admitted that he was pushing the limits of his energy and had to lie down at his home for the whole day before the game." (Here and later, the unattributed quotes are from Suetin's book *Outstanding Soviet Chess Players*.)

No. 263
Suetin – Botvinnik
Moscow 1952, round 19
Annotated by A. Suetin

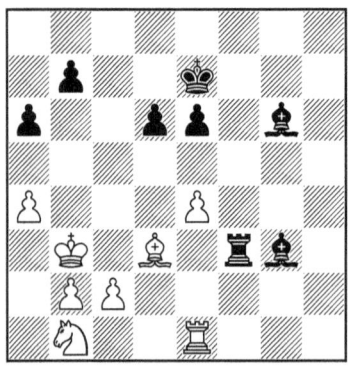

41.♖g1? Black's last move, made in time trouble *(♗e5-g3)*, tempted white to make this mistake. He thought that black had no good defense against the maneuver ♘d2. The simple 41.♖e2 with the subsequent ♘d2 gave white a draw.

"I was quite surprised to see Botvinnik's note to this move in the book *Half a Century in Chess*. Botvinnik thinks that I 'followed the method introduced by Bronstein against him in the 1951 match, hoping that he wouldn't be able to find the right continuation after five hours of play.' Unfortunately, it was all much simpler: I still don't know much about that 'Bronstein method'. However, my perennial flaw, impetuosity, was the simple reason for this mistake.

Of course, I came to the hotel in a gloomy mood. The threat of inevitable loss loomed over me.

Forgetting to rest and eat, I sat doing analysis until midnight. I unexpectedly found a helper, a very strong player. *(Could that have been Taimanov? Why else hide his helper's name?... In addition, Mark's participation in analysis could have explained why he was so sure that the game would end in a draw – see the text at the end of the game.)*

In short, I went to the game tired and hungry in the morning, but my mood was far from defeatist."

41...♗xe4. The sealed move that Botvinnik thought on for 15 minutes. It turned out that the move 41.♖g1 cost white a pawn.

42.♘d2 ♗d5+. White hadn't noticed this check when he made his rash rook move.

43.♔a3 ♖f2 44.♘e4. 44.♖xg3 ♖xd2 45.♖g7+ would objectively have caused black more trouble. But psychologically, the knight move was better because Botvinnik didn't analyze it for long, spent half an hour thinking on this and the next move, and again got into time trouble.

44...♗h2 45.♖g6 ♗xe4. 45... ♖f3 was stronger, retaining the extra pawn and two strong bishops. Now, with opposite-colored bishops, white has great drawing chances.

46.♗xe4 d5 47.♗d3.

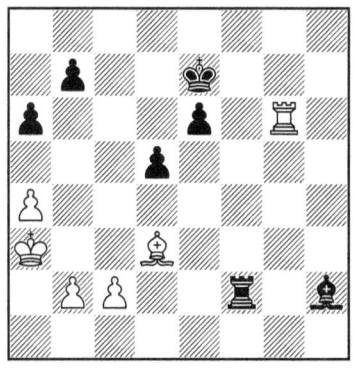

"After the game, Botvinnik admitted that he was pushing the limits of his energy and had to lie down at his home for the whole day before the game." (Suetin)

48.♖g8 ♔d7 49.b4 ♗f6.

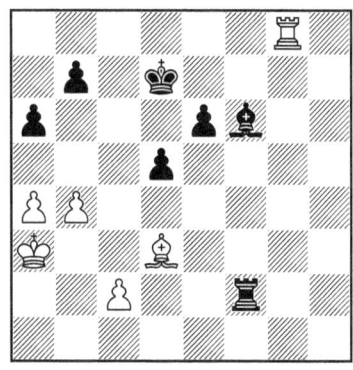

47...♗e5. *"The start of black's misadventure,"* Botvinnik wrote in Analytical and Critical Works. *"The correct move was probably 47...e5 48.♖b6 e4 49.♖xb7+ ♔d6 50.♗xa6 ♖xc2 or 50...e3, with a very dangerous position for black."* But the computer recommends 47... ♗e5, evaluating Botvinnik's line as roughly equal. For instance: *50...♖xc2 51.♖b8 d4 52.♖d8+ ♔e5 53.♗b7 e3 54.♔b3 ♖d2 55.a5 or 50...e3 51.c3 e2 52.♗xe2! ♖xe2 53.a5 etc.*

50.♖g1! The only move, but it's enough to prevent the threat e6-e5. 50...e5 is met with 51.♖d1 and then 52.♗e4 or 52.c4, blocking the onslaught of central pawns.

Let's check: 51...♔e6 52.c4 d4!
53.♗e4 (Botvinnik's line 53.♔b3
♖f3 54.♔c2 ♖e3 is weaker) 53...b6
54.c5 bxc5 55.bxc5 ♖e2 56.♗b7 (or
56.♗d3 ♖e3 57.♔b4 ♖xd3! 58.♖xd3
e4) 56...a5 57.♔b3 e4 etc.

So, Botvinnik is right to call 50...
♖h2 "an inaccuracy": "As soon as I
was able to move the e-pawn, I should
have done it."

50...♖h2 51.♔b3 ♔d6 52.♖d1
♔e7 53.c4! *"Now a draw looks very*
possible, and even though Geller
had already defeated Taimanov at
that point, I realized that I likely
wouldn't catch up with my young
competitor.

'Likely wouldn't' – but what
else could I do, agree to a draw
immediately? And so the game
continued, even though I could only
hope for a miracle." (Botvinnik)

"To my growing surprise, the
draw became increasingly real. The
question was, would I have enough
energy for a prolonged struggle?
By the way, Botvinnik also looked
quite confused and unsure of
himself."

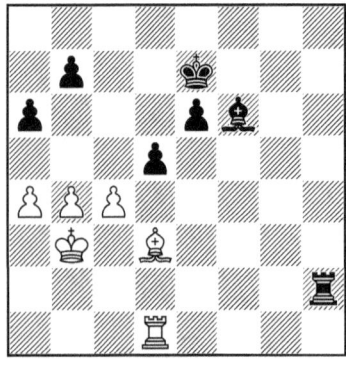

53...♖b2+   54.♔a3   dxc4
55.♗xc4   ♖c2   56.♗b3   ♗b2+
57.♔a2 ♖f2 58.♗c4

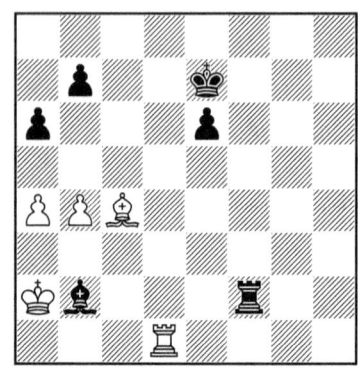

58...a5. The best chance.
Otherwise, after 59.a5 and b4-b5,
white will trade the queenside pawns
with a clear draw.

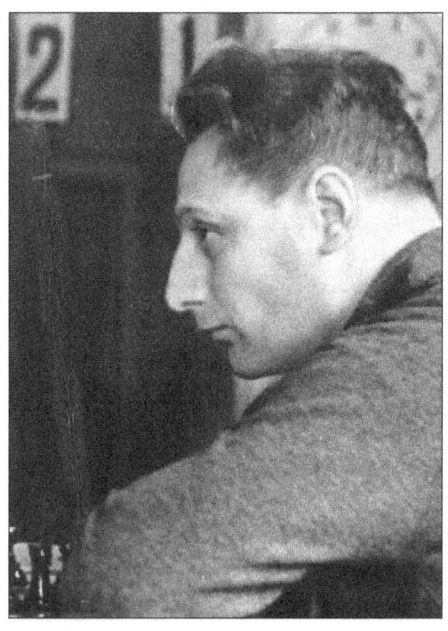

"Botvinnik immediately made a move and
pierced me with such a cold and mistrusting
gaze that I returned and... started blundering."
(Suetin). From the author's archive.

**59.bxa5 ♗c3+ 60.♔b3 ♗xa5
61.♗b5 b6 62.♔c4 ♔f6 63.♔d4
♖f4+ 64.♔e3 ♔e5 65.♖h1 ♖e4+
66.♔d3 ♖g4 67.♖h5+ ♔d6 68.♖h8
♔e5 69.♖h5+ ♔f4 70.♖h3 ♖g8
71.♖h4+ ♔e5 72.♖h5+ ♔d6
73.♖h4.** 73.♖h3 was more precise,
with a drawn position.

73...♖g3+ 74.♔e4. 74.♔d4 or
74.♔e2 were simpler ways to the
draw. "But it seemed that I got too
tired and just hungry at that point...
I decided to go to the cafeteria,
but Botvinnik immediately made
a move and pierced me with such
a cold and mistrusting gaze that I
returned and... started blundering.
By the way, I also noticed that
Botvinnik's usual confidence was
returning to him."

74...♗d2!

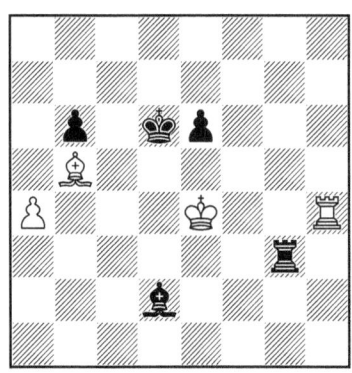

75.♗d3? The threat 75...♖e3+
76.♔d4 e5+ 77.♔c4 ♖c3+ is very
dangerous, but with 75.♖h5 (or
75.♔d4 – Botvinnik), white still
retained great drawing chances.

75...♗g5. Botvinnik gave this
move an exclamation mark, but 75...

— С победой.
— И вас также.

Рисунок И. Александровича

"Congratulations on your win."
"And to you too."
*Before the last round, Taimanov was a point
ahead of Botvinnik, but they "rode" to the
finish together. A Hollywood-like happy
ending! Cartoon by I. Alexandrovich. From
Ogonyok magazine (No. 4, 1953).*

♔c5! was a more precise continuation,
forcing 76.♖h5+ ♗g5 etc.

76.♖h5? This loses immediately.
76.♖h8 was better, but even then,
after 76...♖g4+ and ♖xa4, black
should win.

76...♔c5! White resigned.

*Botvinnik: "An incredibly rare
position! White can escape mate with
77.♖xg5+ or 77.♔e5 ♖xd3 78.♖xg5
♖d5+, but his position is still lost.*

*In the meantime, my competitor
Taimanov and his coach Flohr were
waiting for a draw, watching the
play-off in the Central Railway
Workers House of Culture (where
the championship was held). The
demonstrator came to them from time
to time to recount the latest news. Then,
there was a message: Suetin resigned!
'That is a lie!' both grandmasters
exclaimed at the same time. But when
the demonstrator showed them the
final position, they fell silent."*

Between Heaven and Earth

Match for the Title of Soviet Champion:
Moscow, 25th January – 4th February 1953

And, of course, had Stalin officially
given the battle cry, "Attack the Ki**s!",
none of them would have been left alone.
Maya Plisetskaya. From an interview with Vladimir Pozner

Can you believe it? The first ten Soviet championships ended in 1937, and the next ten in 1953. The peak of repressions – and then the end of the brutal era! Mystic numbers indeed...

I generally like coincidences. I remember being upset at the fact that the 20th championship was played in the dull 1952. And suddenly, there's a bonus: a play-off match that prolonged the tournament until the "necessary" year. Before that, in all the championships where players shared first place (5th, 9th, 16th, and 17th), the matches, despite the regulations, weren't held, and both winners were awarded the champion's titles. It's unknown why they decided to actually play the match this time, but I'm sure that Botvinnik had a hand in that: he wanted to give his offender a "flogging" ("I had to win that match – I didn't like Taimanov's behavior during our championship game") and remind everyone who was top dog. Botvinnik's motivation was essentially the same in 1937, when he challenged Levenfish to a match to restore his champion's status (another coincidence, this time – with the round numbers: the Levenfish match was played after the 10th championship, and this one after the 20th).

The situation was critical. In his book *Half a Century in Chess*, Mikhail Moiseevich wrote, "Since 1948, my results had taken a small dip – I did need to prove that I could still play chess, didn't I?" A "small dip" indeed: instead of a winning streak, there was a match with Bronstein which he barely managed to draw, 5th place in the Soviet Championship (1951) and shared 3rd–4th place in Budapest (1952). When David Ionovich once asked Larsen why Botvinnik disliked him (Bronstein) so much, Larsen answered, "Why, you removed all the gilt from him!"

The situation was made even more dire with the growing antisemitism in the country. In August 1952, after three years of torture and humiliation, prominent members of the Jewish Anti-Fascist Committee were executed, and on 13th January 1953, two weeks before the match, with the TASS news item about the arrest of the "saboteur-doctors" and the *Pravda* article titled

"Vicious Spies and Killers under the Mask of Academic Physicians", the case of the "doctors' plot" started gaining momentum, threatening to turn into a nationwide Jewish pogrom (later, the original manuscript of the article, with Stalin's own notes, was found in the archives).

There were rumors of plans to deport Jews to faraway regions – either to the Jewish Autonomous Oblast in the Far East or, even worse, to the Far North.

Beilin: "On that memorable day, I was reading the materials of a criminal case in the Lvov Oblast court office *(Master Beilin was a defense attorney)*. I wanted to leave Lvov the next morning, so I worked without leaving my room. (...) As I walked into the square, I was yanked out of my numbness by the mighty roar of the street loudspeakers. The news announcer's bass rumbled as he pronounced the Ukrainian

"Traces of crimes". A cartoon by Kukryniksys on the back cover of the Krokodil magazine published at the height of the "doctors' plot" (No. 3, 30ᵗʰ January 1953). The writing in the center says, "The state security organs have exposed a terrorist group of saboteur doctors, hirelings of foreign intelligence services." Which services? The answer is below, on the hat: "American-English intelligence". And "Joint" under the dollar sign refers to the American Jewish Joint Distribution Committee.

words *"shpigunov ta diverrrrsantov" (spies and saboteurs)* and *"infarrrrkt miokarrrrda" (heart attack)*. I stopped and figured out that this was a report about the atrocities of the killer doctors. It was clear that a very important step in the battle against cosmopolitans had been taken. Among the Jewish surnames of the killer professors, those of Egorov and Vinogradov, Stalin's personal physician, were additionally mentioned as a distraction. It seemed that a decisive phase was imminent.

(...) In Moscow, I visited a friend in the evening. His father, a Russian writer and an ethnic Jew, was grim. He said that we had to stock up on sheepskin coats, felt boots and tarpaulin boots. Universal deportation was possible – it had already happened with certain ethnicities." (From the book *Was Not, Was Never a Member, Was Never Indicted.*)

These rumors fell on fertile ground: there had been murmurs about deportation of the Jews ever since 1949, when the JAFC members were arrested shortly after the murder of Mikhoels. It might seem incredible that a country that defeated Nazism under the banner of internationalism could undertake such an openly Nazi action. But if we think a bit, there's nothing too impossible here. Wasn't deporting entire peoples already practiced in the USSR? Why could they deport the Chechens, the Ingush, the Kalmyks, the Crimean Tatars – and not do the same to the Jews? The only difference was in scope. But were tyrants ever stopped by the scope of their undertakings?

The opponents of this version cite the fact that there were no documents mentioning preparations for the deportation, nor lists of persons to be transferred. But, firstly, a lot of documents from that era are still classified, secondly, recollections of people who were warned about deportation did survive, and, thirdly, there were people who saw such lists. And what about the accounts of people from Stalin's inner circle – Mikoyan, Khrushchev, Bulganin? I'm inclined to trust these eyewitness accounts more than the lack of documents. Mikhail Beilin is right: "It's almost impossible to guess what Stalin actually planned. He was an incredible master of unexpected moves and never left any trace if needed."

There are a lot of accounts, but I'll cite only two. Let's start with my father's cousin – the wife of the poet Alexander (Isaak) Sobolev, the author of the famous song "The Alarm Bells of Buchenwald" (in the Soviet times, the poet's name was hushed up and never mentioned together with the name of the author of the music, Muradeli):

> **Tatiana Soboleva** (*nee* Voronkova): "I'm Russian, fair-haired, fair-skinned, green-eyed. And despite all those protective national and racial features, I became the first victim of the Jewish pogrom in the Moscow *Izvestia* office. This ended my journalism career then and there.
>
> At first, they tried to save me from inevitable demise. The concern about me looked very touching: in early 1953, I was confidentially recommended to divorce my husband as soon as possible. Why?! What for?! Because he was a Jew, and there was a plan by the higher-ups to deport Jews from Moscow. This caring warning was given to me by the eminent dame Zinaida Mikhailovna Platkovskaya – the sister of N. M. Shvernik himself, the chairman of the Supreme Soviet Presidium." (From an interview to *My Zdes* magazine, No. 179, 2008.)

Those who saw the Russian language documentary *Interlinear (Podstrochnik)* released in 2009 will probably never forget its heroine –

Lilianna Lungina. A philologist, translator of Boell, Gamsun, Simenon, Astrit Lindgren *(Karlsson on the Roof!)*, the wife of the famous playwright Semyon Lungin ("Sima" in her story), the mother of an even more famous filmmaker Pavel Lungin. Her 15-episode monologue was one of the strongest shocks I felt in recent years. At any rate, you can't describe the film better than Leonid Parfenov: "Lilianna Lungina's fantastic life, which spanned the entire twentieth century and her incredible story about this life crushingly confirms: all that will remain from the horrific Russian twentieth century is its culture."

> **Lilianna Lungina:** "...I was told by a friend, journalist Semyon Berkin: he had prepared a report from Stalingrad – the tractor factory workers unanimously voted for a resolution on the nationwide deportation of the Jews. And Lyonya Agranovich and Senya Listov, our playwright friends, once came to dinner to our home and said that they had written a play for the Soviet Army Theater. It was enthusiastically received, but when the head of the literature department went to the theater director and asked about the fee (they usually received 15–25 thousand 'old' rubles), the director – they called him General Pasha – said, 'Give them three thousand, it'll be enough.' The other man was baffled, and the general explained, '1,500 rubles each will be enough for them to last a month, and then they'll put them into trains and ship them away to Siberia.'
>
> We also received other evidence of what was awaiting us. Dodik Levit worked as head of the production department in Sima's theater. During the war, he worked with the Ministry of the Interior ensemble, toured the front lines with them and still occasionally organized performances of actor brigades in the military units. He told Sima that he recently went on tour to Eastern Siberia, to the middle of nowhere – by the way, Yuri Lyubimov was with him, performing as an actor and reader at these concerts. And the pilot told him at one point, 'Come here' – the planes were small back then. 'Do you see this below?' He pointed to the rows of barracks, built into T-shapes and grouped 8 or 10 meters apart from each other. He said, 'This is all built for you.' Dodik Levit, as you have guessed, was a Jew. 'What do you mean – for us?' 'They'll transport you here. The government has already issued a decree.'
>
> Jews were kicked out of the Central Committee, Moscow City Council, the city and district committees, the state security, the ministries, the newspapers, the research institutes, the universities. (...)
>
> Sima once went to the house management office to get some certificate, and the female clerk who served him said, with malicious joy but still in a somewhat friendly manner, 'Do you see these lists? They make us sit there

in the evening and add more and more names. These are your lists.' Sima
said, 'Ours in what sense?' 'Yours, you're going to be deported. Everything is
written here: who, where, to what train station.'

There were already rumors about the exact manner of the deportation.
Stalin was going to make a speech and say: to save the Jewish people from
the righteous anger of the Russians, they should be transported away from
the big cities where they are in contact with others, settle them separately, in
isolation, that this was a humane act for the sake of saving the Jews. They said
that there was already a schedule for the train stations, trains, buses, that we
could take no more than 15 kilograms of belongings... there was constant talk
like that, and, of course, it was very hard to live with. (...)

I don't doubt even for a minute – and everyone who lived back then
understood that – that hadn't Stalin died, the Jews would have been deported.
This was as real as the deportation of the Kabardians and Ossetians, Crimean
Tatars, Turks, Bulgarians, Greeks, Volga Germans. Do you know how this was
organized? They deported entire nations in 24 hours. We're bad organizers –
notoriously bad, but in such moments, we were genius organizers. I heard in
the Caucasus how the Balkars were deported. The scenario was always the
same: at nightfall or dawn, armed soldiers would surround the region, giving
you two hours to gather your belongings, then they would bring the needed
number of trucks, transported the people to railway sidetracks, with livestock
cars already waiting – brilliant organization. The deportation of Jews from
Moscow or Leningrad would have been the same, there's no doubt about it."
(From Oleg Dorman's book *Interlinear. The Life of Lilianna Lungina as Told
by Her in Oleg Dorman's Film*, Moscow 2016.)

Name Not on the List

The arguments over whether or not deportations were really planned
haven't subsided even now. As though finally learning that no, nothing of the
sort was ever prepared and it was only a rumor would have helped the Jewish
people who lived back then in any way. No, they lived in real terror, the fear
of deportation a non-stop nightmare. It was floating in the air, "hanging over
the city like a black cloud" (Lungina), and all Jewish people, including chess
players, lived under that pressure.

Even though Botvinnik was a "state Jew", it could still have affected
him. The scandal with his removal from the Olympiad team showed that his
support at the top wasn't as strong as before, and his status as first among
equals didn't serve as good protection. Stalin wasn't interested in chess
anymore, and Beria didn't like him.

Mikhail Botvinnik, late 1940s. The drawing's author is unknown.

In Botvinnik's memoir, there's a photocopy of an order signed by Stalin personally, increasing the "limit of gasoline consumption for the automobile allocated for the services of world chess champion Comrade Botvinnik". Well, as it turns out, the glorious leader also helped him to obtain a dacha. The USSR Sports Committee deputy chairman **Dmitry Postnikov**, who oversaw chess back then, recalled:

"When Botvinnik became world champion, he decided to build a dacha. Not just anywhere, but in one of the most prestigious places of the Moscow region – at Nikolina Gora. (...) Nikolina Gora is located near the Moscow River, in the water protection zone of Moscow, and it was controlled by the Ministry of the Interior. Botvinnik sent a letter to 'Interior Minister L. Beria' *(Beria was appointed Deputy Prime Minister of the USSR in March 1946 but the Interior Ministry and Ministry of State Security reported to him)* and asked the Sports Committee Chairman Apollonov for support.

Sometime later, Apollonov ordered Postnikov to call Botvinnik and tell him that Beria had denied his request. Postnikov invited Mikhail Moiseevich to a meeting and relayed the Sports Committee chairman's words to him.

'Allow me to use your government phone,' Botvinnik asked suddenly, and when I allowed him, he quickly dialed a number. It was obvious that he was ready for that turn of events and wasn't going to pull back.

A voice sounded in the receiver. 'Malenkov is on the phone. Whom am I speaking to?'

'Hello, Georgy Maximilianovich! World Champion Botvinnik speaking. Could you please receive me about a small issue?'

At the time (late 1940s), G. Malenkov was one of Stalin's closest associates.

'Where are you calling from?'

'From the Sports Committee.'

'I'll be waiting for you at Staraya Square in twenty minutes. I'll order a pass for you.' (The CPSU Central Committee building was at Staraya Square.)

After saying goodbye to Postnikov, Botvinnik hurried to Staraya Square. And a week later, a telephonogram was sent to the Sports Committee. The contents:

'Concerning the request of Comrade Botvinnik M. M.

To Minister of Forestry Comrade Orlov. Allocate [some specified amount] of cubic meters of wood for Comrade Botvinnik M. M.

To Minister of Railways Comrade Beschev. Ensure transportation of wood to the Nikolina Gora residential area.

To Mossovet Chairman Comrade Popov. Allocate a plot of land in Nikolina Gora for Comrade Botvinnik M. M.'s dacha.

To the Mossovet Main Architecture Department. Provide a standard dacha design project to Comrade Botvinnik M. M.

All expenses to be paid by Comrade Botvinnik M. M.'"

Yuri Averbakh published this story in his book *What the Pieces Don't Mention*, adding, "But the main thing, of course, was the signature: I. Stalin. That's how Botvinnik managed to outplay the all-powerful Beria!" And recently, Yuri Lvovich admitted to me that he omitted the exact words of Beria's refusal in his book (Apollonov mockingly quoted it to his deputy back then). But without these words, you just wouldn't be able to understand the depth of Beria's hostility towards Botvinnik. "A dacha at Nikolina Gora for every sh**head out there?!"

Since, according to Mikoyan, deportation was going to take an "involuntarily voluntary" form, there was an important step in this plan: a letter from famous Jews to the government. Its contents are also still hotly debated. The Russian State Archive of Modern History (RGANI) only holds two later (unsent) versions (dated 29th January and 20th February), with a demand to "punish mercilessly the spying gang of killer doctors", without a single word mentioning deportation. We only know about the contents of the original letter from the words of the people who saw it.

Veniamin Kaverin: "I read the letter: it was like a verdict that immediately confirmed the long-running rumors about barracks being built for a future ghetto in the Russian Far East."

Ilya Ehrenburg (both he and Kaverin were famous Soviet writers of Jewish descent): "The letter contained a most humble request. The killer doctors, those fiends of humanity, are exposed. The anger of the Russian people is righteous. Perhaps Comrade Stalin would deem it possible to show mercy and 'save the Jews from the righteous anger of the Russian people' by transporting them to the margins of the country under protection."

No wonder that this letter was never found: it was probably destroyed right after Stalin's death, given how disgraceful that whole deportation idea would be for the country and how the United States would react. But didn't Stalin realize all that, too?

"Of course he realized that!" **Edvard Radzinsky**, the author of the fundamental work *Stalin* (Moscow 1997), wrote. "Does this mean that he wanted a confrontation for some reason? That he wanted to sever ties with the West completely? (...) As Molotov rightly explained in his dialogues with Chuev, the 1930s terror had a concrete purpose – to prepare the country for war. And the imminent 1950s terror was needed to... Yes, to start a new Great War – a war with the West. The last war that was supposed to finally crush capitalism.

He planned a Patriotic, Holy War – under familiar, understandable slogans: crush the world's evil (capitalism) and its agents (international Jewry). Of course, the propaganda declared America to be the embodiment of this evil. That's why he wanted to provoke a confrontation with the States."

Naturally, when the organizers prepared the letter, they had to include Mikhail Botvinnik among the signatories. The world champion, pride and joy of the whole country. His signature was very important. But did he actually sign the letter?

There were various rumors, but nobody raised the issue in chess literature until recent times. It seems that the first who violated that unspoken taboo was **Garry Kasparov**: "In 1953, when they gathered signatures from famous Jews for the notorious 'doctors' plot', Botvinnik somehow managed to stay away. How he managed that is a mystery: he didn't like to talk about such matters." (From the book *My Great Predecessors*, 2003).

But why didn't he "like to talk about such matters"? If you didn't sign the letter, just say so – you can only be proud of such a deed. Mikhail Moiseevich surely realized that secrecy only begat suspicion? Especially since, as it turned out, he had nothing to hide: no version of the letter kept in RGANI has Botvinnik's signature on it. But how did he manage to avoid it?

I found an answer almost accidentally, in the book *Yuri Razuvaev. Essays* by Sosonko and Gulko. **Boris Gulko** recalls (by the way, he remembered a terrifying detail: they lived in a workers' settlement near Moscow, and his "father kept an axe under his pillow" in case of a pogrom):

"I always wondered what Botvinnik actually did – he was surely asked to sign the letter. Botvinnik was not named among those who refused outright to sign the letter. I couldn't imagine him signing the letter either. To support a death sentence for your family and probably yourself, you have to be very weak-willed. And nobody could have said that about Botvinnik.

Botvinnik told Vaksberg, who made a film *(about Stalin's conspiracy against the Jews)*, that Baturinsky warned him and insistently recommended him to 'disappear' and not pick up the phone while signatures were being gathered. Such advice is worth a lot..."

Internet searches led me to the film *The Reprise*, with a screenplay by well-known journalist and writer **Arkady Vaksberg** (2005). Apart from Botvinnik's story it contained his explanation: "I couldn't go away, I was working, but I hastily took sick leave and didn't touch the phone." But how could he have avoided answering the phone when signatures for the new version of the letter, which was milder because of Ehrenburg's influence, were gathered from 30th January to 1st February, when he was in everyone's sights: the 4th game of the Botvinnik – Taimanov match was played on 31st January on the stage of the Central House of the Soviet Army (TsDSA)?.. Perhaps there was a different reason? After all, another famous "state Jew", news announcer Yuri (Yudka) Levitan, also never signed the letter for some reason!

Well, later I managed to find the full version of this story in Vaksberg's book *From Hell to Paradise and Back. The Jewish Question According to Lenin, Stalin and Solzhenitsyn* (Moscow, 2003):

"Botvinnik angrily refused to talk to me. Angrily – that's what struck me. He asked me not to bother him – he didn't want to return to those 'nightmare days' for all the world. Nightmare – that was his expression. Finally, after my third or fifth attempt (December 1991), he admitted, 'I was being nagged by some academician *(it was probably the historian Isaak Mints)*, who was saying to me: *sign it, everybody else has already signed it*. But it was right during my short match with Taimanov for first place in the Soviet championship – a great excuse to ask that he not disturb me. And I was also warned by Baturinsky (a Colonel of Justice with a leading role in the Soviet Chess Federation) that once the match was over I was not to

Lieutenant Colonel Viktor Baturinsky, back then deputy chief military prosecutor of the USSR, served as Botvinnik's "guardian angel". From the author's archive. Published for the first time.

answer the phone and that it would be better still for me to keep out of sight. I couldn't go away but I didn't pick up the phone either. I didn't know what it was about, but didn't answer the phone just in case. I took Baturinsky's word for it – he was a knowledgeable man and wouldn't have given such advice for nothing. *(It would have been strange for him not to be knowledgeable: he became a "bigwig" in chess only later, but back then he was Deputy Chief Soviet Military Prosecutor!)* My family didn't answer calls either, though the phone rang off the hook incessantly – maybe it was just somebody wanting to congratulate me, but being congratulated was the last thing on my mind at the time.'

Viktor Davydovich Baturinsky (a *Literaturnaya gazeta* correspondent interviewed him at my request) couldn't recall whether or not he had held such a discussion with Botvinnik. But that's not of any relevance. I can imagine the torture that Botvinnik was going through: in 1948 he had written how he welcomed the creation of the state of Israel and the Kremlin's recognition of the state. Signing a letter to *Pravda* could perhaps have softened his guilt for that terrible act, if the time came to face the music. He didn't sign it. Does it matter how he got away with that? He didn't sign it ..."

And finally. Grandmaster Adrian Mikhalchishin wrote to me a few years ago: "I spoke with Beliavsky. He remembers Botvinnik telling him about Stalin's plan to deport the Jews in 1953. Botvinnik called Molotov, who told him: 'Don't worry, you're on the list of those allowed to stay in Moscow.'"

From Beneath the Sands of Time

A paradox: the incumbent world champion played a match, but nobody wrote a separate article about it – neither immediately afterwards nor later (the report given below is part of Ilya Kan's article about the 20th championship). Even the participants themselves, it seems, weren't too eager to remember this match. I think Taimanov only first mentioned it in the book *Remembering the Greatest...*, and only then in connection with the scandal in the tournament game. Botvinnik was also quite cursory in his books. And it's clear why: if not for his opponent's mistakes in the adjourned games, it's hard to say how the match would have ended. At any rate, his win was far from convincing (3.5–2.5). Only one game (the 4th) can be called consistent, and even that was marred by a serious mistake.

The ChessBase Megabase surprised me as well: for one thing, the match was dated 1952, and not a single game was annotated! The match got buried under the sands of time so quickly that even the three-volume book *Chess Games of Botvinnik* states that the match was held from 1st to 16th February.

Where did Baturinsky get these dates from? Maybe from the tournament book? But it only says "February" there. Which is also incorrect, by the way: the match took place from 25th January to 4th February.

And another thing caught my attention as well. Both *Sovietsky Sport* and *Shakhmaty v SSSR* did everything they could to avoid the word "match": "additional competition", "contest", "meeting" – everything but a match. They probably did it to avoid the unneeded allusions: any match against the world champion is a match against the world champion! Years later, when Petrosian and Bronstein shared 1st–2nd place in the 1968 Moscow championship and, in accordance with the regulations, were supposed to play a match to determine the champion, Tigran Vartanovich refused, explaining his decision in the following way: "Bronstein is trying to bypass the existing rules and play a match against the world champion."

Only now do we truly understand the full magnitude of risk that Botvinnik took: losing a match to Taimanov could have tarnished his reputation as a world champion!

From the press: "As we know, M. Botvinnik and M. Taimanov shared 1st and 2nd place at the 20th Soviet Championship. Whom should we consider the 1952 champion?

This will be determined by a competition that started on 25th January in the Central House of the Soviet Army concert hall. Botvinnik and Taimanov will play six games. However, as soon as one of them scores 3.5 or 4 points, the contest will be stopped regardless of the number of remaining games. In the case of a 3–3 score, the competition shall continue until one of the participants wins a game.

The hall is full. The Chief Arbiter, Master M. Kamyshov, starts the chess clock at exactly half past five. Taimanov, who has white, moves the queen's pawn two squares ahead. Botvinnik opts for the Slav Defense. The opponents castle on opposite sides: Botvinnik to the kingside, Taimanov to the queenside. This sets the nature of the struggle. Black concentrates his forces on the queenside, while white tries to create counterplay on the kingside." (*Sovietsky Sport*, 27th January 1953).

Kan: "In the first game, after an idiosyncratic opening, the world champion, who had black, seized the initiative. With inventive and tenacious defense, Taimanov reached a roughly equal position. The game was adjourned. After home analysis, Botvinnik decided against trying to play for a win and planned a safer continuation that guaranteed him a draw but needed certain precision from white.

On the play-off day, the battle ended rather unexpectedly. Taimanov made an elementary miscalculation in his home analysis. As a result, he got into a hopeless pawn endgame and immediately resigned *(see game 264)*.

The second game initially went well for the young grandmaster, and the world champion only managed to equalize and draw the game with subtle maneuvers *(see game 265)*.

The start of the third game leads to a position with mutual chances. However, Botvinnik doesn't play optimally in the middle of the game and even makes a mistake that leads to the loss of the important g7 pawn. The game is adjourned in a critical position for the world champion, but on the play-off day, Taimanov again gives his opponent a 'pleasant surprise': this time, he missed quite a transparent threat by black to win the queen for a rook and bishop in home analysis *(see game 266)*.

From the press: "However, the formidable white passed pawn still gave Taimanov an advantage. Botvinnik had to search for a solution that ensured

If Taimanov hadn't made a gross miscalculation in the analysis of the adjourned first game, we can't say for sure how the match would have gone... Photo by N. Volkov. From V. Chepizhny's archive. Published for the first time.

a peaceful ending to the struggle. The world champion managed to find the right way. Playing very strongly in the endgame, Botvinnik managed to draw on the 56th move. Thus, the score after three games is 2–1 in favor of world champion Botvinnik. Yesterday was a rest day." (*Sovietsky Sport*, 31st January.)

In the fourth game, Botvinnik deployed an important improvement in the opening *(Nimzo-Indian Defense; see game 267)* compared with his game against Taimanov at the 20th championship. Taimanov still managed to create counterplay, and soon white had a choice: either accept a difficult battle faced with black's quickly growing counter-initiative, or go for an interesting piece sacrifice that gave some chances of a strong attack.

Botvinnik chose the second option, and subsequent analysis proved that it was the correct decision. However, there was a moment in the process of attack when Taimanov seemingly could have defended by capturing an apparently invincible pawn. Nevertheless, Taimanov misevaluated the position and quickly lost *(the game was adjourned, but he resigned without resuming play)*.

Once the score reached 3–1 in Botvinnik's favor, there was a real chance that the competition would already end after game 5. However, this didn't happen. On the 13th move, Botvinnik *(now it was he who chose the Nimzo-Indian Defense; see game 268)* made a serious inaccuracy by avoiding trading a bishop for knight. If black went for this trade, he could have got full-blown counterplay that justified his opening structure. Taimanov skillfully exploited Botvinnik's oversight, created a strong kingside attack and deservedly won.

So, the score was 3–2. Botvinnik led by one point and had white in the sixth game.

From the press: "Numerous chess fans filled the TsDSA concert hall to the brim. The spectators had every right to think that the 6th game would be the decisive one. It was enough for Botvinnik to draw to score a match victory. However, Botvinnik didn't go for simplifications. His opponent, who chose the Nimzo-Indian Defense, had to maneuver relentlessly.

Despite all the persistent efforts, neither side managed to break through because all the files were closed off by the pawn chain... During the play-off, the opponents agreed to a draw.

Thus, M. Botvinnik (Moscow, Energia society) won the honorable title of Soviet

М. Ботвинник — чемпион СССР по шахматам

"M. Botvinnik – Soviet chess champion." It's hard to believe, but the portrait of the new Soviet champion was only printed in Sovietsky Sport (7th February 1953). For some reason, there was no photo in Shakhmaty v SSSR, even though a big portrait of Tolush, the winner of the Bucharest tournament, was printed in the same issue (No. 4, 1953).

champion. After six games, he had 3.5 points, and M. Taimanov (Leningrad, Iskra society) had 2.5 points.

After the game, M. Botvinnik was awarded a first-degree diploma and the Soviet Championship gold medal. M. Taimanov received the second-degree diploma." (Ibid., 7th February.)

Evaluating the results of the play-off competition, we should point out that the quality of the games was affected by two factors: the first one is sporting tension caused by the short distance, and the second one is the inadequate length of the break after a difficult tournament that left the players unable to rest and prepare properly.

Taimanov's performance demonstrated that the Leningrad champion is one of our strongest grandmasters. As Botvinnik said at the closing ceremony, Taimanov showed himself to be a first-class chess strategist who was well-prepared theoretically.

The negative aspects of Taimanov's play also manifested themselves: technical miscalculations and insufficiently deep analysis of adjourned positions. We shouldn't doubt that these games against the world champion will help Taimanov to eliminate the shortcomings in his play." (*Shakhmaty v SSSR*, No. 4, 1953.)

Have you noticed? No praise for Botvinnik, as usually happened. They didn't even provide a photo of him, even though they printed a big portrait of Tolush, the winner of the Bucharest tournament (and the portrait of Soviet champion Keres made it to the cover the previous year!). This clearly shows the attitude towards Mikhail Moiseevich at the time. We are mistaken in thinking that he was always the darling of the higher-ups. No, he also had his dark periods...

He Who Makes the Last Mistake

The quality of the match games wasn't solely affected by "sporting tension caused by the short distance" and the "inadequate length of the break after a difficult tournament that left the players unable to rest and prepare properly". Ilya Kan couldn't write about the oppressive atmosphere of fear and uncertainty that surrounded the match and which couldn't help but affect play. Try, as a Jew, to forget everything about the anti-Semitic hysteria and fully concentrate on the games! Therefore, we shouldn't be surprised by the mistakes: we should be surprised that there was so few of them...

Speaking of Taimanov's play, let me remind you of his own words: "Botvinnik clearly set the duration of his 'sentences' and didn't speak with his 'offenders' for a long, long time. My 'sentence' ended about two years later..." And this means that they weren't on speaking terms during the match. And this situation worked in Botvinnik's favor – as we know, he liked to sour relationships with his opponents to prepare himself to fight. The frank, smiling Taimanov, on the other hand, was probably out of his element, even though he never showed his emotions. In the game annotations for the magazine, he calls his opponent just "Botvinnik", while Botvinnik pointedly calls him "Grandmaster Taimanov" or "M. Taimanov", hiding his animosity behind artificial politeness.

A Victim of Routine

Botvinnik writes that "there were a lot of adventures in the match". Very true! However, Taimanov's gross blunder in the play-off of the first game should probably be called a "misadventure". Wouldn't you think that the gross miscalculation in his home analysis served as a warning bell to him, and that he then started studying the adjourned positions in more depth? No, he made a similar mistake in the third game...

No. 264
Taimanov – Botvinnik
Moscow (m/1), 25th January 1953

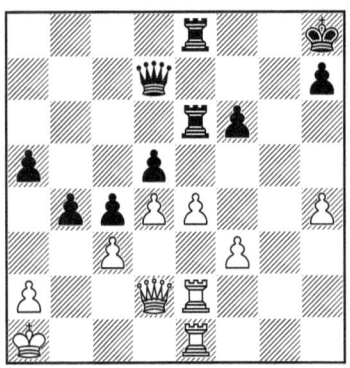

41...♕e7. With his sealed move, black increases the pressure on the e4 pawn to the maximum.

42.e5! In the magazine annotations, Botvinnik only assigned an exclamation mark without commentary. In *Analytical and Critical Works*, we read: "Finalizing the creation of a passed pawn. Black still has some advantage, mainly because in the long term, his king (after the queen trade) can become more active than the white king. Thus, black should go for a rook ending."

42...bxc3 43.♕xc3 ♕b4 44.♕b2?! The correct move was 44.♕xb4 axb4 45.f4 with the idea 45...f5 46.♖g2 ♖h6 47.♖h1 ♖a8 48.♔b1 ♖ha6 49.♖h3 b3 50.♖hh2!= (Botvinnik). But it seemed that Taimanov wanted to wait until black captures the e5 pawn.

44...fxe5 45.♕xb4. Of course, 45.♖xe5? ♕xe1+ is bad, while after 45.dxe5 Botvinnik had prepared 45...♕c5! with the unpleasant threat d5-d4.

45...axb4 46.♖xe5. It still wasn't too late to deviate from the path to disaster: 46.dxe5!? ♔g7 47.f4, even though white's position is already very difficult.

46...♖xe5.

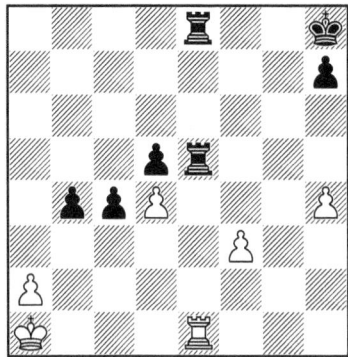

47.♖xe5? "Tantamount to resignation, but after 47.dxe5 ♔g7 black is better as well *(the computer believes that the game is already won)*. Here, Grandmaster Taimanov offered a draw, and it became clear that he was in a pleasant delusion – the result of erroneous home analysis." (Botvinnik)

47...♖xe5 48.dxe5 d4! A rare case when separated passed pawns prove to be stronger than connected ones – Taimanov failed to take account of this "exception"! All other moves miss the win because the white king gets to the c2 square in time.

49.e6 ♔g7 50.f4 ♔f6 51.f5 d3 52.♔b2 h5! White resigned. After 53.♔b1 b3 54.axb3 cxb3 55.♔c1 ♔e7 he's in zugzwang, and one of the black pawns gets promoted.

A Bout Of Cowardice

In the opening, black "got an excellent game", but white managed to "maintain the balance". In the diagram position, Taimanov decided against "unclear play" that gave him some initiative, probably thinking that his task (a draw with black) was complete and deciding to play for a win with white. The next day, after the first game play-off, he probably regretted his pusillanimity!

No. 265
Botvinnik – Taimanov
Moscow (m/2), 26th January 1953
Annotated by M. Taimanov

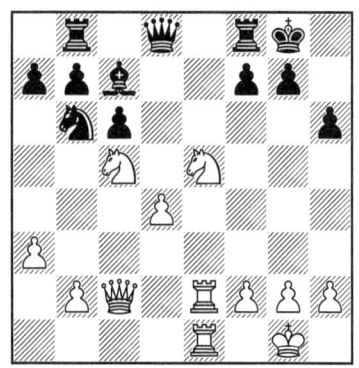

21...♕d5. 21...♕xd4 22.♖d1 ♕h4 23.g3 ♕h5 24.♘ed7 ♖fe8 (24...♘xd7? 25.♖xd7) 25.♖xe8+ ♖xe8 26.♘xb7 led to unclear play.

"Unclear"? After 26...♘xd7 27.♖xd7 ♗xg3!! (Stockfish, you son of a gun!), white loses his queen: 28.fxg3 (otherwise there's checkmate) 28...♖e1+ 29.♔f2 ♕xh2+ and ♕xc2. But instead of 24.♘ed7?!

white had 24.♖de1 ♖fe8 25.♘xc6! ♖xe2 26.♖xe2 bxc6 27.♘a6 ♗xg3! 28.hxg3 with a roughly equal position.

21...♖e8 was a clear error due to 22.♘xf7! ♖xe2 23.♕xe2 ♔xf7 24.♕e6+ ♔f8 25.♖e3 with an unstoppable attack.

And here, our electronic magician also has a surprise: 25...♕xd4!! 26.♖d3 ♕f6 27.♖f3 ♗f4!, and the attack is repelled. Instead of 23.♕xe2, a knight somersault leads to a win:

Position after 21...♖e8 22.♘xf7
♖xe2

23.♘xh6+!! ♔h8 (the best) 24.♘f7+ ♔g8 25.♕xe2! ♔xf7 26.♘e6!, and the bishop cannot be saved. For instance: 26...♕e7 27.♘xc7 ♕xe2 (27...♕xc7 28.♕e6+ ♔f8 29.♖e4!, threatening ♖h4) 28.♖xe2 ♖d8 29.♘e6 ♖e8 30.♘g5+! ♔f8 31.♖xe8+ ♔xe8 32.♘e6 ♔f7 (32...g6 33.♘c5) 33.♘d8+ ♔f6 34.♘xb7 etc.

22.♘f3 ♗d6 23.♕e4. The queen on d5 can't be tolerated for long.

23...♖fd8 24.♕xd5 ♘xd5 25.g3 ♘c7. Draw. Black's position is still somewhat better (the white d4 pawn

is weak), but it's almost impossible to convert such an advantage.

One wonders how they offered draws if they weren't speaking to each other... Through the arbiter, like Alekhine and Capablanca did at the AVRO tournament?

A Hole in Home Analysis

When black failed to find the correct continuation on the 20th move, white seized the initiative and created a strong attack. In the adjourned position, Botvinnik didn't have any chance of saving the game, but then he suddenly got help... from his opponent!

No. 266. Dutch Defense A85
Taimanov – Botvinnik
Moscow (m/3), 28 January 1953
Annotated by M. Taimanov
1.d4 e6 2.c4 f5 3.♘c3 ♘f6 4.e3. This development system in the Dutch Defense was once extensively used by A. Rubinstein. White is trying to position his pieces with the setup ♕c2, ♗d3, ♘ge2, ♗d2.

4...♗b4. This bishop development is the most logical from the point of view of fighting for the center.

5.♕c2 0-0 6.♗d3 d6. *Later, both 6...b6 and the immediate 6... c5 (Taimanov – Kopylov, 1954 Soviet Championship s/f) became fashionable.*

7.♘ge2 c5. This position had already occurred twice in Botvinnik's black games: against Kotov in 1947 *(at the Chigorin Memorial)* and against Bronstein in 1951 *(in the 10th game of the world championship match)*.

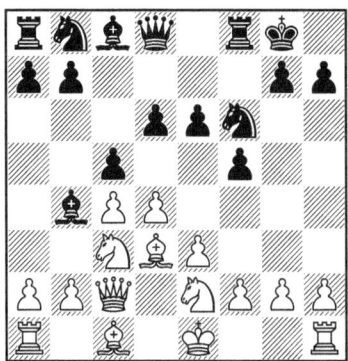

8.a3. Kotov played 8.d5 here, but after 8...♝xc3+! 9.♞xc3 exd5 10.cxd5 ♞g4! 11.0-0 ♞a6 12.♝e2 ♝d7 black got an advantage *(however, only because of white's mistakes on the 18th and 19th moves!)*. The move 8.a3 is stronger and recommended by Botvinnik in his notes to the aforementioned game.

8...♝a5. Without a doubt 8...♝xc3+ 9.♞xc3 *(9.♛xc3!)* 9...♞c6 10.dxc5 dxc5, as played in the Bronstein – Botvinnik game, was better. After the bishop's retreat, white gets a better position.

9.d5! exd5. If now 9...♝xc3+ 10.♞xc3 exd5 11.cxd5 ♞g4 12.0-0 ♞a6, then 13.f4! is very strong.

10.cxd5 ♞g4. Of course, not 10...♞xd5? due to 11.♝c4 ♝e6 12.♛b3.

11.♞f4 ♞e5 12.♝e2 ♛e7 13.0-0 ♞a6 14.b3 ♝d7 15.♝b2 ♞c7 16.♜ad1 b5.

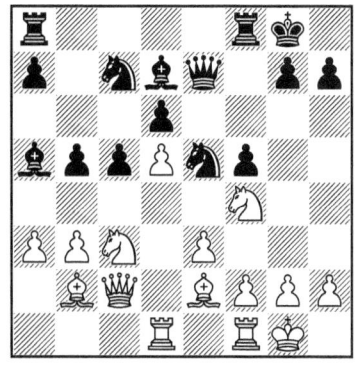

The mobilization of forces is complete. At first sight, black has decent counterplay thanks to the sensible position of his pieces on the queenside. However, as the subsequent play shows, white's chances in the center and on the kingside are more tangible.

17.♞b1! White is planning to transfer his knight to f3 to drive the e5 knight from its strong position and make the dark-squared bishop more "alive".

17.♞e6! was more aggressive, exploiting the pawn's position on b5, so 16...♜ac8 was more resilient.

17...♜ac8   18.♞d2   ♞g6. Perhaps black should have waited until white played ♞f3 to trade the knight off and make the defense easier.

19.♞h5   ♞e8. A serious inaccuracy. 19...♜f7 was better.

The game move is not bad either. Taimanov obviously overestimated his position, and after he played 20.a4?!, he could have even faced serious trouble.

20.a4! An unexpected resource.

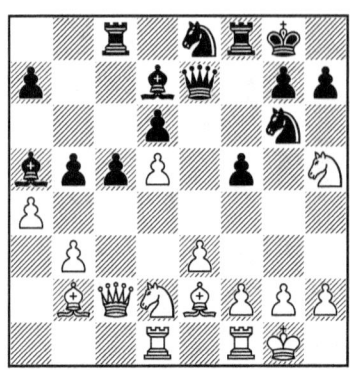

20...♗xd2. It's not easy for black to find a satisfactory continuation.

20...b4 or 20...bxa4 are clearly poor, since the white knight obtains a great outpost on c4. 20...a6 is also bad due to 21.axb5 axb5 22.♖a1, and the disconnected black rooks allow white to seize the a-file.

It was worth considering the attempt to complicate with 20...f4!?, to meet 21.axb5 not with 21...fxe3 22.♘c4 exf2+ 23.♖xf2 ♖xf2 24.♔xf2, which is obviously good for white *(this is questionable due to 24...♗d8!)*, but with the bold 21...♗xd2 22.♕xd2 f3 (proposed by Chekhover). If now 23.♗xf3?, then 23...♖xf3! 24.gxf3 ♘h4 25.♕e2 ♖b8 with a strong attack for black. However, after 23.gxf3! ♗h3 24.♔h1! ♗xf1 25.♖xf1, white, having two pawns for the exchange, active bishops and a strong pawn center, has every chance to win.

Not so: after 23...♕h4! (instead of 23...♗h3?), it's black who "has every chance to win"!

Position after 20...f4 21.axb5 ♗xd2 22.♕xd2 f3 23.gxf3 ♕h4

For example: 24.♘f4 (24.f4 ♕h3 with the threat ♘h4) 24...♘xf4 25.exf4 ♗h3 26.♖fe1 ♖xf4 27.♔h1 (otherwise there's a mate in two) 27...♕xf2 28.♖g1 ♖xf3! or 24.♘g3 ♕h3! 25.♔h1 ♘h4 26.♖g1 ♗g4! 27.♕c2 ♘xf3 28.♖g2 ♘h4 29.♖dg1 (29. ♖gg1? ♖xf2, mating) 29...♘xg2 etc.

21.♕xd2 b4. After this move, white is free to launch kingside operations, but even accepting the sacrifice with 21...bxa4 22.bxa4 ♗xa4 wasn't particularly attractive. For instance: 23.♖a1 ♗b3 24.♖a3 ♖b8 25.♖b1! with various threats.

After 25...♕e4 this loses the d5 pawn. 25.♗c3! is stronger.

22.f4! ♖f7 23.♖de1 ♕f8 24.♗d3. Intending to open the e-file with e3-e4. Another good plan was h2-h3, ♔h2 and g2-g4.

24...♖c7 25.e4. This is not bad, but the preliminary 25.h3! was even stronger.

25...fxe4 26.♗xe4 ♗g4. After 26...♗f5 there could follow 27.♗xf5 ♖xf5 28.g4! ♖ff7 29.f5 and ♘f4.

27.♗f3 ♗xf3 28.♖xf3 ♖ce7

29.♖e6 ♘c7. Passive defense would have left black no chance *(29...♘h4 30.♖f2!)*. The positional threat 30.g4 and 31.f5 is rather unpleasant.

30.♖xd6 ♕e8. Due to the possible rook invasion along the e-file, it seems that black gets some counterchances. However, an unexpected tactical blow destroys these plans. After the game ended, there was an opinion that black could have continued the game by playing 30...♖e2 31.♕xe2 ♕xd6. We can't agree with that. White maintains an obvious advantage with 32.♖d3!.

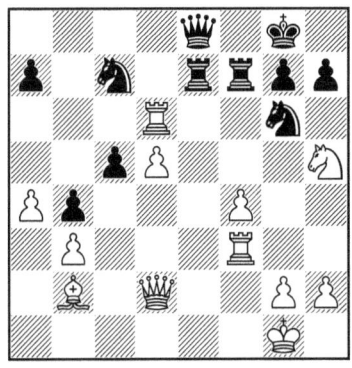

31.♗xg7! ♖e2 (or 31...♖e1+ 32.♔f2) **32.♕d3 ♕e7.** After 32... ♘h4 there was a spectacular mate: 33.♕xh7+! ♔xh7 34.♖h6+ ♔g8 35.♖h8#.

33.♖xg6! hxg6 34.d6 ♖e1+ 35.♔f2 ♕h4+ 36.♘g3. 36.♔g3! won in a simpler way. For instance: 36...♕xh5 37.♔xe1 *(37.dxc7!)* 37... ♔xg7 38.dxc7 ♖xc7 39.♖g5 ♕h6 40.♕d6 etc.

36...♔xg7 37.♔xe1 ♘e6 38.♕e4 ♘d4 39.♖f2 ♕xh2 40.♕e5+

♔h7 **41.♘f1 ♕h5** *(the sealed move)* **42.♘g3 ♕h2.** Of course, 42...♕xe5+ 43.fxe5 ♔g7 44.♘e4! loses.

43.♕xc5 ♖xf4. The only chance. All other moves by black lost immediately. For instance: 43...♘xb3? 44.♕d5 or 43...♕xg3 44.♕xd4 ♕xb3 45.♖f3 etc.

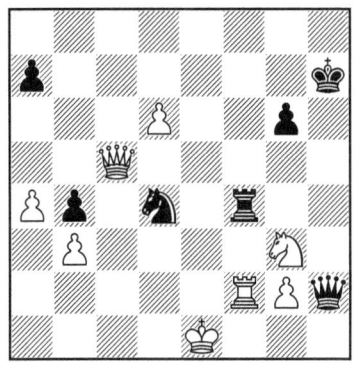

44.♖xf4? A mistake in the home analysis! Looking over this position, white automatically made the move 44...♕xg3+ for his opponent, and the game was subsequently won after 45.♖f2 ♕e3+ 46.♔f1 ♕d3+ 47.♔g1 ♘e2+ 48.♖xe2 ♕xe2 49.♕d4. However, white simply blundered the cunning check on g1. After the Zwischenschach 44.♕c7+! ♔h6 the move 45.♖xf4 led to a simple win.

44...♕g1+! An unpleasant surprise!

45.♘f1 ♘f3+ 46.♖xf3 ♕xc5 47.♖d3. Despite winning the queen for a rook and knight, black's position still looks dangerous because the d6 passed pawn is very strong. Botvinnik finds a subtle maneuver that saves the game.

A spectacular tactical blow, a won adjourned position... and then Taimanov blundered in his home analysis again, effectively sealing the fate of the match. From the author's archives. Published for the first time.

47...♕f5! Very strong. Now white cannot consolidate his pieces and get the king to a safe haven from the checks *(47...♕c2! also led to a draw)*.

48.♖d2 ♕e6+! Again the only move. The white king cannot hide on the queenside because after 49.♔d1 there's 49...♕xb3+.

In fact black had an alternative: 48...♕e4+ 49.♔d1 ♕g4+ 50.♔c1 ♕f4! 51.d7 ♕xf1+ 52.♔c2 ♕f5+ with a draw.

49.♔f2 ♕f5+ 50.♔e2 ♕g4+ 51.♔f2 ♕f5+ 52.♔g1 ♕c5+ 53.♔h2 ♕h5+ 54.♔g1 ♕c5+ 55.♔h1 ♕c1! The only move, but it's enough. After 55...♕h5+, black still risked losing. Now a peaceful finish is inevitable. Draw.

The Flawed Masterpiece

This beautiful victory could have become a gem in Botvinnik's collection, if not for the mutual blindness on move 27. Nevertheless, the world champion's play was superb, and the bold bishop sacrifice was probably well-liked by the fans.

No. 267. Nimzo-Indian Defense E40
Botvinnik – Taimanov
Moscow (m/4), 31st January 1953
1.d4 ♘f6 2.c4 e6 3.♘c3 ♗b4 4.e3 ♘c6. "The favorite line of Grandmaster Taimanov, who often goes for energetic piece play from the very beginning of the game." (Botvinnik)

5.♘ge2 d5 6.a3 ♗e7 7.cxd5 (7.♘g3 h5!? Botvinnik – Taimanov, 1951 Soviet Championship) **7... exd5 8.♘f4.** Improving upon the 20th championship game; after 8.g3?! 0-0 9.♗g2 ♘a5! 10.0-0 c6, black got a comfortable position *(see game 251).*

8...0-0 (later, 8...♗f5 9.♗e2 ♕d7 became popular) **9.♗e2!** Not 9.♗d3 ♖e8 (Levenfish – Taimanov, Leningrad 1952). "Only by developing the plan of attacking the d5 pawn through putting the bishop on f3 can white fight for the initiative." (Taimanov)

9...♗f5?! With the idea 10.♗f3 ♗e4. In Botvinnik's opinion, "9...♘b8 and c7-c6 was safer" and the computer agrees with him. However, 9...♗e6? (Gligoric – Pachman, Saltsjobaden 1952) is bad due to the sudden 10.e4!

10.g4! ♗e6.

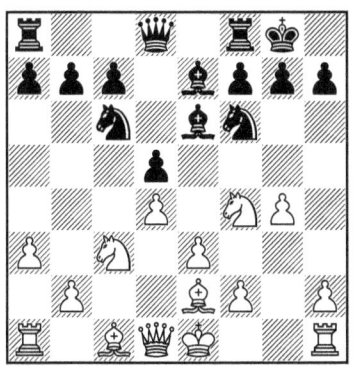

11.♘xe6. With 11.g5! and h2-h4, white got a substantial advantage. Now black manages to stabilize the position.

11...fxe6 12.0-0 ♕d7 13.f4 ♘d8! Botvinnik notes: "Involving the knight in the defense against white's possible kingside attack and threatening to start dangerous queenside counterplay (c7-c5)."

14.♗d3 ♘f7 15.b4. 15.g5 ♘e8 16.♕h5 gives nothing, since after 16...g6 17.♗xg6?! hxg6 18.♕xg6+ ♘g7 19.♗d2 the attack fizzles out and black has a clear plan of counterplay: 19...♘h8 20.♕d3 ♘f5, then ♘g6 and doubling the rooks along the h-file.

15...a5 16.b5 ♘d6. "Black has a good position." (Taimanov)

17.♕f3 (17.a4!? and ♗a3) **17... a4 18.♖a2 c6 19.bxc6 ♕xc6 20.♖c2 ♕d7.** "Now it's black who has a clear advantage on the queenside, he only has to make the prophylactic move g7-g6 before taking decisive action. Therefore, white cannot tarry with his kingside counterplay anymore." (Botvinnik)

21.g5 ♘fe8? Who would have thought that this was the decisive mistake? The computer insists on 21...♘fe4 22.♘xe4 dxe4 23.♗xe4 ♘xe4 24.♕xe4 ♖ac8, and the prospect of creating a passed pawn (after b7-b5) compensates for the pawn loss.

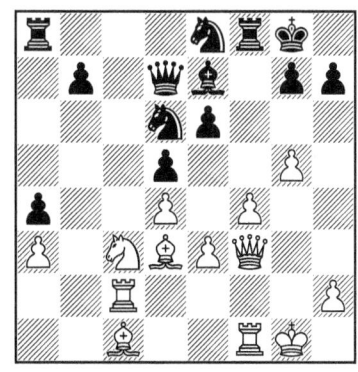

22.♗xh7+! This spectacular blow leads to a forced win. After 22.f5 (22. ♕h3 ♘f5=, while 22.♘xd5?! exd5 23.♕xd5+ ♔h8 is better for black) 22...♘xf5 23.♘xd5 ♕xd5 24.♕xd5 exd5 25.♗xf5 ♖d8 26.♗e6+ ♔h8 there's still a lot of fight in the position.

22...♔xh7 23.♕h3+ ♔g8! "In case of 23...♔g6 24.♘xd5 ♗d8 25.♘b4! the black king's position was quite dangerous due to the threat ♘d3-e5+." (Botvinnik)

24.♘xd5 ♗d8 (24...♗xg5? 25.♘b6, but not 25.fxg5? ♖xf1+ 26.♔xf1 ♕b5+) **25.g6 ♘f6 26.♘xf6+ gxf6.**

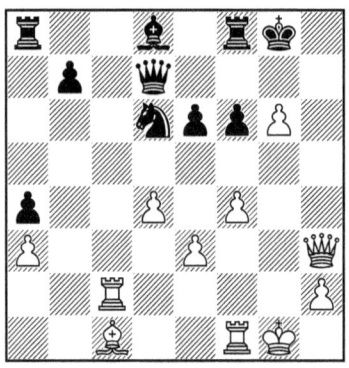

"In this interesting position, the right continuation was 27.♖g2 ♖e8 (27...♘e8 28.d5 gave white a strong attack) 28.g7 ♘f7 29.♖f3 ♖c8!! 30.♗b2 (30.♗d2 ♖c2) 30...♖c7 31.♕h4 (31.♕h5 ♕d5 32.f5 ♕e4!) 31...♕c8 32.♖h3 ♖c1+!, and black draws the game." (Botvinnik)

This approach is actually winning for white. The right way, "found by Czechoslovakian players", was only shown by Botvinnik in his notes for the tournament book.

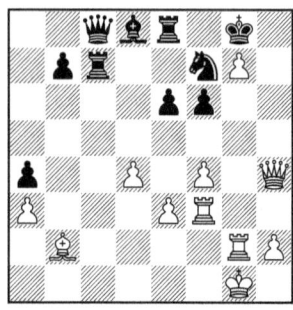

Position after 27.♖g2 ♖e8 28.g7 ♘f7 29.♖f3 ♖c8 30.♗b2 ♖c7 31.♕h4 ♕c8

The problem-like move 32.♗c3!! led to a win. White is threatening the deadly 33.♖h3, and the bishop cannot be captured because of mate: 32...♖xc3 33.♕h8+! ♘xh8 34.gxh8=♕+ ♔xh8 35.♖h3# or 34... ♔f7 35.♖g7#.

27.g7? ♖e8? "A rare case of mutual 'blindness'. Only after the end of the game did we see that black could capture the pawn with the king: in the heat of the battle, both players thought that it was too dangerous... After 27...♔xg7!, white's attempts to attack the black king with 28.♖g2+ ♔f7 or 28.♕h5 ♖f7 are unsuccessful, since the black king can find a safe haven on e7 or e8. However, the continuation 28.f5! ♔f7! 29.e4 ♔e7! 30.♗d2 still gave white some practical chances to save the game." (Botvinnik)

After 30...♗b6!, these chances are minimal (for instance: 31.♔h1 ♖h8

32.♕d3 exf5!, but not 31...♗xd4? 32.fxe6).

28.♕h8+   ♔f7   29.♕h5+! Depriving black of his last illusions. Now the g7 pawn cannot be captured: 29...♔xg7 30.♖g2+ ♔f8 31.♕h8+ ♔e7 32.♖g7+ ♘f7 33.♖xf7+! ♔xf7 34.♕h7+ and ♕xd7.

29...♔g8.

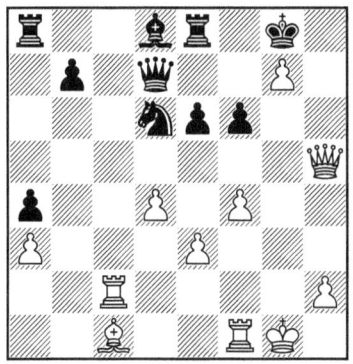

30.♖g2. "It was hard to make that move when I had just 5 minutes to think for 11 moves," Botvinnik revealed in *Analytical and Critical Works*. "However, I really wanted to win this game, which would have practically secured the champion's title. The competitive atmosphere of the match, caused by our unpleasant conflict during the championship tournament game, was also conducive for such an approach. I decided against repeating moves, even though the risk was great."

30...♘f7 31.♖f3! ♖a5 32.♕h4! White only decided to play 30.♖g2 after seeing this move. Taimanov thought for a long time here, but there was no salvation already: 32...f5

33.♕h5 and ♖h3, 32...♕c7 33.♗b2! or 32...♕c6 33.♕h8+! with mate in three.

32...e5 33.♖h3 (33.f5! won more quickly) **33...♕xh3 34.♕xh3 exf4 35.exf4 ♗b6.** After 35...♖e1+ 36.♔f2 ♖xc1, white checkmates with 37.♕h7+!

36.♗b2 ♖b5. The last trap: 37.♕d7? ♖e1+ with a draw (38. ♔f2 ♖xb2+ 39.♔xe1 ♖xg2 40.♕xb7 ♖b2).

37.♔f1 ♗a5 38.♖c2 ♖b3 39.♕d7 ♖be3 40.♕xa4 ♖e1+ 41.♔f2 ♗c7 42.♕xe8+. The game was adjourned here, but black resigned without resuming play.

The Consolation Goal

After losing a game the day before and the catastrophic play-off, a lesser player would have lost heart completely. But Taimanov was different! Exploiting an opening mistake by his opponent, he created a strong attack, executing it with youthful vividness and energy.

No. 268. Nimzo-Indian Defense E58
Taimanov – Botvinnik
Moscow (m/5), 2nd February 1953
Annotated by M. Taimanov
1.d4 ♘f6 2.c4 e6 3.♘c3 ♗b4. A surprise! Botvinnik has very rarely played the Nimzo-Indian Defense in recent years.

"The world champion probably used it out of psychological considerations." (Yudovich)

4.♘f3 c5 5.e3 0-0 6.♗d3 d5 7.0-0 ♘c6 8.a3 ♗xc3. The move 8...♗a5 lost its popularity after the well-known game Novotelnov – Smyslov (19th Soviet Championship), where white played 9.cxd5 exd5 10.dxc5 ♗xc3 11.bxc3 ♕a5 12.c4!

But 11...♗g4!= (Bannik – Petrosian, Tbilisi 1951) is more precise; later, Taimanov himself also used this line several times.

9.bxc3 b6. Another plan is to prepare the liberating pawn push e6-e5 after 9...dxc4 10.♗xc4 ♕c7 *(this became one of the main tabiyas of the Nimzo-Indian Defense).*

10.cxd5 exd5 11.a4. White must strive to open up the position, so that the strength of his bishops tells. The game move also contains the positional threat 12.♗a3 ♘d7 (or 12...♕e7) 13.dxc5 bxc5 14.c4!

Later, Taimanov only played 11.♘e5!? – against Petrosian (Zurich 1953) and Bagirov (1957 Soviet Championship s/f).

11...c4. A committal move, but the most logical one.

It became the most popular, despite the opinions of skeptics who recommended not to hurry with the move c5-c4: "After this move, it's very hard for black to get counterplay on the queenside. White, on the other hand, can now prepare e3-e4 due to the lack of pawn tension in the center." (Yudovich)

12.♗c2 ♗g4. The only move! After other continuations, white could start a typical attack for such positions: ♘d2, f2-f3 and e3-e4.

In game 4 Botvinnik shone in all his glory! In game 6 (pictured) he also had white, and the camera caught the position just before 32...♕d8, ten moves before a draw was agreed and the match ended.

13.♕e1. A good move that first occurred in the game Tolush – Keres (Tallinn 1945).

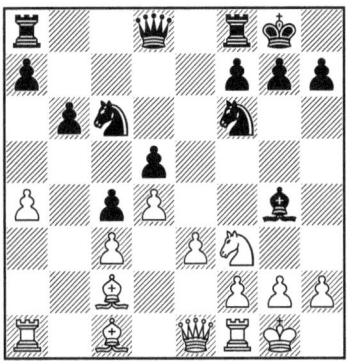

13...♖e8. This natural move turns out to be a serious mistake *("Here, Botvinnik's lack of knowledge of this line obviously told" – Yudovich).* It was necessary to play 13...♗xf3! 14.gxf3 ♕d7. In this case, the knights could successfully fight against the white bishops because of the closed nature of the position. Now black gets into trouble.

It's interesting to note that both Keres in the aforementioned game against Tolush and Bondarevsky in the game against Taimanov (20th Soviet Championship semifinal) made the same mistake (13...♖e8?).

14.♘h4! Tolush played 14.♘d2 here, intending to prepare e3-e4 with 15.f3. Keres, however, managed to neutralize this plan with the maneuver ♗h5-g6!.

The move 14.♘h4! is made for the same purpose – to prepare an attack in the center, but it also plays

another role – it neutralizes the bishop transfer to g6.

14...♗h5. Bondarevsky tried another plan – 14...♘a5 15.f3 ♗c8 16.♗a3 ♘b3, but also failed to equalize.

15.f3 ♗g6 16.♘xg6 hxg6 17.e4! This move secures white's advantage.

17...dxe4 (or else 18.e5 and f3-f4-f5) **18.fxe4.**

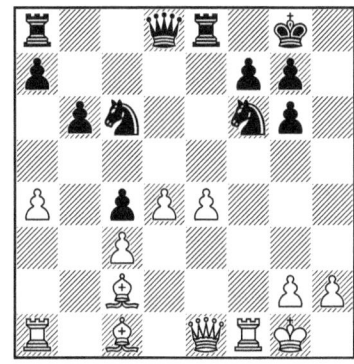

18...♕d7. The attempt to complicate the struggle with 18...♘xe4 19.♗xe4 ♘xd4 (19...f5? 20.♗xc6! ♖xe1 21.♖xe1), intending to get three pawns for the piece after 20.cxd4 ♕xd4+, didn't work. White would have played 20.♕e3! ♘c2 21.♕f3! ♖xe4 22.♕xe4 ♘xa1 23.♗g5!, maintaining his material advantage.

19.♗g5 ♘h7. *The attempt to get three pawns for the piece with 19...♘xd4 20.cxd4 ♕xd4+ 21.♔h1 ♘xe4 again didn't work, due to 22.♖d1! ♕e5 23.♗f4 ♕e6 24.♖d4 (for instance: 24...♘c5 25.♕xe6 ♘xe6 26.♖xc4 or 24...f5 25.♗xe4 fxe4 26.♖d6 ♕e7 27.♖xg6).*

20.♗e3. White's advantage is already so great that black is unlikely to save the game.

20...♘e7 21.♖f3. The signal for decisive operations. White threatens 22.♖h3 and 23.♕h4.

21...f5 22.e5. Now 22.♖h3 gave nothing due to 22...fxe4 23.♕h4 ♘f6.

22...♘f8. Black has no time to make the important defensive move 22...g5, since this is met with 23.♕f1, winning a pawn, and white prevents this altogether with his next move.

23.h4 ♘e6 24.♖d1 ♕d5. Black can't put the knight on this square, since after 24...♘d5 white has a very strong reply 25.h5! *(25...f4 26.♗d2 g5 27.♕e4 or 26...gxh5 27.♖h3).*

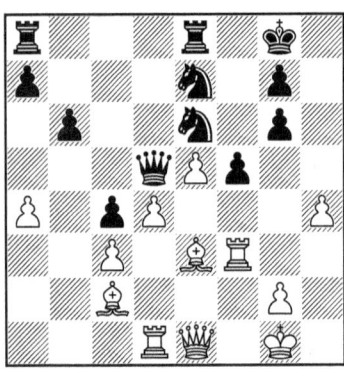

25.♗c1! White transfers the bishop to a3 to attack the e7 knight

– the only defender of the weak g6 pawn. Black's position quickly turns critical.

25...♖f8 26.♗a3 ♖ae8 27.♕g3 g5. After 27...♔h7 black wins with 28.h5!

28.♗xe7 ♖xe7 29.♖xf5 ♖xf5 30.♗xf5 ♘f4. Or 30...gxh4 31.♕xh4 with numerous threats.

31.♕xg5 ♖xe5 32.dxe5 ♕xd1+ 33.♔h2 ♕d2. If the knight retreats white gives mate in a few moves.

34.♗e6+ ♔h7. If 34...♔f8 then 35.♕f5+ ♔e7 36.♕f7+ ♔d8 37.♕f8+ ♔c7 38.♕c8#.

35.♗xc4 g6 36.♗e6! Black resigned.

Landing an immediate return blow, Taimanov shook the world champion a bit, and Botvinnik decided not to tempt fate in game 6: "One of those moments when sporting considerations prevail over creative ones. In a tournament game, white would have probably maintained the tension – he had every reason to continue the game. In the last game of a match, however, when it was enough to draw to secure the win in the competition, white couldn't avoid the temptation to close off the position and essentially end the game with a draw."

Championship Tables

16th Soviet Championship, 1948

#	Players	1	2	3	4	5	6	7	8	9	10	11	12	13	14	15	16	17	18	19	Pts	Place
1	D. Bronstein (Moscow)	◆	=	1	=	1	=	0	=	=	1	=	=	1	=	=	=	1	1	1	12	1–2
2	A. Kotov (Moscow)	=	◆	=	=	0	1	1	1	0	1	=	1	1	0	0	1	1	1	1	12	1–2
3	S. Furman (Leningrad)	0	=	◆	0	0	=	1	1	0	0	1	1	1	1	=	1	1	=	1	11	3
4	S. Flohr (Moscow)	=	=	1	◆	=	=	=	=	=	1	=	1	=	=	1	0	=	=	=	10.5	4
5	A. Tolush (Leningrad)	0	1	1	=	◆	=	=	1	0	1	=	0	1	0	=	1	0	1	=	10	5
6	I. Bondarevsky (Leningrad)	=	0	=	=	=	◆	=	=	=	=	1	=	=	=	0	1	1	0	1	9.5	6–9
7	P. Keres (Tallinn)	1	0	0	=	=	=	◆	0	1	=	=	=	=	=	1	0	=	1	1	9.5	6–9
8	A. Konstantinopolsky (Moscow)	=	1	0	=	0	=	1	◆	=	0	1	1	=	1	0	=	=	=	=	9.5	6–9
9	G. Lisitsin (Leningrad)	=	0	1	0	1	=	0	=	◆	0	1	0	1	=	1	1	=	=	=	9.5	6–9
10	G. Ilivitsky (Sverdlovsk)	0	=	1	=	0	0	=	1	1	◆	0	1	=	0	1	=	=	=	=	9	10–11
11	A. Lilienthal (Moscow)	=	=	0	=	=	0	=	0	0	1	◆	=	1	0	=	=	1	1	1	9	10–11
12	R. Kholmov (Vilnius)	=	0	0	0	1	=	=	0	1	0	=	◆	0	1	1	=	=	=	1	8.5	12
13	Y. Averbakh (Moscow)	0	0	0	=	0	=	=	=	0	=	0	1	◆	=	=	0	1	=	1	8	13–15
14	G. Levenfish (Leningrad)	=	1	0	0	1	1	0	0	=	1	1	0	=	◆	=	1	0	0	0	8	13–15
15	V. Ragozin (Moscow)	=	0	=	1	=	0	1	=	0	0	=	0	=	=	◆	=	=	1	=	8	13–15
16	V. Alatortsev (Moscow)	=	0	0	=	0	0	=	1	0	=	=	=	1	0	=	◆	=	=	1	7.5	16–17
17	V. Panov (Moscow)	0	0	0	=	1	1	0	=	=	=	0	=	0	1	=	=	◆	=	1	7.5	16–17
18	L. Aronin (Moscow Oblast)	0	0	=	=	0	0	0	=	=	=	0	0	=	1	0	=	=	◆	1	6	18–19
19	M. Taimanov (Leningrad)	0	0	0	=	=	=	=	=	=	=	0	=	0	1	=	0	=	0	◆	6	18–19

17th Soviet Championship, 1949

#	Players	1	2	3	4	5	6	7	8	9	10	11	12	13	14	15	16	17	18	19	20	Pts	Place
1	D. Bronstein (Moscow)	♦	0	=	=	=	=	=	1	=	1	=	1	1	=	1	=	1	1	1	=	13	1–2
2	V. Smyslov (Moscow)	1	♦	=	=	=	=	0	=	1	1	1	=	=	1	=	1	1	1	0	1	13	1–2
3	E. Geller (Odessa)	=	=	♦	=	1	1	1	0	=	0	1	0	1	0	=	1	1	1	1	1	12.5	3–4
4	M. Taimanov (Leningrad)	=	=	=	♦	=	=	0	1	1	=	=	1	1	=	1	=	=	1	=	1	12.5	3–4
5	I. Boleslavsky (Sverdlovsk)	=	=	0	=	♦	=	0	=	1	1	=	=	1	=	1	=	1	=	=	1	11.5	5–7
6	A. Kotov (Moscow)	=	=	0	=	=	♦	1	=	0	=	1	0	1	=	0	1	1	1	1	1	11.5	5–7
7	S. Furman (Leningrad)	=	1	0	1	1	0	♦	1	=	=	=	=	0	1	0	1	0	1	1	1	11.5	5–7
8	P. Keres (Tallinn)	0	=	1	0	=	=	0	♦	=	=	=	1	=	1	1	1	1	=	1	0	11	8
9	L. Aronin (Moscow Oblast)	=	0	=	0	0	1	=	=	♦	=	=	=	1	=	1	=	=	=	1	=	10	9–10
10	R. Kholmov (Vilnius)	0	0	1	=	0	=	=	=	=	♦	=	0	1	1	=	=	=	=	1	1	10	9–10
11	S. Flohr (Moscow)	=	0	0	=	=	0	=	=	=	=	♦	=	=	1	=	1	=	=	1	0	9	11
12	A. Sokolsky (Lvov)	0	=	1	0	=	1	=	0	=	1	=	♦	0	=	=	=	=	=	0	=	8.5	12
13	N. Kopylov (Leningrad)	0	=	0	0	0	0	1	=	0	0	=	1	♦	0	1	=	1	1	=	=	8	13–15
14	A. Lilienthal (Moscow)	=	0	1	=	=	=	0	0	=	0	0	=	1	♦	=	0	1	=	=	=	8	13–15
15	V. Mikenas (Vilnius)	0	=	=	0	0	1	1	0	0	=	=	=	0	=	♦	0	1	1	=	=	8	13–15
16	T. Petrosian (Yerevan)	=	0	0	=	=	0	0	0	=	=	0	=	=	1	1	♦	0	0	1	1	7.5	16
17	V. Ragozin (Moscow)	0	0	0	=	0	0	1	0	=	=	=	=	0	0	0	1	♦	1	=	=	6.5	17
18	G. Goldberg (Leningrad)	0	0	0	0	=	0	0	=	=	=	=	=	0	=	0	1	0	♦	1	=	6	18–20
19	G. Levenfish (Leningrad)	0	1	0	=	=	0	0	0	0	0	0	1	=	=	=	0	=	0	♦	1	6	18–20
20	V. Liublinsky (Moscow Oblast)	=	0	0	0	0	0	0	1	=	0	1	=	=	=	=	0	=	=	0	♦	6	18–20

18th Soviet Championship, 1950

#	Players	1	2	3	4	5	6	7	8	9	10	11	12	13	14	15	16	17	18	Pts	Place
1	P. Keres (Tallinn)	•	1	=	=	=	=	0	1	1	1	1	=	0	1	1	=	1	=	11.5	1
2	L. Aronin (Moscow Oblast)	0	•	0	1	1	0	=	1	0	1	1	=	1	=	=	1	1	1	11	2–4
3	I. Lipnitsky (Kiev)	=	1	•	=	0	1	0	=	1	=	=	=	1	1	1	0	1	1	11	2–4
4	A. Tolush (Leningrad)	=	0	=	•	1	=	1	=	0	1	1	=	0	1	=	1	1	1	11	2–4
5	A. Konstantinopolsky (Moscow)	=	0	1	0	•	=	=	1	=	=	=	=	0	1	=	1	1	1	10	5–6
6	V. Smyslov (Moscow)	=	1	0	=	=	•	=	0	=	=	1	1	=	=	0	1	1	1	10	5–6
7	V. Alatortsev (Moscow)	1	=	1	0	=	=	•	0	=	=	0	1	=	=	1	=	1	0	9	7–10
8	I. Boleslavsky (Sverdlovsk)	0	0	=	=	0	1	1	•	1	1	=	0	=	1	=	=	=	=	9	7–10
9	E. Geller (Odessa)	0	1	0	1	=	=	=	0	•	0	=	1	1	1	0	0	1	1	9	7–10
10	S. Flohr (Moscow)	0	0	=	0	=	=	=	0	1	•	1	1	=	=	1	1	=	=	9	7–10
11	V. Mikenas (Vilnius)	0	0	=	0	=	0	1	=	=	0	•	0	1	=	1	1	1	1	8.5	11
12	I. Bondarevsky (Leningrad)	=	=	=	=	=	0	0	1	0	0	1	•	0	1	=	1	=	=	8	12–13
13	T. Petrosian (Moscow)	1	0	0	1	1	=	=	=	0	=	0	1	•	0	1	0	=	=	8	12–13
14	Y. Averbakh (Moscow)	0	=	0	0	0	=	=	0	0	=	=	0	1	•	=	1	1	1	7	14
15	G. Borisenko (Leningrad)	0	=	0	=	=	1	0	=	1	0	0	=	0	=	•	0	=	1	6.5	15–16
16	A. Suetin (Tula)	=	0	1	0	0	0	=	=	1	0	0	0	1	0	1	•	0	1	6.5	15–16
17	V. Liublinsky (Moscow)	0	0	0	0	0	0	0	=	0	=	0	=	=	0	=	1	•	=	4	17–18
18	A. Sokolsky (Lvov)	=	0	0	0	0	0	1	=	0	=	0	=	=	0	0	0	=	•	4	17–18

19th Soviet Championship, 1951

#	Players	1	2	3	4	5	6	7	8	9	10	11	12	13	14	15	16	17	18	Pts	Place
1	P. Keres (Tallinn)	♦	=	1	1	=	=	=	1	=	1	0	0	=	1	1	1	1	1	12	1
2	T. Petrosian (Moscow)	=	♦	=	1	=	=	=	1	=	0	0	1	1	1	=	1	1	1	11.5	2–3
3	E. Geller (Odessa)	0	=	♦	0	1	=	0	1	0	1	1	1	=	1	1	1	1	1	11.5	2–3
4	V. Smyslov (Moscow)	0	0	1	♦	1	0	1	1	1	=	1	=	=	1	=	1	0	1	11	4
5	M. Botvinnik (Moscow)	=	=	0	0	♦	=	1	=	=	1	0	=	=	=	1	1	1	1	10	5
6	Y. Averbakh (Moscow)	=	=	=	1	=	♦	0	0	=	1	=	=	1	=	=	0	1	1	9.5	6–8
7	D. Bronstein (Moscow)	=	=	1	0	0	1	♦	1	=	0	1	0	=	=	=	=	1	1	9.5	6–8
8	M. Taimanov (Leningrad)	0	0	0	0	=	1	0	♦	=	=	1	=	1	=	1	1	1	1	9.5	6–8
9	S. Flohr (Moscow)	=	=	1	0	=	=	=	=	♦	0	=	1	=	=	1	=	0	1	9	9–10
10	L. Aronin (Moscow Oblast)	0	1	0	=	0	0	1	=	1	♦	1	=	0	=	=	1	1	=	9	9–10
11	N. Kopylov (Leningrad)	1	1	0	0	1	=	0	0	=	0	♦	0	1	1	0	1	1	=	8.5	11
12	A. Kotov (Moscow)	1	0	0	=	=	=	1	=	0	=	1	♦	=	=	=	0	1	0	8	12–13
13	I. Bondarevsky (Leningrad)	=	0	=	=	=	0	=	0	=	1	0	=	♦	=	1	0	1	1	8	12–13
14	V. Simagin (Moscow)	0	0	0	0	=	=	=	=	=	=	=	0	=	♦	1	=	1	1	7.5	14
15	O. Moiseev (Moscow)	0	=	0	=	0	=	=	0	0	=	1	=	0	0	♦	=	1	1	6.5	15–16
16	I. Lipnitsky (Kiev)	0	0	0	0	0	1	=	0	=	0	0	1	1	=	=	♦	=	1	6.5	15–16
17	N. Novotelnov (Grozny)	0	0	0	1	0	0	0	0	1	0	0	0	0	0	0	=	♦	=	3	17
18	E. Terpugov (Moscow)	0	0	0	0	0	0	0	0	0	=	=	1	0	0	0	0	=	♦	2.5	18

20th Soviet Championship, 1952

#	Players	1	2	3	4	5	6	7	8	9	10	11	12	13	14	15	16	17	18	19	20	Pts	Place
1	M. Botvinnik (Moscow)	◆	0	1	=	=	=	1	1	=	1	1	=	=	1	=	1	=	1	=	1	13.5	1–2
2	M. Taimanov (Leningrad)	1	◆	0	0	=	1	1	=	=	=	0	1	1	1	1	1	1	=	1	1	13.5	1–2
3	E. Geller (Odessa)	0	1	◆	1	1	=	=	0	0	1	=	=	1	1	1	=	=	1	=	=	12	3
4	I. Boleslavsky (Minsk)	=	1	0	◆	0	=	=	=	=	1	=	1	0	=	=	1	=	1	1	1	11.5	4–5
5	A. Tolush (Leningrad)	=	=	0	1	◆	=	0	1	1	=	=	0	1	=	0	1	1	=	1	1	11.5	4–5
6	V. Korchnoi (Leningrad)	=	0	=	=	=	◆	0	=	1	0	0	1	1	1	=	0	1	1	1	1	11	6
7	D. Bronstein (Moscow)	0	0	=	=	1	1	◆	1	=	=	=	1	1	=	=	=	=	=	0	=	10.5	7–9
8	O. Moiseev (Moscow)	0	=	1	=	0	=	0	◆	=	=	0	=	1	=	1	1	1	=	1	=	10.5	7–9
9	V. Smyslov (Moscow)	=	=	1	0	0	0	=	=	◆	1	1	0	1	1	=	=	=	=	=	1	10.5	7–9
10	P. Keres (Tallinn)	0	=	0	=	=	1	=	=	0	◆	1	=	0	=	=	1	0	1	=	1	9.5	10–11
11	A. Suetin (Tula)	0	1	=	0	=	1	=	1	0	0	◆	=	1	=	=	0	0	1	1	=	9.5	10–11
12	L. Aronin (Moscow Oblast)	=	0	=	1	1	0	0	=	=	=	=	◆	=	0	=	1	=	=	=	=	9	12–13
13	V. Byvshev (Leningrad)	=	0	0	1	0	0	0	0	1	1	0	=	◆	1	0	0	1	1	1	1	9	12–13
14	G. Ilivitsky (Sverdlovsk)	0	0	0	=	=	0	=	=	0	=	=	1	0	◆	1	1	=	=	=	1	8.5	14–15
15	V. Simagin (Moscow)	=	0	0	0	1	=	=	=	0	0	=	=	1	0	◆	1	=	=	=	1	8.5	14–15
16	A. Konstantinopolsky (Moscow)	0	0	=	=	0	1	=	0	=	0	1	0	1	0	0	◆	1	=	=	=	7.5	16
17	I. Lipnitsky (Kiev)	=	0	=	0	0	0	=	0	=	1	1	=	0	=	=	0	◆	1	=	0	7	17
18	I. Kan (Moscow)	0	=	0	0	=	0	=	=	=	0	0	=	0	=	=	=	0	◆	1	1	6.5	18
19	G. Kasparyan (Yerevan)	=	0	=	0	0	0	1	0	=	=	0	=	0	0	=	=	=	0	◆	=	5.5	19
20	B. Goldenov (Minsk)	0	0	=	0	0	0	=	=	0	0	=	=	0	=	0	=	1	0	=	◆	5	20

Match for the Title of Soviet Champion, 1953

Players	1	2	3	4	5	6	Pts
M. Botvinnik (Moscow)	1	=	=	1	0	=	3.5
M. Taimanov (Leningrad)	0	=	=	0	1	=	2.5

Championship Rankings (1939–1952)

Player	Tournaments	W	L	D	Games	Pts	Percentage
Botvinnik	7	66	13	52	131	92	70.2%
Belavenets	1	6	1	10	17	11	64.7%
Geller	4	35	17	20	72	45	62.5%
Smyslov	9	63	25	71	159	98.5	61.9%
Keres	8	59	26	63	148	90.5	61.1%
Furman	2	18	10	9	37	22.5	60.8%
Boleslavsky	8	52	23	71	146	87.5	59.9%
Bronstein	7	42	22	61	125	72.5	58.0%
Korchnoi	1	8	5	6	19	11	57.9%
Chekhover	2	11	7	16	34	19	55.9%
Taimanov	4	27	18	34	79	44	55.7%
Makogonov V.	4	20	13	38	71	39	54.9%
Bondarevsky	8	42	29	73	144	78.5	54.5%
Flohr	6	26	17	63	106	57.5	54.2%
Tolush	7	49	39	35	123	66.5	54.1%
Kotov	7	47	38	38	123	66	53.7%
Lilienthal	7	35	31	62	128	66	51.6%
Veresov	2	13	12	10	35	18	51.4%
Petrosian	3	17	16	20	53	27	50.9%
Kholmov	2	10	10	17	37	18.5	50.0%
Konstantinopolsky	5	22	23	45	90	44.5	49.4%
Lisitsin	4	20	22	28	70	34	48.6%
Aronin	6	27	32	50	109	52	47.7%
Byvshev	1	8	9	2	19	9	47.4%
Petrovs	1	6	7	6	19	9	47.4%
Ilivitsky	2	9	11	17	37	17.5	47.3%
Mikenas	4	20	24	27	71	33.5	47.2%
Moiseev	2	9	11	16	36	17	47.2%
Averbakh	3	13	16	23	52	24.5	47.1%
Rabinovich I.	1	4	5	8	17	8	47.1%
Dubinin	3	13	17	25	55	25.5	46.4%
Lipnitsky	3	15	19	19	53	24.5	46.2%
Ragozin	7	36	46	43	125	57.5	46.0%
Kopylov	2	12	15	9	36	16.5	45.8%
Simagin	2	7	11	18	36	16	44.4%
Suetin	2	11	15	10	36	16	44.4%

Khavin	1	6	8	2	16	7	43.8%
Panov	3	10	17	27	54	23.5	43.5%
Yudovich	2	5	10	21	36	15.5	43.1%
Alatortsev	5	18	31	38	87	37	42.5%
Stolberg	1	5	8	6	19	8	42.1%
Ufimtsev	1	4	7	8	19	8	42.1%
Levenfish	5	20	36	36	92	38	41.3%
Koblencs	1	3	6	8	17	7	41.2%
Rudakovsky	2	8	15	13	36	14.5	40.3%
Sokolsky	3	9	21	22	52	20	38.5%
Borisenko	1	3	7	7	17	6.5	38.2%
Kasparyan	2	8	17	13	38	14.5	38.2%
Pogrebyssky	1	5	9	3	17	6.5	38.2%
Kan	4	12	30	30	72	27	37.5%
Gerstenfeld	1	4	9	6	19	7	36.8%
Ratner	1	3	8	6	17	6	35.3%
Klaman	1	4	10	5	19	6.5	34.2%
Goldenov	2	3	17	18	38	12	31.6%
Romanovsky	2	5	19	10	34	10	29.4%
Chistiakov	1	2	9	6	17	5	29.4%
Ravinsky	1	2	9	5	16	4.5	28.1%
Goldberg	2	4	20	12	36	10	27.8%
Liublinsky	2	3	19	14	36	10	27.8%
Novotelnov	1	2	13	2	17	3	17.6%
Terpugov	1	1	13	3	17	2.5	14.7%

D. Bronstein – 1948, 1949

A. Kotov – 1948

M. Botvinnik – 1952

P. Keres – 1950, 1951

V. Smyslov – 1949

Bibliography

Books and game collections

Asriyan V. A. *Vladimir Makogonov*, 2nd edition, Moscow 2016

Averbakh Y. L. *Centre-Stage and Behind the Scenes (Shakhmaty na stsene i za kulisami)*, Moscow 2003

Averbakh Y. L. *What the Pieces Don't Mention (O chem molchat figury)*, Moscow 2007

Averbakh Y. L. *A Chess Player's Life in the System (Zhizn shakhmatista v sisteme)*, Moscow 2012

Beilin M. A. *My Encounters in the Chess Kingdom (Moi vstrechi v shakhmatnom korolevstve)*, Moscow 2003

Beilin, M. A. *Was Not, Was Never a Member, Was Never Indicted (Ne byl, ne sostoyal, ne privlekalsya)*, Moscow 2008

Botvinnik M. M. *Achieving the Aim (K dostizheniyu tseli)*, Moscow 1978

Botvinnik M. M. *Analytical and Critical Works. 1942–1956 (Analiticheskie i kriticheskie raboty. 1942–1956)*, Moscow 1985

Botvinnik I. Y. (ed.) *Botvinnik – Bronstein Match*, Moscow 2001

Bronstein D. I. *200 Open Games (200 otkrytykh partiy)*, Moscow 1970

Bronstein D. I., Furstenberg T. *Sorcerer's Apprentice (Uchenik charodeya)*, Moscow 2004

Chess Encyclopedia (Shakhmaty. Entsiklopedicheskiy slovar), Moscow 1990

Damsky Y. V. *Grandmaster Geller (Grossmeister Geller)*, Moscow 1976

Dlugolensky Y. N., Zak V. G. *People and Chess (Lyudi i shakhmaty)*, Leningrad 1988

Dvorkovich V. Y. (editor) *Vladas Mikenas*, Moscow 1987

Geller E. P. *At the Chessboard (Za shakhmatnoi doskoy)*, Odessa 1962

Ivanov S., Kentler A., Faibisovich V., Khropov B. *The Chess Annals of Petersburg. 1900–2005. City championships. 2nd edition (Shakhmatnaya letopis Peterburga. 1900–2005. Chempionaty goroda. Izd. 2-e)*, St. Petersburg 2005

Kasparov G. K. (with D. G. Plisetsky) *My Great Predecessors (Moi velikie predshestvenniki), From Euwe to Tal*, Volume 2, Moscow 2003

Keres P. *One Hundred Games (Sto partii)*, Moscow 1966

Konstantinopolsky A. M. *Alexander Konstantinopolsky*, Moscow 1985

Korchnoi V. L. *My 55 Wins with Black (Moi 55 pobed chernymi)*, Moscow 2004

Korchnoi V. L. *Chess Without Mercy (Shakhmaty bez poschady)*, Moscow 2006

Kotov A. A. *Selected Games (Izbrannye partii)*, Moscow 1962

Kotov A. A. *Mastery (Masterstvo)*, Moscow 1975

Lazarev E. M. *Creative Works of Ukrainian Chess Players (Tvorchist shakhistiv Ukrainy)*, Kiev 1982

Levenfish G. Y. *Selected Games and Memories (Izbrannye partii i vospominaniya)*, Moscow 1967

Linder V. I., Linder I. M. *Two Lives of Grandmaster Alatortsev (Dve zhizni grossmeistera Alatortseva)*, Moscow 1994

Malkin F. M. (editor) *Alexander Kotov*, Moscow 1984

Panov V. N. *Forty Years at the Chessboard (Sorok let za shakhmatnoy doskoy)*, Moscow 1966

Pavluchenkov M. N. (editor), Suetin A. S. (general editor) *At Home and Abroad (Doma i za rubezhom)*, Minsk 1968

Radchenko A. P., Allakhverdian S. A. *From Verlinsky to Father Zui (Ot Verlinskogo do Batka Zuya)*, Kiev 2009

Semenko Y. *Chess in Ukraine (Shakhy v Ukraini)*, 2nd ed., Lvov 1993

Shmagin Y. P. (editor) *Georgy Ilivitsky's Chess Odyssey (Shakhmatnaya odisseya Georgia Ilivitskogo)*, Ekaterinburg 2008

Simagin V. P. *Best Games (Luchshie partii)*, Moscow 1963

Smyslov V. V. *Selected Games (Izbrannye partii)*, Moscow 1952

Sosonko G. *Dialogues with the Chess Nostradamus (Dialogi s shakhmatnym Nostradamusom)*, Moscow 2006

Sosonko G., Gulko B. *Yuri Razuvaev. Essays (Yuri Razuvaev. Ocherki)*, Washington 2013

Suetin A. S. *Grandmaster Boleslavsky (Grossmeister Boleslavsky)*, Moscow 1981

Suetin A. S. *Outstanding Soviet Chess Players (Vydayuschiesya sovetskie shakhmatisty)*, Minsk 1984

Suetin A. S. *Chess Through the Prism of Time (Shakhmaty skvoz prizmu vremeni)*, Moscow 1998

Sultanov C. *Chess... and not Only Chess (O shakhmatakh i ne tolko...)*, Baku 2009

Taimanov M. E. *Remembering the Greatest... (Vspominaya samykh-samykh...)*, St. Petersburg 2003

Teplitsky V. I. *Isaak Lipnitsky*, Bat-Yam, 1993

Tolush V. I. (editor) *Alexander Tolush*, Moscow 1983

Vainstein B. S. *Improvisation in the Art of Chess. The Games of Grandmaster Bronstein (Improvizatsiya v shakhmatnom iskusstve. O tvorchestve grossmeistera Bronsteina)*, Moscow 1976

Vasiliev V. L. *A Chess Player's Life (Zhizn shakhmatista)*, Yerevan 1969

Vinogradov V. P. *Soviet Players in Competition for the World Championship (Sovietskie shakhmatisty v borbe za pervenstvo mira)*, Moscow 1954

Voronkov S. B. (editor) *Vladimir Simagin*, Moscow 1981

Voronkov S. B. *Fyodor Bogatyrchuk: the Dr. Zhivago of Soviet Chess (Fyodor Bogatyrchuk. Doktor Zhivago sovetskikh shakhmat)*, Moscow 2013 (2 volumes)

Tournament books and chess yearbooks

Abramov L. Y. (editor) *Chess in 1951–1952 (Shakhmaty za 1951–1952 gg.)*, Moscow 1953

Boleslavsky I. E., Konstantinopolsky A. M. (editors) *18th Soviet Chess Championship (XVIII pervenstvo SSSR po shakhmatam)*, Moscow 1952

Prorvich A. S. (editor) *17th Soviet Chess Championship (XVII pervenstvo SSSR po shakhmatam)*, Moscow 1952

Prorvich A. S. (editor) *19th Soviet Chess Championship (XIX pervenstvo SSSR po shakhmatam)*, Moscow 1953

Ragozin V. V. (editor), Abramov L. Y. (editor) *Chess in 1947–1949 (Shakhmaty za 1947–1949 gg.)*, Moscow 1951

Ragozin V. V. (editor), Abramov L. Y. (editor) *Chess in 1950 (Shakhmaty za 1950 g.)*, Moscow 1952

Yudovich M. M. (editor) *20th Soviet Chess Championship (XX pervenstvo SSSR po shakhmatam)*, Moscow 1954

Magazines, newspapers and tournament bulletins

16th Soviet Championship. Leningrad Semi-Final (XVI Vsesoyuznoe shakhmatnoe pervenstvo. Leningradskiy polufinal), Leningrad 1947

16th Soviet Chess Championship (XVI shakhmatny chempionat SSSR), Moscow 1948

The Four Semi-Finals (Chetyre polufinala), Moscow 1949

17th Soviet Chess Championship (XVII shakhmatny chempionat SSSR), Moscow 1949

18th Soviet Chess Championship Dedicated to the 100th Anniversary of M. I. Chigorin's Birth (XVIII shakhmatny chempionat SSSR, posvyaschenny 100-letiyu so dnya rozhdeniya M. I. Chigorina), Moscow 1950/51

19th Soviet Chess Championship (XIX shakhmatny chempionat SSSR), Moscow 1951/52

20th Soviet Chess Championship (XX shakhmatny chempionat SSSR), Moscow 1952/53

27th Moscow Chess Championship (XXVII Moskovsky shakhmatny chempionat), Moscow 1949

Budapest Match Tournament (Match-turnir v Budapeshte), Moscow 1950
Canadian Chess Chat, Canada, 1950
CHESS, Great Britain, 1948–1950
Chess Review, USA, 1952–1953
Ogonyok, Moscow 1949, 1951
Radyansky Sport, Kiev 1950–1952
Shakhmaty v SSSR, Moscow 1948–1953
Smena, Moscow 1949, 1952
Sovietsky Soyuz, Moscow 1951–1952
Sovietsky Sport, Moscow 1950–1953
Three Tournaments. Semi-Finals of the 16th Soviet Championship (Tri turnira. Polufinaly XVI shakhmatnogo chempionata SSSR), Moscow 1947

www.ingramcontent.com/pod-product-compliance
Lightning Source LLC
Chambersburg PA
CBHW071658120626
46550CB00001B/22